Lecture Notes in Computer Science 10655

Commenced Publication in 1973
Founding and Former Series Editors:
Gerhard Goos, Juris Hartmanis, and Jan van Leeuwen

Editorial Board

More information about this series at http://www.springer.com/series/7410

Máire O'Neill (Ed.)

Cryptography and Coding

16th IMA International Conference, IMACC 2017
Oxford, UK, December 12–14, 2017
Proceedings

 Springer

Editor
Máire O'Neill
Queen's University Belfast
Belfast
UK

ISSN 0302-9743   ISSN 1611-3349 (electronic)
Lecture Notes in Computer Science
ISBN 978-3-319-71044-0   ISBN 978-3-319-71045-7   (eBook)
https://doi.org/10.1007/978-3-319-71045-7

Library of Congress Control Number: 2017958557

LNCS Sublibrary: SL4 – Security and Cryptology

Printed on acid-free paper

This Springer imprint is published by Springer Nature
The registered company is Springer International Publishing AG
The registered company address is: Gewerbestrasse 11, 6330 Cham, Switzerland

Preface

The International Conference on Cryptography and Coding is the biennial conference of the Institute of Mathematics and its Applications (IMA) on cryptography and coding theory. The conference series has been running for more than three decades and the 16th edition was held December 12–14 at St. Catherine's College, University of Oxford. We received 32 submissions from authors all over the world on a diverse set of topics both in cryptography and coding theory. The Program Committee selected 19 of the submissions for presentation at the conference. The review process was double-blind and rigorous. Each submission was reviewed independently by at least two reviewers in an individual review phase, and subsequently considered by the Program Committee in a discussion phase. Feedback from the reviews and discussions was given to the authors and their revised submissions are included in the proceedings.

In addition to the presentations of accepted papers, the conference also featured four keynote talks by internationally leading scientists on their research in the interface of cryptography and coding theory. I am grateful to Daniele Micciancio, Jan Camenisch, Nicolas Sendrier, and Thomas Prest for accepting our invitation and sharing the insights gathered from their exciting research. I am also grateful to Martin Albrecht, who co-chaired a Special Session on Lattice-Based Cryptography Constructions and Architectures, and to the contributing authors, Nina Bindel, Tim Güneysu, Tobias Oder, Francesco Regazzoni, Peter Campbell, and Michael Groves.

Running a conference like IMACC requires the effort of many people and many thanks are due. I would like to thank the Steering Committee for their trust and support. I thank the authors for their submissions and the Program Committee and the external reviewers for their effort in selecting the scientific program. Thanks also goes to the IACR for their cooperation and to the H2020 SAFEcrypto project (www.safecrypto.eu) for providing sponsorship. I appreciate the assistance by Anna Kramer, Abier El-Saeidi and Xavier Mathew from Springer in the production of the proceedings. Finally, I am incredibly thankful to conference officer (general chair) Lizzi Lake and her colleagues at the Institute of Mathematics and its Applications for handling all the practical matters of the conference.

December 2017   Máire O'Neill

IMACC 2017

16th IMA International Conference on Cryptography and Coding

St. Catherine's College, University of Oxford,
December 12–14, 2017

Sponsored by the Institute of Mathematics and its Applications (IMA)
Sponsored by the EU H2020 SAFEcrypto project (www.safecrypto.eu)
In cooperation with the International Association for Cryptologic Research (IACR)

General Chair

Lizzi Lake   Institute of Mathematics and its Applications, UK

Program Chair

Máire O'Neill   Queen's University Belfast, UK

Steering Committee

Liqun Chen	University of Surrey, UK
Bahram Honary	University of Lancaster, UK
Christopher Mitchell	Royal Holloway, University of London, UK
Matthew G. Parker	University of Bergen, Norway
Kenneth G. Paterson	Royal Holloway, University of London, UK
Fred Piper	Royal Holloway, University of London, UK
Martijn Stam	University of Bristol, UK

Program Committee

Martin Albrecht	Royal Holloway, University of London, UK
Marco Baldi	Università Politecnica delle Marche, Italy
Mohammed Benaissa	University of Sheffield, UK
Claude Carlet	University of Paris 8, France
Dooho Choi	ETRI, South Korea
Pooya Farshim	ENS, France
Philippe Gaborit	University of Limoges, France
Guang Gong	University of Waterloo, Canada
Jens Groth	University College London, UK
Cong Ling	Imperial College, UK

Additional Reviewers

Contents

Order Revealing Encryption

Revealing Encryption for Partial Ordering

Helene Haagh[1(✉)], Yue Ji[2], Chenxing Li[2], Claudio Orlandi[1], and Yifan Song[2]

[1] Aarhus University, Aarhus, Denmark
haagh@cs.au.dk
[2] IIIS, Tsinghua University, Beijing, China

Abstract. We generalize the cryptographic notion of *Order Revealing Encryption (ORE)* to arbitrary functions and we present a construction that allows to determine the (partial) ordering of two vectors i.e., given $E(x)$ and $E(y)$ it is possible to learn whether $x = y$, $x > y$, $x < y$ or whether x and y are incomparable. This is the first non-trivial example of a *Revealing Encryption (RE)* scheme with output larger than one bit, and which does not rely on cryptographic obfuscation or multilinear maps.

Keywords: Secret-key cryptography · Order-revealing encryption · Revealing encryption

1   Introduction

Computing on encrypted data is a promising approach to privacy preserving cloud computing. Using techniques such as (fully) homomorphic encryption [RAD78, Gen09], a client can upload sensitive data on a partially untrusted cloud which can perform computation on the data without learning anything about the data, *including* the result of the computation. However in many applications it is desirable for the server to learn the result of the computation, so that the server can make decisions based on this result without further interaction with the client. Imagine as an example a server running an encrypted spam filter: using homomorphic encryption the server can, given an encrypted message, determine whether the message is spam or not but, since the server does not learn this bit, the server is unable to place the encrypted message in the user's spam folder.

Revealing Encryption. To solve the above class of problems a different kind of cryptographic primitive is needed, which we refer to as *revealing encryption* or RE. Intuitively, an RE scheme is an encryption scheme that allows to compute (selected) functions of the plaintexts by having access to the encrypted data only. In other words, given a target function f we want to construct an encryption scheme E and a public function F such that if $X_1 = E(K, x_1)$ and $X_2 = E(K, x_2)$ (for a random key K) then we have that $F(X_1, X_2) = f(x_1, x_2)$.

Work done while visiting Aarhus University.

© Springer International Publishing AG 2017
M. O'Neill (Ed.): IMACC 2017, LNCS 10655, pp. 3–22, 2017.
https://doi.org/10.1007/978-3-319-71045-7_1

Order Preserving Encryption. The first attempt towards building RE was taken by Agrawal et al. [AKSX04] when they introduced *order preserving encryption (OPE)*, which using our language can be phrased as the very special case of RE where both f and F are numeric comparison. The "preserving" part of OPE is both a strength and a weakness: since $f = F$ it is very easy to use OPE in practical applications (a client outsourcing an encrypted database using OPE does not even need to inform the server that the database is encrypted, as the database can compare encrypted data in the exact same way as it would compare plaintext data). Unfortunately preserving numeric ordering implies that OPE cannot achieve strong security guarantees, as shown by [BCLO09,BCO11]. To overcome this limitation order revealing encryption (ORE) was introduced by Boneh et al. [BLR+15]. The main conceptual contributions of this paper is to generalize the notion of ORE to arbitrary functions (the formal definition of RE is given in Sect. 3).

While the first (fully-secure) ORE schemes could only be instantiated using extremely heavy cryptographic tools (see below) and were therefore completely impractical, Chenette et al. [CLWW16] proposed a very elegant and simple construction of ORE which is extremely efficient in practice (at the price of leaking slightly more information than in the ideal case).

Obfuscation & Co. On the other end of the scale, it is trivial to construct secure RE for any function using *ideal circuit obfuscation*. In a nutshell, one can let F be an obfuscated circuit that takes as input two ciphertexts X_1, X_2, contains a (hardwired) secret key K, and outputs

$$F(X_1, X_2) = f(D(K, X_1), D(K, X_2))$$

i.e., the obfuscated program simply outputs the output of f evaluated on the result of the decryption of its inputs.

Unfortunately general purpose *ideal obfuscation* or even *virtual black-box obfuscation* does not exist [BGI+01]. While a weaker notion of obfuscation (called *indistinguishability obfuscation*), might be plausibly instantiated under cryptographic assumptions (as shown by the fascinating research direction started by Garg et al. [GGH+13]), it seems unlikely that this will turn into a practical solution in the foreseeable future. Note that using obfuscation it is possible to instantiate *multi-input functional encryption (MIFE)* [GGG+14, BLR+15,BKS16]: using MIFE, one can implement RE in a similar way as we sketched above, where the obfuscated program is replaced by a MIFE secret key sk_f for the function f.

Note that despite the fact that MIFE implies RE, RE does not imply MIFE[1]. It is therefore plausible that RE can be instantiated *more efficiently* and *under weaker assumptions* than MIFE, and our results show that this is indeed the case.

---

[1] A MIFE scheme must not reveal any information (e.g., satisfy IND-CPA security) until a secret key for a function f is released, while in an RE scheme anyone can compute the authorized function on the encrypted data.

Our Contributions. Given the state of affairs, it is natural to ask:

*For which functions can we construct practically
efficient revealing encryption (RE) schemes?*

In this paper we begin answering the question by showing a construction of revealing encryption for partial order of vectors. This is a naturally interesting function motivated by concrete applications such as *privacy-preserving skyline queries* [BKS01, PTFS03] (or enhancing privacy in any other algorithm based on the partial order relation). In particular, given a dataset of d-dimensional vectors, the goal of a skyline query is to determine the set of dominating vectors. As a classic example, in a skyline query a client (e.g., a department committee) wants to evaluate a number of different offers (e.g., job candidates for a faculty position) based on a set of incomparable parameters (e.g., teaching experience, research output, funding, etc.). In this case the department committee is interested in evaluating all candidates for which there does not exist another candidate who is better qualified *under all parameters*, which is exactly the output of a skyline query. Using RE it is possible to compute the output of a skyline query by performing the partial-comparison directly in the encrypted domain i.e., without having to first decrypt the vectors. We note that there are plenty of protocols and algorithms in the computer science literature which use the partial ordering relation (lattice-based access control, timestamps based on vector clocks, topological ordering, etc.), and we therefore believe that the notion of RE for partial order is as natural as the case of RE for the total order relation.

Note that the notion of revealing encryption has also been independently introduced by Joye and Passelgue [JP16]. (Interestingly, we came to the notion of RE by generalizing ORE while they reached the same notion by simplifying 2-input FE). In their work they present RE constructions for functions different than those considered in this paper, including: comparison (ORE), orthogonality testing and cardinality of intersection.

Technical Overview. The starting point of our solution is the recent ORE scheme of Chenette et al. [CLWW16]. In this scheme, a value $x \in \{0,1\}^n$ is encrypted using n evaluations of a pseudorandom function (PRF) F_K for key K, i.e., for each index $i = 1, \ldots, n$ the encryption algorithm outputs a value

$$c_i = F_K(i, \mathsf{prefix}(x, i-1)) + x_i$$

where $\mathsf{prefix}(x, i)$ is the function that outputs the i most significant bits of x, x_i is the ith most significant bit, and where $+$ is integer addition.

Now, take two values x and y and let i^* be the largest index such that

$$\mathsf{prefix}(x, i^* - 1) = \mathsf{prefix}(y, i^* - 1)$$

i.e., i^* is the smallest index such that $x_{i^*} \neq y_{i^*}$. Then the first $i^* - 1$ ciphertexts will be identical for both x, y (since the PRF is evaluated on exactly the same value, and the added bit is the same), while the i^*-th ciphertext will be "in the right order" (since the PRF is evaluated on exactly the same value but in only one of the two cases 1 will be added) and therefore one can compare x and y by finding the first ciphertext component in which the encryptions differ and perform a simple numerical comparison of this value. For security, note that the bottom $n - i^* - 1$ ciphertexts will be independently random since the PRF is evaluated on different values. Therefore, the scheme reveals the order as well as the first position in which the value differs. A very recent work shows that it is possible to limit this leakage [CLOZ16], but unfortunately their construction requires heavy public key operations (we believe that similar techniques could be applied to our scheme as well).

In a nutshell, we generalize the construction presented by Chenette et al. [CLWW16] in the following way: consider for simplicity the 2-dimensional case $x = (x_1, x_2)$. Then for each pair of indices i, j we compute

$$c_{i,j} = F_K\left(i, j, \mathsf{prefix}(x_1, i - 1), \mathsf{prefix}(x_2, j - 1)\right) + \alpha_{i,j}(x_1, x_2)$$

where $\alpha_{i,j}$ is a carefully chosen function that allows to perform the comparison between two vectors in such a way that no information is leaked when the vectors are incomparable. The main challenge in coming up with the right function α, is that we are trying to encode a non-binary output (i.e., $x = y$, $x > y$, $x < y$, or incomparable) into a binary relation (i.e., the numerical comparison between the scalars $\alpha(x)$ and $\alpha(y)$). Details of the constructions are given in Sect. 4 and in Appendix A we give a performance analysis of our scheme.

Revealing Encryption Beyond Partial Ordering. We think that discovering which functions admit revealing encryption schemes is an exciting and important future research direction. In the full version [HJL+16], we discuss simple (unconditionally secure) examples of revealing encryptions for *absolute distance* and for *hamming distance* (which unfortunately is only secure for a limited number of queries).

Other related work. During recent years, OPE and ORE have been active research areas: Bun and Zhandry [BZ16] have studied the connection between ORE and differentially private learning [DMNS06, KLN+11]. Concurrent with this work, Lewi and Wu [LW16] presented a new and efficient ORE construction based on the work of Chenette et al. [CLWW16]. This construction splits the message in blocks (i.e. a sequence of bits) and the scheme leaks the position of the first block in which the messages differ. Roche et al. [RACY16] proposed a new primitive called *partial order preserving encoding*, which achieves ideal OPE security (IND-OCPA [BCLO09]) while providing fast insertion and search in an encrypted database. Furthermore, *interactive* OPE [PLZ13, KS14, Ker15] was introduced to achieve stronger security guarantees (like ideal security) for OPE schemes. In these schemes, ciphertexts are mutable, meaning that whenever a new value is encrypted the existing ciphertexts can be updated.

During the last couple of decades there has been a long line of work concerning encryption schemes, where either the ciphertexts preserve some information about the underlying messages or it is possible to perform a public test that reveals some information about the encrypted data: *searchable encryption* [SWP00, GSW04, BBO07, BHJP14] allows users to outsource their data in a private manner, while maintaining the possibility to do efficient search over it. Variants of searchable encryption are *public-key encryption with keyword search* [BCOP03, CGKO06], *secure indexes* [Goh03], and *(privacy-preserving) attribute-based searchable encryption* [WLLX13, KHY13, ZXA14, CD15b]. Other related encryption schemes are *prefix preservering encryption* [XFAM02, XY12] and *format preserving encryption* [BRRS09, WRB15], which are concerned with preserving some specific information about the encrypted data. *Property preserving symmetric encryption* [PR12, CD15a] is a generalization of OPE that enables users to learn the properties of a massive data set.

The applications of RE schemes is closely related to the applications of encryption schemes, like *attribute-based encryption* [GPSW06, GVW13], *functional encryption* [BSW11], *predicate encryption* [KSW08], *(anonymous) identity-based encryption* [Sha84, KSW08], and *access control encryption* [DHO16]. All these encryption schemes deal with payload privacy, user privacy, computation on outsourced encrypted data, fine-grained access control on data, etc.

Finally, in the full version [HJL+16], we review the (in)security of some existing systems which offer alternative solutions to *privacy-preserving skyline queries*.

2 Preliminaries

For $n, n_1, n_2 \in \mathbb{N}$, let $[n_1 : n_2]$ be the set $\{n_1, n_1 + 1, \ldots, n_2 - 1, n_2\}$ and $[n]$ be the set $[1 : n]$. For $x \in \mathbb{Z}$, let $|x|$ denote the absolute value of x. Let $x \leftarrow_\$ S$ denote that x is sampled uniform random from the set S.

Definition 1 (Pseudorandom Function). *We say that $F : \{0,1\}^\kappa \times \{0,1\}^* \to \{0,1\}^\kappa$ is a pseudorandom function (PRF) if for all PPT adversaries $\mathcal{A}$*

$$adv_\mathcal{A} = 2 \cdot |\Pr[\mathcal{A}^{\mathcal{O}_b(\cdot)}(1^\kappa) = b] - 1/2| < negl(\kappa)$$

with $\mathcal{O}_0$ a uniform random function and $\mathcal{O}_1 = F_K$ for some key $K \in \{0,1\}^\kappa$.

We interpret $x \in \{0,1\}^n$ both as a string of bits i.e. $x = (x_1, \ldots, x_n)$ and as an integer $x = \sum_{i=0}^{n-1} 2^i x_{n-i}$ i.e., x_1 is the most significant bit of x. Given such an x and an index $i \in [n]$ it is convenient to define the function prefix : $\{0,1\}^n \times [0 : n] \to \{0,1\}^n \times [0 : n]$

$$\mathsf{prefix}(x, i) := (x_1, \ldots, x_i, 0^{n-i}, i)$$

so that $\mathsf{prefix}(x, 0) = (0^n, 0)$, $\mathsf{prefix}(x, 1) = (x_1, 0^{n-1}, 1)$ and so on. Note that prefix has the useful property that for all $x \in \{0,1\}^n$ $\mathsf{prefix}(x, i) \neq \mathsf{prefix}(x, j)$ if $i \neq j$. Given a d-dimensional vector $\boldsymbol{m} = (x_1, \ldots, x_d) \in (\{0,1\}^n)^d$ we define prefix to output the vector[2]

$$\mathsf{prefix}(\boldsymbol{m}, (i_1, \ldots, i_d)) := (\mathsf{prefix}(x_\mathbf{1}, i_1), \ldots, \mathsf{prefix}(x_\mathbf{d}, i_d)).$$

---

[2] To ease the notation we use bold subscripts to indicate the entries in the vector.

Given two strings $x, y \in \{0,1\}^n$ we define $\mathsf{pos}(x,y)$ to return the largest i such that $\mathsf{prefix}(x, i-1) = \mathsf{prefix}(y, i-1)$ or equivalently the smallest i such that $x_i \neq y_i$. If $x = y$, then we define $\mathsf{pos}(x,y)$ to output $n+1$. Given two d-dimensional vectors $\boldsymbol{m}^{(1)} = (x_1^{(1)}, \ldots, x_d^{(1)}), \boldsymbol{m}^{(2)} = (x_1^{(2)}, \ldots, x_d^{(2)})$ we define pos to output the vector

$$\mathsf{pos}(\boldsymbol{m}^{(1)}, \boldsymbol{m}^{(2)}) := (\mathsf{pos}(x_1^{(1)}, x_1^{(2)}), \ldots, \mathsf{pos}(x_d^{(1)}, x_d^{(2)})).$$

3   Revealing Encryption

In this section we formally define Revealing Encryption (RE).

Authorized Function. Let $\mathcal{M}$ be the input space and $\mathcal{I}$ the output space, then a RE scheme is parametrized by ℓ-ary authorized function

$$f : \mathcal{M}^\ell \to \mathcal{I}.$$

Revealing Encryption. Given an authorized function f, a RE scheme for f is a triple of algorithms $\Pi_f = (\mathsf{Setup}, \mathsf{Enc}, \mathsf{Eval})$ defined as follows:

Setup: On input the security parameter κ, the randomized algorithm Setup outputs a secret key sk and the public parameters pp.

Encryption: On input a message $m \in \mathcal{M}$ and a secret key sk, the randomized algorithm Enc outputs a ciphertext c.

Eval: On input ℓ ciphertexts $\{c_i = \mathsf{Enc}(sk, m_i)\}_{i \in [\ell]}$ and the public parameters pp, the Eval algorithm outputs $f(m_1, \ldots, m_\ell) \in \mathcal{I}$.

Remark 1. Note that here and in the rest of the paper we do not mention the decryption algorithm, since any RE can be enhanced to allow for decryption by appending an IND-CPA secure encryption to the RE ciphertext.

Definition 2 (Correctness). *Let f be an authorized function and κ be the security parameter. Let $\Pi_f = (\mathsf{Setup}, \mathsf{Enc}, \mathsf{Eval})$ be a RE scheme for f. We say that Π_f is correct if for all messages $\{m_i\}_{i \in [\ell]} \in \mathcal{M}^\ell$ the following probability*

$$\Pr\left[\mathsf{Eval}\left(pp, \{\mathsf{Enc}(sk, m_i)\}_{i \in [\ell]}\right) \neq f\left(\{m_i\}_{i \in [\ell]}\right)\right]$$

is negligible in κ, where $(sk, pp) \leftarrow \mathsf{Setup}(1^\kappa)$ and the probabilities are taken over the random coins of all algorithms.

Leakage Function. Following the work of Chenette et al. [CLWW16], our definition also allows for a leakage function $\mathcal{L} : \mathcal{M}^* \to \{0,1\}^*$ that exactly characterizes the information leaked by our constructions. In the best case $\mathcal{L}(\{m_i\}_{i \in [q]})$ outputs $f(\{m_j\}_{j \in S})$ for every subset $S \subset [q]$ of size ℓ, and in this case we talk about *optimal leakage*. Note that the work of Chenette et al. leaks extra information as well (the first digit at which two integers x, y are different) and our main construction inherits this leakage.

Definition 3 (Security, [CLWW16]). *Let κ be the security parameter, let $q \in \mathbb{N}$, and let f be an authorized function. Let $\Pi_f = (\mathsf{Setup}, \mathsf{Enc}, \mathsf{Eval})$ be a RE scheme for f. Consider the following experiments, where $\mathcal{A} = (\mathcal{A}_1, \ldots, \mathcal{A}_q)$ is an adversary, $\mathcal{S} = (\mathcal{S}_0, \ldots, \mathcal{S}_q)$ is a simulator, and $\mathcal{L}(\cdot)$ is a leakage function.*

Security Experiments	
$\mathsf{REAL}_{\mathcal{A}}^{\Pi_f}(\kappa)$:	$\mathsf{IDEAL}_{\mathcal{A},\mathcal{S},\mathcal{L}}^{\Pi_f}(\kappa)$:
1. $(sk, pp) \leftarrow \mathsf{Setup}(1^\kappa)$;	1. $(\mathsf{st}_\mathcal{S}, pp) \leftarrow \mathcal{S}_0(1^\kappa)$;
2. $(m_1, \mathsf{st}_\mathcal{A}) \leftarrow \mathcal{A}_1(1^\kappa, pp)$;	2. $(m_1, \mathsf{st}_\mathcal{A}) \leftarrow \mathcal{A}_1(1^\kappa, pp)$;
3. $c_1 \leftarrow \mathsf{Enc}(sk, m_1)$;	3. $(c_1, \mathsf{st}_\mathcal{S}) \leftarrow \mathcal{S}_1(\mathsf{st}_\mathcal{S}, \mathcal{L}(m_1))$;
4. for $2 \leq i \leq q$;	4. for $2 \leq i \leq q$;
a. $(m_i, \mathsf{st}_\mathcal{A}) \leftarrow \mathcal{A}_i(\mathsf{st}_\mathcal{A}, c_1, \ldots, c_{i-1})$;	a. $(m_i, \mathsf{st}_\mathcal{A}) \leftarrow \mathcal{A}_i(\mathsf{st}_\mathcal{A}, c_1, \ldots, c_{i-1})$;
b. $c_i \leftarrow \mathsf{Enc}(sk, m_i)$;	b. $(c_i, \mathsf{st}_\mathcal{S}) \leftarrow \mathcal{S}_i(\mathsf{st}_\mathcal{S}, \mathcal{L}(m_1, \ldots, m_i))$;
5. output $(c_1, \ldots, c_q)$ and $\mathsf{st}_\mathcal{A}$;	5. output $(c_1, \ldots, c_q)$ and $\mathsf{st}_\mathcal{A}$;

We say that Π_f is a q-secure RE scheme wrt $\mathcal{L}(\cdot)$ if for all adversaries $\mathcal{A}$ that makes no more than q queries, there exists a simulator $\mathcal{S}$ such that the output distributions of the two experiments are computationally indistinguishable

$$\mathsf{REAL}_{\mathcal{A}}^{\Pi_f}(\kappa) \sim^c \mathsf{IDEAL}_{\mathcal{A},\mathcal{S},\mathcal{L}}^{\Pi_f}(\kappa)$$

We say a scheme is simply secure if it is q-secure for every $q = poly(\kappa)$.

Definition 3 captures the requirement that given an a priori bounded number of ciphertexts, the adversary should not be able to learn more than the allowed leakage. The security experiments formalize this requirement by creating the challenge ciphertexts either as real encryptions of the adversarial chosen plaintexts or simulated based on the allowed leakage of the adversarial chosen plaintexts. Note that the output of the experiment contains an arbitrary output from the adversary (i.e., $\mathsf{st}_\mathcal{A}$), which is a very conservative way of allowing the adversary to output any information that might be useful to distinguish between the ideal experiment and the real experiment.

4   Partial Order Revealing Encryption (PORE)

In this section, we present a construction of revealing encryption for partial ordering of vectors. For the sake of presentation, we will start by showing our construction in the 2-dimensional case (which already requires a significant amount of notation and indices). In the full version [HJL+16], we generalize to the multidimensional case. Let $\mathcal{M} = \{0, 1\}^n \times \{0, 1\}^n$ be the message domain, and the authorized function for a 2-dimensional PORE is

$$f : \mathcal{M} \times \mathcal{M} \rightarrow \{(0, 0), (0, 1), (1, 0), (1, 1)\}$$

For $\boldsymbol{m}^{(1)} = (x^{(1)}, y^{(1)}) \in \mathcal{M}$ and $\boldsymbol{m}^{(2)} = (x^{(2)}, y^{(2)}) \in \mathcal{M}$ we define a function that determines the order

$$\mathsf{ord}(\boldsymbol{m}^{(1)}, \boldsymbol{m}^{(2)}) := \begin{cases} 1 & \text{if } x^{(1)} \leq x^{(2)} \wedge y^{(1)} \leq y^{(2)} \\ 0 & \text{otherwise} \end{cases}$$

Then we can define the authorized function as

$$f(\boldsymbol{m}^{(1)}, \boldsymbol{m}^{(2)}) := (\text{ord}(\boldsymbol{m}^{(1)}, \boldsymbol{m}^{(2)}), \text{ord}(\boldsymbol{m}^{(2)}, \boldsymbol{m}^{(1)}))$$

which means that

$$f(\boldsymbol{m}^{(1)}, \boldsymbol{m}^{(2)}) := \begin{cases} (1,1) & \text{if } \boldsymbol{m}^{(1)} = \boldsymbol{m}^{(2)} \\ (1,0) & \text{if } \boldsymbol{m}^{(1)} < \boldsymbol{m}^{(2)} \\ (0,1) & \text{if } \boldsymbol{m}^{(1)} > \boldsymbol{m}^{(2)} \\ (0,0) & \text{if they are incomparable} \end{cases}$$

We will prove the security of our scheme with respect to the following leakage function (with f as defined above and pos as defined in Sect. 2):

$$\mathcal{L}(\boldsymbol{m}^{(1)}, \cdots, \boldsymbol{m}^{(q)}) = \left\{ f(\boldsymbol{m}^{(i)}, \boldsymbol{m}^{(j)}), \text{pos}(\boldsymbol{m}^{(I)}, \boldsymbol{m}^{(j)}) \mid i, j \in [q] \right\}$$

i.e. the construction reveals the order as well as the first position in which each coordinate differ.

Given a pseudorandom function $F : \{0,1\}^\kappa \times \{0,1\}^* \to \{0,1\}^\kappa$, we define the following four functions:

$$F_{1,K}, F_{2,K} : \mathcal{M} \times [n+1]^2 \to \{0,1,2\}$$
$$F_{3,K}, F_{4,K} : \{0,1\}^n \times [n] \to \{0,1\}$$

where given a plaintext $\boldsymbol{m} = (x, y) \in \mathcal{M}$ and two indices $i, j \in [n+1]$ we define

$$F_{1,K}(\boldsymbol{m}, (i,j)) = F_K(1, \text{prefix}(x, i-1), \text{prefix}(y, j-1)) \mod 3$$
$$F_{2,K}(\boldsymbol{m}, (i,j)) = F_K(2, \text{prefix}(x, i-1), \text{prefix}(y, j-1)) \mod 3$$
$$F_{3,K}(x, i) = F_K(3, \text{prefix}(x, i-1)) \mod 2$$
$$F_{4,K}(y, j) = F_K(4, \text{prefix}(y, j-1)) \mod 2$$

On a high level, the construction works as follows: given a point $\boldsymbol{m} = (x, y)$ and a key K for the pseudorandom function F, then the ciphertext consist of a two-dimensional matrix $\boldsymbol{cm} \in \{0,1,2\}^{(n+1)\times(n+1)}$ and two bit strings $bx, by \in \{0,1\}^n$ (i.e. one bit string for each entry in the point). These bit strings are constructed to fulfil the property: given encryptions of two points, we can for each entry (x and y) determine at which position they differ, but without revealing the order. These positions can then be used to look up an entry in the matrix $\boldsymbol{cm}$, which will determine the partial order of the two points.

Construction 1. *Fix a security parameter $\kappa \in \mathbb{N}$. We define a PORE scheme for two dimensions $\Pi_{\mathsf{PORE}} = (\mathsf{Setup}, \mathsf{Enc}, \mathsf{Eval})$ as follows*

Setup: On input $\kappa \in \mathbb{N}$, sample and output a key $K \leftarrow_\$ \{0,1\}^\kappa$.
Encryption: Given a point $\boldsymbol{m} = (x, y) \in \mathcal{M}$ and a secret key K compute for all $i, j \in [n+1]$

$$cm_{i,j} = F_{2,K}(\boldsymbol{m}, (i,j)) + \alpha(\boldsymbol{m}, (i,j)) \mod 3$$

where α is a function defined as follows

$$\alpha\left(\boldsymbol{m},(i,j)\right) := \begin{cases} 0 & \text{if } (x_i, y_j) = (0,0) \\ 1 & \text{if } (x_i, y_j) = (1,1) \\ x_i & \text{if } i \leqslant n, j = n+1 \\ y_j & \text{if } i = n+1, j \leqslant n \\ 0 & \text{if } i = n+1, j = n+1 \\ z_{i,j} & \text{otherwise} \end{cases}$$

where $z_{i,j} = F_{1,K}(\boldsymbol{m},(i,j))$. Next, we compute for all $i, j \in [n]$

$$bx_i = F_{3,K}(x,i) + x_i \mod 2$$
$$by_j = F_{4,K}(y,j) + y_j \mod 2$$

Then, output the ciphertext $C = (\boldsymbol{cm}, bx, by)$, where

$$\boldsymbol{cm} := (cm_{i,j})_{i,j\in[n+1]} \in \{0,1,2\}^{(n+1)\times(n+1)}$$
$$bx := (bx_1, \ldots, bx_n) \in \{0,1\}^n$$
$$by := (by_1, \ldots, by_n) \in \{0,1\}^n$$

Evaluation: On input two ciphertexts

$$C^{(1)} = (\boldsymbol{cm}^{(1)}, bx^{(1)}, by^{(1)}) = \mathsf{Enc}(K, \boldsymbol{m}^{(1)})$$
$$C^{(2)} = (\boldsymbol{cm}^{(2)}, bx^{(2)}, by^{(2)}) = \mathsf{Enc}(K, \boldsymbol{m}^{(2)})$$

Compute $\mathsf{pos}(bx^{(1)}, bx^{(2)}) = \ell_x$ and $\mathsf{pos}(by^{(1)}, by^{(2)}) = \ell_y$. If $\ell_x = n+1$ and $\ell_y = n+1$, the algorithm outputs $(1,1)$ (since $\boldsymbol{m}^{(1)} = \boldsymbol{m}^{(2)}$). Otherwise, lookup the two entries $cm^{(1)}_{\ell_x,\ell_y}$ and $cm^{(2)}_{\ell_x,\ell_y}$ and compute

$$t = cm^{(1)}_{\ell_x,\ell_y} - cm^{(2)}_{\ell_x,\ell_y} \mod 3$$

Next, the algorithm branches on the value of t:
  If $t = -1$, output $(1,0)$ (since $\boldsymbol{m}^{(1)} < \boldsymbol{m}^{(2)}$);
  If $t = 1$, output $(0,1)$ (since $\boldsymbol{m}^{(1)} > \boldsymbol{m}^{(2)}$);
  Otherwise output $(0,0)$, since the two points are *incomparable*.

Correctness. Let $\boldsymbol{m}^{(1)} = (x^{(1)}, y^{(1)})$ and $\boldsymbol{m}^{(2)} = (x^{(2)}, y^{(2)})$ be two plaintexts such that

$$\mathsf{pos}(\boldsymbol{m}^{(1)}, \boldsymbol{m}^{(2)}) = (\ell_x, \ell_y)$$

(i.e. $x^{(1)}$ and $x^{(2)}$ differ at position ℓ_x and $y^{(1)}$ and $y^{(2)}$ differ at position ℓ_y). We consider the encryptions of these messages

$$C^{(1)} = (\boldsymbol{cm}^{(1)}, bx^{(1)}, by^{(1)}) = \mathsf{Enc}(K, \boldsymbol{m}^{(1)})$$
$$C^{(2)} = (\boldsymbol{cm}^{(2)}, bx^{(2)}, by^{(2)}) = \mathsf{Enc}(K, \boldsymbol{m}^{(2)})$$

We first argue that $bx_i^{(1)} = bx_i^{(2)}$ for $i < \ell_x$. This is easy to see:

$$
\begin{aligned}
bx_i^{(1)} &= F_{3,K}(x^{(1)}, i) + x_i^{(1)} \quad \mathrm{mod}\ 2 \\
&= F_K(3, \mathsf{prefix}(x^{(1)}, i-1)) + x_i^{(1)} \quad \mathrm{mod}\ 2 \\
&= F_K(3, \mathsf{prefix}(x^{(2)}, i-1)) + x_i^{(2)} \quad \mathrm{mod}\ 2 \\
&= bx_i^{(2)}
\end{aligned}
$$

Since by definition of ℓ_x we know that $\forall i < \ell_x$, $\mathsf{prefix}(x^{(1)}, i-1) = \mathsf{prefix}(x^{(2)}, i-1)$ and $x_i^{(1)} = x_i^{(2)}$. The same can be argued about the y part. We then argue that if $\ell_x < n + 1$, then there $\exists i < n + 1$ such that $bx_i^{(1)} \neq bx_i^{(2)}$. This is easy to see since by definition of ℓ_x the output of prefix is the same but $x_{\ell_x}^{(1)} \neq x_{\ell_x}^{(2)}$.

So, we turn our attention to the comparison between $cm_{\ell_x,\ell_y}^{(1)}$ and $cm_{\ell_x,\ell_y}^{(2)}$ by computing

$$
t = cm_{\ell_x,\ell_y}^{(1)} - cm_{\ell_x,\ell_y}^{(2)} \quad \mathrm{mod}\ 3
$$

Note that by definition of ℓ_x, ℓ_y, the output of prefix is the same for both ciphertexts and therefore the output of $F_{2,K}$ is the same so we can rewrite this as

$$
t = \alpha(m^{(1)}, (\ell_x, \ell_y)) - \alpha(m^{(2)}, (\ell_x, \ell_y)) \quad \mathrm{mod}\ 3
$$

We now have the following cases:

1. $\ell_x < n + 1 \wedge \ell_y < n + 1$: In this case we know that $x_{\ell_x}^{(1)} \neq x_{\ell_x}^{(2)} \wedge y_{\ell_y}^{(1)} \neq y_{\ell_y}^{(2)}$, which means that we are either in the case (comparable)

$$
\begin{aligned}
(x_{\ell_x}^{(1)}, y_{\ell_y}^{(1)}) = (0,0), \quad (x_{\ell_x}^{(2)}, y_{\ell_y}^{(2)}) = (1,1) \quad &\text{or} \\
(x_{\ell_x}^{(1)}, y_{\ell_y}^{(1)}) = (1,1), \quad (x_{\ell_x}^{(2)}, y_{\ell_y}^{(2)}) = (0,0)
\end{aligned}
$$

or (incomparable)

$$
\begin{aligned}
(x_{\ell_x}^{(1)}, y_{\ell_y}^{(1)}) = (0,1), \quad (x_{\ell_x}^{(2)}, y_{\ell_y}^{(2)}) = (1,0) \quad &\text{or} \\
(x_{\ell_x}^{(1)}, y_{\ell_y}^{(1)}) = (1,0), \quad (x_{\ell_x}^{(2)}, y_{\ell_y}^{(2)}) = (0,1)
\end{aligned}
$$

In the comparable case we have that one of the α is 1 and the other is 0. When we are in the case $m^{(1)} < m^{(2)}$ (i.e. the first of the two comparable cases), then we have that $\alpha(m^{(1)}, (\ell_x, \ell_y)) = 0$ and $\alpha(m^{(2)}, (\ell_x, \ell_y)) = 1$, thus $t = -1$ and the evaluation algorithm will output $(1,0)$ meaning that $m^{(1)} < m^{(2)}$. Similar, we argue that the evaluation algorithm correctly outputs $(0,1)$ (since $t = 1$) when $m^{(1)} > m^{(2)}$.

In the incomparable case we have that $t = 0$ since the value $z_{i,j}$ is the same in both cases (since as argued before prefix's output is the same and so is $F_{1,K}$'s output).

2. $\ell_x = n + 1 \wedge \ell_y < n + 1$: following a similar reasoning in this case $x_{\ell_x}^{(1)} = x_{\ell_x}^{(2)} \wedge y_{\ell_y}^{(1)} \neq y_{\ell_y}^{(2)}$ therefore $t = y_{\ell_y}^{(1)} - y_{\ell_y}^{(2)} = -1$ when $\boldsymbol{m}^{(1)} < \boldsymbol{m}^{(2)}$, and $t = 1$ when $\boldsymbol{m}^{(1)} > \boldsymbol{m}^{(2)}$.

3. $\ell_x < n + 1 \wedge \ell_y = n + 1$: following a similar reasoning in this case $x_{\ell_x}^{(1)} \neq x_{\ell_x}^{(2)} \wedge y_{\ell_y}^{(1)} = y_{\ell_y}^{(2)}$ therefore $t = x_{\ell_y}^{(1)} - x_{\ell_y}^{(2)} = -1$ when $\boldsymbol{m}^{(1)} < \boldsymbol{m}^{(2)}$, and $t = 1$ when $\boldsymbol{m}^{(1)} > \boldsymbol{m}^{(2)}$.

4. $\ell_x = n + 1 \wedge \ell_y = n + 1$: by the definition of the pos function this means that $\boldsymbol{m}^{(1)} = \boldsymbol{m}^{(2)}$, and by definition the evaluation algorithm will output $(1, 1)$ meaning that the two messages are equal.

4.1   Security

To prove the security of the construction, we present a simulator that constructs the ciphertexts based on information provided by the leakage function and the previous generated ciphertext.

On a high level the simulator works as follows: each component of the ciphertext $C^{(i)}$ is generated using the leakage $\mathcal{L}(\boldsymbol{m}^{(1)}, \ldots, \boldsymbol{m}^{(i)})$. For each $j < i$, the leakage reveals at which position ℓ_x (resp. ℓ_y) the messages $\boldsymbol{m}^{(i)}$ and $\boldsymbol{m}^{(j)}$ differ for coordinate x (resp. y) and the partial order of the messages. Given this information, we can construct the entries $cm_{\ell_x,\ell_y}^{(i)}$, $bx_{\ell_x}^{(i)}$ and $by_{\ell_y}^{(i)}$ in $\boldsymbol{cm}^{(i)}$, $\boldsymbol{bx}^{(i)}$ and $\boldsymbol{by}^{(i)}$ such that they reveal the order. Next, for each entry $cm_{s,t}^{(i)}$, $bx_s^{(i)}$ and $by_t^{(i)}$ with $s < \ell_x$ and $t < \ell_y$, the content of the entry will be equivalent to (some of) the previous generated ciphertexts (which are contained in the state of the simulator), since the encryption algorithm uses a pseudorandom function. Finally, for each entry $cm_{s,t}^{(i)}$, $bx_s^{(i)}$ and $by_t^{(i)}$ with $s > \ell_x$ and $t > \ell_y$, the content of the entry will be generated uniformly at random, since the corresponding input to the pesudorandom function has never been used before.

Simulator. Denote the adversarial chosen message as $\boldsymbol{m}^{(1)}, \cdots, \boldsymbol{m}^{(q)}$, where $\boldsymbol{m}^{(i)} = (x^{(i)}, y^{(i)}) \in \mathcal{M}$. Initially, simulator $\mathcal{S}_0$ is empty and $\mathcal{S}_1$ sets $C^{(1)} = (\boldsymbol{cm}^{(1)}, \boldsymbol{bx}^{(1)}, \boldsymbol{by}^{(1)})$, where $\boldsymbol{cm}^{(1)}, \boldsymbol{bx}^{(1)}, \boldsymbol{by}^{(1)}$ are all drawn uniformly at random. Furthermore, it sets the state $\mathsf{st}_{\mathcal{S}} = (C^{(1)})$. Next, define the simulator $\mathcal{S}_i$ (for $2 \leq i \leq q$) as in Fig. 1.

Theorem 1. *The RE scheme Π_{PORE} from Construction 1 is secure with leakage function $\mathcal{L}$.*

The complete proof of Theorem 1 is presented in the full version of the paper [HJL+16].

$$(C^{(i)}, \mathsf{st}_\mathcal{S}) \leftarrow \mathcal{S}_i(\mathsf{st}_\mathcal{S}, \mathcal{L}(\boldsymbol{m}^{(1)}, \dots, \boldsymbol{m}^{(i)}))$$

For all $j < i$ we have that $\mathsf{pos}(\boldsymbol{m}^{(i)}, \boldsymbol{m}^{(j)}) = (\ell_x^{(j)}, \ell_y^{(j)})$ is provided by $\mathcal{L}(\boldsymbol{m}^{(1)}, \dots, \boldsymbol{m}^{(i)})$.

For each $s, t \in [n+1]$ define entry $cm_{s,t}^{(i)} \in \boldsymbol{cm}^{(i)}$ as:

1. If $\exists j < i$ such that $\ell_x^{(j)} > s$ and $\ell_y^{(j)} > t$, then set $cm_{s,t}^{(i)} := cm_{s,t}^{(j)}$.
2. Else if $\exists j < i$ such that $\ell_x^{(j)} = s$ and $\ell_y^{(j)} = t$, then
   - if $\boldsymbol{m}^{(i)} > \boldsymbol{m}^{(j)}$, set $cm_{s,t}^{(i)} := cm_{s,t}^{(j)} + 1 \mod 3$;
   - if $\boldsymbol{m}^{(i)} < \boldsymbol{m}^{(j)}$, set $cm_{s,t}^{(i)} := cm_{s,t}^{(j)} - 1 \mod 3$;
   - if they are incomparable, set $cm_{s,t}^{(i)} := cm_{s,t}^{(j)}$.
3. Else set $cm_{s,t}^{(i)} \leftarrow_\$ \{0, 1, 2\}$.

For each $s \in [n]$ define entry $bx_s^{(i)} \in \boldsymbol{bx}^{(i)}$ as:

4. If $\exists j < i$ such that $\ell_x^{(j)} > s$, then set $bx_s^{(i)} := bx_s^{(j)}$.
5. Else if $\exists j < i$ such that $\ell_x^{(j)} = s$, then set $bx_s^{(i)} := bx_s^{(j)} + 1 \mod 2$.
6. Else set $bx_s^{(i)} \leftarrow_\$ \{0, 1\}$.

For each $t \in [n]$ define entry $by_t^{(i)} \in \boldsymbol{by}^{(i)}$ as:

7. If $\exists j < i$ such that $\ell_y^{(j)} > t$, then set $by_t^{(i)} := by_t^{(j)}$.
8. Else if $\exists j < i$ such that $\ell_y^{(j)} = t$, then set $by_t^{(i)} := by_t^{(j)} + 1 \mod 2$.
9. Else set $by_t^{(i)} \leftarrow_\$ \{0, 1\}$.

Output $C^{(i)} = (\boldsymbol{cm}^{(i)}, bx^{(i)}, by^{(i)})$ and $\mathsf{st}_\mathcal{S} = (C^{(1)}, \dots, C^{(i)})$.

Fig. 1. Simulator $\mathcal{S}_i$ (for $2 \leq i \leq q$) for 2-dimensional PORE.

5 Conclusion

In this work, we introduced a generalization of order-revealing encryption (ORE) called revealing encryption (RE), which is an encryption scheme that allows to compute a (selected) function f of the plaintexts given only the encrypted data. We adopt the simulation-based security notion presented by Chenette et al. [CLWW16], which define security with respect to a leakage function. This enables one to determine the exact information that the ciphertexts leak about the underlying messages (which will always include the function f evaluated on all possible ciphertexts).

Revealing encryption is of special interest in relation to applications like computation or queries on outsourced encrypted data. However, these encryption schemes leak potentially sensitive information about the encrypted data depending on the actual application in which RE is used. This means that before using RE in a concrete application one should make a proper analysis to understand whether the leakage provided is problematic or not. A recent line of work has been concerned with attacking applications built on top of this kind of encryption schemes [NKW15, DDC16, GSB+17].

Acknowledgements. This research received funding from the Danish National Research Foundation and The National Science Foundation of China (grant 61361136003) for the Sino-Danish Center for the Theory of Interactive Computation (CTIC), the Danish Independent Research Council under Grant-ID DFF-6108-00169 (FoCC), and the European Union's Horizon 2020 research and innovation programme under grant agreement No 731583 (SODA).

Appendices

A   Efficiency of PORE

In this section we analyze the efficiency of our PORE construction.

A.1   Theoretical Efficiency

Let κ be the security parameter, d the number of dimensions and n the bit length of each entry. Then we can compute the storage and computational complexity of our scheme.

Storage Complexity. The bit length of a ciphertext in our PORE scheme is exactly:

$$1.6(n+1)^d + nd = O(n^d)$$

Computational Overhead. Performing an encryption requires

$$2(n+1)^d + nd = O(n^d)$$

calls to a PRF (with unbounded domain). Note that running the evaluation algorithm requires no invocation of the PRF (only d binary searches into vectors of n bits each and a single addition modulo 3).

A.2   Implementation Choices

In this section we describe the result of our experimental validation of the efficiency of our PORE scheme.

Plaintext Space. We have implemented our scheme for a range of parameters d and n. We report here the results for all combinations (d, n) with $d \in \{2, \ldots, 8\}$ and $n = 2^i$ for $i \in \{1, \ldots, 13\}$ s.t. the ciphertext size is less than 20 MB.

PRF Choice. We implement the PRF $F : \{0,1\}^\kappa \times \{0,1\}^* \to \{0,1\}^\kappa$ using AES-CBC mode, with key size $\kappa = 128$ bits. This is a particularly convenient choice thanks to the AES native instruction in modern CPUs.

Note that in the theoretical analysis we stated that the complexity of the encryption is $O(n^d)$ when measured as the number of calls to a PRF with unbounded domain. However in practice, when instantiating F with AES in CBC mode the running time (in terms of number of calls to AES) grows linearly with the number of blocks needed for the plaintext, namely $\lceil dn/128 \rceil$. Therefore, a naïve implementation would be significantly slower than promised. We notice, however, that thanks to the special structure of the inputs of our PRF it is possible to get rid of this extra factor. In particular, we note that in our matrix of ciphertexts we evaluate the PRF on inputs of the form

$$F_K(\mathsf{prefix}(x_1, i_1), \ldots, \mathsf{prefix}(x_d, i_d))$$

where each value $\mathsf{prefix}(x_k, i_k)$ is given as input to n different PRFs. Therefore we modify the way we evaluate the PRF by first precomputing

$$u_{k,i} = F_K^k(\mathsf{prefix}(x_k, i)) \; \forall k \in [d], i \in [n]$$

and then implement

$$F_K(\mathsf{prefix}(x_1, i_1), \ldots, \mathsf{prefix}(x_d, i_d)) = F_K^0(u_{1,i_1} \oplus \cdots \oplus u_{d,i_d})$$

so that the inputs to F_K^0 is of fixed length 128. Therefore (even adding the $O(n^2 d)$ extra AES invocations on "long" n-bit values used to precompute the u's), the total number of calls to AES and hence the running time is $O(n^d)$ as initially promised.

Note, the XOR operation over d strings takes $O(d)$ time. However, the points which are in the same position in the first k dimensions shares the value $u_{1,i_1} \oplus \cdots \oplus u_{k,i_k}$. By making these values reusable, we can reduce the amortized complexity to $\sum_{i=1}^d \frac{1}{n^{i-1}} = O(1)$.

A.3 Experimental Setup

The reported encryption timings (Table 1) are the average taken over 100 executions of the encryption algorithm. For the evaluation timings (Table 2), we randomly pick 500 pairs from the 100 ciphertexts and take the average of the 500 executions of the evaluation algorithm. To measure the size of the ciphertexts (Table 3), we keep track of the size of the required space each time the encryption algorithm applies the memory.

Hardware. The experiments were executed on a machine with the following characteristics:

- OS: Linux TitanX1 3.19.0-15-generic #15-Ubuntu SMP
- CPU: Intel(R) Xeon(R) CPU E5-2675 v3   1.80 GHz
- Memory: 128 GB
- GCC: gcc version 4.9.2 (Ubuntu 4.9.2-10ubuntu13) (Compile option -O2)

Table 1. Encryption time and standard deviation

d \ n	2	3	4	5
2	2.0 (±0.42) μs	4.0 (±0.61) μs	18.2 (±4.56) μs	45.1 (±7.53) μs
4	7.0 (±0.76) μs	23.9 (±1.98) μs	100.2 (±4.81) μs	411.4 (±36.60) μs
8	16.2 (±0.98) μs	107.5 (±4.31) μs	749.3 (±95.20) μs	5.6 (±0.60) ms
16	49.2 (±1.81) μs	622.3 (±63.24) μs	7.6 (±1.12) ms	110.6 (±6.49) ms
32	154.8 (±5.05) μs	3.5 (±0.37) ms	93.0 (±6.40) ms	3.2 (±0.01) s
64	546.8 (±47.95) μs	21.9 (±2.21) ms	1.4 (±0.01) s	
128	1.8 (±0.22) ms	162.5 (±8.32) ms		
256	6.5 (±0.83) ms	1.3 (±0.02) s		
512	21.8 (±2.53) ms			
1024	83.3 (±5.95) ms			
2048	326.5 (±7.58) ms			
4096	1.3 (±0.02) s			
8192	5.3 (±0.03) s			

d \ n	6	7	8	
2	124.1 (±7.18) μs	342.8 (±25.00) μs	744.3 (±21.90) μs	
4	1.6 (±0.22) ms	7.4 (±1.03) ms	33.7 (±4.03) ms	
8	39.3 (±0.59) ms	358.0 (±12.67) ms		
16	1.9 (±0.01) s			

A.4 Results

Encryption Complexity. Table 1 shows how long it takes to encrypt a single plaintext for different values of d and n. As expected, we observe that the encryption time grows as the dimension d and bit lengths n increases.

Evaluation Complexity. Note that the theoretically complexity of the evaluation algorithm is $O(d)$. However, the actual running time of the evaluation algorithm from Table 2 indicates that the algorithm is so fast that for most choices of parameters it is hard to appreciate the theoretical complexity.

When the combined size of all 100 ciphertext from the experiments does not exceed 6MB (i.e. each ciphertext does not exceed 60 kB), then all ciphertexts fits inside the L2 cache of the CPU. By observing the variation of the evaluation timings in Table 2 and the ciphertext size in Table 3, we can conclude that there is a tendency that when the ciphertexts fits inside the L2 cache, then the variation stays below 0.07 μs (this observation is indicated in the tables by splitting the columns in two).

Table 2. Evaluation time and standard deviation (μs)

d \ n	2	3	4	5
2	0.27 (±0.02)	0.56 (±0.05)	0.59 (±0.05)	0.62 (±0.06)
4	0.54 (±0.05)	0.57 (±0.05)	0.61 (±0.05)	0.54 (±0.06)
8	0.54 (±0.05)	0.58 (±0.06)	0.43 (±0.05)	0.37 (±0.05)
16	0.55 (±0.05)	0.42 (±0.05)	0.35 (±0.04)	0.91 (±0.57)
32	0.43 (±0.04)	0.32 (±0.02)	0.30 (±0.22)	0.35 (±0.28)
64	0.42 (±0.05)	0.56 (±0.51)	0.95 (±0.79)	
128	0.37 (±0.04)	0.71 (±0.62)		
256	0.30 (±0.04)	0.80 (±0.73)		
512	0.39 (±0.31)			
1024	0.40 (±0.35)			
2048	0.52 (±0.60)			
4096	0.50 (±0.44)			
8192	0.24 (±0.02)			

d \ n	6	7	8
2	0.61 (±0.06)	0.64 (±0.73)	0.48 (±0.06)
4	0.49 (±0.07)	0.41 (±0.06)	3.78 (±3.24)
8	0.91 (±0.53)	1.40 (±0.76)	
16	1.27 (±0.78)		

Table 3. The size of a ciphertext

d \ n	2	3	4	5	6	7	8
2	32 B	84 B	232 B	668 B	1.9 kB	5.7 kB	17.1 kB
4	48 B	212 B	1016 B	4.9 kB	24.4 kB	122.1 kB	610.4 kB
8	80 B	660 B	5.7 kB	51.3 kB	461.3 kB	4.1 MB	
16	144 B	2.3 kB	38.4 kB	652.5 kB	10.8 MB		
32	536 B	17.0 kB	561.5 kB	18.1 MB			
64	1.5 kB	99.0 kB	6.3 MB				
128	5.1 kB	650.1 kB					
256	18.1 kB	4.5 MB					
512	68.3 kB						
1024	264.5 kB						
2048	1.0 MB						
4096	4.0 MB						
8192	16.1 MB						

References

[AKSX04] Agrawal, R., Kiernan, J., Srikant, R., Xu, Y.: Order-preserving encryption for numeric data. In: Proceedings of the ACM SIGMOD International Conference on Management of Data, Paris, France, 13–18 June 2004, pp. 563–574 (2004)

[BBO07] Bellare, M., Boldyreva, A., O'Neill, A.: Deterministic and efficiently searchable encryption. In: Advances in Cryptology – CRYPTO 2007, 27th Annual International Cryptology Conference, Santa Barbara, CA, USA, 19–23 August 2007, Proceedings, pp. 535–552 (2007)

[BCLO09] Boldyreva, A., Chenette, N., Lee, Y., O'Neill, A.: Order-preserving symmetric encryption. In: Advances in Cryptology - EUROCRYPT 2009, 28th Annual International Conference on the Theory and Applications of Cryptographic Techniques, Cologne, Germany, 26–30 April 2009, Proceedings, pp. 224–241 (2009)

[BCO11] Boldyreva, A., Chenette, N., O'Neill, A.: Orderpreserving encryption revisited: improved security analysis and alternative solutions. In: Advances in Cryptology - CRYPTO 2011 - 31st Annual Cryptology Conference, Santa Barbara, CA, USA, 14–18 August 2011, Proceedings, pp. 578–595 (2011)

[BCOP03] Boneh, D., Di Crescenzo, G., Ostrovsky, R., Persiano, G.: Public key encryption with keyword search. IACR Cryptology ePrint Archive, 2003:195 (2003)

[BGI+01] Barak, B., Goldreich, O., Impagliazzo, R., Rudich, S., Sahai, A., Vadhan, S.P., Yang, K.: On the (Im)possibility of obfuscating programs. In: Advances in Cryptology - CRYPTO 2001, 21st Annual International Cryptology Conference, Santa Barbara, California, USA, 19–23 August 2001, Proceedings, pp. 1–18 (2001)

[BHJP14] Bösch, C., Hartel, P.H., Jonker, W., Peter, W.: A survey of provably secure searchable encryption. ACM Comput. Surv. $47(2)$, 18:1–18:51 (2014)

[BKS01] Börzsönyi, S., Kossmann, D., Stocker, K.: The skyline operator. In: Proceedings of the 17th International Conference on Data Engineering, 2–6 April 2001, Heidelberg, Germany, pp. 421–430 (2001)

[BKS16] Brakerski, Z., Komargodski, I., Segev, G.: Multi-input functional encryption in the private-key setting: stronger security from weaker assumptions. In: Advances in Cryptology - EUROCRYPT 2016 - 35th Annual International Conference on the Theory and Applications of Cryptographic Techniques, Vienna, Austria, 8–12 May 2016, Proceedings, Part II, pp. 852–880 (2016)

[BLR+15] Boneh, D., Lewi, K., Raykova, M., Sahai, A., Zhandry, M., Zimmerman, J.: Semantically secure order-revealing encryption: multi-input functional encryption without obfuscation. In: Oswald, E., Fischlin, M. (eds.) EUROCRYPT 2015. LNCS, vol. 9057, pp. 563–594. Springer, Heidelberg (2015). https://doi.org/10.1007/978-3-662-46803-6_19

[BRRS09] Bellare, M., Ristenpart, T., Rogaway, P., Stegers, T.: Format-preserving encryption. In: Selected Areas in Cryptography, 16th Annual International Workshop, SAC 2009, Calgary, Alberta, Canada, 13–14 August 2009, Revised Selected Papers, pp. 295–312 (2009)

[BSW11] Boneh, D., Sahai, A., Waters, B.: Functional encryption: definitions and challenges. In: Ishai, Y. (ed.) TCC 2011. LNCS, vol. 6597, pp. 253–273. Springer, Heidelberg (2011). https://doi.org/10.1007/978-3-642-19571-6_16

[BZ16] Bun, M., Zhandry, M.: Order-revealing encryption and the hardness of private learning. In: Kushilevitz, E., Malkin, T. (eds.) TCC 2016. LNCS, vol. 9562, pp. 176–206. Springer, Heidelberg (2016). https://doi.org/10.1007/978-3-662-49096-9_8

[CD15a] Chatterjee, S., Das, M.P.L.: Property preserving symmetric encryption revisited. In: Iwata, T., Cheon, J.H. (eds.) ASIACRYPT 2015. LNCS, vol. 9453, pp. 658–682. Springer, Heidelberg (2015). https://doi.org/10.1007/978-3-662-48800-3_27

[CD15b] Chaudhari, P., Das, M.: Privacy-preserving attribute based searchable encryption. Cryptology ePrint Archive, Report 2015/899 (2015). http://eprint.iacr.org/2015/899

[CGKO06] Curtmola, R., Garay, J.A., Kamara, S., Ostrovsky, R.: Searchable symmetric encryption: improved definitions and efficient constructions. In: Proceedings of the 13th ACM Conference on Computer and Communications Security, CCS 2006, Alexandria, VA, USA, October 30– November 3 2006, pp. 79–88 (2006)

[CLOZ16] Cash, D., Liu, F.-H., O'Neill, A., Zhang, C.: Reducing the leakage in practical order-revealing encryption. Cryptology ePrint Archive, Report 2016/661 (2016). http://eprint.iacr.org/2016/661

[CLWW16] Chenette, N., Lewi, K., Weis, S.A., Wu, D.J.: Practical order-revealing encryption with limited leakage. In: Peyrin, T. (ed.) FSE 2016. LNCS, vol. 9783, pp. 474–493. Springer, Heidelberg (2016). https://doi.org/10.1007/978-3-662-52993-5_24

[DDC16] Betül Durak, F., DuBuisson, T.M., Cash, D.: What else is revealed by order-revealing encryption? In: Proceedings of the 2016 ACM SIGSAC Conference on Computer and Communications Security, Vienna, Austria, 24–28 October 2016, pp. 1155–1166 (2016)

[DHO16] Damgård, I., Haagh, H., Orlandi, C.: Access control encryption: enforcing information flow with cryptography. In: Theory of Cryptography - 14th International Conference, TCC 2016-B, Beijing, China, October 31– November 3 2016, Proceedings, Part II, pp. 547–576 (2016)

[DMNS06] Dwork, C., McSherry, F., Nissim, K., Smith, A.: Calibrating noise to sensitivity in private data analysis. In: Halevi, S., Rabin, T. (eds.) TCC 2006. LNCS, vol. 3876, pp. 265–284. Springer, Heidelberg (2006). https://doi.org/10.1007/11681878_14

[Gen09] Gentry, C.: Fully homomorphic encryption using ideal lattices. In: Proceedings of the 41st Annual ACM Symposium on Theory of Computing, STOC 2009, Bethesda, MD, USA, May 31–June 2 2009, pp. 169–178 (2009)

[GGG+14] Goldwasser, S., Dov Gordon, S., Goyal, V., Jain, A., Katz, J., Liu, F.-H., Sahai, A., Shi, E., Zhou, H.-S.: Multiinput functional encryption. In: Advances in Cryptology - EUROCRYPT 2014 - 33rd Annual International Conference on the Theory and Applications of Cryptographic Techniques, Copenhagen, Denmark, 11–15 May 2014, Proceedings, pp. 578–602 (2014)

[GGH+13] Garg, S., Gentry, C., Halevi, S., Raykova, M., Sahai, A., Waters, B.: Candidate indistinguishability obfuscation and functional encryption for all circuits. In: 54th Annual IEEE Symposium on Foundations of Computer Science, FOCS 2013, Berkeley, CA, USA, 26–29 October 2013, pp. 40–49 (2013)

[Goh03] Goh, E.-J.: Secure indexes. Cryptology ePrint Archive, Report 2003/216 (2003). http://eprint.iacr.org/2003/216

[GPSW06] Goyal, V., Pandey, O., Sahai, A., Waters, B.: Attribute-based encryption for fine-grained access control of encrypted data. In: Proceedings of the 13th ACM Conference on Computer and Communications Security, CCS 2006, Alexandria, VA, USA, October 30–November 3 2006, pp. 89–98 (2006)

[GSB+17] Grubbs, P., Sekniqi, K., Bindschaedler, V., Naveed, M., Ristenpart, T.: Leakage-abuse attacks against order-revealing encryption. In: 2017 IEEE Symposium on Security and Privacy, SP 2017, San Jose, CA, USA, 22–26 May 2017, pp. 655–672 (2017)

[GSW04] Golle, P., Staddon, J., Waters, B.: Secure conjunctive keyword search over encrypted data. In: Jakobsson, M., Yung, M., Zhou, J. (eds.) ACNS 2004. LNCS, vol. 3089, pp. 31–45. Springer, Heidelberg (2004). https://doi.org/10.1007/978-3-540-24852-1_3

[GVW13] Gorbunov, S., Vaikuntanathan, V., Wee, H.: Attribute-based encryption for circuits. In: Symposium on Theory of Computing Conference, STOC 2013, Palo Alto, CA, USA, 1–4 June 2013, pp. 545–554 (2013)

[HJL+16] Haagh, H., Ji, Y., Li, C., Orlandi, C., Song, Y.: Revealing encryption for partial ordering. Cryptology ePrint Archive, Report 2016/972 (2016). http://eprint.iacr.org/2016/972

[JP16] Joye, M., Passelgue, A.: Function-revealing encryption. Cryptology ePrint Archive, Report 2016/622 (2016). http://eprint.iacr.org/2016/622

[Ker15] Kerschbaum, F.: Frequency-hiding order-preserving encryption. In: Proceedings of the 22nd ACM SIGSAC Conference on Computer and Communications Security, Denver, CO, USA, 12–16 October 2015, pp. 656–667 (2015)

[KHY13] Koo, D., Hur, J., Yoon, H.: Secure and efficient data retrieval over encrypted data using attribute-based encryption in cloud storage. Comput. Elec. Eng. **39**(1), 34–46 (2013)

[KLN+11] Kasiviswanathan, S.P., Lee, H.K., Nissim, K., Raskhodnikova, S., Smith, A.D.: What can we learn privately? SIAM J. Comput. **40**(3), 793–826 (2011)

[KS14] Kerschbaum, F., Schröpfer, A.: Optimal average-complexity ideal-security order-preserving encryption. In: Proceedings of the 2014 ACM SIGSAC Conference on Computer and Communications Security, Scottsdale, AZ, USA, 3–7 November 2014, pp. 275–286 (2014)

[KSW08] Katz, J., Sahai, A., Waters, B.: Predicate encryption supporting disjunctions, polynomial equations, and inner products. In: Smart, N. (ed.) EUROCRYPT 2008. LNCS, vol. 4965, pp. 146–162. Springer, Heidelberg (2008). https://doi.org/10.1007/978-3-540-78967-3_9

[LW16] Lewi, K., Wu, D.J.: Order-revealing encryption: new constructions, applications, and lower bounds. In: Proceedings of the 2016 ACM SIGSAC Conference on Computer and Communications Security, Vienna, Austria, 24–28 October 2016, pp. 1167–1178 (2016)

[NKW15] Naveed, M., Kamara, S., Wright, C.V.: Inference attacks on property-preserving encrypted databases. In: Proceedings of the 22nd ACM SIGSAC Conference on Computer and Communications Security, Denver, CO, USA, 12–16 October 2015, pp. 644–655 (2015)

[PLZ13] Popa, R.A., Li, F.H., Zeldovich, N.: An ideal-security protocol for order-preserving encoding. In: 2013 IEEE Symposium on Security and Privacy, SP 2013, Berkeley, CA, USA, 19–22 May 2013, pp. 463–477 (2013)

[PR12] Pandey, O., Rouselakis, Y.: Property preserving symmetric encryption. In: Pointcheval, D., Johansson, T. (eds.) EUROCRYPT 2012. LNCS, vol. 7237, pp. 375–391. Springer, Heidelberg (2012). https://doi.org/10.1007/978-3-642-29011-4_23

[PTFS03] Papadias, D., Tao, Y., Fu, G., Seeger, B.: An optimal and progressive algorithm for skyline queries. In: Proceedings of the 2003 ACM SIGMOD International Conference on Management of Data, San Diego, California, USA, 9–12 June 2003, pp. 467–478 (2003)

[RACY16] Roche, D.S., Apon, D., Choi, S.G., Yerukhimovich, A.: POPE: partial order preserving encoding. In: Proceedings of the 2016 ACM SIGSAC Conference on Computer and Communications Security, Vienna, Austria, 24–28 October 2016, pp. 1131–1142 (2016)

[RAD78] Rivest, R.L., Adleman, L., Dertouzos, M.L.: On data banks and privacy homomorphisms. Found. Sec. Somput. 4(11), 169–180 (1978)

[Sha84] Shamir, A.: Identity-based cryptosystems and signature schemes. In: Blakley, G.R., Chaum, D. (eds.) CRYPTO 1984. LNCS, vol. 196, pp. 47–53. Springer, Heidelberg (1985). https://doi.org/10.1007/3-540-39568-7_5

[SWP00] Song, D.X., Wagner, D., Perrig, A.: Practical techniques for searches on encrypted data. In: 2000 IEEE Symposium on Security and Privacy, Berkeley, California, USA, May 14–17, 2000, pp. 44–55 (2000)

[WLLX13] Wang, C., Li, W., Li, Y., Xu, X.: A ciphertext-policy attribute-based encryption scheme supporting keyword search function. In: Wang, G., Ray, I., Feng, D., Rajarajan, M. (eds.) CSS 2013. LNCS, vol. 8300, pp. 377–386. Springer, Cham (2013). https://doi.org/10.1007/978-3-319-03584-0_28

[WRB15] Weiss, M., Rozenberg, B., Barham, M.: Practical solutions for format-preserving encryption. CoRR, abs/1506.04113 (2015)

[XFAM02] Xu, J., Fan, J., Ammar, M.H., Moon, S.B.: Prefix-preserving IP address anonymization: measurement-based security evaluation and a new cryptography-based scheme. In: 10th IEEE International Conference on Network Protocols (ICNP 2002), 12–15 November 2002, Paris, France, Proceedings, pp. 280–289 (2002)

[XY12] Xiao, L., Yen, I.-L.: Security analysis and enhancement for prefix-preserving encryption schemes. IACR Cryptology ePrint Archive, 2012:191 (2012)

[ZXA14] Zheng, Q., Xu, S., Ateniese, G.: VABKS: verifiable attribute-based keyword search over outsourced encrypted data. In: 2014 IEEE Conference on Computer Communications, INFOCOM 2014, Toronto, Canada, April 27–May 2 2014, pp. 522–530 (2014)

Homomorphic Encryption
and Secure Computation

Dynamic Multi Target Homomorphic Attribute-Based Encryption

Ryo Hiromasa$^{(\boxtimes)}$ and Yutaka Kawai

Mitsubishi Electric, Kamakura, Japan
Hiromasa.Ryo@ajMitsubishiElectric.co.jp,
Kawai.Yutaka@daMitsubishiElectric.co.jp

Abstract. We propose multi target homomorphic attribute-based encryption (MT-HABE) with *dynamic* homomorphic evaluation: it can take as input *arbitrary* additional ciphertexts during homomorphic computation. In the previous MT-HABE of Brakerski et al. (TCC 2016-B), the output of homomorphic computation, which is related to a policy set, cannot be computed with a fresh ciphertext whose attribute does not satisfy any policy in the set. This is because the underlying multi-key fully homomorphic encryption (MKFHE) is single-hop: some keys are related to the output of homomorphic computation, which cannot be combined with ciphertexts encrypted under other keys. To implement dynamic homomorphic evaluations, we construct MT-HABE from a dual variant of multi-hop MKFHE proposed by Peikert and Shiehian (TCC 2016-B).

1 Introduction

Fully homomorphic encryption (FHE) allows us to evaluate any function over encrypted data by only using public information. Since the breakthrough work by Gentry [Gen09a, Gen09b], many different varieties of FHE have been proposed [DGHV10, BV11b, BV11a, BGV12, Bra12, LTV12, GSW13, CLT14]. FHE can be used, for example, to outsource computations to remote servers (e.g., cloud servers) without compromising privacy.

A cloud server may be used by multiple users, so it is required to set access permission among them. Attribute-based encryption (ABE) is a special type of public key encryption to accomplish this requirement. In key-policy ABE scheme, a (master) public key mpk is used to generate a ciphertext of a message μ, which is labeled with a public attribute $x \in \{0, 1\}^\ell$. The secret key sk_f is associated to a policy $f : \{0, 1\}^\ell \to \{0, 1\}$ and it can only decrypt ciphertexts that satisfy $f(x) = 0$. Previously, several ABE schemes under the learning with errors (LWE) assumption have been proposed [GVW13, BGG+14, BV16], and it was known that from [GSW13, GVW13] we can construct homomorphic ABE (HABE). The HABE scheme enables us to both set access permission and homomorphically evaluate on the ciphertexts, but the homomorphism is somewhat limited: the scheme can correctly evaluate only on the ciphertexts with the same attribute. In [CM16], Clear and McGoldrick proposed a way to compile the above HABE to an HABE with non-leveled homomorphism, but the resulting scheme still has the limitation over the attributes.

© Springer International Publishing AG 2017
M. O'Neill (Ed.): IMACC 2017, LNCS 10655, pp. 25–43, 2017.
https://doi.org/10.1007/978-3-319-71045-7_2

In [BCTW16], Brakerski et al. proposed target HABE (T-HABE) that enables cross-attribute homomorphic evaluations. A syntactical difference between T-HABE and HABE is in the homomorphic evaluation algorithm. In T-HABE, a homomorphic evaluation algorithm takes as input a set of policies $F = \{f_i\}_i$, an operation g, and some ciphertexts $\{(ct_j, x_j)\}$, where each ciphertext encrypts μ_j. If for any x_j there exists f_i such that $f_i(x_j) = 0$, the algorithm outputs a ciphertext $ct_F^{(g)}$ that can be decrypted by using all of the secret keys $\{sk_{f_i}\}_i$, and the result of the decryption is $g(\{\mu_j\}_j)$ with high probability. The paper proposed two types of T-HABE, single target HABE (ST-HABE) and multi target HABE (MT-HABE). ST-HABE is an T-HABE that can homomorphically evaluate between the ciphertexts each of whose attributes satisfy a certain single policy, i.e., T-HABE in which $F = \{f\}$ for a single policy f. In MT-HABE, a set of policies is related to the homomorphic computation, which can be processed between ciphertexts whose attribute satisfies some policy in the set. The MT-HABE of [BCTW16] is constructed from the ST-HABE and multi-key FHE (MKFHE) of [CM15, MW16].

The MT-HABE proposed in [BCTW16] is *static* (i.e., single-hop for policies): the output of ciphertexts, which depends on a certain policy set F, cannot be homomorphically evaluated with the fresh ciphertext whose attribute does not satisfy any policy in F. This forces the evaluator to know all the involved policies before the computation begins.

1.1 Our Results

We construct *dynamic* MT-HABE (i.e., which is multi-hop for policies): it can take as input *arbitrary* additional ciphertexts during homomorphic computation. This enables us both dynamic cross-attribute homomorphic computations and setting access permissions.

In the previous MT-HABE of [BCTW16], the output of homomorphic computation is related to a policy set F, and it cannot be computed with a fresh ciphertext whose attribute does not satisfy any policy in F. This is because the underlying multi-key fully homomorphic encryption (MKFHE) is single-hop: some keys are related to the output of homomorphic computation, which cannot be combined with ciphertexts encrypted under other keys. To implement dynamic homomorphic evaluation algorithms, we construct MT-HABE from a dual variant of multi-hop MKFHE proposed by Peikert and Shiehian [PS16].

The security of the proposed MT-HABE is proven under the same assumption as [BCTW16]: the LWE assumption with sub-exponential modulus to noise ratio in the random oracle model. A comparison of key and ciphertext size between the MT-HABE of [BCTW16] and our scheme is shown in Table 1, which tells that the size of the public key of our scheme is almost the same as [BCTW16] ignoring the logarithmic factor.

1.2 Our Techniques

For the notation of this section, we refer the reader to the first paragraph of Sect. 2. Let n, q be LWE parameters, $m = O(n \log q)$, $N := n\lceil \log q \rceil$, $M := (m + N + 1)\lceil \log q \rceil$, and $\mathbf{g}^T := (1, 2, 2^2, \ldots, 2^{\lceil \log q \rceil})$. In the following, we use the notation $x \approx y$ to represent

Table 1. Comparison of key and ciphertext size between the previous MT-HABE [BCTW16] and our dynamic MT-HABE. The parameter n is the LWE dimension, ℓ is the maximal number of inputs of policies, $d_{\mathsf{BCTW}} = d_{\mathcal{F}} + d_{\mathcal{G}} \log d$, and $d_{\mathsf{ours}} = d \log d + d_{\mathcal{G}} + d_{\mathcal{F}} \log \ell$, where d represents the bound on the number of involved policies on homomorphic computations, and $d_{\mathcal{F}}$ and $d_{\mathcal{G}}$ denote the maximal depths of policies and operations, respectively. The left and right hand sides of the notation $\rightarrow$ represent the size of a fresh and evaluated ciphertext.

	Key size	Ciphertext size
[BCTW16]	$\tilde{O}(n^2 d_{\mathsf{BCTW}}^2 \ell)$	$\tilde{O}(\ell n^4 d_{\mathsf{BCTW}}^6) \rightarrow \tilde{O}(d^2 n^2 d_{\mathsf{BCTW}}^4)$
Ours	$\tilde{O}(n^2 d_{\mathsf{ours}}^2 \ell)$	$\tilde{O}(n^3(\ell + d_{\mathsf{ours}})d_{\mathsf{ours}}^6) \rightarrow \tilde{O}(n^3 d_{\mathsf{ours}}^7)$

the noisy equation $x = y + e$ for some noise term e. The starting point of the proposed scheme is the MKFHE scheme of [PS16].

Multi-hop MKFHE of [PS16]. A ciphertext of the MKFHE is a triple of matrices $(\mathbf{C}, \mathbf{F}, \mathbf{D}) \in \mathbb{Z}_q^{n \times N} \times \mathbb{Z}_q^{n \times N} \times \mathbb{Z}_q^{nm \times N\lceil \log q \rceil}$ such that for a secret key vector $\mathbf{t} \in \mathbb{Z}_q^n$,

$$\mathbf{t}^T \mathbf{C} \approx \mu(\mathbf{t}^T \otimes \mathbf{g}^T), \quad \mathbf{F} = \hat{\mathbf{F}} + \mu(\mathbf{I}_n \otimes \mathbf{g}^T), \quad (\mathbf{I}_m \otimes \mathbf{t}^T)\mathbf{D} \approx (\mathbf{R} \otimes \mathbf{g}),$$

where $\hat{\mathbf{F}} = \mathbf{AR} \in \mathbb{Z}_q^{m \times N}$ for a random public matrix $\mathbf{A} \in \mathbb{Z}_q^{n \times m}$ and a random binary matrix $\mathbf{R} \in \mathbb{Z}_q^{m \times N}$. To achieve dynamic homomorphism on the ciphertexts, the MKFHE has an algorithm to expand a ciphertext $\mathbf{C}$ under $\mathbf{t}$ into a ciphertext $\mathbf{C}' \in \mathbb{Z}_q^{(n+n) \times (n+n)\lceil \log q \rceil}$ under $\mathbf{t}' = [\mathbf{t}, \mathbf{t}^*] \in \mathbb{Z}_q^{n+n}$ for an additional key $\mathbf{t}^* \in \mathbb{Z}_q^n$, where $\mathbf{C}$ and $\mathbf{C}'$ encrypts the same message. The expanded ciphertext $\mathbf{C}'$ is generated by

$$\mathbf{C}' := \begin{bmatrix} \mathbf{C} & \mathbf{X} \\ & \mathbf{F} \end{bmatrix},$$

for a matrix $\mathbf{X} \in \mathbb{Z}_q^{n \times N}$ that satisfies $\mathbf{t}^T \mathbf{X} + \mathbf{t}^T \mathbf{AR} \approx \mathbf{0}$. Since it holds that $\mathbf{t}'^T \mathbf{C}' \approx \mu(\mathbf{t}'^T \otimes \mathbf{g}^T)$, which is the approximate eigenvector relation as in [GSW13], we can homomorphically evaluate on these expanded ciphertexts.

ST-HABE of [BCTW16]. A public parameter contains random matrices $\mathbf{A}, \mathbf{B}_0, \mathbf{B}_1, \ldots,$ $\mathbf{B}_\ell \in \mathbb{Z}_q^{n \times m}$ and a random vector $\mathbf{v} \in \mathbb{Z}_q^n$. We define $\mathbf{B}_x := [\mathbf{B}_1, \ldots, \mathbf{B}_\ell]$, and $x\mathbf{G} := [x_1(\mathbf{I}_n \otimes \mathbf{g}^T), \ldots, x_\ell(\mathbf{I}_n \otimes \mathbf{g}^T)]$ for an attribute $x \in \{0, 1\}^\ell$. A ciphertext of the ST-HABE consists of the following two matrices

$$\mathbf{C} \approx \begin{bmatrix} \mathbf{A}^T \\ \mathbf{B}_0^T \\ \mathbf{v}^T \end{bmatrix} \cdot \mathbf{S} + \mu(\mathbf{I}_{m+N+1} \otimes \mathbf{g}^T) \in \mathbb{Z}_q^{(m+N+1) \times M},$$

$$\mathbf{C}_x \approx (\mathbf{B}_x - x\mathbf{G})^T \cdot \mathbf{S} \in \mathbb{Z}_q^{\ell N \times M}$$

for some random matrix $\mathbf{S}$. Let $f : \{0, 1\}^\ell \rightarrow \{0, 1\}$ be a policy and $\mathbf{B}_f$ be a matrix generated upon f. The secret key for f is a vector $\mathbf{r}_f$ such that $\mathbf{r}_f^T \mathbf{A}^T + \mathbf{r}_f'^T(\mathbf{B}_0 + \mathbf{B}_f)^T + \mathbf{v}^T = \mathbf{0}$ for a random binary vector $\mathbf{r}_f'$, which is generated by the random oracle in the MT-HABE of [BCTW16]. There exists a matrix $\mathbf{H}$ such that $\mathbf{B}_f - f(x)(\mathbf{I}_n \otimes \mathbf{g}^T) = (\mathbf{B}_x -$

$x\mathbf{G})\mathbf{H}$. In homomorphic evaluations, the ST-HABE generates the functioned ciphertext for the policy f by computing $\hat{\mathbf{C}}_f := \mathbf{C} + [\mathbf{0}_{M\times m}, \mathbf{C}_x^T\mathbf{H}, \mathbf{0}_M]^T$. If $f(x) = 0$ holds, then the functioned ciphertext satisfies the approximate eigenvector relation of [GSW13] with $\mathbf{t}_f^T = [\mathbf{r}_f^T, \mathbf{r}_f'^T, 1]$.

Our Scheme. We construct dynamic MT-HABE by making the multi-hop MKFHE [PS16] attribute-based. To this end, we consider a dual variant of [PS16]: set $\mathbf{C}$ in the same way as [BCTW16] and $\hat{\mathbf{F}} = [\mathbf{A}, \mathbf{B}, \mathbf{v}]^T\mathbf{R} + \mathbf{E} \approx [\mathbf{A}, \mathbf{B}, \mathbf{v}]^T\mathbf{R} \in \mathbb{Z}_q^{(m+N+1)\times M}$ for a random matrix $\mathbf{B} \in \mathbb{Z}_q^{n\times N}$. In the scheme of [PS16], the matrix $\mathbf{F}$ contains a message μ, so $\hat{\mathbf{F}}$ must be indistinguishable from uniform to ensure the security. The matrix $\hat{\mathbf{F}}$ of [PS16] is set to be $\mathbf{AR}$, and so statistically indistinguishable from uniform by the leftover hash lemma (LHL). In our scheme, $\hat{\mathbf{F}}$ is computationally indistinguishable from uniform by the LWE assumption.

In the proposed MT-HABE, the functioned ciphertext is computed in a similar way to [BCTW16], and it consists of the following three matrices such that for a secret key $\mathbf{t}$,

$$\mathbf{t}^T\mathbf{C} \approx \mu(\mathbf{t}^T \otimes \mathbf{g}^T), \quad \mathbf{F} \approx \begin{bmatrix}\mathbf{A}^T\\\mathbf{B}^T\\\mathbf{v}^T\end{bmatrix} \cdot \mathbf{R} + \mu(\mathbf{I}_{m+N+1} \otimes \mathbf{g}^T), \quad (\mathbf{I}_N \otimes \mathbf{t}^T)\mathbf{D} \approx (\mathbf{R} \otimes \mathbf{g}),$$

where $m = O(n\log^2 q)$ for the security reason. To dynamically evaluate on this ciphertext, we need to implement the ciphertext expansion algorithm, which transforms the ciphertext $\mathbf{C}$ under the key $\mathbf{t}$ to the ciphertext $\mathbf{C}'$ under $[\mathbf{t}, \mathbf{t}_f]$ for an additional policy f. The algorithm must compute a matrix $\mathbf{X}$ such that $\mathbf{t}^T\mathbf{X} + \mathbf{t}_f^T\mathbf{F} \approx \mu(\mathbf{t}_f^T \otimes \mathbf{g}^T)$, which is in other words $\mathbf{t}^T\mathbf{X} + \mathbf{t}_f^T[\mathbf{A}, \mathbf{B}, \mathbf{v}]^T \cdot \mathbf{R} \approx \mathbf{0}$. However, the term $\mathbf{r}_f^T\mathbf{A}$, which is from expanding $\mathbf{t}_f^T[\mathbf{A}, \mathbf{B}, \mathbf{v}]^T$, cannot be known because $\mathbf{r}_f$ is a part of the secret key. To overcome this problem, our algorithm instead computes $\mathbf{X}$ such that $\mathbf{t}^T\mathbf{X} \approx \mathbf{r}_f'^T(\mathbf{B}_0 + \mathbf{B}_f - \mathbf{B})^T \cdot \mathbf{R}$, where $\mathbf{r}_f'^T$ is obtained from the random oracle, the matrices $\mathbf{B}_0$ and $\mathbf{B}$ are the public matrices, and $\mathbf{B}_f$ can publicly be generated from f. Then, it holds that

$$\mathbf{t}^T\mathbf{X} + \mathbf{t}_f\mathbf{F} \approx \mathbf{r}_f'^T \cdot (\mathbf{B}_0 + \mathbf{B}_f - \mathbf{B})^T \cdot \mathbf{R} + [\mathbf{r}_f^T, \mathbf{r}_f'^T, 1]\begin{bmatrix}\mathbf{A}^T\\\mathbf{B}^T\\\mathbf{v}^T\end{bmatrix} \cdot \mathbf{R} + \mu(\mathbf{t}_f^T \otimes \mathbf{g}^T)$$

$$= [\mathbf{r}_f^T, \mathbf{r}_f'^T, 1]\begin{bmatrix}\mathbf{A}^T\\\mathbf{B}_0^T + \mathbf{B}_f^T\\\mathbf{v}^T\end{bmatrix} \cdot \mathbf{R} + \mu(\mathbf{t}_f^T \otimes \mathbf{g}^T)$$

$$= \mu(\mathbf{t}_f^T \otimes \mathbf{g}^T).$$

1.3 Organization

In Sect. 2, we introduce mathematical preliminaries used in this paper. In Sect. 3, we show the construction of the proposed dynamic MT-HABE.

2 Preliminaries

Notations. We denote the set of natural numbers by $\mathbb{N}$, and the set of integers by $\mathbb{Z}$. For any positive integer $d > 0$, we represent $\{1, 2, \ldots, d\}$ by $[d]$. Let S be a set and $\mathcal{P}$

be a probability distribution over S. Then, we denote by $a \leftarrow S$ that $a \in S$ is chosen uniformly at random from S, and by $b \leftarrow \mathcal{P}$ that $b \in S$ is sampled from $\mathcal{P}$. The notation $\mathsf{negl}(\lambda)$ represents the set of negligible functions for $\lambda \in \mathbb{N}$.

Vectors are in column form and written by bold lower-case letters (e.g., $\mathbf{x}$). The i-th element of the vector $\mathbf{x}$ is represented by x_i. We denote the ℓ_∞ norm (max norm) of the vector $\mathbf{x}$ by $\|\mathbf{x}\|_\infty$. The inner-product of two vectors is written by $\langle \mathbf{x}, \mathbf{y} \rangle$. We denote matrices as the bold capital letters (e.g., $\mathbf{X}$) and the i-th column vector of the matrix $\mathbf{X}$ is represented by $\mathbf{X}[i]$. For matrix $\mathbf{X} \in \mathbb{R}^{m \times n}$, the ℓ_∞ norm of $\mathbf{X}$ is defined as $\|\mathbf{X}\|_\infty := \max_{i \in [n]}\{\|\mathbf{X}[i]\|_\infty\}$ The notation $\mathbf{X}^T \in \mathbb{R}^{n \times m}$ represents the transpose of $\mathbf{X}$. For two matrices $\mathbf{A} \in \mathbb{R}^{m \times n_1}$ and $\mathbf{B} \in \mathbb{R}^{m \times n_2}$, $[\mathbf{A}, \mathbf{B}] \in \mathbb{R}^{m \times (n_1 + n_2)}$ is the matrix generated by concatenating $\mathbf{A}$ and $\mathbf{B}$. Let $\mathbf{I}_n$ be the $n \times n$ identity matrix, and $\mathbf{0}_{n \times m}$ be the $n \times m$ matrix all of whose entries are 0. For any $i \in [n]$, $\mathbf{u}_i \in \{0, 1\}^n$ represents the i-th standard basis vector of dimension n.

Tensor Products. The tensor product of an $m_1 \times n_1$ matrix $\mathbf{A}$ and $m_2 \times n_2$ matrix $\mathbf{B}$ over a commutative ring $\mathcal{R}$ is the $m_1 m_2 \times n_1 n_2$ matrix consisting of $m_2 \times n_2$ blocks whose (i, j)-th block is $a_{i,j}\mathbf{B}$, where $a_{i,j}$ is the (i, j)-th element of $\mathbf{A}$.

For any scalar $r \in \mathcal{R}$, we have

$$r(\mathbf{A} \otimes \mathbf{B}) = (r\mathbf{A}) \otimes \mathbf{B} = \mathbf{A} \otimes (r\mathbf{B}).$$

We heavily use the mixed product property of tensor products, which says

$$(\mathbf{A} \otimes \mathbf{B}) \cdot (\mathbf{C} \otimes \mathbf{D}) = (\mathbf{A}\mathbf{C}) \otimes (\mathbf{B}\mathbf{D})$$

for any matrices $\mathbf{A}, \mathbf{B}, \mathbf{C}, \mathbf{D}$ with compatible dimensions. In particular, it holds that

$$\mathbf{A} \otimes \mathbf{B} = (\mathbf{A} \otimes \mathbf{I}_{height(\mathbf{B})}) \cdot (\mathbf{I}_{width(\mathbf{A})} \otimes \mathbf{B})$$
$$= (\mathbf{I}_{height(\mathbf{A})} \otimes \mathbf{B}) \cdot (\mathbf{A} \otimes \mathbf{I}_{width(\mathbf{B})}).$$

Noisy Equations. In this paper, we consider the noisy equations, and we use the notation $\approx$ to say that the two sides of the equation are approximately equal within some additive error. For example,

$$x \approx y \quad (\text{error: } B)$$

represents $x = y + e$ for some $e \in [-B, B]$.

2.1   Target Homomorphic Attribute-Based Encryption

In [BCTW16], Brakerski et al. first introduced the notion of target homomorphic attribute based encryption (T-HABE), which is an homomorphic encryption whose homomorphic operations depend on policies. We here define the syntax of T-HABE and then define its correctness and security.

Definition 1 (Target Homomorphic Attribute Based Encryption (T-HABE)). *A target homomorphic attribute based encryption scheme consists of the following five algorithms* THABE = THABE.{Setup, Enc, Keygen, Dec, EvalNAND}.

- THABE.Setup(1^λ): *takes as input a security parameter λ (additionally, the algorithm can take parameters that specify classes of policies or admissible operations), and outputs a public parameter* pp *and master secret key* msk.
- THABE.Enc$_{pp}(\mu, x)$: *takes as input a public parameter* pp, *plaintext μ, and attribute x, and outputs a tuple of a ciphertext and attribute* (ct, x).
- THABE.Keygen$_{msk}(f)$: *takes as input a master secret key* msk *and policy f, and outputs a secret key* sk$_f$.
- THABE.EvalNAND$_{pp}(\mathsf{ct}^{(1)}, \mathsf{ct}^{(2)})$: *takes as input a public parameter* pp, *and two ciphertexts $\mathsf{ct}^{(1)}, \mathsf{ct}^{(2)}$, and outputs a ciphertext* $\mathsf{ct}^{\mathsf{NAND}}$.
- THABE.Dec$_{\mathsf{sk}_F}(\mathsf{ct})$: *takes as input a secret key* sk$_F$ (sk$_F = \{sk_f : f \in F\}$) *and ciphertext* ct, *and outputs a plaintext $\mu \in \{0, 1\}$.*

As well as the definition of multi-hop MKFHE in [PS16], we consider the algorithm EvalNAND, which homomorphically evaluates the NAND gate for two input ciphertexts, to capture multi-hop property in the above definition. The circuit evaluation algorithm Eval($\{\mathsf{ct}^{(i)}\}_i, \{f_j\}_j \subseteq \mathcal{F}, g \in \mathcal{G}$) takes as input an operation g composed of NAND gates of two inputs and one output, and computes each gate by EvalNAND on ciphertexts associated to the inputs of the gate. Each gate evaluation depends on the policies related only with the input ciphertexts, which makes the homomorphic evaluation multi-hop for policies.

The correctness of T-HABE guarantees that the ciphertext is correctly decrypted to the intended value with high probability when given all the keys for the policies involved in the homomorphic computation.

Definition 2 (Correctness). *Let $\{\mathcal{F}_\lambda\}_{\lambda \in \mathbb{N}}$ be a class of policies, and $\{\mathcal{G}_\lambda\}_{\lambda \in \mathbb{N}}$ be a class of operations. The dynamic T-HABE scheme* THABE = THABE.{Setup, Enc, Keygen, Eval, Dec} *is correct if the following holds.*

Let (pp, msk) $\leftarrow$ THABE.Setup(1^λ). *Consider a set of* poly(λ) *policy $F \subseteq \mathcal{F}_\lambda$, set of the corresponding secret keys* sk$_F := \{sk_f : f \in F\}$, *a sequence of $k \geq 1$ messages and attributes $\{(\mu^{(i)} \in \{0, 1\}, x^{(i)} \in \{0, 1\}^*)\}_{i \in [k]}$ such that $\forall x^{(i)}, \exists f \in F, f(x^{(i)}) = 0$, and their ciphertexts $\{\mathsf{ct}^{(i)} \leftarrow$ THABE.Enc$_{pp}(\mu^{(i)}, x^{(i)})\}_{i \in [k]}$. Then, computing $\mathsf{ct}^g :=$ THABE.Eval$_{pp}(F, \mathsf{ct}^{(1)}, \ldots, \mathsf{ct}^{(k)}, g)$ for some $g \in \mathcal{G}$, it holds that*

$$\Pr[\text{THABE.Dec}_{sk_f}(\mathsf{ct}^g) \neq g(\mu^{(1)}, \ldots, \mu^{(k)})] = \mathsf{negl}(\lambda),$$

where the probability is take over the randomness in the experiment.

The security is defined in the same way as standard (key-policy) ABE.

Definition 3 (Security). *Let* THABE *be a T-HABE scheme described in the above, and consider the following game between the challenger and adversary.*

1. *The adversary sends an attribute x^* to the challenger.*
2. *The challenger generates* (msk, pp) $\leftarrow$ THABE.Setup(1^λ) *and sends* pp *to the adversary.*
3. *The adversary makes arbitrary many key generation queries by sending f_i (represented as circuits) to the challenger. Upon receiving such functions, the challenger creates a key* sk$_{f_i}$ $\leftarrow$ THABE.Keygen$_{msk}(f_i)$ *and sends* sk$_{f_i}$ *if $f_i(x^*) = 1$, and sends $\perp$ otherwise.*

4. The adversary sends a pair of messages μ_0, μ_1 to the challenger. The challenger chooses $b \leftarrow \{0, 1\}$ uniformly at random, and computes $\mathsf{ct}^* \leftarrow$ THABE.Enc$_{\mathsf{pp}}(\mu_b, x^*)$. It sends ct^* to the challenger.
5. The adversary makes arbitrary many key generation queries as in Step 3.
6. The adversary outputs $b' \in \{0, 1\}$.

The above game is called the selective security game, and the advantage of the adversary in this game is defined by $\mathsf{Adv}_{\mathcal{A}}^{\mathsf{SS-THABE}}(\lambda) := |\Pr[b' = b] - 1/2|$, where b and b' are generated in the game. The scheme THABE is selectively secure if for any PPT adversary $\mathcal{A}$, it holds that $\mathsf{Adv}_{\mathcal{A}}^{\mathsf{SS-THABE}}(\lambda) = \mathsf{negl}(\lambda)$.

As well as the previous attribute-based encryption from lattices, we allow decryption when $f(x) = 0$, and all of the queries must satisfy $f_i(x^*) = 1$.

2.2 Learning with Errors (LWE)

The *Learning with errors (LWE)* assumption was first introduced by Regev [Reg05]. The decision version of the LWE problem is called Decisional LWE (DLWE) and defined as follows.

Definition 4 (DLWE). *For a security parameter λ, let $n := n(\lambda)$ be an integer lattice dimension, $q := q(\lambda) \geq 2$ be an integer modulus, and $\chi := \chi(\lambda)$ be an error distribution over $\mathbb{Z}$. DLWE$_{n,q,\chi}$ is the problem that for any $m = \mathsf{poly}(\lambda)$, letting $\mathbf{A} \leftarrow \mathbb{Z}_q^{m \times n}$, $\mathbf{s} \leftarrow \mathbb{Z}_q^n$, $\mathbf{e} \leftarrow \chi^m$, and $\mathbf{u} \leftarrow \mathbb{Z}_q^m$, distinguishes the two distributions $(\mathbf{A}, \mathbf{As} + \mathbf{e})$ and $(\mathbf{A}, \mathbf{u})$. DLWE$_{n,q,\chi}$ assumption states that DLWE$_{n,q,\chi}$ is intractable for any PPT adversary.*

By letting χ be a discrete Gaussian distribution over $\mathbb{Z}$ with parameter $r = \alpha q \geq 2\sqrt{n}$ (represented by $D_{\mathbb{Z},r}$) for some $0 < \alpha < 1$, there exists a quantum reduction [Reg05] between DLWE$_{n,q,\chi=D_{\mathbb{Z},r}}$ and approximating a short vector over n dimensional lattices within factor of $\tilde{O}(n/\alpha)$[1]. Additionally, it is known that there exists the classical reductions [Pei09, BLP+13] for other parameters.

2.3 Gadget Matrix and Bit Decomposition

Let $\mathbf{g}^T := (1, 2, \ldots, 2^{\lceil \log q \rceil})$ be a vector consisting of the powers of 2. The operation $\mathbf{g}^{-1} : \mathbb{Z}_q \to \{0, 1\}^{1 \times \lceil \log q \rceil}$ takes as input $x \in \mathbb{Z}_q$, and outputs $\mathbf{y}$ such that $\langle \mathbf{y}, \mathbf{g} \rangle = x \in \mathbb{Z}_q$. For example, $\mathbf{g}^{-1}$ is the operation to decompose x into its binary representation. Symmetrically, $\mathbf{g}^{-T} : \mathbb{Z}_q \to \{0, 1\}^{\lceil \log q \rceil}$ transforms an element in $\mathbb{Z}_q$ into the column vector of its binary representation. More generally, the operation $(\mathbf{I}_n \otimes \mathbf{g}^{-T})(\cdot)$ generates $n \cdot \lceil \log q \rceil$ dimensional vector with coefficients of $\{0, 1\}$ by applying $\mathbf{g}^{-T}$ to every element of the vector in $\mathbb{Z}_q^n$. Then the following holds

$$(\mathbf{I}_n \otimes \mathbf{g}^T) \cdot (\mathbf{I}_n \otimes \mathbf{g}^{-T})(\mathbf{x}) = \mathbf{x}.$$

It is clear that this operation can be generalized to matrices.

---

[1] Approximating a short vector over n dimensional lattices within factor of γ takes $2^{\tilde{\Omega}(n/\log \gamma)}$ computations [Sch87].

2.4   Lattice Trapdoors and Discrete Gaussian Distributions

Consider a matrix $\mathbf{A} \in \mathbb{Z}_q^{n \times m}$. For all $\mathbf{V} \in \mathbb{Z}_q^{n \times m'}$ and for any probability distribution P over $\mathbb{Z}^m$, let $\mathbf{A}_P^{-1}(\mathbf{V})$ be the random variable whose distribution is P conditioned on $\mathbf{A} \cdot \mathbf{A}_P^{-1}(\mathbf{V}) = \mathbf{V}$. A P-trapdoor for $\mathbf{A}$ is an algorithm that can efficiently sample from a distribution within 2^{-n} statistical distance of $\mathbf{A}_P^{-1}(\mathbf{V})$ for any $\mathbf{V}$. We denote the P-trapdoor by $\mathbf{A}_P^{-1}$, and $\mathbf{A}_P^{-1} = \mathbf{A}_\tau^{-1}$ in the case where P is a Gaussian distribution with parameter τ.

In the following, we introduce the procedures to generate an almost uniform $\mathbf{A}$ with a trapdoor for sampling from the Gaussian distribution.

Corollary 1 (Generating Trapdoors [Ajt99, GPV08, MP12, BLP+13]). *There exists an efficient algorithm* TrapGen($1^n, q, m$) *that outputs* $(\mathbf{A}, \mathbf{A}_{\tau_0}^{-1})$, *where* $\mathbf{A} \in \mathbb{Z}_q^{n \times m}$ *for any* $m \geq m_0$ *for* $m_0 = O(n \log q)$, $\mathbf{A}$ *is statistically close to uniform over* $\mathbb{Z}_q^{n \times m}$ *within* 2^{-n} *distance, and* $\tau_0 = O(\sqrt{n \log q \log n})$. *Given* $\mathbf{A}_{\tau_0}^{-1}$, *one can obtain* $\mathbf{A}_\tau^{-1}$ *for any* $\tau \geq \tau_0$.

Corollary 2 (Gaussian-Binary Sampler [LW15]). *Let* n, m, q *be such that* $m \geq n\lceil \log q \rceil$. *With all but* $O(2^{-n})$ *probability over the choice of* $\mathbf{A} \leftarrow \mathbb{Z}_q^{n \times m}$, *for all* $\mathbf{R} \in \mathbb{Z}^{m \times N}$ *with* $N = n\lceil \log q \rceil$, *one can obtain* $[\mathbf{A}, \mathbf{AR} + (\mathbf{I}_n \otimes \mathbf{g}^T)]_P^{-1}$ *with* $P = D_{\mathbb{Z}^m, \tau} \times \{0, 1\}^N$ *for* $\tau = O(N\sqrt{mn} \cdot \|\mathbf{R}\|_\infty)$. *Furthermore, for all* $\mathbf{v}$, *it holds that the marginal distribution of the last N coordinates of* $[\mathbf{A}, \mathbf{AR} + (\mathbf{I}_n \otimes \mathbf{g}^T)]_P^{-1}(\mathbf{v})$ *is statistically close to uniform over* $\{0, 1\}^N$ *within* 2^{-n} *distance.*

2.5   Homomorphic Operations

Here we define the procedure used for homomorphic evaluations in our scheme.

Definition 5. *Let* $n, q, \ell \in \mathbb{N}$ *and* $N := n\lceil \log q \rceil$. *Consider* $\mathbf{B}_1, \ldots, \mathbf{B}_\ell \in \mathbb{Z}_q^{n \times N}$, *and denote* $\mathbf{B} := [\mathbf{B}_1, \ldots, \mathbf{B}_\ell]$. *Let* f *be a Boolean circuit of depth d that computes a function* $\{0, 1\}^\ell \rightarrow \{0, 1\}$ *and consists only of NAND gates. We define* $\mathbf{B}_f := \mathsf{Eval}(\mathbf{B}, f)$ *recursively: associate* $\mathbf{B}_1, \ldots, \mathbf{B}_\ell$ *with the ℓ input wires of f. For every wire* $w \in f$, *let* u, v *be its predecessors and define*

$$\mathbf{B}_w := (\mathbf{I}_n \otimes \mathbf{g}^T) - \mathbf{B}_u \cdot (\mathbf{I}_n \otimes \mathbf{g}^{-T})(\mathbf{B}_v).$$

Finally, $\mathbf{B}_f$ *is the matrix associated with the output wire of f.*

The following fact represents the properties of the above homomorphic evaluation algorithm.

Fact 21. *Consider* $\mathbf{B}_1, \ldots, \mathbf{B}_\ell \in \mathbb{Z}_q^{n \times N}$ ($N = n\lceil \log q \rceil$). *Letting* $\mathbf{B} := [\mathbf{B}_1, \ldots, \mathbf{B}_\ell]$, *and* $x\mathbf{G} := [x_1(\mathbf{I}_n \otimes \mathbf{g}^T), \ldots, x_\ell(\mathbf{I}_n \otimes \mathbf{g}^T)]$, *there exists a polynomial time algorithm* $\mathsf{EvRelation}$ *such that if* $\mathbf{H} := \mathbf{H}_{f,x,\mathbf{B}} := \mathsf{EvRelation}(f, x, \mathbf{B})$, *then* $\|\mathbf{H}\|_\infty \leq (N + 1)^d$ *and*

$$(\mathbf{B}_f - f(x)(\mathbf{I}_n \otimes \mathbf{g}^T))^T = \mathbf{H}^T \cdot [\mathbf{B} - x\mathbf{G}]^T,$$

where $\mathbf{B}_f = \mathsf{Eval}(f, \mathbf{B})$.

In particular, if $\mathbf{B}_i := \mathbf{AR}_i + x_i(\mathbf{I}_n \otimes \mathbf{g}^T)$, *that is,* $\mathbf{B} = \mathbf{AR} + x\mathbf{G}$ *for* $\mathbf{R} := [\mathbf{R}_1, \ldots, \mathbf{R}_\ell]$, *then* $\mathbf{B}_f = \mathbf{AR}_f + f(x)(\mathbf{I}_n \otimes \mathbf{g}^T)$ *for* $\mathbf{R}_f = \mathbf{R} \cdot \mathbf{H}_{f,x,\mathbf{B}}$.

We can see that this fact holds by verifying that for the NAND operation in Definition 5,

$$\mathsf{EvRelation}(\mathsf{NAND}, (x_u, x_v), [\mathbf{B}_u, \mathbf{B}_v]) = \begin{bmatrix} -(\mathbf{I}_n \otimes \mathbf{g}^{-T})(\mathbf{B}_v) \\ -x_u \mathbf{I}_{N \times N} \end{bmatrix}.$$

3 Dynamic MT-HABE

In this section, we construct dynamic MT-HABE (i.e., which is multi-hop for keys) from the multi-hop MKFHE scheme of [PS16]. The proposed MT-HABE can take as input arbitrary additional ciphertexts during homomorphic computations. We show the construction in Sect. 3.1 except for homomorphic evaluation algorithms, which are described in Sect. 3.2.

3.1 Construction

Let $\mathcal{F} \subseteq \{0, 1\}^\ell \to \{0, 1\}$ be a class of policies computed by depth-$d_\mathcal{F}$ circuits only from NAND gates, and $\mathcal{G} \subseteq \{0, 1\}^* \to \{0, 1\}$ be a class of operations computed by depth-$d_\mathcal{G}$ circuits only from NAND gates. Let $\mathsf{PRF}.\{\mathsf{Gen}, \mathsf{Eval}\}$ be a pseudorandom function, and d be the designed bound on the number of involved policies on homomorphic computations.

- $\mathsf{dMTHABE.Setup}(1^\lambda, 1^\ell, 1^{d_\mathcal{F}}, 1^{d_\mathcal{G}}, 1^d)$: choose DLWE parameters n, q, χ as described in Appendix A.1. Let B be a bound of samples from error distribution χ. Let $m = O(n \log^2 q)$, $N := n\lceil \log q \rceil$, and $M := (m + N + 1)\lceil \log q \rceil$. Generate $(\mathbf{A}, \mathbf{A}_{\tau_0}^{-1}) \leftarrow \mathsf{TrapGen}(1^n, q, m)$, where $\mathbf{A} \in \mathbb{Z}_q^{n \times m}$ and $\tau_0 = O(\sqrt{n \log q} \log n)$ from Corollary 1. Sample random matrices $\mathbf{B}, \mathbf{B}_0, \mathbf{B}_1, \ldots, \mathbf{B}_\ell \leftarrow \mathbb{Z}_q^{n \times N}$, and let $\mathbf{B}_x := [\mathbf{B}_1, \ldots, \mathbf{B}_\ell]$. Sample a random vector $\mathbf{v} \leftarrow \mathbb{Z}_q^n$. Choose a PRF seed $\sigma \leftarrow \mathsf{PRF.Gen}(1^\lambda)$. Let $H : \mathbb{Z}_q^{n \times m} \times \mathcal{F} \to \{0, 1\}^N$ be a hash function implemented by the random oracle. Output $\mathsf{pp} := (\mathbf{A}, \mathbf{B}, \mathbf{B}_0, \mathbf{B}_x, \mathbf{v}, H)$ and $\mathsf{msk} := (\mathbf{A}_{\tau_0}^{-1}, \sigma)$.
- $\mathsf{dMTHABE.Enc}_{\mathsf{pp}}(\mu \in \{0, 1\}, x \in \{0, 1\}^\ell)$: sample a random matrix $\mathbf{S} \leftarrow \mathbb{Z}_q^{n \times M}$, error matrix $\mathbf{E}_A \leftarrow \chi^{m \times M}$, and error vector $\mathbf{e}_v \leftarrow \chi^M$. For every $i \in \{0, 1, \ldots, \ell\}$ and $j \in [M]$, sample $\mathbf{R}_{i,j} \leftarrow \{0, 1\}^{m \times N}$, define $\mathbf{E}_i[j] := \mathbf{R}_{i,j}^T \mathbf{E}_A[j]$, and compute

$$\mathbf{C} := \begin{bmatrix} \mathbf{A}^T \\ \mathbf{B}_0^T \\ \mathbf{v}^T \end{bmatrix} \cdot \mathbf{S} + \begin{bmatrix} \mathbf{E}_A \\ \mathbf{E}_0 \\ \mathbf{e}_v^T \end{bmatrix} + \mu(\mathbf{I}_{m+N+1} \otimes \mathbf{g}^T) \in \mathbb{Z}_q^{(m+N+1) \times M}$$

$$\mathbf{C}_x := (\mathbf{B}_x - x\mathbf{G})^T \cdot \mathbf{S} + \begin{bmatrix} \mathbf{E}_1 \\ \vdots \\ \mathbf{E}_\ell \end{bmatrix} \in \mathbb{Z}_q^{\ell N \times M}.$$

Choose a random matrix $\mathbf{R} \leftarrow \mathbb{Z}_q^{n \times M}$ and sample a noise matrix $\mathbf{E}_A^{(F)} \leftarrow \chi^{m \times M}$. For every $j \in [M]$, choose $\mathbf{R}_j^{(F)} \leftarrow \{0, 1\}^{m \times N}$ and define $\mathbf{E}^{(F)}[j] := (\mathbf{R}_j^{(F)})^T \mathbf{E}_A^{(F)}[j]$.

Sample $\mathbf{e}_v^{(F)} \leftarrow \chi^M$, and compute

$$\mathbf{F} := \begin{bmatrix} \mathbf{A}^T \\ \mathbf{B}^T \\ \mathbf{v}^T \end{bmatrix} \cdot \mathbf{R} + \begin{bmatrix} \mathbf{E}_A^{(F)} \\ \mathbf{E}^{(F)} \\ (\mathbf{e}_v^{(F)})^T \end{bmatrix} + \mu(\mathbf{I}_{m+N+1} \otimes \mathbf{g}^T) \in \mathbb{Z}_q^{(m+N+1)\times M}$$

$$\approx \begin{bmatrix} \mathbf{A}^T \\ \mathbf{B}^T \\ \mathbf{v}^T \end{bmatrix} \cdot \mathbf{R} + \mu(\mathbf{I}_{m+N+1} \otimes \mathbf{g}^T) \quad \text{(error: } mB\text{).}$$

For every $i \in \{0, 1, \ldots, \ell\}$, $j \in [M]$, and $k \in [N]$, sample $\mathbf{E}_A^{(k)} \leftarrow \chi^{m\times M}$ and $\mathbf{e}_v^{(k)} \leftarrow \chi^M$, compute $\mathbf{E}_i^{(k)}[j] := \mathbf{R}_{i,j}^T \mathbf{E}_A^{(k)}[j]$, and set $\mathbf{E}^{(k)} := [(\mathbf{E}_A^{(k)})^T, (\mathbf{E}_0^{(k)})^T, \mathbf{e}_v^{(k)}]^T$. Sample $\mathbf{S}^{(1)}, \ldots, \mathbf{S}^{(N)} \leftarrow \chi^{n\times M}$, and compute

$$\mathbf{D} := \left(\mathbf{I}_N \otimes \begin{bmatrix} \mathbf{A}^T \\ \mathbf{B}_0^T \\ \mathbf{v}^T \end{bmatrix} \right) \cdot \begin{bmatrix} \mathbf{S}^{(1)} \\ \vdots \\ \mathbf{S}^{(N)} \end{bmatrix} + \begin{bmatrix} \mathbf{E}^{(1)} \\ \vdots \\ \mathbf{E}^{(N)} \end{bmatrix} + \mathbf{R} \otimes \mathbf{g} \otimes \mathbf{u}_{m+N+1} \in \mathbb{Z}_q^{(m+N+1)N\times M},$$

$$\mathbf{D}_x^{(k)} := (\mathbf{B}_x - x\mathbf{G})^T \cdot \mathbf{S}^{(k)} + \begin{bmatrix} \mathbf{E}_1^{(k)} \\ \vdots \\ \mathbf{E}_\ell^{(k)} \end{bmatrix} \in \mathbb{Z}_q^{\ell N\times M}.$$

Output $\mathsf{ct} := (x, \mathbf{C}, \mathbf{C}_x, \mathbf{F}, \mathbf{D}, \{\mathbf{D}_x^{(k)}\}_k)$.

– dMTHABE.Keygen$_{\mathsf{msk}}(f \in \mathcal{F})$: compute $\mathbf{B}_f := \mathsf{Eval}(f, \mathbf{B}_x)$ from f and $\mathbf{B}_x$. Generate $\mathbf{r}_f' = H(\mathbf{A}, f) \in \{0, 1\}^N$ by using the random oracle. Sample $\mathbf{r}_f \leftarrow \mathbf{A}_\tau^{-1}(-(\mathbf{B}_0 + \mathbf{B}_f)\mathbf{r}_f' - \mathbf{v}; \rho)$ with randomness $\rho \leftarrow \mathsf{PRF.Eval}(\sigma, f)$, where $\tau = O(\sqrt{mn} \cdot N^2\ell(N+1)^{d_{\mathcal{F}}}) \geq \tau_0$. Then, it holds that

$$[\mathbf{r}_f^T, \mathbf{r}_f'^T, 1] \begin{bmatrix} \mathbf{A}^T \\ (\mathbf{B}_0 + \mathbf{B}_f)^T \\ \mathbf{v}^T \end{bmatrix} = \mathbf{0}_{1\times n}.$$

Output $\mathsf{sk}_f := \mathbf{r}_f$.

– dMTHABE.ApplyF$_{\mathsf{pp}}(\mathsf{ct}, f \in \mathcal{F})$: when given ct and f, first compute a matrix $\mathbf{H} := \mathsf{EvRelation}(f, x, \mathbf{B}_x)$. Then set $\mathbf{C}_f := \mathbf{H}^T\mathbf{C}_x$, and compute

$$\hat{\mathbf{C}}_f := \mathbf{C} + \begin{bmatrix} \mathbf{0}_{m\times M} \\ \mathbf{C}_f \\ \mathbf{0}_{1\times M} \end{bmatrix}.$$

By Fact 21, it holds that for a secret key $\mathbf{t}_f^T := [\mathbf{r}_f^T, \mathbf{r}_f'^T, 1]$ with related to f,

$$\mathbf{t}_f^T \cdot \hat{\mathbf{C}}_f \approx \mu(\mathbf{t}_f^T \otimes \mathbf{g}^T) \quad \text{(error: } \|\mathbf{t}_f\|_\infty \cdot ((N+1)^{d_{\mathcal{F}}} \cdot \ell N + 1) \cdot mB\text{).}$$

For every $k \in [N]$, compute $\mathbf{D}_f^{(k)} := \mathbf{H}^T\mathbf{D}_x^{(k)}$ and let

$$\mathbf{D}_f := [\mathbf{0}_{M\times m}, (\mathbf{D}_f^{(1)})^T, \mathbf{0}_M, \ldots, \mathbf{0}_{M\times m}, (\mathbf{D}_f^{(N)})^T, \mathbf{0}_M]^T.$$

Compute $\hat{\mathbf{D}}_f := \mathbf{D} + \mathbf{D}_f$. Similar to $\hat{\mathbf{C}}_f$, it holds that for the secret key $\mathbf{t}_f$,

$$(\mathbf{I}_N \otimes \mathbf{t}_f^T) \cdot \hat{\mathbf{D}}_f \approx \mathbf{R} \otimes \mathbf{g} \in \mathbb{Z}_q^{N \times M} \quad (\text{error: } \|\mathbf{t}_f\|_\infty \cdot ((N+1)^{d_F} \cdot \ell N + 1) \cdot mB).$$

Output the functioned ciphertext $\mathsf{ct}^{(f)} := (\hat{\mathbf{C}}_f, \mathbf{F}, \hat{\mathbf{D}}_f)$.

- dMTHABE.Eval$(\mathsf{ct}^{(1)}, \ldots, \mathsf{ct}^{(k)}, F := \{f_1, \ldots, f_d\} \subseteq \mathcal{F}, g \in \mathcal{G})$: for fresh ciphertext $\mathsf{ct}^{(i)}$, compute functioned ciphertext $\mathsf{ct}^{(f_i)} := \mathsf{dMTHABE.ApplyF}_{\mathsf{pp}}(\mathsf{ct}^{(i)}, f_j)$, where $f_j \in F$ such that $f_j(x_i) = 0$. Then homomorphically evaluate g between the ciphertexts, and output $\mathsf{ct}^{(F)}$.

- dMTHABE.Dec$_{\mathsf{sk}_{f_1}, \ldots, \mathsf{sk}_{f_d}}(\mathsf{ct}^{(F)})^2$: given secret keys $\mathsf{sk}_{f_1}, \ldots, \mathsf{sk}_{f_d}$ for every policy in $F = \{f_1, \ldots, f_d\}$, and an ciphertext $\mathsf{ct}^{(F)} = (\hat{\mathbf{C}}_F, \mathbf{F}, \hat{\mathbf{D}}_F)$ for F, first, for all $j \in [d]$, obtain $\mathbf{r}'_{f_j} := H(\mathbf{A}, f_j)$ by using the random oracle. Construct the concatenated key $\mathbf{t}_F^T := [\mathbf{r}_{f_1}^T, \mathbf{r}_{f_1}'^T, 1, \ldots, \mathbf{r}_{f_d}^T, \mathbf{r}_{f_d}'^T, 1]$, and compute a vector $\mathbf{c} := \mathbf{t}_F^T \hat{\mathbf{C}}_F$. Let $\mathbf{u}^T := (0, \ldots, 0, \lfloor q/2 \rfloor) \in \mathbb{Z}^{1 \times d(m+N+1)}$. Compute $\tilde{\mu} := \mathbf{c}^T \cdot (\mathbf{I}_{d(m+N+1)} \otimes \mathbf{g}^{-T})(\mathbf{u})$, and output 0 if $|\tilde{\mu}| < q/4$, and 1 otherwise.

Correctness and security of this scheme are discussed in Appendix A.

3.2 The Algorithm Eval

We here describe the algorithms used in homomorphic evaluation of Eval.

Suppose that we obtain a functioned ciphertext $\mathsf{ct}^{(f)} := (\hat{\mathbf{C}}_f, \mathbf{F}, \hat{\mathbf{D}}_f)$ by applying dMTHABE.ApplyF for a policy $f \in \mathcal{F}$ to a fresh ciphertext $\mathsf{ct} := (x, \mathbf{C}, \mathbf{C}_x, \mathbf{F}, \mathbf{D}, \{\mathbf{D}_x^{(k)}\}_k)$. Then the functioned ciphertext $\mathsf{ct}^{(f)}$ satisfies the following three noisy equations with a secret key $\mathbf{t}_f \in \mathbb{Z}_q^{m+N+1}$ for f and small random matrix $\mathbf{R} \in \mathbb{Z}_q^{n \times M}$. For ease of notation, let B_C, B_F, B_D be bounds of errors included in $\hat{\mathbf{C}}_f, \mathbf{F}$, and $\hat{\mathbf{D}}_f$, respectively.

$$\mathbf{t}_f^T \hat{\mathbf{C}}_f \approx \mu(\mathbf{t}_f^T \otimes \mathbf{g}^T) \qquad (\text{error: } B_C) \qquad (1)$$

$$\mathbf{F} \approx \begin{bmatrix} \mathbf{A}^T \\ \mathbf{B}^T \\ \mathbf{v}^T \end{bmatrix} \mathbf{R} + \mu(\mathbf{I}_{m+N+1} \otimes \mathbf{g}^T) \quad (\text{error: } B_F) \qquad (2)$$

$$(\mathbf{I}_N \otimes \mathbf{t}_f^T) \cdot \hat{\mathbf{D}}_f \approx \mathbf{R} \otimes \mathbf{g} \qquad (\text{error: } B_D). \qquad (3)$$

Ciphertext Expansion. We describe a way to expand ciphertexts so that they can be decrypted by the concatenation of all the keys related to the target policies. This expansion method is very similar to that of [PS16]. Given ciphertext $(\hat{\mathbf{C}}, \mathbf{F}, \hat{\mathbf{D}})$ that satisfies the three relations (1), (2), and (3) for secret key $\mathbf{t} \in \mathbf{Z}_q^{n'}$ ($n' = k(m+N+1)$ for some positive integer k) and random matrix $\mathbf{R} \in \mathbb{Z}_q^{n \times M}$, generate $(\tilde{\mathbf{C}}, \tilde{\mathbf{F}}, \tilde{\mathbf{D}})$ that satisfies the relations (1), (2), and (3) for the concatenated secret key $\tilde{\mathbf{t}} := [\mathbf{t}, \mathbf{t}_f]$ constructed from $\mathbf{t}$ and $\mathbf{t}_f := [\mathbf{r}_f^T, \mathbf{r}_f'^T, 1]^T \in \mathbb{Z}_q^{m+N+1}$, and random matrix $\tilde{\mathbf{R}}$:

---

[2] The algorithm can take as input fresh ciphertext ct (and the single secret key sk_f for $f \in \mathcal{F}$ such that $f(x) = 0$) by generating the functioned ciphertext $\mathsf{ct}^{(F)} := \mathsf{dMTHABE.ApplyF}_{\mathsf{pp}}(\mathsf{ct}, f)$ before the computation begins.

– $\mathbf{F}$ and $\mathbf{R}$ are not changed. That is, $\tilde{\mathbf{F}} := \mathbf{F}$ and $\tilde{\mathbf{R}} := \mathbf{R}$. This preserves the relation (2).

– $\tilde{\mathbf{D}}$ is computed as

$$\tilde{\mathbf{D}} := \left(\mathbf{I}_N \otimes \begin{bmatrix} \mathbf{I}_{n'} \\ \mathbf{0}_{(m+N+1) \times n'} \end{bmatrix} \right) \cdot \hat{\mathbf{D}}.$$

Then, since the following holds, the relation (3) is preserved.

$$(\mathbf{I}_N \otimes \tilde{\mathbf{t}}^T) \cdot \tilde{\mathbf{D}} = (\mathbf{I}_N \otimes \mathbf{t}^T) \cdot \hat{\mathbf{D}}$$
$$\approx \mathbf{R} \otimes \mathbf{g} \qquad \text{(error: } B_{\mathbf{D}}\text{)}.$$

– We define

$$\tilde{\mathbf{C}} := \begin{bmatrix} \hat{\mathbf{C}} \ \mathbf{X} \\ \mathbf{F} \end{bmatrix},$$

where $\mathbf{X}$ is a matrix computed by the following procedure. Let $\mathbf{B}, \mathbf{B}_0 \in \mathbb{Z}_q^{n \times N}$ be matrices included in the public parameter, generate $\mathbf{r}'_f = H(\mathbf{A}, f) \in \{0, 1\}^N$, and compute $\mathbf{B}_f := \mathsf{Eval}(\mathbf{B}, f)$. Define

$$\mathbf{s} := (\mathbf{I}_n \otimes \mathbf{g}^{-T})((\mathbf{B}_0 + \mathbf{B}_f - \mathbf{B})\mathbf{r}'_f) \in \{0, 1\}^N$$
$$\mathbf{X} := (\mathbf{s}^T \otimes \mathbf{I}_{n'}) \cdot \hat{\mathbf{D}}.$$

Then, by construction of $\mathbf{X}$, it holds that

$$\mathbf{t}^T \mathbf{X} = \mathbf{t}^T \cdot (\mathbf{s}^T \otimes \mathbf{I}_{n'}) \cdot \hat{\mathbf{D}}$$
$$= (\mathbf{s}^T \otimes 1) \cdot (\mathbf{I}_N \otimes \mathbf{t}^T) \cdot \hat{\mathbf{D}}$$
$$\approx \mathbf{s}^T \cdot \mathbf{R} \otimes \mathbf{g} \qquad \text{(error: } N \cdot B_{\mathbf{D}}\text{)}$$
$$= \mathbf{s}^T \cdot (\mathbf{I}_n \otimes \mathbf{g}) \cdot (\mathbf{R} \otimes 1)$$
$$= \mathbf{r}'^T_f \cdot (\mathbf{B}_0 + \mathbf{B}_f - \mathbf{B})^T \cdot \mathbf{R}.$$

From

$$\mathbf{t}^T \mathbf{X} + \mathbf{t}_f \mathbf{F}$$

$$\approx \mathbf{r}'^T_f \cdot (\mathbf{B}_0 + \mathbf{B}_f - \mathbf{B})^T \cdot \mathbf{R} + [\mathbf{r}^T_f, \mathbf{r}'^T_f, 1] \begin{bmatrix} \mathbf{A}^T \\ \mathbf{B}^T \\ \mathbf{v}^T \end{bmatrix} \cdot \mathbf{R} + \mu(\mathbf{t}^T_f \otimes \mathbf{g}^T)$$

$$\text{(error: } N \cdot B_{\mathbf{D}} + \|\mathbf{t}_f\|_\infty \cdot (m + N + 1) \cdot B_{\mathbf{F}}\text{)}$$

$$= [\mathbf{r}^T_f, \mathbf{r}'^T_f, 1] \begin{bmatrix} \mathbf{A}^T \\ \mathbf{B}^T_0 + \mathbf{B}^T_f \\ \mathbf{v}^T \end{bmatrix} \cdot \mathbf{R} + \mu(\mathbf{t}^T_f \otimes \mathbf{g}^T)$$

$$= \mu(\mathbf{t}^T_f \otimes \mathbf{g}^T)$$

we have

$$\tilde{\mathbf{t}}^T \tilde{\mathbf{C}} \approx \mu(\tilde{\mathbf{t}}^T \otimes \mathbf{g}^T) \qquad \text{(error: } B_{\mathbf{C}} + N \cdot B_{\mathbf{D}} + \|\mathbf{t}_f\|_\infty \cdot (m + N + 1) \cdot B_{\mathbf{F}}\text{)},$$

and so the relation (1) is preserved for $\tilde{\mathbf{C}}$.

Homomorphic Operations. We here describe a way to evaluate homomorphic addition and multiplication. Consider two ciphertexts $(\mathbf{C}_1, \mathbf{F}_1, \mathbf{D}_1)$ and $(\mathbf{C}_2, \mathbf{F}_2, \mathbf{D}_2)$ that encrypt $\mu_1, \mu_2 \in \{0, 1\}$ under the secret key $\mathbf{t} \in \mathbb{Z}_q^{n'}$. The two ciphertexts satisfy the relations (1), (2), and (3) for two random matrices $\mathbf{R}_1, \mathbf{R}_2$, respectively.

- Homomorphic addition: to homomorphically add the ciphertexts, we just add the corresponding matrices:

$$(\mathbf{C}_{\mathrm{add}}, \mathbf{F}_{\mathrm{add}}, \mathbf{D}_{\mathrm{add}}) := (\mathbf{C}_1 + \mathbf{C}_2, \mathbf{F}_1 + \mathbf{F}_2, \mathbf{D}_1 + \mathbf{D}_2).$$

  It is immediate that the relations (1), (2), and (3) are preserved for message $\mu_{\mathrm{add}} := \mu_1 + \mu_2$ and random matrix $\mathbf{R}_{\mathrm{add}} := \mathbf{R}_1 + \mathbf{R}_2$.
- Homomorphic multiplication: to homomorphically multiply the ciphertexts, we compute the ciphertext consisting of the matrices computed as follows:

$$\mathbf{C}_{\mathrm{mult}} := \mathbf{C}_1 \cdot (\mathbf{I}_{n'} \otimes \mathbf{g}^{-T})(\mathbf{C}_2)$$

$$\mathbf{F}_{\mathrm{mult}} := \mathbf{F}_1 \cdot (\mathbf{I}_{m+N+1} \otimes \mathbf{g}^{-T})(\mathbf{F}_2)$$

$$\mathbf{D}_{\mathrm{mult}} := \mathbf{D}_1 \cdot (\mathbf{I}_{m+N+1} \otimes \mathbf{g}^{-T})(\mathbf{F}_2) + (\mathbf{I}_N \otimes \mathbf{C}_1) \cdot (\mathbf{I}_{n'N} \otimes \mathbf{g}^{-T})(\mathbf{D}_2).$$

We now show that the ciphertext output by the homomorphic multiplication procedure satisfies the relations (1), (2), and (3). Since $\mathbf{C}_{mult}$ is the ciphertext output by the homomorphic multiplication of GSW FHE [GSW13], it is easy to see that the relation (1) is preserved. If we let $B_{\mathbf{C}_i}$ be a upper bound of the noise included in $\mathbf{C}_i (i = 1, 2)$, then we have

$$\mathbf{t}^T \mathbf{C}_{\mathrm{mult}} \approx \mu_1 (\mathbf{t}^T \otimes \mathbf{g}^T) \cdot (\mathbf{I}_{n'} \otimes \mathbf{g}^{-T})(\mathbf{C}_2) \quad (\text{error: } n' \lceil \log q \rceil B_{\mathbf{C}_1})$$

$$= \mu_1 \mathbf{t}^T \mathbf{C}_2$$

$$\approx \mu_1 \mu_2 (\mathbf{t}^T \otimes \mathbf{g}^T) \qquad (\text{error: } \mu_1 B_{\mathbf{C}_2}).$$

Let $\mathbf{R}_{\mathrm{mult}} := \mathbf{R}_1 \cdot (\mathbf{I}_{m+N+1} \otimes \mathbf{g}^{-T})(\mathbf{F}_2) + \mu_1 \mathbf{R}_2$ and $\mu_{\mathrm{mult}} := \mu_1 \mu_2$. Then the relation (2) is also preserved for $\mathbf{F}_{\mathrm{mult}}$:

$$\mathbf{F}_{\mathrm{mult}} = \mathbf{F}_1 \cdot (\mathbf{I}_{m+N+1} \otimes \mathbf{g}^{-T})(\mathbf{F}_2)$$

$$\approx \left(\begin{bmatrix} \mathbf{A}^T \\ \mathbf{B}^T \\ \mathbf{v}^T \end{bmatrix} \cdot \mathbf{R}_1 + \mu_1 (\mathbf{I}_{m+N+1} \otimes \mathbf{g}^T) \right) (\mathbf{I}_{m+N+1} \otimes \mathbf{g}^{-T})(\mathbf{F}_2) \qquad (\text{error: } M \cdot B_{\mathbf{F}_1})$$

$$\approx \begin{bmatrix} \mathbf{A}^T \\ \mathbf{B}^T \\ \mathbf{v}^T \end{bmatrix} \cdot (\mathbf{R}_1 \cdot (\mathbf{I}_{m+N+1} \otimes \mathbf{g}^{-T})(\mathbf{F}_2) + \mu_1 \mathbf{R}_2) + \mu_1 \mu_2 (\mathbf{I}_{m+N+1} \otimes \mathbf{g}^T) \qquad (\text{error: } \mu_1 B_{\mathbf{F}_2})$$

$$= \begin{bmatrix} \mathbf{A}^T \\ \mathbf{B}^T \\ \mathbf{v}^T \end{bmatrix} \cdot \mathbf{R}_{\mathrm{mult}} + \mu_{\mathrm{mult}} (\mathbf{I}_{m+N+1} \otimes \mathbf{g}^T).$$

We check that the relation (3) is also preserved. First, we can see that

$$(\mathbf{I}_N \otimes \mathbf{t}) \cdot \mathbf{D}_1 \cdot (\mathbf{I}_{m+N+1} \otimes \mathbf{g}^{-T})(\mathbf{F}_2)$$

$$\approx (\mathbf{R}_1 \otimes \mathbf{g}) \cdot (\mathbf{I}_{m+N+1} \otimes \mathbf{g}^{-T})(\mathbf{F}_2) \qquad (\text{error: } M \cdot B_{\mathbf{D}_1})$$

$$= (\mathbf{R}_1 \cdot (\mathbf{I}_{m+N+1} \otimes \mathbf{g}^{-T})(\mathbf{F}_2)) \otimes \mathbf{g}.$$

In addition, the following holds:

$$(\mathbf{I}_N \otimes \mathbf{t})(\mathbf{I}_N \otimes \mathbf{C}_1) \cdot (\mathbf{I}_{n'N} \otimes \mathbf{g}^{-T})(\mathbf{D}_2)$$
$$= (\mathbf{I}_N \otimes \mathbf{t}\mathbf{C}_1) \cdot (\mathbf{I}_{n'N} \otimes \mathbf{g}^{-T})(\mathbf{D}_2)$$
$$\approx \mu_1(\mathbf{I}_N \otimes \mathbf{t}^T \otimes \mathbf{g}^T) \cdot (\mathbf{I}_{n'N} \otimes \mathbf{g}^{-T})(\mathbf{D}_2) \qquad (\text{error: } n'\lceil \log q \rceil B_{\mathbf{C}_1})$$
$$= \mu_1(\mathbf{I}_N \otimes \mathbf{t}^T) \cdot \mathbf{D}_2$$
$$\approx (\mu_1 \mathbf{R}) \otimes \mathbf{g} \qquad\qquad\qquad (\text{error: } \mu_1 B_{\mathbf{D}_2}).$$

Hence, by

$$(\mathbf{I}_N \otimes \mathbf{t}^T)\mathbf{D}_{\text{mult}} \approx \mathbf{R}_{\text{mult}} \otimes \mathbf{g} \quad (\text{error: } M \cdot B_{\mathbf{D}_1} + n'\lceil \log q \rceil B_{\mathbf{C}_1} + \mu_1 B_{\mathbf{D}_2}),$$

$\mathbf{D}_{\text{mult}}$ satisfies the relation (3).

A Correctness and Security

In this section, we discuss about correctness and security of the proposed MT-HABE described in Sect. 3. In Appendix A.1, we consider parameter settings of the proposed scheme for the correctness and security, and the proofs of them are described in Appendix A.2.

A.1 Parameter Settings

The DLWE parameters n, q, χ are chosen according to the conditions decided by the correctness and security.

It is required to set $n \geq \lambda$ and $q \leq 2^n$. We also set $\ell, d = \text{poly}(\lambda)$. We estimate the worst-case noise growth when homomorphically evaluating a depth-$d_{\mathcal{G}}$ circuit consisting only of the NAND gate under d different policies of depth at most $d_{\mathcal{F}}$. We define the max error B_{max} of the ciphertext $(\mathbf{C}, \mathbf{F}, \mathbf{D})$ output by the algorithm ApplyF or Eval:

$$B_{\max} := \max(B_{\mathbf{C}}, B_{\mathbf{F}}, B_{\mathbf{D}}).$$

From Sect. 3.2, the ciphertext generated by homomorphically evaluating a NAND gate has noise at most

$$M \cdot B_{\mathbf{D}_1} + d(m + N + 1)\lceil \log q \rceil B_{\mathbf{C}_1} + \mu_1 B_{\mathbf{D}_2}$$
$$\leq \{M \cdot (d + 1) + 1\} \cdot B_{\max}$$
$$= \text{poly}(d, n, \lceil \log q \rceil) \cdot B_{\max}.$$

for some polynomial $\text{poly}(\cdot)$. The ciphertext generated by the ciphertext expansion algorithm described in Sect. 3.2 also has noise at most

$$B_{\mathbf{C}} + N \cdot B_{\mathbf{D}} + \|\mathbf{t}_f\|_\infty \cdot (m + N + 1) \cdot B_{\mathbf{F}}$$
$$\leq (1 + N + \|\mathbf{t}_f\|_\infty \cdot (m + N + 1)) \cdot B_{\max}$$
$$= \text{poly}'(n, \lceil \log q \rceil) \cdot B_{\max}.$$

for some polynomial $\mathsf{poly}'(\cdot)$.

Since the max error $B_{\max}$ of fresh functioned ciphertexts is at most $\|\mathbf{t}_f\|_\infty \cdot ((N+1)^{d_{\mathcal{F}}} \cdot \ell N + 1)mB$, the noise of the evaluated ciphertexts obtained by homomorphic evaluation of a depth-$d_{\mathcal{G}}$ circuit under different d policies is at most

$$\mathsf{poly}(d, n, \lceil \log q \rceil)^d \cdot \mathsf{poly}'(n, \lceil \log q \rceil)^{d_{\mathcal{G}}} \cdot \|\mathbf{t}_f\|_\infty \cdot ((N+1)^{d_{\mathcal{F}}} \cdot \ell N + 1)mB$$

$$\leq \mathsf{poly}(d, n, \lceil \log q \rceil)^d \cdot \mathsf{poly}'(n, \lceil \log q \rceil)^{d_{\mathcal{G}}} \cdot O(\ell^2 m^2 \sqrt{n} N^3 (N+1)^{2d_{\mathcal{F}}})B.$$

For the correctness and security, we select the parameters so that the above quantity by a factor of eight is less than 2^{n^ϵ} for some $0 < \epsilon < 1$. To hold this, we set $n = \tilde{O}(d \cdot \log d + d_{\mathcal{G}} + d_{\mathcal{F}} \cdot \log \ell)^{1/\epsilon}$ and choose q and χ so that they satisfy $q/B \geq 2^{n^\epsilon}$, where B is the upper bound of the noise distribution χ. Selecting such parameters leads the reduction from the $\mathsf{DLWE}_{n,q,\chi}$ problem to approximate a short vector on the n dimensional lattice by a factor of $\tilde{O}(n \cdot 2^{n^\epsilon})$.

A.2   Proofs

Correctness and security of our dMTHABE scheme can be proven in a very similar way to [BCTW16].

Theorem 1 (Correctness). *The scheme* dMTHABE *with parameters* $\ell, d_{\mathcal{F}}, d_{\mathcal{G}}, d$ *is correct for policy class* $\mathcal{F}_{\ell,d_{\mathcal{F}}}$ *and homomorphism class* $\mathcal{G}_{d_{\mathcal{G}}}$.

Proof. Let $(\mathsf{pp}, \mathsf{msk}) \leftarrow \mathsf{dMTHABE.Setup}(1^\lambda, 1^\ell, 1^{d_{\mathcal{F}}}, 1^{d_{\mathcal{G}}}, 1^d)$. Consider k ciphertexts $\mathsf{ct}^{(i)} \leftarrow \mathsf{dMTHABE.Enc}_{\mathsf{pp}}(\mu_i, x_i)$ of message $\mu_i \in \{0, 1\}$ with attribute $x_i \in \{0, 1\}^\ell$. For a set of d policies $F := \{f_i\}_{i \in [d]} \subseteq \mathcal{F}_{\ell,d_{\mathcal{F}}}$ and operation $g \in \mathcal{G}_{d_{\mathcal{G}}}$, consider an evaluated ciphertext

$$\mathsf{ct}^{(F)} := (\hat{\mathbf{C}}_F, \mathbf{F}_F, \hat{\mathbf{D}}_F) := \mathsf{dMTHABE.Eval}(\{\mathsf{ct}^{(i)}\}_{i \in [k]}, F, g).$$

By the process of Eval in Sect. 3.2, it holds that

$$\mathbf{c} := \mathbf{t}_F \hat{\mathbf{C}}_F \approx \mu_g (\mathbf{t}_F^T \otimes \mathbf{g}^T)$$

for $\mu_g := g(\mu_1, \ldots, \mu_k)$ and $\mathbf{t}_F^T := [\mathbf{t}_{f_1}^T, \ldots, \mathbf{t}_{f_d}^T]$ where $\mathbf{r}_{f_i} \leftarrow \mathsf{dMTHABE.Keygen}_{\mathsf{msk}}(f_i)$, $\mathbf{r}'_{f_i} = H(\mathbf{A}, f_i)$, and $\mathbf{t}_{f_i}^T := [\mathbf{r}_{f_i}^T, \mathbf{r}'^T_{f_i}, 1]$. Let $\mathbf{u}^T := (0, \ldots, 0, \lfloor q/2 \rfloor)$, then

$$\tilde{\mu} := \mathbf{c}^T (\mathbf{I}_{d(m+N+1)} \otimes \mathbf{g}^{-T})(\mathbf{u}) \approx \mu_g \lfloor q/2 \rfloor.$$

Choosing the parameters as described in Appendix A.1, the noise in $\hat{\mathbf{C}}_F$ is of size at most $q/8$. Hence, it holds that

$$\Pr[\mathsf{dMTHABE.Dec}_{\mathsf{sk}_{f_1}, \ldots, \mathsf{sk}_{f_d}}(\mathsf{ct}^{(F)}) \neq \mu_g] = \mathsf{negl}(\lambda).$$

Theorem 2 (Security). *The scheme* dMTHABE *scheme is selectively secure for function classes* $\mathcal{F}, \mathcal{G}$ *in the random oracle model if the* $\mathsf{DLWE}_{n,q,\chi}$ *assumption holds.*

Proof. In a similar way to [BCTW16], we prove this theorem by considering about the indistinguishability of a column vector in the challenge ciphertext $\mathbf{C}, \mathbf{C}_{x^*}, \mathbf{F}$, $\mathbf{D}, \{\mathbf{D}_{x^*}^{(k)}\}_{k \in [N]}$, where we let x^* be the challenge attribute. That is, we consider the game in which the adversary is given the following vectors

$$\mathbf{c} := \begin{bmatrix} \mathbf{A}^T \\ \mathbf{B}_0^T \\ \mathbf{v}^T \end{bmatrix} \cdot \mathbf{s} + \begin{bmatrix} \mathbf{e}_A \\ \mathbf{e}_0 \\ \mathbf{e}_v \end{bmatrix}, \mathbf{c}_{x^*} := (\mathbf{B}_{x^*} - x^*\mathbf{G})^T \cdot \mathbf{s} + \begin{bmatrix} \mathbf{e}_1 \\ \vdots \\ \mathbf{e}_\ell \end{bmatrix}, \quad \mathbf{f} := \begin{bmatrix} \mathbf{A}^T \\ \mathbf{B}^T \\ \mathbf{v}^T \end{bmatrix} \cdot \mathbf{r} + \begin{bmatrix} \mathbf{e}_A^{(F)} \\ \mathbf{e}^{(F)} \\ \mathbf{e}_v^{(F)} \end{bmatrix}$$

$$\begin{bmatrix} \mathbf{d}^{(1)} \\ \vdots \\ \mathbf{d}^{(N)} \end{bmatrix} := \mathbf{d} = \left(\mathbf{I}_N \otimes \begin{bmatrix} \mathbf{A}^T \\ \mathbf{B}_0^T \\ \mathbf{v}^T \end{bmatrix} \right) \cdot \begin{bmatrix} \mathbf{s}^{(1)} \\ \vdots \\ \mathbf{s}^{(N)} \end{bmatrix} + \begin{bmatrix} \mathbf{e}^{(1)} \\ \vdots \\ \mathbf{e}^{(N)} \end{bmatrix}, \mathbf{d}_{x^*}^{(k)} := (\mathbf{B}_{x^*} - x^*\mathbf{G})^T \cdot \mathbf{s}^{(k)} + \begin{bmatrix} \mathbf{e}_1^{(k)} \\ \vdots \\ \mathbf{e}_\ell^{(k)} \end{bmatrix} \quad (\forall k \in [N]).$$

or the uniformly random vectors, and distinguishes them. We call this game *column game*, and define the advantage of the adversary in this game as $\mathsf{Adv}_{\mathcal{A}}^{\mathsf{column}}(\lambda)$. Without loss of generality, we can prove the security in the column game instead of proving the selective security game defined in Definition 3.

We now consider the following sequence of games. Let $\mathsf{Adv}_{\mathcal{A}}^{\mathsf{Game}_i}(\lambda)$ be the advantage of the adversary $\mathcal{A}$ in Game_i.

- Game_0: This game is the same as the column game, so it holds that

$$\mathsf{Adv}_{\mathcal{A}}^{\mathsf{column}}(\lambda) = \mathsf{Adv}_{\mathcal{A}}^{\mathsf{Game}_0}(\lambda).$$

- Game_1: This game is the same as Game_0 except that the challenger aborts if the adversary sends the random oracle query $(\mathbf{D}, f)$ such that $\mathbf{D} = \mathbf{A}$ and $f(x^*) = 1$ before the challenger outputs the challenge attribute x^*.
  Since the probability that the adversary sends such query is $\mathsf{negl}(\lambda)$, we have

$$|\mathsf{Adv}_{\mathcal{A}}^{\mathsf{Game}_1}(\lambda) - \mathsf{Adv}_{\mathcal{A}}^{\mathsf{Game}_0}(\lambda)| = \mathsf{negl}(\lambda).$$

- Game_2: This game is the same as Game_1 except that for every Keygen query the challenger uniformly chooses the randomness and use it for $\mathbf{A}_{\tau_0}^{-1}$ instead of generating the randomness for $\mathbf{A}_{\tau_0}^{-1}$ by using PRF. To answer the oracle query consistently, the challenger stores the Keygen query and its secret key to the table. By the property of the PRF, this game is indistinguishable from Game_1:

$$|\mathsf{Adv}_{\mathcal{A}}^{\mathsf{Game}_2}(\lambda) - \mathsf{Adv}_{\mathcal{A}}^{\mathsf{Game}_1}(\lambda)| = \mathsf{negl}(\lambda).$$

- Game_3: This game is the same as Game_2 except for the generation of the public parameters $\mathbf{B}, \mathbf{B}_0, \mathbf{B}_1, \dots, \mathbf{B}_\ell$. Here, there exist matrices $\mathbf{R}_0, \mathbf{R}_1, \dots, \mathbf{R}_\ell$ such that they are distributed uniformly over $\{0, 1\}^{m \times N}$ and satisfies $\mathbf{e}_i = \mathbf{R}_i^T \mathbf{e}_A$ and $\mathbf{e}_i^{(k)} = \mathbf{R}_i^T \mathbf{e}_A^{(k)}$. There exists a matrix $\mathbf{R}^{(F)}$ such that it is distributed uniformly over $\{0, 1\}^{m \times N}$ and satisfies $\mathbf{e}^{(F)} = (\mathbf{R}^{(F)})^T \mathbf{e}_A^{(F)}$. In this game, the public matrices $\mathbf{B}, \mathbf{B}_0, \mathbf{B}_1, \dots, \mathbf{B}_\ell$ are computed as $\mathbf{B} := \mathbf{A}\mathbf{R}^{(F)}, \mathbf{B}_0 := \mathbf{A}\mathbf{R}_0, \mathbf{B}_i := \mathbf{A}\mathbf{R}_i + x_i^*(\mathbf{I}_n \otimes \mathbf{g}^T) \; (\forall i \in [\ell])$ instead of choosing them uniformly at random. By the leftover hash lemma, every distribution of $\mathbf{B}, \mathbf{B}_0, \mathbf{B}_1, \dots, \mathbf{B}_\ell$ is indistinguishable from uniform over $\mathbb{Z}_q^{n \times N}$. Hence we have

$$|\mathsf{Adv}_{\mathcal{A}}^{\mathsf{Game}_3}(\lambda) - \mathsf{Adv}_{\mathcal{A}}^{\mathsf{Game}_2}(\lambda)| = \mathsf{negl}(\lambda).$$

– Game_4: This game is the same as Game_3 except that the return sk_f for the key generation query $(\mathbf{A}, f)$ is generated without using the trapdoor $\mathbf{A}_\tau^{-1}$.

Without loss of generality, we can assume that the tuple $(\mathbf{A}, f)$ is queried to the Keygen oracle before querying to the random oracle. By the definition of selective security, the policy f satisfies $f(x^*) = 1$ for the challenge attribute x^*, and $[\mathbf{r}_f, \mathbf{r}'_f]$ is generated as $\mathbf{r}'_f \leftarrow \{0, 1\}^N$ and $\mathbf{r}_f \leftarrow \mathbf{A}_\tau^{-1}(-\mathbf{v} - (\mathbf{B}_0 + \mathbf{B}_f)\mathbf{r}'_f)$.

Let $\mathbf{H} := \mathsf{EvRelation}(f, x^*, \mathbf{B}_{x^*})$. Then it holds that $\mathbf{B}_f - f(x^*)(\mathbf{I}_n \otimes \mathbf{g}^T) = (\mathbf{B}_{x^*} - x^*\mathbf{G})\mathbf{H}$. From $f(x^*) = 1$, we have $\mathbf{B}_f = \mathbf{A}\mathbf{R}\mathbf{H} + (\mathbf{I}_n \otimes \mathbf{g}^T)$. Hence we have $[\mathbf{A}, \mathbf{B}_0 + \mathbf{B}_f] = [\mathbf{A}, \mathbf{A}(\mathbf{R}_0 + \mathbf{R}\mathbf{H}) + (\mathbf{I}_n \otimes \mathbf{g}^T)]$. By Corollary 2, when given $\mathbf{R}_0$, $\mathbf{R}$ and $\mathbf{H}$, for any $\tau \geq \tau' = O(\sqrt{mn} \cdot N \cdot \|(\mathbf{R}_0 + \mathbf{R}\mathbf{H})\|_\infty)$, we can sample from $[\mathbf{A}, \mathbf{B}_0 + \mathbf{B}_f]_P^{-1}$ for $P = D_{\mathbb{Z}^m, \tau} \times \{0, 1\}^N$.

We generate $[\mathbf{r}_f, \mathbf{r}'_f]$ by $[\mathbf{r}_f, \mathbf{r}'_f] \leftarrow [\mathbf{A}, \mathbf{B}_0 + \mathbf{B}_f]_P^{-1}(-\mathbf{v})$. Then, $\mathbf{r}'_f$ is stored as the reply for the random oracle query $(\mathbf{A}, f)$. By Corollary 2, the marginal distribution of $\mathbf{r}'_f$ is statistically indistinguishable from uniform over $\{0, 1\}^N$, and the probability distribution of $\mathbf{r}_f$ conditioned on $\mathbf{r}'_f$ is a discrete Gaussian distribution over the appropriate coset of the integer lattice. Since the view of the adversary in this game is statistically indistinguishable from that of Game_3, we have

$$|\mathsf{Adv}_{\mathcal{A}}^{\mathsf{Game}_4}(\lambda) - \mathsf{Adv}_{\mathcal{A}}^{\mathsf{Game}_3}(\lambda)| = \mathsf{negl}(\lambda).$$

– Game_5: This game is the same as Game_4 except for the way to choose $\mathbf{A}$. The challenger chooses random $\mathbf{A}$ from $\mathbb{Z}_q^{n \times m}$ instead of generating it by using $\mathsf{TrapGen}$. By Corollary 1, the distribution of the matrix $\mathbf{A}$ generated by $\mathsf{TrapGen}$ is statistically indistinguishable from uniform over $\mathbb{Z}_q^{n \times m}$, so we have

$$|\mathsf{Adv}_{\mathcal{A}}^{\mathsf{Game}_5}(\lambda) - \mathsf{Adv}_{\mathcal{A}}^{\mathsf{Game}_4}(\lambda)| = \mathsf{negl}(\lambda).$$

– Game_6: We change the contents of the challenge ciphertexts as follows:

$$\mathbf{u}_A^{(C)} := \mathbf{A}^T\mathbf{s} + \mathbf{e}_A, u_v^{(C)} := \mathbf{v}^T\mathbf{s} + e_v, \quad \mathbf{u}_A^{(F)} := \mathbf{A}^T\mathbf{r} + \mathbf{e}_A^{(F)},$$

$$u_v^{(F)} := \mathbf{v}^T\mathbf{r} + e_v^{(F)}, \mathbf{u}_A^{(D,k)} := \mathbf{A}^T\mathbf{s}^{(k)} + \mathbf{e}_A^{(k)}, \quad u_v^{(D,k)} := \mathbf{v}^T\mathbf{s}^{(k)} + e_v^{(k)}.$$

The challenge ciphertexts can be rewritten as

$$\mathbf{c} := \begin{bmatrix} \mathbf{u}_A^{(C)} \\ \mathbf{R}_0^T\mathbf{u}_A^{(C)} \\ u_v^{(C)} \end{bmatrix}, \mathbf{c}_{x^*} := \begin{bmatrix} \mathbf{R}_1^T\mathbf{u}_A^{(C)} \\ \vdots \\ \mathbf{R}_\ell^T\mathbf{u}_A^{(C)} \end{bmatrix}, \quad \mathbf{f} := \begin{bmatrix} \mathbf{u}_A^{(F)} \\ (\mathbf{R}^{(F)})^T\mathbf{u}_A^{(F)} \\ u_v^{(F)} \end{bmatrix},$$

$$\mathbf{d}^{(k)} := \begin{bmatrix} \mathbf{u}_A^{(D,k)} \\ \mathbf{R}_0^T\mathbf{u}_A^{(D,k)} \\ u_v^{(D,k)} \end{bmatrix}, \mathbf{d}_{x^*}^{(k)} := \begin{bmatrix} \mathbf{R}_1^T\mathbf{u}_A^{(D,k)} \\ \vdots \\ \mathbf{R}_\ell^T\mathbf{u}_A^{(D,k)} \end{bmatrix} \quad (\forall k \in [N]).$$

This game is equivalent to Game_5, so we have

$$\mathsf{Adv}_{\mathcal{A}}^{\mathsf{Game}_6}(\lambda) = \mathsf{Adv}_{\mathcal{A}}^{\mathsf{Game}_5}(\lambda).$$

– Game$_7$: We change the distribution of $\mathbf{u}_A^{(C)}, u_v^{(C)}, \mathbf{u}_A^{(F)}, u_v^{(F)}, \mathbf{u}_A^{(D,k)}, u_v^{(D,k)}$ to the uniform distribution. By the $\mathsf{DLWE}_{n,q,\chi}$ assumption, this change cannot be distinguished by the adversary $\mathcal{A}$ and so we have

$$|\mathsf{Adv}_{\mathcal{A}}^{\mathsf{Game}_7}(\lambda) - \mathsf{Adv}_{\mathcal{A}}^{\mathsf{Game}_6}(\lambda)| = \mathsf{negl}(\lambda).$$

– Game$_8$: In this game, we change the distribution of the challenge ciphertexts to the uniform. By the leftover hash lemma, the view of the adversary in this game is statistically indistinguishable from Game$_7$, so we have

$$|\mathsf{Adv}_{\mathcal{A}}^{\mathsf{Game}_8}(\lambda) - \mathsf{Adv}_{\mathcal{A}}^{\mathsf{Game}_7}(\lambda)| = \mathsf{negl}(\lambda).$$

The advantage of the adversary in this game is 0, that is, $\mathsf{Adv}_{\mathcal{A}}^{\mathsf{Game}_8}(\lambda) = 0$.

From the above sequences of the games, we can see that $\mathsf{Adv}_{\mathcal{A}}^{\mathsf{column}}(\lambda) = \mathsf{negl}(\lambda)$, and therefore the proposed MT-HABE is selectively secure.

References

[Ajt99] Ajtai, M.: Generating hard instances of the short basis problem. In: ICALP, pp. 1–9 (1999)

[BCTW16] Brakerski, Z., Cash, D., Tsabary, R., Wee, H.: Targeted homomorphic attribute-based encryption. In: Hirt, M., Smith, A. (eds.) TCC 2016, Part II. LNCS, vol. 9986, pp. 330–360. Springer, Heidelberg (2016). https://doi.org/10.1007/978-3-662-53644-5_13

[BGG+14] Boneh, D., Gentry, C., Gorbunov, S., Halevi, S., Nikolaenko, V., Segev, G., Vaikuntanathan, V., Vinayagamurthy, D.: Fully key-homomorphic encryption, arithmetic circuit ABE and compact garbled circuits. In: Nguyen, P.Q., Oswald, E. (eds.) EUROCRYPT 2014. LNCS, vol. 8441, pp. 533–556. Springer, Heidelberg (2014). https://doi.org/10.1007/978-3-642-55220-5_30

[BGV12] Brakerski, Z., Gentry, C., Vaikuntanathan, V.: (leveled) Fully homomorphic encryption without bootstrapping. In: ITCS, pp. 309–325 (2012)

[BLP+13] Brakerski, Z., Langlois, A., Peikert, C., Regev, O., Stehlé, D.: Classical hardness of learning with errors. In: STOC, pp. 575–584 (2013)

[Bra12] Brakerski, Z.: Fully homomorphic encryption without modulus switching from classical GapSVP. In: Safavi-Naini, R., Canetti, R. (eds.) CRYPTO 2012. LNCS, vol. 7417, pp. 868–886. Springer, Heidelberg (2012). https://doi.org/10.1007/978-3-642-32009-5_50

[BV11a] Brakerski, Z., Vaikuntanathan, V.: Efficient fully homomorphic encryption from (standard) LWE. In: FOCS, pp. 97–106 (2011)

[BV11b] Brakerski, Z., Vaikuntanathan, V.: Fully homomorphic encryption from Ring-LWE and security for key dependent messages. In: Rogaway, P. (ed.) CRYPTO 2011. LNCS, vol. 6841, pp. 505–524. Springer, Heidelberg (2011). https://doi.org/10.1007/978-3-642-22792-9_29

[BV16] Brakerski, Z., Vaikuntanathan, V.: Circuit-ABE from LWE: unbounded attributes and semi-adaptive security. In: Robshaw, M., Katz, J. (eds.) CRYPTO 2016, Part III. LNCS, vol. 9816, pp. 363–384. Springer, Heidelberg (2016). https://doi.org/10.1007/978-3-662-53015-3_13

[CLT14] Coron, J.-S., Lepoint, T., Tibouchi, M.: Scale-Invariant Fully Homomorphic Encryption over the Integers. In: Krawczyk, H. (ed.) PKC 2014. LNCS, vol. 8383, pp. 311–328. Springer, Heidelberg (2014). https://doi.org/10.1007/978-3-642-54631-0_18

[CM15] Clear, M., McGoldrick, C.: Multi-identity and multi-key leveled FHE from learning with errors. In: Gennaro, R., Robshaw, M. (eds.) CRYPTO 2015, Part II. LNCS, vol. 9216, pp. 630–656. Springer, Heidelberg (2015). https://doi.org/10.1007/978-3-662-48000-7_31

[CM16] Clear, M., McGoldrick, C.: Attribute-based fully homomorphic encryption with a bounded number of inputs. In: Pointcheval, D., Nitaj, A., Rachidi, T. (eds.) AFRICACRYPT 2016. LNCS, vol. 9646, pp. 307–324. Springer, Cham (2016). https://doi.org/10.1007/978-3-319-31517-1_16

[DGHV10] van Dijk, M., Gentry, C., Halevi, S., Vaikuntanathan, V.: Fully homomorphic encryption over the integers. In: Gilbert, H. (ed.) EUROCRYPT 2010. LNCS, vol. 6110, pp. 24–43. Springer, Heidelberg (2010). https://doi.org/10.1007/978-3-642-13190-5_2

[Gen09a] Gentry, C.: A fully homomorphic encryption scheme. Ph.D. thesis, Stanford University (2009). http://crypto.stanford.edu/craig

[Gen09b] Gentry, C.: Fully homomorphic encryption using ideal lattices. In: STOC, pp. 169–178 (2009)

[GPV08] Gentry, C., Peikert, C., Vaikuntanathan, V.: How to use a short basis: trapdoors for hard lattices and new cryptographic constructions. In: STOC, pp. 197–206 (2008)

[GSW13] Gentry, C., Sahai, A., Waters, B.: Homomorphic encryption from learning with errors: conceptually-simpler, asymptotically-faster, attribute-based. In: Canetti, R., Garay, J.A. (eds.) CRYPTO 2013, Part I. LNCS, vol. 8042, pp. 75–92. Springer, Heidelberg (2013). https://doi.org/10.1007/978-3-642-40041-4_5

[GVW13] Gorbunov, S., Vaikuntanathan, V., Wee, H.: Attribute-based encryption for circuits. In: STOC, pp. 545–554 (2013)

[LTV12] López-Alt, A., Tromer, E., Vaikuntanathan, V.: On-the-fly multiparty computation on the cloud via multikey fully homomorphic encryption. In: STOC, pp. 1219–1234 (2012)

[LW15] Lyubashevsky, V., Wichs, D.: Simple lattice trapdoor sampling from a broad class of distributions. In: Katz, J. (ed.) PKC 2015. LNCS, vol. 9020, pp. 716–730. Springer, Heidelberg (2015). https://doi.org/10.1007/978-3-662-46447-2_32

[MP12] Micciancio, D., Peikert, C.: Trapdoors for lattices: simpler, tighter, faster, smaller. In: Pointcheval, D., Johansson, T. (eds.) EUROCRYPT 2012. LNCS, vol. 7237, pp. 700–718. Springer, Heidelberg (2012). https://doi.org/10.1007/978-3-642-29011-4_41

[MW16] Mukherjee, P., Wichs, D.: Two round multiparty computation via multi-key FHE. In: Fischlin, M., Coron, J.-S. (eds.) EUROCRYPT 2016, Part II. LNCS, vol. 9666, pp. 735–763. Springer, Heidelberg (2016). https://doi.org/10.1007/978-3-662-49896-5_26

[Pei09] Peikert, C.: Public-key cryptosystems from the worst-case shortest vector problem. In: STOC, pp. 333–342 (2009)

[PS16] Peikert, C., Shiehian, S.: Multi-key FHE from LWE, revisited. In: Hirt, M., Smith, A. (eds.) TCC 2016, Part II. LNCS, vol. 9986, pp. 217–238. Springer, Heidelberg (2016). https://doi.org/10.1007/978-3-662-53644-5_9

[Reg05] Regev, O.: On lattices, learning with errors, random linear codes, and cryptography. In: STOC, pp. 84–93 (2005)

[Sch87] Schnorr, C.-P.: A hierarchy of polynomial time lattice basis reduction algorithm. Theor. Comput. Sci. **53**(2–3), 201–224 (1987)

Practical Homomorphic Encryption Over the Integers for Secure Computation in the Cloud

James Dyer[1]([⊠]), Martin Dyer[2], and Jie Xu[2]

[1] School of Computer Science, University of Manchester, Manchester, UK
james.dyer@postgrad.manchester.ac.uk
[2] School of Computing, University of Leeds, Leeds, UK
{m.e.dyer,j.xu}@leeds.ac.uk

Abstract. We present novel homomorphic encryption schemes for integer arithmetic, intended primarily for use in secure single-party computation in the cloud. These schemes are capable of securely computing arbitrary degree polynomials homomorphically. In practice, ciphertext size and running times limit the polynomial degree, but this appears sufficient for most practical applications. We present four schemes, with increasing levels of security, but increasing computational overhead. Two of the schemes provide strong security for high-entropy data. The remaining two schemes provide strong security regardless of this assumption. These four algorithms form the first two levels of a hierarchy of schemes which require linearly decreasing entropy. We have evaluated these four algorithms by computing low-degree polynomials. The timings of these computations are extremely favourable by comparison with even the best of existing methods, and dramatically out-perform running times of directly comparable schemes by a factor of up to 1000, and considerably more than that for fully homomorphic schemes, used in the same context. The results clearly demonstrate the practical applicability of our schemes.

Keywords: Cryptography · Symmetric encryption · Homomorphic encryption · Computing on encrypted data · Secure computation in the cloud

1 Introduction

With services like Amazon's Elastic MapReduce and Microsoft's HDInsight offering large-scale distributed cloud computing environments, computation in the cloud is becoming increasingly more available. Such services allow for computation on large volumes of data to be performed without the large investment in local computing resources. However, where the data that is processed is sensitive, such as financial or medical data, then uploading such data in its raw form to such a third-party service becomes problematic.

© Springer International Publishing AG 2017
M. O'Neill (Ed.): IMACC 2017, LNCS 10655, pp. 44–76, 2017.
https://doi.org/10.1007/978-3-319-71045-7_3

To take advantage of these cloud services, we require a means to process the data securely on such a platform. We designate such a computation, *secure computation in the cloud* (SCC). SCC should not expose input or output data to any other party, including the cloud service provider. Furthermore, the details of the computation should not allow any other party to deduce its inputs and outputs. Cryptography seems the natural approach to this problem.

However, it should be noted that van Dijk and Juels [23] show that cryptography alone cannot realise secure *multi-party* computation in the cloud. Since our approach is via homomorphic encryption, we will restrict our attention to what we will call *secure single-party computation in the cloud* (SSCC).

Homomorphic encryption (HE) seems to offer a solution to the SSCC problem. First defined by Rivest et al. [50] in 1978, HE allows a function to be computed on encrypted inputs without ever decrypting the inputs. A *somewhat HE* scheme (SWHE) is a scheme which is homomorphic for only limited inputs and functions. *Fully HE* (FHE) is a scheme that is homomorphic for all functions and inputs. This was first realised by Gentry in 2009 [30], and appeared to be the ideal HE scheme.

However, despite the clear advantages of FHE, and many significant advances [12,13], it remains largely impractical. Two implementations of FHE schemes, HELib [34] and FHEW [24], both perform very poorly in practice, both in their running time and space requirements (see Sect. 2.6). Therefore, we take the view in this paper that only SWHE is, for the forseeable future, of practical interest. Our goal is to develop new SWHE schemes which are practically useful, and which we have tested with a realistic implementation.

In this paper, we present four novel SWHE schemes for encryption of integers that are additively and multiplicatively homomorphic. These schemes are capable of computing arbitrary degree polynomials. In Sect. 2, we present our usage scenario, a summary of our results, and a discussion of related work. We present our initial homomorphic scheme in Sect. 3, in two variants, HE1 and HE1N. HE1 (Sect. 3.1) provides strong security for integers distributed with sufficient entropy. This security derives from the assumed hardness of the *partial approximate common divisor problem* (PACDP). HE1N (Sect. 3.2) guarantees strong security for integers not distributed with sufficient entropy or where the distribution is not known, by adding an additional "noise" term. In addition to the hardness assumption, we prove that HE1N is IND-CPA secure [5]. Section 4 describes a further two variants, HE2 and HE2N, which increase the entropy of the plaintext by adding a dimension to the ciphertexts, which are 2-vectors. This further increases the security of these schemes by effectively doubling the entropy. HE2 (Sect. 4.1) deals with integers of sufficient entropy, HE2N (Sect. 4.2) with integers without the required entropy or of unknown distribution. HE2N also satisfies IND-CPA. We describe this in some detail, since it appears to be practically useful, and is the simplest version of our general scheme. We have performed extensive experimental evaluation of the four schemes presented in this paper. We report on this in Sect. 5. Our results are extremely favourable when compared with other methods. In some cases, our algorithms outperform the running times of directly comparable schemes by a factor of up to 1000, and considerably more than that for fully homomorphic schemes, used in the same context. Finally, in Sect. 6, we conclude the paper.

This paper also contains three appendices. In Appendix A, we generalise HE2 and HE2N from 2-vectors to k-vectors, for arbitrary k, in the scheme HEk, with noisy variant HEkN. These schemes may also be practical for small enough k. In Appendix B, we provide proofs of all theorems and lemmas in this paper. Finally, in Appendix C, we provide the derivation of the bounds on the security parameters discussed in Sect. 3.1.

2   Background

2.1   Scenario

As introduced above, our work concerns secure single-party computation in the cloud. In our scenario, a secure client wishes to compute a function on a large volume of data. This function could be searching or sorting the data, computing an arithmetic function of numeric data, or any other operation. We consider here the case where the client wishes to perform arithmetic computations on numeric data. This data might be the numeric fields within a record, with non-numeric fields being treated differently.

The client delegates the computation to the cloud. However, while the data is in the cloud, it could be subject to snooping, including by the cloud provider. The client does not wish to expose the input data, or the output of the computation, to possible snooping in the cloud. A snooper here will be a party who may observe the data and the computation in the cloud, but cannot, or does not, change the data or insert spurious data. (In our setting data modification would amount to pointless vandalism.) The snooping may be casual, displaying an uninvited interest, or malicious, intending to use data for the attacker's own purposes.

To obtain the required data privacy, the client's function will be computed homomorphically on an encryption of the data. The client encrypts the source data using a secret key and uploads the encryption to the cloud, with a homomorphic equivalent of the target computation. The cloud environment performs the homomorphic computation on the encrypted data. The result of the homomorphic computation is returned to the client, who decrypts it using the secret key, and obtains the output of the computation.

In this scenario, the source data is never exposed in the cloud, but encryptions of it are. A snooper may observe the computation of the equivalent homomorphic function in the cloud environment. As a result, they may be able to deduce what operations are performed, even though they do not know the inputs. A snooper may also be able to inspect the (encrypted) working data generated by the cloud computation, and even perform side computations of their own. However, snoopers have no access to the secret key, so cannot make encryptions of their own.

2.2 Definitions and Notation

$x \xleftarrow{\$} S$ denotes a value x chosen uniformly at random from the discrete set S.

KeyGen : $S \to \mathcal{K}$ denotes the key generation function operating on the security parameter space S and whose range is the secret key space $\mathcal{K}$.

Enc : $\mathcal{M} \times \mathcal{K} \to \mathcal{C}$ denotes the symmetric encryption function operating on the plaintext space $\mathcal{M}$ and the secret key space $\mathcal{K}$, whose range is the ciphertext space $\mathcal{C}$.

Dec : $\mathcal{C} \times \mathcal{K} \to \mathcal{M}$ denotes the symmetric decryption function operating on the ciphertext space $\mathcal{C}$ and the secret key space $\mathcal{K}$, whose range is the plaintext space $\mathcal{M}$.

Add : $\mathcal{C} \times \mathcal{C} \to \mathcal{C}$ denotes the homomorphic addition function whose domain is $\mathcal{C}^2$ and whose range is $\mathcal{C}$.

Mult : $\mathcal{C} \times \mathcal{C} \to \mathcal{C}$ denotes the homomorphic multiplication function whose domain is $\mathcal{C}^2$ and whose range is $\mathcal{C}$.

$m, m_1, m_2, \ldots$ denote plaintext values, and $c, c_1, c_2, \ldots$ denote ciphertext values.

If $k^* = \binom{k+1}{2}$, $\boldsymbol{v}_\star = [v_1\ v_2\ \ldots\ v_{k^*}]^T$ denotes a k^*-vector which augments the k-vector $\boldsymbol{v} = [v_1\ v_2\ \ldots\ v_k]^T$ by appending elements $v_i = f_i(v_1, \ldots, v_k)$ ($i \in [k+1, k^*]$), for a linear function f_i. (All vectors are column vectors throughout.)

e_i denotes the ith unit vector ($i = 1, 2, \ldots$), with size determined by the context.

$[x, y]$ denotes the integers between x and y inclusive, and $[x, y)$ denotes $[x, y] \setminus \{y\}$.

log denotes $\log_e$ and lg denotes $\log_2$.

If λ is a security parameter, "with high probability" will mean with probability $1 - 2^{-\epsilon\lambda}$, for some constant $\epsilon > 0$.

Polynomial time or space will mean polynomial in the security parameter λ.

2.3 Formal Model of Scenario

We have n integer inputs $m_1, m_2, \ldots, m_n$ distributed in $[0, M)$ according to a probability distribution $\mathcal{D}$. If X is a random integer sampled from $\mathcal{D}$, let $\Pr[X = i] = \xi_i$, for $i \in [0, M)$. We will consider three measures of the *entropy* of X, measured in bits:

Shannon: $H_1(X) = -\sum_{i=0}^{M-1} \xi_i \lg \xi_i$, Collision: $H_2(X) = -\lg\left(\sum_{i=0}^{M-1} \xi_i^2\right)$, Min: $H_\infty(X) = -\lg\left(\max_{i=0}^{M-1} \xi_i\right)$.

It is known that $H_1(X) \geq H_2(X) \geq H_\infty(X)$, with equality if and only if X has the uniform distribution on $[0, M)$, in which case all three are $\lg M$. We will denote $H_\infty(X)$ by ρ, so it also follows that $H_1(X), H_2(X) \geq \rho$. We use the term "entropy" without qualification to mean min entropy, $H_\infty(X)$. Note that $H_\infty(X) = \rho \geq \lg M$ implies $\xi_i \leq 2^{-\rho}$, $i \in [0, M)$, and that $M \geq 2^\rho$.

We wish to compute a multivariate polynomial P of degree d on these inputs. A secure client A selects an instance $\mathcal{E}_K$ of the encryption algorithm $\mathcal{E}$ using the secret parameter set K. A encrypts the n inputs by computing $c_i = \mathcal{E}_K(m_i)$, for

$i \in [1, n]$. A uploads $c_1, c_2, \ldots, c_n$ and P' to the cloud computing environment, where P' is the homomorphic equivalent of P in the ciphertext space. The cloud environment computes $P'(c_1, c_2, \ldots, c_n)$. A retrieves $P'(c_1, c_2, \ldots, c_n)$ from the cloud, and computes

$$P(m_1, m_2, \ldots, m_n) = \mathcal{E}_K^{-1}(P'(c_1, c_2, \ldots, c_n)).$$

A snooper is only able to inspect $c_1, c_2, \ldots, c_n$, the function P', and the computation of $P'(c_1, c_2, \ldots, c_n)$, including subcomputations and working data, and perform side-computations on these.[1] Thus the snooper is *passive* or *honest-but-curious* [31].

2.4   Observations from Scenario

Our encryption schemes are essentially symmetric key encryption, though there is no key escrow or distribution problem. The public parameters of our schemes are exposed to the cloud, but they do not provide an encryption oracle.

Note that the n inputs do not necessarily need to be uploaded at once, but n is an upper bound on the total number of inputs. For example, if the polynomial is separable we might compute it in separate stages, and this might be useful in more dynamic situations.

This model is clearly susceptible to certain attacks. We consider ciphertext only, brute force, and cryptanalytic attacks. To avoid cryptanalytic attacks, we must choose the parameters of the system carefully. Here, a brute force attack will mean guessing the plaintext associated with a ciphertext. In our encryption schemes, it will be true that a guess can be verified. Since $\xi_i \leq 2^{-\rho}$ for $i \in [0, M)$, the expected number μ of guesses before making a correct guess satisfies $\mu \geq 2^\rho$. Massey [43] gave a corresponding result in terms of the Shannon entropy $H_1(X)$.

Similarly, probability of any correct guess in $2^{\rho/2}$ guesses is at most $2^{-\rho/2}$. This bound holds if we need only guess one of n inputs, $m_1, m_2, \ldots, m_n$, even if these inputs are not independent. Therefore, if ρ is large enough, a brute force attack is infeasible. An example of high entropy data is salaries for a large national or multinational business. Low entropy data might include enumerated types, such as gender.

In our model, known plaintext attack (KPA) is possible only by brute force, and not through being given a sample of plaintext, ciphertext pairs. Chosen plaintext attack (CPA) or chosen ciphertext attack (CCA) do not appear relevant to our model. Since $\mathcal{E}_K$ is never exposed in the cloud, there is no realistic analogue of an encryption or decryption oracle, as required by these attacks. In public key encryption, an encryption algorithm is available as part of the system, so CPA should be forestalled, though failure to satisfy IND-CPA [6] does not imply that we can break the system.

Following [5], it is common in studying symmetric key encryption to suppose that, in most practical settings, defence against CPA or CCA is necessary.

---

[1] However, note that our "N" schemes below provide security even against more malicious snooping.

While IND-CPA and IND-CCA are clearly desirable properties for a cryptosystem, their necessity, in the symmetric-key context, seems hard to justify. Both [4, 9] provide examples intended to support this convention. However, these examples are unconvincing. Nevertheless, we show that the "N" variants of our HE schemes below do satisfy IND-CPA.

We note that observation of the function P', which closely resembles P, might leak some information about its inputs. However, we assume that this information is far too weak to threaten the security of the system, as is common in the HE literature. However, if the threat is significant, "garbled circuits" [31] are a possible solution.

Finally, we note that our model of SSCC is very similar to the model of *private single-client computing*, described in [23]. Furthermore, they describe an example practical application, a privacy preserving tax return preparation program, which computes the relevant statistics on government servers without revealing the client's inputs. Another example, cited in [42], is a device which collects health data which is streamed to the cloud. Statistics are computed on the data and reported back to the device. To protect the patient's privacy this data is encrypted by the device and the computations are performed homomorphically. Erkin et al. [27] employ a similar scenario in the description of their privacy-preserving face recognition algorithm.

2.5   Our Results

We describe new practical HE schemes for the encryption of integers, to be employed in a SSCC system inspired by the HE scheme CryptDB [46]. CryptDB encrypts integers using the Paillier cryptosystem [45] which is additively homomorphic[2]. Similar systems [52, 53] use ElGamal [26] to support multiplications. The "unpadded" versions of these schemes must be used. These are not secure under CPA [32], reducing the advantage of a public-key system. These schemes do not support both addition and multiplication. Computing the inner product function requires re-encrypting the data once the multiplications have been done, so that the additions can be performed. In a SSCC system, this requires shipping the data back to the initiator for re-encryption, a significant communication overhead. We aim to support both addition and multiplication without this overhead. It should also be noted that a hybrid scheme of Paillier and ElGamal, for a given modulus, will be limited in the degree of polynomials that can be computed. Should a product or sum exceed the modulus then the result cannot be successfully decrypted.

Our scheme is inspired by the SWHE scheme of van Dijk et al. that is used as the basis for a public-key system. As in their system, we add multiples of integers to the plaintext to produce a ciphertext. However, [22] supports only arithmetic mod 2. We generalise their scheme to larger moduli.

---

[2] Paillier supports computation of linear functions with known coefficients homomorphically by repeated addition.

We showed above that the input data must have sufficient entropy to negate brute force attacks. If the data lacks sufficient entropy, we will introduce more in two ways. The first adds random "noise" of sufficient entropy to the ciphertext, to "mask" the plaintext. This approach is employed in [22]. In our "N" variants below, we add a random multiple (from 0 to κ) of a large integer, κ, to the ciphertext, such that $m_i < \kappa$, for all $i \in [1, N]$. If the entropy of the original data was ρ, it becomes $\rho + \lg \kappa$. Therefore, if κ is large enough, our data has sufficient entropy. But there is a downside. If the noise term grows too large, the ciphertext cannot be decrypted successfully. So we are restricted to computing polynomials of bounded degree, but this does not appear to be a practical problem.

The other technique will be to increase the dimension of the ciphertext. We represent the ciphertext as a k-vector, where each element is a linear function of the plaintext. Addition and multiplication of ciphertexts use linear algebra. The basic case $k = 1$ is described in Sect. 3.1. Then we can increase the entropy by creating a k-vector ciphertext. Then we must guess k plaintexts to break the system. Assuming that the inputs $m_1, m_2, \ldots, m_n$ are chosen independently from $\mathcal{D}$, and the entropy is ρ, the entropy of a k-tuple $(m_1, m_2, \ldots, m_k)$ is $k\rho$. Thus the k-vectors effectively have entropy $k\rho$. If k is chosen large enough, we have sufficient entropy to prevent brute force attack. The assumption of independence among $m_1, m_2, \ldots, m_n$ can be relaxed, to allow some correlation, but we will not discuss the details. On the upside, some cryptanalytic attacks for $k = 1$ do not seem to generalise even to $k = 2$. The downside is that ciphertexts are k times larger, and each homomorphic multiplication requires $\Omega(k^3)$ time and space. For very large k, this probably renders the methods impractical. Therefore, we consider the case $k = 2$ in Sect. 4. The general case is considered in Appendix A.

Our work here supports computing arbitrary degree multivariate polynomials on integer data. However, we expect that for many practical applications, computing low-degree polynomials will suffice. See [42] for a discussion regarding this. In this paper, we present four variants of our scheme. Two provide strong security under the assumption that the input data has high entropy. The other two provide strong security regardless of this assumption. Appendix A generalises these four schemes to dimension k ciphertexts.

2.6   Related Work

A comprehensive survey of somewhat and fully HE schemes is presented in [1]. In this section, we discuss those most related to our own work. Some related work [46,52,53] has already been discussed in Sect. 2.5.

Our scheme is inspired by that of van Dijk et al. [22]. In their paper they produce an FHE scheme over the integers, where a simple SWHE scheme for modulo 2 arithmetic is "bootstrapped" to FHE. Our scheme HE1N below (Sect. 3.2) may be regarded as a generalisation of theirs to arbitrary prime moduli. In van Dijk et al. [22], their symmetric scheme is transformed into a public key scheme. Though we could do this, we will not do so, since public key systems appear to have little application to our model. In [19], Coron et al. develop a similar encryption scheme, where the sum term in the ciphertext is quadratic rather than linear.

Several implementations of SWHE and FHE schemes have been produced. Lauter et al. [42] implement the SWHE scheme from [12]. However, they give results only for degree two polynomials. Our schemes are capable of computing degree three and four polynomials for practical key and ciphertext sizes. HELib [34] is an implementation of the BGV [13] FHE scheme. HELib-MP [48] is an adaptation of HELib to support multi-precision moduli. At the current time, it only supports basic SWHE features. The *Homomorphic Encryption Applications and Technology* (HEAT) project's *Homomorphic Encryption Application Programming Interface* (HE-API) [56] has currently integrated HELib and FV-NFLib [20], an implementation of the Fan and Vercauteren (FV) [28] SWHE scheme, under a single API. The authors appear to have made significant improvements in circuit evaluation times, but few details have been made available [10]. Microsoft's SEAL library [41] also implements the FV scheme, albeit, in a modified form. FHEW [25] implements the FHE scheme described in [24]. The performance of these implementations is discussed in Sect. 5.

Erkin et al. [27] exploit the linearly-homomorphic properties of Paillier to compute feature vector matches in their privacy-preserving face recognition algorithm. Our schemes can likewise compute known linear functions, simply by not encrypting the coefficients of the function.

Catalano et al. [15] aim to extend a linearly-homomorphic system, such as Paillier [45], to compute multivariate quadratics homomorphically. However, their extension relies on pre-computing a product for each pair of plaintexts and then applying a linear function on the encryption of these products. As such, it does not extend the underlying linear encryption scheme and is not multiplicatively homomorphic. They claim that their system can compute any degree 2 polynomial with at most one multiplication. However, it is not clear how they would compute the polynomial $m_1 \cdot (m_2 + \ldots + m_n)$ without performing $n - 1$ offline multiplications. By contrast, our scheme would only require one multiplication. In [14], Catalano et al. extend their approach to cubics.

Zhou and Wornell [59] construct a scheme based on integer vectors, similar, in some respects, to our HE2 (Sect. 4.1) and HEk (Appendix A) schemes. Bogos et al. [8] demonstrate that the system displays some theoretical insecurities. However, the question of whether these are of practical importance is not addressed.

The symmetric MORE scheme [39] uses linear transformations, as do our schemes but in a different way. MORE has been shown [57] to be insecure against KPA, at least as originally proposed. However, whether KPA is relevant in applications of the scheme is unclear.

Recent work on *functional encryption* [33] should also be noted. While these results are of great theoretical interest, the scenario where such schemes might be applied is rather different from our model. Also, the methods of [33] seem too computationally expensive to be of practical interest in the immediate future.

3   Initial Homomorphic Scheme

3.1   Sufficient Entropy (HE1)

We have integer inputs $m_1, m_2, \ldots, m_n \in [0, M)$. (Negative integers can be handled as in van Dijk et al. [22], by taking residues in $[-(p-1)/2, (p-1)/2)$, rather than $[0, p)$.) We wish to compute a polynomial P of degree d in these inputs. The inputs are distributed with entropy ρ, where ρ is large enough, as discussed in Sect. 2.3 above. In practical terms, $\rho \geq 32$ will provide sufficient entropy for strong security, since breaking the system would require more than a billion guessses. Our HE scheme is the system (KeyGen, Enc, Dec, Add, Mult).

Key Generation. Let λ be a security parameter, measured in bits. Let p and q be randomly chosen large distinct primes such that $p \in [2^{\lambda-1}, 2^{\lambda}]$, and $q \in [2^{\eta-1}, 2^{\eta}]$, where $\eta \approx \lambda^2/\rho - \lambda$. Here λ must be large enough to negate direct factorisation of pq (see [40]), and p and q are chosen to negate Coppersmith's attack [18]. We will also require $p > (n+1)^d M^d$ to ensure that $P(m_1, m_2, \ldots, m_n) < p$, so that the result of the computation can be successfully decrypted. Our bounds are worst case, allowing for polynomials which contain all possible monomial terms. For some applications, they will be much larger than required to ensure that $P(m_1, m_2, \ldots, m_n) < p$ and smaller bounds will suffice. Our function KeyGen will randomly select p and q according to these bounds. Then p is the private symmetric key for the system and pq is the modulus for arithmetic performed by Add and Mult. pq is a public parameter of the system. We assume that the entropy $\rho \gg \lg \lambda$, so that a brute force attack cannot be carried out in polynomial time.

Security Parameters. We can easily set the security parameters λ and η to practical values. If $n \approx \sqrt{M}$, $M \approx 2^{\rho}$ then we may take $\lambda \approx 3d\rho/2$ and $\eta \approx 3d\lambda/2 - \lambda$ (see Appendix C). For, example, if $\rho = 32$, $d = 4$, we can take any $\lambda > 192$, $\eta > 960$.

Encryption. We encrypt a plaintext integer m as

$$\mathsf{Enc}(m, p) = m + rp \pmod{pq}, \text{ where } r \overset{\$}{\leftarrow} [1, q).$$

Decryption. We decrypt the ciphertext c by $\mathsf{Dec}(c, p) = c \pmod{p}$.

Addition. The sum modulo pq of two ciphertexts, $c = m + rp$ and $c' = m' + r'p$, is

$$\mathsf{Add}(c, c') = c + c' = m + m' + (r + r')p \pmod{pq}.$$

This decrypts to $m + m'$, provided $m + m' < p$.

Multiplication. The product modulo pq of two ciphertexts, $c = m + rp$ and $c' = m' + r'p$, is

$$\mathsf{Mult}(c, c') = cc' = mm' + (rm' + r'm + rr'p)p \pmod{pq},$$

which decrypts to mm', provided $mm' < p$.

Security. Security of the system is provided by the *partial approximate common divisor problem* (PACDP), first posed by Howgrave-Graham [36], but can be formulated [16,17] as:

Definition 1. *(Partial approximate common divisor problem.) Suppose we are given one input x_0, of the form pr_0, and n inputs x_i, of the form $pr_i + m_i$, $i \in [1, n]$, where p is an unknown constant integer and the m_i and r_i are unknown integers. We have a bound B such that $|m_i| < B$ for all i. Under what conditions on the m_i and r_i, and the bound B, can an algorithm be found that can uniquely determine p in time polynomial in the total bit length of the numbers involved?*

A straightforward attack on this problem is by brute force. Consider x_1. Assuming that m_1 is sampled from $\mathcal{D}$, having entropy ρ, we successively try values for m_1 and compute $\gcd(x_0, x_1 - m_1)$ in polynomial time until we find a divisor that is large enough to recover p. Then we can recover m_i as $(x_i \bmod p)$ for $i \in [2, n]$. As discussed in Sect. 2.3, the search will requires 2^ρ gcd operations in expectation. Note that publicly known constants, need not, and should not be encrypted. Encrypting them provides an obvious guessing attack.

Several attempts have been made to solve the PACDP [16,17,36], resulting in theoretically faster algorithms for some cases of the problem. The paper [16] gives an algorithm requiring only $\sqrt{M}$ polynomial time operations if $\mathcal{D}$ is the uniform distribution on $[0, M)$, and hence $\rho = \lg M$. No algorithm running in time subexponential in ρ is known for this problem, so the encryption will be secure if ρ is large enough. See [29] for a survey and evaluation of attacks on PACDP.

Our system is a special case of PACDP, since we use the residues modulo a distinct semiprime. A semiprime is a natural number that is the product of two primes. A distinct semiprime is a semiprime where the primes are distinct. We call this the *semiprime partial approximate common divisor problem* (SPACDP). It is a restriction, but there is no reason to believe that it is any easier than PACDP.

Definition 2. *(Semiprime factorisation problem.) Given a semiprime s, the product of primes p and q, can p and q be determined in polynomial time?*

The computational complexity of this problem, which lies at the heart of the widely-used RSA cryptosystem, is open, other than for quantum computing, which currently remains impractical. We will show that breaking HE1 is equivalent to semiprime factorisation. Therefore, our scheme is at least as secure as unpadded RSA [49].

Theorem 1. *An attack against HE1 is successful in polynomial time if and only if we can factorise a distinct semi-prime in polynomial time.*

With low entropy plaintexts, there is a brute force attack on this system, which we call a *collision attack*. Suppose we have a pair of equal plaintexts $m_1 = m_2$. The difference between their encryptions $(c_1 - c_2)$ is an encryption of 0, and KPA is possible. In fact, for n plaintexts $m_1, m_2, \ldots, m_n$, if there exist $i, j \in [1, n]$ with $m_i = m_j$, then $\prod_{1 \leq i < j \leq n}(c_j - c_i)$ is an encryption of 0. However, if there is sufficient entropy, this attack is not possible.

Lemma 1. *If the inputs m have entropy ρ then, for any two independent inputs m_1, m_2, $\Pr(m_1 = m_2) \leq 2^{-\rho}$.*

Thus, for n inputs, $m_1, m_2, \ldots, m_n$ the probability that there exist $i, j \in [1, n]$ with $m_i = m_j$ is at most $\binom{n}{2}2^{-\rho}$. If $n < 2^{-\rho/3}$, this probability is at most $2^{-\rho/3}$. Hence, for large enough λ, collision attack is infeasible.

3.2   Insufficient Entropy (HE1N)

Suppose now that the integer inputs $m_i, i \in [1, n]$, are distributed with entropy ρ, where ρ is not large enough to negate a brute force guessing attack. Therefore, we increase the entropy of the plaintext by adding an additional "noise" term to the ciphertext. This will be a multiple s (from 0 to κ) of an integer κ, chosen so that the entropy $\rho' = \rho + \lg \kappa$ is large enough to negate a brute force guessing attack. As a result of the extra linear term in the ciphertext, we compute $P(m_1, \ldots, m_n, \kappa)$ instead. We can easily retrieve $P(m_1, \ldots, m_n)$ from $P(m_1, \ldots, m_n, \kappa)$.

Key Generation. KeyGen now randomly chooses p and q as in HE1, but with $\eta = \lambda^2/\rho' - \lambda$, and $p > (n+1)^d (M + \kappa^2)^d$ so that $P(m_1 + s_1\kappa, m_2 + s_2\kappa, \ldots, m_N + s_n\kappa) < p$, when $s_1, s_2, \ldots, s_n \in [0, \kappa)$. **KeyGen** also randomly chooses κ, where $\kappa > (n+1)^d M^d$, so that $P(m_1, m_2, \ldots, m_n) < \kappa$. The secret key, **sk**, is now (κ, p).

Security Parameters. Again, we can set the security parameters λ and η to practical values. If we assume $M \approx 2^\rho$ and large enough n, as in Sect. 3.1, then we may take $\lg \kappa > d(\lg n + \rho)$, $\rho' = \rho + \lg \kappa$, $\lambda > d(\lg n + 2 \lg \kappa)$. Then, for example, if $d = 3$, $\lg n = 16$, $\rho = 8$, then $\lg \kappa > 72$, $\rho' = 80$, $\lambda > 480$, $\eta > 2400$. In the extreme case that the inputs are bits, so $\rho = 1$, and $d = 3$, $\lg n = 16$, then we can take $\lg \kappa \approx 51$ and $\rho' \approx 52$, and we have $\lambda > 354$, $\eta > 2056$, which is only 15% smaller than for $\rho = 8$.

Encryption. We encrypt plaintext m as $\mathsf{Enc}(m, \mathsf{sk}) = m + s\kappa + rp \pmod{pq}$, where $r \overset{\$}{\leftarrow} [1, q]$ and $s \overset{\$}{\leftarrow} [0, \kappa)$.

Decryption. We decrypt ciphertext c as $\mathsf{Dec}(c, \mathsf{sk}) = (c \bmod p) \bmod \kappa$.

Arithmetic. Addition and multiplication of ciphertexts is as above.

Security. The use of random noise gives the encryption the following "indistinguishability" property, which implies that the system satisfies IND-CPA [5,6].

Theorem 2. *For any encryption c, $c \bmod \kappa$ is polynomial time indistinguishable from the uniform distribution on $[0, \kappa)$. Thus HE1N satisfies IND-CPA, under the assumption that SPACDP is not polynomial time solvable.*

Therefore, HE1N is resistant to both the "guessing" and "collision" attacks discussed in Sect. 3.1.

Hybrid Scheme. Note that mixed data, some of which has high entropy and some low, can be encrypted with a hybrid of HE1 and HE1N. More generally, we can choose s to be smaller for higher entropy and larger for lower entropy, say $s \in [0, \chi_i)$, where $0 \leq \chi_i < \kappa$, for the ith data type, rather than $[0, \kappa)$. However, κ itself remains the same for all i, or we cannot decrypt. Then the entropy increases to $\rho_i + \lg \chi_i$ for data type i. The advantage is a smaller blow-up in the noise. A possible disadvantage is that this mixed scheme may not necessarily have the IND-CPA property of Theorem 2. The same idea can be applied to HE2 and HE2N below, and to the HEkN schemes, for $k > 2$, described in the appendix.

4   Adding a Dimension

In this section we discuss adding an additional dimension to the ciphertext, which becomes a 2-vector. The purpose of this is to increase the level of security beyond HE1 and HE1N. In both schemes presented below, HE2 and HE2N, we add a further vector term, with two further secret parameters. The two schemes presented below have a constant factor overhead for arithmetic operations. An addition operation in the plaintext space requires two additions in the ciphertext space, and a multiplication in the plaintext space requires nine multiplications and four additions in the ciphertext space.

4.1   Sufficient Entropy (HE2)

As with HE1, it is assumed that the inputs m_i ($i \in [1, n]$) are of sufficient entropy.

Key Generation. p and q are randomly chosen by **KeyGen** according to the bounds given in Sect. 3.1. **KeyGen** sets $\boldsymbol{a} = [a_1 \ a_2]^T$, where $a_i \xleftarrow{\$} [1, pq)$ ($i \in [1, 2]$) such that $a_1, a_2, a_1 - a_2 \neq 0$ (mod p and mod q).[3] **KeyGen** also sets R, the re-encryption matrix (see "Multiplication") as

$$\begin{bmatrix} 1 - 2\alpha_1 & \alpha_1 & \alpha_1 \\ -2\alpha_2 & \alpha_2 + 1 & \alpha_2 \end{bmatrix},$$

where

$$\alpha_1 = \beta^{-1}(\sigma a_1 + \varrho p - a_1^2), \qquad \alpha_2 = \beta^{-1}(\sigma a_2 + \varrho p - a_2^2), \tag{1}$$

such that $\beta = 2(a_2 - a_1)^2$, $\varrho \xleftarrow{\$} [0, q]$ and $\sigma \xleftarrow{\$} [0, pq)$.

The secret key **sk** is $(p, \boldsymbol{a})$ and the public parameters are pq and R.

Encryption. We encrypt a plaintext integer m as the 2-vector $\boldsymbol{c}$,

$$\boldsymbol{c} = \mathsf{Enc}(m, \mathsf{sk}) = (m + rp)\mathbf{1} + s\boldsymbol{a} \quad (\text{mod } pq),$$

where $\mathbf{1} = [1 \ 1]^T$, $r \xleftarrow{\$} [0, q)$, and $s \xleftarrow{\$} [0, pq)$. r and s are independent. We note that two encryptions of the same plaintext are different with very high probability.

Theorem 3. *The encryption scheme produces ciphertexts with components which are random integers modulo pq.*

Note, however, that the components of the ciphertexts are correlated, and this may be a vulnerability. We discuss this later in this section ("Cryptanalysis").

Decryption. To decrypt, we eliminate s from $\boldsymbol{c}$ (modulo p), giving

$$\mathsf{Dec}(\boldsymbol{c}, \mathsf{sk}) = \boldsymbol{\gamma}^T \boldsymbol{c} \quad \text{mod } p,$$

where $\boldsymbol{\gamma}^T = (a_2 - a_1)^{-1}[a_2 \ -a_1]$. We call $\boldsymbol{\gamma}$ the *decryption vector*.

Addition. We define the addition operation on ciphertexts as the vector sum modulo pq of the two ciphertext vectors $\boldsymbol{c}$ and $\boldsymbol{c}'$,

$$\mathsf{Add}(\boldsymbol{c}, \boldsymbol{c}') = \boldsymbol{c} + \boldsymbol{c}' \quad (\text{mod } pq).$$

Therefore, if inputs m, m' encrypt as $(m + rp)\mathbf{1} + s\boldsymbol{a}$, $(m' + r'p+)\mathbf{1} + s'\boldsymbol{a}$,

$$\mathsf{Add}(\boldsymbol{c}, \boldsymbol{c}') = \boldsymbol{c} + \boldsymbol{c}' = (m + m' + (r + r')p)\mathbf{1} + (s + s')\boldsymbol{a}.$$

which is a valid encryption of $m + m'$.

---

[3] The condition $a_1, a_2, a_1 - a_2 \neq 0$, (mod p, mod q) fails with exponentially small probability $3(1/p + 1/q)$. Thus, a_1 and a_2 are indistinguishable in polynomial time from $a_1, a_2 \xleftarrow{\$} [0, pq)$.

Multiplication. If $c = [c_1\ c_2]^T$, we construct the augmented ciphertext vector, $c_\star = [c_1\ c_2\ c_3]^T$, where $c_3 = 2c_1 - c_2$. Thus, $c_3 = (m + rp) + sa_3 \mod pq$, for $a_3 = 2a_1 - a_2$. So,

$$\text{Mult}(c, c') = c \cdot c' = R(c_\star \circ c'_\star) \quad (\text{mod } pq),$$

where $\cdot$ is a product on $\mathbb{Z}_{pq}^2$ and $c_\star \circ c'_\star$ is the Hadamard product modulo pq of the two augmented ciphertext vectors $c_\star$ and $c'_\star$.

Theorem 4. *If c is an encryption of m and c' is an encryption of m' then $R(c_\star \circ c'_\star)$ (mod pq) is an encryption of mm'.*

Observe that α_1, α_2 in R are public, but give only two equations for the four parameters of the system $a_1, a_2, \sigma, \varrho p$. These equations are quadratic mod pq, and solving them is as hard as semiprime factorisation in the worst case [47].

Also, observe that, independently of a,

$$Rc_\star = (m + rp)R1_\star + sRa_\star = (m + rp)\mathbf{1} + sa = c,$$

for any ciphertext c. Hence re-encrypting a ciphertext gives the identity operation, and discloses no information.

Hardness. We can show that this system is at least as hard as SPACDP. In fact,

Theorem 5. *SPACDP is of equivalent complexity to the special case of HE2 where $\delta = a_2 - a_1$ $(0 < \delta < q)$ is known.*

Without knowing the parameter $\delta = a_2 - a_1$, HE2 cannot be reduced to SPACDP in this way, so HE2 is more secure than HE1.

Cryptanalysis. Each new ciphertext c introduces two new unknowns r, s and two equations for c_1, c_2. Thus we gain no additional information from a new ciphertext. However, if we can guess, m, m' for any two ciphertexts c, c', we can determine

$$(c_1 - m) = rp + sa_1, \qquad (c_2 - m) = rp + sa_2,$$
$$(c'_1 - m') = r'p + s'a_1, \qquad (c'_2 - m') = r'p + s'a_2,$$
$$\text{so } (c_1 - m)(c'_2 - m') - (c_2 - m)(c'_1 - m') = (a_2 - a_1)(rs' - r's)p \quad (\text{mod } pq)$$

Since $a_2 \neq a_1$, and $sr' \neq s'r$ with high probability, this is a nonzero multiple of p, νp say. We may assume $\nu < q$, so $p = \gcd(\nu p, pq)$. We can now solve the linear system $\gamma^T[c\ c'] = [m\ m'] \mod p$ to recover the decryption vector. This effectively breaks the system, since we can now decrypt an arbitrary ciphertext. We could proceed further, and attempt to infer a_1 and a_2, but we will not do so.

Note that to break this system, we need to guess two plaintexts, as opposed to one in HE1. The entropy of a pair (m, m') is 2ρ, so we have effectively squared the number of guesses needed to break the system relative to HE1. So HE2 can tolerate smaller entropy than HE1. We note further that HE2 does not seem immediately vulnerable to known cryptanalytic attacks on HE1 [16,17,36].

4.2 Insufficient Entropy (HE2N)

In this section we extend HE1N above (Sect. 3.2) to two dimensions.

Key Generation. KeyGen randomly chooses p, q and κ according to the bounds given in Sect. 3.2. **1** is defined as in Sect. 4.1. $\boldsymbol{a}$, and R are generated as in Sect. 4.1. The secret key is $(\kappa, p, \boldsymbol{a})$, and the public parameters are pq and R, defined in Sect. 4.1.

Encryption. We encrypt a plaintext integer $m \in [0, M)$ as a 2-vector $\boldsymbol{c}$,

$$\mathsf{Enc}(m, \mathsf{sk}) = \boldsymbol{c} = (m + rp + s\kappa)\mathbf{1} + t\boldsymbol{a} \quad \bmod pq,$$

where r is as in Sect. 4.1, $s \xleftarrow{\$} [0, \kappa)$, and $t \xleftarrow{\$} [0, pq)$.

Decryption. We decrypt a ciphertext $\boldsymbol{c}$ by $\mathsf{Dec}(\boldsymbol{c}, \mathsf{sk}) = (\boldsymbol{\gamma}^T \boldsymbol{c} \bmod p) \bmod \kappa$, where $\boldsymbol{\gamma}^T$ is defined as in Sect. 4.1.

Arithmetic. Addition and multiplication of ciphertexts are as in Sect. 4.1.

Security. HE2N has all the properties of HE1N. However, it is more secure, since there is an additional unknown parameter in the ciphertext. We also note that HE2N satisfies Theorem 2, so it inherits the IND-CPA property.

4.3 Generalisation of HE2 and HE2N to k Dimensions

The integer vector based approach of HE2 and HE2N can be generalised to vectors of dimension k. We do not have space to present this material here, but it may be found in Appendix A.

5 Experimental Results

HE1, HE1N, HE2, and HE2N have been implemented in pure unoptimised Java using the JScience mathematics library [21]. Secure pseudo-random numbers are generated using the ISAAC algorithm [37], seeded using the Linux /dev/random source. This prevents the weakness in ISAAC shown by Aumasson [3].

The evaluation experiment generated 24,000 encrypted inputs and evaluated a polynomial homomorphically on the inputs, using a Hadoop MapReduce (MR) algorithm. On the secure client side, the MR input is generated as pseudo-random ρ-bit integers which are encrypted and written to a file with d inputs per line, where d is the degree of the polynomial to be computed. The security parameters λ and η were selected to be the minimum values required to satisfy the conditions give in Sects. 3.1, 3.2, 4.1, and 4.2. In addition, the unencrypted result

Table 1. Timings for each experimental configuration ($n = 24000$ in all cases, $\lambda > 96$). *Init* is the initialisation time for the encryption algorithm, *Enc* is the mean time to encrypt a single integer, *Exec* is the total MR job execution time, *Prod* is the mean time to homomorphically compute the product of two encrypted integers, *Sum* is the mean time to homomorphically compute the sum of two encrypted integers.

Alg.	Parameters			Encryption		MR Job			Decrypt
	d	ρ	ρ'	Init(s)	Enc(μs)	Exec(s)	Prod(μs)	Sum(μs)	(ms)
HE1	2	32	n/a	0.12	13.52	23.82	54.41	9.06	0.21
HE1	2	64	n/a	0.12	16.24	23.85	60.38	8.04	0.49
HE1	2	128	n/a	0.15	25.73	23.77	84.69	8.43	0.28
HE1	3	32	n/a	0.17	22.98	23.65	87.75	11.46	0.35
HE1	3	64	n/a	0.19	34.63	24.72	95.68	12.37	0.45
HE1	3	128	n/a	0.42	54.83	26.05	196.71	14.07	0.55
HE1	4	32	n/a	0.28	43.36	24.48	108.72	13.75	0.5
HE1	4	64	n/a	0.53	58.85	26.41	227.44	15.85	3.59
HE1	4	128	n/a	1.36	104.95	28.33	484.95	16.92	5.67
HE1N	2	1	32	0.22	32.99	22.94	88.38	8.53	3.35
HE1N	2	1	64	0.39	52.63	26.24	168.54	12.39	3.56
HE1N	2	1	128	1.2	89.01	26.18	226.2	13.16	8.1
HE1N	2	8	32	0.6	57.88	25.9	177.36	11.17	7.18
HE1N	2	8	64	0.32	43.93	26.53	96.78	12.18	2.27
HE1N	2	8	128	1.13	78.11	24.42	212.75	11.07	8.4
HE1N	2	16	64	0.33	53.97	27.15	168	13.67	4.47
HE1N	2	16	128	0.63	68.73	25.22	194.42	11.01	7.65
HE1N	3	1	32	8.54	183.19	24.24	522.07	12.06	9.09
HE1N	3	1	64	3.67	125	29.49	467.36	18.22	11.43
HE1N	3	1	128	27.84	313.76	26.94	1235.77	15.04	11.75
HE1N	3	8	32	115	462.45	32.61	1556.17	21.11	19.79
HE1N	3	8	64	9.75	180.08	25.87	500.62	15.03	10.39
HE1N	3	8	128	36.05	259.15	30.1	836.27	20.68	11.45
HE1N	3	16	64	30.96	378.99	28.24	1338.33	15.51	13.3
HE1N	3	16	128	8.13	226.32	27.92	621.95	18.01	10.89
HE2	2	32	n/a	0.16	85.79	26.82	305.52	11.68	4.83
HE2	2	64	n/a	0.17	95.92	29.71	354.79	16.9	3.26
HE2	2	128	n/a	0.22	132.53	32.84	540.78	22.83	4.92
HE2	3	32	n/a	0.23	130.3	31.18	513.93	23.77	6.52
HE2	3	64	n/a	0.29	145.62	32.84	615.9	24.61	6.3
HE2	3	128	n/a	0.52	249.47	29.54	1443.82	16.56	18.34
HE2	4	32	n/a	0.39	175.63	29.5	733.23	20.69	6.01
HE2	4	64	n/a	0.7	255.3	29.55	1578.39	18.29	16.24
HE2	4	128	n/a	2.7	465.51	37.47	2943.91	22.15	15.41

(continued)

Table 1. (*continued*)

Alg.	Parameters			Encryption		MR Job			Decrypt
	d	ρ	ρ'	Init(s)	Enc(μs)	Exec(s)	Prod(μs)	Sum(μs)	(ms)
HE2N	2	1	32	0.27	147.83	29.74	571.94	16.58	5.66
HE2N	2	1	64	0.43	202.74	33.36	1291.68	18.3	13.23
HE2N	2	1	128	1.58	354.19	33.76	1977.51	17.13	12.46
HE2N	2	8	32	0.59	234.83	31.42	1413.31	15.21	14.92
HE2N	2	8	64	0.33	163.78	27.42	635.64	13.6	6.18
HE2N	2	8	128	0.9	307.68	36.32	1850.83	21.71	15.79
HE2N	2	16	64	0.42	208.1	29.96	1230.56	13.41	13.16
HE2N	2	16	128	0.73	274.48	30.82	1585.1	14.85	15.04
HE2N	3	1	32	5.72	651.1	36.49	3438.96	18.67	19.05
HE2N	3	1	64	4.45	477.52	35.33	3073.46	18.75	19.77
HE2N	3	1	128	26.83	1192.79	43.23	6416.43	22.48	25.12
HE2N	3	8	32	87.38	1658.36	49.63	8139.19	23.71	27.24
HE2N	3	8	64	5.21	607.75	36.54	3337.1	22.28	17.39
HE2N	3	8	128	17.14	945.64	40.49	4620.69	25.91	22.41
HE2N	3	16	64	39.19	1368.18	44.88	7005.7	24.1	28.3
HE2N	3	16	128	11.39	774.07	36.05	3845.1	20.29	20.74

of the computation is computed so that it may checked against the decrypted result of the homomorphic computation. On the Hadoop cluster side, each mapper processes a line of input by homomorphically multiplying together each input on a line and outputs this product. A single reducer homomorphically sums the products. The MR algorithm divides the input file so that each mapper receives an equal number of lines of input, ensuring maximum parallelisation. Finally, on the secure client side, the MR output is decrypted.

Our test environment consisted of a single secure client (an Ubuntu Linux VM with 16 GB RAM) and a Hadoop 2.7.3 cluster running in a heterogeneous OpenNebula cloud. The Hadoop cluster consisted of 17 Linux VMs, one master and 16 slaves, each allocated 2 GB of RAM. Each experimental configuration of algorithm, polynomial degree (d), integer size (ρ), and effective entropy of inputs after adding "noise" (ρ', for the 'N' variant algorithms only), was executed 10 times. The means are tabulated in Table 1.

There are some small anomalies in our data. JScience implements arbitrary precision integers as an array of Java `long` (64-bit) integers. This underlying representation may be optimal in some of our test configurations and suboptimal in others, causing anomalous results. Another possibility is that the unexpected results are due to garbage collection in the JVM heap, which may be more prevalent in certain test configurations.

We may compare these results with those reported in the literature. Our results compare extremely favourably with Table 2 of [42]. For encryption, our results are, in the best case, 1000 times faster than those presented there, and, in the worst case, 10 times faster. For decryption, our results are comparable. However, it should be noted that to decrypt our results we take the moduli for large primes rather than 2 as in [42], which is obviously less efficient. For homomorphic sums and products, our algorithms perform approximately 100 times faster. [42] only provides experimental data for computing degree 2 polynomials. We provide experimental results for higher degree polynomials.

Similarly, compared with Fig. 13 of Popa et al. [46], our encryption times for a 32-bit integer are considerably faster. While a time for computing a homomorphic sum on a column is given in Fig. 12, it is unclear how many rows exist in their test database. Nevertheless, our results for computing homomorphic sums compare favourably with those given. Since CryptDB [46] only supports homomorphic sums and cannot compute an inner product, we can only compare the homomorphic sum timings.

Table 1 of [52] is unclear whether the timings are aggregate or per operation. Even assuming that they are aggregate, our results are approximately 100 times faster for homomorphic sum and product operations. Crypsis [52] uses two different encryption schemes for integers, ElGamal [26] and Paillier [45], which only support addition or multiplication but not both. No discussion of computation of an inner product is made in [52] but we expect that the timings would be considerably worse as data encrypted using ElGamal to compute the products would have to be shipped back to the secure client to be re-encrypted using Paillier so that the final inner product could be computed.

Varia et al. [55] present experimental results of applying their HETest framework to HELib [35]. Varia et al. show timings 10^4 to 10^6 times slower than that of computations on unencrypted data. Although it is unclear exactly which circuits are being computed, the timings given are in seconds, so we believe that HELib will not be a serious candidate for SSCC in the immediate future.

As reported in [24], the current performance of FHEW [25] is poor compared with unencrypted operations. The authors report that FHEW processed a single homomorphic NAND operation followed by a re-encryption in 0.69 s and using 2.2 GB of RAM. Therefore, we also believe that FHEW is not a candidate for SCCC, as it currently stands.

Although claims regarding its performance have been made in the press [54], no benchmarking statistics have been made publicly available for Microsoft's SEAL library [41]. However, in [2], it is reported that, for SEAL v1, the time to perform one multiplication is approximately 140 ms.

With regard to FV-NFLib [20], Bonte et al. [10] recently reported a significant decrease in the time to evaluate a four layer *Group Method of Data Handling* (GMDH) neural network [11] from 32 s to 2.5 s, as a result of their novel encoding of the inputs.

Aguilar-Melchor et al. [2] report their experimental findings regarding HELib-MP [48]. They show that HELib-MP outperforms FV-NFLib for large (2048-bit) plaintexts. They further go on to benchmark HELib-MP by computing RSA-2048 and ECC-ElGamal-P256. An exponentiation in RSA-2048 takes between 157 ms and 1.8 s depending on the window size and number of multiplications required. For ECC-ElGamal-P256, an elliptic curve multiplication takes between 96 ms and 242 ms depending on window size and number of elliptic curve additions.

Catalano et al. [15] provide experimental results for their work. For 128-bit plaintexts, our algorithms are approximately 10 to 1000 times faster at performing a multiplication operation and our most complex algorithm, HE2N, is roughly equal to their fastest, an extension of Joye-Libert [38], for additions.

Yu et al. [58] give experimental results for their implementation of the Zhou and Wornell scheme [59]. From their Figs. 3, 4 and 5, it is hard to compare our scheme with theirs directly but it would appear that our vector based schemes are at least comparable in performance to theirs.

6 Conclusion

In this paper we have presented several new homomorphic encryption schemes intended for use in a practical SSCC system. We envisage that the majority of computation on integer big data, outside of scientific computing, will be computing low degree polynomials on integers, or fixed-point decimals which can be converted to integers. Our somewhat homomorphic schemes are perfectly suited to these types of computation.

Our evaluation has only concerned one- or two-dimensional ciphertexts and polynomials of degree up to four. We intend to investigate higher degree polynomials in future work. We believe that HE1N and HE2N provide strong security, even for low-entropy data, as they satisfy the desirable IND-CPA property. If a user has a high confidence in the entropy of the input data, HE2 may provide sufficient security.

As they are only somewhat homomorphic, each of these schemes require that the computational result cannot grow bigger than the secret modulus. In the case of the "noise" variants, we also have to consider the noise term growing large. So, as they stand, these schemes can only compute polynomials of suitably bounded degree. However, we believe this is adequate for most practical purposes.

The schemes presented in Sects. 3 and 4 extend to a hierarchy of systems, HEk, with increasing levels of security. These are presented in Appendix A and may be investigated further in future work.

We have implemented and evaluated the HE1, HE1N, HE2 and HE2N schemes as part of an SSCC system as discussed in Sect. 5. Our results are extremely favourable by comparison with existing methods. In some cases, they outperform those methods by a factor of 1000. This clearly demonstrates the practical applicability of our schemes. Furthermore, our MapReduce job execution times remain low even when using the largest set of parameters for HE2N. We believe that this demonstrates the advantages of our schemes for encrypted computations on fixed-point data in the cloud.

A   Generalisation to k Dimensions

In this appendix, we generalise HE2 and HE2N to k-vectors. HE1 and HE1N are the cases for $k = 1$ and HE2 and HE2N are the cases for $k = 2$.

A.1   Sufficient Entropy (HEk)

We generalise HE2 to k dimensions.

Key Generation. KeyGen randomly chooses p and q according to the bounds given in Sect. 4.1. KeyGen sets $a_j \overset{\$}{\leftarrow} [1, pq)^k$, $\forall j \in [1, k-1]$, and R (detailed in "Multiplication" below). The secret key sk is $(p, a_1, \ldots, a_{k-1})$, and the public parameters are pq and R.

Computational Overhead. The computational overhead increases, the number of arithmetic operations per plaintext multiplication is $O(k^3)$, and the space requirement per ciphertext is $O(k)$, by comparison with HE1.

Encryption. A plaintext, $m \in [0, M]$, is enciphered as

$$\mathsf{Enc}(m, \mathsf{sk}) = c = (m + rp)\mathbf{1} + \sum_{j=1}^{k-1} s_j a_j \quad \bmod pq$$

where c is a k-vector, $r \overset{\$}{\leftarrow} [0, q)$, and $\forall j, s_j \overset{\$}{\leftarrow} [0, pq)$. Let $a_0 = \mathbf{1}$, and $A_k = [a_0 \ a_1 \ \ldots \ a_{k-1}]$. We wish the columns of A_k to be a basis for $\mathbb{Z}_{pq}^k$. We can show that they do so with high probability. If they do not, we generate new vectors until they do.

Lemma 2. $\Pr(a_0, a_1, \ldots, a_{k-1}$ *do not form a basis*$) \leq (k-1)(1/p + 1/q)$.

We extend our definition of an augmented vector $v_\star$, for a k-vector, v, such that $v_\star$ is a $\binom{k+1}{2}$-vector, with components v_i $(1 \leq i \leq k)$ followed by $2v_i - v_j$ $(1 \leq i < j \leq k)$. In general, for $\ell > k$, $v_\ell = 2v_i - v_j$, where $\ell = \binom{i}{2} + k + j - 1$. Note that $v_\star = U_k v$ for a $\binom{k+1}{2} \times k$ matrix with entries $0, \pm 1, 2$, and whose first k rows form the $k \times k$ identity matrix I_k. Note that $v_\star = U_k v$ implies that $\mathbf{1}_\star$ is the $\binom{k+1}{2}$ vector of 1's, and that $\star$ is a linear mapping, i.e. $(r_1 v_1 + r_2 v_2)_\star = r_1 v_{1\star} + r_2 v_{2\star}$.

Decryption. $\mathsf{Dec}(c, \mathsf{sk}) = \gamma^T c \bmod p$, where $\gamma^T = (A_k^{-1})_1$ is the first row of A_k^{-1}. We call γ the *decryption vector*, as in HE2.

Addition. Addition is the vector sum of the ciphertext vectors as in HE2.

Multiplication. Consider the Hadamard product of two augmented ciphertext vectors, $c_\star \circ c'_\star$. For notational brevity, let $\tilde{m} = m + rp$.

$$
\begin{aligned}
c_\star \circ c'_\star &= \left(\tilde{m}\mathbf{1}_\star + \sum_{j=1}^{k-1} s_j a_{\star j}\right) \circ \left(\tilde{m}'\mathbf{1}_\star + \sum_{j=1}^{k-1} s'_j a_{\star j}\right) \\
&= \tilde{m}\tilde{m}'\mathbf{1}_\star + \sum_{j=1}^{k-1}(\tilde{m}s'_j + \tilde{m}'s_j)a_{\star j} + \sum_{j=1}^{k-1} s_j s'_j a_{\star j} \circ a_{\star j} \\
&\quad + \sum_{1 \le i < j \le k-1}(s_i s'_j + s'_i s_j)a_{\star i} \circ a_{\star j},
\end{aligned}
$$

since $\mathbf{1}_\star \circ v_\star = v_\star$ for any v. There are $\binom{k}{2}$ product vectors, which we must eliminate using the re-encryption matrix R, a $k \times \binom{k+1}{2}$.

Lemma 3. *Let $A_{\star k} = [a_{\star 0}\ a_{\star 1}\ \ldots\ a_{\star,k-1}]$, where the columns of A_k form a basis for $\mathbb{Z}_{pq}^k$. If $RA_{\star k} = A_k$, then $Rv_\star = v$ for all $v \in \mathbb{Z}_{pq}^k$.*

The condition $RA_{\star k} = A_k$ can be written more simply, since it is $RU_k A_k = A_k$. Postmultiplying by A_k^{-1} gives $RU_k = I_k$. Now, since $RA_{\star k} = A_k$, we have

$$
R(c_\star \circ c'_\star) = (mm' + \hat{r}p)\mathbf{1} + \sum_{j=1}^{k-1} \hat{s}_j a_j + \sum_{1 \le i \le j \le k-1} \hat{s}_{ij} R(a_{\star i} \circ a_{\star j}),
$$

where $\hat{r}$, $\hat{s}_j$ and $\hat{s}_{ij}$ $(1 \le i < j \le k-1)$ are some integers.

There are $k(\binom{k+1}{2} - k) = k\binom{k}{2}$ undetermined parameters $R_{i\ell}$, $1 \le i \le k$, $k < \ell \le \binom{k+1}{2}$. We now determine these by setting

$$
R(a_{\star i} \circ a_{\star j}) = \varrho_{ij}p\mathbf{1} + \sum_{l=1}^{k-1} \sigma_{ijl} a_l \tag{2}
$$

Thus we have $k\binom{k}{2}$ new unknowns, the ϱ's and σ's, and $k\binom{k}{2}$ linear equations for the $k\binom{k}{2}$ unassigned $R_{i\ell}$'s. Let $A_{\star k}^{\circ 2}$ be the $\binom{k+1}{2} \times \binom{k+1}{2}$ matrix with columns $a_{\star i} \circ a_{\star j}$ $(0 \le i < j < k)$, and let C_k be the $k \times \binom{k}{2}$ matrix with columns $\varrho_{ij}p\mathbf{1} + \sum_{l=1}^{k-1} \sigma_{ijl} a_l$ $(0 < i < j < k)$. Then the equations for the $R_{i\ell}$ can be written as

$$
RA_{\star k}^{\circ 2} = [A_k \mid C_k]. \tag{3}
$$

giving $k\binom{k+1}{2}$ linear equations for the $k\binom{k+1}{2}$ $R_{i\ell}$'s in terms of quadratic functions of the $k(k-1)$ a_{ij}'s $(1 \le i \le k, 1 \le j \le k-1)$, which are undetermined. Thus the system has $k(k-1)$ parameters that cannot be deduced from R.

The system of equations (3) has a solution provided that $A_{\star k}^{\circ 2}$ has an inverse mod pq. We prove that this is true with high probability. Again, in the unlikely event that this is not true, we generate new vectors $a_1, \ldots, a_{k-1}$ until it is.

Theorem 6. *$A_{\star k}^{\circ 2}$ has no inverse mod pq with probability at most $(k^2-1)(1/p+1/q)$.*

Note that Theorem 6 subsumes Lemma 2, since the first k columns of $A_{\star k}^{\circ 2}$ contain A_k as a submatrix, and must be linearly independent.

Each c introduces k new parameters $rp, s_1, \ldots, s_{k-1}$ and k equations, so the number of undetermined parameters is always $k(k-1)$.

Cryptanalysis. Note that p can be determined from m_i for k ciphertexts. Let

$$C = [c_1 - m_1 1 \ \ldots \ c_k - m_k 1], \quad A_k = [1 \ a_1 \ \ldots \ a_{k-1}]$$

and let

$$W = \begin{bmatrix} r_1 p & r_2 p & \cdots & r_k p \\ s_{1,1} & s_{2,1} & \cdots & s_{k,1} \\ \vdots & & & \vdots \\ s_{1,k-1} & s_{2,k-1} & \cdots & s_{k,k-1} \end{bmatrix}, \quad W' = \begin{bmatrix} r_1 & r_2 & \cdots & r_k \\ s_{1,1} & s_{2,1} & \cdots & s_{k,1} \\ \vdots & & & \vdots \\ s_{1,k-1} & s_{2,k-1} & \cdots & s_{k,k-1} \end{bmatrix},$$

where r_i, s_{ij} refer to c_i. Then $C = A_k W$, and so $\det C = \det A_k \det W$. Note that $\det W = p \det W'$, so $\det C$ is a multiple of p. Now $\det C$ can be determined in $O(k^3)$ time and, if it is nonzero, p can be determined as $\gcd(\det C, pq)$.

Lemma 4. $\Pr(\det C = 0 \bmod pq) \leq (2k - 1)(1/p + 1/q)$.

Once we have recovered p, we can use the known m_i to determine the decryption vector γ, by solving linear equations. Let $C_0 = [c_1 \ c_2 \ \ldots \ c_k]$, $m^T = [m_1 \ m_2 \ \ldots \ m_k]$.

Lemma 5. $\Pr(\det C_0 = 0 \bmod pq) \leq (2k - 1)(1/p + 1/q)$.

Thus, with high probability, we can uniquely solve the system $\gamma^T C_0 = m^T$ mod p, to recover γ and enable decryption of an arbitrary ciphertext. However, encryption of messages is not possible, since we gain little information about $a_1, \ldots, a_k$. Note also that, if we determined p by some means other than using k known plaintexts, it is not clear how to recover γ.

To break this system, we need to guess k plaintexts. The entropy of a k-tuple of plaintexts $(m_1, m_2, \ldots, m_k)$ is $k\rho$, so effectively we need μ^k guesses, where μ is the number of guesses needed to break HE1. So HEk can tolerate much smaller entropy than HE1, provided k is large enough. If k is sufficiently large, the scheme appears secure without adding noise, but does not have the other advantages of adding noise.

Fixing an Insecurity for $k > 2$. The decryption vector for HEk is $\gamma^T = (A_k^{-1})_1$. Note that $\gamma^T 1 = 1$ and $\gamma^T a_i = 0$ ($i \in [1, k - 1]$), since $\gamma^T a_i = I_{1i}$ ($i \in [0, k - 1]$).

The equations $\quad R(a_{\star i} \circ a_{\star j}) = p\varrho_{ij} 1 + \sum_{l=1}^{k-1} \sigma_{ijl} a_l,$

$$(4)$$

define a product $\cdot$ on $\mathbb{Z}_{pq}^k$ so that $c \cdot c' = R(c_\star \circ c'_\star)$. This product is linear, commutative and distributive, since R and $\star$ are linear operators, and $\circ$ is commutative and distributive. So we have an algebra $\mathcal{A}_k$, with unit element 1 [51]. The $\varrho_{ij}, \sigma_{ijl}$ ($i, j, l \in [1, k - 1]$) are the *structure constants* of the algebra. In general, $\mathcal{A}_k$ will not be associative, i.e. we can have $(c_1 \cdot c_2) \cdot c_3 \neq c_1 \cdot (c_2 \cdot c_3)$ This leads to a potential insecurity. We must have

$$\gamma^T ((c_1 \cdot c_2) \cdot c_3) = \gamma^T (c_1 \cdot (c_2 \cdot c_3)) \pmod{p}, \quad (5)$$

in order to have correct decryption. The *associator* for $\mathcal{A}_k$ is

$$[c_i, c_j, c_l] \; = c_i \cdot (c_j \cdot c_l) - (c_i \cdot c_j) \cdot c_l = rp\mathbf{1} + \sum_{l=1}^{k-1} s_l c_l \qquad (\text{mod } pq).$$

Thus $[c_i, c_j, c_l]$ is an encryption of 0. If we can find k associators from $c_1, \ldots, c_n$ which violate (5), with high probability we have k linearly independent associators. We can use these to make a collision attack on HEk, similar to that described in Sect. 3.1. We use the gcd method to determine p, and then γ, as described in Sect. A.1. In fact all we need is that (5) holds for any associator. That is, for all c_1, c_2, c_3, we need

$$\gamma^T((c_1 \cdot c_2) \cdot c_3) \; = \; \gamma^T(c_1(\cdot c_2 \cdot c_3)) \qquad (\text{mod } pq),$$

or, equivalently, using the Chinese Remainder Theorem,

$$\gamma^T((c_1 \cdot c_2) \cdot c_3) \; = \; \gamma^T(c_1 \cdot (c_2 \cdot c_3)) \qquad (\text{mod } q). \qquad (6)$$

By linearity, (6) holds if and only if it holds for all basis elements, excluding the identity. That is, for all $i, j, l \in [1, k-1]$, we need

$$\gamma^T(a_i \cdot (a_j \cdot a_l)) \; = \; \gamma^T((a_i \cdot a_j) \cdot a_l) \qquad (\text{mod } q). \qquad (7)$$

The associator for $\mathcal{A}_k$ is

$$[a_i, a_j, a_l] \; = a_i \cdot (a_j \cdot a_l) - (a_i \cdot a_j) \cdot a_l = rp\mathbf{1} + \sum_{l=1}^{k-1} s_l a_l \qquad (\text{mod } pq),$$

for some integers $r, s_1, \ldots, s_{k-1}$, and so $\gamma^T[a_i, a_j, a_l] = rp$.

If $\mathcal{A}_k$ is associative, the problem does not arise, since (7) will be satisfied automatically. Associativity holds if $k \leq 2$. All we have to check is that $a \cdot (a \cdot a) = (a \cdot a) \cdot a$, which is true by commutativity. Thus HE1, HE2 cannot be attacked in this way.

Requiring associativity in $\mathcal{A}_k$ overconstrains the system, imposing $k\binom{k+1}{2}$ equations on the $k\binom{k+1}{2}$ structure constants. With only $k(k-1)$ undetermined parameters, this is too much. But all we need is that (7) holds. We have

Lemma 6. *Equation* (7) *holds if and only if* $\sum_{t=1}^{k-1} \sigma_{jlt} \varrho_{it} \; = \; \sum_{t=1}^{k-1} \sigma_{ijt} \varrho_{lt}$ (mod q), $\forall i, j, l \in [1, k-1]$.

Now we can ensure (7) by giving the ϱ_{ij} a multiplicative structure.

Lemma 7. *Let* $\tau, \varrho_i \overset{\$}{\leftarrow} [0, q)$ $(i \in [1, k-1])$, *let* $\varrho_{ij} = \varrho_i \varrho_j \mod q$, *and let the* σ_{ijl} *satisfy* $\sum_{l=1}^{k-1} \sigma_{ijl} \varrho_l = \tau \varrho_i \varrho_j$ (mod q) *for all* $i, j \in [1, k-1]$. *Then, for all* $i, j, \ell \in [1, k-1]$, $\gamma^T(a_i \cdot (a_j \cdot a_l)) = \tau \varrho_i \varrho_j \varrho_l \mod q$, *the symmetry of which implies* (7).

Thus the conditions of Lemma 7 are sufficient to remove the insecurity. The price is that we now have $(k-1)\binom{k}{2} + (k-1) + k(k-1) = (k+1)\binom{k}{2} + k - 1$ parameters and $k\binom{k}{2}$ equations. There are $\binom{k}{2} + (k-1) = (k+2)(k-1)/2$ independent parameters. This is fewer than the original $k(k-1)$, but remains $\Omega(k^2)$.

A.2   Insufficient Entropy (HEkN)

We generalise HE2N to k dimensions.

Key Generation. KeyGen, randomly chooses κ, p and q as outlined in Sect. 4.2, and sets $a_j\ \forall j$ and R as in Sect. A.1. The secret key, sk, is $(\kappa, p, a_1, \ldots, a_{k-1})$, and the public parameters are pq and R. Note that, as a result of adding the "noise" term, defence against non-associativity is not required.

Encryption. A plaintext, $m \in [0, M]$, is enciphered as

$$\mathsf{Enc}(m, \mathsf{sk}) = c = (m + rp + s\kappa)\mathbf{1} + \textstyle\sum_{j=1}^{k-1} t_j a_j \quad (\mathrm{mod}\ pq)$$

where r, s are as in Sect. 4.2, and $t_j \overset{\$}{\leftarrow} [0, pq)\ \forall j \in [1, k)$.

Decryption. If γ^T is defined as in Sect. A.1, a ciphertext is deciphered by,

$$\mathsf{Dec}(c, \mathsf{sk}) = (\gamma^T c \quad \mathrm{mod}\ p) \quad \mathrm{mod}\ \kappa.$$

Arithmetic. Addition and multiplication of ciphertexts are as in Sect. A.1.

Security. The effective entropy of HEkN is $\rho' = k(\rho + \lg \kappa)$. Thus, as we increase k, the "noise" term can be made smaller while still providing the requisite level of entropy.

Clearly HEkN also inherits the conclusions of Theorem 2, so this system also satisfies IND-CPA.

B   Proofs

Theorem 1. *An attack against HE1 is successful in polynomial time if and only if we can factorise a distinct semi-prime in polynomial time.*

Proof. Suppose that we have an unknown plaintext m, encrypted as $c = m + rp$ mod pq, where $r \overset{\$}{\leftarrow} [1, q)$.

If we can factor pq in polynomial time, we can determine p and q in polynomial time, since we know $p < q$. Therefore, we can determine $m = c$ mod p.

If we can determine m given c for arbitrary m, then we can determine $rp = c - m$. We are given qp, and we know $0 < r < q$, so $\gcd(rp, qp)$ must be p, and we can compute p in polynomial time. Now, given p, we can determine q as qp/p. Hence, we can factorise pq in polynomial time. □

Lemma 1. *If the inputs m have entropy ρ then, for any two independent inputs m_1, m_2, $\Pr(m_1 = m_2) \leq 2^{-\rho}$.*

Proof. $\Pr(m_1 = m_2) = \sum_{i=0}^{M-1} \xi_i^2 = 2^{-H_2} \le 2^{-\rho}$, since $H_2 \ge H_\infty = \rho$. $\square$

Theorem 2. *For any encryption c, $c \bmod \kappa$ is polynomial time indistinguishable from the uniform distribution on $[0, \kappa)$. Thus HE1N satisfies IND-CPA, under the assumption that SPACDP is not polynomial time solvable.*

Proof.

$$c = m + s\kappa + rp = m + rp \quad \bmod \kappa,$$

where $r \xleftarrow{\$} [1, q)$. Thus, for $i \in [0, \kappa)$,

$$\begin{aligned}
\Pr\left(c \bmod \kappa = i\right) &= \Pr(m + rp = i \bmod \kappa) \\
&= \Pr\left(r = p^{-1}(i - m) \bmod \kappa\right) \\
&\in \left\{\lfloor q/\kappa \rfloor 1/q, \lceil q/\kappa \rceil 1/q\right\} \\
&\in [1/\kappa - 1/q, 1/\kappa + 1/q],
\end{aligned}$$

where the inverse p^{-1} of $p \bmod \kappa$ exists since p is a prime. Hence the total variation distance from the uniform distribution is

$$\frac{1}{2}\sum_{i=0}^{\kappa-1} |\Pr\left(c \bmod \kappa = i\right) - 1/\kappa| < \kappa/q.$$

This is exponentially small in the security parameter λ of the system, so the distribution of $c \bmod \kappa$ cannot be distinguished in polynomial time from the uniform distribution. Note further that $c_1 \bmod \kappa$, $c_2 \bmod \kappa$ are independent for any two ciphertexts $c_i = m_i + s_i\kappa + r_ip$ $(i = 1, 2)$, since r_1, r_2 are independent.

To show IND-CPA, suppose now that known plaintexts $\mu_1, \ldots, \mu_n$ are encrypted by an oracle for HE1N, giving ciphertexts $c_1, \ldots, c_n$. Then, for $r_i \xleftarrow{\$} [0, q)$, $s_i \xleftarrow{\$} [0, \kappa)$, we have an SPACDP with ciphertexts $c_i = m_i + s_i\kappa + r_ip$, and the approximate divisor p cannot be determined in polynomial time in the worst case. However, the offsets in this SPACDP are all of the form $\mu_i + s_i\kappa$, for known m_i, and we must make sure this does not provide information about p. To show this, we rewrite the SPACDP as

$$c_i = \mu_i + s_i\kappa + r_ip = \mu_i' + s_i'\kappa, \quad (i = 1, 2, \ldots, n), \tag{8}$$

where $s_i' = s_i + \lfloor (m_i + r_ip)/\kappa \rfloor$, and $\mu_i' = \mu_i + r_ip \pmod{\kappa}$. Now we may view (8) as an ACDP, with "encryptions" μ_i' of the μ_i, and approximate divisor κ. Since ACDP is at least as hard as SPACDP, and the offsets μ_i' are polynomial time indistinguishable from uniform $[0, \kappa)$, from above, we will not be able to determine κ in polynomial time. Now, the offsets m_1', m_2' of any two plaintexts m_1, m_2 are polynomial time indistinguishable from m_2', m_1', since they are indistinguishable from two independent samples from uniform $[0, \kappa)$. Therefore, in polynomial time, we will not be able to distinguish between the encryption c_1 of m_1 and the encryption c_2 of m_2. $\square$

Theorem 3. *The encryption scheme produces ciphertexts with components which are random integers modulo pq.*

Proof. Consider a ciphertext vector which encrypts the plaintext, m, and the expression $m + rp + sa \bmod pq$ which represents one of its elements. Then $r \xleftarrow{\$} [0, q)$, $s \xleftarrow{\$} [0, pq)$.

Consider first $m + sa$. We know that $a^{-1} \bmod pq$ exists because $a \neq 0$ $(\bmod\ p$ and $\bmod\ q)$. Thus, conditional on r,

$$\Pr[m + rp + sa = i \bmod\ pq] =$$
$$\Pr[s = a^{-1}(i - m - rp) \bmod\ pq] = \frac{1}{pq}.$$

Since this holds for any $i \in [0, pq)$, $m + ra + sp \bmod pq$ is a uniformly random integer from $[0, pq)$. □

Theorem 4. *If c is an encryption of m and c' is an encryption of m' then $R(c_\star \circ c'_\star) \pmod{pq}$ is an encryption of mm'.*

Proof. Consider the Hadamard product modulo pq, $c_\star \circ c'_\star$, of the two augmented ciphertext vectors $c_\star$ and $c_\star'$:

$$z_\star = c_\star \circ c'_\star = \begin{bmatrix} c_1 c'_1 \\ c_2 c'_2 \\ c_3 c'_3 \end{bmatrix} \quad \bmod pq$$

Therefore, if inputs m, m' are encrypted as $(m+rp)\mathbf{1} + sa$, $(m'+r'p)\mathbf{1} + s'a$, we first calculate

$$z_\star = (m + rp)(m' + r'p)\mathbf{1}_\star + [(m + rp)s' + (m' + r'p)s]a_\star$$
$$+ ss'a_\star^{\circ 2} = (mm' + r_1 p)\mathbf{1}_\star + s_1 a_\star + ss'a_\star^{\circ 2} \quad \bmod pq,$$

where $r_1 = mr' + m'r + rr'p$, $s_1 = (m + rp)s' + (m' + r'p)s$, and $a_\star^{\circ 2} = [a_1^2\ a_2^2\ a_3^2]^T$.

As we can see, $z_\star$ is not a valid encryption of mm'. We need to re-encrypt this product to eliminate the $a_\star^{\circ 2}$ term.

We achieve this by multiplying $z_\star$ by R. It is easy to check that $R\mathbf{1}_\star = 1$ and $Ra_\star = a$, independently of a_1, a_2. Now

$$(Ra_\star^{\circ 2})_1 = (1 - 2\alpha_1)a_1^2 + \alpha_1 a_2^2 + \alpha_1(2a_1 - a_2)^2$$
$$= a_1^2 + \alpha_1((2a_1 - a_2)^2 + a_2^2 - 2a_1^2)$$
$$= a_1^2 + 2\alpha_1(a_2 - a_1)^2$$
$$= a_1^2 + \alpha_1 \beta$$
$$= \varrho p + \sigma a_1$$
$$(Ra_\star^{\circ 2})_2 = -2\alpha_2 a_1^2 + (\alpha_2 + 1)a_2^2 + \alpha_2(2a_1 - a_2)^2$$
$$= a_2^2 + \alpha_2((2a_1 - a_2)^2 + a_2^2 - 2a_1^2)$$

$$= a_2^2 + 2\alpha_2(a_2 - a_1)^2$$
$$= a_2^2 + \alpha_2\beta$$
$$= \varrho p + \sigma a_2$$

Thus, we obtain the identity $Ra_*^{\circ 2} = \varrho p\mathbf{1} + \sigma\mathbf{a}$.

So, applying R to z_*, i.e. $z' = Rz_*$, gives

$$z' = (mm' + r_1p)R\mathbf{1} + s_1R\mathbf{a} + ss'R\mathbf{a}^{\circ 2}$$
$$= (mm' + r_1p)\mathbf{1} + s_1\mathbf{a} + ss'(\sigma\mathbf{a} + \varrho p\mathbf{1})$$
$$= (mm' + r_2p)\mathbf{1} + (s_1 + \sigma rr')\mathbf{a}$$
$$= (mm' + r_2p)\mathbf{1} + s_2\mathbf{a} \qquad (\text{mod } pq)$$

for some integers r_2, s_2. So z' is a valid encryption of mm'. □

Theorem 5. *SPACDP is of equivalent complexity to the special case of HE2 where $\delta = a_2 - a_1$ $(0 < \delta < q)$ is known.*

Proof. Suppose we have a system of n approximate prime multiples, $m_i + r_ip$ $(i = 1, 2, \ldots, n)$. Then we generate values $a, s_1, s_2, \ldots, s_n \overset{\$}{\leftarrow} [0, pq)$, and we have an oracle set up the cryptosystem with $a_1 = a$, $a_2 = a + \delta$. The oracle has access to p and provides us with R, but no information about its choice of ϱ and σ. We then generate the ciphertexts c_i $(i = 1, 2, \ldots, n)$:

$$\begin{bmatrix} c_{i1} \\ c_{i2} \end{bmatrix} = \begin{bmatrix} m_i + r_ip + s_ia \\ m_i + r_ip + s_i(a + \delta) \end{bmatrix} \quad (\text{mod } pq). \qquad (9)$$

Thus $c_{i1} - s_ia = c_{i2} - s_i(a + \delta) = m_i + r_ip$. Thus finding the m_i in (9) in polynomial time solves SPACDP in polynomial time.

Conversely, suppose we have any HE2 system with $a_2 = a_1 + \delta$. The ciphertext for m_i $(i = 1, 2, \ldots, n)$ is as in (9). so $s_i = \delta^{-1}(c_{i2} - c_{i1})$. Since $0 < \delta < q < p$, δ is coprime to both p and q, and hence δ^{-1} mod pq exists. Thus breaking the system is equivalent to determining the m_i mod p from $m_i + \delta^{-1}(c_{i2} - c_{i1})a + r_ip$ $(i = 1, 2, \ldots, n)$. Determining the $m_i + \delta^{-1}(c_{i2} - c_{i1})a$ from the $m_i + \delta^{-1}(c_{i2} - c_{i1})a + r_ip$ $(i = 1, 2, \ldots, n)$ can be done using SPACDP. However, we still need to determine a in order to determine m_i. This can be done by "deciphering" R using SPACDP. We have

$$2\delta^2\alpha_1 = \sigma a - a^2 + \varrho p, \qquad 2\delta^2\alpha_2 = \sigma(a + \delta) - (a + \delta)^2 + \varrho p,$$

so $\sigma = 2\delta^2(\alpha_2 - \alpha_1) - 2ka - \delta^2$. Now a can be determined by first determining $m_0 = a(2\delta^2(\alpha_2 - \alpha_1) - (2\delta + 1)a - \delta^2)$ from $m_0 + \varrho p = 2\delta^2\alpha_1$. This can be done using SPACDP. Then a can be determined by solving the quadratic equation $m_0 = a(2\delta^2(\alpha_2 - \alpha_1) - (2\delta + 1)a - \delta^2)$ mod p for a. This can be done probabilistically in polynomial time using, for example, the algorithm of Berlekamp

[7]. So the case $\boldsymbol{a} = [a \ \ a + \delta]^T$, with known δ, can be attacked using SPACDP on the system

$$m_0 + \varrho p, \ m_1 + \delta^{-1}(c_{11} - c_{12})a + r_1 p,$$
$$\ldots, \ m_n + \delta^{-1}(c_{n1} - c_{n2})a + r_n p.$$

$\square$

Lemma 2. $\Pr(\boldsymbol{a}_0, \boldsymbol{a}_1, \ldots, \boldsymbol{a}_{k-1} \ \textit{do not form a basis}) \leq (k-1)(1/p + 1/q)$.

Proof. The $\boldsymbol{a}$'s are a basis if A_k^{-1} exists, since then $\boldsymbol{v} = A_k \boldsymbol{r}$ when $\boldsymbol{r} = A_k^{-1}\boldsymbol{v}$, for any $\boldsymbol{v}$. Now A_k^{-1} exists mod pq if $(\det A_k)^{-1} \mod pq$ exists, by constructing the adjugate of A_k. Now $(\det A_k)^{-1} \mod pq$ exists if $\det A_k \neq 0 \mod p$ and $\det A_k \neq 0 \mod q$. Now $\det A_k$ is a polynomial of total degree $(k-1)$ in the a_{ij} $(0 < i \leq k, 0 < j < k)$, and is not identically zero, since $\det A_k = 1$ if $\boldsymbol{a}_i = \boldsymbol{e}_{i+1}$ $(1 < i < k)$. Also $a_{ij} \overset{\$}{\leftarrow} [0, pq)$ implies $a_{ij} \mod p \overset{\$}{\leftarrow} [0, p)$ and $a_{ij} \mod q \overset{\$}{\leftarrow} [0, q)$. Hence, using the Schwartz-Zippel Lemma (SZL) [44], we have $\Pr(\det A_k = 0 \mod p) \leq (k-1)/p$ and $\Pr(\det A_k = 0 \mod q) \leq (k-1)/q$, and it follows that $\Pr(\nexists (\det A_k)^{-1} \mod pq) \leq (k-1)(1/p + 1/q)$. $\square$

Lemma 3. *Let* $A_{\star k} = [\boldsymbol{a}_{\star 0} \ \boldsymbol{a}_{\star 1} \ \cdots \ \boldsymbol{a}_{\star, k-1}]$, *where the columns of* A_k *form a basis for* $\mathbb{Z}_{pq}^k$. *If* $RA_{\star k} = A_k$, *then* $R\boldsymbol{v}_\star = \boldsymbol{v}$ *for all* $\boldsymbol{v} \in \mathbb{Z}_{pq}^k$.

Proof. We have $\boldsymbol{v} = A_k \boldsymbol{r}$ for some $\boldsymbol{r} \in \mathbb{Z}_{pq}^k$. Then $A_{\star k} = U_k A_k$ and $\boldsymbol{v}_{\star k} = U_k \boldsymbol{v}$, so $R\boldsymbol{v}_\star = RU_k \boldsymbol{v} = RU_k A_k \boldsymbol{r} = RA_{\star k} \boldsymbol{r} = A_k \boldsymbol{r} = \boldsymbol{v}$. $\square$

Theorem 6. $A_{\star k}^{\circ 2}$ *has no inverse* mod pq *with probability at most* $(k^2 - 1)(1/p + 1/q)$.

Proof. We use the same approach as in Lemma 2. Thus $A_{\star k}^{\circ 2}$ is invertible provided $\det A_{\star k}^{\circ 2} \neq 0 \mod p$ and $\det A_{\star k}^{\circ 2} \neq 0 \mod q$. Let $\boldsymbol{A}$ denote the vector of a_{ij}'s, $(a_{ij} : 1 \leq i \leq k, 1 \leq j < k)$. The elements of $A_{\star k}^{\circ 2}$ are quadratic polynomials over $\boldsymbol{A}$, except for the first column, which has all 1's, and columns $2, 3, \ldots, k$ which are linear polynomials. So $\det A_{\star k}^{\circ 2}$ is a polynomial over $\boldsymbol{A}$ of total degree $2\binom{k}{2} + k - 1 = k^2 - 1$. Thus, unless $\det A_{\star k}^{\circ 2}$ is identically zero as a polynomial over $\boldsymbol{A}$, the SZL [44] implies $\Pr(\nexists (\det A_{\star k}^{\circ 2})^{-1} \mod p) \leq (k^2 - 1)/p$ and $\Pr(\nexists (\det A_{\star k}^{\circ 2})^{-1} \mod q) \leq (k^2 - 1)/q$. Therefore we have $\Pr(\nexists (\det A_{\star k}^{\circ 2})^{-1} \mod pq) \leq (k^2 - 1)(1/p + 1/q)$.

It remains to prove that $\det A_{\star k}^{\circ 2}$ is not identically zero as a polynomial over $\boldsymbol{A}$ in either $\mathbb{Z}_p$ or $\mathbb{Z}_q$. We prove this by induction on k. Consider $\mathbb{Z}_p$, the argument for $\mathbb{Z}_q$ being identical. Since $\mathbb{Z}_p$ is a field, $\det A_{\star k}^{\circ 2}$ is identically zero if and only if it has rank less than $\binom{k+1}{2}$ for all $\boldsymbol{A}$. That is, there exist $\lambda_{ij}(\boldsymbol{A}) \in \mathbb{Z}_p$ $(0 \leq i \leq j < k)$, not all zero, so that

$$\mathcal{L}(\boldsymbol{A}) = \sum_{0 \leq i \leq j}^{k-1} \lambda_{ij} \boldsymbol{a}_{\star i} \circ \boldsymbol{a}_{\star j}$$
$$= \boldsymbol{\alpha} + \boldsymbol{a}_{\star, k-1} \circ \boldsymbol{\beta} + \lambda_{k-1, k-1} \boldsymbol{a}_{\star, k-1}^{\circ 2} = 0,$$

where $\alpha = \sum_{0 \leq i \leq j}^{k-2} \lambda_{ij} \mathbf{a}_{\star i} \circ \mathbf{a}_{\star j}$ and $\beta = \sum_{i=0}^{k-2} \lambda_{i,k-1} \mathbf{a}_{\star i}$ are independent of $\mathbf{a}_{\star, k-1}$.

Clearly $\lambda_{k-1,k-1} = 0$. Otherwise, whatever α, β, we can choose values for $\mathbf{a}_k$ so that $\mathcal{L} \neq 0$, a contradiction. Now suppose $\lambda_{i,k-1} \neq 0$ for some $0 \leq i < k-1$. The matrix $\hat{A}_\star$ with columns $\mathbf{a}_{\star i}$ ($0 \leq i < k-1$) contains A_{k-1} as a submatrix, which has rank $(k-1)$ with high probability by Lemma 2. Thus $\beta \neq \mathbf{0}$ and, whatever α, we can choose values for $\mathbf{a}_k$ so that $\mathcal{L} \neq 0$. Thus $\lambda_{i,k-1} = 0$ for all $0 \leq i < k$. Thus $\lambda_{ij} \neq 0$ for some $0 \leq i \leq j < k-1$. Now the matrix $\hat{A}_\star^{\circ 2}$ with $\binom{k}{2}$ columns $\mathbf{a}_{\star i} \circ \mathbf{a}_{\star j}$ ($0 \leq i \leq j < k-1$) contains $A_{\star, k-1}^{\circ 2}$ as a submatrix, and therefore has rank $\binom{k}{2}$ by induction. Hence $\alpha \neq \mathbf{0}$, implying $\mathcal{L} \neq 0$, a contradiction. □

Lemma 4. $\Pr(\det C = 0 \bmod pq) \leq (2k-1)(1/p + 1/q)$.

Proof. From Lemma 2, $\det A = 0 \bmod p$ or $\det A = 0 \bmod q$ with probability at most $(k-1)(1/p + 1/q)$. So $\det A$ is not zero or a divisor of zero $\bmod pq$. The entries of W' are random $[0, pq)$, and $\det W'$ is a polynomial of total degree k in its entries. It is a nonzero polynomial, since $W' = I_k$ is possible. Hence, using the SZL [44], $\Pr(\det W' = 0 \bmod p) \leq k/p$ and $\Pr(\det W' = 0 \bmod q) \leq k/q$. So $\det W'$ is zero or a divisor of zero $\bmod pq$ with probability at most $k(1/p + 1/q)$. So $\det A \det W' = 0 \bmod pq$ with probability at most $(2k-1)(1/p + 1/q)$. So $\det C \neq 0$ with high probability. □

Lemma 5. $\Pr(\det C_0 = 0 \bmod pq) \leq (2k-1)(1/p + 1/q)$.

Proof. Note that $C_0 = C$ if $m_1 = m_2 = \cdots = m_k = 0$. Since Lemma 4 holds in that case, the result follows. □

Lemma 6. *Equation* (7) *holds if and only if* $\sum_{t=1}^{k-1} \sigma_{jlt} \varrho_{it} = \sum_{t=1}^{k-1} \sigma_{ijt} \varrho_{lt}$ (mod q), $\forall i, j, l \in [1, k-1]$.

Proof. Since $\gamma^T \mathbf{1} = 1$ and $\gamma^T \mathbf{a}_i = 0$, $i \in [1, k-1]$, $\gamma^T(\mathbf{a}_i \cdot \mathbf{a}_j) = \gamma^T(p\varrho_{ij}\mathbf{1} + \sum_{l=1}^{k-1} \sigma_{ijl} \mathbf{a}_l) = p\varrho_{ij}$. Thus

$$\mathbf{a}_i \cdot (\mathbf{a}_j \cdot \mathbf{a}_l) = \mathbf{a}_i \cdot \left(p\varrho_{jl}\mathbf{1} + \sum_{t=1}^{k-1} \sigma_{jlt}\mathbf{a}_t \right)$$

$$= p\varrho_{jl}\mathbf{a}_i + \sum_{t=1}^{k-1} \sigma_{jlt}\mathbf{a}_i \cdot \mathbf{a}_t,$$

and hence $\gamma^T[\mathbf{a}_i \cdot (\mathbf{a}_j \cdot \mathbf{a}_l)] = p\sum_{t=1}^{k-1} \sigma_{jlt}\varrho_{it}$. Similarly $\gamma^T[(\mathbf{a}_i \cdot \mathbf{a}_j) \cdot \mathbf{a}_l] = p\sum_{t=1}^{k-1} \sigma_{ijt}\varrho_{lt}$, and the lemma follows. □

Lemma 7. *Let* $\tau, \varrho_i \overset{\$}{\leftarrow} [0, q)$ ($i \in [1, k-1]$), *let* $\varrho_{ij} = \varrho_i \varrho_j \bmod q$, *and let the* σ_{ijl} *satisfy* $\sum_{l=1}^{k-1} \sigma_{ijl} \varrho_l = \tau \varrho_i \varrho_j$ (mod q) *for all* $i, j \in [1, k-1]$. *Then, for all* $i, j, \ell \in [1, k-1]$, $\gamma^T(\mathbf{a}_i \cdot (\mathbf{a}_j \cdot \mathbf{a}_l)) = \tau \varrho_i \varrho_j \varrho_l \bmod q$, *the symmetry of which implies* (7).

Proof. We have $\gamma^T(\mathbf{a}_j \cdot \mathbf{a}_l) = p\varrho_{ij} = p\varrho_j\varrho_l$ for all $j, \ell \in [1, k-1]$. Hence, mod q,

$$
\begin{aligned}
\gamma^T(\mathbf{a}_i \cdot (\mathbf{a}_j \cdot \mathbf{a}_l)) &= p \sum_{t=1}^{k-1} \sigma_{jlt}\varrho_{it} \\
&= p \sum_{t=1}^{k-1} \sigma_{jlt}\varrho_i\varrho_t \\
&= p\varrho_i \sum_{t=1}^{k-1} \sigma_{jlt}\varrho_t \\
&= p\varrho_i\tau\varrho_j\varrho_l = p\tau\varrho_i\varrho_j\varrho_l.
\end{aligned}
$$

$\square$

C Derivation of Bounds

To recap, n is the number of inputs, M is an exclusive upper bound on the inputs, d is the degree of the polynomial we wish to calculate. We take $p \approx 2^\lambda$ and then $q \approx 2^\eta$, where $\eta = \lambda^2/\rho - \lambda$, to guard against the attacks of [17,36].

For HE1, we assume $M \approx 2^\rho$, $n \le \sqrt{M}$. Therefore,

$$ p > (n+1)^d M^d \approx (nM)^d \text{for large } n. $$

So, we may take

$$ p = 2^\lambda > M^{3d/2} \approx 2^{3d\rho/2} \quad \text{i.e. } \lambda \approx 3d\rho/2 $$
$$ \text{and } \eta \approx \frac{\lambda^2}{\rho} - \lambda = \frac{3d\lambda}{2} - \lambda = \frac{3d\rho}{2}\left(\frac{3d}{2} - 1\right) $$

For HE1N, we assume $M \approx 2^\rho$, and we have $\rho' = \rho + \lg\kappa$. Now,

$$ \kappa > (n+1)^d M^d \approx (nM)^d \text{ for large } n, \quad \text{i.e. } \lg\kappa \approx d(\lg n + \rho) $$

Therefore, since $\rho = \rho' - \lg\kappa$,

$$ \lg\kappa > d\lg n + d(\rho' - \lg\kappa) \quad \text{i.e. } \lg\kappa \approx \frac{d(\lg n + \rho')}{d+1} $$

Since κ is much larger than M, we also have

$$ p = 2^\lambda > (n+1)^d(M + \kappa^2)^d \approx (n\kappa^2)^d \text{ for large } n \quad \text{i.e. } \lambda \approx d(\lg n + 2\lg\kappa), $$
$$ \text{and } \eta \approx \frac{\lambda^2}{\rho'} - \lambda = \frac{3d\lambda}{2} - \lambda = \frac{3d\rho'}{2}\left(\frac{3d}{2} - 1\right) $$

Then we can calculate η as for HE1 above. Note that, in both HE1 and HE1N, λ scales linearly with d, and η scales quadratically. These bounds carry over to HE2, HE2N, HEk and HEkN.

References

1. Acar, A., et al.: A survey on homomorphic encryption schemes: theory and implementation (2017). arXiv:1704.03578 [cs.CR]
2. Aguilar-Melchor, C., et al.: A comparison of open-source homomorphic libraries with multi-precision plaintext moduli, WHEAT 2016, July 2016. https://wheat2016.lip6.fr/ricosset.pdf
3. Aumasson, J.-P.: On the pseudo-random generator ISAAC. Cryptology ePrint Archive: 2006/438 (2006)
4. Bellare, M., Rogaway, P.: Introduction to Modern Cryptography. Lecture Notes (2005)
5. Bellare, M., et al.: A concrete security treatment of symmetric encryption. In: Proceedings of FOCS 1997, pp. 394–403 (1997)
6. Bellare, M., Desai, A., Pointcheval, D., Rogaway, P.: Relations among notions of security for public-key encryption schemes. In: Krawczyk, H. (ed.) CRYPTO 1998. LNCS, vol. 1462, pp. 26–45. Springer, Heidelberg (1998). https://doi.org/10.1007/BFb0055718
7. Berlekamp, E.R.: Factoring polynomials over large finite fields. Math. Comput. **24**(111), 713–735 (1970)
8. Bogos, S., et al.: Cryptanalysis of a Homomorphic Encryption Scheme. Cryptology ePrint Archive: 2016/775 (2016)
9. Boneh, D., Shoup, V.: A Graduate Course in Applied Cryptography. Draft 0.2 (2015)
10. Bonte, C., et al.: Faster homomorphic function evaluation using non-integral base encoding. Cryptology ePrint Archive: 2017/333 (2017)
11. Bos, J.W., et al.: Privacy-friendly Forecasting for the Smart Grid using Homomorphic Encryption and the Group Method of Data Handling. Cryptology ePrint Archive: 2016/1117 (2016)
12. Brakerski, Z., Vaikuntanathan, V.: Fully homomorphic encryption from Ring-LWE and security for key dependent messages. In: Rogaway, P. (ed.) CRYPTO 2011. LNCS, vol. 6841, pp. 505–524. Springer, Heidelberg (2011). https://doi.org/10.1007/978-3-642-22792-9_29
13. Brakerski, Z., et al.: (Leveled) Fully homomorphic encryption without bootstrapping. In: Proceedings of ITCS 2012, pp. 309–325 (2012)
14. Catalano, D., Fiore, D.: Boosting linearly-homomorphic encryption to evaluate degree-2 functions on encrypted data. Cryptology ePrint Archive: 2014/813 (2014)
15. Catalano, D., Fiore, D.: Using linearly-homomorphic encryption to evaluate degree-2 functions on encrypted data. In: Proceedings of CCS 2015, pp. 1518–1529. ACM (2015)
16. Chen, Y., Nguyen, P.Q.: Faster algorithms for approximate common divisors: breaking fully homomorphic encryption challenges over the integers. In: Proceedings of EUROCRYPT 2012, pp. 502–519 (2012)
17. Cohn, H., Heninger, N.: Approximate common divisors via lattices. In: Proceedings of ANTSX, vol. 1, pp. 271–293 (2012)
18. Coppersmith, D.: Small solutions to polynomial equations, and low exponent RSA vulnerabilities. J. Cryptol. **10**(4), 233–260 (1997)
19. Coron, J.-S., Mandal, A., Naccache, D., Tibouchi, M.: Fully homomorphic encryption over the integers with shorter public keys. In: Rogaway, P. (ed.) CRYPTO 2011. LNCS, vol. 6841, pp. 487–504. Springer, Heidelberg (2011). https://doi.org/10.1007/978-3-642-22792-9_28

20. CryptoExperts. FV-NFLib. https://github.com/CryptoExperts/FV-NFLlib
21. Dautelle, J.-M.: JScience. Version 4.3.1, September 2014. http://jscience.org
22. van Dijk, M., Gentry, C., Halevi, S., Vaikuntanathan, V.: Fully homomorphic encryption over the integers. In: Gilbert, H. (ed.) EUROCRYPT 2010. LNCS, vol. 6110, pp. 24–43. Springer, Heidelberg (2010). https://doi.org/10.1007/978-3-642-13190-5_2
23. van Dijk, M., Juels, A.: On the impossibility of cryptography alone for privacy-preserving cloud computing. In: Proceedings of HotSec 2010, pp. 1–8 (2010)
24. Ducas, L., Micciancio, D.: FHEW: bootstrapping homomorphic encryption in less than a second. In: Oswald, E., Fischlin, M. (eds.) EUROCRYPT 2015. LNCS, vol. 9056, pp. 617–640. Springer, Heidelberg (2015). https://doi.org/10.1007/978-3-662-46800-5_24
25. Ducas, L., Micciancio, D.: FHEW. A fully homomorphic encryption library. https://github.com/lducas/FHEW
26. ElGamal, T.: A public key cryptosystem and a signature scheme based on discrete logarithms. In: Blakley, G.R., Chaum, D. (eds.) CRYPTO 1984. LNCS, vol. 196, pp. 10–18. Springer, Heidelberg (1985). https://doi.org/10.1007/3-540-39568-7_2
27. Erkin, Z., Franz, M., Guajardo, J., Katzenbeisser, S., Lagendijk, I., Toft, T.: Privacy-preserving face recognition. In: Goldberg, I., Atallah, M.J. (eds.) PETS 2009. LNCS, vol. 5672, pp. 235–253. Springer, Heidelberg (2009). https://doi.org/10.1007/978-3-642-03168-7_14
28. Fan, J., Vercauteren, F.: Somewhat practical fully homomorphic encryption. Cryptology ePrint Archive: 2012/144 (2012)
29. Galbraith, S.D., et al.: Algorithms for the approximate common divisor problem. LMS J. Comput. Math. 19(A), 58–72 (2016)
30. Gentry, C.: Fully homomorphic encryption using ideal lattices. In: Proceedings of STOC 2009, pp. 169–178 (2009)
31. Goldreich, O., et al.: How to play ANY mental game. In: Proceedings of STOC 1987, pp. 218–229 (1987)
32. Goldwasser, S., Micali, S.: Probabilistic encryption. J. Comput. Syst. Sci. 28(2), 270–299 (1984)
33. Goldwasser, S., et al.: Reusable garbled circuits and succinct functional encryption. In: Proceedings of STOC 2013, pp. 555–564 (2013)
34. Halevi, S., Shoup, V.: Bootstrapping for HElib. In: Oswald, E., Fischlin, M. (eds.) EUROCRYPT 2015. LNCS, vol. 9056, pp. 641–670. Springer, Heidelberg (2015). https://doi.org/10.1007/978-3-662-46800-5_25
35. Halevi, S., Shoup, V.: HELib. https://github.com/shaih/HElib
36. Howgrave-Graham, N.: Approximate integer common divisors. In: Silverman, J.H. (ed.) CaLC 2001. LNCS, vol. 2146, pp. 51–66. Springer, Heidelberg (2001). https://doi.org/10.1007/3-540-44670-2_6
37. Jenkins, B.: ISAAC: a fast cryptographic random number generator (1996). http://burtleburtle.net/bob/rand/isaacafa.html
38. Joye, M., Libert, B.: Efficient cryptosystems from 2^k-th power residue symbols. In: Proceedings of EUROCRYPT 2013, pp. 76–92 (2013)
39. Kipnis, A., Hibshoosh, E.: Efficient methods for practical fully homomorphic symmetrickey encryption, randomization and verification. Cryptology ePrint Archive: 2012/637 (2012)
40. Kleinjung, T., et al.: Factorization of a 768-Bit RSA modulus. In: Rabin, T. (ed.) CRYPTO 2010. LNCS, vol. 6223, pp. 333–350. Springer, Heidelberg (2010). https://doi.org/10.1007/978-3-642-14623-7_18

41. Laine, K., et al.: Simple Encrypted Arithmetic Library - SEAL. Version 2.2 (2017). https://sealcrypto.codeplex.com/
42. Lauter, K., et al.: Can homomorphic encryption be practical? In: Proceedings of CCSW 2011, pp. 113–124 (2011)
43. Massey, J.L.: Guessing and entropy. In: Proceedings of ISIT 1994, p. 204 (1994)
44. Moshkovitz, D.: An alternative proof of the Schwartz-Zippel lemma. In: Electronic Colloquium on Computational Complexity (ECCC), p. 96 (2010)
45. Paillier, P.: Public-key cryptosystems based on composite degree residuosity classes. In: Stern, J. (ed.) EUROCRYPT 1999. LNCS, vol. 1592, pp. 223–238. Springer, Heidelberg (1999). https://doi.org/10.1007/3-540-48910-X_16
46. Popa, R.A., et al.: CryptDB: protecting confidentiality with encrypted query processing. In: Proceedings of SOSP 2011, pp. 85–100 (2011)
47. Rabin, M.O.: Digitalized signatures and public-key functions as intractable as factorization. Technical report. MIT/LCS/TR-212, p. 12 (1979)
48. Ricosset, T.: HElib-MP. https://github.com/tricosset/HElib-MP
49. Rivest, R.L., et al.: A method for obtaining digital signatures and public-key cryptosystems. Commun. ACM 21(2), 120–126 (1978)
50. Rivest, R.L., et al.: On data banks and privacy homomorphisms. Found. Secure Comput. 4(11), 169–180 (1978)
51. Schafer, R.D.: An Introduction to Nonassociative Algebras, vol. 22. Dover, New York (1966)
52. Stephen, J.J., et al.: Practical confidentiality preserving big data analysis. In: Proceedings of HotCloud 2014, p. 10 (2014)
53. Tetali, S.D., et al.: MRCrypt: static analysis for secure cloud computations. In: Proceedings of OOPSLA 2013, pp. 271–286 (2013)
54. Thomson, I.: Microsoft researchers smash homomorphic encryption speed barrier, 9 February 2016. https://www.theregister.co.uk/2016/02/09/researchers_break_homomorphic_encryption/
55. Varia, M., et al.: HETest: a homomorphic encryption testing framework. Cryptology ePrint Archive: 2015/416 (2015)
56. Vivek, S.: Homomorphic encryption API software library, 21 February 2017. http://heat-h2020-project.blogspot.co.uk/2017/02/homomorphic-encryptionapi-software.html
57. Vizár, D., Vaudenay, S.: Cryptanalysis of chosen symmetric homomorphic schemes. Stud. Sci. Math. Hung. 52(2), 288–306 (2015)
58. Yu, A., et al.: Efficient integer vector homomorphic encryption (2015). https://courses.csail.mit.edu/6.857/2015/files/yu-lai-payor.pdf
59. Zhou, H., Wornell, G.: Efficient homomorphic encryption on integer vectors and its applications. In: Proceedings of ITA 2014, pp. 1–9 (2014)

When It's All Just Too Much: Outsourcing MPC-Preprocessing

Peter Scholl[1], Nigel P. Smart[2(✉)], and Tim Wood[2]

[1] Department of Computer Science, Aarhus University, Aarhus, Denmark
[2] Department of Computer Science, University of Bristol, Bristol, UK
nigel@cs.bris.ac.uk

Abstract. Many modern actively secure multi-party computation protocols make use of a function- and input-independent pre-processing phase. This pre-processing phase is tasked with producing some form of correlated randomness and distributing it to the parties. Whilst the "online" phase of such protocols is exceedingly fast, the bottleneck comes in the pre-processing phase. In this paper we examine situations in which the computing parties in the online phase may want to outsource the pre-processing phase to another set of parties, or to a sub-committee. We examine how this can be done, and also describe situations where this may be a benefit.

1 Introduction

Secure multi-party computation (MPC) is the idea of allowing multiple parties to compute on their combined inputs in a "secure" manner. We use the word secure to mean that the interaction provides no party with any information on the secret inputs of the other parties, bar what can be learned from the output (a property called *privacy* or *secrecy*). In this paper we will focus on protocols which can tolerate a majority of the parties being corrupted. In such a situation we know there is no hope that the honest parties can always obtain the correct output, so we usually require that either the honest parties obtain the correct result, or they abort (with overwhelming probability in the security parameter, λ).

For a long time, MPC remained a theoretical exercise and implementations were impractical. However, much work has recently been undertaken on developing practical MPC protocols in the so-called *pre-processing model*. In this model, the protocol is split up into an offline (a.k.a. pre-processing) phase and an online phase. In the offline phase, the parties execute a protocol which emulates a *trusted dealer* who distributes "raw material" (pre-processed data) to parties; this data is then used up in the online phase as the circuit is evaluated. The advantage of doing this is that the pre-processing involves expensive public key operations which can be isolated to the pre-processing phase. In addition, pre-processed data can be made independent of both the inputs and the circuit, so it can be computed at any point prior to the evaluation of the circuit. The online phase is then executed with (essentially) information theoretic primitives, and is thus very fast.

© Springer International Publishing AG 2017
M. O'Neill (Ed.): IMACC 2017, LNCS 10655, pp. 77–99, 2017.
https://doi.org/10.1007/978-3-319-71045-7_4

This protocol idea goes back to Beaver [Bea96]. It was first used in a practical (and implemented) MPC system in the VIFF protocol [DGKN09], which was a protocol system built for the case of honest majority MPC. Modern dishonest majority MPC protocols make use of information theoretic MACs to achieve active security, an idea which stems from [RBO89] In the last five years, combining the pre-processed triple idea of Beaver with these protocols has resulted in a step change in what can be implemented efficiently by MPC protocols.

The first protocol in this area was BDOZ [BDOZ11], which demonstrated that if the number of parties was constant and the parties had access to a functionality which would provide the pre-processed data then the overhead of computing an arithmetic circuit over a large finite field securely is only a constant factor times the work required to compute it in the clear. The SPDZ [DPSZ12] protocol showed that the mere constant factor overhead encountered in the BDOZ protocol holds for any number of parties. Further improvements were presented in [DKL+13] to the SPDZ protocol. In the BDOZ and SPDZ protocols, the pre-processing is produced using forms of homomorphic encryption, and so the protocols are more suited to MPC over a large finite field. In TinyOT [NNOB12], similar results in the two-party case for Boolean circuits were given, where the pre-processing was implemented using oblivious transfer (OT) extension. In [LOS14,BLN+15], the TinyOT protocol was extended to the multi-party case, and the online phase was made consistent (in terms of computational pattern) with that of the SPDZ protocol from [DKL+13]. Further unification of these protocol families occurred with the replacement of the homomorphic encryption based pre-processing phase of SPDZ with an OT based pre-processing [KOS16], forming what is known as the MASCOT protocol. To simplify exposition, since all of these protocols are essentially the same at a high level, in this paper we shall refer to the collective as the "SPDZ family".

As already remarked, the SPDZ family of protocols has an efficient online phase; indeed, the online phase has a number of interesting properties:

- **Computational Efficiency:** Since the online phase is made up of information theoretic primitives, the basic arithmetic operations are incredibly simple, requiring only a constant multiplicative factor increase in the number of operations when compared to evaluating the function in the clear. Before every output operation, the execution of a PRF is also required for MAC checking, but for a large computation this is negligible when measuring performance.
- **Communication Efficiency:** The basic protocol requires interaction for each multiplication operation[1]. This interaction need only be conducted over authenticated channels, rather than private channels, and the communication required grows linearly in the number of players.
- **Deterministic:** Given the correlated randomness from the offline phase, the function to be computed, and the parties' inputs, the online phase is essen-

---

[1] For simplicity of expression we assume the MPC functionality is evaluating an arithmetic circuit over a finite field. This is purely for exposition: in practice the usual MPC tricks to remove the need for circuit based computation will be used.

tially deterministic. Only a small amount of "random data" per party is needed to ensure that dishonest parties are detected in the MAC checking protocol. Indeed this random data can be created in the offline phase and then stored for later use.

The simplicity and efficiency of the online phase, however, comes with a penalty in the offline phase. Using either method (i.e. the homomorphic encryption of SPDZ or the OT method of MASCOT) to generate the pre-processed data, the offline phase requires expensive public key machinery, and in practice is a couple of orders of magnitude slower than the online phase. In some instances, while the online phase is computationally cheap enough to be executed by a relatively low powered computing device, the same device would not be sufficiently powerful to perform the associated offline phase efficiently. This can cause a problem when there are parties in a network with very different computing power. Similarly the offline phase requires the transmission of a larger amount of data per multiplication gate than the online phase. Again, this can be a problem in practice if certain parties are on a slow part of the network.

The offline phase also requires each party to input a large amount of randomness, and it is well known that one of the major challenges of running any cryptography in the real world is the generation of randomness. Small hardware devices may not have the capability of producing random values easily, as they usually have very limited access to good sources of entropy: for example, devices such as mobile phones and tablets still have problems with good entropy sources. Moreover, it does not suffice simply to be able to generate pseudo-random numbers: in many cryptographic applications (including MPC) it is necessary that it be "high quality" randomness. This has led to high-end applications requiring expensive dedicated hardware to generate entropy; however, such dedicated hardware may not be available to all computers in a network. Thus, even in the case of high-end servers executing the MPC protocol, it may easily not be the case that all have access to a sufficient entropy source.

For these reasons, we propose a method of outsourcing the offline pre-processing for the SPDZ family of protocols to a different set of parties. We will let Q denote the set of n_q parties who are to run the online phase; the set Q will outsource the computation of the pre-processing to a set of parties R of size n_r. This set R may be a strict subset of Q, or they could be a completely different set all together, or even a mix of parties who will later be involved in computation and parties who will not. The idea is that Q is unable to execute the pre-processing as an n_q-party protocol, due to some limitation of resources (computation, bandwidth, or randomness, for example), whereas R is "more able" to execute the pre-processing as an n_r-party protocol. Our protocol to perform this outsourcing will also aim to minimise the communication needed to transfer the pre-processing data from the set R to the set Q.

Of course, for this to make sense it is important that the set Q trust the set R to perform this task, and that the protocol respect this trust relationship. In particular, our protocol will assume an adversary which can corrupt a majority of parties in Q and a majority of parties in R, but that the adversary can neither corrupt all parties in R nor all parties in Q: indeed, in such a situation we clearly would not even be *expected* to guarantee any security. In particular, this means that each honest party in Q believes that there is at least one honest party in R, but they may not know which one is honest.

The fact that the parties do not know which parties in the other network are honest has security implications for the way pre-processing is passed from one network to the other. The naïve method of sending on the pre-processed data (in the case of $n_r \leq n_q$) would be to partition Q into n_r subsets, and then for each party in R to send their data to one set in the partition; it turns out that this method is insecure (using our redistribution procedure), though it only requires minor modification to make it secure. Our protocol creates a cover of Q, $\{Q_i\}_{i \in R}$, using $|R|$ sets, not necessarily disjoint, and associates each subset with a party in R; namely, party $i \in R$ is assigned the set Q_i. The association merely defines the network of secure channels by which secret-shared data amongst the parties in R is reshared amongst the parties in Q. Note that there is no assumption of trust of parties in Q for parties in R they are associated to (i.e. with respect to the cover): the only assumption of trust is that at least one party in each of R and Q is honest. Our protocol will be secure if there is at least one pair (i, Q_i) for which $i \in R$ is an honest party in R and Q_i contains at least one honest party from Q. This raises (at least) three potential ways for the subsets to arise:

- If $R \subseteq Q$ then for each $i \in R$, we can just ensure that Q_i contains i. Then since R and Q each contain an honest party, there must be at least one pair containing (the same) honest party.
- It may be the case that every party in Q trusts at least one party in R already. In this case, our cover, $\{Q_i\}_{i \in R}$, can be produced by letting parties in Q elect which parties in R they want to be associated with. Security will follow because in particular, at least one honest party in R believes there is at least one honest party in Q.
- If no prior trust relation is known then the cover must be defined either deterministically or probabilistically. If deterministically, to satisfy the requirement above we must choose $Q_i = Q$ for all i. This guarantees a pair (i, Q_i) as described above, but results in an inefficient network topology (since each party in R needs a secure channel to each party in Q). Alternatively, we make a probabilistic assignment and derive bounds on n_q and n_r which ensure that the assignment preserves security with overwhelming probability: see Sect. 4 for details.

The first case above is a reasonably likely scenario. Consider an (n, t)-threshold access structure, in which any set of $t + 1$ parties contains an honest party. In this case any set of $t + 1$ parties can form the network R and undertake the pre-processing. To pass the data on, these parties need to be associated to the remaining $n - t - 1$ parties. Thus each party in R must send to $(n - t - 1)/(t + 1)$ parties on average. For example, if $n = 20$ and $t = 14$, then any 15 parties perform the pre-processing and each sends to all of the remaining 5 parties. For a multiplication performed in the production of a single triple in

MASCOT amongst 20 parties, assuming a full-threshold access structure, the required communication is essentially $20 \times 19 = 380$ oblivious transfers (OTs). If we no longer assume full-threshold and instead suppose that any set of 15 parties contains an honest party, we need only $15 \times 14 = 210$ OTs plus $15 \times 5 = 75$ field elements to be sent per triple. In light of the real-world applications of MPC in which full-threshold is sometimes too strong an assumption, and the fact that the number of OTs required for a multiplication is $O(n^2)$, any reduction in the assumed fraction of corruptions t/n provides significant improvements in communication efficiency via our protocol, since we require only $O(t^2)$ OTs plus $O(t \cdot (n - t))$ field elements transmitted.

In the case where we use a probabilistic assignment, and where the parties generating the pre-processing are not later involved in the computation, our protocol is less efficient. For example, using our protocol and the probabilistic algorithm we describe later, if there are 5 parties in R of which at most 2 are corrupt, and 50 parties in Q of which at most 25 are corrupt (and R and Q are disjoint), each party in R need only send to 23 parties in Q for the cover to be statistically secure (in the sense that the adversary cannot with probability greater than $1 - 2^{-80}$), instead of the 25 required for information-theoretic security.

Besides the ability of the protocol we describe to enable localising the generation of pre-processed data, another potential application of the protocol is to increase the number of parties involved in a given instance of the SPDZ protocol dynamically (i.e. during the online phase). For example, suppose a set of parties already running an instance of the SPDZ protocol want to (efficiently and securely) allow another set of parties to join them during a reactive computation. It may make more sense to transform the already pre-processed data (or even just a few pre-processed values) via our protocol to a form that is amenable for use by a larger number of parties, and then distribute it to the parties who want to join in on the computation, instead of requiring that the parties halt the computation and then engage in a new round of pre-processing. This would only make sense if the parties joining the computation trusted at least one of the pre-existing parties, which is likely to be the case in any reasonable application of this use-case. The set of parties already performing the computation becomes the set R, and so we are in the first use-case above.

At its heart our technique can be described as follows. We let $\mathcal{F}_{\text{Prep}}^{\mathcal{P},\mathcal{A}}$ denote the SPDZ offline functionality for a set of parties $\mathcal{P}$ of size n with set of corrupt parties $\mathcal{A}$. Suppose now that we have a set of parties indexed by the set $[n]$ and (not necessarily disjoint) subsets $R, Q \subset [n]$ so that $R \cup Q = [n]$, and a subset $A \subset R \cup Q$ indexing corrupt parties. We then define a cover $\{Q_i\}_{i \in R}$ of Q such that there is at least one pair (i, Q_i) for which $i \in R$ is an honest party in R, and Q_i contains at least one honest party from Q. The cover provides a description of therequired network: each party in Q_i must be connected by a *secure* channel to the associated party i in R. Just as (i, Q_i) associated a subset $Q_i \subset Q$ to a party $i \in R$, we also let $R_j \subset R$ be the set of parties in R associated to a party $j \in Q$. We then extend A to a set $\overline{A} \subset R \cup Q$ by setting $\overline{A} = A \cup \{j \in Q : R_j \subset A\}$. The set $\overline{A}$ contains all corrupt parties and additionally what we refer to as *effectively corrupt honest parties* with respect to the online phase of the protocol. In brief, these are parties whose pre-processed data is entirely determined by the adversary – while these parties execute the online protocol honestly, the deterministic dependence on pre-processed data means the adversary can decide what values these parties hold for their shares. Our protocol realises the functionality $\mathcal{F}_{\mathrm{Prep}}^{Q,Q \cap \overline{A}}$ in the $\mathcal{F}_{\mathrm{Prep}}^{R,R \cap \overline{A}}$-hybrid model.

The main idea of the protocol is conceptually quite simple, and is essentially a standard "re-sharing" technique similar to [BOGW88]. The main novelty is in showing that this can be efficiently applied to the SPDZ protocol, without the need for any expensive zero-knowledge proofs. In doing this, the difficulty comes in proving that the protocol is actually secure in the UC framework, and also in creating and analysing an (efficient) algorithm for assigning a cover to the network so that the adversary can only win with negligible probability in the security parameter in the case where we randomly assign the covers.

Related Work. There is a long line of works on scalable secure computation with a large number of parties [DI06, HN06, DKMS14, BCP15] (to name a few), which use similar techniques to ours. These works often divide the parties into random *committees* (or *quorums*) to distribute the workload of the computation. Most of these papers target asymptotic efficiency, and strong models such as adaptive security, asynchronicity and RAM computation. This gives interesting theoretical results, but the practicality of these techniques has not been demonstrated. In contrast, our work focuses on applying simple techniques to modern, practical MPC protocols. Furthermore, we give a concrete analysis and examples of parameters that can be used for different numbers of parties in real-world settings, at a given security level.

2   Preliminaries

In this section, we describe the notation used in subsequent sections, formally define *secure cover*, and give an overview of the SPDZ protocol, and the offline phase in particular.

General Concepts and Notation. Parties in the network are indexed by $[n] = \{1, ..., n\}$, where n is the total number of parties. We consider the complete network of parties as the union of two parts, which we call R and Q (so each is a subset of n and they are not necessarily disjoint). To avoid confusion, we will index parties in R by the letter i, and parties in Q by the letter j. We let n_r (resp. n_q) denote the number of parties in R (resp. Q). We let $A \subseteq R \cup Q$ denote the indexing set of corrupt parties in the complete network, and $\overline{A}$ denote the superset of A which possibly contains additional honest parties in Q, called *effectively corrupt honest parties* from the introduction. We assume there is a complete network of authenticated channels amongst the parties in R, and similarly amongst the parties in Q. We define a *secure cover* $\{Q_i\}_{i \in R}$ of Q by R in the following way:

Definition 1. *Let $[n]$ be the indexing set of a set of parties in a given network and suppose we are also given subsets $R, Q \subset [n]$ of sizes n_r and n_q respectively. Each party in the network is either corrupt or honest. We call a set $\{Q_i\}_{i \in R}$ of (non-empty but not necessarily disjoint) subsets of Q a secure cover if the following hold:*

- *All parties in Q_i are connected to player $i \in R$ via a secure channel.*
- *The subsets cover Q, i.e. $Q = \bigcup_{i \in R} Q_i$.*
- *There is at least one pair (i, Q_i) where $i \in R$ is an honest party in R, and Q_i contains at least one honest party from Q.*

We will also let R_j denote the set of parties in R which are connected to party $j \in Q$. Note that $\{R_j\}_{j \in Q}$ is necessarily a cover of R since $Q_i \neq \varnothing$ for all i, so each i is in at least one R_j. We will use λ to denote the security parameter, and we will say an event occurs with overwhelming probability in the security parameter λ if it occurs with probability at least $1 - 2^\lambda$. We denote by $\mathbb{F}_q$ the finite field of order q, a (large) prime power. A function $\nu \in \mathbb{Z}[x]$ is called negligible if for every polynomial $p \in \mathbb{Z}[x]$, there exists a $C \in \mathbb{Z}$ such that $\nu(x) \leq 1/p(x)$ for all $x > C$. We write $\alpha \leftarrow \mathbb{F}_q$ to mean that α is sampled uniformly at random from the field $\mathbb{F}_q$. We denote by $\lceil a \rceil$ the smallest integer $b \in \mathbb{Z}$ such that $b \geq a$.

In Sect. 6, we discuss the different network topologies of secure channels between our parties in R and parties in Q. In particular, we explore the different ways by which to define the cover $\{Q_i\}_{i \in R}$, taking into account, for example, the fact that the Q_i's are not necessarily all the same size. Section 4 then builds on these considerations by providing concrete methods of creating the cover and analysing the resulting protocols. This involves, for example, examining how the likelihood of the cover being secure changes (if we define it probabilistically) as we change the value of ℓ if we require that all parties in R send to the same number ℓ of parties in Q.

Our main theorem is given in the Universally Composability (UC) framework. The power of UC is well demonstrated in the pre-processing model, since it allows the functionality to be split up into separate independent parts and their corresponding individual protocols to be proved secure independently, such that they remain secure even when run concurrently or sequentially. In this model, we define some functionality $\mathcal{F}_{\text{Prep}}$ for the pre-processing and a separate functionality $\mathcal{F}_{\text{Online}}$ for the online phase. A protocol is designed for each, Π_{Prep} and Π_{Online}, the protocol Π_{Prep} is shown to implement $\mathcal{F}_{\text{Prep}}$ securely, and finally Π_{Online} is shown to implement $\mathcal{F}_{\text{Online}}$ securely in the $\mathcal{F}_{\text{Prep}}$-hybrid model. This is particularly useful in our situation where we only want to change how pre-processing is done since we only need to revamp the pre-processing, and can leave the online phase unchanged, avoiding the need to reprove security.

SPDZ Overview. In general, computation will be done over a finite field $\mathbb{F} = \mathbb{F}_q$ where q is a (large) prime power. The protocol called MACCheck in the SPDZ paper [DPSZ12] requires that the field be large enough to make MAC forgery unfeasible by pure guessing. In particular this means that $1/q$ must be negligible in λ. For smaller finite fields, and in particular the important case of binary circuits, adaptions to the MACCheck protocol can be made; see [LOS14], for example. For this paper we will assume the simpler case of large q for ease of exposition. The SPDZ MPC protocol allows parties to compute an arithmetic circuit on their combined secret input. More specifically, for an arbitrary set of parties $\mathcal{P}$ and a subset set of corrupt parties $\mathcal{A} \subset \mathcal{P}$, the SPDZ protocol implements the functionality $\mathcal{F}_{\mathrm{MPC}}^{\mathcal{P},\mathcal{A}}$ described in Fig. 1, provided $\mathcal{P} \setminus \mathcal{A} \neq \varnothing$.

The Functionality $\mathcal{F}_{\mathrm{MPC}}^{\mathcal{P},\mathcal{A}}$.

The superscript $\mathcal{P}$ denotes the set of parties involved in the protocol, and $\mathcal{A} \subsetneq \mathcal{P}$ is the set of corrupt parties.

Initialise: On input (Initialise, $\mathbb{F}$) from all parties in $\mathcal{P}$, store $\mathbb{F}$.
Input: On input (Input, i, id, x) from party i and (Input, i, id) from all other parties, with id a fresh identifier and $x \in \mathbb{F}$, store (id, x).
Add: On command (Add, $\mathrm{id}_1, \mathrm{id}_2, \mathrm{id}_3$) from all parties in $\mathcal{P}$ (where id_1 and id_2 are present in memory), retrieve (id_1, x) and (id_2, y) and store ($\mathrm{id}_3, x + y$).
Multiply: On command (Multiply, $\mathrm{id}_1, \mathrm{id}_2, \mathrm{id}_3$) from all parties in $\mathcal{P}$ (where id_1 and id_2 are present in memory), retrieve (id_1, x) and (id_2, y) and store ($\mathrm{id}_3, x \cdot y$).
Output: On input (Output, id) from all honest parties (where id is present in memory), retrieve (id, z), output z to the adversary. If the adversary responds with OK then output the value z to all parties, otherwise output Abort to all parties.

Fig. 1. The Functionality $\mathcal{F}_{\mathrm{MPC}}^{\mathcal{P},\mathcal{A}}$.

The main motivation for this paper is that the "standard" protocols which implement $\mathcal{F}_{\mathrm{MPC}}^{\mathcal{P},\mathcal{A}}$ in the pre-processing model (for some set of parties $\mathcal{P}$ and corrupt parties $\mathcal{A}$) require a lot of work by the parties in $\mathcal{P}$ during pre-processing. Our goal is to implement $\mathcal{F}_{\mathrm{MPC}}^{\mathcal{P},\mathcal{A}}$ using a (possibly larger) set of parties in which some specified set of parties execute the expensive pre-processing part of the protocol and only the parties in $\mathcal{P}$ who are interested in the computation itself execute the cheap online part of the protocol. In our terminology, the parties in Q outsource the pre-processing to a set of parties R (which possibly includes some parties in R) and then compute using the data.

We will elaborate a little here; in what follows we use the notation and functionalities of the latest version of the SPDZ protocol, based on OT, called MASCOT [KOS16]. We will describe the SPDZ offline functionality $\mathcal{F}_{\mathrm{Prep}}^{\mathcal{P},\mathcal{A}}$ and online protocol $\Pi_{\mathrm{Online}}^{\mathcal{P},\mathcal{A}}$ for an arbitrary set of parties $\mathcal{P}$; at the end of this section, we give the conversion protocol $\Pi_{\mathrm{Prep}}^{R \to Q, \overline{\mathcal{A}}}$. In the initialisation stage, the parties sample (and keep private) random shares α_i, one for each party, whose sum is taken to be a global (secret) MAC key α, i.e. $\alpha = \sum_{i \in \mathcal{P}} \alpha_i$.

A value $x \in \mathbb{F}_q$ is secret shared among the parties in $\mathcal{P}$ by sampling $(x_i)_{i \in \mathcal{P}} \leftarrow \mathbb{F}_q^{|\mathcal{P}|}$ subject to $x = \sum_{i \in \mathcal{P}} x_i$, with party i holding the value x_i. In addition, we sample $(\gamma(x)_i)_{i \in \mathcal{P}} \leftarrow \mathbb{F}_q^{|\mathcal{P}|}$ subject to $\sum_{i \in \mathcal{P}} \gamma(x)_i = \alpha \cdot x$ and party i holding the share $\gamma(x)_i$. Thus $\gamma(x)_i$ is a sharing of the MAC $\gamma(x) := \alpha \cdot x$ of x. We write the following to denote that x is a secret value, where party $i \in \mathcal{P}$ holds x_i and $\gamma(x)_i$.

$$\langle x \rangle := ((x_i)_{i \in \mathcal{P}}, (\gamma(x)_i)_{i \in \mathcal{P}}))$$

Since this sharing scheme is linear, linear operations on secret values comes "for free", in the sense that adding secret values or multiplying them by a public constant requires no communication. Crucially, since the MAC is linear, the same operations applied to the corresponding MAC shares will result in MACs on the result of the said linear computation.

Unfortunately, multiplication of secret values requires a little more work, and is the reason data must be generated offline. At its heart SPDZ uses Beaver's method [Bea96] to multiply secret-shared values, which we outline here. In the offline phase, a large number of multiplication triples are generated, which are triples $(\langle a \rangle, \langle b \rangle, \langle c \rangle)$ such that $c = a \cdot b$. Note that while other forms of pre-processing can help in various computations, such as shared squares and shared bits, in this paper we focus on the basic form of pre-processing and leave the interested reader to consult [DKL+13] and [KSS13]. To multiply secret-shared elements $\langle x \rangle$ and $\langle y \rangle$ in the online phase, we take a triple $(\langle a \rangle, \langle b \rangle, \langle c \rangle)$ and partially open $\langle x \rangle - \langle a \rangle$ and $\langle x \rangle - \langle b \rangle$ to obtain $\varepsilon := \langle x \rangle - \langle a \rangle$ and $\delta := \langle y \rangle - \langle b \rangle$. By "partially open $\langle x \rangle - \langle a \rangle$", we mean that each party i sends the value $x_i - a_i$ to every other party, but does not send the corresponding MAC share. Then

$$\langle z \rangle = \langle c \rangle + \varepsilon \cdot \langle b \rangle + \delta \cdot \langle a \rangle + \varepsilon \cdot \delta$$

is a correct secret sharing of $z = x \cdot y$, and since the triple is never opened, no information about x or y is revealed. A similar use of pre-processed data is used for the parties to enter their inputs into the computation.

As remarked earlier our paper is focused on turning SPDZ preprocessing produced by one set of parties into preprocessing for another set of parties. Thus we do not discuss the online phase in detail. There is a minor tweak to the proof of security of the online phase, due to our minor tweak to the preprocessing functionality. For the interested reader we include the details in Sect. 5.

SPDZ Preprocessing. To formalise things a little more, we now discuss the functionality $\mathcal{F}_{\mathrm{Prep}}^{\mathcal{P}, \mathcal{A}}$, given in Fig. 2, which implements the necessary pre-processing. The superscripts denote parameters of the functionality, where $\mathcal{P}$ denotes the indexing set of parties involved in the computation, and $\mathcal{A} \subset \mathcal{P}$ is a set of parties in $\mathcal{P}$ under the control of the adversary. As explained in the introduction, if we have a set of parties $\mathcal{P}$ and our cover produces *effectively corrupt honest parties*, which are those nominally honest parties which receive

---

The Offline Functionality $\mathcal{F}_{\text{Prep}}^{\mathcal{P},\mathcal{A}}$ for SPDZ.

The set $\mathcal{A} \subset \mathcal{P}$ indexes the corrupt parties in $\mathcal{P}$.

Initialise: On input $(\text{Initialise}, q)$ from all players and the adversary, the functionality does the following:

1. The functionality samples $\alpha \leftarrow \mathbb{F}_q$ to be the global MAC key.
2. The functionality receives some error Δ_α from the adversary and, for each corrupted player $i \in \mathcal{A}$, a share α_i.
3. The functionality samples at random α_i for each $i \notin \mathcal{A}$ subject to $\sum_{i \in \mathcal{P}} \alpha_i = \alpha + \Delta_\alpha$.
4. The functionality sends α_i to party i, for all $i \in \mathcal{P}$.

Macro: $\text{Angle}(x)$ The following will be run by the functionality at several points to create $\langle \cdot \rangle$ representations:

1. The functionality accepts $(\{x_i, \gamma(x)_i\}_{i \in \mathcal{A}}, \Delta_x, \Delta_\gamma)$ from the adversary.
2. The functionality samples at random $\{x_i, \gamma(x)_i\}_{i \notin \mathcal{A}}$ subject to $\sum_{i \in \mathcal{P}} x_i = x + \Delta_x$ and $\sum_{i \in \mathcal{P}} \gamma(x)_i = \alpha \cdot x + \Delta_\gamma$.
3. The functionality is left with $((x_i)_{i \in \mathcal{P}}, (\gamma(x)_i)_{i \in \mathcal{P}})$.

Computation: On input $(\text{DataGen}, DataType)$ from all players and the adversary, the functionality executes the data generation procedures specified below.

- On input $DataType = \text{InputPrep}$ and a party $i \in \mathcal{P}$,
  1. If $i \notin \mathcal{A}$, the functionality samples $r^{(i)} \leftarrow \mathbb{F}_q$. Otherwise $i \in \mathcal{A}$ so the functionality accepts $r^{(i)}$ from the adversary.
  2. The functionality runs $\text{Angle}(r^{(i)})$.
  3. For each $j \in \mathcal{P}$, the functionality sends party j the pair $(r_j^{(i)}, \gamma(r^{(i)})_j)$.
  4. Additionally, to party i, the functionality sends $r^{(i)}$.

  Thus the parties obtain a sharing $\langle r^{(i)} \rangle$ of a value $r^{(i)}$ known only to party i.

- On input $DataType = \text{Triple}$,
  1. The functionality samples $a, b \in \mathbb{F}_p$ and computes $c = a \cdot b$.
  2. The functionality calls $\text{Angle}(a)$, $\text{Angle}(b)$ and $\text{Angle}(c)$.
  3. For each $i \in \mathcal{P}$, the functionality sends $((a_i, \gamma(a)_i), (b_i, \gamma(b)_i), (c_i, \gamma(c)_i))$ to party i.

Fig. 2. The Offline Functionality $\mathcal{F}_{\text{Prep}}^{\mathcal{P},\mathcal{A}}$ for SPDZ.

reshares from only corrupt parties, the set $\mathcal{A}$ will include these parties. If the parties generate the pre-processing themselves and do not make use of our protocol, this set is exactly the set of corrupt parties; when the pre-processing is outsourced, then we have to worry about (the possibility of) effectively corrupt parties.

The functionality is a little more general than the functionality presented in [KOS16] as we allow the corrupt parties to introduce more errors: the standard SPDZ offline functionality only allows errors to be introduced into the MAC shares and not the data shares, whereas this new functionality allows errors on both. It is fairly intuitive that we will retain a security using this functionality as opposed to the standard one, as an adversary winning having changed shared values and MACs needs to have forged the same MAC equation as an adversary winning after just altering MAC values. The extra ability of altering share values gives him no advantage, a fact which we will prove shortly.

In [KOS16] the following theorem is (implicitly) proved, where $\mathcal{F}_{OT}$ and $\mathcal{F}_{Rand}$ are functionalities implementing OT and shared randomness for the parties.

Theorem 1. *There is a protocol $\Pi_{Prep}^{\mathcal{P},\mathcal{A}}$ that securely implements $\mathcal{F}_{Prep}^{\mathcal{P},\mathcal{A}}$ against static, active adversaries in the $\mathcal{F}_{OT}, \mathcal{F}_{Rand}$-hybrid model, where $\mathcal{P}$ is the complete set of parties and $\mathcal{A}$ the set of corrupt parties in $\mathcal{P}$.*

We do not give the definition of the $\Pi_{Prep}^{\mathcal{P},\mathcal{A}}$ protocol here as it is identical to MASCOT when based on OT, or identical to the original SPDZ pre-processing when based on homomorphic encryption (in spite of the slight difference in functionalities). Note that the paper [KOS16] proves the above theorem by giving a number of different protocols which, when combined, securely implement the required functionality $\mathcal{F}_{Prep}^{\mathcal{P},\mathcal{A}}$.

3   Feeding One Protocol from Another

In this section we give our main result on feeding pre-processed data from the parties in R to the parties in Q, assuming a set of corruptions in the latter which includes effectively corrupt honest parties. In notation, we are instantiating an instance of $\mathcal{F}_{Prep}^{Q, Q \cap \overline{A}}$ from an instance of $\mathcal{F}_{Prep}^{R, R \cap \overline{A}}$ via the protocol $\Pi_{Prep}^{R \to Q, \overline{A}}$. Note that $R \cap \overline{A} = R \cap A$. We assume we have a *secure cover* $\{Q_i\}_{i \in R}$ of Q. We emphasise that the actual execution of $\Pi_{Prep}^{R \to Q, \overline{A}}$ is independent of the set of corrupted parties; we only use the superscript $\overline{A}$ notation to indicate the relation between the corrupted parties in the protocol and in the different functionalities.

Method of Redistributing Data. Recall the parties in R will be performing the offline phase on behalf of the parties in Q. The parties in Q will share data in the standard manner (see Sect. 2), and the same will happen for parties in R. To avoid confusion, a data item $x \in \mathbb{F}$ secret shared amongst partes in Q will be denoted by $\langle x \rangle_Q$, whilst the same data item shared amongst parties in R will be denoted by $\langle x \rangle_R$, where implicitly we are assuming the *same* MAC key α is shared amongst the parties in R and the parties in Q.

When parties in Q want to evaluate a circuit amongst themselves, they follow the online protocol, in Fig. 5, and whenever they require a pre-processed data-item, they will ask R to provide one[2]. Thus we simply require a methodology to

---

[2] Of course, Q could ask R for these to be obtained all in one go in a form of outsourced pre-processing.

translate $\langle x \rangle_R$ sharings into $\langle x \rangle_Q$ sharings. Recall a shared value in the network R is denoted by

$$\langle x \rangle_R = ((x_i)_{i \in R}, (\gamma(x)_i)_{i \in R})$$

The principal idea of the protocol is, for each $i \in R$, to take the value x_i held by i and sample a set $\{x_i^j\}_{j \in Q_i}$ subject to $x_i = \sum_{j \in Q_i} x_i^j$ and define $x^j \leftarrow \sum_{i \in R_j} x_i^j$ so that

$$\sum_{i \in R} x_i = \sum_{i \in R} \sum_{j \in Q_i} x_i^j = \sum_{j \in Q} \sum_{i \in R_j} x_i^j = \sum_{j \in Q} x^j$$

which holds because, by definition,

$$\{(i,j) : i \in R, \ j \in Q_i\} = \{(i,j) : j \in Q, i \in R_j\}.$$

If we do the same for the MAC shares, and at initialisation also share the global MAC key α in the same way, we obtain the same secret value x under the same global MAC key but shared instead amongst the parties in Q, which we denote by

$$\langle x \rangle_Q = ((x^j)_{j \in Q}, (\gamma(x)^j)_{j \in Q}).$$

It is hopefully now clear how to define a feeding protocol to send shares from the R parties to the Q parties. We do this by providing a protocol $\Pi_{\text{Prep}}^{R \to Q}$ which assumes the existence of the functionality $\mathcal{F}_{\text{Prep}}^{R, R \cap \overline{A}}$.

It is important to note that honest parties use incoming shares in an entirely deterministic manner; as such, observe that if some party $j \in Q$ is honest but it receives shares from only corrupt parties in R, the adversary has complete control over what this party's share will look like. For this reason, we consider them as "effectively" corrupt, contained in the extended adversary set $\overline{A}$. This is why in the online protocol, run by the parties in Q, we need to consider the set of adversaries as being $Q \cap \overline{A}$.

The Protocol. The idea of the protocol is to convert the pre-processing generated by the parties in R to pre-processing that can be used by the parties in Q. Our goal, then, is to show that if the set of parties $R \cup Q$ is provided with the functionality $\mathcal{F}_{\text{Prep}}^{R, R \cap \overline{A}}$ and the parties engage in the protocol $\Pi_{\text{Prep}}^{R \to Q}$ to send their pre-processing to the parties in Q, then this "looks the same" to the parties in Q as a functionality $\mathcal{F}_{\text{Prep}}^{Q, Q \cap \overline{A}}$. The protocol is given in Fig. 3.

Main Theorem. Before we give the statement of the theorem, we briefly give some intuition as to why our construction gives us the desired security. Recall that we are given a cover $\{Q_i\}_{i \in R}$ of Q, indexed by parties in R, so that each party in R is associated to the set $Q_i \neq \varnothing$ of parties in Q. We defined a cover to be secure if there is at least one pair (i, Q_i) where i is honest and Q_i contains at least one honest party. If a cover is not secure, it means that for every i, we have that i is corrupt, or i is honest but Q_i contains no honest parties. In this case, given a secret value v, for each $i \in R$ the adversary either has share v_i

(when $i \in R$ is corrupt), or all "reshares", $\{v_i^j\}_{j \in Q_i}$ (when $i \in R$ is honest but all $j \in Q_i$ are corrupt); using these shares and reshares, the adversary can construct v and hence he breaks secrecy: thus a secure cover is necessary. Conversely, if the cover is secure then at "worst", the adversary obtains all reshares but one; then since all reshares were sampled uniformly at random so that they summed to individual shares, and these shares were sampled so that they summed to the secret, this set of shares is indistinguishable from a uniformly randomly sampled set. Our main theorem (for which the proof is in the full version) is as follows.

Theorem 2. *The construction* $\Pi_{Prep}^{R \to Q, \overline{A}}$ *securely implements the functionality* $\mathcal{F}_{Prep}^{Q, Q \cap \overline{A}}$ *in the presence of static, active adversaries in the* $\mathcal{F}_{Prep}^{R, R \cap \overline{A}}$*-hybrid model assuming a secure cover of* Q *is given.*

4   Creating a Secure Cover

In the introduction, we assumed three potential use-cases. We now consider how to assign a cover securely for each scenario.

1. $R \subseteq Q$. In this case, for each i we define Q_i to be any subset of Q containing i and ensure that their union covers.
2. Each party in Q knows a subset of parties in R in which it believes there is an honest party. The cover is created respecting this knowledge.
3. There is no prior trust relationship.

In this last scenario we have two choices: either to set each covering subset Q_i equal to the whole set Q, or to assign the players randomly to subsets of Q whose union is the whole. In this section we provide an algorithm creating a cover and analyse the security it provides.

Recall that, when creating the secure cover, is necessary to ensure that at least one honest party in Q receives a share from at least one honest party in R with overwhelming probability in the security parameter λ. If this is not true, the adversary is able to reconstruct the share.

Let t_r and t_q be the number of corrupt parties in R and Q respectively. We set $\epsilon_r = t_r/n_r$ and $\epsilon_q = t_q/n_q$ to be the associated ratios. To help with the analysis, and for efficiency and load-balancing reasons, we will assume that each party in R sends to the same number of parties $\ell \geq \lceil n_q/n_r \rceil$ in Q. Note, any assignment of sets to parties in R which covers Q where $\ell = t_q + 1$ is automatically secure, since every party in R necessarily sends to at least one honest party in Q. We will see how small ℓ can be to provide statistical security for a given security parameter.

To assign a cover randomly in such a situation we use the algorithm in Fig. 4. The high-level idea of the algorithm is the following:

1. For each party in Q, we assign a random party in R, until each party in R has $\lceil n_q/n_r \rceil$ parties in Q assigned to it (or, equivalently, until the sets of parties in Q assigned to parties in R forms a disjoint cover). For ease of exposition, we assume $n_r | n_q$.

Protocol $\Pi_{\text{Prep}}^{R \to Q, \overline{A}}$

Parties in R have ideal access to an instance of $\mathcal{F}_{\text{Prep}}^{R, R \cap \overline{A}}$.

Initialise: On input (Initialise, q) from all parties in Q,
1. The parties in R execute $\mathcal{F}_{\text{Prep}}^{R, R \cap \overline{A}}$.**Initialise:**
   (a) The functionality samples some $\alpha \leftarrow \mathbb{F}_q$.
   (b) From each corrupt party $i \in R \cap \overline{A}$, the functionality receives $(\alpha_i, \Delta_{\alpha,i})$.
   (c) The functionality samples $\{\alpha_i\}_{i \in R \setminus \overline{A}}$ uniformly subject to the constraint that $\sum_{i \in R} \alpha_i = \alpha + \sum_{i \in R \cap \overline{A}} \Delta_{\alpha,i}$.
   (d) For each $i \in R$, the functionality sends α_i to party i.
2. The parties run FeedValue(α) below to share the global MAC key amongst Q.

Macro: FeedValue(v) On input an element $v \in \mathbb{F}_q$ shared amongst the parties as $v = \sum_{i \in R} v_i$ with party $i \in R$ holding v_i,
1. For each $i \in R$, party i samples $\{v_i^j\}_{j \in Q_i}$ subject to $\sum_{j \in Q_i} v_i^j = v_i$.
2. For each $i \in R$, for each $j \in Q_i$, party i sends v_i^j to party j.
3. For each $j \in Q$, party j sets $v^j = \sum_{i \in R_j} v_i^j$.

Computation: On input (DataGen, $DataType$) from all players in Q,
   – On input $DataType = $ InputPrep and a value $j \in Q$,
      1. For each $i \in R_j$,
         (a) The parties call $\mathcal{F}_{\text{Prep}}^{R, R \cap \overline{A}}$.**Computation**(DataGen, InputPrep) with input i:
            i. If $i \notin R \cap \overline{A}$, the functionality will sample some $r^{(i)} \leftarrow \mathbb{F}$, and otherwise will accept $r^{(i)}$ as input from the corrupt party.
            ii. In the execution of Angle, the corrupt parties $k \in R \cap \overline{A}$ each give the functionality some $r_k^{(i)}$ and $\gamma(r^{(i)})_k$ and errors $\Delta_{r^{(i)},k}$ and $\Delta_{\gamma(r^{(i)}),k}$. The functionality samples $\{r_k^{(i)}, \gamma(r_k^{(i)}) : k \in R \setminus \overline{A}\}$ such that $\sum_{k \in R} r_k^{(i)} = r^{(i)} + \sum_{k \in R \setminus \overline{A}} \Delta_{r^{(i)},k}$ and $\sum_{k \in R} \gamma(r^{(i)})_k = \alpha \cdot r^{(i)} + \sum_{k \in R \setminus \overline{A}} \Delta_{\gamma(r^{(i)}),k}$.
            iii. For each $k \in R$, the functionality sends party k the pair $(r_k^{(i)}, \gamma(r^{(i)})_k)$.
            iv. Additionally, the functionality sends $r^{(i)}$ to party i.
         (b) The parties run FeedValue($r^{(i)}$) and FeedValue($\gamma(r^{(i)})$) to get $\langle r^{(i)} \rangle_Q$.
         (c) Party i sends $r^{(i)}$ to party j.
      2. Party j computes $r_{(j)} \leftarrow \sum_{i \in R_j} r^{(i)}$.
      3. The parties in Q then fix $\langle r_{(j)} \rangle_Q \leftarrow \sum_{i \in R_j} \langle r^{(i)} \rangle_Q$.
   – On input $DataType = $ Triple by parties in Q,
      1. The parties call $\mathcal{F}_{\text{Prep}}^{R, R \cap \overline{A}}$.**Computation**(DataGen, Triple) to obtain a triple $(\langle a \rangle_R, \langle b \rangle_R, \langle c \rangle_R)$.
      2. The parties in R now run FeedValue on a, b and c and their MACs.

Fig. 3. Protocol $\Pi_{\text{Prep}}^{R \to Q, \overline{A}}$

2. For each party in R, we assign random parties in Q until each party in R has ℓ total parties which it sends to.

Note that in practice, the parties may want to run this algorithm using a trusted source of randomness (such as a blockchain or lottery), or execute a coin-tossing protocol to generate the necessary randomness.

Algorithm for randomly assigning elements of a cover of Q to parties in R.

For ease of notation, we label parties in R as i_k for $k \in [n_r]$ and parties in Q as j_l for $l \in [n_q]$; then the output array M is a binary $n_r \times n_q$ matrix with a 1 in the $(k, l)^{\text{th}}$ position if and only if i_k in R sends to j_l in Q.

Inputs: n_r, n_q, $n = n_r + n_q$, ℓ, and sets $R, Q \subset [n]$ whose disjoint union is $[n]$.

Outputs: Matrix $M \in \mathbb{F}_2^{n_r \times n_q}$.

Method: (Note that ℓ is a constant, whereas l is an index.)

1. Set $M[1..n_r, \ 1..n_q] \leftarrow \{\{0, 0, \ldots, 0\}, \ldots, \{0, 0, \ldots, 0\}\}$
2. Set NoOfOnes$[1..n_r] \leftarrow \{0, \ldots, 0\}$
3. For $l \in [n_q]$,
   - Do
     - $k \leftarrow \mathcal{F}_{\text{Rand}}([n_r])$
   - Until NoOfOnes$[k] < \lceil n_q/n_r \rceil$ and $M[k, l] = 0$
   - $M[k, l] \leftarrow 1$, NoOfOnes$[k] \leftarrow$ NoOfOnes$[k] + 1$
4. For $k \in [n_r]$,
   (a) While NoOfOnes$[k] < \ell$,
     - Do
       - $l \leftarrow \mathcal{F}_{\text{Rand}}([n_q])$
     - Until $M[k, l] = 0$
     - $M[k, l] \leftarrow 1$, NoOfOnes$[k] \leftarrow$ NoOfOnes$[k] + 1$
5. Output matrix M.

Fig. 4. Algorithm for randomly assigning elements of a cover of Q to parties in R.

The algorithm allows different parties in Q to receive from different numbers of parties in R, whilst parties in R always send to the same number of parties in Q. Over $\mathbb{Z}$, each row of the matrix we generate, M, sums to ℓ, whilst the array NoOfOnes records how many parties in Q the i_k^{th} party in R sends to. Step 3 assigns all parties in Q to a party in R: this is the part of the algorithm which ensures we have a cover. In fact, this is done in such a way that each party in R sends to the *same* number of parties in Q, namely $\lceil n_q/n_r \rceil$. The reason for doing this is that it lends itself better to analysis of relevant probabilities below. Step 4 assign parties in Q to parties in R at random until each party in R is assigned ℓ parties in Q.

In the worst case, there is only one honest party in each of R and Q. Since we ensure that each party in R is assigned the same number of parties, the probability we obtain a secure cover is given by:

$1 - \Pr[\text{Every good party in } R \text{ is assigned only dishonest parties in Step 3}]$

$\quad \cdot \Pr[\text{Every good party in } R \text{ is assigned only dishonest parties in Step 4}]$

When performing Step 3, the probability that the first good party in R is assigned only dishonest parties is the number of ways of choosing $\lceil n_q/n_r \rceil$ parties from the t_q corrupt parties divided by the number of ways of choosing $\lceil n_q/n_r \rceil$ parties from all n_q parties:

$$\frac{\binom{t_q}{\lceil n_q/n_r \rceil}}{\binom{n_q}{\lceil n_q/n_r \rceil}}$$

Thus the first $\lceil n_q/n_r \rceil$ corrupt parties in Q have been assigned. Then the probability that the next honest party in R is also assigned only corrupt parties from the remaining $t_q - \lceil n_q/n_r \rceil$ corrupt parties, out of the $n_q - \lceil n_q/n_r \rceil$ remaining parties in Q, is:

$$\frac{\binom{t_q - \lceil n_q/n_r \rceil}{\lceil n_q/n_r \rceil}}{\binom{n_q - \lceil n_q/n_r \rceil}{\lceil n_q/n_r \rceil}}.$$

This continues until all the $n_r - t_r - 1$ honest parties in R have been assigned parties in Q.

Each party in R has been assigned $\lceil n_q/n_r \rceil$ parties in Q so that each party in Q has been assigned to exactly one party in R. In Step 4 of the algorithm, each party in R is randomly assigned parties in Q until all parties in R have ℓ parties assigned to them; they are thus each assigned $\ell - \lceil n_q/n_r \rceil$ more parties in Q. For a given party in R, this is the number of ways of choosing $\ell - \lceil n_q/n_r \rceil$ dishonest parties from the remaining $n_q - \lceil n_q/n_r \rceil$ parties in Q such that they too are all dishonest – i.e. they are from the $t_q - \lceil n_q/n_r \rceil$ remaining dishonest parties:

$$\frac{\binom{t_q - \lceil n_q/n_r \rceil}{\ell - \lceil n_q/n_r \rceil}}{\binom{n_q - \lceil n_q/n_r \rceil}{\ell - \lceil n_q/n_r \rceil}}$$

The choice of parties in Q is *with* replacement since the algorithm is oblivious to the choice of other parties in Step 4 (since Step 3 ensured the cover).

Then the probability that we obtain a secure cover is given by:

$$1 - \left(\frac{\binom{t_q}{\lceil n_q/n_r \rceil} \cdot \binom{t_q - \lceil n_q/n_r \rceil}{\lceil n_q/n_r \rceil} \cdot \ldots \cdot \binom{t_q - (n_r - t_r - 1)\lceil n_q/n_r \rceil}{\lceil n_q/n_r \rceil}}{\binom{n_q}{\lceil n_q/n_r \rceil} \cdot \binom{n_q - \lceil n_q/n_r \rceil}{\lceil n_q/n_r \rceil} \cdot \ldots \cdot \binom{n_q - (n_r - t_r - 1)\lceil n_q/n_r \rceil}{\lceil n_q/n_r \rceil}} \right) \cdot \left(\frac{\binom{t_q - \lceil n_q/n_r \rceil}{\ell - \lceil n_q/n_r \rceil}}{\binom{n_q - \lceil n_q/n_r \rceil}{\ell - \lceil n_q/n_r \rceil}} \right)^{n_r - t_r}$$

After some simplification we find that this is equal to

$$1 - \frac{t_q! \cdot (n_q - (n_r - t_r)\lceil n_q/n_r \rceil)!}{n_q! \cdot (t_q - (n_r - t_r)\lceil n_q/n_r \rceil)!} \cdot \left(\frac{\binom{t_q - \lceil n_q/n_r \rceil}{\ell - \lceil n_q/n_r \rceil}}{\binom{n_q - \lceil n_q/n_r \rceil}{\ell - \lceil n_q/n_r \rceil}} \right)^{n_r - t_r} \tag{1}$$

To see what happens in the extreme case where all but one party is corrupt in each of R and Q, we set $t_q = n_q - 1$ and $t_r = n_r - 1$. Then the probability that we obtain a secure cover is given by

$$1 - \frac{(n_q - 1)! \cdot (n_q - \lceil n_q/n_r \rceil)!}{(n_q)! \cdot (n_q - 1 - \lceil n_q/n_r \rceil)!} \cdot \frac{\binom{(n_q-1)-\lceil n_q/n_r \rceil}{\ell - \lceil n_q/n_r \rceil}}{\binom{n_q - \lceil n_q/n_r \rceil}{\ell - \lceil n_q/n_r \rceil}}$$

$$= 1 - \frac{n_q - \lceil n_q/n_r \rceil}{n_q} \cdot \frac{n_q - \ell}{n_q - \lceil n_q/n_r \rceil} = \frac{\ell}{n_q}.$$

When ℓ is equal to n_q, i.e. each party in R sends to every party in Q, we obtain a secure cover. For any other choice of ℓ with this high proportion of corruptions, we do not obtain a sufficiently high probability of obtaining a secure cover. Thus our protocol will not be secure for any size of R.

When ℓ is at least $t_q + 1$, then every party in R necessarily sends to at least one honest party. For small numbers of parties, the parties in R must send to all parties in Q because chance of the cover being insecure is too great. However, as we increase the total number of parties, the probability that the cover is not secure decreases. For example, if there are 5 parties in R of which at most 2 are corrupt, and 50 parties in Q of which at most 25 are corrupt, each party in R must be assigned $\ell = 23$ parties in Q to ensure at least one honest party in R sends to one honest party in Q with probability at least $1 - 2^{-80}$, instead of the 25 parties we would require to *guarantee* the cover is secure.

For the data in Table 1, we fix the number of parties in R at 5, fix the number of allowable corruptions to be at most 3, and compute the lower bound on the size of Q (i.e. on n_q) to guarantee that the adversary cannot win even where ℓ is fixed as the smallest number of connections necessary to make $\{Q_i\}_{i \in R}$ to cover Q, and vary the number of corruptions we allow in Q. In other words, ℓ need be no larger to provide 80-bit security than it need be for enabling the partition to be an exact cover (i.e. each party in Q sent to by at most one party in R).

We stress that while the idea of completely outsourcing the pre-processing to an independent set of parties often does not result in an efficient protocol, the best use-case of our protocol is when $R \subset Q$; i.e., if there is some subset of parties trusted by all other parties in the network which can do all of the pre-processing and then distribute it to the other parties.

Table 1. We fix $n_r = 5$, $t_r = 3$ and vary the fraction of corruptions in Q; the last column in the table is the least n_q such that the cover is secure even if each party in R only sends to $\ell = \lceil n_q/n_r \rceil$ parties.

n_r	t_r	t_q/n_q	Min. n_q for $\lambda = 80$ and $\ell = \lceil n_q/n_r \rceil$
5	3	1/2	336
5	3	1/3	201
5	3	1/4	148
5	3	1/5	125

5   SPDZ Online Protocol

The SPDZ online protocol is given in Fig. 5 which itself uses the subprocedure MACCheck presented in Fig. 6, which itself makes use of a commitment functionality given in Fig. 7. It has been shown that UC commitment schemes in the plain model cannot exist, though they do exist in the *common reference string model* (in which one assumes the existence of common string known to all parties) [CF01], or, alternatively, the *random oracle model* (e.g. [HMQ04]).

The SPDZ Online Protocol $\Pi_{\text{Online}}^{\mathcal{P},\mathcal{A}}$.

The set $\mathcal{P}$ is the complete set of parties, and the set $\mathcal{A} \subset \mathcal{P}$ the set of corrupt parties in $\mathcal{P}$.

Initialise: The parties call $\mathcal{F}_{\text{Prep}}^{\mathcal{P},\mathcal{A}}$ for the handles of enough multiplication triples $(\langle a \rangle, \langle b \rangle, \langle c \rangle)$ and enough input mask values $(r_i, \langle r_i \rangle)$ as are needed for the function being evaluated. If $\mathcal{F}_{\text{Prep}}^{\mathcal{P},\mathcal{A}}$ aborts then the parties output $\perp$ and abort.

Input: To share an input x_i, party $i \in \mathcal{P}$ takes an available unused input mask value $(r_i, \langle r_i \rangle)$ and does the following:

1. Broadcast $\varepsilon \leftarrow x_i - r_i$.
2. The parties compute $\langle x_i \rangle \leftarrow \langle r_i \rangle + \varepsilon$.

Add: On input $(\langle x \rangle, \langle y \rangle)$, locally compute $\langle x + y \rangle \leftarrow \langle x \rangle + \langle y \rangle$.

Multiply: On input $(\langle x \rangle, \langle y \rangle)$, the parties do the following:

1. Take one multiplication triple $(\langle a \rangle, \langle b \rangle, \langle c \rangle)$, compute $\langle \varepsilon \rangle \leftarrow \langle x \rangle - \langle a \rangle$ and $\langle \rho \rangle \leftarrow \langle y \rangle - \langle b \rangle$ and partially open these shares to obtain ε and ρ respectively. Partially opening a sharing $\langle x \rangle$ consists of each party $i \in \mathcal{P}$ sending its share x_i to every other party $j \in \mathcal{P}$ and computing the sum of all of these shares, including the party's own. The values of $\gamma(x)_i$ are kept secret.
2. Set $\langle z \rangle \leftarrow \langle c \rangle + \varepsilon \cdot \langle b \rangle + \rho \cdot \langle a \rangle + \varepsilon \cdot \rho$.

Output: To output a share $\langle y \rangle$, do the following:

1. Check all partially opened values since the last MACCheck in the following manner.
   (a) The parties have some id's $\text{id}_1, \ldots, \text{id}_k$ for some k, and corresponding partially opened values $x_1, \ldots, x_k$.
   (b) The players agree on a random vector $\mathbf{r} \leftarrow \mathcal{F}_{\text{Rand}}(\mathbb{F}_q^k)$.
   (c) Party i in $\mathcal{P}$ computes $z \leftarrow \sum_{j=1}^{k} r_j \cdot x_j$ and $\gamma(z)_i \leftarrow \sum_{j=1}^{k} r_j \cdot \gamma(x_j)_i$ where $\gamma(x_j)_i$ denotes the MAC share held by party $i \in \mathcal{P}$ on x_j.
   (d) The parties now run MACCheck on z, with party i inputting z and $\gamma(z)_i$.
2. If the check fails, output $\perp$ and abort.
3. Open the value by each party $i \in \mathcal{P}$ sending y_i to all other parties $j \in \mathcal{P}$ to compute $y \leftarrow \sum_{j \in \mathcal{P}} y_i$, and then run MACCheck once more, so party $i \in \mathcal{P}$ inputs y and $\gamma(y)_i$, to verify $\langle y \rangle$. If this check fails, output $\perp$ and abort; otherwise, accept y as a valid output.

Fig. 5. The SPDZ Online Protocol $\Pi_{\text{Online}}^{\mathcal{P},\mathcal{A}}$.

The MACCheck Protocol from SPDZ/MASCOT.

On input an opened value s, a MAC share $\gamma(s)_i$ and a MAC key share α_i from each party i and a session id sid, each party i does the following:

1. Compute $\sigma_i \leftarrow \gamma(s)_i - s \cdot \alpha_i$ and call $\mathcal{F}_{\mathrm{Commit}}.\mathsf{Commit}(\sigma_i, i, \mathsf{sid})$ to commit to this, and receive the handle τ_i.
2. When commitments are output by all parties call $\mathcal{F}_{\mathrm{Commit}}.\mathsf{Open}(i, \mathsf{sid}, \tau_i)$ to open the commitments.
3. If $\sum_{i=1}^{n} \sigma_i \neq 0$, output $\bot$ and abort; otherwise, continue.

Fig. 6. The MACCheck Protocol from SPDZ/MASCOT.

Commitment Functionality $\mathcal{F}_{\mathrm{Commit}}$.

Commit: On input $\mathsf{Commit}(v, i, \mathsf{sid})$ by party i, where v is the value to committed, sample a handle τ_v and send $(i, \mathsf{sid}, \tau_v)$ to all parties.
Open: On input $\mathsf{Open}(i, \mathsf{sid}, \tau_v)$ by party i, output $(v, i, \mathsf{sid}, \tau_v)$ to all parties. If some party P_i is corrupt and the adversary inputs $(\mathsf{Abort}, i, \mathsf{sid}, \tau_v)$, the functionality outputs $(\bot, i, \mathsf{sid}, \tau_v)$ to all parties.

Fig. 7. Commitment Functionality $\mathcal{F}_{\mathrm{Commit}}$.

The MAC check passes if the MAC is correct for the corresponding share. Importantly, the check fails if the MAC is incorrect for the shared value, which occurs if the MAC *or* the value it authenticates (or both) is incorrect. Proofs can be found in [KOS16, App. B] and [DPSZ12, App. D3]. It is precisely because MACCheck detects errors in either the MAC value or share value or both that we can use an offline phase which introduces errors into the share values themselves, and not restrict ourselves to an offline phase in which only errors on MACs are allowed (as in the original SPDZ papers). For clarity, we show this more explicitly in the proof of the next theorem:

Theorem 3. *The protocol* $\Pi_{Online}^{\mathcal{P},\mathcal{A}}$ *securely implements the functionality* $\mathcal{F}_{MPC}^{\mathcal{P},\mathcal{A}}$ *in the* $\mathcal{F}_{Prep}^{\mathcal{P},\mathcal{A}}$, $\mathcal{F}_{Commit}$, $\mathcal{F}_{Rand}$-*hybrid model.*

Proof. The proof is identical to that in [DPSZ12], except that the pre-processing may now introduce errors into the share values as well as the MAC values. To prove the theorem, we must show that no environment can distinguish between an adversary interacting as in the protocol $\Pi_{Prep}^{\mathcal{P},\mathcal{A}}$ and a simulator interacting with the functionality $\mathcal{F}_{Prep}^{\mathcal{P},\mathcal{A}}$. Thus the proof runs exactly as in [DPSZ12, App. D3], except that when we run the MACCheck protocol, the error can now be on the value in the share or the MAC. However, the security game presented in [DPSZ12] already allowed the adversary to introduce errors on the shares, so the original protocol already offers the stronger guarantee that no error can occur on either the MAC or the value of the share it authenticated (or both). Note that if the adversary can alter the share and the MAC and have MACCheck pass, then in particular this is equivalent to tweaking some share a_i by t to obtain $a_i' \leftarrow a_i + t$ and then choosing the correct tweak τ on the MAC share, $\gamma(a')_i \leftarrow \gamma(a_i) + \tau$ so that the check passes. However, this means the adversary has successfully guessed $\alpha = \tau/t$, the global MAC key, which it can only do successfully with probability $1/q$. (Since q is expontial in the security parameter λ, this probability is negligible.)   □

6   Communication Between Subnetworks

Here we discuss the topology of the network of secure channels between the subnetworks R and Q. Recall that Q has been partitioned into sets $\{Q_i\}_{i \in R}$ and party $i \in R$ assigned the set Q_i, and each Q_i is assumed to be of size ℓ. The topology depends primarily on the choice for the size ℓ of each set Q_i. We assume Q_i is the same size for all i, and note that obviously ℓ is lower-bounded by $\lceil n_q/n_r \rceil$ (so that $\ell \cdot n_r \geq n_q$), since $\{Q_i\}_{i \in R}$ together need to cover Q.

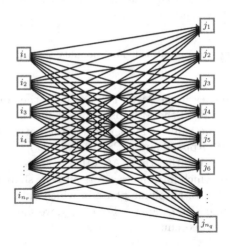

Fig. 8. Complete bipartite graph

6.1   Complete

A naïve approach to connecting the two graphs with bilateral secure channels would be to form the complete bipartite graph between them (so $\ell = n_q$). This topology requires $n_r \cdot n_q$ secure connections and is shown in Fig. 8. If there is at least one honest party in each of R and Q then an adversary controlling any number of other parties still can never recover the MAC key. Unfortunately, there is a big communication overhead. Additionally, each party in R must compute

n_q reshares for their share. If we assume the adversary is able to corrupt at most some t of the n total parties, we can clearly improve efficiency by instead requiring each party in R to send to $t+1$ parties in Q, since then it is guaranteed each party, and in particular at least one honest party, sends to an honest party in Q.

6.2 Load-Balanced

To aim for a load-balanced solution, we could instead ask each party $i \in R$ to reshare its share into $\ell = k \cdot \lceil n_q/n_r \rceil$ shares for some integer $k \geq 1$, and sending these to some set Q_i of ℓ parties in Q. If we have a secure cover, then the intuition is that there exist shares held by only honest players which are independent of all shares held by the adversary and are necessary for reconstructing the secret. This is discussed in more detail in the proof of our main theorem (see the full version). Figure 9 shows an example of our load-balanced topology for when $n_q \approx 2n_r$ and $k = 1$. Note that it is not necessarily the case that each party in Q receive the same number of shares, even though we require each party in R to reshare to the same number of parties in Q.

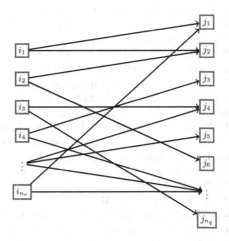

Fig. 9. Load-balanced topology

Acknowledgements. This work has been supported in part by ERC Advanced Grant ERC-2015-AdG-IMPaCT, by EPSRC via grant EP/N021940/1, by Defense Advanced Research Projects Agency (DARPA) and Space and Naval Warfare Systems Center, Pacific (SSC Pacific) under contract No. N66001-15-C-4070, and by the European Union's Horizon 2020 programme under grant No. 731583 (SODA).

References

[BCP15] Boyle, E., Chung, K.-M., Pass, R.: Large-scale secure computation: multi-party computation for (Parallel) RAM programs. In: Gennaro, R., Robshaw, M. (eds.) CRYPTO 2015. LNCS, vol. 9216, pp. 742–762. Springer, Heidelberg (2015). https://doi.org/10.1007/978-3-662-48000-7_36

[BDOZ11] Bendlin, R., Damgård, I., Orlandi, C., Zakarias, S.: Semi-homomorphic encryption and multiparty computation. In: Paterson, K.G. (ed.) EUROCRYPT 2011. LNCS, vol. 6632, pp. 169–188. Springer, Heidelberg (2011). https://doi.org/10.1007/978-3-642-20465-4_11

[Bea96] Beaver, D.: Correlated pseudorandomness and the complexity of private computations. In: 28th ACM STOC, pp. 479–488. ACM Press, May 1996

[BLN+15] Burra, S.S., Larraia, E., Nielsen, J.B., Nordholt, P.S., Orlandi, C., Orsini, E., Scholl, P., Smart, N.P.: High performance multi-party computation for binary circuits based on oblivious transfer. Cryptology ePrint Archive, Report 2015/472 (2015), http://eprint.iacr.org/2015/472

[BOGW88] Ben-Or, M., Goldwasser, S., Wigderson, A.: Completeness theorems for non-cryptographic fault-tolerant distributed computation (extended abstract). In: 20th ACM STOC, pp. 1–10. ACM Press, May 1988

[CF01] Canetti, R., Fischlin, M.: Universally composable commitments. In: Kilian, J. (ed.) CRYPTO 2001. LNCS, vol. 2139, pp. 19–40. Springer, Heidelberg (2001). https://doi.org/10.1007/3-540-44647-8_2

[DGKN09] Damgård, I., Geisler, M., Krøigaard, M., Nielsen, J.B.: Asynchronous multiparty computation: theory and implementation. In: Jarecki, S., Tsudik, G. (eds.) PKC 2009. LNCS, vol. 5443, pp. 160–179. Springer, Heidelberg (2009). https://doi.org/10.1007/978-3-642-00468-1_10

[DI06] Damgård, I., Ishai, Y.: Scalable secure multiparty computation. In: Dwork, C. (ed.) CRYPTO 2006. LNCS, vol. 4117, pp. 501–520. Springer, Heidelberg (2006). https://doi.org/10.1007/11818175_30

[DKL+13] Damgård, I., Keller, M., Larraia, E., Pastro, V., Scholl, P., Smart, N.P.: Practical covertly secure MPC for dishonest majority – or: breaking the SPDZ limits. In: Crampton, J., Jajodia, S., Mayes, K. (eds.) ESORICS 2013. LNCS, vol. 8134, pp. 1–18. Springer, Heidelberg (2013). https://doi.org/10.1007/978-3-642-40203-6_1

[DKMS14] Dani, V., King, V., Movahedi, M., Saia, J.: Quorums quicken queries: efficient asynchronous secure multiparty computation. In: Chatterjee, M., Cao, J., Kothapalli, K., Rajsbaum, S. (eds.) ICDCN 2014. LNCS, vol. 8314, pp. 242–256. Springer, Heidelberg (2014). https://doi.org/10.1007/978-3-642-45249-9_16

[DPSZ12] Damgård, I., Pastro, V., Smart, N., Zakarias, S.: Multiparty computation from somewhat homomorphic encryption. In: Safavi-Naini, R., Canetti, R. (eds.) CRYPTO 2012. LNCS, vol. 7417, pp. 643–662. Springer, Heidelberg (2012). https://doi.org/10.1007/978-3-642-32009-5_38

[HMQ04] Hofheinz, D., Müller-Quade, J.: Universally composable commitments using random oracles. In: Naor, M. (ed.) TCC 2004. LNCS, vol. 2951, pp. 58–76. Springer, Heidelberg (2004). https://doi.org/10.1007/978-3-540-24638-1_4

[HN06] Hirt, M., Nielsen, J.B.: Robust multiparty computation with linear communication complexity. In: Dwork, C. (ed.) CRYPTO 2006. LNCS, vol. 4117, pp. 463–482. Springer, Heidelberg (2006). https://doi.org/10.1007/11818175_28

[KOS16] Keller, M., Orsini, E., Scholl, P.: MASCOT: faster malicious arithmetic secure computation with oblivious transfer. In: Weippl, E.R., Katzenbeisser, S., Kruegel, C., Myers, A.C., Halevi, S. (eds.) ACM CCS 2016, pp. 830–842. ACM Press, October 2016

[KSS13] Keller, M., Scholl, P., Smart, N.P.: An architecture for practical actively secure MPC with dishonest majority. In: Sadeghi, A.-R., Gligor, V.D., Yung, M. (eds.) ACM CCS 2013, pp. 549–560. ACM Press, November 2013

[LOS14] Larraia, E., Orsini, E., Smart, N.P.: Dishonest majority multi-party computation for binary circuits. In: Garay, J.A., Gennaro, R. (eds.) CRYPTO 2014. LNCS, vol. 8617, pp. 495–512. Springer, Heidelberg (2014). https://doi.org/10.1007/978-3-662-44381-1_28

[NNOB12] Nielsen, J.B., Nordholt, P.S., Orlandi, C., Burra, S.S.: A new approach to practical active-secure two-party computation. In: Safavi-Naini, R., Canetti, R. (eds.) CRYPTO 2012. LNCS, vol. 7417, pp. 681–700. Springer, Heidelberg (2012). https://doi.org/10.1007/978-3-642-32009-5_40

[RBO89] Rabin, T., Ben-Or, M.: Verifiable secret sharing and multiparty protocols with honest majority (extended abstract). In: 21st ACM STOC, pp. 73–85. ACM Press, May 1989

Coding Theory

Chapter Three

On the Probability of Incorrect Decoding for Linear Codes

Marco Frego$^{(\boxtimes)}$

University of Trento, Trento, Italy
marco.frego@unitn.it

Abstract. In the literature of Error Correcting Codes (ECC) there are many probabilistic characterizations of different events that happen in the decoding process. Historically, the most considered parameters in the performance of a linear code are the Probability of Undetected Error and the probability of incorrect decoding, also known as Probability of Miscorrected Error. While there is agreement about the first, starting from the Seventies, basically four definitions of the Probability of Miscorrected Error are present in literature; aim of this work is to show that they are equivalent and, although different in the mathematical formulation, they yield exactly the same result. The gap of this missing proof is herein fulfilled and two examples with interesting properties are given.

Keywords: Linear code · Error probability · Miscorrected error · Error detection · Bounded distance decoding · Decoding error probabilities

1 Introduction

The performance of a (linear) error correcting code can be evaluated on the basis of many parameters. Depending on the application studied, one can focus on the distance of the code, its dimension, the information rate; or one can investigate what happens when the number of errors in transmission is greater than the correction capability of the code. Those events are studied in terms of error probabilities. In the decoding process, the events of major interest have an associated probability, in particular, the Probability of Correct Decoding ($\mathbb{P}_{CD}$), the Probability of Undetected Error ($\mathbb{P}_{UE}$) and the Probability of Miscorrected Error ($\mathbb{P}_{ME}$), [15]. The presence of an undetected error is especially important when related to safety, e.g. when the codewords represent a feedback for danger. A miscorrected error can have heavy consequences when the wrong information can corrupt a whole set of data, that is, the cost of incorrect decoding is high, for example in data storage applications or in the 3D reconstruction of a human body [1].

There are four formulations for the $\mathbb{P}_{ME}$ and they have been derived by different authors from different points of view, also the mathematical expression is not the same but after a computer implementation and evaluation of the four formulas, it becomes clear that they give the same result. Therefore it is interesting to prove their equivalence, which is missing in literature.

© Springer International Publishing AG 2017
M. O'Neill (Ed.): IMACC 2017, LNCS 10655, pp. 103–115, 2017.
https://doi.org/10.1007/978-3-319-71045-7_5

The work has this structure: Sect. 2 gives a short review of the names, conventions and standard use of symbols for ECC that will be useful for Sect. 3, where the four formulations of $\mathbb{P}_{\text{ME}}$ are stated and the equivalence theorem is proved. Section 4 presents a comparison of the results of bruteforce decoding (maximum likelihood) with the theoretical results of the probability of miscorrected error. Section 5 contains comments and conclusions on those four different formulas proposed in literature.

2   Background and Framework

Let $\mathcal{C}$ be an $[n, k, d]$ linear code over $\mathbb{F}_q$ with weight distribution $A_0, A_1, \ldots, A_n$ and let the symbol error probability on a $q-$ary alphabet be p. The probability that a symbol is correctly transmitted over the channel is then $1 - p$. Assume that if an error does occur, then each of the $q - 1$ symbols aside from the correct symbol is equally likely to be received, with probability $\frac{p}{q-1}$ each. This hypothetical channel is called the $q-$ary symmetric channel or $q - \text{SC}$ for short, [4]. This is a standard framework in ECC.

Let τ be the number of errors that occurred in transmission. If $\tau = 0$ the decoder does not detect any error and does not decode the received vector, as it is in the code already. If $1 \leq \tau \leq t$, where $t := \lfloor \frac{d-1}{2} \rfloor$, the decoder detects the error and corrects it to the unique codeword at distance less than t from the received vector. However, if $\tau > t$ three models of decoder must be considered: the ideal bounded distance decoder, the maximum likelihood decoder and other types (e.g. Berlekamp-Massey, etc.). If more than t errors occur, two situations can happen: (a) there is a unique codeword at distance at most t from the received vector; (b) there is no codeword at a distance lower than $t + 1$ from the received vector. In case (a), every decoder will clearly correct the vector to that unique codeword, and the correction will be wrong, see Fig. 1. In case (b), the decoders exhibit different behaviours: the ideal bounded distance decoder will not attempt to correct the vector and will raise a flag of decoding failure; the maximum likelihood decoder will correct the vector to its closest codeword (which may not be unique); for other decoders the behaviour is not specified, see Figure 2.

Remark 1. As a remark, notice that the algorithm of Berlekamp-Massey can be approximated with an ideal decoder. This algorithm is based on the error locator polynomial, which has the properties that its roots give the locations of the errors occurred in transmission (for instance [3] for a Gröbner Basis derivation). For a number of errors $\tau \leq t$ the roots of the locator polynomial are valid positions and the correction is unambiguous. If there are more than t errors, the following cases can happen: 1. there exists a codeword at distance lower than t from the received vector and this produces a wrong correction; 2a. there does not exist any codeword at distance lower than $t + 1$ from the received vector and the decoder corrects wrong, 2b. as in 2a but the decoder corrects to the sent codeword, 2c. there does not exist any codeword at distance lower than $t + 1$

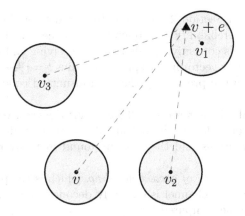

Fig. 1. Suppose to send v and receive $v + e$, i.e. the triangle inside the decoding sphere of v_1, in this case every decoder will correct $v + e$ to v_1 thus making a correction error.

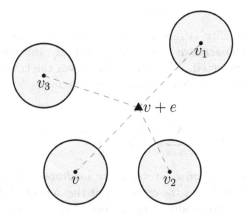

Fig. 2. Suppose to send v and receive $v+e$, i.e. the triangle outside any decoding sphere (in gray around each codeword). In this case the ideal decoder will raise a message of decoding failure, whereas the maximum likelihood decoder will decode to the closest codeword around $v + e$, that is v_2 in that picture.

from the received vector, but not all the roots of the locator polynomial are valid positions, the decoder sends a message of decoding failure. The case 2b cannot happen in practice because in this instance the locator polynomial will have a degree higher than t, but in an implementation, the decoding process will be stopped after degree t.

After these considerations about the decoders, we are interested in the probability of the miscorrected error for bounded distance decoders. It is important to notice that this decoding scheme is incomplete because not all possible received vectors will have a distance less than t from a codeword, that is, inside a decoding sphere, [12]. An example where the sent codeword is outside of any decoding sphere is presented in Section 4, see also [10] for details about the decoding sphere. Consider the reliability of a bounded distance decoder. A codeword c sent over the channel is correctly decoded at the receiving end by the decoder if the decoder receives any vector in the sphere of radius $t = \lfloor \frac{d-1}{2} \rfloor$ around c, yielding a lower bound on the probability that a transmitted codeword is correctly decoded.

There are several different ways to characterize the error detecting and correcting capabilities of codes at the output of the channel decoder. Those are widely accepted definitions and they can be found in many references e.g. in [2,5,7,11,14].

$\mathbb{P}_{CD}(p)$ is the *probability of correct decoding*, which is the probability that a codeword c sent over the channel is correctly decoded at the receiving end by the decoder, and can be computed by:

$$\mathbb{P}_{CD}(p) = \sum_{i=0}^{t} \binom{n}{i} p^i (1-p)^{n-i}.$$

Note that this probability is independent of the size of the alphabet. $\mathbb{P}_{UE}(p)$ is the *probability of undetected error*, the probability that errors occurring in a codeword are not detected. An error vector moves the transmitted codeword into another codeword, and this probability is therefore

$$\mathbb{P}_{UE}(p) = \sum_{i=d}^{n} A_i \left(\frac{p}{q-1} \right)^i (1-p)^{n-i}.$$

$\mathbb{P}_E(w)$ is the *probability of miscorrected error conditioned to an error of weight* w. This is the probability that the codeword at the output of the decoder is not the same as the codeword produced by the encoder, with the condition that an error of weight w occurred. $\mathbb{P}_{ME}(p)$ is the *probability of miscorrected error*. This is the probability that the decoder outputs a wrong codeword. It depends only on the code (it is important to note that knowledge of the weight distribution is required) and on the channel.

Whereas for the probabilities of correct decoding and undetected error there is agreement in the definition among all authors, the situation is very different for the $\mathbb{P}_{ME}$. In the literature there are four definitions of $\mathbb{P}_{ME}$, only one of them (proposed by [5]) involves the definition of $\mathbb{P}_E(w)$, the others directly assume the presence of the $q-$ary symmetric channel. The study of the $\mathbb{P}_{ME}$ in terms of the $\mathbb{P}_E(w)$ brings more insight in what happens when the number of errors increases, therefore it is herein briefly summarized.

In order to proceed, define the quantity $N(\ell, w; s)$ as the number of vectors of weight w that are at distance s from a fixed codeword of weight ℓ. If w is not such that $\ell - s \leq w \leq \ell + s$, then $N(\ell, w; s) = 0$. $N(\ell, w; s)$ is independent of the given codeword of weight ℓ and is hence well defined ([5]). For $s \leq t$, spheres of radius s about codewords are disjoint and hence the number of vectors of weight w at distance exactly s from a codeword of weight ℓ is $A_\ell \cdot N(\ell, w; s)$.

Now received vectors which will be improperly decoded are those which lie within a sphere of radius t about some codeword other than that which was sent. Call C_w the number of these vectors, clearly

$$C_w = \sum_{\ell=0}^{n} A_\ell \sum_{s=0}^{t} N(\ell, w; s) \quad \text{for } t+1 \le w \le n.$$

This leads easily to the next lemma.

Lemma 1. *The probability $\mathbb{P}_E(w)$ is the probability of miscorrected error conditioned to an error of weight w and is characterized by*

$$\mathbb{P}_E(w) = \frac{C_w}{(q-1)^w \binom{n}{w}}.$$

Proof. $\mathbb{P}_E(w)$ is given by the ratio of the *decodable* vectors of weight w (i.e. C_w) by all possible vectors of weight w, which are $(q-1)^w \binom{n}{w}$.

The following lemma finds out the number $N(\ell, w; s)$.

Lemma 2. *The number $N(\ell, w; s)$ of vectors of weight w that are at distance s from a fixed codeword of weight ℓ is zero if w is not such that $\ell - s \le w \le \ell + s$, otherwise is*

$$N(\ell, w; s) = \sum_{r=r_1}^{r_2} \binom{\ell}{\ell - s + r} \binom{s - r}{w - \ell + s - 2r} \binom{n - \ell}{r} (q-2)^{w-\ell+s-2r} (q-1)^r,$$

where $r_1 := \max\{0, w-\ell\}$ and $r_2 := \lfloor \frac{w-\ell+s}{2} \rfloor$. Note that $\lfloor x \rfloor$ is the larger integer less than or equal to x and that $\binom{x}{y}$ is zero if $y \notin \mathbb{N}$.

Proof. See [5]. $\square$

Corollary 1. *In the case of binary linear codes $q = 2$ and the previous lemma simplifies to*

$$N(\ell, w; s) = \begin{cases} \binom{n-\ell}{\frac{s+w-\ell}{2}} \binom{\ell}{\frac{s-w+\ell}{2}} & \text{if } |w - \ell| \le s \\ \\ 0 & \text{if } |w - \ell| > s. \end{cases}$$

Once the weight distribution of C and $\mathbb{P}_E(w)$ are known, the formula for the probability that the decoder outputs a wrong codeword is given by the next theorem.

Theorem 1. *The probability of miscorrected error $\mathbb{P}_{ME}(p)$ depends only on the code C and on the channel ϕ, and is*

$$\mathbb{P}_{ME}(p) := \mathbb{P}_{ME}(C, \phi) = \sum_{w=t+1}^{n} \mathbb{P}_E(w) \phi(w), \tag{1}$$

where $\phi(w)$ is the probability of w errors in transmission. In the case of the $q-$ary symmetric channel $\phi(w)$ has the classic form

$$\phi(w) = \binom{n}{w}(q-1)^w \left(\frac{p}{q-1}\right)^w (1-p)^{n-w}.$$

Corollary 2. *In the $q-$ary symmetric channel, the probability of miscorrected error* (1) *simplifies to*

$$\mathbb{P}_{\mathrm{ME}}(\mathcal{C}, q-\mathrm{SC}) = \sum_{w=t+1}^{n} C_w \left(\frac{p}{q-1}\right)^w (1-p)^{n-w}.$$

It may be difficult to compute exactly this probability because the weight distribution of a linear code (or even just the minimum distance) is in general not known, [9]. In these cases the weight distribution can be approximated by suitable estimates and (1) becomes a bound.

3   Unified Probability of Miscorrected Error

This section collects the four formulations of the $\mathbb{P}_{\mathrm{ME}}$ found from different authors in literature. They are reported in four lemmas identified with the letters A, B, C and D. The corresponding expression for the $\mathbb{P}_{\mathrm{ME}}$ has a superscript with the matching letter. In the previous section the approach of [5] was presented, which turns out to be the most followed (Lemma 5), maybe because it was the first proposed. In [2] there is a historical description and bibliography of the papers and previous results that yield to [5]. With the aim of keeping the paper contained, the derivation of the four characterizations is skipped, but can be easily retrieved in each of the cited references.

Lemma 3 ([13]).

$$\mathbb{P}_{\mathrm{ME}}^A(p) = \sum_{\ell=2t+1}^{n} A_\ell \sum_{s=0}^{t} \sum_{r=0}^{t-s} \binom{n-\ell}{s}\binom{\ell}{r}$$
$$\cdot (q-1)^{r-\ell}\left(1-\frac{p}{q-1}\right)^r (1-p)^{n-\ell-s} p^{\ell+s-r}.$$

Lemma 4 ([8,12,14]).

$$\mathbb{P}_{\mathrm{ME}}^B(p) = \sum_{\ell=2t+1}^{n} A_\ell \sum_{s=0}^{t} \sum_{r=0}^{s} \binom{n-\ell}{r}\binom{\ell}{s-r}$$
$$\cdot \left(\frac{p}{q-1}\right)^{\ell-s+r}\left(1-\frac{p}{q-1}\right)^{s-r} (1-p)^{n-\ell-r} p^r.$$

Lemma 5 ($[2,5,6]$). *For r_1 and r_2 as defined in Lemma 2,*

$$\mathbb{P}_{ME}^C(p) = \sum_{\ell=0}^{n} A_\ell \sum_{s=0}^{t} \sum_{w=t+1}^{n} \sum_{r=r_1}^{r_2} \binom{n-\ell}{r}$$
$$\cdot \binom{\ell}{\ell-s+r}\binom{s-r}{w-\ell+s-2r}\left(\frac{p}{q-1}\right)^w (1-p)^{n-w}$$
$$\cdot (q-2)^{w-\ell+s-2r}(q-1)^r.$$

Lemma 6 ($[11]$).

$$\mathbb{P}_{ME}^D(p) = \sum_{w=t+1}^{n} \left(\frac{p}{q-1}\right)^w (1-p)^{n-w}$$
$$\sum_{\ell=\max(w-t,d)}^{\min(w+t,n)} A_\ell \sum_{s=|l-w|}^{t} \sum_{r=0}^{s} \binom{\ell}{r}\binom{n-\ell}{r+w-\ell}\binom{\ell-r}{s+\ell-w-2r}$$
$$\cdot (q-2)^{s+\ell-w-2r}(q-1)^{r+w-\ell}.$$

A final technical lemma is needed in order to prove the main theorem of this section.

Lemma 7. *The following identity holds:*

$$\sum_{j=0}^{s-r} \binom{s-r}{j}(q-2)^j (1-p)^{s-r-j}(q-1)^{r-s}$$
$$= \sum_{j=0}^{s-r} \binom{s-r}{j}\left(\frac{p}{q-1}\right)^j (q-2)^j (1-p)^{s-r-j},$$

which, in particular, is equal to $\left(\frac{q-p-1}{q-1}\right)^{s-r}$.

Proof. Follows easily with Newton's Binomial Theorem. $\qquad\square$

Theorem 2 (Unified Error Probability). *The four Lemmas 3, 4, 5 and 6 are equivalent.*

Proof. The proof is divided in three parts: Lemma 3 $\iff$ Lemma 4, then Lemma 5 $\iff$ Lemma 6 and finally Lemma 4 $\iff$ Lemma 5. First consider the equivalence of Lemma 3 and Lemma 4. The outer sum over ℓ is the same in (3) and (4), hence look at the inner part only. Starting from the binomial part of equation (4), the first observation is that $s \leq t$ and $r \leq s$, otherwise the binomial $\binom{\ell}{s-r}$ would become zero because of $s - r < 0$. It is possible to rewrite (4) as

$$\sum_{\ell=2t+1}^{n} A_\ell \sum_{s=0}^{t} \sum_{r=0}^{t} \binom{n-\ell}{r}\binom{\ell}{s-r}\left(\frac{p}{q-1}\right)^{\ell-s+r}\left(1-\frac{p}{q-1}\right)^{s-r}(1-p)^{n-\ell-r}p^r$$

and the swap r with s yields

$$\sum_{\ell=2t+1}^{n} A_\ell \sum_{s=0}^{t} \sum_{r=0}^{t} \binom{n-\ell}{s}\binom{\ell}{r-s}\left(\frac{p}{q-1}\right)^{\ell-r+s}\left(1-\frac{p}{q-1}\right)^{r-s}(1-p)^{n-\ell-s}p^s$$

Observing that the terms of the sum for the index $r = 0, 1, \ldots, s-1$ are zero, the previous expression is simplified (with the index substitution $k = r - s$, $r = k + s$) in

$$\sum_{\ell=2t+1}^{n} A_\ell \sum_{s=0}^{t} \sum_{k=0}^{t-s} \binom{n-\ell}{s}\binom{\ell}{k} \cdot (q-1)^{k-\ell}\left(1-\frac{p}{q-1}\right)^{k}(1-p)^{n-\ell-s}p^{\ell+s-k}.$$

After relabelling k with r, the result is exactly the same as $\mathbb{P}^A_{ME}(p)$ given in (3). Thus Lemma B is equivalent to Lemma A.

Equivalence of Lemmas 5 and 6. Consider now Lemma 5, a preventive simplification shows that the index of the outer sum over ℓ can be made start from $d = 2t+1$ because for $\ell = 0$ the binomial term $\binom{\ell}{\ell-s+r} = 0$. Then for $\ell = 1, \ldots, 2t$ the weights A_ℓ of the code are all zero. The same binomial can be substituted by symmetry with $\binom{\ell}{s-r}$. With similar reasoning on the binomials, it is possible to make the summation over r run from $r_1 = w - l$ or 0 to $r_2 = w - l + s$. In fact, e.g. for r_2, the binomial $\binom{s-r}{(w-l+s)-2r}$ will have a negative argument and thus is zero. Similarly, when r_1 is negative the first binomial has a negative argument, and for $0 \le r_1 < |w-l|$ the last binomial is zero. Hence the bounds r_1 and r_2 by [5] are very accurate and reduce the effort of computation over dummy indexes. Rewrite Lemma 5 as

$$\mathbb{P}^C_{ME}(p) = \sum_{\ell=2t+1}^{n} A_\ell \sum_{s=0}^{t} \sum_{w=t+1}^{n} \sum_{r=w-l}^{w-l+s} \binom{n-\ell}{r}\binom{\ell}{s-r}\binom{s-r}{w-\ell+s-2r}$$
$$\cdot\left(\frac{p}{q-1}\right)^{w}(1-p)^{n-w}\cdot(q-2)^{w-\ell+s-2r}(q-1)^r. \tag{2}$$

In the formula (6) of Lemma 6, notice that $r, s \le t$ so that $r + s < 2t + 1 = d$. The sum over ℓ can run just over $\ell = d, \ldots, n$, because if $\ell - w > t$ the binomial $\binom{n-\ell}{r+w-\ell} = \binom{n-l}{r-(l-w)}$ will have a negative argument and is therefore zero, when $\ell - w < -t$, the third binomial has a negative argument. Thus it is possible to swap the sum over ℓ with the sum over w and obtain,

$$\mathbb{P}^D_{ME}(p) = \sum_{\ell=2t+1}^{n} A_\ell \sum_{w=t+1}^{n} \sum_{s=|l-w|}^{t} \sum_{r=0}^{s} \binom{\ell}{r}\binom{n-\ell}{r+w-\ell}\binom{\ell-r}{s+\ell-w-2r}$$
$$\cdot\left(\frac{p}{q-1}\right)^{w}(1-p)^{n-w}\cdot(q-2)^{s+\ell-w-2r}(q-1)^{r+w-\ell}.$$

Now with the change of variable $r \rightarrow r + w - \ell$ the new sum over r runs from $w - \ell$ to $s + w - l$, and the first binomial becomes, by symmetry, $\binom{\ell}{w - \ell}$. Observe then that the index s runs from t to zero, therefore it is possible to reorder the sum for $s = 0, \ldots, t$. Those simplifications lead to

$$
\mathbb{P}_{\mathrm{ME}}^D(p) = \sum_{\ell=2t+1}^n A_\ell \sum_{w=t+1}^n \sum_{s=0}^t \sum_{r=w-\ell}^{s+w-\ell} \binom{\ell}{w-r} \binom{n-\ell}{r} \binom{w-r}{s+w-\ell-2r}
$$
$$
\left(\frac{p}{q-1} \right)^w (1-p)^{n-w} \cdot (q-2)^r (q-1)^{s+w-\ell-2r},
$$

which resembles equation (2) apart from the role of w in the three binomials. After a sharp look, it is possible to substitute the missing s with the w without changing the result, because of a combined simplification of the binomials, in particular:

$$
\binom{n-\ell}{r} \binom{\ell}{w-r} \binom{w-r}{s+w-\ell-2r} = \binom{n-\ell}{r} \binom{\ell}{s-r} \binom{s-r}{w-\ell+s-2r},
$$

which can be easily verified expanding with factorials. Therefore $\mathbb{P}_{\mathrm{ME}}^C(p) = \mathbb{P}_{\mathrm{ME}}^D(p)$.

The last part of the proof is that Lemma 4 is equivalent to Lemma 5: in Lemma 4 consider the quantity $1 - p/(q-1)$, it can be recast into $[(q-2) + (1-p)]/(q-1)$. Therefore, with Newton's Binomial Theorem, $[1 - p/(q-1)]^{s-r}$ becomes

$$
\frac{1}{(q-1)^{s-r}} \sum_{j=0}^{s-r} \binom{s-r}{j} (q-2)^j (1-p)^{s-r-j}.
$$

Hence, Lemma 4 can be expanded as,

$$
\mathbb{P}_{\mathrm{ME}}^B(p) = \sum_{\ell=2t+1}^n A_\ell \sum_{s=0}^t \sum_{r=0}^s \sum_{j=0}^{s-r} \binom{n-\ell}{r} \binom{\ell}{s-r} \binom{s-r}{j}
$$
$$
\cdot \left(\frac{p}{q-1} \right)^{\ell-s+r} (q-1)^{r-s} (q-2)^j (1-p)^{n-\ell-2r+s-j} p^r,
$$

where, after collecting terms,

$$
\mathbb{P}_{\mathrm{ME}}^B(p) = \sum_{\ell=2t+1}^n A_\ell \sum_{s=0}^t \sum_{r=0}^s \binom{n-\ell}{r} \binom{\ell}{s-r}
$$
$$
\cdot \left(\frac{p}{q-1} \right)^{\ell-s+2r} (q-1)^r (1-p)^{n-\ell-r}
$$
$$
\cdot \sum_{j=0}^{s-r} \binom{s-r}{j} (q-1)^{r-s-j} (q-2)^j (1-p)^{s-r-j}.
$$

It is now possible to make use of Lemma 7 and substitute the last sum over j as follows:

$$\mathbb{P}^B_{ME}(p) = \sum_{\ell=2t+1}^{n} A_\ell \sum_{s=0}^{t} \sum_{r=0}^{s} \sum_{j=0}^{s-r} \binom{n-\ell}{r} \binom{\ell}{s-r} \binom{s-r}{j}$$
$$\cdot \left(\frac{p}{q-1}\right)^{j+\ell-s+2r} (q-1)^r (q-2)^j (1-p)^{n-(j+\ell-s+2r)}.$$

The substitution $w = j + \ell - s + 2r$ yields something that is almost equal to the modified version of Lemma 5 in equation (2):

$$\sum_{\ell=d}^{n} A_\ell \sum_{s=0}^{t} \sum_{r=0}^{s} \sum_{w=\ell-s+2r}^{\ell+r} \binom{n-\ell}{r} \binom{\ell}{s-r} \binom{s-r}{w-\ell+s-2r}$$
$$\cdot \left(\frac{p}{q-1}\right)^{w} (q-1)^r (q-2)^{w-\ell+s-2r} (1-p)^{n-w}.$$

The differences with (2) are the order of the inner sums. To exchange the sum over r with the sum over w, the new indexes must be $w = \ell - s, \ldots, \ell + s$ and $r = w - \ell, \ldots, w - \ell + s$, where the upper limit of r was simplified using the same consideration on the third binomial discussed above for r_2. With similar considerations it is possible to extend the range of w to $w = t+1, \ldots, n$, because for values smaller than $\ell - s$ the first binomial will have a negative r and for values greater than $\ell + s$ the other binomials will have negative argument. The result is exactly $\mathbb{P}^C_{ME}(p)$ and the proof is complete.   □

4   An Application with Numerical Results

$\mathbb{P}_D(p)$ is the *probability of detected codeword error*, the probability that one or more errors occurring in a codeword are detected. $\mathbb{P}_F(p)$ is the *probability of decoder failure*, which is the probability that the decoder is unable to decode the received vector (and is able to determine that it cannot decode). The following check is performed: comparison between the theoretical $\mathbb{P}_E(w)$ and the "real" one, obtained by bruteforce decoding, this last identified as $\mathbb{P}^r_E(w)$. Suppose to send the zero codeword, if an arbitrary error occurs, it is possible to receive every possible vector of $(\mathbb{F}_q)^n$. After the correction, five cases can happen:

1. the received vector lies in the correct decoding sphere and is decoded to the sent word;
2. the received vector lies in a wrong decoding sphere and is decoded to a wrong codeword;
3. the vector is outside of any decoding sphere but is close to only one codeword and is decoded to the sent word;
4. the vector is outside of any decoding sphere but is close to only one codeword and is decoded to a wrong codeword;

5. the vector is outside of any decoding sphere and there are more codewords at the same distance, so a decoding failure happens.

In the next examples all decoded vectors (according to the weight w of the error) are divided in three sets: the set D_w of the vectors correctly decoded (cases 1 and 3), the set S_w of the miscorrected vectors (cases 2 and 4), and the set of the failures F_w (case 5). The number C_w gives the number of elements of case 2, hence they are expected to be $|S_w| \geq C_w$. Furthermore $|S_0|, \ldots, |S_t|$ should be all zero. The next two toy examples show a case on $\mathbb{F}_2$ where $|S_w| = C_w$ and a case on $\mathbb{F}_3$ where $|S_w| > C_w$.

4.1   Example over $\mathbb{F}_2$

Let C be the linear code $[5, 2, 3]$ over $\mathbb{F}_2$ with generator matrix

$$G = \begin{pmatrix} 1\,0\,1\,0\,1 \\ 0\,1\,0\,1\,1 \end{pmatrix}.$$

In this example there is no difference between the theorical formula and the bruteforce, see Table 1.

Table 1. Results for the linear code $[5, 2, 3]$ over $\mathbb{F}_2$. A_w is the weight distribution, $|D_w|$ is the number of the vectors correctly decoded, $|F_w|$ the number of failures, $|S_w|$ the number of miscorrected vectors, $|C_w|$ the number of vectors in the wrong decoding sphere.

w	A_w	$|D_w|$	$|F_w|$	$|S_w|$	C_w	$\mathbb{P}_E^r(w)$	$\mathbb{P}_E(w)$
0	1	1	0	0	(1)	0	0
1	0	5	0	0	(5)	0	0
2	0	0	4	6	6	3/5	3/5
3	2	0	4	6	6	3/5	3/5
4	1	0	0	5	5	1	1
5	0	0	0	1	1	1	1

4.2   Example over $\mathbb{F}_3$

Let C be the linear code $[5, 2, 3]$ over $\mathbb{F}_3$ with generator matrix

$$G = \begin{pmatrix} 1\,0\,1\,2\,0 \\ 0\,1\,0\,1\,1 \end{pmatrix}$$

In this example there are some vectors outside the decoding spheres, the results are collected in Table 2. Notice that $|S_w| > C_w$ and so $\mathbb{P}_E^r(w) \geq \mathbb{P}_E(w)$.

Table 2. Results for the linear code $[5, 2, 3]$ over $\mathbb{F}_3$. A_w is the weight distribution, $|D_w|$ is the number of the vectors correctly decoded, $|F_w|$ the number of failures, $|S_w|$ the number of miscorrected vectors, $|C_w|$ the number of vectors in the wrong decoding sphere.

w	A_w	$|D_w|$	$|F_w|$	$|S_w|$	C_w	$\mathbb{P}_E^r(w)$	$\mathbb{P}_E(w)$
0	1	1	0	0	(1)	0	0
1	0	10	0	0	(10)	0	0
2	0	8	20	12	12	3/10	3/10
3	4	0	16	64	24	4/5	3/10
4	2	0	28	52	36	13/20	9/20
5	2	0	8	24	16	3/4	1/2

5   Comments and Conclusions

In the literature of ECC there are at least four different formulations of the probability of miscorrected error. They have been presented in Lemmas 3, 4, 5 and 6, with some comments for Lemma 5, probably the most known. It has been proved that they are equivalent, hence it is useful to point out what is the most practical formula in terms of complexity. The complexity of Lemmas 3 and 4 is the same, the number of iterations of the sums required to evaluate the $\mathbb{P}_{ME}(p)$ is $\gamma = \frac{1}{2}(n-2t)(t+2)(t+1) \leq n^3$, whereas for Lemmas 5 and 6 a rough estimate is $\gamma(n-t) \leq n^4$, which is one factor greater. Nevertheless, formulation of $\mathbb{P}_{ME}^C(p)$ gives information on the $\mathbb{P}_E(w)$ which can be useful in some applications, where the number of errors beyond t has importance.

References

1. Biasi, N., Setti, F., Del Bue, A., Tavernini, M., Lunardelli, M., Fornaser, A., Da Lio, M., De Cecco, M.: Garment-based motion capture (gamocap): high-density capture of human shape in motion. Mach. Vis. Appl. **26**(7–8), 955–973 (2015)
2. Blahut, R.E.: Theory and Practice of Error Control Codes. Addison-Wesley Pub. Co., Massachusetts (1983)
3. Caruso, F., Orsini, E., Sala, M., Tinnirello, C.: On the shape of the general error locator polynomial for cyclic codes. IEEE Trans. Inf. Theor. **63**(6), 3641–3657 (2017)
4. Faldum, A., Lafuente, J., Ochoa, G., Willems, W.: Error probabilities for bounded distance decoding. Des. Codes Crypt. **40**(2), 237–252 (2006)
5. Huntoon, Z., Michelson, A.: On the computation of the probability of post-decoding error events for block codes (corresp.). IEEE Trans. Inf. Theor. **23**(3), 399–403 (1977)
6. Kim, M.G., Lee, J.H.: Decoder error probability of binary linear block codes and its application to binary primitive bch codes. IEICE Trans. Fundam. Electron. Commun. Comput. Sci. **E79–A**(4), 592–599 (1996)

7. McWilliams, F.J., Sloane, N.J.A.: The Theory of Error-correcting Codes. North-Holland, Amsterdam (1977)
8. Moon, T.K.: Error Correction Coding: Mathematical Methods and Algorithms. Wiley-Interscience, Hoboken (2005)
9. Piva, M., Sala, M.: A new bound for cyclic codes beating the roos bound. In: Muntean, T., Poulakis, D., Rolland, R. (eds.) CAI 2013. LNCS, vol. 8080, pp. 101–112. Springer, Heidelberg (2013). https://doi.org/10.1007/978-3-642-40663-8_11
10. Roman, S.: Introduction to Coding and Information Theory. Undergraduate Texts in Mathematics. Springer, New York (1997)
11. Torrieri, D.J.: Principles of Spread-Spectrum Communication Systems. Springer, Cham (2005)
12. Vanstone, S.A., van Oorschot, P.C.: An Introduction to Error Correcting Codes with Applications. Kluwer International Series in Engineering and Computer Science: Communications and Information Theory. Springer, New York (1989)
13. Wicker, S.B.: Reed-solomon error control coding for rayleigh fading channels with feedback. IEEE Trans. Veh. Technol. 41(2), 124–133 (1992)
14. Wicker, S.B.: Error Control Systems for Digital Communication and Storage. Prentice Hall, New Jersey (1995)
15. Xia, S.-T., Fu, F.-W.: Undetected error probability of q-ary constant weight codes. Des. Codes Crypt. 48(2), 125–140 (2008)

Improvement on Minimum Distance
of Symbol-Pair Codes

Han Zhang$^{(\boxtimes)}$ ⓘ

Northwest University, Xuefu Dadao, Xi'an 710127, China
`micohanzhang@hotmail.com`

Abstract. Symbol-pair codes were first introduced by Cassuto and Blaum (2010). The minimum pair distance of a code is a criterion that characterises the error correcting capability of the code with respect to pair errors. The codes that achieve the optimal minimum pair distance (for given codeword length, code book size and alphabet) are called Maximum Distance Separable (MDS) symbol-pair codes. A way to study the minimum pair distance of a code is through its connection to the minimum Hamming distance of the code. For certain structured codes, these two types of distances can be very different. Yaakobi et al. (2016) showed that for a binary cyclic code, the minimum pair distance is almost three halves of its minimum Hamming distance. We extend this connection to q-ary (q is a prime power) constacyclic codes. The extension involves non-trivial usage of the double counting technique in combinatorics. Such a connection naturally yields a constructive lower bound on the minimum pair distance of q-ary symbol-pair codes. For some choices of the code parameters, this lower bound matches the Singleton type upper bound, yielding q-ary MDS symbol-pair codes.

Keywords: Coding theory · Symbol-pair codes · Cyclic codes · Constacyclic codes · MDS symbol-pair codes

1 Introduction

In [1], Cassuto and Blaum introduced a new coding model in which reading from the channel is performed as overlapping pairs of symbols. In other words, each channel read involves the contribution from two adjacent symbols, called pair-read symbols. For example, if the recorded sequence is $(0, 1, 1)$, then the output of the symbol-pair read channel would be $[(0, 1), (1, 1), (1, 0)]$. The symbol-pair weight of the word $(0, 1, 1)$ is the Hamming weight of its pair-read vector $[(0, 1), (1, 1), (1, 0)]$, which is 3. The pair distance of two words is the symbol-pair weight of the difference of the two words. A symbol-pair code is a set of words, where instead of Hamming distance, pair distance is considered. To distinguish the notations, we use d_H to denote the minimum Hamming distance and d_p to denote the minimum pair distance. It was shown in [1] that if a code has minimum pair distance d_p, then it can correct up to $\lfloor (d_p - 1)/2 \rfloor$ symbol-pair errors. In this case, we want to construct symbol-pair codes with a large minimum pair

© Springer International Publishing AG 2017
M. O'Neill (Ed.): IMACC 2017, LNCS 10655, pp. 116–124, 2017.
https://doi.org/10.1007/978-3-319-71045-7_6

distance. For a fixed code length n, it would be good if both the code size M and the minimum pair distance d_p could be as large as possible. However, there is a trade-off between these two parameters. Chee *et al.* in [2] established a Singleton-type bound on symbol-pair codes and constructed classes of symbol-pair codes with respect to d_p which meet the Singleton-type bound, called MDS symbol-pair codes. Recently, constacyclic codes over finite fields have been used to construct quantum MDS code [8]. Kai *et al.* [4] constructed MDS symbol-pair codes from cyclic codes and almost MDS constacyclic codes.

The relation between the minimum Hamming distance d_H and minimum pair-distance d_p of a code is usually exploited in the study of the d_p. Cassuto *et al.* [1] established a relation between the minimum Hamming distance d_H of an error-correcting code and the minimum pair distance d_p, and obtained lower and upper bounds on d_p in terms of d_H. In particular, they showed that $d_H + 1 \leq d_p \leq 2d_H$. They also showed that the pair distance of cyclic codes is at least $d_H + 2$ and if instead the length is restricted and for any code, using Hartmann-Tzeng Bound (Theorem 11 [1]), the relation can be improved into $d_H + 3$. In a follow-up paper, Kai *et al.* [4] considered a slightly larger class, the constacyclic codes and obtained the same relation.

Yaakobi [3] *et al.* proved that, for binary linear cyclic codes the minimum pair distance d_p is at least $d_H + \lceil \frac{d_H}{2} \rceil$. In this paper, we first generalize this relation from binary cyclic symbol-pair codes to q-ary cyclic symbol-pair codes. The extension involves non-trivial usage of the double counting technique in combinatorics. As cyclic codes are a subclass of constacyclic codes, this naturally motivates one to consider symbol-pair codes from constacyclic codes. We then further extend the relation from q-ary cyclic codes to q-ary constacyclic codes. This relation over q-ary alphabet becomes $d_p \geq d_H + \lceil \frac{d_H}{2(q-1)} \rceil$ (for both cyclic and consta-cyclic). Using this relation and known lower bounds on d_H, we naturally obtained lower bounds on the minimum pair distance of q-ary symbol-pair codes. We show for some choices of parameters, this lower bound matches the Singleton type upper bound, yielding q-ary MDS symbol-pair codes.

The rest of the paper is organized as follows. In Sect. 2, we introduce the basic definition and notations as well as results of symbol-pair codes and Singleton-type bound. We also review the definition and lower bounds of cyclic codes and constacyclic codes. In Sect. 3, we deduce a relation between minimum pair distance and Hamming distance of linear cyclic codes from binary to q-ary. In Sect. 4, we derive some MDS symbol-pair codes with certain parameters.

From now on, $\mathbb{F}_q$ denotes a finite field with q elements, where q is a power of a prime number p.

2   Preliminaries

2.1   Symbol Pair Code

In this section, basic notations and results of *symbol − pair codes* are provided.

Let Σ denote a symbol alphabet, each element in Σ is called a *symbol*. Let $\boldsymbol{x} = (x_0, x_1, \cdots, x_{n-1})$ be a vector in Σ^n. Then the symbol-pair read vector of $\boldsymbol{x}$ is defined as

$$\pi(\boldsymbol{x}) = [(x_0, x_1), (x_1, x_2), \cdots, (x_{n-2}, x_{n-1}), (x_{n-1}, x_0)].$$

Note that $\pi(\boldsymbol{x}) \in (\Sigma \times \Sigma)^n$, and for $\boldsymbol{x}, \boldsymbol{y} \in \Sigma$,

$$\pi(\boldsymbol{x} + \boldsymbol{y}) = \pi(\boldsymbol{x}) + \pi(\boldsymbol{y}).$$

We say a symbol pair (a, b) differs from (c, d) if $a \neq c$ or $b \neq d$, or both. The all-zeros, all-ones vector is denoted by $\boldsymbol{0}, \boldsymbol{1}$, respectively. The minimum Hamming distance between two vectors $\boldsymbol{x}, \boldsymbol{y} \in \Sigma^n$ is denoted by $d_H(\boldsymbol{x}, \boldsymbol{y})$, and the Hamming weight of a vector $\boldsymbol{x}$ is denoted by $w_H(\boldsymbol{x})$. The pair-distance between $\boldsymbol{x}$ and $\boldsymbol{y}$ is defined as

$$d_p(\boldsymbol{x}, \boldsymbol{y}) = d_H(\pi(\boldsymbol{x}), \pi(\boldsymbol{y})).$$

For any vector $\boldsymbol{x} \in \Sigma^n$, the pair weight of $\boldsymbol{x}$ is $w_p(\boldsymbol{x}) = w_H(\pi(\boldsymbol{x}))$. A code $\mathcal{C}$ over Σ of length n is a nonempty set $\mathcal{C} \subseteq \Sigma^n$. Define the minimum pair-distance of $\mathcal{C}$ as

$$d_p(\mathcal{C}) = \min\{d_p(\boldsymbol{x}, \boldsymbol{y}) | \boldsymbol{x}, \boldsymbol{y} \in \mathcal{C}, \boldsymbol{x} \neq \boldsymbol{y}\}.$$

A code of length n over Σ is called an $(n, M, d_p)_q$-symbol-pair code if its size is M and the minimum pair distance is d_p.

It has been shown in [2] that an $(n, M, d)_q$-symbol-pair code must satisfy the following version of the Singleton-type bound.

Proposition 1. *(Singleton Bound) Let $q \geq 2$ and $2 \leq d_H \leq n$. If $\mathcal{C}$ is an $(n, M, d_H)_q$-symbol-pair code, then $M \leq q^{n-d_H+2}$.*

An $(n, M, d_H)_q$-symbol-pair code attains the Singleton-type bound, i.e., $M = q^{n-d_H+2}$, is said to be an maximum distance separable (MDS) symbol-pair code. On account of no code of length n with size M has a higher minimum pair distance than an MDS symbol-pair code, it is desirable to construct MDS symbol-pair code in theory and practice.

In Cassuto [1], it was shown that if a code has minimum pair distance d_p, then it can correct up to $\lfloor (d_p - 1)/2 \rfloor$ symbol-pair errors. For this reason, the purpose of constructing codes in symbol-pair read channels is to find a high minimum pair distance.

Cassuto and Blaum [1] provided two ways to construct symbol-pair codes. One is *interleaving* method, while codes constructed by interleaving method can obtain optimal pair-distance for their Hamming distance, but they have poor Hamming distance themselves. So it came out the second method: *linear cyclic codes*, which is the main focus of this paper.

2.2   Cyclic Codes and Constacyclic Codes

We know that cyclic codes are the special case of constacyclic codes. In this section, we start with general definitions and notations for *linear constacyclic codes* over finite fields.

Let q be a prime power and $\mathbb{F}_q$ be the finite field with q elements. If, in addtion, $\mathcal{C}$ is a linear subspace over $\mathbb{F}_q$ of $\mathbb{F}_q^n$, then $\mathcal{C}$ is called a *linear code*. A q-ary linear code of length n is a subspace of $\mathbb{F}_q^n$. For a nonzero element η in $\mathbb{F}_q$, the η-constacyclic shift τ_η on $\mathbb{F}_q^n$ is the shift

$$\tau_\eta(c_0, c_1, \ldots, c_{n-1}) = (\eta c_{n-1}, c_0, \ldots, c_{n-2})$$

A linear code $\mathcal{C}$ is said to be η-*constacyclic* if $\mathcal{C}$ is a τ_η-invariant subspace of $\mathbb{F}_q^n$, i.e., $\tau_\eta(\mathcal{C}) = \mathcal{C}$. It is obvious that if $\eta = 1$, then $\mathcal{C}$ is just the usual *cyclic code*.

In [3], Yaakobi *et al.* focused on binary vectors, i.e., $\Sigma = \{0, 1\}$, they deduced an improved lower bound on the minimum pair distance of linear cyclic codes by showing a relation between d_p and d_H. In order to give the improved lower bound, they first give a glance of the method to determine the pair weight of a vector $\boldsymbol{x}$. As we calculate the number of non-zero symbols, it can be obtained that the condition $(x_{i-1}, x_i) = (0, 1)$ contributes two new non-zero symbols to $\pi(\boldsymbol{x})$, and the condition $(x_{i-1}, x_i) = (1, 1)$ or $(x_{i-1}, x_i) = (1, 0)$ contributes one new non-zero symbol. Obviously, in order to determine the weight of $\pi(x)$, we need to know the number of $(x_{i-1}, x_i) = (0, 1)$ in the vector $\boldsymbol{x}$.

For $\boldsymbol{x} = (x_0, x_1, \ldots, x_{n-1})$, we define

$$\boldsymbol{x}' = (x_0 + x_1, x_1 + x_2, \ldots, x_{n-1} + x_0).$$

The next lemma gives a method to calculate the pair weight of any vector $\boldsymbol{x} \in \Sigma^n$.

Lemma 1. *([3]) For any $\boldsymbol{x} \in \Sigma^n$, $\omega_p(\boldsymbol{x}) = \omega_H(\boldsymbol{x}) + \omega_H(\boldsymbol{x}')/2$.*

Using the Lemma above, Yaakobi *et al.* deduced an improved lower bound on the minimum pair distance of linear cyclic codes.

Lemma 2. *([3]) Let $\mathcal{C}$ be a linear cyclic code of dimension greater than one. Then,*

$$d_p(\mathcal{C}) \geq d_H(\mathcal{C}) + \lceil \frac{d_H(\mathcal{C})}{2} \rceil.$$

Since the result of Yaakobi *et al.* is for the binary field, we will next generalize their lower bound to the q-ary case.

3   Lower Bounds on the Minimum Pair Distance of q-ary Linear Cyclic Codes and Constacyclic Codes

In this section, we give a lower bound on the minimum pair distance over q-ary vectors, and extend the result to constacyclic codes.

In order to determine the weight of $\pi(\boldsymbol{x})$, we need to determine the number of occurrences of the sequences $(x_{i-1}, x_i) = (0, \alpha)$ in the vector $\boldsymbol{x}$, where $\alpha \in \mathbb{F}_q^*$.

For $\boldsymbol{x} = (x_0, x_1, \cdots, x_{n-1})$, we define

$$\boldsymbol{x}_\lambda' = (x_0 + \lambda x_1, x_1 + \lambda x_2, \cdots, x_{n-1} + \lambda x_0), \lambda \in \mathbb{F}_q^*. \tag{1}$$

We now derive a lower bound on the minimum pair distance of q-ary cyclic codes.

Theorem 1. *Let $\mathcal{C}$ be a q-ary linear cyclic code of dimension greater than one. Then,*

$$d_p(\mathcal{C}) \geq d_H(\mathcal{C}) + \lceil \frac{d_H(\mathcal{C})}{2(q-1)} \rceil.$$

Proof. For any $\boldsymbol{x} \in \Sigma^n$, let $\boldsymbol{x} = (x_0, x_1, \cdots, x_{n-1})$ be a codeword in $\mathcal{C}$. Here, without loss of generality, first we assume that $\boldsymbol{x} \neq \boldsymbol{\alpha}, \alpha \in \mathbb{F}_q^*$. Since the code is cyclic, $(x_1, \cdots, x_{n-1}, x_0) \in \mathcal{C}$. Thus for any $\lambda \in \mathbb{F}_q^*$,

$$\boldsymbol{x}_\lambda' = (x_0, x_1, \cdots, x_{n-1}) + \lambda(x_1, \cdots, x_{n-1}, x_0) \in \mathcal{C}.$$

Now let

$$S_\alpha = \{i | (x_i, x_{i+1}) \neq (0, 0), x_i = \alpha\}, \alpha \in \mathbb{F}_q.$$

For $\alpha, \beta \in \mathbb{F}_q, \alpha \neq \beta$, one has $S_\alpha \cap S_\beta = \emptyset$ and $w_p(\boldsymbol{x}) = \sum_{\alpha \in \mathbb{F}_q} |S_\alpha| = w_H(x) + |S_0|$. In order to get $|S_0|$, we use the trick of double counting to calculate $\sum_{\lambda \in \mathbb{F}_q^*} w_H(\boldsymbol{x}_\lambda')$.

If there exists a sequence $(x_{i-1}, x_i) = (0, \alpha)$, then there must exist a sequence $(x_{j-1}, x_j) = (\beta, 0)$. We can deduce that the i-th place of $\boldsymbol{x}'$ could not be zero for any $\alpha, \beta \in \mathbb{F}_q^*$. Hence, each element of S_0 contributes two new non-zero symbols for each $\lambda \in \mathbb{F}_q^*$. For each element $(\alpha, \beta) \in S_\alpha, \alpha, \beta \in \mathbb{F}_q^*$, the equation $\alpha + \lambda\beta = 0$ has exact one root in $\mathbb{F}_q^*$. It follows that each element $(\alpha, \beta) \in S_\alpha$ with $\alpha, \beta \in \mathbb{F}_q^*$ contributes $q - 2$ non-zero symbols when q runs through $\mathbb{F}_q^*$. Thus, one has

$$\sum_{\lambda \in \mathbb{F}_q^*} w_H(\boldsymbol{x}_\lambda') = 2(q-1)|S_0| + (q-2) \sum_{\lambda \in \mathbb{F}_q^*} |S_\alpha|$$

$$= 2(q-1)|S_0| + (q-2)w_H(\boldsymbol{x}).$$

Then we can deduce that

$$|S_0| = \frac{1}{2(q-1)} \sum_{\lambda \in \mathbb{F}_q^*} w_H(\boldsymbol{x}_\lambda') - \frac{q-2}{2(q-1)} w_H(\boldsymbol{x}).$$

It follows that

$$
\begin{aligned}
w_p(\boldsymbol{x}) &= w_H(x) + |S_0| \\
&= \frac{1}{2(q-1)} \sum_{\lambda \in \mathbb{F}_q^*} w_H(\boldsymbol{x}_\lambda') - \frac{q-2}{2(q-1)} w_H(\boldsymbol{x}) + w_H(\boldsymbol{x}) \\
&\geq \frac{d_H}{2} - \frac{q-2}{2(q-1)} d_H + d_H \\
&= \frac{d_H}{2(q-1)} + d_H
\end{aligned}
$$

Hence,

$$
w_p(\boldsymbol{x}) \geq \lceil \frac{d_H}{2(q-1)} \rceil + d_H.
$$

Remark 1. If $q = 2$, we can recover the same result from [3].

In the next theorem, as cyclic codes are a subclass of constacyclic codes, we deduce that for a nonzero element η in $\mathbb{F}_q$, a η-constacyclic code $\mathcal{C}$ of length n also holds the similar result as Thoerem 1.

Theorem 2. *Let $\mathcal{C}$ be a q-ary η-constacyclic code of dimension greater than one. Then,*

$$
d_p(\mathcal{C}) \geq d_H(\mathcal{C}) + \lceil \frac{d_H(\mathcal{C})}{2(q-1)} \rceil.
$$

Proof. Let $\boldsymbol{x} = (x_0, x_1, \cdots, x_{n-1})$ be a codeword in $\mathcal{C}$. We know that

$$
\tau_\eta(\boldsymbol{x}) = (\eta x_{n-1}, x_0, \cdots, x_{n-2}) \in \mathcal{C}.
$$

We define

$$
\begin{aligned}
\boldsymbol{x}_{\eta\lambda} &= \boldsymbol{x} + \tau_\eta(\boldsymbol{x}) \\
&= (x_0 + \lambda \eta x_{n-1}, x_1 + \lambda x_0, \cdots, x_{n-1} + \lambda x_0).
\end{aligned}
$$

For any nonzero $\lambda \in \mathbb{F}_q^*$, we can deduce that

$$
\sum_{\lambda \in \mathbb{F}_q^*} w_H(\boldsymbol{x}_{\eta\lambda}) = 2(q-1)|S_0| + (q-2)w_H(\boldsymbol{x}).
$$

Then, from Thoerem 1 we can derive

$$
d_p(\mathcal{C}) \geq d_H(\mathcal{C}) + \lceil \frac{d_H(\mathcal{C})}{2(q-1)} \rceil.
$$

In [9](Theorem 1.1), Chen *et al.* presented a lower bound for the minimum pair distance of constacyclic codes. Let $\mathcal{C}$ be an $[n, k, d_H]$ constacyclic code over $\mathbb{F}_q$ with $2 \leq d_H \leq n$. Then they deduced the following.

(1) $d_p(\mathcal{C}) \geq d_H + 2$ if and only if $\mathcal{C}$ is not an MDS code, i.e., $k < n - d_H + 1$. Equivalently, $d_p(\mathcal{C}) = d_H + 1$ if and only if $\mathcal{C}$ is an MDS codes, i.e., $k = n - d_H + 1$.

(2) If $k > 1$ and $n - d_H \geq 2k - 1$, then $d_p(\mathcal{C}) \geq d_H + 3$.

Compared with the results above, it can be seen that if we have sufficiently large d_H and sufficiently small q in Theorem 1, our result $d_H + \lceil \frac{d_H}{2(q-1)} \rceil$ improves the result $d_H + 3$ in [1].

So far, we derive lower bounds of cyclic codes and constacyclic codes, next section we use them to construct some MDS symbol-pair codes with certain parameters.

4   Some Specific MDS Symbol-Pair Codes Constructed by Constacyclic Codes

Cyclic codes were used to construct symbol-pair codes and gave a good pair-error correctability. In the former sections, we deduce a lower bound for codes over q-ary. As cyclic codes are a subclass of constacyclic codes, in this section, we yield some classes of new MDS symbol-pair codes with certain parameters by constacyclic codes with respect to Hamming distance.

Example 1.   (1) Let $\mathcal{C}$ be a $[23, 3, 19]_5$ η-constacyclic code, there exists an MDS $[23, 22]_5$-symbol-pair code. (2) Let $\mathcal{C}$ be a $[11, 5, 6]$ η-constacyclic code over $\mathbb{F}_3$, there exists an MDS $(11, 8)_3$-symbol-pair code.

Put the certain parameters d, q into $d_p(\mathcal{C}) \geq d_H + \lceil \frac{d_H}{2(q-1)} \rceil$, we obtain $d_p(\mathcal{C}) \geq 22$, it meets the Singleton Bound of symbol-pair codes when equality holds, so we construct a MDS symbol-pair code.

Note that a linear $[n, k, n - k]$-code over $\mathbb{F}_q$ is called an almost MDS code [5]. Therefore, the code $[11, 5, 6]_3$ is an almost MDS code.

5   Conclusion

In this paper, we study the symbol-pair codes and deduce a lower bound on the minimum pair distance of q-ary constacyclic codes. It has enabled us to construct some q-ary MDS symbol-pair codes with certain parameters by using constacyclic codes over $\mathbb{F}_q$. Comparing with the construction methods before, our MDS symbol-pair codes have been constructed directly from both constasyclic codes and almost MDS codes.

Clearly, the result in this paper can just construct some MDS symbol-pair codes with certain parameters but not a class of MDS symbol-pair codes. Furthermore, it is not clear whether the lower bound on the minimum pair-distance of a constacyclic code can be improved. Finally, several other topics relating to symbol-pair codes have not been explored, such as tight upper bounds, and optimal code constructions by using constacyclic codes.

Acknowledgment. The author expresses her gratitude to Liming Ma and Fuchun Lin for their instructive and useful suggestions of this paper.

Appendix

For better understanding,we give detailed proof of Lemma 1.

Proof. Let $\boldsymbol{x} = (x_0, x_1, \cdots, x_{n-1}) \in \Sigma^n$. Our goal is to calculate $w_p(\boldsymbol{x})$, namely,

$$w_p(\boldsymbol{x}) = wt\{(x_0, x_1), (x_1, x_2), \cdots, (x_{n-1}, x_0)\}.$$

Now we let

$S_0 = \{i : (x_i, x_{i+1}) \neq (0, 0) \text{ and } x_i = 1\}$,
$S_1 = \{i : (x_i, x_{i+1}) = (0, 1)\}$.

In the cases above, S_0 contains all the pairs $(1, 0)$ and $(1, 1)$. S_1 contains all the pairs $(0, 1)$. Hence, $|S_0| = \omega_H(\boldsymbol{x})$, $S_0 \cap S_1 = \emptyset$, and $\omega_p(\boldsymbol{x}) = |S_0| + |S_1|$. For all $0 \leq i \leq n - 1$, $i \in S_1$ if and only if $x_{i+1} = 1$ and $x_i = 0$. Thus, $x_i + x_{i+1} = 1$ or $x'_{i+1} = 1$, where $x_i = 0$. Hence, we get

$$|S_1| = |\{i : x_{i+1} = 1 \text{ and } x_i = 0\}|.$$

Note that for any $\boldsymbol{x} \in \Sigma^n$,

$$|\{i : x_{i+1} = 1 \text{ and } x_i = 0\}| = |\{i : x_{i+1} = 0 \text{ and } x_i = 1\}|,$$

and the sum of the cardinality of the two sets is $\omega_H(\boldsymbol{x}')$. Hence, $S_1 = \frac{\omega_H(\boldsymbol{x}')}{2}$ and

$$\omega_p(\boldsymbol{x}) = |S_0| + |S_1| = \omega_H(\boldsymbol{x}) + \frac{\omega_H(\boldsymbol{x}')}{2}.$$

References

1. Cassuto, Y., Blaum, M.: Codes for symbol-pair read channels. Trans. Inf. Theory **57**(12), 8011–8020 (2011)
2. Chee, Y.M., Kiah, H. M., Wang, C.: Maximum distance separable symbol-pair codes. In: Proceedings of International Symposium Information Theory, Cambridge, MA, USA, pp. 2886–2890 (2012)
3. Yaakobi, E., Bruck. J., Siegel, P.H.: Construction and decoding of cyclic codes over *b*-symbol read channels. IEEE Trans. Inf. Theory **62**(4) (2016)
4. Kai, X.S., Zhu, S.X., Li, P.: A construction of new MDS symbol-pair codes. IEEE Trans. Inf. Theory **61**(11) (2015)
5. De Boer, M.A.: Almost MDS codes. Designs Codes Cryptogr. **9**(2), 143–155 (1996)
6. Chee, Y.M., Ji, L., Kiah, H.M., Wang, C., Yin, J.: Maximum distance separable codes for symbol-pair read channels. IEEE Trans. Inf. Theory **59**(11), 7259–7267 (2013)
7. Chen, B., Lin, L., Liu, H.: Constacyclic symbol-pair codes: lower bounds and optimal constructions. arXiv:1605. 03460v1 [cs. IT] (2016)
8. Kai, X.S., Zhu, S.X., Li, P.: Constacyclic codes and some new quantum MDS codes. IEEE Trans. Inf. Theory **60**(4), 2080–2086 (2014)
9. Chen, B., Ling, S., Zhang, G.: Application of constacyclic codes to quantum MDS codes. IEEE Trans. Inf. Theory **61**(3), 1474–1484 (2015)

10. Cassuto, Y., Blaum, M.: Codes for symbol-pair read channels. In: Proceedings of International Symposium Information Theory, Austin, TX, USA, pp. 988–992 (2010)
11. Cassuto, Y., Litsyn, S.: Symbol-pair codes: algebraic constructions and asymptotic bounds. In: Proceedings of International Symposium Information Theory, St. Petersburg, Russia, pp. 2348–2352 (2011)
12. Chee, Y.M., Kiah, H.M., Wang, C.: Maximum distance separable symbol-pair codes. In: Proceedings of International Symposium Information Theory, Cambridge, MA, USA, pp. 2886–2890 (2012)
13. Yaakobi, E., Bruck, J., Siegel, P.H.: Decoding of Cyclic Codes over Symbol-Pair Read Channels. In: Proceedings of International Symposium Information Theory, Cambridge, MA, USA, pp. 2891–2895 (2012)
14. Li, S.X., Ge, G.N.: Constructions of maximum distance separable symbol-pair codes using cyclic and constacyclic codes. Des. Codes Crytogr. **84**, 359–372 (2017). https://doi.org/10.1007/s10623-016-0271-y

Bilinear and Multilinear Maps

Bilinear Cryptography Using Groups of Nilpotency Class 2

Ayan Mahalanobis$^{(\boxtimes)}$ and Pralhad Shinde

Indian Institute of Science Education and Research Pune,
Dr. Homi Bhabha Road, Pashan, Pune, India
ayan.mahalanobis@gmail.com

Abstract. In this paper, we develop a novel idea of a bilinear cryptosystem using the discrete logarithm problem in matrices. These matrices come from a linear representation of a group of nilpotency class 2. We discuss an example at the end.

1 Introduction

Simply stated, this paper is an application of nilpotency class 2 groups in bilinear public-key cryptography to build a secure bilinear cryptosystem. Bilinear or pairing based cryptosystems are used in many practical situations such as the following:

- Identity based encryption: In this case the user's public-key is based on his own identity, like his email address or phone number, see [4].
- Short signatures: Signature schemes where the signature is short, about half the size of the original signatures, see [3].
- Key exchange: Tripartite Diffie-Hellman key exchange [2,8].
- And others.

We are not going to survey all of pairing-based cryptographic protocols but will refer the reader to [6]. However, we briefly talk about the tripartite Diffie-Hellman key exchange protocol purely as a motivation to our paper.

2 A Brief Introduction to Bilinear Public-Key Cryptography

The origin of pairing based cryptosystems is in the MOV attack [10] on the elliptic curve discrete logarithm problem. The attack was first envisioned by Gerhard Frey. The idea was to use the bilinear properties of the Weil pairing to reduce a discrete logarithm problem in an elliptic curve over a finite field $\mathbb{F}_q$ to a discrete logarithm problem in $\mathbb{F}_{q^k}$. It is known [1] that most of the time for non super-singular curves, this k, the embedding degree is very large.

This research was supported by a NBHM and a SERB research grant.

M. O'Neill (Ed.): IMACC 2017, LNCS 10655, pp. 127–134, 2017.
https://doi.org/10.1007/978-3-319-71045-7_7

The Weil or the Tate pairing is a bilinear map

$$B : G \times G \to \mathbb{F}_{q^k}.$$

Where G is the (abelian) group of the elliptic curve written additively. Then the discrete logarithm problem in G to the base $g \in G$ is given g and αg find α. It was Joux [8] who first noticed that one can manipulate the bilinear map to deliver a one-round tripartite Diffie-Hellman key exchange protocol. The idea of using a bilinear map can also be traced back to the work of Dan Boneh on the decisional Diffie-Hellman problem. Let $\mathcal{A}, \mathcal{B}$ and $\mathcal{C}$ be three users who want to set up a common secret key among themselves. Then choose three integers α, β and γ respectively and keep it a secret. They then compute αg, βg and γg respectively from the public information $G = \langle g \rangle$ and broadcast this information over the public channel. The user $\mathcal{A}$ on receiving βg, γg can compute $B(\beta g, \gamma g)^{\alpha}$ using his private key α. The same thing can be computed by $\mathcal{B}$ and $\mathcal{C}$ by using the public information of the other two users and his private information. The common key becomes $B(g, g)^{\alpha \beta \gamma}$. All is well and nice in what we just said, except that B being a alternate(skew-symmetric) map, $B(g, g) = 1$. There are many approaches to solve that problem, one was proposed by Joux [8] and the other using a distortion map. In the interest of brevity of this paper we won't go into further details of pairing based cryptosystems using elliptic curve. We will just have to comment on a few things. There are lots of issues with elliptic curve pairing. The most important of those are, how to find curves with right embedding degree and what is the right embedding degree?

3   A Brief Introduction to Nilpotency Class 2 Groups and Commutator Identities

For any group G we can define the lower-central series as follows:

$$G := \gamma_0(G) \trianglerighteq \gamma_1(G) \trianglerighteq \cdots \trianglerighteq \gamma_k(G) \cdots$$

Where $\gamma_i(G) = [\gamma_{i-1}(G), G]$, $i > 1$. Let x, y be elements of a group G, we follow the usual definition of a commutator as $[x, y] = x^{-1} y^{-1} xy$. For two subgroups, H and K of G we define $[H, K] = \langle [h, k] \mid h \in H, k \in K \rangle$. If the central series stops at identity, then we call that group a nilpotent group. If the length of the series is c, i.e., $\gamma_{c+1}(G) = 1$, then we call it a nilpotent group of class c. This c is also often referred to as the nilpotency class of a group or simply the class. In this paper we refer the nilpotent class simply as the class. It is not hard to show that if G is a group of class c, then any commutator $[x_1, x_2, ..., x_{c+1}]$ of weight $c + 1$ is the identity.

Nilpotent groups of class 2 have many properties similar to that of abelian groups. We state without proof a well known lemma about groups of class 2.

Lemma 1. *Let $x, y \in G$ and assume that both x and y commute with $[x, y]$ then:*

(a) $[x, y]^n = [x^n, y] = [x, y^n]$ *for all integer n*

(b) $(xy)^n = x^n y^n [y, x]^{\frac{n(n-1)}{2}}$ *for all* $n \geq 0$

For a proof see Rotman [12, Lemma 5.42]. The above lemma is a restatement of the fact, that in a nilpotent group of class 2, the map $x \mapsto [a, x]$ for a fixed a is a linear map. This gives rise to the fact that $(x, y) \mapsto [x, y]$ is a bilinear map from $G \times G \to G$. This is the central idea that we are going to use next. However, at this point we are obliged to report that in the case of groups of class 2, the bilinear map is from the group to the same group. Unlike the case of elliptic curves, where the bilinear map is from the group of an elliptic curve to a finite field. This change can have a profound effect on bilinear cryptography, especially in designing protocols.

4   The Central Idea

Let G be a group of nilpotency class 2. As discussed earlier, there are three users – $\mathcal{A}$, $\mathcal{B}$ and $\mathcal{C}$ with private exponent α, β and γ respectively. The main formula on which this key-exchange protocol is based an identity in a nilpotent group of class 2.

$$[x, y]^n = [x^n, y] = [x, y^n] \tag{1}$$

As with the tripartite Diffie-Hellman key exchange, the users $\mathcal{A}$ and $\mathcal{B}$ and $\mathcal{C}$ transmits in public x^α, y^α; x^β, y^β and x^γ, y^γ respectively in public.

Key Exchange. The tripartite key-exchange is as follows: On receiving x^β, y^γ through the public channel, the user $\mathcal{A}$ can compute $[x^\beta, y^\gamma]^\alpha = [x, y]^{\alpha\beta\gamma}$. On receiving x^α, y^γ through the public channel, the user $\mathcal{B}$ can compute $[x^\alpha, y^\gamma]^\beta = [x, y]^{\alpha\beta\gamma}$. On receiving x^α, y^β through the public channel, the user $\mathcal{C}$ can compute $[x^\alpha, y^\beta]^\gamma = [x, y]^{\alpha\beta\gamma}$. The common key is $[x, y]^{\alpha\beta\gamma}$.

4.1   The Primary Security Concerns

The primary security concerns are as follows:

- Given x and x^α find α. The same can be said for y. This is the classic discrete logarithm problem.
- From the information x^α and y, one can compute $[x^\alpha, y] = [x, y]^\alpha$. Then it turns out to be the discrete logarithm problem in $[x, y]$.
- Note that $[x^\alpha, y^\beta] = [x, y]^{\alpha\beta}$. Clearly $[x, y]^{\alpha\beta}$ can be easily computed and so is $[x, y]^\gamma$ from $[x, y^\gamma]$. The key-exchange is also broken, if we can compute $[x, y]^{\alpha\beta\gamma}$ from $[x, y]^{\alpha\beta}$ and $[x, y]^\gamma$. This is the classic Diffie-Hellman problem, also known as the computational Diffie-Hellman problem.

Bilinear cryptography described in previous section works in any nilpotent group of class 2. It is well known that every finite p-group is nilpotent. There are plenty of finite p-groups. So, it is a natural choice to investigate p-groups of class 2 for the purpose of bilinear cryptography. From now on we shall be concerned with finite p-groups of class 2. In order to build an effective and secure bilinear cryptosystem using finite p-groups of class 2, users needs to choose the private exponents cleverly. Here we shed some light on the choices of private exponents.

Exponent Semigroup. Let G be a group, define $\mathcal{E}(G) = \{n \in \mathbb{Z} \mid (xy)^n = x^n y^n$ for all $x, y \in G\}$. The semigroup $\mathcal{E}(G)$ is called the exponent semigroup and is of independent interest in group theory, see [9, 11]. We state without proof a proposition which describes the structure of $\mathcal{E}(G)$.

Proposition 1 [11, Proposition 3.2]. *Let G be a finite p-group, $|G| = p^m$ and $\exp(G/Z(G))=p^e$. Then there exist a nonnegative integer r such that $\mathcal{E}(G) = p^{e+r}\mathbb{Z} \cup (p^{e+r}\mathbb{Z}+1)$.*

Let G be a finite p-group of class 2 and $|G| = p^m$. Let $x, y \in G$ such that $\text{ord}(x)=p^i$, $\text{ord}(y)=p^j$ where $1 < i, j \leq m$. The private exponents α, β, γ used in tripartite key-exchange protocol are independent of each other. In order to have a successful key-agreement it is necessary to have $[x, y]^{\alpha\beta\gamma} \neq 1$. Thus, α, β, γ must be choosen relatively prime to p, otherwise we could have $[x, y]^{\alpha\beta\gamma} = 1$. Henceforth, we can assume that the private exponents $\alpha, \beta, \gamma < p^m$ and are relatively prime to p. Recall that $(xy)^n = x^n y^n [y, x]^{\frac{n(n-1)}{2}}$ for all $n \geq 0$. If $[y, x]^{\frac{n(n-1)}{2}} = 1$ for all $x, y \in G$, implies $n \in \mathcal{E}(G)$. Thus, by above proposition $n = ap^{e+r}$ or $n = ap^{e+r} + 1$, where $1 \leq a < p^{m-e-r}$. Therefore, we must avoid choosing private exponents α, β or γ in $\mathcal{E}(G) = p^{e+r}\mathbb{Z} \cup (p^{e+r}\mathbb{Z}+1)$. If all α, β, γ is in $\mathcal{E}(G)$, then $\alpha\beta\gamma$ belongs to $\mathcal{E}(G)$ and by computing integers of the form ap^{e+r} or $ap^{e+r}+1$ where $1 \leq a < p^{m-e-r}$ recover the private key $\alpha\beta\gamma$. However, this attack is not of much concern because α, β and γ are chosen independent of one another and is a secret, so it is not likely that all three of these will belong to $\mathcal{E}(G)$. When there is no prior information on whether α, β and γ belongs to $\mathcal{E}(G)$ is available, there is no guarantee that $\alpha\beta\gamma$ will belong to $\mathcal{E}(G)$ and the attack then is just a mere exhaustive search.

We now hope that there is a convincing argument that our central idea runs parallel to the pairing based cryptosystems currently being studied. There is a lot that can be said about protocols using the above idea. A lot can be said about "provable" or semantic security of those cryptosystems. It can be an active field of study to design proper protocols using the above idea in an appropriate security model. However, this paper is not about "provable" or semantic security. It is about finding the right group in which the above mentioned scheme works nicely and securely. As we know the security of the discrete logarithm problem depends on the presentation of the group. There are three most commonly used presentations of finite groups.

- Permutation presentation.
- Polycyclic presentation.
- Matrix presentation.

5   Finding a Right Group

From the above discussion it is clear that the stepping stone to bring this idea to light is to look at 2-generator p-groups of nilpotency class 2. Fortunately there is a lot known about 2-generator p-groups of class 2, these groups have even been classified. The automorphism group of these groups are somewhat known but there is no mention in the literature on the linear representations of these groups. Our idea simply is to find suitable representations of these 2-generator p-groups of class 2 and then use it in the ideas described above. In particular, for the purpose of an exposition, we are interested in the extra-special p groups.

5.1   Extra-Special p-groups

Let G be a finite p-group. Then G is defined to be special if either G is elementary abelian or G is of class 2 and $G' = \Phi(G) = Z(G)$ is elementary abelian. If G is a non-abelian special group with $|Z(G)| = p$, then G is said to be extraspecial. For example, dihedral group D_8 and quaternion group Q_8 are extraspecial. An example of our interest is the following: For $\alpha \geq \beta \geq \gamma \geq 1$,

$$G = \langle a, b | a^{p^\alpha} = b^{p^\beta} = [a,b]^{p^\gamma} = 1, [a,b,a] = [a,b,b] = 1 \rangle.$$

It is clear that G is a two-generator p-group of nilpotency class 2. It is not hard to see that the derived subgroup G' is cyclic and of order p^γ. Furthermore G/G' is isomorphic to $C_{p^\gamma} \oplus C_{p^\beta}$. Here C_n is the cyclic group of order n.

Here our main goal is to find suitable linear representations for the above mentioned group. The following theorem will be very useful for our study.

Theorem 1. *Every extraspecial p-group G is the central product of extraspecial groups of order p^3. Irreducible representations of G are all obtained as tensor product of irreducible representations of the individual factors of G.*

We now give some examples of p-groups that we will use for our study. The modular p-group $Mod_n(p)$ is given by the generators and relations

$$Mod_n(p) = \langle a, b | a^{p^{n-1}} = b^p = 1, a^b = a^{1+p^{n-2}} \rangle. \tag{2}$$

And the group

$$M(p) = \langle a, b | a^p = b^p = [a,b]^p = 1, [a,b,a] = [a,b,b] = 1 \rangle. \tag{3}$$

In light of the above theorem we will study the linear representations of extraspecial p-groups of order p^3. The following theorem characterize the non-abelian groups of order p^3.

Theorem 2. *A non-abelian p-group G of order p^3 is extraspecial and is isomorphic to one of the groups $Mod_3(p)$, $M(p)$, D_8 or Q_8.*

For the purpose of bilinear cryptography we will look for the irreducible faithful linear representations of $Mod_3(p)$ over a finite field. As we know that [7, Theorem 5.5], if G be an extraspecial p-group of order p^{2r+1} and F be a field of characteristic 0 or prime to p which contains a primitive p^2-root of unity. Then the faithful representation of G over F are all of degree p^r. Throughout we will assume that p and s are odd primes and $q = s^r$. Let ζ be a primitive m^{th} root of unity in $\overline{\mathbf{F}}_s$ and let k be a positive integer with $|k|_m = n$. Where $|k|_m$ is the order of k in the multiplicative groups of units mod m.

Lemma 2 [5, Lemma 2.2]. *The Frobenius automorphism τ on $\overline{\mathbf{F}}_s$ defined by $\tau(x) = x^q$ permutes the elements of $\{\zeta, \zeta^k, \cdots, \zeta^{q^{n-1}}\}$ iff $q \equiv k^i \pmod{m}$ for some $0 \le i \le n-1$.*

Theorem 3 [5, Theorem 2.5]. *Let $G = \langle a, b | a^m = 1 = b^n, b^{-1}ab = a^k \rangle$ where $|k|_m = n$. Let ρ be the representation of $\langle a \rangle$ defined by $\rho(a) = \zeta$ where ζ is a primitive m^{th} root of unity in $\overline{\mathbf{F}}_s$, $(s, m) = 1$. Then the induced representation ρ^G is realizable over $\mathbf{F}_q$ iff $q \equiv k^i \pmod{m}$ for some $0 \le i \le n-1$.*

Observe that if we choose $m = p^2$, $n = p$, and $k = p+1$ in the above theorem then $G = Mod_3(p)$ as $(p+1)^p \equiv 1 \pmod{p^2}$. Now as we know that by [5, Proposition 2.1] ρ^G is irreducible over $\overline{\mathbf{F}}_s$ iff $|k|_m$ is equal to the order of b. Observe that $\zeta, \zeta^q, \cdots, \zeta^{q^{n-1}}$ are distinct and $\zeta^{q^n} = \zeta$ whence $|q|_{p^2} = p$. By [5, Lemma 2.2], $q \equiv (p+1)^i \pmod{p^2}$ for some i. As $|q|_{p^2} = |p+1|_{p^2}$ implies that i and p are co-prime. Hence, letting $c = b^i$ we have $G = \langle a, c | a^m = 1 = c^n, c^{-1}ac = a^q \rangle$. The induced representation ρ^G using coset representatives $1, c, c^2, \cdots, c^{p-1}$ is given by

$$\rho^G(c) = \begin{pmatrix} 0 & 0 & \cdots & 0 & 1 \\ 1 & 0 & \cdots & 0 & 0 \\ 0 & 1 & \cdots & 0 & 0 \\ \vdots & \vdots & \cdots & \vdots & \vdots \\ 0 & 0 & \cdots & 1 & 0 \end{pmatrix}$$

$$\rho^G(a) = \begin{pmatrix} \zeta & & & 0 \\ & \zeta^q & & \\ & & \ddots & \\ 0 & & & \zeta^{q^{p-1}} \end{pmatrix}$$

Again by [5, Lemma 2.2] we can see that $V^{-1}\rho^G(a)V = X$ and $V^{-1}\rho^G(c)V = Y \in M_p(\mathbf{F}_q)$ where V and X(the companion matrix of $f(x) = \prod_{i=1}^{p-1}(x - \zeta^{q^i})$) are as follows:

$$V = \begin{pmatrix} 1 & \zeta_0 & \cdots & \zeta_0^{p-1} \\ 1 & \zeta_1 & \cdots & \zeta_1^{p-1} \\ \vdots & \vdots & \cdots & \vdots \\ 1 & \zeta_{p-1} & \cdots & \zeta_{p-1}^{p-1} \end{pmatrix},$$

$$X = \begin{pmatrix} 0 & 0 & \cdots & 0 & -a_0 \\ 1 & 0 & \cdots & 0 & -a_1 \\ 0 & 1 & \cdots & 0 & -a_2 \\ \vdots & \vdots & \cdots & \vdots & \vdots \\ 0 & 0 & \cdots & 1 & \zeta^{q^{p-1}} \end{pmatrix},$$

$$Y = \begin{pmatrix} 1 & & & \\ & \zeta^p & & \\ & & \ddots & \\ & & & \zeta^{(p-1)p} \end{pmatrix}$$

where $\zeta_i = \zeta^{q^i}$, $0 \le i \le n-1$. Here we have $f(x) = x^p - \zeta^p$, hence we get the equivalent representation σ of ρ^G which is given by:

$$\sigma(a) = \begin{pmatrix} 0 & 0 & \cdots & 0 & \zeta^p \\ 1 & 0 & \cdots & 0 & 0 \\ 0 & 1 & \cdots & 0 & 0 \\ \vdots & \vdots & \cdots & \vdots & \vdots \\ 0 & 0 & \cdots & 1 & 0 \end{pmatrix},$$

$$\sigma(c) = \begin{pmatrix} 1 & & & & \\ & \zeta^p & & & \\ & & \zeta^{2p} & & \\ & & & \ddots & \\ & & & & \zeta^{(p-1)p} \end{pmatrix}$$

Note that $\sigma(ac) = \begin{pmatrix} 0 & 0 & \cdots & 0 & 1 \\ 1 & 0 & \cdots & 0 & 0 \\ 0 & \zeta^p & \cdots & 0 & 0 \\ \vdots & \vdots & \cdots & \vdots & \vdots \\ 0 & 0 & \cdots & \zeta^{(p-2)p} & 0 \end{pmatrix}$

The characteristic polynomial of $\sigma(a)$ and $\sigma(ac)$ is same which is $x^p - \zeta^p$.

Now consider the tensor product of representation σ with itself. If the characteristic polynomials of A and B factor as $P_A(x) = \prod_{i=1}^{n}(x - \lambda_i)$ and $P_B(x) = \prod_{i=1}^{m}(x - \mu_j)$, then the characteristic polynomial of $A \otimes B$ is $P_{A \otimes B}(x) = \prod_{i=1}^{n}\prod_{i=1}^{m}(x - \lambda_i \mu_j)$. Thus characteristic polynomial of $\sigma(a)$, $\sigma(ac)$ is $(x^p - \zeta^p)^p$. Observe that the polynomial $(x^p - \zeta^p)$ is irreducible over F where F is a subfield of F_q with $\zeta^p \in F$.

6   Conclusion

In this short note, we introduced a novel idea of pairing based cryptosystem using matrices. The idea is simple, use linear representation of groups of class 2.

As a test case we looked at the extraspecial p-group of exponent p^2. For this particular group, the set of parameters is not encouraging. From [5], it follows that the only possible matrices that we can come up with is matrices of size p over $\mathbb{Z}_p$. The most security this can provide is the security in the finite field $\mathbb{F}_{p^p}$. However, since the size of the field and the size of the matrix must be the same, this is of little practical value. The size of the matrix is too large. However, we hope, that there are other groups of class 2 for which we can get better parameters.

References

1. Balasubramanian, R., Koblitz, N.: The improbability than an elliptic curve has subexponential discrete log problem under the Menezes-Okamoto-Vanstone algorithm. J. Cryptology **11**(2), 141–145 (1998)
2. Barua, R., Dutta, R., Sarkar, P.: Extending Joux's protocol to multi party key agreement. In: Johansson, T., Maitra, S. (eds.) INDOCRYPT 2003. LNCS, vol. 2904, pp. 205–217. Springer, Heidelberg (2003). doi:10.1007/978-3-540-24582-7_15
3. Boneh, D., Shacham, H., Lynn, B.: Short signatures from the Weil pairing. J. Cryptology **17**(4), 297–319 (2004)
4. Chatterjee, S., Sarkar, P.: Identity-Based Encryption. Springer, Boston (2011)
5. Chebolu, S., Mináč, J., Reis, C.: Reciprocity laws for representations of finite groups. Ann. Math. Québec **34**(1), 37–61 (2010)
6. Dutta, R., Barua, R., Sarkar, P.: Pairing based cryptographic protocols: A survey. http://eprint.iacr.org/2004/064
7. Gorenstein, D.: Finite Groups. AMS Chelsea Publishing (1980)
8. Joux, A.: A one round protocol for Diffie-Hellman. In: Proceedings of the 4th International Symposium on Algorithmic Number Theory, pp. 385–394 (2000)
9. Kobayashi, Y.: On the structure of exponent semigroups. J. Algebra **78**, 1–19 (1982)
10. Menezes, A., Okamoto, T., Vanstone, S.: Reducing elliptic curve logarithms to logarithms in a finite field. IEEE Trans. Inf. Theor. **39**(5), 1639–1646 (1993)
11. Moravec, P.: Schur multipliers and power endomorphisms of groups. J. Algebra **308**(1), 12–25 (2007)
12. Rotman, J.J.: An Introduction to the Theory of Groups, 4th edn. Springer, New York (1994)

Notes on GGH13 Without the Presence of Ideals

Martin R. Albrecht[(✉)], Alex Davidson[(✉)], and Enrique Larraia

Royal Holloway, University of London, Egham, UK
{martin.albrecht,alex.davidson.2014}@rhul.ac.uk

Abstract. We investigate the merits of altering the Garg, Gentry and Halevi (GGH13) graded encoding scheme to remove the presence of the ideal $\langle g \rangle$. In particular, we show that we can alter the form of encodings so that effectively a new g_i is used for each source group $\mathbb{G}_i$, while retaining correctness. This would appear to prevent all known attacks on IO candidates instantiated using GGH13. However, when analysing security in a simplified branching program model, we present an IO distinguishing attack that does not use $\langle g \rangle$. This result opens a counterpoint with the work of Halevi (EPRINT 2015) which stated that the core computational hardness problem underpinning GGH13 is computing a basis of this ideal. Our attempts seem to suggest that there is a structural vulnerability in the way that GGH13 encodings are constructed that lies deeper than the presence of $\langle g \rangle$. Tangentially, we observe that our attack is prevented when considering all the added machinery of IO candidates.

1 Introduction

The work of Garg, Gentry and Halevi [GGH13a] initiated the study of candidate *multilinear maps* (MMAPs). In short, a multilinear map $e : \mathbb{G}_1 \times \cdots \times \mathbb{G}_\kappa \mapsto \mathbb{G}_T$ maps κ elements $g_i \in \mathbb{G}_i$ to a single target element $g_T \in \mathbb{G}_T$ in target group $\mathbb{G}_T$.[1] More accurately, [GGH13a] constructed a *graded encoding scheme* (GES), informally defining intermediate bilinear maps between the source groups and thus allowing group operations on intermediate 'levels'. The actual construction provides 'noisy' approximations to the functionality of MMAPs and subsequent candidates [CLT13, GGH15] follow in the same vein. In fact, the common interface that we assume of a GES is similar to that of a levelled FHE scheme except that decryption is replaced with a public 'zero-testing' procedure. This allows the evaluator to learn whether a particular computation over encodings is equal to zero or not provided that the result is encoded at the top level of a computation hierarchy (e.g. after κ multiplications).

M.R. Albrecht and E. Larraia were supported by the EPSRC grant EP/L018543/1 "Multilinear Maps in Cryptography". A. Davidson was supported by the EPSRC and the UK Government as part of the Centre for Doctoral Training in Cyber Security at Royal Holloway, University of London (EP/K035584/1).

[1] Here we describe an asymmetric MMAP, we can equally describe a symmetric variant where $\mathbb{G}_1 = \cdots = \mathbb{G}_\kappa = \mathbb{G}$.

© Springer International Publishing AG 2017
M. O'Neill (Ed.): IMACC 2017, LNCS 10655, pp. 135–158, 2017.
https://doi.org/10.1007/978-3-319-71045-7_8

The importance of graded encoding schemes for theoretical cryptography has solidified with applications including semantically-secure, order-revealing encryption [BLR+15], attribute-based encryption for circuits [GGH+13c] and low-overhead broadcast encryption [BWZ14] to name a few. Although, perhaps the most important application is that of constructing candidates for indistinguishability obfuscation (IO) [GGH+13b, BGK+14, GMM+16]. All-known constructions of IO obfuscators require usage of a GES or MMAP, and analyse security in generic graded encoding models.

Unfortunately, the three candidates of GES [GGH13a, CLT13, GGH15] (denoted as GGH13, CLT13 and GGH15 respectively) have been shown to be vulnerable to a wide-range of attacks; e.g. 'zeroizing' [HJ16, CLR15, CLLT16, CLT14, CLLT17], 'overstretched' NTRU assumption [ABD16, CJL16, KF17] and using algebraic dependencies [MSZ16a, ADGM16, CGH17]. Zeroizing attacks are largely avoided in the realm of IO since they rely on lower-level encodings of zero being made available [HJ16, CLR15, CLLT16] or highly structured branching program constructions [CLLT17]. Attacks on 'overstretched' NTRU assumptions only affect GGH13, but can be avoided by increasing parameters. Finally, algebraic dependency attacks affect specific 'BGK-style' IO candidates (e.g. [AGIS14, BGK+14, BMSZ15, MSW14, PST14]) instantiated with the GGH13 GES and rely on circuits outputting a sufficient number of zeroes. In short, the presence of a common generator g in all GGH13 encodings allows an adversary in an IO security game to create a basis for the ideal $\langle g \rangle$. This basis is then used in a distinguishing attack on the obfuscated circuit. We provide a background on algebraically dependent sets of polynomials in finite fields in Appendix E.

Recently, there have been attempts to develop 'immunised' IO constructions such as [GMM+16] (a combination of original proposals [GMS16, MSZ16b]). These immunisations construct branching programs that make finding algebraic dependences on zero-tested encodings (as described by [MSZ16a, ADGM16]) much more difficult, and analyse security in a weakened graded encoding model.[2] However, the cryptanalysis of Chen et al. [CGH17] seems to offer attacks that are still effective, even for these immunisations.[3]

This Work. Our analysis is motivated by the cryptanalysis of [CGH17] and its applicability against 'immunised' IO candidates. We focus on algebraic dependency (or annihilation) attacks on IO candidates instantiated with GGH13, and their propensity to find representatives of the ideal $\langle g \rangle$. We investigate the possibility of making changes at the GES level to avoid the attacks described previously, rather than using ad-hoc fixes to IO constructions. In particular, we derive

---

[2] This model allows all the same operations as the generic graded encoding model along with an additional step where the adversary is allowed to submit certain polynomial evaluations on the results of zero-testing.

[3] They are thwarted only by the usage of dual-input branching programs which are external to the security model considered. In fact, they note that parts of their attack take place externally to the WGEM and thus suggest that the model is incomplete.

a variant of GGH13 where the common generator g is removed such that encodings on different levels i are cosets of the form $\alpha + I_i$ for κ ideals I_i. Concretely, we replace the usage of the short g in GGH13 with larger elements β_i that also depends on the level that the encoding is associated with (See Sect. 3 for more details). The correctness of zero-testing is achieved since the magnitude of the result is completely determined by the presence of the β_i's — the number of which differ in zero and non-zero encodings. The result is a GES that has no structural ideals that can easily be computed by a PPT adversary.

At first sight, this prevents all known attacks that require an annihilation phase. On the other hand, it should be noted that, similarly to GGH13, our variant is trivially susceptible to zeroizing attacks and thus is immediately short of providing full MMAP functionality. As such, our alteration would only be a plausible candidate in situations where *multilinear jigsaw puzzle* (MJP) functionality is sufficient (e.g. IO [GGH+13b], order-revealing encryption [BLR+15]).

However, we find that our derived GES is still vulnerable, in a simplified IO security game, to a variation of the annihilation attack given in [MSZ16a]. While we remove the ability of an adversary to learn ideals from our MJP scheme, we detail an attack that side-steps these measures and distinguishes based on the magnitude of zero-tested encodings. We interpret this result as a counter-point to the work of Halevi [Hal15] where it is stated that the core computational hardness problem underpinning GGH13 is to establish a basis of $\langle g \rangle$. Given the similarity between our encodings and those of GGH13, our attack seems to highlight a structural fault that is exploitable even if the ideal testing capability of adversaries is removed. However, we stress that the attack is only possible because of distribution of our elements β_i that we use to replace g.

Finally, while our attack works in a simplified branching program model, the added machinery used in candidate obfuscators (such as 'multiplicative bundling' scalars and Kilian randomisation) render the attack *apparently* useless. This applies even for BGK-style obfuscators and seems to imply that our GES could still be used as a valid alternative for instantiating obfuscation candidates — even those that are believed insecure for GGH13. This may indicate a logical separation between the structure of the GGH13 MJP scheme and the variant proposed here. Unfortunately, a BGK-style obfuscator based on our GES still comes with no security guarantees and merely appears to resist currently available attacks in the weakened graded encoding model.

Layout. Section 2 details the notation that we will use and a recap of rings, branching programs and definitions on algebraic dependence — we also cover additional preliminaries on MJPs and rings in the Appendix. In Sect. 3 we describe the changes we can make to GGH13 to remove the dependency on the ideal $\langle g \rangle$. In Sect. 4 we provide an analysis of the security of this variant when applied in differing IO security settings. In Sect. 5 we provide a final discussion of our results and possible future avenues for research. For a background on GGH13 and how it is susceptible to the annihilation attacks introduced by [MSZ16a] see Appendix D.

2 Preliminaries

2.1 Notation and Rings

We may denote sets of the form $\{1,\ldots,n\}$ by $[n]$. For matrices M, we refer to the entry in row i and column j as $M[i,j]$. For ring elements x we also use the square-bracket notation $[x]_{\mathcal{S}}$ to represent an encoding of x with respect to some index set $\mathcal{S}$. For an algorithm A, we use the notation $w \leftarrow A(x,y,z)$ to denote that A outputs w on inputs x,y,z. For a set $\mathcal{X}$ we use the notation $x \leftarrow_{\$} \mathcal{X}$ to indicate that x is sampled from $\mathcal{X}$ using the uniform distribution. For elements $y \in R_q$ for some polynomial ring R_q, when referring to the *'magnitude'* of y we will mean $\|y\|_{\infty}$. For some distribution Y, we write $\mathsf{poly}(Y^n)$ to denote sampling a degree n polynomial with coefficients sampled from Y.

We will be working over rings $R := \mathbb{Z}[x]/\langle \phi(x)\rangle$ and $R_q := R/qR$ for some degree $n = n(\lambda)$ integer polynomial $\phi(x) \in \mathbb{Z}[x]$ and a prime integer $q = q(\lambda) \in \mathbb{Z}$ — notably R_q is isomorphic to the ring $\mathbb{Z}_q[x]/\langle \phi(x)\rangle$. We perform addition in these rings component-wise in the coefficients of the polynomial elements and multiplication is performed via polynomial multiplication modulo $\phi(x)$ and, if applicable, q. An element in R (respectively R_q) can be viewed as a degree $(n-1)$ polynomial over $\mathbb{Z}$ (respectively $\mathbb{Z}_q$). We can represent such an element using the vector of its n coefficients (where these will be in the range $\{-\lfloor q/2\rfloor,\ldots,\lfloor q/2\rfloor\}$ for elements in R_q). We work with the polynomial $\phi(x) = x^N + 1$ with N a power of two. In particular, $\mathbb{Z}[x]/\langle \phi(x)\rangle$ is isomorphic to the ring of integers of the $2N$-th cyclotomic field.

2.2 Branching Programs

Let $L = L(\lambda)$, $\nu = \nu(\lambda)$ and $d = d(\lambda)$ be parameters dependent on the security parameter λ. Let $\mathsf{inp} : [L] \mapsto [\nu]^d$ be some 'input' function. Let $\{M_{(b_1,\ldots,b_d),l}\}$ be a set of matrices individually sampled from $\mathbb{Z}_q^{5\times 5}$ for $b_1,\ldots,b_d \in \{0,1\}$ and $l \in [L]$. Let $M_0 \in \mathbb{Z}_q^{5\times 1}$, $M_{L+1} \in \mathbb{Z}_q^{1\times 5}$ be two vectors, these are known as 'bookends' and are used for guaranteeing a single element output. Define

$$\mathcal{M} := (L,\nu,d,\mathsf{inp},\{M_{x_{\mathsf{inp}(l)},l}\}_{l\in[L]}, M_0, M_{L+1}) \tag{1}$$

to be a matrix branching program (MBP) of length L, input width ν and arity d. We can evaluate $\mathcal{M}$ on inputs $x \in 2^{\nu}$ where $x_s = x[s]$ and we denote such an evaluation by $\mathcal{M}(x)$.[4] The input function inp chooses the bits in the input x that are examined at each layer l of the branching program. Clearly $|\mathsf{inp}(i)| = d$ where $\mathsf{inp}(i)[y]$ is equal to the yth component of $\mathsf{inp}(i)$. In total, we have that the branching program contains $2^d L + 2$ matrices. Let $x_{\mathsf{inp}(l)} = (x_{\mathsf{inp}(l)[1]},\ldots,x_{\mathsf{inp}(l)[d]})$, we evaluate the branching program on an input x by computing

$$\mathcal{M}(x) := M_0 \cdot \left(\prod_{l=1}^{L} M_{x_{\mathsf{inp}(l)},l}\right) \cdot M_{L+1}. \tag{2}$$

---

[4] We use 5×5 matrices as these are sufficient for Barrington's theorem [Bar89].

Using Barrington's theorem we can associate a circuit C with a branching program $\mathcal{M}_C$. We have that the branching program (without bookend vectors) evaluates to the identity matrix on an input x if and only if $C(x) = 0$. Since this theorem is commonly used in the construction of IO candidates this formulation of correctness applies to our situation. It is common to structure a branching program $\mathcal{M}_C$ such that $\mathcal{M}(x) = 0$ when $C(x) = 0$. To ensure this, we can construct a dummy branching program that contains only identity matrices with the same bookend vectors as in the functional branching program. We then compute the dummy branch on the same input as the functional branch and subtract the dummy output from the functional output. All current obfuscators only consider branching programs that take either single [GGH+13b] or dual [BGK+14] inputs i.e. cases where $d = 1$ or $d = 2$.

Definition 1 (Functional equivalence). *Let $\mathcal{X}$ be the set of valid inputs for two branching programs $\mathcal{M}_0, \mathcal{M}_1$ of length L, input length ν and arity d. We say that $\mathcal{M}_0, \mathcal{M}_1$ are* functionally equivalent *(or $\mathcal{M}_0 \equiv \mathcal{M}_1$) if, for any input $x \in \mathcal{X}$ then:*

$$\mathcal{M}_0(x) = 0 \text{ if and only if } \mathcal{M}_1(x) = 0.$$

As above, we can alter the branching program computation to ensure that only a single value is output rather than matrices.

Remark 1. Note that we can pad the length of the branching program to any required length by simply appending the required number of identity matrices to the end of the branching program. These matrices clearly do not alter the result of the program evaluation.

2.3   IO from Branching Programs

The majority of current IO candidates make use of branching programs when constructing an obfuscated version of a circuit $C(\cdot)$. This generalised approach is developed from the randomised branching program model used by [MSZ16a] — using Barrington's theorem to convert a fan-in 2 circuit, C, of depth D into a branching program $\mathcal{M}$ of the form above with length $L = O(4^D)$. The construction we detail here is heavily generalised but follows the BGK-style obfuscation candidates of [AGIS14, BGK+14, BMSZ15, MSW14, PST14]. Obfuscators such as [GGH+13b, GMM+16] use more complicated randomisation procedures.

To obfuscate the program, we apply Kilian's randomisation technique [Kil88] by randomly sampling invertible matrices $\mathcal{R}_0, \ldots, \mathcal{R}_{L+1}$, sampling $2L$ random non-zero scalars $\epsilon_{b,l} \leftarrow_{\$} \mathbb{Z}_q$ and then constructing randomised matrices

$$\widetilde{M}_{b,l} = \epsilon_{b,l} \cdot \mathcal{R}_{l-1}^{-1} M_{b,l} \mathcal{R}_l$$

along with bookend vectors

$$\widetilde{M}_0 = \epsilon_0 \cdot M_0 \mathcal{R}_0, \quad \text{and} \quad \widetilde{M}_{L+1} = \epsilon_{L+1} \cdot \mathcal{R}_{L+1}^{-1} M_{L+1}.$$

Notice that the following holds:

$$\widetilde{M}_0 \cdot \left(\prod_{l=1}^{L} \widetilde{M}_{x_{\mathsf{inp}(l)},l} \right) \cdot \widetilde{M}_{L+1} = \tilde{\epsilon} \cdot M_0 \cdot \left(\prod_{l=1}^{L} M_{x_{\mathsf{inp}(l)},l} \right) \cdot M_{L+1}$$

for the multiplicative bundling scalar $\tilde{\epsilon} = \epsilon_0 \epsilon_{L+1} \prod_{i=1}^{L} \epsilon_{x_{\mathsf{inp}(i)},i}$. This means that, if we replace the matrices in the branching program with the randomised matrices then we still compute the same function. These randomisations procedures prevent 'partial evaluation' and 'input mixing' attacks on obfuscated programs. Similarly to the work of [BGK+14], we could make use of a straddling set structure when encoding elements to prevent further algebraic attacks. However, this is unnecessary for the security model that we consider.

Finally, the entries of each matrix $\widetilde{M}_{b,l}$ are encoded using an MJP scheme with respect to a source index set $\mathcal{S}_{b,l}$. Security of the construction is then analysed in the generic graded encoding model as in previous work. This limits an adversary to computing multilinear operations and zero-testing top-level encodings. We denote the encoded matrices by $\widehat{M}_{b,l}$, the bookend vectors by $\widehat{M}_0, \widehat{M}_{L+1}$ and the obfuscated branching program by $\widehat{\mathcal{M}}$. The index sets are define such that the output of $\widehat{\mathcal{M}}$ is an encoding with respect to a top-level set $\mathcal{U}$.

Evaluation. When evaluating the branching program on an input x the bookend vectors and a dummy program execution ensure that a single element is propagated from the computation. Using the randomised branching program

$$\widehat{\mathcal{M}} := (L, \nu, d, \mathsf{inp}, \{\widehat{M}_{x_{\mathsf{inp}(l)},l}\}_{l \in [L]}, \widehat{M}_0, \widehat{M}_{L+1})$$

we learn a top-level encoded element where the encoded value is 0 if and only if the circuit that was obfuscated also evaluates to 0 on x.[5] That is, $\widehat{\mathcal{M}}_C(x) = [0]_{\mathcal{U}}$ iff $C(x) = 0$ and, since $[0]_{\mathcal{U}}$ is a top-level encoding, we can use the zero-test procedure to learn the output of the obfuscated circuit.

3   GGH13 Without Ideals

The main component of this note is our analysis of the security of IO candidates when instantiated with a variant of GGH13 where ideals cannot be efficiently found. In the following we give an overview of our adapted scheme without ideals. In Appendix A we define a multilinear jigsaw puzzle formally, and in Appendix B we give a formal MJP realisation of our construction.

---

[5] The bundling scalars ensure that inputs x satisfying $C(x) = 1$ satisfies $\widehat{\mathcal{M}}_C(x) \neq [0]_{\mathcal{U}}$.

3.1   Overview of Encodings

Let $R = \mathbb{Z}[x]/\langle\phi(x)\rangle$ be a ring and $R_q = R/qR$ be the quotient ring for a large prime q, with an accompanying error distribution $\chi = \bar{D}_{\mathbb{Z}^n,\sigma}$ for parameter σ. The ring R_q will define the space of encodings.

Let $\alpha \in R_q$ be some non-zero polynomial with small coefficients. Sample a polynomial $r \leftarrow_\$ \mathsf{poly}(\chi)$ with small coefficients and sample z_i uniformly from R_q for $1 \leq i \leq \kappa$. Finally, sample β_i such that $\sqrt[\kappa+1]{q} < \|\beta_i\|_\infty < \sqrt[\kappa]{q}$. We refer the reader to Appendix C for more details on how to sample the β_i.

A level 1 encoding of α with respect to some set $\mathcal{S}_i$ takes the form:

$$[v]_q = \frac{\alpha + r/\beta_i}{z_i} \quad \bmod q \tag{3}$$

where the values z_i, β_i enforce the leveled structure that we require from the specification of an MJP scheme. It is easy to see that β_i^{-1} corresponds to using a different g_i in GGH13. We reiterate that β_i has to be sampled in a different way (e.g. no longer as small elements) to ensure correctness for zero-testing.

Remark 2. It is possible to sample higher-level encodings by encoding with respect to $\prod_{i\in\mathcal{S}} z_i$ and $\prod_{i\in\mathcal{S}} \beta_i$ for some index set $\mathcal{S}$. We do not require this functionality for a MJP scheme.

3.2   Operations

Let $\mathcal{U}$ refer to the top-level index where zero-testing can take place.

Addition of Encodings. Let v_1, v_2 be encodings with respect to the same index set $\mathcal{S} \subseteq \mathcal{U}$. Then we can compute additions of these encodings by simply computing $v = v_1 + v_2$, the result is an encoding of the form

$$[v]_q = \frac{\alpha_1 + \alpha_2 + (r_1 + r_2)/\beta_\mathcal{S}}{z_\mathcal{S}} \quad \bmod q$$

Multiplication of Encodings. Let v_1, v_2 be encodings with respective index sets $\mathcal{S}_i$ and $\mathcal{S}_j$ such that $\mathcal{S}_i \cup \mathcal{S}_j \subseteq \mathcal{U}$. A multiplication of these encodings is calculated by multiplying the encodings directly, i.e. $v = v_1 \cdot v_2$ which creates an encoding of the form

$$[v]_q = \frac{\alpha_1 \cdot \alpha_2 + \tilde{r}/(\beta_i \cdot \beta_j)}{z_i \cdot z_j} \quad \bmod q \tag{4}$$

where $\tilde{r} = \alpha_1 \cdot r_2 \cdot \beta_j + \alpha_2 \cdot r_1 \cdot \beta_i + (r_1 \cdot r_2)$.

As with GGH13, operations can only take place while the noise stays smaller than a set upper bound (in this case $\sqrt[\kappa]{q}$). We choose parameters such that κ multiplications can be computed without overflowing this boundary.

Zero-Testing. To enable zero-testing on encodings $v_\mathcal{U}$ that are indexed at the top-level we follow procedures set in previous GE schemes and publish a zero-testing parameter p_{zt}. We consider top-level encodings that are constructed via a sequence of multiplications of encodings indexed with each of the sets $\mathcal{S}_i$ and thus they take the form:

$$[v_\mathcal{U}]_q = \frac{\tilde{\alpha} + \tilde{r}/\beta_\mathcal{U}}{z_\mathcal{U}}$$

where $\beta_\mathcal{U} = \prod_{i=1}^\kappa \beta_i$, $z_\mathcal{U} = \prod_{i=1}^\kappa z_i$ and $\tilde{\alpha}$ is a polynomial of underlying α values. Finally, $\tilde{r}$ is a polynomial taking the form $\hat{r} + \beta^{(1)} + \beta^{(2)} + \ldots + \beta^{(\kappa-1)}$ where we stratify the polynomial into the components $\beta^{(h)}$, containing all monomials of degree h in the β_i elements, and $\hat{r}$ representing a polynomial in the r_j values from each of the underlying encodings v_j. Notice that the polynomial structure of $\hat{r}$ exactly mirrors the polynomial that has been calculated over the encodings as a whole. The zero-test parameter is defined as

$$p_{zt} = \prod_{i=1}^\kappa \beta_i \cdot z_i$$

and an encoding $v_\mathcal{U}$ is zero-tested by first computing $\delta = p_{zt} \cdot v_\mathcal{U} \mod q$ and then we state that $v_\mathcal{U}$ encodes the value '0' if δ is 'small' and encodes a non-zero value if δ is 'big'. For example, we have

$$\delta_1 = \prod_{i=1}^\kappa \beta_i \cdot \tilde{\alpha} + \hat{r} + \beta^{(1)} + \beta^{(2)} + \ldots + \beta^{(\kappa-1)} \tag{5}$$

for non-zero encodings ($\tilde{\alpha} \neq 0$) and so for an encoding of zero ($\tilde{\alpha} \neq 0$) we have

$$\delta_0 = \hat{r} + \beta^{(1)} + \beta^{(2)} + \ldots + \beta^{(\kappa-1)}. \tag{6}$$

The difference between Eqs. (5) and (6) is the loss of a factor of $\prod_{i=1}^\kappa \beta_i$, in Eq. (6) we have monomials in the β_i of maximum degree $\kappa - 1$.

Observe that the value of the encoding is now stored in the MSB of the final output — in GGH13 the value is stored in the LSB. Therefore, zero-testing requires more involved distinguishing in our case than in GGH13. We discuss this in detail below.

CORRECTNESS. Correctness of zero-testing follows providing that

$$q^{\kappa-1/\kappa} < \|\delta_1\|_\infty < q, \quad \text{and} \quad q^{\kappa-2/\kappa} < \|\delta_0\|_\infty < q^{\kappa-1/\kappa}.$$

For δ_0, $\beta^{(1)} + \beta^{(2)} + \ldots + \beta^{(\kappa-1)}$ is a sum of monomials dominated by the term $\beta^{\kappa-1}$. In this particular term, we have a sum of monomials of degree $\kappa - 1$ over variables β_i, sampled such that $\|\beta_i\|_\infty < \sqrt[\kappa]{q}$. The coefficients of these monomials are made up of polynomials in the α, r elements from underlying encodings and are thus small. Therefore, providing that $\kappa \ll q$, we have that $q^{\kappa-2/\kappa} < \|\beta^{\kappa-1}\|_\infty < q^{\kappa-1/\kappa}$. Therefore, by appropriate choice of q, κ, we have

$$q^{\kappa-2/\kappa} < \|\beta^{(1)} + \beta^{(2)} + \ldots + \beta^{(\kappa-1)}\|_\infty < q^{\kappa-1/\kappa}.$$

Again, since $\hat{r}_x$ is a monomial made up of variable sampled as small elements from R_q, then we have that δ_0 satisfies the relation above. Finally, since δ_1 contains a product of all β_i values then $q^{\kappa-1/\kappa} \leq \|\delta_1\|_\infty \leq q$.

We could set out tighter bounds for correctness but we are more concerned with the analysis of this scheme in the IO setting. As a consequence we merely state that it is possible to choose parameters such that distinguishing non-zero and zero encodings given how we sample each β_i.

4   Security Analysis in IO Setting

In this section we demonstrate flaws in the encoding scheme from Sect. 3 via an annihilation attack in a simplified security model. Our attack does not depend on finding representations of any ideals. We will then highlight explicit machinery in IO constructions that may prevent the attack and may allow us to instantiate BGK-style obfuscators where annihilation attacks are not possible.

4.1   Simplified Security Model

In the attacks that we propose we prefer to talk explicitly in a game-based representation of the IO game. In particular, the scope of the weakened graded encoding model is unnecessarily wide since our attacks only occur during the post-zero-testing query phase. As a result we propose two interactive distinguishing security games. In the first, **IND-$\mathcal{M}$**, the adversary chooses functionally equivalent (Definition 1) branching programs to be encoded and then has oracle access for querying inputs on the branching program and receiving zero-tested outputs. In the second, **IND-OBF**, the branching programs are also randomised using the techniques (Kilian randomisation and multiplicative bundling scalars) discussed in Sect. 2.3 before encoding takes place — noting else is changed. In the weakened graded encoding model, the adversary is able to interact with random handles that represent encodings after operations have taken place.

The advantage of the adversary in **IND-$\mathcal{M}$** (Fig. 1) is written as:

$$\mathsf{Adv}_{\mathcal{A}}^{\mathbf{IND}\text{-}\mathcal{M}}(\lambda) = \left| \Pr\left[1 \leftarrow \mathcal{A}(\lambda, \widehat{\mathcal{M}_0})\right] - \Pr\left[1 \leftarrow \mathcal{A}(\lambda, \widehat{\mathcal{M}_1})\right] \right|$$

and the security game is satisfied if $\mathsf{Adv}_{\mathcal{A}}^{\mathbf{IND}\text{-}\mathcal{M}}(\lambda) = \mathsf{negl}(\lambda)$.

The advantage of the adversary in **IND-OBF** (Fig. 2) is written as:

$$\mathsf{Adv}_{\mathcal{A}}^{\mathbf{IND}\text{-}\mathbf{OBF}}(\lambda) = \left| \Pr\left[1 \leftarrow \mathcal{A}(\lambda, \widehat{\mathcal{M}_0})\right] - \Pr\left[1 \leftarrow \mathcal{A}(\lambda, \widehat{\mathcal{M}_1})\right] \right|$$

and the security game is satisfied if $\mathsf{Adv}_{\mathcal{A}}^{\mathbf{IND}\text{-}\mathbf{OBF}}(\lambda) = \mathsf{negl}(\lambda)$. We use iO to denote the oracle that the challenger uses for performing the BGK-style obfuscation of a branching program.

4.2   Analysis of (in)security in IND-$\mathcal{M}$ Game

Let $\widehat{\mathcal{M}_b}$ be the encoded branching program that $\mathcal{A}_1$ receives in the **IND-$\mathcal{M}$** security game. Then let $\mathcal{X} = \{0,1\}^L$ be the set of valid inputs to $\widehat{\mathcal{M}_b}$ and let $\kappa = L + 2$ be the total degree of multilinearity (due to encoding of bookends as well). Let $\mu_x = \widehat{\mathcal{M}_b}(x)$ be the output of $\widehat{\mathcal{M}_b}$ on some input $x \in \{0,1\}^L$ and let $\delta_x = \mathcal{O}_{zt}(\mu_x)$. Assuming that μ_x is honestly computed then δ_x should be meaningful.

Here we show that if μ_x is generated honestly and that if $\mathsf{JTest}(\delta_x) = 1$ then it is possible to distinguish which branching program has been encoded. Our analysis uses an annihilation attack that is very similar in spirit to the original given in [MSZ16a]. Let $\widehat{M}_{x_{\mathsf{inp}(l)},l}$ be a matrix at level l in $\widehat{\mathcal{M}_b}$. Let $\alpha_{i,j,l}^{x_{\mathsf{inp}(l)}} = M_{x_{\mathsf{inp}(l)},l}[i][j]$ in the original branching program $\mathcal{M}_b$. Recall that the corresponding entry $\widehat{M}_{x_{\mathsf{inp}(l)},l}[i][j]$ after encoding has taken place takes the form:

$$v_{i,j,l}^{x_{\mathsf{inp}(l)}} = (\alpha_{i,j,l}^{x_{\mathsf{inp}(l)}} + r_{i,j,l}^{x_{\mathsf{inp}(l)}}/\beta_l)/z_l.$$

Game **IND-$\mathcal{M}^{\mathcal{A}}(\lambda)$**:	Oracle $\mathcal{O}_{zt}(x)$:
1. $(\mathsf{sk}, \mathsf{prms}, \mathsf{evk}, \mathsf{ztk}) \leftarrow \mathsf{JInstGen}(1^\lambda, 1^\kappa)$	1. if init, $q \leftarrow 0$; else, $q \leftarrow q + 1$
2. $(st, \mathcal{M}_0, \mathcal{M}_1) \leftarrow \mathcal{A}_0(l, \mathsf{prms}, \mathsf{evk})$	2. if $q > \mathcal{Q}$, $\delta \leftarrow \bot$
3. $b \leftarrow \{0,1\}$	3. else:
4. $\widehat{\mathcal{M}_b} \leftarrow \mathsf{JEnc}(\mathsf{sk}, \mathsf{prms}, \{\mathcal{S}_i\}_{i\in[\kappa]}, \mathcal{M}_b)$	4. $(\mathcal{U}, \mu_x) \leftarrow \widehat{\mathcal{M}_b}(x)$
5. $b' \leftarrow \mathcal{A}_1^{\mathcal{O}_{zt}}(st)$	5. $\delta_x \leftarrow \mathsf{JZTParam}(\mathsf{prms}, \mathsf{ztk}, (\mathcal{U}, \mu_x))$
6. output $(b' = b)$	6. return δ_x

Fig. 1. Left: The **IND-$\mathcal{M}$** game. An adversary $\mathcal{A} = (\mathcal{A}_0, \mathcal{A}_1)$ is legitimate if $\mathcal{A}_0$ outputs two branching programs $(\mathcal{M}_0, \mathcal{M}_1)$ of the same size that compute functionally equivalent circuits. We abuse notation and write $\mathsf{JEnc}(\mathsf{sk}, \mathsf{prms}, \{\mathcal{S}_i\}_{i\in[\kappa]}, \mathcal{M}_b)$ to denote the encoding of the ith level of matrices in $\mathcal{M}_b$ with respect to the index set $\mathcal{S}_i$. **Right:** Oracle for computing inputs on the encoded branching program $\widehat{\mathcal{M}_b}$ and outputting zero-tested results.

Game **IND-$\mathcal{M}^{\mathcal{A}}(\lambda)$**:	Oracle $\mathcal{O}_{zt}(x)$:
1. $(\mathsf{sk}, \mathsf{prms}, \mathsf{evk}, \mathsf{ztk}) \leftarrow \mathsf{JInstGen}(1^\lambda, 1^\kappa)$	1. if init, $q \leftarrow 0$; else, $q \leftarrow q + 1$
2. $(st, \mathcal{M}_0, \mathcal{M}_1) \leftarrow \mathcal{A}_0(l, \mathsf{prms}, \mathsf{evk})$	2. if $q > \mathcal{Q}$, $\delta \leftarrow \bot$
3. $b \leftarrow \{0,1\}$	3. else:
4. $\widehat{\mathcal{M}_b} \leftarrow \mathsf{iO}(\mathsf{sk}, \mathsf{prms}, \{\mathcal{S}_i\}_{i\in[\kappa]}, \mathcal{M}_b)$	4. $(\mathcal{U}, \mu_x) \leftarrow \widehat{\mathcal{M}_b}(x)$
5. $b' \leftarrow \mathcal{A}_1^{\mathcal{O}_{zt}}(st)$	5. $\delta_x \leftarrow \mathsf{JZTParam}(\mathsf{prms}, \mathsf{ztk}, (\mathcal{U}, \mu_x))$
6. output $(b' = b)$	6. return δ_x

Fig. 2. Left: The **IND-OBF** game. Same as above, except that the oracle iO takes a branching program as input and outputs an obfuscation of the branching program, as defined in Sect. 2.3. The ith level of matrices is still encoded with respect to $\mathcal{S}_i$. **Right:** Oracle for computing inputs on the encoded branching program $\widehat{\mathcal{M}_b}$ and outputting zero-tested results.

In the attack we treat the variables $r_{i,j,l}^{x_{\mathrm{inp}(l)}}$ as formal variables and show that, for enough inputs x, we can compute a polynomial Q that annihilates these variables. Let r^x denote the set of all variables $r_{i,j,l}^{x_{\mathrm{inp}(l)}}$ that are used in computing $\widehat{\mathcal{M}}_b(x)$.

Firstly notice that the form of δ_x is the following:

$$\delta_x = \hat{r}_x + \beta^{(1)} + \beta^{(2)} + \ldots + \beta^{(\kappa-1)}$$

recalling that $\hat{r}_x$ is a polynomial dependent only on r_j values from encodings and $\beta^{(\ell)}$ is the sum of all monomials in the terms $\{\beta_i\}_{i \in [\kappa]}$ of degree ℓ. In this analysis we focus on the term $\beta^{(\kappa-1)}$, which has coefficients in the $\alpha_{i,j,l}^{x_{\mathrm{inp}(l)}}, r_{i,j,l}^{x_{\mathrm{inp}(l)}}$ terms. The adversary $\mathcal{A}$ knows the values $\alpha_{i,j,l}^{x_{\mathrm{inp}(l)}}$ as they are the entries from one of the original branching programs. The values β_i are the same in both branching programs so we can view $\beta^{(\kappa-1)}$ as a linear polynomial in the set of variables $r^{(x)}$.

Now, consider two bit strings x, x' where there is only a single bit difference between the two at position $t \neq 1$. Let $x_l = x_{\mathrm{inp}(l)} = x'_{\mathrm{inp}(l)}$ and consider the monomials in the matrix entries $r_{i,j,1}^{x_{\mathrm{inp}(1)}}$. Notice that the coefficients will only change in the values $\alpha_{i,j,t}^{x_{\mathrm{inp}(t)}}$ — since the β_l variables are fixed at level l. Let $c_{i,j,1}^{x_{\mathrm{inp}(1)}}$, $c'^{x_{\mathrm{inp}(1)}}_{i,j,1}$ denote the coefficients of $r_{i,j,1}^{x_{\mathrm{inp}(1)}}$ after computing $\delta_x \leftarrow \mathsf{JZTParam}(\widehat{\mathcal{M}}_b(x))$ and $\delta_{x'} \leftarrow \mathsf{JZTParam}(\widehat{\mathcal{M}}_b(x'))$, respectively. Then, as long as $\mathsf{JTest}(\delta_x) = \mathsf{JTest}(\delta_{x'}) = 1$, notice that if we compute

$$c'^{x_{\mathrm{inp}(1)}}_{i,j,1} \delta_x - c_{i,j,1}^{x_{\mathrm{inp}(1)}} \delta_{x'} = \tilde{\delta}.$$

we remove the monomial in the variable $r_{i,j,1}^{x_{\mathrm{inp}(1)}}$. To see this, note that by multiplying through the coefficient of $r_{i,j,1}^{x_{\mathrm{inp}(1)}}$ with the coefficient from the opposing output gives equal monomials in both expressions. Subtracting the two scaled outputs removes this monomial entirely, all other monomials are scaled by the coefficient that is multiplied through.

The power of this attack is that it only requires four inputs to remove all monomials that are linear in some $r_{i,j,l}^{x_{\mathrm{inp}(l)}}$ for any program length L. That is, we iterate over the possible four choices for the first two input bits and fix the remaining $L - 2$ input bits. Recall, that we are only interested in annihilating the monomials that are linear in the variables $r_{i,j,l}^{x_{\mathrm{inp}(l)}}$. Moreover, the annihilation is performed on the polynomial evaluations that arise after computing the branching program on these four different inputs. Let $x \in \{00, 01, 10, 11\}$ describe the four varying inputs and notice that, for any $r_{i,j,l'}^{x_{\mathrm{inp}(l')}}$ for $l' \notin \{1, 2\}$, then the coefficient of the monomial in δ_x changes only in the values of $\alpha_{i,j,l_x}^{x_{\mathrm{inp}(l_x)}}$ for $l_x \in \{1, 2\}$ — which are known the adversary. Moreover, for the monomials in entries $r_{i,j,l_x}^{x_{\mathrm{inp}(l_x)}}$, precisely two of the polynomial evaluations contain monomials with differing coefficients. Therefore, we have at least two polynomials containing each variable $r_{i,j,l}^{x_{\mathrm{inp}(l)}}$; thus the problem essentially becomes solving a set of linear simultaneous equations of rank less than four. By performing operations over these polynomial evaluations to reduce the rank of the system from four to three then we create a polynomial where all monomials $r_{i,j,l}^{x_{inp}(l)}$ are annihilated. There are $25(L + 2) + 10$ variables that need to be annihilated which is linear in the length of the branching program — the attack needs to be applied this many times but this is clearly efficient.[6]

Thus, once an equation is solved a distinguishing attack in the **IND-$\mathcal{M}$** game can be launched. The final result is a term δ that is noticeably smaller than all previous outputs δ_x since the only monomials that are left have degree $\leq \kappa - 2$ in the variables β_i. The β_i variables are the largest components of δ_x and so the magnitude noticeably decreases. Notice, that the attack only works for the choice of one branching program, i.e. the attack works in the case where $\widehat{\mathcal{M}_0}$ is encoded rather than $\widehat{\mathcal{M}_1}$ (without loss of generality). Therefore, if the attack fails (i.e. the magnitude of δ is no smaller) then $\mathcal{A}$ outputs $b' = 1$; if it does work they output $b' = 0$. The attack works with probability 1 and so we have no security when analysing our MJP scheme in the **IND-$\mathcal{M}$** game.

4.3   Initial Analysis of Security in IND-OBF game

Recall that the **IND-OBF** game adds extra randomisation details to the branching program that are commonplace in most IO constructions. Importantly, it mimics the structure of BGK-style obfuscated branching programs. In this setting, instantiating using GGH13 is insecure due to the attacks of [CGH17, MSZ16a, ADGM16] and as such these attacks also work in our simplified model. We show that there is an observable difference between our MJP scheme and that of GGH13 since the multiplicative bundling scalars introduced in **IND-OBF** seem to render our previous attack useless. However, we stress that it is likely a variant of the attack could be used to still distinguish easily in the game.

Concretely, the adversary in **IND-OBF** receives $\widehat{M_0}, \widehat{M_{x_{inp}(l),l}}, \widehat{M_{L+1}}$ that are, respectively, encodings of the following matrices:

- $\epsilon_0 M_0 \cdot \mathcal{R}_0$;
- $\epsilon_{x_{inp}(l),l} \mathcal{R}_{l-1}^{-1} \cdot M_{x_{inp}(l),l} \cdot \mathcal{R}_l$;
- $\epsilon_{L+1} \mathcal{R}_L^{-1} \cdot M_{L+1}$.

Recall, $\mathcal{R}_0, \ldots, \mathcal{R}_L$ are randomly sampled invertible matrices used to implement Kilian's randomisation technique and $\epsilon_0, \{\epsilon_{x_{inp}(l),l}\}_{l \in [L]}, \epsilon_{L+1}$ are random multiplicative bundling scalars taken from R_q. There are other techniques that are used for protecting constructions of indistinguishability obfuscation (such as encoding with respect to a straddling sets structure), but for simplicity we only consider these randomisation measures.

Indeed, it appears that the randomisation matrices obscure the encoded values to the adversary. However, we can write each encoded matrix at level l as:

$$\widehat{M_{x_{inp}(l),l}} = \epsilon_{x_{inp}(l),l} \mathcal{R}_{l-1}^{-1} \cdot M_{x_{inp}(l),l} \cdot \mathcal{R}_l + E_{x_{inp}(l),l}/\beta_l$$

---

[6] After each iteration the output is also scaled by the coefficients used previously so these need to be taken account for in further operations.

where $E_{x_{inp(l)},l}$ is a matrix containing the entries $r_{i,j,l}^{x_{inp(l)}}$.[7] However, a change of variables transformation allows us to rewrite the encodings as

$$\widehat{M}_{x_{inp(l)},l} = \epsilon_{x_{inp(l)},l} \mathcal{R}_{l-1}^{-1} \cdot (M_{x_{inp(l)},l} + E_{x_{inp(l)},l}/\beta_l) \cdot \mathcal{R}_l$$

which lets us assume that the adversary still has knowledge of the encoded values. This technique was first used by Miles et al. [MSZ16a] in justifying their annihilation attack scenario. Thus, while Kilian randomisation procedures are still regarded as an important facet of IO candidates, it would appear that they do very little to prevent known attacks.[8]

The reason that our attack no longer works trivially is due to the introduction of the multiplicative bundling scalars. These act as unknown variables in the final output when computing δ_x as the zero-tested output of $\widehat{\mathcal{M}}_b(x)$. Consider the monomials that are linear in some random variable $r_{i,j,l}^{x_{inp(l)}}$; we previously annihilated any such monomial by picking two inputs x, x' differing only on one input bit in position t. The outputs δ_x, δ'_x would now also include different scalars $\epsilon_{x_t,t}$ that are unknown to the adversary. This means that the previous technique for annihilating the monomial in variable $r_{i,j,l}^{x_{inp(l)}}$ is no longer possible since it would also require scaling by $\epsilon_{x_t,t}$.

There are $2L + 2$ input mixing scalars and a total $50L + 10$ matrix entries $r_{i,j,l}^{x_{inp(l)}}$. It is, in principle, possible (by a corollary of Theorem 2 of Kayal [Kay09]) to carry out a generic annihilation attack since there are 2^L possible inputs. Such an attack would require finding annihilating polynomials for each of the monomials (degree $\kappa + 1$) in the variables $r_{i,j,l}^{x_{inp(l)}}, \{\epsilon_{x_{inp(l)},l}\}_l, \epsilon_0, \epsilon_{L+1}$ for an input x. Computing general annihilating polynomials is believed to be a $\#P$-hard problem and indeed there are some sets of cubic polynomials for which the annihilating polynomial cannot be expressed by a poly-depth circuit [MSZ16a, Kay09]. As such, the distinguishing attack above no longer seems to apply, though we stress that we cannot prove hardness under any reasonable assumption.

Thus, it appears that our encoding scheme may still be able to be used in instantiating BGK-style obfuscators in our security model, even though these obfuscators are insecure when instantiated via GGH13. Exploring the possibility of attacks that could distinguish in this setting would be valuable in further ascertaining the relationship between our encodings and original GGH13.

5   Discussion of Findings

Finally, we summarise and address the key points arising from our analysis and give points that may warrant further attention.

---

[7] We ignore the usage of each z_l in the encodings for now as these are removed after zero-testing.

[8] It may be wise to no longer think of these random invertible matrices as offering any security when analysing IO candidates.

Structural Faults in GGH13. Our main focus is to highlight that the GGH13 GES bears structural faults that are vulnerable even when a natural variant where the ideals are removed is constructed. All previous attacks exploit the presence of the generator g in each encoding to learn a basis of the ideal $\langle g \rangle$. We show that removing the capability to learn this ideal does not prevent distinguishing attacks in a simplified Security model.

These faults appear to be mitigated by considering more complete obfuscation techniques in our security model, though we fully expect a more sophisticated attack to be viable via the annihilating polynomial route. In order to make security more concrete we would need to reduce the hardness of finding annihilating polynomials for our case back to a plausible hard problem. This may take into account the hardness of finding an annihilating polynomial for a general set of algebraically dependent polynomials in R_q.

CGH Attacks. The attacks of Chen, Gentry and Halevi [CGH17] use a variant of an annihilation attack, along with knowledge of the ratios of input mixing scalars to launch powerful attacks on various IO candidates (including recent immunisations). These attacks can be prevented using input authentication methods [FRS16], however these prevention methods lie outside scope of the weakened graded encoding model.

It is not completely clear whether a variant of the CGH attack can be leveraged on an IO candidate using our MJP scheme. This is because it explicitly launches a distinguishing attack based on the ideal $\langle g \rangle$. It would be valuable to investigate whether a variant of their attack can be used to break our MJP scheme as well. Such a result would add weight to the fact that structural faults in 'GGH-like' encodings are to be blamed rather than the presence of g explicitly.

Thus, it might be preferable to instantiate immunised IO candidates with our MJP scheme rather than GGH13 as our encodings provide no natural way of finding a basis of representative ideals. Furthermore, immunised constructions seem to prevent MSZ-like attacks on the underlying encoding schemes and thus also prevent the simplified attack that we described in Sect. 4.2. However, this should not be construed as having confidence in the security of our scheme. It is an interesting open question if the attacks in [CGH17] can be generalised to our case.

A   Multilinear Jigsaw Puzzles

Typically, IO candidates are instantiated via multilinear jigsaw puzzles (MJPs) — a restricted variant of a GES where lower-level encodings of zero are not permitted and only certain types of multilinear form can be computed. From now on we will use the following MJP formalisation when referring to the functionality required for constructing IO rather than the wider GES framework.

Definition 2 (MJP Scheme). *A multilinear jigsaw puzzle consists of two algorithms* (JGen, JVer) *that generate the puzzle and verify a solution to the puzzle, respectively. We explain the algorithms in detail.*

Puzzle generation: *The algorithm* JGen *comprises the triple of sub-algorithms* (JInstGen, JEnc, JGenPuzz) *described as such:*

- JInstGen($1^\lambda, 1^\kappa$) : *On input the security parameter λ and multilinearity κ, this algorithm outputs a set of private parameters* sk *needed to encode ring elements, and a set of public parameters* pp = (prms, evk, ztk). *The last two components of the public tuple are necessary to perform algebraic operations over the encodings, and for zero-testing, respectively. The system-wide parameters* prms *include a prime q defining the working ring, a set universe $\mathcal{U}$, and a partition $\{\mathcal{S}_1, \ldots, \mathcal{S}_\kappa\}$ of $\mathcal{U}$.*

- JEnc(prms, sk, $\mathcal{S}, a$) : *On input* sk, *a set $\mathcal{S} \subset \mathcal{U}$ and $a \in \mathbb{Z}_q$, this algorithm outputs an encoding v relative to the set $\mathcal{S}$.*

- JGenPuzz($1^\lambda, 1^\kappa, l, A$) : *Takes as input the security and multilinearity parameters, $l \in \mathbb{N}$ and a set $A = (A_1, \ldots, A_l)$, where A_i is a set of values $\{a_j\}_{j \in [m_i]}$ that will be encoded with respect to index set $\mathcal{S}_i$. First it runs* JInstGen($1^\lambda, 1^\kappa$) *to receive system parameters* (sk, pp = (prms, evk, ztk)). *It then runs* JEnc *on inputs* (prms, sk) *and each element $(\mathcal{S}_i, a_j) \in A_i$ to receive encodings $(\mathcal{S}_i, v_j) \in C_i$.*

  Let puzzle = $(C_1, \ldots, C_l)$ *and let $X = ((\mathcal{S}_1, v_1), \ldots, (\mathcal{S}_l, v_l))$, then we define (X, puzzle) as the output of* JGen *where X is kept secret and* puzzle *is the public output.*

Puzzle verification: *Algorithm* JVer *takes as input the public parameters* pp = (prms, evk, ztk), *the public output* puzzle *of* JGen *and some multilinear form F (the solution to the puzzle). It outputs either acceptance or rejection. More formally, following [MSZ16a], we split the verification into three sub-algorithms* JVer = (JCompute, JZTParam, JTest). *This helps in capturing the weakened grading encoding security model [MSZ16a, GMM+16].*

- JCompute(prms, evk, puzzle, F) : *On input the encodings in* puzzle *and some* valid *multilinear form F, outputs the encoding $(\mathcal{S}, v) = F(\text{puzzle})$ for $\mathcal{S} \subseteq \mathcal{U}$. We will sometimes abuse notation and simply write the output of the algorithm as $F(\text{puzzle})$.*

- JZTParam(prms, ztk, $(\mathcal{S}, v)$) : *On input encoding $(\mathcal{S}, v)$ it first checks if $\mathcal{S} = \mathcal{U}$ and if not aborts. If true, it outputs the ring element δ. In an honest execution we have that $(\mathcal{S}, v) \leftarrow$ JCompute(puzzle, F).*

- JTest(prms, δ) : *On input ring element δ it returns 1 or 0. In an honest execution we have that $\delta \leftarrow$ JZTParam(prms, ztk, $(\mathcal{U}, v)$).*

In the above definition, by *valid* multilinear form, we mean some sort of computation that respects the computation laws of a graded encoding scheme and outputs a top-level encoding [GGH+13b]. For instance, for any encodings $(\mathcal{S}_1, v_1), (\mathcal{S}_2, v_2)$ we have an addition operation that is defined when $\mathcal{S} = \mathcal{S}_1 = \mathcal{S}_2$ and outputs the encoding $(\mathcal{S}, v_1 + v_2)$. We also have multiplication that is defined when $\mathcal{S}_1 \cap \mathcal{S}_2 = \emptyset$ and results in an encoding $(\mathcal{S}, v_1 \cdot v_2)$ for $\mathcal{S} = \mathcal{S}_1 \cup \mathcal{S}_2$. The output of these operations is said to be a top-level encoding when $\mathcal{S} = \mathcal{U}$.

Definition 3 (MJP Correctness). *A jigsaw verifier* JVer *is correct for a tuple* (pp, $(X, \text{puzzle}), F$) *if either $F(X) = (\mathcal{U}, 0)$ and* JVer(puzzle, F) = 1 *or $F(X) \neq (\mathcal{U}, 0)$ and* JVer(puzzle, F) = 0. *Otherwise it is incorrect on F.*

We specifically require that JVer is correct on all but negligibly many forms (see [GGH+13b] for an explanation of the requirement).

Security. Characterising the security that should be offered by a MJP is one of the difficulties confronted by constructions of IO. In short, constructions of IO are proven secure in a generic model where encodings are treated as random handles and all operations that can be performed are interacted with via oracle calls. Yet, as discussed above, current MJP constructions do not justify the use of such a model, i.e. they are broken by attacks which fall our side of this model. See [MSZ16a, GMM+16] for more details.

B   MJP from Our Encoding Scheme

Using the encodings that we describe in Sect. 3.1 we can now construct an MJP scheme. Note that we refer to jigsaw generation and verification as both algorithms and as specific roles within a computation interchangeably.

B.1   Setup

Instance Generation. (JInstGen): On input the security parameter 1^λ, and perceived multilinearity κ the algorithm does the following:

- Samples the prime integer q
- Samples κ uniform polynomials z_i from the ring R_q
- Samples κ polynomials β_i fulfilling the requirements set out in Sect. 3
- Outputs $(\mathsf{sk}, \mathsf{pp}) = ((\beta_i, z_i), (\{\mathcal{S}_i\}_{i \in [\kappa]}, q))$

Encoding. (JEnc): This algorithm takes as input some value α, an index set $\mathcal{S}_i$ and a pair $(\beta_i, z_i) = \mathsf{sk}$ sampled from JInstGen and:

- Samples a small element r uniformly from the error distribution χ
- Computes $v = \frac{\alpha + r/\beta_i}{z_i}$ as an encoding of the value α

Jigsaw Generation. (JGen): Takes as input an index set $\mathcal{S}_i$, the pair (β_i, z_i) for $i \in [\kappa]$ and associated encoded values $(\alpha_1, \ldots, \alpha_{m_i})$ for each of these pairs, where m_i is the number of values to be encoded with respect to $\mathcal{S}_i$. Then this algorithm performs the following:

- Inputs each tuple $(\mathcal{S}_i, \alpha_j)$ for $j \in [m_i]$ to the encode algorithm JEnc and receives back the κ sets C_i where C_i consists of all pairs $(\mathcal{S}_i, v_j)$ for $1 \le j \le m_i$.
- Generates the zero-testing parameter p_{zt} by computing

$$p_{zt} = \prod_{i=1}^{\kappa} \beta_i \cdot z_i$$

– Creates

$$\mathsf{puzzle} = (q, \{C_1, \ldots, C_\kappa\}, p_{zt}) \tag{7}$$

as the public output. Let $\boldsymbol{\alpha}^{(i)}$ be the set of values $\{\alpha_1, \ldots, \alpha_{m_i}\}$ that are encoded with respect to $\mathcal{S}_i$ — then the private output is defined as

$$X = (\boldsymbol{\alpha}^{(1)}, \ldots, \boldsymbol{\alpha}^{(\kappa)}).$$

Note that the values r, β and z are all kept secret in order to preserve the secrecy of the encoded values. Public access to each β_i and z_i is granted in the form of the zero-test parameter p_{zt}, though it should be impossible to decompose this into the individual factors.

B.2   Jigsaw Verification

As before, we note that the zero-test procedure is split into three separate algorithms to accurately model the security setting that we consider. These three algorithms are defined as the following:

Computation. (JCompute): Takes as input the encodings $v_j^{(i)}$ with respect to each index set $\mathcal{S}_i$ and a multilinear form, F, and outputs

$$v^* = F(v_1^{(1)}, \ldots, v_{m_1}^{(1)}, \ldots, v_1^{(\kappa)}, \ldots, v_{m_\kappa}^{(\kappa)})$$

where v^* is a top-level encoding as shown in Equation (4).

Zero-Testing. (JZTParam): Takes as input an encoding v^* resulting from the JCompute algorithm and p_{zt} from puzzle and output $\delta = p_{zt} \cdot v^*$

Zero-Test Output. (JTest): Takes δ as an output from the JZTParam algorithm and checks the magnitude of the element. If it has magnitude greater than $\prod_{i=1}^\kappa \beta_i$ then output 1 (encoded value is zero). Otherwise output 0 (encoded value is non-zero).

Finally the overarching JVer algorithm defined previously simply runs these three algorithms in sequence and outputs the result of JTest.

B.3   Correctness of Construction

The homomorphic properties of our encodings as shown in the previous section enable us to evaluate the multilinear forms that are input to the JCompute algorithm. Correctness is lost post-zero-testing if wrap-around modulo q occurs for a top-level encoding, or if an encoding of zero exceeds $q^{\frac{\kappa-1}{\kappa}}$. Since we specifically sample the β_i elements from R_q such that we satisfy these requirements and since each of the sampled elements are small.

C   Additional Ring Preliminaries

Canonical Embeddings. Let ζ_m denote a primitive m-th root of unity. The m-th cyclotomic number field $Q = \mathbb{Q}(\zeta_m)$ is the field extension of $\mathbb{Q}$ obtained by adjoining ζ_m. Let n be the degree of K over $\mathbb{Q}$, then there are n embeddings σ_i of $K \to \mathbb{C}$. These n embeddings correspond precisely to evaluation in each of the n distinct roots α_i of $\phi(x)$. In our case, $\psi(x)$ has $2 \cdot s_2 = n$ complex conjugate roots. Order the roots such that $\overline{\alpha_k} = \alpha_{s_2+k}$ for $k = 1, \ldots, s_2$. The *canonical embedding* $\sigma : K \to \mathbb{C}^n$ is defined as

$$a \mapsto (\sigma_1(a), \ldots, \sigma_{s_s}(a), \overline{\sigma_1}(a), \ldots, \overline{\sigma_{s_2}}(a)).$$

The canonical embedding maps into a space $H \subset \mathbb{C}^n$ given by

$$H = \{(x_1, \ldots, x_n) \in \mathbb{C}^n : \overline{x_j} = x_{s_2+j}, \forall 1 \le j \le s_2\}$$

which is isomorphic to $\mathbb{R}^n$ and we can represent the coordinates of $\sigma(a)$ by a real vector [CIV16]

$$(\tilde{a}_1, \ldots, \tilde{a}_n) \propto (\Re(\sigma_1(a)), \ldots, \Re(\sigma_{s_2}(a)), \Im(\sigma_1(a)), \ldots, \Im(\sigma_{s_2}(a))).$$

This naturally induces a geometry on K with ℓ_2-norm $\|\cdot\|_2$ and ℓ_∞-norm $\|\cdot\|_\infty$:

$$\|a\|_2 = \|\sigma(a)\|_2 = \left(\sum_{i=1}^{n} |\tilde{a}_i|^2\right)^{1/2} \quad \text{and}$$

$$\|a\|_\infty = \|\sigma(a)\|_\infty = \max_i |\tilde{a}_i|.$$

Bounded Distributions. When sampling our encodings we are required to define a B-bounded distribution, where all elements sampled from this distribution have an l_∞ norm that is bounded by B. In this section we will formally define such a distribution.

Definition 4 *(B-bounded element).* *An element $p \in R$ is called B-bounded if $\|p\|_\infty \le B$.*

Definition 5 *(B-bounded distribution).* *A distribution ensemble $\{\chi_\lambda\}_{\lambda \in \mathbb{N}}$, supported over R, is called B-bounded (for $B = B(\lambda)$) if for all p in the support of χ_λ, we have $\|p\|_\infty < B$. In other words, a B-bounded distribution over R outputs a B-bounded polynomial.*

Lemma 1 *([LTV12]). Let $n \in \mathbb{N}$, let $\phi(x) = x^n + 1$ and let $R = \mathbb{Z}[x]/\langle\phi(x)\rangle$. For any $s, t \in R$,*

$$\|s \cdot t\| \le \sqrt{n} \cdot \|s\| \cdot \|t\| \quad \text{and} \quad \|s \cdot t\|_\infty \le \|s\|_\infty \cdot \|t\|_\infty$$

Corollary 1 *([LTV12]). Take $n, \phi(x), R$ as before. Let $s_1, \ldots, s_k \leftarrow_s \chi$ where χ is a B-bounded distribution over the ring R. Then $s := \prod_{i=1}^{k} s_i$ is $(n^{k-1}B^k)$-bounded.*

Gaussian Sampling. For any real $r > 0$ the *Gaussian function* on $\mathbb{R}^n$ centred at $\mathbf{c}$ with parameter r is defined as:

$$\forall \mathbf{x} \in \mathbb{R}^n \quad : \quad \rho_{r,c}(\mathbf{x}) := e^{-\pi||\mathbf{x}-\mathbf{c}||^2/r^2}$$

Definition 6. *For any $n \in N$ and for any $\mathbf{c} \in \mathbb{R}^n$ and real $r > 0$, the Discrete Gaussian distribution over $\mathbb{Z}^n$ with standard deviation r and centred at $\mathbf{c}$ is defined as:*

$$\forall \mathbf{x} \in \mathbb{Z} : D_{\mathbb{Z}^n, r, \mathbf{c}} := \frac{\rho_{r,c}(\mathbf{x})}{\rho_{r,c}(\mathbb{Z}^n)}$$

where $\rho_{r,c}(\mathbb{Z}^n) := \sum\limits_{\mathbf{x} \in \mathbb{Z}^n} \rho_{r,c}(\mathbf{x})$ is a normalisation factor.

The work of [MR04] showed that the discrete Gaussian distribution over $\mathbb{Z}^n$ with standard deviation r outputs elements that are $(r\sqrt{n})$-bounded with high probability $(\geq 1 - 1/2^{-n+1})$. We can then define the *truncated* Gaussian distribution that is $(r\sqrt{n})$-bounded and is statistically close to the discrete Gaussian.

The truncated Gaussian with standard deviation r and centred at $\mathbf{c}$ will be denoted by $\bar{D}_{\mathbb{Z}^n, r, \mathbf{c}}$ and can be defined by sampling polynomials according to the discrete Gaussian ($D_{\mathbb{Z}^n, r, \mathbf{c}}$) and repeating any samples that are not $(r\sqrt{n})$-bounded. We note that this distribution is statistically close to $D_{\mathbb{Z}^n, r, \mathbf{c}}$ as shown in [LTV12]. For the case where $\mathbf{c} = 0$ we will simply write $\bar{D}_{\mathbb{Z}^n, r}$.

Our GES (Sect. 3) relies on distinguishing between products of $\kappa - 1$ and κ elements. For this, we sample real vectors $(\tilde{a}_1, \ldots, \tilde{a}_n)$ with each coordinate sampled from a Gaussian distribution conditioned on a minimum size through rejection sampling. Mapping these real vectors to elements in K produces the desired distribution in K. We then discretise, i.e. randomised round each coordinate to an integer to obtain elements in $\mathbb{Z}[x]/\langle \phi(x) \rangle$ as usual.

Thus, we may infer the magnitude of elements that are sampled from certain distributions and latterly what the magnitude of such an element is expected to be after multiplying any number of these elements is. We can use this information to make statements on the size of encodings that are made up of elements sampled from such B-bounded distributions.

D   GGH13 and Annihilation Attacks

D.1   GGH13 Overview

The space for GGH13 encodings is $R_q = R/qR$ where q is some big integer and $R = \mathbb{Z}[x]/(x^m + 1)$ for $m \in \mathbb{N}$. The plaintext ring is defined by $R_g = R/gR$ where g is a small element in the ring. A GGH13 encoding takes the form $v = (\alpha + rg)/z$ mod q where z is some uniformly random value — z and g are secret — α is the encoded plaintext value and r is some small random value, all these values are sampled from some error distribution, χ, over R_q.

The denominators z enforce the levels of the GES, where we can sample one global z for the symmetric case and $z_1, \ldots, z_\kappa$ in the asymmetric case, we will consider the asymmetric case unless otherwise stated. Where an encoding v has a denominator z_i we will say that v is encoded at level $\mathcal{S}_i$ where there are κ such index sets. Additions and multiplications are carried out by simply adding and multiplying encodings directly. Clearly, additions of encodings indexed at the same level results in another encoding at that level. Multiplying two encodings, indexed by z_1 and z_2 respectively, results in an encoding at level $\mathcal{S}_1 \cup \mathcal{S}_2$.

Finally, there is a public zero-test parameter

$$p_{zt} = \frac{h \cdot \prod\limits_{i=1}^{\kappa} z_i}{g}$$

for some 'smallish' $h \in R_q$.[9] We can learn whether an encoding $(\mathcal{U}, v)$ (e.g. top-level with denominator $z_1 \cdots z_\kappa$) encodes zero or not by computing $p_{zt} \cdot v$ and seeing if the result is small.

The functionality described can be adapted to construct a correct MJP scheme [GGH+13b].

D.2   Annihilation Attacks on GGH13

Let $\widehat{\mathcal{M}}$ be a randomised branching program that has entries encoded as GGH13 elements and each pair of matrices $\widehat{M}_{b,l}$ and bookends $\widehat{M}_0, \widehat{M}_{L+1}$ are encoded with respect to the levels $l \in \{0, \ldots, L+1\}$. Let $x \in \mathcal{X}$ be some valid input for $\widehat{\mathcal{M}}$ and let $\mu_x \leftarrow \widehat{\mathcal{M}}(x)$ be the output. Finally denote $\delta_x = p_{zt} \cdot \mu_x = \mathsf{JZTParam}(\mu_x)$ as the zero-tested output.

A top-level GGH13 encoding will have the following form:

$$\delta_x = \widetilde{\alpha}_x \cdot g^{-1} + \gamma_{1,x} + \gamma_{2,x} \cdot g + \ldots + \gamma_{\kappa,x} \cdot g^{\kappa-1} \qquad (8)$$

after zero-testing has occurred. The target of the annihilation attacks is the polynomial $\gamma_{1,x}(\alpha, r)$ which is linear in the unknown sampled elements r_j from each encoding v_j. Using a change of variables in the branching program it is possible to assume that the adversary has knowledge of the values α_j that are encoded in each of the matrices [MSZ16a] (see Sect. 4.3 for more details). By choosing enough inputs x such that $\alpha_x = 0$, the adversary is able to guarantee that there exists an annihilating polynomial Q for the set of $\gamma_{1,x}$ polynomials [Kay09]. In fact, the work of [MSZ16a] explicitly gives a description of Q for a given single-input branching program $\mathcal{M}$.

Consequently, the result $\rho_x \leftarrow Q(\{\delta_x\}_x)$ results in some output where the $\gamma_{1,x}$ polynomials are eliminated. In particular, this means that $\rho_x \in \langle g \rangle$. By computing enough outputs, an adversary can heuristically construct a basis of $\langle g \rangle$. The attack concludes by specifying a functionally equivalent $\mathcal{M}'$ where the set of polynomials $\gamma'_{1,x}$ are not annihilated by Q. The work of [MSZ16a] show that it is

---

[9] The exact magnitude is not important for the attack in [MSZ16a] as long as $h \ll q$.

possible to construct $\mathcal{M}, \mathcal{M}'$ such that a PPT adversary with obfuscated access to either of the circuits can first construct a basis of $\langle g \rangle^{10}$ and then secondly distinguish between the circuits. Distinguishing is possible since $\rho'_x \leftarrow \widehat{\mathcal{M}}'(x)$ is not in $\langle g \rangle$ and so they are able to distinguish using the basis computed in the first step.

E   Algebraic Dependence

Here, we list definitions and key results taken from the work of [Kay09] that we use in the security analysis of our MJP scheme. In short, we articulate the formalisation of expressing algebraic dependencies for a set of polynomials sampled from a particular field.

Definition 7. *Let $f = (f_1, \ldots, f_k)$ be a vector of k polynomials (of degree $\leq d$) where each $f_i \in \mathbb{F}[y_1, \ldots, y_n]$ is an n-variate polynomial over the field $\mathbb{F}$. A non-zero polynomial $A(t_1, \ldots, t_k) \in \mathbb{F}[t_1, \ldots, t_k]$ is said to be an annihilating polynomial for f if $A(f_1, \ldots, f_k) = 0$. The polynomials $f_1, \ldots, f_k$ are said to be algebraically dependent if such an annihilating polynomial exists.*

Definition 8. *Let $f = (f_1, \ldots, f_k)$ be a vector of k polynomials as above where f' represents some subset of algebraically independent polynomials of maximal size k (i.e. for any $f_{k+1} \in \mathbb{F}[y_1, \ldots, y_n]$ then the set $f' \cup f_{k+1}$ is algebraically dependent). Then the algebraic rank of the set of polynomials f is k.*

Theorem 1 (Theorem 2 [Kay09]). *Let $f_1, \ldots, f_k \in \mathbb{F}[x_1, \ldots, x_n]$ be a set of k polynomials in n variables over the field $\mathbb{F}$. Then this set of polynomials has algebraic rank k if and only if the Jacobian matrix, $Jf(x)$, has rank k.*

Corollary 2 ([Kay09, BS83]). *There exists a randomized polynomial time algorithm that on input a set of k arithmetic circuits over a field $\mathbb{F}$, determines if the polynomials computed by these arithmetic circuits are algebraically dependent or not.*

Remark 3. The algorithm mentioned by Corollary 2 essentially requires submitting random values in place of the variables in the Jacobian matrix $Jf(x)$. By the Schwarz-Zippel lemma, the rank of the symbolic matrix is likely to be the same as the rank of the matrix evaluated on random inputs with high probability. As such we can calculate the algebraic rank for a given system of polynomials.

References

[ABD16] Albrecht, M., Bai, S., Ducas, L.: A subfield lattice attack on overstretched NTRU assumptions. In: Robshaw, M., Katz, J. (eds.) CRYPTO 2016. LNCS, vol. 9814, pp. 153–178. Springer, Heidelberg (2016). https://doi. org/10.1007/978-3-662-53018-4_6

---

[10] It is possible to find inputs for both circuits that allow the adversary to construct a basis of $\langle g \rangle$.

156   M.R. Albrecht et al.

[ADGM16] Apon, D., Döttling, N., Garg, S., Mukherjee, P.: Cryptanalysis of indistinguishability obfuscations of circuits over GGH13. Cryptology ePrint Archive, Report 2016/1003 (2016). http://eprint.iacr.org/2016/1003

[AGIS14] Ananth, P.V., Gupta, D., Ishai, Y., Sahai, A.: Optimizing obfuscation: avoiding Barrington's theorem. In: Ahn, G.-J., Yung, M., Li, N. (eds.), ACM CCS 2014, pp. 646–658. ACM Press, November 2014

[Bar89] Barrington, D.A.M.: Bounded-width polynomial-size branching programs recognize exactly those languages in nc^1. J. Comput. Syst. Sci. **38**(1), 150–164 (1989)

[BGK+14] Barak, B., Garg, S., Kalai, Y.T., Paneth, O., Sahai, A.: Protecting obfuscation against algebraic attacks. In: Nguyen, P.Q., Oswald, E. (eds.) EUROCRYPT 2014. LNCS, vol. 8441, pp. 221–238. Springer, Heidelberg (2014). https://doi.org/10.1007/978-3-642-55220-5_13

[BLR+15] Boneh, D., Lewi, K., Raykova, M., Sahai, A., Zhandry, M., Zimmerman, J.: Semantically secure order-revealing encryption: multi-input functional encryption without obfuscation. In: Oswald, E., Fischlin, M. (eds.) EUROCRYPT 2015. LNCS, vol. 9057, pp. 563–594. Springer, Heidelberg (2015). https://doi.org/10.1007/978-3-662-46803-6_19

[BMSZ15] Badrinarayanan, S., Miles, E., Sahai, A., Zhandry, M.: Post-zeroizing obfuscation: the case of evasive circuits. Cryptology ePrint Archive, Report 2015/167 (2015). http://eprint.iacr.org/2015/167

[BS83] Baur, W., Strassen, V.: The complexity of partial derivatives. Theor. Comput. Sci. **22**, 317–330 (1983)

[BWZ14] Boneh, D., Waters, B., Zhandry, M.: Low overhead broadcast encryption from multilinear maps. In: Garay and Gennaro [GG14], pp. 206–223

[CGH17] Chen, Y., Gentry, C., Halevi, S.: Cryptanalyses of candidate branching program obfuscators. In: Coron, J.-S., Nielsen, J.B. (eds.) EUROCRYPT 2017. LNCS, vol. 10212, pp. 278–307. Springer, Cham (2017). https://doi.org/10.1007/978-3-319-56617-7_10

[CIV16] Castryck, W., Iliashenko, I., Vercauteren, F.: Provably weak instances of ring-LWE revisited. In: Fischlin and Coron [FC16], pp. 147–167

[CJL16] Cheon, J.H., Jeong, J., Lee, C.: An algorithm for NTRU problems and cryptanalysis of the GGH multilinear map without a low-level encoding of zero. LMS J. Comput. Math. **19**(A), 255–266 (2016)

[CLLT16] Coron, J.-S., Lee, M.S., Lepoint, T., Tibouchi, M.: Cryptanalysis of GGH15 multilinear maps. In: Robshaw and Katz [RK16], pp. 607–628

[CLLT17] Coron, J.-S., Lee, M.S., Lepoint, T., Tibouchi, M.: Zeroizing attacks on indistinguishability obfuscation over CLT13. In: Fehr, S. (ed.) PKC 2017. LNCS, vol. 10174, pp. 41–58. Springer, Heidelberg (2017). https://doi.org/10.1007/978-3-662-54365-8_3

[CLR15] Cheon, J.H., Lee, C., Ryu, H.: Cryptanalysis of the new CLT multilinear maps. Cryptology ePrint Archive, Report 2015/934 (2015). http://eprint.iacr.org/2015/934

[CLT13] Coron, J.-S., Lepoint, T., Tibouchi, M.: Practical multilinear maps over the integers. In: Canetti, R., Garay, J.A. (eds.) CRYPTO 2013. LNCS, vol. 8042, pp. 476–493. Springer, Heidelberg (2013). https://doi.org/10.1007/978-3-642-40041-4_26

[CLT14] Coron, J.-S., Lepoint, T., Tibouchi, M.: Cryptanalysis of two candidate fixes of multilinear maps over the integers. Cryptology ePrint Archive, Report 2014/975 (2014). http://eprint.iacr.org/2014/975

[FC16] Fischlin, M., Coron, J.-S. (eds.): EUROCRYPT 2016, Part I. LNCS, vol. 9665. Springer, Heidelberg (2016)

[FRS16] Fernando, R., Rasmussen, P.M.R., Sahai, A.: Preventing CLT zeroizing attacks on obfuscation. Cryptology ePrint Archive, Report 2016/1070 (2016). http://eprint.iacr.org/2016/1070

[GG14] Garay, J.A., Gennaro, R. (eds.): CRYPTO 2014, Part I. LNCS, vol. 8616. Springer, Heidelberg (2014)

[GGH13a] Garg, S., Gentry, C., Halevi, S.: Candidate multilinear maps from ideal lattices. In: Johansson, T., Nguyen, P.Q. (eds.) EUROCRYPT 2013. LNCS, vol. 7881, pp. 1–17. Springer, Heidelberg (2013). https://doi.org/10.1007/978-3-642-38348-9_1

[GGH+13b] Garg, S., Gentry, C., Halevi, S., Raykova, M., Sahai, A., Waters, B.: Candidate indistinguishability obfuscation and functional encryption for all circuits. In: 54th FOCS, pp. 40–49. IEEE Computer Society Press, October 2013

[GGH+13c] Garg, S., Gentry, C., Halevi, S., Sahai, A., Waters, B.: Attribute-based encryption for circuits from multilinear maps. In: Canetti, R., Garay, J.A. (eds.) CRYPTO 2013. LNCS, vol. 8043, pp. 479–499. Springer, Heidelberg (2013). https://doi.org/10.1007/978-3-642-40084-1_27

[GGH15] Gentry, C., Gorbunov, S., Halevi, S.: Graph-induced multilinear maps from lattices. In: Dodis, Y., Nielsen, J.B. (eds.) TCC 2015. LNCS, vol. 9015, pp. 498–527. Springer, Heidelberg (2015). https://doi.org/10.1007/978-3-662-46497-7_20

[GMM+16] Garg, S., Miles, E., Mukherjee, P., Sahai, A., Srinivasan, A., Zhandry, M.: Secure obfuscation in a weak multilinear map model. In: Hirt, M., Smith, A. (eds.) TCC 2016. LNCS, vol. 9986, pp. 241–268. Springer, Heidelberg (2016). https://doi.org/10.1007/978-3-662-53644-5_10

[GMS16] Garg, S., Mukherjee, P., Srinivasan, A.: Obfuscation without the vulnerabilities of multilinear maps. Cryptology ePrint Archive, Report 2016/390 (2016). http://eprint.iacr.org/2016/390

[Hal15] Halevi, S.: Graded encoding, variations on a scheme. Cryptology ePrint Archive, Report 2015/866 (2015). http://eprint.iacr.org/2015/866

[HJ16] Hu, Y., Jia, H.: Cryptanalysis of GGH map. In: Fischlin and Coron [FC16], pp. 537–565

[Kay09] Kayal, N.: The complexity of the annihilating polynomial. In: Proceedings of the 24th Annual IEEE Conference on Computational Complexity, CCC 2009, Paris, France, 15–18 July 2009, pp. 184–193. IEEE Computer Society (2009)

[KF17] Kirchner, P., Fouque, P.-A.: Revisiting lattice attacks on overstretched NTRU parameters. In: Coron, J.-S., Nielsen, J.B. (eds.) EUROCRYPT 2017. LNCS, vol. 10210, pp. 3–26. Springer, Cham (2017). https://doi.org/10.1007/978-3-319-56620-7_1

[Kil88] Kilian, J.: Zero-knowledge with log-space verifiers. In: 29th FOCS, pp. 25–35. IEEE Computer Society Press, October 1988

[LTV12] López-Alt, A., Tromer, E., Vaikuntanathan, V.: On-the-fly multiparty computation on the cloud via multikey fully homomorphic encryption. In: Karloff, H.J., Pitassi, T. (eds.), 44th ACM STOC, pp. 1219–1234. ACM Press, May 2012

[MR04] Micciancio, D., Regev, O.: Worst-case to average-case reductions based on Gaussian measures. In: 45th FOCS, pp. 372–381. IEEE Computer Society Press, October 2004

[MSW14] Miles, E., Sahai, A., Weiss, M.: Protecting obfuscation against arithmetic attacks. Cryptology ePrint Archive, Report 2014/878 (2014). http://eprint.iacr.org/2014/878

[MSZ16a] Miles, E., Sahai, A., Zhandry, M.: Annihilation attacks for multilinear maps: cryptanalysis of indistinguishability obfuscation over GGH13. In: Robshaw and Katz [RK16], pp. 629–658

[MSZ16b] Miles, E., Sahai, A., Zhandry, M.: Secure obfuscation in a weak multilinear map model: a simple construction secure against all known attacks. Cryptology ePrint Archive, Report 2016/588 (2016). http://eprint.iacr.org/2016/588

[PST14] Pass, R., Seth, K., Telang, S.: Indistinguishability obfuscation from semantically-secure multilinear encodings. In: Garay and Gennaro [GG14], pp. 500–517

[RK16] Robshaw, M., Katz, J. (eds.): CRYPTO 2016, Part II. LNCS, vol. 9815. Springer, Heidelberg (2016)

Signatures

Attribute-Based Signatures
with User-Controlled Linkability
Without Random Oracles

Ali El Kaafarani[1(✉)] and Essam Ghadafi[2]

[1] University of Oxford, Oxford, UK
ali.elkaafarani@maths.ox.ac.uk
[2] University of the West of England, Bristol, UK
essam.ghadafi@uwe.ac.uk

Abstract. Attribute-Based Signatures (ABS) are a versatile crypto-graphic primitive and have many applications. They are a generalization of many widely-used signature-related notions such as group, ring and mesh signatures. Attribute-Based Signatures with User-Controlled Link-ability (ABS-UCL) add the notion of user-controlled linkability to ABS thus allowing users to anonymously and at will maintain a session with a verifier. In this work, we provide the first constructions of ABS-UCL dispensing with heuristic assumptions such as random oracles. We start by providing a generic construction which avoids some of the inefficiency pitfalls of existing constructions. We then provide efficient instantiations supporting expressive signing policies. We also give a concrete construc-tion for threshold policies yielding constant-size signatures. Some of the building blocks we construct might be of independent interest.

Keywords: Attribute-based signatures · User-controlled linkability · Standard model

1 Introduction

Attribute-Based Signatures (ABS), introduced by Maji et al. [28], are a promis-ing, versatile primitive that allows signers to authenticate messages while enjoy-ing fine-grained control over identifying information. In ABS, users sign messages w.r.t. policies satisfied by a set of attributes they possess. The verifier of a sig-nature is convinced that a signer with a set of attributes satisfying the policy in question signed the message but learns neither the identity of the signer nor the exact attributes used to satisfy the policy in question. ABS are a generalization of many prominent notions such as group [11], ring [31] and mesh [8] signa-tures. They have numerous applications including trust negotiation, e.g. [18], attribute-based messaging, e.g. [5], and leaking secrets.

ABS schemes can be categorized according to the expressiveness the policies they support. In threshold ABS (tABS), proposed by Shahandashti and Safavi-Naini [33], the policy is restricted to proving possession of at least t out of

© Springer International Publishing AG 2017
M. O'Neill (Ed.): IMACC 2017, LNCS 10655, pp. 161–184, 2017.
https://doi.org/10.1007/978-3-319-71045-7_9

n attributes. Constructions of tABS schemes include [19,24,27]. ABS schemes supporting more expressive policies, i.e. monotonic access structures, were first given by Maji et al. [28]. Okamoto and Takashima [29,30] gave constructions supporting non-monotonic access structures. Note that any scheme supporting monotonic access structures could be extended to support non-monotonic access structures in a straightforward manner by doubling the universe of attributes. ABS schemes for circuits were given by Tang et al. [34] and Sakai et al. [32]. Practical features such as decentralization [30], user-controlled linkability [15], traceability [16,17,21], and controllable-linkability [35] have been added to ABS schemes resulting in various ABS notions.

El Kaafarani et al. [15] introduced the notion of Attribute-Based Signatures with User-Controlled Linkability (ABS-UCL), which analogously to the Direct Anonymous Attestation (DAA) protocol [9], which is a standardized protocol deployed in practice, it adds the user-controlled linkability feature to standard ABS schemes. More precisely, the user can at her discretion choose to make some of her signatures aimed at a particular verifier linkable without sacrificing her anonymity. Thus, the user-controlled linkability feature allows anonymous users to establish and maintain sessions with particular verifiers. For instance, consider a potential buyer of age-restricted products who wishes to convince the seller that she indeed satisfies the policy in place for buying such products but without revealing her identity. In this scenario, the user may also wish to link her current transaction to some of her earlier anonymous ones, e.g. to benefit from discounts. Another useful application of the controlled-linkability feature is resuming interrupted or lost authentication sessions between communicating parties. The more recent notion of DAA with attributes (DAA-A) [12] can also be viewed as a variant of ABS-UCL where the signer is split into a trusted (computationally-constrained) TPM and a more powerful but not necessarily trusted host. Note that unlike in DAA, where the signature attests to the fact that the user belongs to a particular group, and thanks to the expressiveness of the policies with which signatures in ABS schemes are associated, ABS-UCL allows the user to attest to much broader statements than merely proving she belongs to a particular group. Also, note that ABS-UCL is very different from the notion of Attribute-Based Signatures with Controllable Linkability [35] in which a designated authority (equipped with a secret key) is able to check if two signatures originated from the same signer. Traceable ABS (TABS) [17] and Decentralized Traceable ABS (DTABS) schemes [16,21] add the traceability feature to ABS schemes by granting a designated opener a special tracing key using which she can revoke anonymity when the need arises.

To the best of our knowledge, currently there exist no constructions of anonymous signature schemes offering the user-controlled linkability feature and supporting attributes which do not rely on random oracles. The constructions in [15] as well as the more recent variants in [12] all rely on heuristic assumptions for their security.

Our Contribution. We give a generic construction of ABS-UCL supporting expressive policies, i.e. monotone access structures (and hence non-monotone access structures) and 3 efficient concrete constructions. The first two are instantiations of the generic construction whereas the third construction is a concrete one supporting threshold policies and yielding constant-size signatures. Our generic construction is tailored towards avoiding some of the inefficiency pitfalls of existing ones. Our instantiations are efficient and constitute the first constructions not relying on random oracles [2] and compare favourably to existing related constructions offering different features. As a special case of our constructions, i.e. when the user-controlled linkability requirement is dropped, we obtain efficient instantiations of standard ABS schemes which compare favourably to existing ones. As a building block for some of our constructions, we construct a new efficient partially structure-preserving signature scheme [22], which might be of independent interest.

Paper Organization. In Sect. 2, we give some preliminaries. In Sect. 3, we present the building blocks we use. We define ABS-UCL in Sect. 4. In Sects. 5 and 6, we present our constructions of ABS-UCL.

2 Preliminaries

In this section we present some preliminaries.

2.1 Bilinear Groups

A bilinear group is a tuple $\mathcal{P} := (\mathbb{G}, \mathbb{H}, \mathbb{G}_T, p, G, \tilde{H}, e)$ where $\mathbb{G} := \langle G \rangle, \mathbb{H} := \langle \tilde{H} \rangle$ and $\mathbb{G}_T$ are groups of a prime order p. The function e is a non-degenerate bilinear map $\mathbb{G} \times \mathbb{H} \longrightarrow \mathbb{G}_T$. We focus on Type-III bilinear groups [20], where $\mathbb{G} \neq \mathbb{H}$ and no efficient isomorphisms between $\mathbb{G}$ and $\mathbb{H}$ are known in either direction, since it is well-known it is more efficient than the other settings.

2.2 Intractability Assumptions

We will use the following existing intractability assumptions:

DDH. Given $(G, G^a, G^b, G^c) \in \mathbb{G}^4$ for $a, b, c \leftarrow \mathbb{Z}_p$, where $\mathbb{G} = \langle G \rangle$ is of a prime order p, it is hard to decide whether or not $c = ab \pmod{p}$.
SXDH. This requires that the DDH assumption holds in both groups $\mathbb{G}$ and $\mathbb{H}$.
q-**SDH** [7]. Given $(G, G^x, \ldots, G^{x^q})$ for $x \leftarrow \mathbb{Z}_p$, where $\mathbb{G} = \langle G \rangle$ is of a prime order p, it is hard to output a pair $(c, G^{\frac{1}{x+c}})$, where $c \in \mathbb{Z}_p \backslash \{-x\}$.
q-**DDHI** [6]. Given $(G, G^x, \ldots, G^{x^q})$ for $x \leftarrow \mathbb{Z}_p$, where $\mathbb{G} = \langle G \rangle$ is of a prime order p, it is hard to distinguish $G^{\frac{1}{x}}$ from a random element of $\mathbb{G}$.
(ℓ, m, t)-**aMSE-CDH** [25]. Given $\mathcal{P} := (\mathbb{G}, \mathbb{H}, \mathbb{G}_T, p, G, \tilde{H}, e)$ and $\boldsymbol{x} = (x_1, \cdots, x_{\ell+m}) \leftarrow (\mathbb{Z}_p^\times)^{\ell+m}$, $g_1(X) = \prod_{i=1}^{\ell}(X + x_i)$ and $g_2(X) = \prod_{i=\ell+1}^{\ell+m}(X + x_i)$ for some $\ell, m, t \in \mathbb{N}$. The assumption states that it is infeasible to compute $e(G, \tilde{H})^{\kappa g_1(\gamma)}$ given:

$$G, G^\gamma, \ldots, G^{\gamma^{\ell+t-2}}, G^{\kappa \gamma g_1(\gamma)} \quad (1) \qquad G^{\omega\gamma}, G^{\omega\gamma^2}, \ldots, G^{\omega\gamma^{\ell+t-2}} \quad (2)$$

$$G^\alpha, G^{\alpha\gamma}, \ldots, G^{\alpha\gamma^{\ell+t}} \quad (3) \qquad \tilde{H}, \tilde{H}^\gamma, \ldots, G^{\gamma^{m-2}}, \tilde{H}^{\kappa g_2(\gamma)} \quad (4)$$

$$\tilde{H}^\omega, \tilde{H}^{\omega\gamma}, \ldots, G^{\omega\gamma^{m-1}} \quad (5) \qquad \tilde{H}^\alpha, \tilde{H}^{\alpha\gamma}, \ldots, G^{\alpha\gamma^{2(m-t)+3}} \quad (6)$$

3 Building Blocks

In this section, we present the building blocks we use; this includes a new partially structure-preserving signature scheme that we construct.

3.1 Partially Structure-Preserving Signature Schemes

Ghadafi [22] defined Partially Structure-Preserving Signature (PSPS) schemes as a variant of structure-preserving signature schemes [1] where the only deviation from the definition of the latter is that some part of the message might be field elements rather than group elements. In this work we will use 2 PSPS schemes the first of which is new.

A New PSPS Scheme for the Message Space $\mathbb{G}^n \times \mathbb{Z}_p^{n'}$. We give here a PSPS scheme for the message space $\mathbb{G}^n \times \mathbb{Z}_p^{n'}$. It is an extension of the single-message structure-preserving scheme of Chatterjee and Menezes [10]. The new scheme is as follows:

- KeyGen($\mathcal{P}$):Choose $x_1, \ldots, x_n, y_1, \ldots, y_{n'}, z \leftarrow \mathbb{Z}_p, \tilde{X}_i := \tilde{H}^{x_i}, \tilde{Y}_i := \tilde{H}^{y_i}, \tilde{Z} := \tilde{H}^z$. Return (sk $:= (x_1, \ldots, x_n, y_1, \ldots, y_{n'}, z)$, vk $:= (\tilde{X}_1, \ldots, \tilde{X}_n, \tilde{Y}_1, \ldots, \tilde{Y}_{n'}, \tilde{Z})$).

- Sign$\Big($sk, $\big(U = (U_1, \ldots, U_n), m = (m_1, \ldots, m_{n'})\big) \in \mathbb{G}^n \times \mathbb{Z}_p^{n'}\Big)$: Choose $r \leftarrow \mathbb{Z}_p$. Set $R := G^r$, $\tilde{R} := \tilde{H}^r$, and $S := \prod_{i=1}^n U_i^{x_i} \cdot G^{\sum_{i=1}^{n'} m_i y_i + r^2 + z}$. Return $\sigma := \big(\tilde{R}, R, S\big) \in \mathbb{H} \times \mathbb{G}^2$.

- Verify$\Big($vk, $\big(U = (U_1, \ldots, U_n), m = (m_1, \ldots, m_{n'})\big), \sigma = (\tilde{R}, R, S)\Big)$: Return 1 iff $\tilde{R} \in \mathbb{H}$, $R, S \in \mathbb{G}$, $U_i \in \mathbb{G}$, and the following two equations hold:

$$e(R, \tilde{H}) = e(G, \tilde{R}),$$

$$e(S, \tilde{H}) = \prod_{i=1}^n e(U_i, \tilde{X}_i) \prod_{i=1}^{n'} e(G^{m_i}, \tilde{Y}_i) e(R, \tilde{R}) e(G, \tilde{Z}) \cdot$$

- Randomize$\left(\mathsf{vk}, (\boldsymbol{U} = (U_1, \ldots, U_n), \boldsymbol{m} = (m_1, \ldots, m_{n'})), \sigma = (\tilde{R}, R, S)\right)$:
  Choose $r' \leftarrow \mathbb{Z}_p$, Set $R' := R \cdot G^{r'}, \tilde{R}' := \tilde{R} \cdot \tilde{H}^{r'}$, and $S' := S \cdot R^{2r'} \cdot G^{r'^2}$.
  Return $\sigma' := (\tilde{R}', R', S')$.

Correctness of the scheme is easy to verify. The signatures are perfectly randomizable as the distribution of randomized signatures is identical to that of fresh signatures on the same message. We now prove the following theorem.

Theorem 1. *The signature scheme is existentially unforgeable against a chosen-message attack in the generic group model.*

Proof. We prove that no linear combinations of the elements available to the adversary produce Laurent polynomials corresponding to a forgery on a message that was not queried to the sign oracle.

Public elements in $\mathbb{H}$ are $\tilde{H}, \tilde{X}_1, \ldots, \tilde{X}_n, \tilde{Y}_1, \ldots, \tilde{Y}_{n'}, \tilde{Z}$ which correspond to the discrete logarithms $1, x_1, \ldots, x_n, y_1, \ldots, y_{n'}, z$, respectively. Thus, this means that at the it-h sign query on $(\boldsymbol{U}_i, \boldsymbol{m}_i)$, $U_{i,j}$ (for $j = 1, \ldots, n$) can only be a linear combination of $G, \{R_k\}_{k=1}^{i-1}, \{S_k\}_{k=1}^{i-1}$. Thus, we have

$$u_{i,j} = a_{u_{i,j}} + \sum_{k=1}^{i-1} b_{u_{i,j,k}} r_k + \sum_{k=1}^{i-1} c_{u_{i,j,k}} (\sum_{l=1}^n u_{k,l} x_l + \sum_{l=1}^{n'} m_{k,l} y_l + r_k^2 + z),$$

After q signing queries, $\boldsymbol{u}^*$, which is the discrete logarithm of the forged vector $\boldsymbol{U}^*$ must be of the form

$$u_i^* = a_{u_i} + \sum_{k=1}^q b_{u_{i,k}} r_k + \sum_{k=1}^q c_{u_{i,k}} (\sum_{l=1}^n u_{k,l} x_l + \sum_{l=1}^{n'} m_{k,l} y_l + r_k^2 + z), \text{ for } i = 1, \ldots, n$$

Similarly, the (R^*, S^*) components part of the forgery can only be a linear combination of the group elements from $\mathbb{G}$, i.e. a linear combination of $G, \{R_i\}_{i=1}^q$ and $\{S_i\}_{i=1}^q$ and therefore we have

$$r^* = a_r + \sum_{k=1}^q b_{r_k} r_k + \sum_{k=1}^q c_{r_k} (\sum_{l=1}^n u_{k,l} x_l + \sum_{l=1}^{n'} m_{k,l} y_l + r_k^2 + z)$$

$$s^* = a_s + \sum_{k=1}^q b_{s_k} r_k + \sum_{k=1}^q c_{s_k} (\sum_{l=1}^n u_{k,l} x_l + \sum_{l=1}^{n'} m_{k,l} y_l + r_k^2 + z)$$

Analogously, the $\tilde{R}^*$ part of the forgery can only be a linear combination of the elements from $\mathbb{H}$. Therefore, we have

$$\tilde{r}^* = a_{\tilde{r}} + \sum_{k=1}^q b_{\tilde{r}_k} \tilde{r}_k + \sum_{i=1}^n c_{\tilde{r}_i} x_i + \sum_{i=1}^{n'} d_{\tilde{r}_i} y_i + e_{\tilde{r}} z$$

For the forgery to be a valid signature, r^*, $\tilde{r}^*$ and s^* must satisfy

$$r^* = \tilde{r}^* \tag{7}$$

$$s^* = \sum_{l=1}^{n} u_l^* x_l + \sum_{l=1}^{n'} m_l^* y_l + r^{*2} + z \tag{8}$$

By (7), we must have $e_{\tilde{r}} = 0$ and $c_{\tilde{r}_i} = d_{\tilde{r}_i} = 0$ for all $i \in [n]$. Also, we must have $a_{\tilde{r}} = a_r$, $b_{\tilde{r}_k} = b_{r_k}$ for all k, and $c_{r_k} = 0$ for all $k \in [q]$. Therefore, we have

$$r^* = \tilde{r}^* = a_r + \sum_{k=1}^{q} b_{r_k} r_k$$

By (8), we must have

$$a_s + \sum_{k=1}^{q} b_{s_k} r_k + \sum_{k=1}^{q} c_{s_k} \left(\sum_{l=1}^{n} u_{k,l} x_l + \sum_{l=1}^{n'} m_{k,l} y_l + r_k^2 + z \right)$$

$$= \sum_{l=1}^{n} u_l^* x_l + \sum_{l=1}^{n'} m_l^* y_l + r^{*2} + z$$

Thus, we must have

$$a_s + \sum_{k=1}^{q} b_{s_k} r_k + \sum_{k=1}^{q} c_{s_k} \left(\sum_{l=1}^{n} u_{k,l} x_l + \sum_{l=1}^{n'} m_{k,l} y_l + r_k^2 + z \right)$$

$$= \sum_{l=1}^{n} u_l^* x_l + \sum_{l=1}^{n'} m_l^* y_l + \left(a_r + \sum_{k=1}^{q} b_{r_k} r_k \right)^2 + z$$

Note that on the left-hand side there is no term in $r_j r_k$ for all $k \neq j$. This means that on the right-hand side we must have $b_{r_j} b_{r_k} = 0$ for all $k \neq j$. This implies that there is only one value of j such that $b_{r_j} \neq 0$, whereas $b_{r_k} = 0$ for all $k \neq j$. Thus, we have

$$a_s + \sum_{k=1}^{q} b_{s_k} r_k + \sum_{k=1}^{q} c_{s_k} \left(\sum_{l=1}^{n} u_{k,l} x_l + \sum_{l=1}^{n'} m_{k,l} y_l + r_k^2 + z \right)$$

$$= \sum_{l=1}^{n} u_l^* x_l + \sum_{l=1}^{n'} m_l^* y_l + \left(a_r + b_{r_j} r_j \right)^2 + z$$

Thus, we have

$$a_s + \sum_{k=1}^{q} b_{s_k} r_k + \sum_{k=1}^{q} c_{s_k} \left(\sum_{l=1}^{n} u_{k,l} x_l + \sum_{l=1}^{n'} m_{k,l} y_l + r_k^2 + z \right)$$

$$= \sum_{l=1}^{n} u_l^* x_l + \sum_{l=1}^{n'} m_l^* y_l + a_r^2 + 2 a_r b_{r_j} r_j + b_{r_j}^2 r_j^2 + z$$

Re-writing the left-hand side we have

$$a_s + b_{s_j} r_j + c_{s_j} \sum_{l=1}^{n} u_{j,l} x_l + c_{s_j} \sum_{l=1}^{n'} m_{j,l} y_l + c_{s_j} r_j^2 + c_{s_j} z$$

$$= \sum_{l=1}^{n} u_l^* x_l + \sum_{l=1}^{n'} m_l^* y_l + a_r^2 + 2a_r b_{r_j} r_j + b_{r_j}^2 r_j^2 + z$$

The monomial z implies $c_{s,j} = 1$. Therefore, we have

$$a_s + b_{s_j} r_j + \sum_{l=1}^{n} u_{j,l} x_l + \sum_{l=1}^{n'} m_{j,l} y_l + r_j^2 + z$$

$$= \sum_{l=1}^{n} u_l^* x_l + \sum_{l=1}^{n'} m_l^* y_l + a_r^2 + 2a_r b_{r_j} r_j + b_{r_j}^2 r_j^2 + z$$

By the monomial x_l, it is clear that we must have $u_{j,l} = u_l^*$ for all $l \in [n]$ and some $j \in [q]$. Similarly, the monomial y_l implies we must have $m_{j,l} = m_l^*$ for all $l \in [n']$ and some $j \in [q]$. This means the forgery is on vectors which have been queried to the sign oracle and therefore the adversary does not win.

This concludes the proof.   □

PSPS Scheme for a Diffie-Hellman Pair [22]. We also use the recent efficient PSPS scheme by Ghadafi [22] which signs a Diffie-Hellman pair and a vector from $\mathbb{Z}_p^n$. It suffices for our case to have $n = 1$. The scheme from [22] is as follows, where as in [22], we let $\widehat{\mathbb{GH}}$ denote the set of Diffie-Hellman pairs, i.e. $\widehat{\mathbb{GH}} = \{(U, \tilde{V}) | (U, \tilde{V}) \in \mathbb{G} \times \mathbb{H}, e(U, \tilde{H}) = e(G, \tilde{V})\}$.

- KeyGen($\mathcal{P}$): Select $x, y_1, \ldots, y_n, z \leftarrow \mathbb{Z}_p^\times$. Set $\tilde{X} := \tilde{H}^x$, $\tilde{Y}_i := \tilde{H}^{y_i}$ for all $i \in [n]$, $\tilde{Z} := \tilde{H}^z$. Set $\mathsf{sk} := (x, y_1, \ldots, y_n, z)$ and $\mathsf{vk} := (\tilde{X}, \tilde{Y}_1, \ldots, \tilde{Y}_n, \tilde{Z})$.
- Sign$\left(\mathsf{sk}, ((U, \tilde{V}), \boldsymbol{m} = (m_1, \ldots, m_n))\right)$: To sign $(U, \tilde{V}) \in \widehat{\mathbb{GH}}$ and a vector $(m_1, \ldots, m_n) \in \mathbb{Z}_p^n$, select $r \leftarrow \mathbb{Z}_p^\times$, and set $R := G^r$, $S := \left(U^r \cdot G^{r(x+\sum_{i=1}^{n} m_i y_i)}\right)^{\frac{1}{z}}$. Return $\sigma := (R, S) \in \mathbb{G}^2$.
- Verify$\left(\mathsf{vk}, ((U, \tilde{V}), \boldsymbol{m}), \sigma = (R, S)\right)$: Return 1 iff $R \in \mathbb{G}^\times$, $(U, \tilde{V}) \in \widehat{\mathbb{GH}}$, and

$$e(S, \tilde{Z}) = e(R, \tilde{V}) e(R, \tilde{X}) \prod_{i=1}^{n} e(R, \tilde{Y}_i^{m_i}) .$$

- Randomize$\left(\mathsf{vk}, ((U, \tilde{V}), \boldsymbol{m}), \sigma = (R, S)\right)$: Select $r' \leftarrow \mathbb{Z}_p^\times$, and set $R' := R^{r'}$, $S' := S^{r'}$. Return $\sigma' := (R', S')$.

3.2   Groth-Sahai Proofs

Groth-Sahai (GS) proofs [23] are non-interactive proofs in the CRS model. We will use GS proofs that are secure under the SXDH assumption.

For clarity, when describing the statements to be proven, we underline the variables which are part of the witness. The language for the proofs is of the form

$$\mathcal{L} := \{\text{statement} \mid \exists\, \text{witness} : E(\text{statement}, \text{witness}) \text{ holds}\},$$

where $E(\text{statement}, \cdot)$ is one of the four types as described in [23].

The system consists of the algorithms (GSSetup, GSProve, GSVerify, GSExtract, GSSimSetup, GSSimProve).

GSSetup takes as input the description of a bilinear group $\mathcal{P}$ and outputs a *binding* reference string crs and an extraction key xk. GSProve takes as input the string crs, a set of equations statement and a witness, and outputs a proof Ω for the satisfiability of the equations. GSVerify takes as input a set of equations, a string crs and a proof Ω and outputs 1 if the proof is valid, and 0 otherwise. GSExtract takes as input a binding crs, the extraction key xk and a valid proof Ω, and outputs the witness used for the proof. GSSimSetup, on input a bilinear group $\mathcal{P}$, outputs a *hiding* string crs_{Sim} and a trapdoor key tr that allows to simulate proofs. GSSimProve takes as input crs_{Sim}, a statement and the trapdoor tr and produces a simulated proof Ω_{Sim} without a witness.

The system can either be instantiated using a binding CRS crs (produced by GSSetup) or a hiding CRS crs_{Sim} (produced by GSSimSetup). The distributions of strings crs and crs_{Sim} are computationally indistinguishable and simulated proofs are indistinguishable from real proofs. The proof system has perfect completeness, (perfect) soundness, composable witness-indistinguishability/composable zero-knowledge.

Formal definitions of those properties are provided below, where y denotes the statement whereas x denotes the witness.

(Perfect) Completeness: $\forall \lambda \in \mathbb{N}$, $\forall (x, y) \in \mathcal{R}_{\mathcal{L}}$, we have

$$\Pr\left[(\text{crs}, \text{xk}) \leftarrow \text{GSSetup}(1^{\lambda}); \pi \leftarrow \text{GSProve}(\text{crs}, x, y) : \text{GSVerify}(\text{crs}, y, \pi) = 1\right] = 1$$

Soundness: $\forall \lambda \in \mathbb{N}$, $\forall y \notin \mathcal{L}$, we have for all adversaries $\mathcal{F}$

$$\Pr\left[(\text{crs}, \text{xk}) \leftarrow \text{GSSetup}(1^{\lambda}); \pi \leftarrow \mathcal{F}(\text{crs}, y) : \text{GSVerify}(\text{crs}, y, \pi) = 1\right] \leq 2^{-\lambda}$$

If the above probability is 0, we say the system has *perfect soundness*.

Knowledge Extraction: A proof system is a *Proof of Knowledge* if there exists an efficient extractor algorithm GSExtract which can extract the witness from any proof the adversary outputs. Note that if a proof system is a proof of knowledge then it is sound. More formally, for all adversaries $\mathcal{F}$, we have

$$\Pr\Big[(\text{crs}, \text{xk}) \leftarrow \text{GSSetup}(1^{\lambda}); (y, \pi) \leftarrow \mathcal{F}(\text{crs}); x \leftarrow \text{GSExtract}(\text{crs}, \text{xk}, y, \pi)$$
$$: \text{GSVerify}(\text{crs}, y, \pi) = 0 \ \lor \ (x, y) \in \mathcal{R}_{\mathcal{L}}\Big] \leq 1 - \nu(\lambda)$$

If the above probability is 1, we say the system has *perfect knowledge extraction*.

Witness Indistinguishability: The system is *witness indistinguishable* if for all PPT adversaries $\mathcal{F}$, we have

$$\Pr\left[\begin{array}{l}(\mathsf{crs},\mathsf{xk}) \leftarrow \mathsf{GSSetup}(1^\lambda); (\mathsf{st}_{\mathsf{find}}, y, x_0, x_1) \leftarrow \mathcal{F}_{\mathsf{find}}(\mathsf{crs}); b \leftarrow \{0,1\}; \\ \pi \leftarrow \mathsf{GSProve}(\mathsf{crs}, x_b, y); b^* \leftarrow \mathcal{F}_{\mathsf{guess}}(\mathsf{st}_{\mathsf{find}}, \pi) \\ \quad : (x_0, y) \in \mathcal{R}_\mathcal{L} \ \wedge \ (x_1, y) \in \mathcal{R}_\mathcal{L} \ \wedge \ b = b^*\end{array}\right] = \frac{1}{2} + \nu(\lambda) \ .$$

If $\nu(\lambda) = 0$, we say the system has *perfect witness indistinguishability*.

Zero-Knowledge: The system is *zero-knowledge* if $\forall (x, y) \in \mathcal{R}_\mathcal{L}$, we have for all PPT adversaries $\mathcal{F}$

$$\Pr\left[(\mathsf{crs}_{\mathsf{sim}}, \mathsf{tr}) \leftarrow \mathsf{GSSimSetup}(1^\lambda) : \mathcal{F}^{\mathsf{GSSim}(\mathsf{crs}_{\mathsf{sim}}, \mathsf{tr}, \cdot, \cdot)}(\mathsf{crs}_{\mathsf{sim}}) = 1\right]$$

$$\approx \Pr\left[(\mathsf{crs}, \mathsf{xk}) \leftarrow \mathsf{GSSetup}(1^\lambda) : \mathcal{F}^{\mathsf{GSProve}(\mathsf{crs}, \cdot, \cdot)}(\mathsf{crs}) = 1\right],$$

where $\mathsf{GSSim}(\mathsf{crs}_{\mathsf{sim}}, \mathsf{tr}, x, y)$ outputs $\mathsf{GSSimProve}(\mathsf{crs}_{\mathsf{sim}}, \mathsf{tr}, y)$ if $(x, y) \in \mathcal{R}_\mathcal{L}$ or $\perp$ otherwise.

3.3 Linkable Indistinguishable Tag

A Linkable Indistinguishable Tag (LIT) scheme [3,4] is defined w.r.t. a one-way function PK such that a tag created with a secret key sk can be verified using $\mathsf{PK}(\mathsf{sk})$. LIT consists of the algorithms $(\mathsf{KeyGen}, \mathsf{Tag}, \mathsf{Verify})$ defined as follows:

$\mathsf{KeyGen}(1^\lambda)$: produces a secret key sk.
$\mathsf{Tag}(\mathsf{sk}, m)$: outputs a tag τ on the message m.
$\mathsf{Verify}(\mathsf{PK}(\mathsf{sk}), m, \tau)$: verifies that the tag τ is valid on the message m returning $0/1$ accordingly.

Besides correctness, the security of LIT [3,4] requires linkability and f-indistinguishability. Informally, the former requires that an adversary who is allowed to control both the secret key and the message cannot produce identical tags unless they are on the same message/key pair. Indistinguishability, which is defined w.r.t. a one-way function f of the secret key, requires that an adversary who gets $f(\mathsf{sk})$ and access to a tag oracle, cannot determine whether or not a new tag on a message of her choice was produced using the same key used by the tag oracle.

As in [3], we instantiate LIT in the standard model with the function underlying the weak Boneh-Boyen signature scheme [7]. The instantiation is secure under the q-DDHI assumption.

4 Definition and Security of ABS-UCL

In this section, we recall the syntax and security of Attribute-Based Signatures with User-Controlled Linkability (ABS-UCL) [15]. An ABS-UCL scheme consists of the following algorithms, where pp output by Setup is an implicit input to the rest of the algorithms:

Setup(1^λ) on input a security parameter, it returns public parameters pp.

AASetup(aid) is run by attribute authority AA_{aid} to generate her public/secret key pair (vk_{AA}, sk_{AA}).

UKeyGen(id) is run by user id to generate her personal secret key usk_{id}.

AttKeyGen(sk_{AA}, id, $f(usk_{id}), a$) is run by attribute authority AA (managing attribute a), where f is an injective one-way function, it gives user id the secret key $sk_{id,a}$.

Sign($usk_{id}, \{sk_{id,a}\}_{a \in \mathcal{A}}, m, \mathbb{P}, recip$) user id with attributes $\mathcal{A}$ s.t. $\mathbb{P}(\mathcal{A}) = 1$ uses this algorithm to sign a message m w.r.t. signing policy $\mathbb{P}$ and the recipient tag recip. The algorithm returns a signature σ.

Verify($\sigma, \{vk_{AA_i}\}_i, \mathbb{P}, m, recip$) checks if the signature σ is valid on the message m w.r.t. (the possibly empty) recipient tag recip and the policy $\mathbb{P}$ returning $1/0$.

Link($\sigma_0, m_0, \{vk_{AA_i}\}_i, \mathbb{P}_0, \sigma_1, m_1, \{vk_{AA_j}\}_j, \mathbb{P}_1, recip$) checks if the two signatures on their respective messages and w.r.t. recip $\neq \perp$ and their respective signing policies were produced by the same user, outputting $0/1$ accordingly.

Identify($sk, \sigma, m, recip, \{vk_{AA_i}\}_i, \mathbb{P}$) is only used in the security model for capturing linkability. It checks whether the valid signature σ (w.r.t. the signing policy $\mathbb{P}$) on the message m and recip $\neq \perp$ was produced by the secret key sk, outputting $0/1$ accordingly.

Security Requirements. Besides correctness, the security of ABS-UCL [15] requires unforgeability, linkability and anonymity which we define below.

UNFORGEABILITY. This property guarantees that users cannot output signatures on (message, recipient tag) pairs w.r.t a signing policy that is not satisfied by their set of attributes, even if they collude, ensuring collusion-resistance. It also ensures that an adversary cannot produce a signature which links to a signature by an honest user even if everyone else in the system is corrupt.

Definition 1 (Unforgeability). *An* ABS-UCL *scheme is unforgeable if for all security parameters $\lambda \in \mathbb{N}$, for all PPT adversaries the advantage in winning the following game is negligible:*

Setup: *The challenger runs* Setup *and gives* pp *to the adversary.*

Play: *The adversary can ask for attribute authorities to be created and get hold of their secret keys. She can also ask for honest users to be created and get hold of their personal secret keys. Moreover, the adversary can ask for keys for attributes for users and signatures on tuples $(m, \mathbb{P}, recip)$ of her choice on behalf of honest users.*

Output: *The adversary outputs either of the following:*

    ⋆ *A valid signature σ on m and* recip *w.r.t. $\mathbb{P}$, where $(m, recip, \mathbb{P})$ was not queried to the signing oracle, and there exists no subset of attributes $\mathcal{A}^*$ whose keys have been revealed to the adversary or managed by corrupt attribute authorities such that $\mathbb{P}(\mathcal{A}^*) = 1$.*

    ⋆ *A tuple $(m_0, \sigma_0, \{vk_{AA_i}\}_i, \mathbb{P}_0, m_1, \sigma_1, \{vk_{AA_j}\}_j, \mathbb{P}_1, recip \neq \perp, id)$, where σ_i is valid on m_i and* recip *w.r.t. $\mathbb{P}_i$, user id is honest,* Link($\sigma_0, m_0, \{vk_{AA_i}\}_i, \mathbb{P}_0, \sigma_1, m_1, \{vk_{AA_j}\}_j, \mathbb{P}_1, recip$) $= 1$ *and either*

$(\text{id}, m_0, \text{recip}, \mathbb{P}_0)$ *or* $(\text{id}, m_1, \text{recip}, \mathbb{P}_1)$ *was not queried to the signing oracle.*

LINKABILITY. This property ensures that only valid signatures directed at the same recipient and which were produced by the same user link.

Definition 2 (Linkability). *An* ABS-UCL *scheme is linkable if for all security parameters* $\lambda \in \mathbb{N}$, *for all PPT adversaries the advantage in winning the following game is negligible:*

Setup: *The challenger runs* Setup *and gives* pp *to the adversary.*
Play: *The adversary can choose all the secret keys of all users and attribute authorities.*
Output: *The adversary outputs* $(\sigma_1, \text{recip}_1, m_1, \{\text{vk}_{\text{AA}_i}\}_i, \mathbb{P}_1, \text{sk}_1)$ *and* $(\sigma_2, \text{recip}_2, m_2, \{\text{vk}_{\text{AA}_j}\}_j, \mathbb{P}_2, \text{sk}_2)$. *She wins if* σ_i *is valid (w.r.t.* $\mathbb{P}_i$) *on* m_i *and* recip_i, *for* $i = 1, 2$ *and either of the following holds:*

  ⋆ σ_1 *was produced by* sk_1 *and* σ_2 *was produced by* sk_2 *where* $\text{sk}_1 = \text{sk}_2$ *and* recip = recip_1 = $\text{recip}_2 \neq \perp$ *but* $\text{Link}(\sigma_1, m_1, \{\text{vk}_{\text{AA}_i}\}_i, \mathbb{P}_1, \sigma_2, m_2, \{\text{vk}_{\text{AA}_j}\}_j, \mathbb{P}_2, \text{recip}) = 0$.
  ⋆ σ_1 *was produced by* sk_1 *and* σ_2 *was produced by* sk_2 *where* $\text{sk}_1 = \text{sk}_2$ *and* $\text{Link}(\sigma_1, m_1, \{\text{vk}_{\text{AA}_i}\}_i, \mathbb{P}_1, \sigma_2, m_2, \{\text{vk}_{\text{AA}_j}\}_j, \mathbb{P}_2, \text{recip}_k) = 1$ *for* $k \in \{1, 2\}$ *and either* $\text{recip}_k = \perp$ *or* $\text{recip}_1 \neq \text{recip}_2$.
  ⋆ σ_1 *was produced by* sk_1 *and* σ_2 *was produced by* sk_2 *where* $\text{sk}_1 \neq \text{sk}_2$ *and* recip = recip_1 = $\text{recip}_2 \neq \perp$ *and* $\text{Link}(\sigma_1, m_1, \{\text{vk}_{\text{AA}_i}\}_i, \mathbb{P}_1, \sigma_2, m_2, \{\text{vk}_{\text{AA}_j}\}_j, \mathbb{P}_2, \text{recip}) = 1$.

ANONYMITY. This ensures that neither the identity of the signer, nor the attributes used in the signing are revealed by the signature.

Definition 3 (Anonymity). *An* ABS-UCL *scheme is anonymous if for all security parameters* $\lambda \in \mathbb{N}$, *for all PPT adversaries the advantage in winning the following game is negligibly close to* $\frac{1}{2}$:

Setup: *The challenger runs* Setup *and gives* pp *to the adversary.*
Play I: *The adversary has full control over all attribute authorities. She can also get hold of the secret keys of signers of her choice; those signers automatically become corrupt users. Moreover, the adversary can get hold of the secret key of any attribute and signatures on tuples* $(m, \mathbb{P}, \text{recip})$ *of her choice on behalf of honest users.*
Challenge: *The adversary outputs* $(m, \text{id}_0, \mathcal{A}_0, \text{id}_1, \mathcal{A}_1, \mathbb{P}, \text{recip})$ *where* $\mathbb{P}(\mathcal{A}_i) = 1$ *for* $i = 0, 1$. *If* recip $\neq \perp$, *we require that both* id_0 *and* id_1 *are honest users. The challenger sends back a signature* σ_b *generated using* $(\text{id}_b, \mathcal{A}_b)$, *for* $b \leftarrow \{0, 1\}$.
Play II: *Same as in play I with the additional condition that if* recip $\neq \perp$, *the adversary can corrupt neither* id_0 *nor* id_1.
Output: *The adversary outputs her guess* b^* *and wins if* $b^* = b$.

5   Efficient ABS-UCL Constructions for Expressive Policies

Here we give efficient constructions for monotone access policies. By doubling the attribute space, we also cover non-monotone access policies. Our construction is a modified and improved variant of the generic construction in [15]. We describe the idea of our construction generically and then give specific efficient instantiations. When producing the zero-knowledge proofs part of the signature, we use a span program [26] to represent the signing policy. Refer to [26] for more information about span programs.

The personal secret key of user id is a secret key $uskid \in \mathcal{SK}$ for a linkable indistinguishable tag scheme LIT. Let $f : \mathcal{SK} \to \mathcal{F}$ and $PK : \mathcal{SK} \to \mathcal{PK}$ be two one-way injective functions. In our instantiations, f and PK are exponentiations of $uskid$ in groups $\mathbb{G}$ and $\mathbb{H}$, respectively. We make $f(uskid)$ public whereas $PK(uskid)$ is only known to the user.

Since our main goal is to design efficient schemes while dispensing with heuristic assumptions, unlike the generic construction of [15] and other similar constructions of variants of standard-model attribute-based signature schemes, e.g. [16,21], which do not offer the user-controlled linkability feature, we use an existentially unforgeable randomizable partially structure-preserving signature scheme (RPSPS) [22] to issue attribute credentials to users. Unlike e.g. [16,21], we have weakened the requirement we need from the signature scheme from being structure-preserving [1] to being partially structure-preserving [22]. This serves to improve the efficiency of the construction. We also require a second existentially unforgeable signature scheme DS whose public verification key is part of the public parameters of the system whereas its secret key is not known to any party.

The credential $skid,a$ for attribute a to user id is a RPSPS signature on $(f(uskid), a)$ using sk_{AAaid} which is the secret key of the authority managing a.

To sign a message m w.r.t. a signing policy $\mathbb{P}$ where the signer possesses credentials $\{sk'_{id,a}\}_{a \in \mathcal{A}}$ for a set of attributes $\mathcal{A}$ satisfying $\mathbb{P}(\mathcal{A}) = 1$, the signer first re-randomizes $sk'_{id,a}$ into $sk_{id,a}$ for all $a \in \mathcal{A}$ so that the new randomized credentials are unlinkable to the original credentials $sk'_{id,a}$. Another deviation from the construction in [15] is that we only need to hide the components of the user's attribute credentials $sk_{id,a}$ which depend on the user's secret key $uskid$ and publicly release the remaining components. When signing a message m w.r.t. a signing policy $\mathbb{P}$ and a non-empty recipient tag recip, the user produces a proof of knowledge π to prove that she either has enough credentials for a set of attributes $\mathcal{A}$ such that $\mathbb{P}(\mathcal{A}) = 1$ or has a DS signature on $\mathcal{H}(m, \mathbb{P}, recip)$ for some collision-resistant hash function $\mathcal{H} : \{0,1\}^* \to \mathcal{M}_{DS}$. Following the literature, we refer to the latter as a pseudo-attribute. Since in this case the signature is linkable, the NIZK proof π additionally proves that the tag τ on recip verifies w.r.t. the same user secret key $uskid$ with which the attribute credentials are associated. To prove the latter, let IsConsistent : $\mathcal{F} \times \mathcal{PK} \to \{0,1\}$ be a predicate where $\mathcal{F}$

and $\mathcal{PK}$ are the ranges of the functions f and PK respectively. In our instantiations, IsConsistent requires checking that the pair is a Diffie-Hellman pair. For all remaining attributes in the policy $\mathbb{P}$ that the signer is not going to use, i.e. the set of attributes $a \in \mathbb{P} \setminus \mathcal{A}$, the user chooses random dummy credentials $\boxed{\mathsf{sk}_{\mathsf{id},a}}$. For all attributes $a \in \mathcal{A}$, we parse $\mathsf{sk}_{\mathsf{id},a}$ as $(\widehat{\mathsf{sk}}_{\mathsf{id},a}, \check{\mathsf{sk}}_{\mathsf{id},a})$, where $\check{\mathsf{sk}}_{\mathsf{id},a}$ are independent of $\mathsf{usk}_{\mathsf{id}}$. Similarly, for all attributes $a \in \mathbb{P} \setminus \mathcal{A}$, parse $\boxed{\mathsf{sk}_{\mathsf{id},a}}$ as $\left(\boxed{\widehat{\mathsf{sk}}_{\mathsf{id},a}}, \check{\mathsf{sk}}_{\mathsf{id},a} \right)$.

Let $\boxed{\mathsf{sk}_{\mathsf{id},a_{\mathrm{psdo}}}}$ be the credential for the pseudo-attribute, i.e. the DS signature on $\mathcal{H}(m, \mathbb{P}, \mathsf{recip})$. We parse $\boxed{\mathsf{sk}_{\mathsf{id},a_{\mathrm{psdo}}}}$ as $\left(\boxed{\widehat{\mathsf{sk}}_{\mathsf{id},a_{\mathrm{psdo}}}}, \check{\mathsf{sk}}_{\mathsf{id},a_{\mathrm{psdo}}} \right)$, where $\widehat{\mathsf{sk}}_{\mathsf{id},a_{\mathrm{psdo}}}$ is independent of the message of DS. Since the signing key of DS is only known to the challenger in the security reduction, we can safely reveal the component $\boxed{\widehat{\mathsf{sk}}_{\mathsf{id},a_{\mathrm{psdo}}}}$ in the clear since it does not reveal whether $\mathsf{sk}_{\mathsf{id},a_{\mathrm{psdo}}}$ is a valid signature on $\mathcal{H}(m, \mathbb{P}, \mathsf{recip})$ or a fake dummy signature. If $\mathsf{recip} = \perp$, then we set $\tau = \perp$ and π excludes the latter part concerning proving correctness of the tag τ. The signature Σ is then $\left(\pi, \tau, \{\widehat{\mathsf{sk}}_{\mathsf{id},a}\}_{a \in \mathcal{A}} \cup \{ \boxed{\widehat{\mathsf{sk}}_{\mathsf{id},a}} \}_{a \in \mathbb{P} \setminus \mathcal{A}} \cup \widehat{\mathsf{sk}}_{\mathsf{id},a_{\mathrm{psdo}}} \right)$.

To verify the signature, it suffices to just verify the proof π. To link two signatures, one checks that tag components of the two valid signatures are identical.

Details of the construction are given in Fig. 1, where $\boldsymbol{z}$ and $\mathbf{M}$ are the secret vector and the public span matrix used in the span program, respectively. The languages associated with the NIZK system are as follows. For clarity we underline the witnesses:

$$\mathcal{L}: \left\{ \begin{array}{l} \left(\left(\tau, \mathsf{recip}, \{\mathsf{vk}_{\mathsf{AA}_{\mathsf{aid}(a)}}\}_{a \in \mathbb{P}} \cup \mathsf{svk}, \{\widehat{\mathsf{sk}}_{\mathsf{id},a}\}_{a \in \mathring{\mathbb{P}}} \right), \left((\underline{f(\mathsf{usk}_{\mathsf{id}})}, \mathsf{PK}(\mathsf{usk}_{\mathsf{id}})), \boldsymbol{z}, \{\check{\mathsf{sk}}_{\mathsf{id},a}\}_{a \in \mathring{\mathbb{P}}} \right) \right) \\ : \underline{\boldsymbol{z}}\mathbf{M} = [1, 0, \ldots, 0] \wedge \mathsf{LIT.Verify}(\mathsf{PK}(\mathsf{usk}_{\mathsf{id}}), \mathsf{recip}, \tau) = 1 \wedge \mathsf{IsConsistent}(\underline{f(\mathsf{usk}_{\mathsf{id}})}, \mathsf{PK}(\mathsf{usk}_{\mathsf{id}})) = 1 \\ \wedge_{i=1}^{|\mathbb{P}|} \text{ if } \underline{z_i} \neq 0 \Rightarrow \mathsf{RPSPS.Verify}\left(\mathsf{vk}_{\mathsf{AA}_{\mathsf{aid}(a_i)}}, \left((\underline{f(\mathsf{usk}_{\mathsf{id}})}, \mathsf{PK}(\mathsf{usk}_{\mathsf{id}})), a_i \right), \left(\widehat{\mathsf{sk}}_{\mathsf{id},a_i}, \underline{\check{\mathsf{sk}}_{\mathsf{id},a_i}} \right) \right) = 1 \\ \wedge \text{ if } \underline{z_{|\mathbb{P}|+1}} \neq 0 \Rightarrow \mathsf{DS.Verify}\left(\mathsf{svk}, \mathcal{H}(m, \mathbb{P}, \mathsf{recip}), \left(\widehat{\mathsf{sk}}_{\mathsf{id},a_{\mathrm{psdo}}}, \underline{\check{\mathsf{sk}}_{\mathsf{id},a_{\mathrm{psdo}}}} \right) \right) = 1 \end{array} \right\}.$$

$\mathcal{L}'$ is similar to $\mathcal{L}$ but without $\mathsf{LIT.Verify}(\underline{\mathsf{PK}(\mathsf{usk}_{\mathsf{id}})}, \mathsf{recip}, \tau) = 1$ and $\mathsf{IsConsistent}(\underline{f(\mathsf{usk}_{\mathsf{id}})}, \underline{\mathsf{PK}(\mathsf{usk}_{\mathsf{id}})}) = 1$.

Theorem 2. *The construction in Fig. 1 is a secure ABS-UCL scheme.*

Proof. Correctness is straightforward and is easy to verify. Also, linkability follows from that of the LIT scheme and is easy to verify.

Lemma 1. *The construction satisfies anonymity if* NIZK *is zero-knowledge and* LIT *is f-indistinguishable.*

Proof. Note that all public parts of the attribute credentials including that for the pseudo-attribute are independent of the witness of the NIZK proof.

We proceed by defining a sequence of games such that the last game is independent of the bit b used in the anonymity game. We prove that an adversary against anonymity behaves differently in any two consecutive games only with a negligible probability.

Setup(1^λ)

- (crs, xk) ← NIZK.Setup(1^λ). (svk, ssk) ← DS.KeyGen(1^λ).
- Choose a collision-resistant hash function $\mathcal{H} : \{0,1\}^* \to \mathcal{M}_{DS}$. Return pp := $(1^\lambda, \text{crs}, \mathcal{H}, \text{svk})$.

AASetup(pp, aid)

- $(\text{vk}_{\text{AA}_{aid}}, \text{sk}_{\text{AA}_{aid}})$ ← RPSPS.KeyGen(1^λ). Return $(\text{vk}_{\text{AA}_{aid}}, \text{sk}_{\text{AA}_{aid}})$.

UKeyGen(pp)

- usk_{id} ← LIT.KeyGen(1^λ). Return usk_{id}.

AttKeyGen(id, $f(\text{usk}_{id})$, a, $\text{sk}_{\text{AA}_{aid}(a)}$)

- $\text{sk}'_{id,a}$ ← RPSPS.Sign$\big(\text{sk}_{\text{AA}_{aid}(a)}, ((f(\text{usk}_{id}), \cdot), a)\big)$. Return $\text{sk}'_{id,a}$.

Sign(m, $\mathbb{P}$, usk_{id}, $\{\text{sk}'_{id,a}\}_{a \in \mathcal{A}}$, recip)

- Return $\perp$ if $\mathbb{P}(\mathcal{A}) = 0$.
- Let $a_{psdo} := \mathcal{H}(m, \mathbb{P}, \text{recip})$ and $\hat{\mathbb{P}} := \mathbb{P} \vee a_{psdo}$.
- For each $a \in \mathcal{A}$, compute $\text{sk}_{id,a}$ ← RPSPS.Randomize $\big(\text{vk}_{\text{AA}_{aid}(a)}, (((f(\text{usk}_{id}), \text{PK}(\text{usk}_{id})), a), \text{sk}'_{id,a}\big)$.
- For each $a \in \mathbb{P} \setminus \mathcal{A}$, choose a random dummy credential $\boxed{\text{sk}_{id,a}}$.
- Choose a random dummy credential $\boxed{\text{sk}_{id,a_{psdo}}}$ for the pseudo-attribute a_{psdo}.
- Parse $\text{sk}_{id,\alpha}$ as $(\hat{\text{sk}}_{id,a}, \check{\text{sk}}_{id,a})$, where $\check{\text{sk}}_{id,a}$ are independent of usk_{id}.
- Similarly, parse $\boxed{\text{sk}_{id,a}}$ as $(\boxed{\hat{\text{sk}}_{id,a}}, \check{\text{sk}}_{id,a})$, and $\boxed{\text{sk}_{id,a_{psdo}}}$ as $(\boxed{\hat{\text{sk}}_{id,a_{psdo}}}, \check{\text{sk}}_{id,a_{psdo}})$.
- If recip $= \perp$ Then
  - Set $\tau := \perp$, $\Omega := (\{\text{vk}_{\text{AA}_{aid}(a)}\}_{a \in \hat{\mathbb{P}}} \cup \text{svk}, \{\hat{\text{sk}}_{id,a}\}_{a \in \mathcal{A}} \cup \{\boxed{\hat{\text{sk}}_{id,a}}\}_{a \in \hat{\mathbb{P}} \setminus \mathcal{A}})$.
  - π ← NIZK.Prove $\Big(\text{crs}, \big((f(\text{usk}_{id}), \text{PK}(\text{usk}_{id})), z, \{\check{\text{sk}}_{id,a}\}_{a \in \mathcal{A}} \cup \{\boxed{\check{\text{sk}}_{id,a}}\}_{a \in \hat{\mathbb{P}} \setminus \mathcal{A}}\big) : \Omega \in \mathcal{L}'\Big)$.
- Else
  - τ ← LIT.Tag(usk_{id}, recip).
  - $\Omega := (\tau, \text{recip}, \{\text{vk}_{\text{AA}_{aid}(a)}\}_{a \in \hat{\mathbb{P}}} \cup \text{svk}, \{\hat{\text{sk}}_{id,a}\}_{a \in \mathcal{A}} \cup \{\boxed{\hat{\text{sk}}_{id,a}}\}_{a \in \hat{\mathbb{P}} \setminus \mathcal{A}})$.
  - π ← NIZK.Prove(crs, $\big((f(\text{usk}_{id}), \text{PK}(\text{usk}_{id})), z, \{\check{\text{sk}}_{id,a}\}_{a \in \mathcal{A}} \cup \{\boxed{\check{\text{sk}}_{id,\alpha}}\}_{a \in \hat{\mathbb{P}} \setminus \mathcal{A}}\big) : \Omega \in \mathcal{L}$).
- Return $\Sigma := \Big(\pi, \tau, \{\hat{\text{sk}}_{id,a}\}_{a \in \mathcal{A}} \cup \{\boxed{\hat{\text{sk}}_{id,a}}\}_{a \in \hat{\mathbb{P}} \setminus \mathcal{A}}\Big)$.

Verify(Σ, $\{\text{vk}_{\text{AA}_{aid}(a)}\}_{a \in \mathbb{P}}$, $\mathbb{P}$, m, recip)

- Parse Σ as $\Big(\pi, \tau, \{\hat{\text{sk}}_{id,a}\}_{a \in \hat{\mathbb{P}}}\Big)$ and pp as $(1^\lambda, \text{crs}, \text{svk}, \mathcal{H})$. Return NIZK.Verify(crs, π).

Link$\big(\text{recip}, (m_i, \{\text{vk}_{\text{AA}_{aid}(a)}\}_{a \in \mathbb{P}_i}, \mathbb{P}_i, \Sigma_i)_{i=1,2}\big)$

- Parse Σ_i as $\Big(\pi_i, \tau_i, \{\hat{\text{sk}}_{id,a}\}_{a \in \hat{\mathbb{P}}_i}\Big)$ and pp as $(1^\lambda, \text{crs}, \text{svk}, \mathcal{H})$.
- Return 0 if recip $= \perp$ or $\exists i \in \{1, 2\}$ s.t. Verify(Σ_i, $\{\text{vk}_{\text{AA}_{aid}(a)}\}_{a \in \mathbb{P}_i}$, $\mathbb{P}_i$, m_i, recip) = 0 .
- If $\tau_1 = \tau_2 \neq \perp$ Then Return 1 Else Return 0.

Identify(sk, Σ, m, recip, $\{\text{vk}_{\text{AA}_{aid}(a)}\}_{a \in \mathbb{P}}$, $\mathbb{P}$)

- Parse Σ as $\Big(\pi, \tau, \{\hat{\text{sk}}_{id,a}\}_{a \in \hat{\mathbb{P}}}\Big)$ and pp as $(1^\lambda, \text{crs}, \text{svk}, \mathcal{H})$.
- If recip $= \perp$ or Verify(Σ, $\{\text{vk}_{\text{AA}_{aid}(a)}\}_{a \in \mathbb{P}}$, $\mathbb{P}$, m, recip) = 0 Then Return 0.
- If LIT.Tag(sk, recip) = τ Then Return 1 Else Return 0.

Fig. 1. Our generic construction of ABS-UCL

Let $\eta(\lambda)$ be a polynomial representing an upper bound on the number of users the adversary is allowed to create in the game. We let Game 0 be the original anonymity game but where we randomly guess the challenge user used by randomly choosing $\bar{\text{id}}$ from the set $\{1, \ldots, \eta(\lambda)\}$ and aborting if the challenge user chosen is different from $\bar{\text{id}}$. We have a probability of $\frac{1}{\eta(\lambda)}$ of guessing the challenge user correctly. If the advantage of the adversary against the original anonymity game is non-negligible then so is her advantage against Game 0 since $\eta(\lambda)$ is polynomial in λ.

Let Game 1 be the same as Game 0 but now the CRS crs used for the NIZK is chosen as a hiding string. By the security of the NIZK system, the difference between games Game 0 and Game 1 is negligible.

Let Game 2 be the same as Game 1 but now proof π part of the signature is a simulated proof rather than a real proof. By the zero-knowledge property of NIZK, the difference between games Game 1 and Game 2 is negligible.

Let Game 3 be the same as Game 2 but now every time the game answers a signature on behalf of user $\bar{\mathsf{id}}$ (via a signing or a challenge query) for a recipient tag recip $\neq\bot$, if such a recipient tag has already been queried on behalf of the same user, we return the same tag τ; otherwise, we choose a random user key $\mathsf{usk_{id}} \in \mathcal{SK}$ and use it to produce a tag τ on recip. We can use a hybrid argument and a reduction to the f-indistinguishability of the LIT scheme to argue that the difference between games Game 3 and Game 2 is negligible. Let $\gamma(\lambda)$ be a polynomial representing an upper bound on the total number of signing and challenge queries involving user $\bar{\mathsf{id}}$ on non-empty recipient names recip $\neq\bot$. We define a sequence of games $\mathsf{GM}_{i=0}^{\gamma(\lambda)}$ where in game GM_j we answer the first j queries on non-empty recipient tags using the key for user $\bar{\mathsf{id}}$ and from the $(j+1)$-th query onwards we use tags under random keys. If the adversary behaves differently in any two subsequent games with a non-negligible probability, we can use her to break the f-indistinguishability of the LIT scheme. We have $\mathsf{GM}_0 =$ Game 3 and $\mathsf{GM}_{\gamma(\lambda)} =$ Game 2. By the f-indistinguishability of LIT we have that the difference between games Game 3 and Game 2 is negligible.

Now note that Game 3 is independent of the bit b used in the anonymity game and therefore the adversary has a negligible advantage against anonymity.   □

Lemma 2. *The construction satisfies unforgeability if* NIZK *is sound,* RPSPS *and* DS *are existentially unforgeable, and the hash function* $\mathcal{H}$ *is collision-resistant.*

Proof. By the collision-resistance of the hash function $\mathcal{H}$ used in the pseudo-attribute a_{psdo}, the adversary has a negligible probability in finding two different tuples $(m, \mathbb{P}, \mathsf{recip}) \neq (m', \mathbb{P}', \mathsf{recip}')$ where $\mathcal{H}(m, \mathbb{P}, \mathsf{recip}) = \mathcal{H}(m', \mathbb{P}', \mathsf{recip}')$.

By choosing the CRS crs for NIZK as a binding one, the proofs are perfectly sound and we are guaranteed to be able to extract a valid witness from the proof π^* part of the forged signature Σ^*. The underlying witness would be either a valid signature on a new pseudo-attribute $(m, \mathbb{P}, \mathsf{recip})$ which was not queried to the sign oracle or a set of credentials on a one-way function of a user secret key $\mathsf{usk_{id}}$ where some of the valid credentials were not obtained from the AttKeyGen oracle. In the former case, we can reduce unforgeability to the existential unforgeability of signature scheme DS used for the pseudo-attribute, whereas in the latter case, by guessing which attribute authority (with probability $\frac{1}{\eta(\lambda)}$, where $\eta(\lambda)$ is a polynomial representing an upper bound on the number of attribute authorities the adversary can create in the unforgeability game) managing a forged credential, we can reduce unforgeability to the existential unforgeability of signature scheme RPSPS used in issuing attribute credentials to users.   □

5.1   Instantiations

In both instantiations below, we instantiate NIZK using the Groth-Sahai system (secure under SXDH) and instantiate the signature scheme DS using the full Boneh-Boyen signature scheme [7] (secure under q-SDH). We instantiate the LIT scheme LIT using the weak Boneh-Boyen signature [7] as in [3] (secure under q-DDHI). The only difference between the two instantiations lies in how we instantiate the signature scheme RPSPS. In the following, we let $F = f(\mathsf{usk_{id}}) = G^{\mathsf{usk_{id}}}$ and $\tilde{F} = \mathsf{PK}(\mathsf{usk_{id}}) = \tilde{H}^{\mathsf{usk_{id}}}$.

Instantiation I. Here we instantiate RPSPS using the efficient partially structure-preserving signature scheme from [22] as shown in Sect. 3.1.

Below we detail the Groth-Sahai NIZK proofs required for the instantiation.

Let $\mathbf{M} \in \mathbb{Z}_p^{|\hat{\mathbb{P}}|,\beta}$ be the span program for $\hat{\mathbb{P}} := \mathbb{P} \vee a_{\mathsf{psdo}}$. The proof π part of the signature is a proof for the following:

- To prove $\mathbf{zM} = [1, 0, \dots, 0]$, the signer proves:

$$\sum_{i=1}^{|\hat{\mathbb{P}}|}(\underline{z}_i M_{i,1}) = 1 \qquad\qquad \sum_{i=1}^{|\hat{\mathbb{P}}|}(\underline{z}_i M_{i,j}) = 0, \text{ for } j = 2, \dots, \beta$$

- For each $a_i \in \{1, \dots, |\mathbb{P}|\}$, we have $\mathsf{sk}'_{\mathsf{id},a_i} = (R'_i, S'_i) \in \mathbb{G}^2$ where $\widehat{\mathsf{sk}}'_{\mathsf{id},a_i} = R'_i$ and $\check{\mathsf{sk}}'_{\mathsf{id},a_i} = S'_i$. The signer re-randomizes $\mathsf{sk}'_{\mathsf{id},a_i}$ by choosing $r' \leftarrow \mathbb{Z}_p^\times$ and computing $\mathsf{sk}_{\mathsf{id},a_i} := (R_i, S_i) = (R'^{r'}_i, S'^{r'}_i)$.

  To prove if $\underline{z}_i \neq 0 \Rightarrow \mathsf{RPSPS}.\mathsf{Verify}\Big(\mathsf{vk}_{\mathsf{AA}_{\mathsf{aid}(a_i)}}, ((F, \tilde{F}), a_i),$ $(\widehat{\mathsf{sk}}_{\mathsf{id},a_i}, \check{\mathsf{sk}}_{\mathsf{id},a_i})\Big) = 1$, where $\mathsf{vk}_{\mathsf{AA}_{\mathsf{aid}(a_i)}} = (\tilde{X}_i, \tilde{Y}_i, \tilde{Z}_i) \in \mathbb{H}^3$. Note that R_i is independent of R'_i and $(F, \tilde{F})$. The signer then proves the following:

$$\check{S}_i = S_i^{\underline{z}_i} \qquad \check{R}_i = R_i^{\underline{z}_i} \qquad e(\check{S}_i, \tilde{Z}_i) = e(\check{R}_i, \tilde{F})e(\check{R}_i, \tilde{X}_i)e(\check{R}_i^{\alpha_i}, \tilde{Y}_i)$$

  Note that since R_i is public, the verifier can verify that $R_i \neq 1_{\mathbb{G}}$. The verifier can on her own compute a Groth-Sahai commitment to the value $\check{R}_i^{a_i}$ by computing $\mathcal{C}_{\check{R}_i}^{a_i}$, where $\mathcal{C}_{\check{R}_i}$ is the Groth-Sahai commitment (which is ElGamal ciphertext) to $\check{R}_i$. Such an observation improves the efficiency. Also, we only need to commit to the elements of the vector $\mathbf{z}$ in $\mathbb{H}$, which further improves the efficiency.

- For the pseudo-attribute a_{psdo}, we have $\boxed{\widehat{\mathsf{sk}}_{\mathsf{id},a_{\mathsf{psdo}}}} = r_{\mathsf{FBB}}$, $\boxed{\check{\mathsf{sk}}_{\mathsf{id},a_{\mathsf{psdo}}}} = \sigma_{\mathsf{FBB}}$ and $\mathsf{svk} = (\tilde{X}_{\mathsf{FBB}}, \tilde{Y}_{\mathsf{FBB}})$, the signer proves that

$$\check{\sigma}_{\mathsf{FBB}} = \sigma_{\mathsf{FBB}}^{\underline{z}_{|\mathbb{P}|+1}} \qquad \check{G} = G^{\underline{z}_{|\mathbb{P}|+1}} \qquad e(\check{\sigma}_{\mathsf{FBB}}, \tilde{X}_{\mathsf{FBB}} \cdot \tilde{Y}_{\mathsf{FBB}}^{r_{\mathsf{FBB}}} \cdot \tilde{G}^{a_{\mathsf{psdo}}})e(\check{G}, \tilde{H}) = 1$$

The signature size of this instantiation is $(15|\mathbb{P}|+15)\cdot|\mathbb{G}|+(14|\mathbb{P}|+22)\cdot|\mathbb{H}|+(\beta+3)\cdot|p|$ which is much more efficient than the traceable constructions in [16,21].

Instantiation II. Here we instantiate RPSPS with our new partially structure-preserving signature scheme from Sect. 3.1. The only difference from the details of the NIZK proof π from that of instantiation I is in the part that proves possession of credentials for attributes used in the signing which we detail below. The rest of the details of the proof π and hence the signature are identical to those of instantiation I.

For each $a_i \in \{1, \ldots, |\mathbb{P}|\}$, we have $\mathsf{sk}'_{\mathsf{id},a_i} = (R'_i, S'_i, \tilde{R}'_i) \in \mathbb{G}^2 \times \mathbb{H}$ where $\widehat{\mathsf{sk}}'_{\mathsf{id},a_i} = (R'_i, \tilde{R}'_i)$ and $\check{\mathsf{sk}}'_{\mathsf{id},a_i} = S'_i$. The signer re-randomizes $\mathsf{sk}'_{\mathsf{id},a_i}$ by choosing $r' \leftarrow \mathbb{Z}_p^\times$ and computing $\mathsf{sk}_{\mathsf{id},a_i} := (R_i, \tilde{R}_i, S_i) = (R'_i \cdot G^{r'}, \tilde{R}'_i \cdot \tilde{H}^{r'}, S'_i \cdot R'^{2r'}_i \cdot G'^{r'^2})$. To prove if $\check{z}_i \neq 0 \Rightarrow \mathsf{RPSPS.Verify}\left(\mathsf{vk}_{\mathsf{AAaid}(a_i)}, (F, a_i), (\widehat{\mathsf{sk}}_{\mathsf{id},a_i}, \check{\mathsf{sk}}_{\mathsf{id},a_i})\right) = 1$, where $\mathsf{vk}_{\mathsf{AAaid}(a_i)} = (\tilde{X}_i, \tilde{Y}_i, \tilde{Z}_i) \in \mathbb{H}^3$. The signer proves the following:
$$\check{S}_i = S_i^{\check{z}_i} \qquad \check{F}_i = F^{\check{z}_i} \qquad \check{R}_i = R_i^{\check{z}_i} \qquad \check{G}_i = G^{\check{z}_i}$$
$$e(\check{S}_i, \tilde{H}) = e(\check{F}, \tilde{X}_i) e(\check{G}_i^{\alpha_i}, \tilde{Y}_i) e(\check{R}_i, \tilde{R}_i) e(\check{G}_i, \tilde{Z}_i)$$

Note that since $(R_i, \tilde{R}_i)$ are independent of $\mathsf{vk}_{\mathsf{AAaid}(a_i)}$ and thus when choosing dummy credentials for attributes in $\mathbb{P} \setminus \mathcal{A}$, any one can choose such a pair satisfying $e(R_i, \tilde{H}) = e(G, \tilde{R}_i)$.

The verifier can on her own compute a Groth-Sahai commitment to the value $\check{G}_i^{a_i}$ by computing $\mathcal{C}_{\check{G}_i}^{a_i}$, where $\mathcal{C}_{\check{G}_i}$ is the Groth-Sahai commitment (which is ElGamal ciphertext) to $\check{G}_i$. Such an observation improves the efficiency. In addition, we only need to commit to the elements of the vector z in $\mathbb{H}$, which further improves the efficiency. When verifying the signature, one additionally checks that $e(R_i, \tilde{H}) = e(G, \tilde{R}_i)$.

The signature size of this instantiation is $(19|\mathbb{P}| + 15) \cdot |\mathbb{G}| + (21|\mathbb{P}| + 22) \cdot |\mathbb{H}| + (\beta + 3) \cdot |p|$ which is again more efficient than the traceable constructions in [16,21].

6   Construction of ABS-UCL for Threshold Policies

We give here an ABS-UCL construction supporting threshold policies and a single authority. The scheme is based on an improved variant of the ABS scheme in [24].

$\mathsf{Setup}(1^\lambda, n)$: Generate a bilinear group $\mathcal{P} := (\mathbb{G}, \mathbb{H}, \mathbb{T}, G, \tilde{H}, p, e)$ and choose a collision-resistant hash function $\mathcal{H} : \{0,1\}^* \rightarrow \{0,1\}^k$, and a coding map $\zeta : \mathcal{A} \rightarrow \mathbb{Z}_p^*$. Define a set of pairwise different elements of $\mathbb{Z}_p^*$, $D = \{d_1, \cdots, d_{n-1}\}$ where D_i represents the first i elements of D, i.e. $D_i = \{d_1, \cdots, d_i\}$. These values correspond to $n - 1$ dummy attributes that should be different from all attributes appearing in $\mathcal{A}$. Generate a CRS crs for the Groth-Sahai NIZK system and the secret/verification keys $(\mathsf{ssk}, \mathsf{svk})$ of a signature scheme (Full Boneh-Boyen) which will be used to sign a special attribute called the pseudo-attribute which is needed in the security proofs to simulate signing queries and to bind a signature to the message.

The public parameters is $\mathsf{pp} = (\mathcal{A}, n, \lambda, \mathcal{P}, G', \tilde{H}', \mathsf{crs}, \mathcal{H}, D, \mathsf{svk})$, where $e(G, \tilde{H}') = e(G', \tilde{H})$.

AASetup(pp): this is run by the attribute authority. It randomly chooses $\alpha, \gamma \in \mathbb{Z}_p^*$, and sets $U = G^{\alpha\gamma}$, and $V = e(G, \tilde{H})^\alpha$. The master secret key is $\mathsf{gmsk} = (\alpha, \gamma)$ whereas the master public key is $\mathsf{gmpk} = (U, V, G^\alpha, \{\tilde{H}^{\alpha\gamma^i}\}_{i=0,\cdots,2n-1})$.

AttKeyGen(pp, gmpk, $I, F, \tilde{F}$): given a set of attributes $I \subset \mathcal{A}$ and $F = (G')^{\mathsf{uskid}}$, and $\tilde{F} = (\tilde{H}')^{\mathsf{uskid}}$. It picks $r \leftarrow \mathbb{Z}_p^*$ at random and returns

$$\mathsf{sk}_{\mathsf{id},I} = \left(\{(G \cdot F)^{\frac{r}{\gamma + \zeta(a)}}\}_{a \in I}, \{(\tilde{H} \cdot \tilde{F})^{r\gamma^i}\}_{i=0,\cdots,n-2}, (\tilde{H} \cdot \tilde{F})^{\frac{r-1}{\gamma}} \right)$$

.

Sign(pp, gmpk, $\mathsf{sk}_{\mathsf{id},I}$, uskid, $M, \mathbb{P}$, recip): Given a message $M \in \{0,1\}^*$, a policy $\mathbb{P}(t, S)$, for which $t \leq |S| = s \leq n$. If $|S \cap I| < t$, return $\perp$. Otherwise, fix the signing set of attributes as $I_S \subseteq I$ where $|I_S| = t$ and compute the following:

- Let $C_1 = (G \cdot F)^{z_1} \leftarrow \mathsf{Aggregate}(\{(G \cdot F)^{\frac{r}{\gamma + \zeta(a)}}\}_{a \in I_S}, I_S)$, where[1]

$$z_1 = \frac{r}{\prod_{a \in I_S}(\gamma + \zeta(a))}$$

- Define the sets $W = S \cup D_{n+t-1-s}$ and $R = W \setminus I_S$ and compute $z_2 = \prod_{a \in R}(\zeta(a))$. Then compute $T_1 = C_1^{1/z_2}$.
- Define the following polynomial in γ where $\deg(P(\gamma)) = n - 2$

$$P(\gamma) = \frac{1}{\gamma}\left(\prod_{a \in R}(\gamma + \zeta(a)) - \prod_{a \in R}(\zeta(a)) \right).$$

Using the second part of the secret key as an input to a Lagrange interpolation algorithm, one can efficiently compute $\tilde{H}_1 = (\tilde{H} \cdot \tilde{F})^{rP(\gamma)}$. We actually need to compute the following value;

$$\tilde{T}_2 = (\tilde{H} \cdot \tilde{F})^{\frac{r-1}{\gamma}} \cdot \tilde{H}_1^{\frac{1}{\prod_{a \in R}(\zeta(a))}}$$

- If recip $\neq \perp$, set $\tau = \chi^{\frac{1}{\mathsf{recip} + \mathsf{uskid}}}$, where $\chi \in \mathbb{G}$. Otherwise, $\tau = \perp$.
- Let $\tilde{H}_2 = \tilde{H}^{\alpha \cdot \prod_{a \in W}(\gamma + \zeta(a))}$, which can be computed from gmpk.
- When recip $\neq \perp$, the signer proves that either she has enough attributes to satisfy the policy $\mathbb{P}$ or she has a signature on the pseudo-attribute $a_{\mathsf{psdo}} = \mathcal{H}(M, \mathbb{P}, \mathsf{recip})$. This is realized by a GS NIZK proof for the following language:

$$\mathcal{L}: \left\{ \begin{array}{l} \left((\tau, \mathsf{recip}, \mathsf{pp}), \left((f(\mathsf{uskid}), \mathsf{PK}(\mathsf{uskid})), \tilde{T}_2, T_1, G'', \tilde{H}'' \right) \right): \\ e(U^{-1}, \tilde{T}_2) \cdot e(T_1, \tilde{H}_2) = e(G^\alpha, \tilde{H}'') \cdot e(G^\alpha, \tilde{F}) \\ \wedge F = (G')^{\mathsf{uskid}} \wedge e(\sigma_{\mathsf{FBB}}^r, \tilde{X}_{\mathsf{FBB}} \cdot \tilde{Y}_{\mathsf{FBB}}^{\tau \mathsf{FBB}} \cdot \tilde{G}^{a_{\mathsf{psdo}}}) = e(\underline{G''}, \tilde{H}) \\ \wedge e(\underline{G''} \cdot G^{-1}, \tilde{H}'' \cdot \tilde{H}^{-1}) = 1 \wedge e(\tau, \tilde{H}^{\mathsf{uskid}}) \cdot e(\tau, \tilde{H}^{\mathsf{recip}}) = e(\underline{\chi}, \tilde{H}) \\ \wedge e(G, \tilde{F}) = e(G', \tilde{H}^{\mathsf{uskid}}) \end{array} \right\},$$

---

[1] **Aggregate** was originally defined in [13], and is based on the fact that a product of inverses of coprime polynomials can be written as a sum of inverses of affine polynomials, as described and used in [14]. More details on **Aggregate** can be found in [13].

- When recip $= \bot$, everything stays the same except that we remove the last two equations from the NIZK language and change the pseudo-attribute to $a_{\mathrm{psdo}} = \mathcal{H}(M, \mathbb{P})$.

The signature is $\sigma = (\pi_{\mathsf{GS}}, \tau)$ which is of size $27 \cdot |\mathbb{G}| + 28 \cdot |\mathbb{H}|$.

Verify(pp, gmpk, $M, \mathbb{P}, \sigma$, recip): Compute $H_2 = \tilde{H}^{\alpha \cdot \Pi_{a \in W} (\gamma + \zeta(a))}$ and verify the GS proof π_{GS}.

Link(pp, gmpk, $\sigma_1, \sigma_2, M_1, M_2, \mathbb{P}_1, \mathbb{P}_2$, recip): If σ_1 or σ_2 are invalid, return 0. Otherwise, parse σ_i as $(\pi_{\mathsf{GS}_i}, \tau_i)$ and return 1 if both τ_1 and τ_2 are non-trivial and $\tau_1 = \tau_2 \neq \bot$, return 0 otherwise.

Efficiency comparison with Herranz et al. results in [24]. The two schemes that are presented in [24] employ the less efficient pairing setting, i.e. symmetric pairing. The sizes of the schemes' signatures are 15 and 3 group elements. The latter comes at the cost of having longer secret keys. Our scheme, even after adding the user-controlled linkability feature, is still comparable to the first scheme in terms of the size of the secret key and the size of the signature (as the group elements in our scheme are much smaller). However, the public parameters in our scheme are shorter (by k group elements, where k is the bit length of the output of the hash function used in the sheme). We get this improvement by using the pseudo-attribute idea to bind the message to the signature. Moreover, using our technique to bind the message, and if we were to drop the user-linkability property from our scheme, we would get a standard ABS for threshold policies that has the same signature size as [24], but with much shorter public keys.

The proof of the following theorem is in Appendix A.

Theorem 3. *The construction above is a secure tABS-UCL.*

Acknowledgement. The first author was funded by a research grant from the UK government.

Appendix

A   Single Authority tABS-UCL: Security Proofs

Theorem 4 (Anonymity). *If the NIZK proof system NIZK is zero-knowledge, the linkable indistinguishable tag scheme LIT is indistinguishable, and the hash function $\mathcal{H}$ is collision-resistance then the tABS-UCL is anonymous.*

Proof. We will prove the anonymity of tABS-UCL by showing that a sequence of games are only negligibly indistinguishable from one another. The technique is similar to [3]; the challenger will beforehand guess the challenge user that will be chosen by the adversary $\mathcal{F}$ during the game, and will abort if they are not the same. If the adversary has advantage ϵ in winning the unchanged game, than $\mathcal{F}$ will have an advantage $\epsilon/\eta(\lambda)$ in winning the second game, where $\eta(\lambda)$, a polynomial in λ, is the upper bounds of number of users that an adversary can create. The sequence of games will start with a game where the challenger guesses correctly the challenger user and end with a game that is independent of challenger user. If we can prove that $\mathcal{F}$'s behaviour changes only with negligible probability, then our tABS-UCL is anonymous.

We start with the first game Game 0 where the challenger guesses a particular user $\text{id}^* \leftarrow [1, \eta(\lambda)]$, and aborts the game if in the challenge call we have $\text{id}_b \neq \text{id}^*$. In *Game-1*, we replace the crs of the NIZK proof by the hiding crs, i.e. we run GSSimSetup instead of GSSetup.

By the Zero-knowledge property of the NIZK, we have that Game 0 and Game 1 differ only negligibly from each other.

In Game 2, we don't use usk_{id}^* while replying to KeyGen oracle queries. This game is only negligibly different from *Game-1* as the generated keys are always randomized with a fresh uniform random r and therefore are indistinguishable from random group elements.

In Game 3, for any Sign or Challenge queries that involve id^*, if the recip is new, we use independent uniformly random keys to produce the tags, i.e. σ_{UCL}, otherwise, we use the same tag that has been used before.

From Game 2 to Game 3, we will have a series of sub-games, where each two consecutive ones are indistinguishable by the indistinguishability of the LIT, i.e. they differ from each other by a single construction of a LIT tag. We start by answering all queries related to the selected signer id^* using its secret key usk_{id}^*, then we move from a sub-game to another by answering one of these queries using a random key sk. We end up in the last sub-game where we answer all those queries using a key sk chosen uniformly at random. We have $\mu(\lambda)$ sub-games, where each two consecutive ones differ from each other by a negligible value, i.e. the advantage against the indistinguishability of the LIT. One can easily see that the last game is now independent of the challenge user used in answering challenge query, and hence the anonymity of tABS-UCL.   □

Theorem 5 (Unforgeability). *if (ℓ, m, t)-aMSE-CDH holds, $\mathcal{H}$ is collision-resistance and the NIZK system is sound then our tABS-UCL is unforgeable.*

Proof. First, by the collision-resistance of $\mathcal{H}$ the adversary has a negligible probability in finding two different tuples $(m, \mathbb{P}, \text{recip}) \neq (m', \mathbb{P}', \text{recip}')$ where $\mathcal{H}(m, \mathbb{P}, \text{recip}) = \mathcal{H}(m', \mathbb{P}', \text{recip}')$.

Now, we take as input a problem instance of (ℓ, m, t)-aMSE-CDH. We denote the generators used in the given instance by $G_0, \tilde{H}_0$. Given an attacker $\mathcal{F}_1$ that can break the unforgeability of our tABS-UCL scheme, we will build an attacker $\mathcal{F}_2$ that can use $\mathcal{F}_1$ as a subroutine to solve (ℓ, m, t)-aMSE-CDH. The attacker gives the policy that he wants to be challenged on $\mathbb{P}^*(t^*, S^*)$ where $|S^*| = s^*$. We can set $n - s^* = \ell, n + t^* - 1 = m$ and $t^* + 1 = t$. The adversary $\mathcal{F}_2$ will then simulate the different algorithms of tABS-UCL as follows:

Setup.

- Define the attribute encoding ζ as follows:

$$\zeta(a) = \begin{cases} -x_i, \text{where } g_1(x_i) = 0 & \text{if } a \in \mathcal{P} \backslash S^* \\ -x_j, \text{where } g_2(x_j) = 0 & \text{if } a \in S^* \text{or } a \in D_1 = D_{n+t^*-1-s^*} \\ d, d \leftarrow Z_p & \text{if } a \in D \backslash D_1 \end{cases}$$

- Use the elements of line (1) to compute $G_0^{g_1(\gamma)}$, set $G := G_0^{g_1(\gamma)}$ and $\tilde{H} := \tilde{H}_0$.
- Sample $x, y \leftarrow Z_p^*$ and set $F_1 = G^x$ and $F_2 = \tilde{H}^y$.
- Use line (3) to compute $u = G^{\alpha\gamma} = G_0^{\alpha\gamma g_1(\gamma)}$ and $v = e(G, \tilde{H})^\alpha = e(G_0^{g_1(\gamma)\alpha}, \tilde{H}_0)$.
- Use line (6) to get $\{h^{\alpha\gamma^i}\}_{i=0,\dots,2n-1}$. Then generate $(\mathsf{svk}, \mathsf{ssk})$ for the pseudo-attribute and crs for GS proofs in the soundness setting.

Key Generation. On input $\mathbb{P}(\Omega, t)$, if $|\Omega_S = \Omega \cap S^*| \geq t^*$, return $\perp$, otherwise it generates the key corresponding to S as follows: The first step is to compute

$$\left(\left\{ G^{\frac{r}{\gamma+\zeta(a)}} \right\}_{a\in\Omega}, \left\{ \tilde{H}^{r\gamma^i} \right\}_{i=0,\dots,n-2}, \tilde{H}^{\frac{r-1}{\gamma}} \right)$$

and the second step is to compute:

$$\mathsf{sk}_\Omega = \left(\left\{ \left(G^{\frac{r}{\gamma+\zeta(a)}} \right)^{x\mathsf{sk}_{sid}+1} \right\}_{a\in\Omega}, \left\{ \left(\tilde{H}^{r\gamma^i} \right)^{y\mathsf{sk}_{sid}+1} \right\}_{i=0,\dots,n-2}, \left(\tilde{H}^{\frac{r-1}{\gamma}} \right)^{y\mathsf{sk}_{sid}+1} \right)$$

The second step can be easily done as the challenger knows of x, y, sk_{id}. For the first step, here are the details (similar to [24]):

- Let where $\lambda_\Omega = \left(\prod_{a\in\Omega_S} \zeta(a) \right)^{-1}$, $r = (\omega y_\Omega \gamma + 1)Q_\Omega(\gamma)$. Define

$$Q_\Omega(X) = \begin{cases} 1 & \text{if } X = \gamma \text{ and } |\Omega_S| = 0 \\ \lambda_\Omega \cdot \prod_{a\in\Omega_S}(X + \zeta(a)) & \text{otherwise} \end{cases}$$

- Define

$$L_a(X) = \begin{cases} \frac{Q_\Omega(X)}{X+\zeta(a)} & \text{if } a \in \Omega_S \\ \frac{g_1(X)}{X+\zeta(a)} & \text{if } a \in \Omega\setminus\Omega_S \end{cases}$$

- For $a \in \Omega_S$, use the line (1) and (2) to compute $G^{\frac{r}{\gamma+\zeta(a)}} = G_0^{g_1(\gamma)\omega y_\Omega\gamma L_a(\gamma)} \cdot G_0^{g_1(\gamma)L_a(\gamma)}$. For $a \in \Omega\setminus\Omega_S$, compute $G^{\frac{r}{\gamma+\zeta(a)}} = G_0^{L_a(\gamma)\omega y_\Omega\gamma Q_\Omega(\gamma)} \cdot G_0^{Q_\Omega(\gamma)L_a(\gamma)}$.
- Use the lines (4) and (5) to compute $\left\{ \tilde{H}^{r\gamma^i} \right\}_{i=0,\cdots,n-2}$.
- Use the line (4) to compute $\tilde{H}^{\frac{Q_\Omega(\gamma)-1}{\gamma}}$ and (5) to compute $\tilde{H}^{Q_\Omega(\gamma)\omega y_\omega}$. Their product will give $\tilde{H}^{\frac{r-1}{\gamma}}$.

Signing Queries. Use the pseudo-attribute secret key ssk to sign any message of the attacker's choice.

Forgery. The adversary now outputs a valid signature. By the extractability of the GS proofs, $\mathcal{F}_2$ can either extract T_1 and T_2 or a valid signature on the pseudo-attribute. In the first case, we note that $\mathcal{F}_2$ knows of x, y and sk_{id}, and therefore can compute $T_1' = T_1^{\frac{1}{x\mathsf{sk}_{id}+1}}, T_2' = T_2^{\frac{1}{y\mathsf{sk}_{id}+1}}$. Using the lines (4) and (5), $\mathcal{F}_2$ can finally compute

$$e(T_1', \tilde{H}_0^{\kappa g_2(\gamma)}) \cdot e(G^{-\kappa\gamma g_1(\gamma)}, T_2') = e(G_0, \tilde{H}_0)^{\kappa g_1(\gamma)}$$

and therefore solve (ℓ, m, t)-aMSE-CDH. In the second case, the forgery on tABS-UCL will directly give a forgery on the underlying digital signature used to sign the pseudo-attributes (i.e. the Full Boneh-Boyen signature). $\qquad \square$

Theorem 6 (User-controlled linkability). *The threshold attribute based signatures is User controlled linkable if the Linkable Indistinguishable tag scheme* LIT *is linkable.*

Proof. We will first deal with the case in which an adversary produces two supposedly linkable signatures, but when testing them with Link, it says they are not. Given that an adversary C has full control over the secret keys so he can generate secret keys to any user that he wants to be challenged on, say id_{Link}. He should also pick the verifier's name recip as a part of the challenge. At the end, he needs to produce two signatures, σ_1 and σ_2 on behalf of the user id_{Link}, for which $\sigma_1 = (\sigma_{ABS_1}, \sigma_{UCL_1})$ and $\sigma_2 = (\sigma_{ABS_2}, \sigma_{UCL_2})$. He wins if both signatures σ_1 and σ_2 verify correctly and $Link(\sigma_1, \sigma_2, recip) = 0$. The contradiction is straight forward here, non-linkable signatures would lead to $\sigma_{UCL1} \neq \sigma_{UCL2}$, where the fact that both signatures verify correctly against the same recipient name recip, would lead to $\sigma_{UCL1} = \sigma_{UCL2}$. In the second case, the adversary aims to break the soundness of the linking algorithm Link by producing supposedly non-linkable signatures (σ_1, σ_2) and yet Link tells that they are linkable. This case can be easily reduced to breaking the linkability property of the LIT scheme, as this can only be done by having $(sk_1, recip_1) \neq (sk_2, recip_2)$. □

References

1. Abe, M., Fuchsbauer, G., Groth, J., Haralambiev, K., Ohkubo, M.: Structure-preserving signatures and commitments to group elements. In: Rabin, T. (ed.) CRYPTO 2010. LNCS, vol. 6223, pp. 209–236. Springer, Heidelberg (2010). https://doi.org/10.1007/978-3-642-14623-7_12
2. Bellare, M., Rogaway, P.: Random oracles are practical: a paradigm for designing efficient protocols. In: ACM CCS, pp. 62–73. ACM (1993)
3. Bernhard, D., Fuchsbauer, G., Ghadafi, E.: Efficient signatures of knowledge and DAA in the standard model. In: Jacobson, M., Locasto, M., Mohassel, P., Safavi-Naini, R. (eds.) ACNS 2013. LNCS, vol. 7954, pp. 518–533. Springer, Heidelberg (2013). https://doi.org/10.1007/978-3-642-38980-1_33
4. Bernhard, D., Fuchsbauer, G., Ghadafi, E., Smart, N.P., Warinschi, B.: Anonymous attestation with user-controlled linkability. Int. J. Inf. Secur. **12**(3), 219–249 (2013)
5. Bobba, R., Fatemieh, O., Khan, F., Gunter, C.A., Khurana, H.: Using attribute-based access control to enable attribute-based messaging. In: ACSAC. IEEE CS, pp. 403–413 (2006)
6. Boneh, D., Boyen, X.: Efficient selective-ID secure identity-based encryption without random oracles. In: Cachin, C., Camenisch, J.L. (eds.) EUROCRYPT 2004. LNCS, vol. 3027, pp. 223–238. Springer, Heidelberg (2004). https://doi.org/10.1007/978-3-540-24676-3_14
7. Boneh, D., Boyen, X.: Short signatures without random oracles and the SDH assumption in bilinear groups. J. Cryptology **21**(2), 149–177 (2008)
8. Boyen, X.: Mesh signatures. In: Naor, M. (ed.) EUROCRYPT 2007. LNCS, vol. 4515, pp. 210–227. Springer, Heidelberg (2007). https://doi.org/10.1007/978-3-540-72540-4_12
9. Brickell, E., Camenisch, J., Chen, L.: Direct anonymous attestation. In: ACM CCS, pp. 132–145. ACM (2004)

10. Chatterjee, S., Menezes, A.: Type 2 structure-preserving signature schemes revisited. In: Iwata, T., Cheon, J.H. (eds.) ASIACRYPT 2015. LNCS, vol. 9452, pp. 286–310. Springer, Heidelberg (2015). https://doi.org/10.1007/978-3-662-48797-6_13

11. Chaum, D., van Heyst, E.: Group signatures. In: Davies, D.W. (ed.) EUROCRYPT 1991. LNCS, vol. 547, pp. 257–265. Springer, Heidelberg (1991). https://doi.org/10.1007/3-540-46416-6_22

12. Chen, L., Urian, R.: DAA-A: direct anonymous attestation with attributes. In: Conti, M., Schunter, M., Askoxylakis, I. (eds.) Trust 2015. LNCS, vol. 9229, pp. 228–245. Springer, Cham (2015). https://doi.org/10.1007/978-3-319-22846-4_14

13. Delerablée, C., Paillier, P., Pointcheval, D.: Fully collusion secure dynamic broadcast encryption with constant-size ciphertexts or decryption keys. In: Takagi, T., Okamoto, T., Okamoto, E., Okamoto, T. (eds.) Pairing 2007. LNCS, vol. 4575, pp. 39–59. Springer, Heidelberg (2007). https://doi.org/10.1007/978-3-540-73489-5_4

14. Delerablée, C., Pointcheval, D.: Dynamic threshold public-key encryption. In: Wagner, D. (ed.) CRYPTO 2008. LNCS, vol. 5157, pp. 317–334. Springer, Heidelberg (2008). https://doi.org/10.1007/978-3-540-85174-5_18

15. El Kaafarani, A., Chen, L., Ghadafi, E., Davenport, J.: Attribute-based signatures with user-controlled linkability. In: Gritzalis, D., Kiayias, A., Askoxylakis, I. (eds.) CANS 2014. LNCS, vol. 8813, pp. 256–269. Springer, Cham (2014). https://doi.org/10.1007/978-3-319-12280-9_17

16. El Kaafarani, A., Ghadafi, E., Khader, D.: Decentralized traceable attribute-based signatures. In: Benaloh, J. (ed.) CT-RSA 2014. LNCS, vol. 8366, pp. 327–348. Springer, Cham (2014). https://doi.org/10.1007/978-3-319-04852-9_17

17. Escala, A., Herranz, J., Morillo, P.: Revocable attribute-based signatures with adaptive security in the standard model. In: Nitaj, A., Pointcheval, D. (eds.) AFRICACRYPT 2011. LNCS, vol. 6737, pp. 224–241. Springer, Heidelberg (2011). https://doi.org/10.1007/978-3-642-21969-6_14

18. Frikken, K.B., Li, J., Atallah, M.J.: Trust negotiation with hidden credentials, hidden policies, and policy cycles. In: NDSS, pp. 157–172 (2006)

19. Gagné, M., Narayan, S., Safavi-Naini, R.: Short pairing-efficient threshold-attribute-based signature. In: Abdalla, M., Lange, T. (eds.) Pairing 2012. LNCS, vol. 7708, pp. 295–313. Springer, Heidelberg (2013). https://doi.org/10.1007/978-3-642-36334-4_19

20. Galbraith, S.D., Paterson, K.G., Smart, N.P.: Pairings for cryptographers. Discrete Appl. Math. **156**(16), 3113–3121 (2008)

21. Ghadafi, E.: Stronger security notions for decentralized traceable attribute-based signatures and more efficient constructions. In: Nyberg, K. (ed.) CT-RSA 2015. LNCS, vol. 9048, pp. 391–409. Springer, Cham (2015). https://doi.org/10.1007/978-3-319-16715-2_21

22. Ghadafi, E.: More efficient structure-preserving signatures - or: bypassing the type-III lower bounds. In: Foley, S.N., Gollmann, D., Snekkenes, E. (eds.) ESORICS 2017. LNCS, vol. 10493, pp. 43–61. Springer, Cham (2017). https://doi.org/10.1007/978-3-319-66399-9_3

23. Groth, J., Sahai, A.: Efficient noninteractive proof systems for bilinear groups. SIAM J. Comput. **41**(5), 1193–1232 (2012)

24. Herranz, J., Laguillaumie, F., Libert, B., Ràfols, C.: Short attribute-based signatures for threshold predicates. In: Dunkelman, O. (ed.) CT-RSA 2012. LNCS, vol. 7178, pp. 51–67. Springer, Heidelberg (2012). https://doi.org/10.1007/978-3-642-27954-6_4

25. Herranz, J., Laguillaumie, F., Ràfols, C.: Constant size ciphertexts in threshold attribute-based encryption. In: Nguyen, P.Q., Pointcheval, D. (eds.) PKC 2010. LNCS, vol. 6056, pp. 19–34. Springer, Heidelberg (2010). https://doi.org/10.1007/978-3-642-13013-7_2

26. Karchmer, M., Wigderson, A.: On span programs. In: IEEE Structure in Complexity Theory, pp. 102–111 (1993)

27. Li, J., Au, M.H., Susilo, W., Xie, D., Ren, K.: Attribute-based signature and its applications. In: ASIACCS, pp. 60–69. ACM (2010)

28. Maji, H.K., Prabhakaran, M., Rosulek, M.: Attribute-based signatures. In: Kiayias, A. (ed.) CT-RSA 2011. LNCS, vol. 6558, pp. 376–392. Springer, Heidelberg (2011). https://doi.org/10.1007/978-3-642-19074-2_24

29. Okamoto, T., Takashima, K.: Efficient attribute-based signatures for non-monotone predicates in the standard model. In: Catalano, D., Fazio, N., Gennaro, R., Nicolosi, A. (eds.) PKC 2011. LNCS, vol. 6571, pp. 35–52. Springer, Heidelberg (2011). https://doi.org/10.1007/978-3-642-19379-8_3

30. Okamoto, T., Takashima, K.: Decentralized attribute-based signatures. In: Kurosawa, K., Hanaoka, G. (eds.) PKC 2013. LNCS, vol. 7778, pp. 125–142. Springer, Heidelberg (2013). https://doi.org/10.1007/978-3-642-36362-7_9

31. Rivest, R.L., Shamir, A., Tauman, Y.: How to leak a secret. In: Boyd, C. (ed.) ASIACRYPT 2001. LNCS, vol. 2248, pp. 552–565. Springer, Heidelberg (2001). https://doi.org/10.1007/3-540-45682-1_32

32. Sakai, Y., Attrapadung, N., Hanaoka, G.: Attribute-based signatures for circuits from bilinear map. In: Cheng, C.-M., Chung, K.-M., Persiano, G., Yang, B.-Y. (eds.) PKC 2016. LNCS, vol. 9614, pp. 283–300. Springer, Heidelberg (2016). https://doi.org/10.1007/978-3-662-49384-7_11

33. Shahandashti, S.F., Safavi-Naini, R.: Threshold attribute-based signatures and their application to anonymous credential systems. In: Preneel, B. (ed.) AFRICACRYPT 2009. LNCS, vol. 5580, pp. 198–216. Springer, Heidelberg (2009). https://doi.org/10.1007/978-3-642-02384-2_13

34. Tang, F., Li, H., Liang, B.: Attribute-based signatures for circuits from multilinear maps. In: Chow, S.S.M., Camenisch, J., Hui, L.C.K., Yiu, S.M. (eds.) ISC 2014. LNCS, vol. 8783, pp. 54–71. Springer, Cham (2014). https://doi.org/10.1007/978-3-319-13257-0_4

35. Urquidi, M., Khader, D., Lancrenon, J., Chen, L.: Attribute-based signatures with controllable linkability. In: Yung, M., Zhang, J., Yang, Z. (eds.) INTRUST 2015. LNCS, vol. 9565, pp. 114–129. Springer, Cham (2016). https://doi.org/10.1007/978-3-319-31550-8_8

How Low Can You Go? Short Structure-Preserving Signatures for Diffie-Hellman Vectors

Essam Ghadafi[✉]

University of the West of England, Bristol, UK
`essam.ghadafi@uwe.ac.uk`

Abstract. Structure-Preserving Signatures (SPSs) are an important tool for the design of modular cryptographic protocols. It has been proven that such schemes in the most efficient Type-3 bilinear group setting have a lower bound of 3-element signatures, which must include elements from both base groups, and a verification overhead of at least 2 Pairing-Product Equations (PPEs). Very recently, Ghadafi (ESORICS 2017) showed that by restricting the message space to the set of Diffie-Hellman pairs (which does not hinder applicability of the schemes), some of the existing lower bounds for the single message case can be circumvented. However, the case of signing multiple messages, which is required for many applications, was left as an open problem since the techniques used for signing single messages do not seem to lend themselves to the multi-message setting. In this work we investigate this setting and answer the question in the affirmative. We construct schemes that sign vectors of messages and which yield shorter signatures than optimal schemes for vectors of unilateral messages. More precisely, we construct 2 fully randomiazble schemes that sign vectors of Diffie-Hellman pairs yielding signatures consisting of only 2 elements regardless of the size of the vector signed. We also construct a unilateral scheme that signs a pair of messages yielding signatures consisting of 3 elements from the shorter base group. All of our schemes require a single PPE for verification (not counting the cost of verifying the well-formedness of the messages). Thus, all of our schemes compare favourably to all existing schemes with respect to signature size and verification overhead. Even when considering single messages, our first 2 schemes compare favourably to the best existing schemes in many aspects including the verification overhead and the key size.

Keywords: Digital signatures · Structure-preserving signatures · Type-3 groups

1 Introduction

Structure-Preserving Signatures (SPSs) [3] are pairing-based signature schemes where the message, the verification key and the signature consist of only group

© Springer International Publishing AG 2017
M. O'Neill (Ed.): IMACC 2017, LNCS 10655, pp. 185–204, 2017.
https://doi.org/10.1007/978-3-319-71045-7_10

elements from one or both base groups, and signature verification requires evaluating Pairing-Product Equations (PPEs). Due to their elegant structure and the fact that they compose nicely with existing widely used tools such as ElGamal encryption [20] and Groth-Sahai proofs [34], SPS schemes are an ideal building block for designing cryptographic protocols not relying on random oracles [22].

The notion has numerous applications which include group signatures, e.g [3,38], blind signatures, e.g. [3,25], attribute-based signatures, e.g. [21], tightly secure encryption, e.g. [2,35], malleable signatures, e.g. [9], anonymous credentials, e.g. [16,24], network coding, e.g. [9], oblivious transfer, e.g. [31], direct anonymous attestation, e.g. [13,28], and e-cash, e.g. [10].

Related Work. The term "structure-preserving signature" was first formally introduced by Abe et al. [3] but earlier schemes conforming to the definition were given in [31,32]. The notion has received a significant amount of attention and many studies on the notion have been published. Constructions of such schemes in the Type-3 setting (cf. Section 2.1) include [3,4,6,19,27,33]. The vast majority of those constructions rely on security proofs in the generic group model [40,41]. Abe et al. [4] proved that signatures of any scheme in the Type-3 bilinear group setting must contain at least 3 elements, which must include elements from both base groups, and require at least 2 PPEs for verification. This rules out the existence of schemes with unilateral signatures, i.e. where all components of the signature are from the same group.

Constructions relying on standard assumptions, e.g. DLIN and DDH, were given by [1,2,15,18,36–38]. Abe et al. [5] proved that it is impossible to base the security of an optimal Type-3 scheme on non-interactive intractability assumptions. Their result guarantees that schemes based on non-interactive intractability assumptions can never be as efficient as their counterparts relying on interactive assumptions or those proven secure directly in the generic group model. In fact all existing constructions based on standard (static) assumptions are far less efficient than existing optimal schemes.

Recently, Ghadafi [28] gave a randomizable scheme yielding signatures consisting of 3 elements from the shorter base group which signs a single Diffie-Hellman (cf. Section 2.1) pair. Signatures of his scheme are shorter than those of optimal schemes for unilateral messages since the bit size of the elements of the second base group are at least twice that of those from the first base group. Verification in his scheme requires, besides checking the well-formedness of the message, the evaluation of 2 PPEs. However, his scheme is only capable of signing a single message and it is unclear whether it can be extended (or even if that is at all possible) to signing multiple messages while preserving the signature size. More recently, Ghadafi [29] defined the notion of unilateral structure-preserving signatures on Diffie-Hellman pairs and gave constructions for a single Diffie-Hellman pair yielding signatures consisting of only 2 elements from the shorter base group. Ghadafi argued that restricting the message space to the set of Diffie-Hellman pairs does not restrict applicability of the schemes and used direct anonymous attestation [14], which is a protocol deployed in practice, and attribute-based signatures [39] as an example. Even though Ghadafi [29] gave a partially structure-preserving scheme which can sign a vector of field elements along the single Diffie-Hellman pair, it was left as an open problem to investigate the case of structure-preserving signatures for a vector of group elements.

Constructions in the Type-2 setting (where there is an efficiently computable homomorphism between the base groups in one direction) were given in [7,11,19]. Fully structure-preserving schemes where even the secret key consists of only group elements from the base groups were recently given by [8,33,42].

Numerous applications require signing a vector of group elements, e.g. when certifying the public key of an encryption/signature scheme, without hindering the structure of the messages, i.e. without hashing. This is particularly important when the aim is to avoid relying on random oracles. Therefore, the design of efficient signature schemes conforming to those requirements would have implications for various applications. Note that SPS schemes for Diffie-Hellman tuples proved useful for many applications see e.g. [3,13,24,27,29].

Our Contribution. We construct 3 new fully randomizable structure-preserving schemes for vectors of messages which yield shorter signatures than all existing schemes for vectors of unilateral messages. Our first 2 schemes yield signatures consisting of 2 elements and requiring 1 PPE for verification. Our third scheme which signs a vector of size 2 yield (unilateral) signatures consisting of 3 elements from the shorter base group and require 1 PPE for verification. The verification overhead of our schemes also compares favourably to exiting schemes, in particular, when verifying multiple signatures on the same message vector, which is what a number of applications require.

Even when signing single messages, our first 2 schemes compare favourably in many measures, e.g. the key size and verification overhead, to the best existing scheme [29].

Paper Organization. We provide some preliminary definitions in Sect. 2. In Sect. 3 we give two new fully randomizable schemes for signing arbitrary vectors of messages. In Sect. 4 we give a scheme for signing a pair of messages. In Sect. 5 we compare the efficiency of our constructions with that of existing ones.

Notation. We write $y = A(x; r)$ when algorithm A on input x and randomness r outputs y. We write $y \leftarrow A(x)$ for the process of setting $y = A(x; r)$ where r is sampled at random. We also write $y \leftarrow S$ for sampling y uniformly at random from a set S. A function $\nu(.) : \mathbb{N} \to \mathbb{R}^+$ is negligible (in n) if for every polynomial $p(.)$ and all sufficiently large values of n, it holds that $\nu(n) < \frac{1}{p(n)}$. By PPT we mean running in probabilistic polynomial time in the relevant security parameter. We use $[k]$ to denote the set $\{1, \ldots, k\}$. We use capital letters for group elements and small letters for field elements.

2 Preliminaries

In this section we provide some preliminary definitions.

2.1 Bilinear Groups

A bilinear group is a tuple $\mathcal{P} := (\mathbb{G}, \mathbb{H}, \mathbb{T}, p, G, \tilde{H}, e)$ where $\mathbb{G}$, $\mathbb{H}$ and $\mathbb{T}$ are groups of a prime order p, and G and $\tilde{H}$ generate $\mathbb{G}$ and $\mathbb{H}$, respectively. The function e is a non-degenerate bilinear map $e : \mathbb{G} \times \mathbb{H} \longrightarrow \mathbb{T}$. For clarity, elements of $\mathbb{H}$ will be accented with $\tilde{\ }$. We use multiplicative notation for all the groups. We let $\mathbb{G}^\times := \mathbb{G} \setminus \{1_{\mathbb{G}}\}$ and $\mathbb{H}^\times := \mathbb{H} \setminus \{1_{\mathbb{H}}\}$. In this paper, we work in the efficient Type-3 setting [26], where $\mathbb{G} \neq \mathbb{H}$ and there is no efficiently computable homomorphism between the groups in either direction. We assume there is an algorithm $\mathcal{BG}$ that on input a security parameter κ, outputs a description of bilinear groups.

The message space of the schemes we consider is the set of elements of the subgroup $\widehat{\mathbb{GH}}$ of $\mathbb{G} \times \mathbb{H}$ defined as the image of the map $\psi : x \longmapsto (G^x, \tilde{H}^x)$ for $x \in \mathbb{Z}_p$. One can efficiently test whether $(M, \tilde{N}) \in \widehat{\mathbb{GH}}$ by checking

$$e(M, \tilde{H}) = e(G, \tilde{N}) \cdot$$

Such pairs were called Diffie-Hellman pairs in [3,23]. An important observation here is that techniques used for batch verification, e.g. [12,17], can be applied when verifying the well-formedness of a vector of Diffie-Hellman pairs. This reduces the cost for verifying a vector of ℓ pairs from 2ℓ pairings to 2 pairings.

2.2 Digital Signatures

A digital signature scheme $\mathcal{DS}$ over a bilinear group $\mathcal{P}$ generated by $\mathcal{BG}$ for a message space $\mathcal{M}$ consists of the following algorithms:

KeyGen($\mathcal{P}$) on input $\mathcal{P}$, it outputs a pair of secret/verification keys (sk, vk).
Sign(sk, m) on input sk and a message $m \in \mathcal{M}$, it outputs a signature σ.
Verify(vk, m, σ) outputs 1 if σ is a valid signature on m w.r.t. vk and 0 otherwise.

Besides the usual correctness requirement, we require existential unforgeability.

Definition 1 (Existential Unforgeability). *A signature scheme $\mathcal{DS}$ over a bilinear group generator $\mathcal{BG}$ is* Existentially-Unforgeable against adaptive Chosen-Message Attack (EUF-CMA) *if for all $\kappa \in \mathbb{N}$ for all PPT adversaries $\mathcal{A}$, the following is negligible (in κ)*

$$\Pr \left[\begin{array}{c} \mathcal{P} \leftarrow \mathcal{BG}(1^\kappa); (\mathsf{sk}, \mathsf{vk}) \leftarrow \mathsf{KeyGen}(\mathcal{P}); (\sigma^*, m^*) \leftarrow \mathcal{A}^{\mathsf{Sign}(\mathsf{sk}, \cdot)}(\mathcal{P}, \mathsf{vk}) \\ : \mathsf{Verify}(\mathsf{vk}, m^*, \sigma^*) = 1 \wedge m^* \notin Q_{\mathsf{Sign}} \end{array} \right],$$

where Q_{Sign} is the set of messages queried to Sign.

Strong Existential Unforgeability against adaptive Chosen-Message Attack (sEUF-CMA) requires that the adversary cannot even output a new signature on a message that was queried to the sign oracle.

A weaker variant of EUF-CMA is *Existential Unforgeability against a Random-Message Attack (EUF-RMA)* in which the sign oracle samples a message uniformly from the message space and returns the message and a signature on it. In one-time signatures, the adversary is restricted to a single signing query.

We consider schemes which are publicly re-randomizable where there is an algorithm Randomize that on input (vk, m, σ) outputs a new signature σ' on m. A desirable property for such class of schemes is that randomized signatures are indistinguishable from fresh signatures.

Definition 2 (Randomizability). *A signature scheme $\mathcal{DS}$ over a bilinear group generator $\mathcal{BG}$ is* randomizable *if for all $\kappa \in \mathbb{N}$ for all stateful adversaries $\mathcal{A}$ the following probability is negligibly close to $\frac{1}{2}$.*

$$\Pr \left[\begin{array}{l} \mathcal{P} \leftarrow \mathcal{BG}(1^\kappa); (\mathsf{sk}, \mathsf{vk}) \leftarrow \mathsf{KeyGen}(\mathcal{P}); (\sigma^*, m^*) \leftarrow \mathcal{A}(\mathcal{P}, \mathsf{sk}, \mathsf{vk}); \sigma_0 \leftarrow \mathsf{Sign}(\mathsf{sk}, m^*); \\ \sigma_1 \leftarrow \mathsf{Randomize}(\mathsf{vk}, m^*, \sigma^*); b \leftarrow \{0,1\} : \mathsf{Verify}(\mathsf{vk}, m^*, \sigma^*) = 1 \wedge \mathcal{A}(\sigma_b) = b \end{array} \right]$$

When the above is exactly $\frac{1}{2}$, we say the scheme has *Perfect Randomizability*.

2.3   Structure-Preserving Signatures

Structure-preserving signatures [3] are signature schemes defined over bilinear groups where the messages, the verification key and signatures are all group elements from either or both base groups, and verifying signatures only involves deciding group membership of the signature components and evaluating PPEs of the form of Equation (1).

$$\prod_i \prod_j e(A_i, \tilde{B}_j)^{c_{i,j}} = 1_{\mathbb{T}}, \tag{1}$$

where $A_i \in \mathbb{G}$ and $\tilde{B}_j \in \mathbb{H}$ are group elements appearing in $\mathcal{P}, m, \mathsf{vk}, \sigma$, whereas $c_{i,j} \in \mathbb{Z}_p$ are constants.

Generic Signer. We refer to a signer that can only decide group membership, evaluate the bilinear map e, compute the group operations in groups $\mathbb{G}, \mathbb{H}$ and $\mathbb{T}$, and compare group elements as a *generic signer*.

3   Constant-Size Schemes for Diffie-Hellman Vectors

In this section, we give 2 new schemes for signing a vector of Diffie-Hellman pairs.

3.1   Scheme I

Given the description of Type-3 bilinear groups $\mathcal{P}$ output by $\mathcal{BG}(1^\kappa)$, the scheme is as follows:

- KeyGen($\mathcal{P}$): Select $x_1, \ldots, x_\ell, y \leftarrow \mathbb{Z}_p$. Set $X_i := G^{x_i}$ for all $i \in [\ell]$, $\tilde{Y} := \tilde{H}^y$, sk $:= (x_1, \ldots, x_\ell, y)$ and vk $:= (X_1, \ldots, X_\ell, \tilde{Y}) \in \mathbb{G}^\ell \times \mathbb{H}$.
- Sign $\Big(\text{sk}, \big((M_1, \tilde{N}_1), \ldots, (M_\ell, \tilde{N}_\ell)\big)\Big)$: To sign $\big((M_1, \tilde{N}_1), \ldots, (M_\ell, \tilde{N}_\ell)\big) \in \widehat{\mathbb{GH}}^\ell$, select $r \leftarrow \mathbb{Z}_p$ and set $R := G^r$, and $\tilde{S} := (\prod_{i=1}^\ell \tilde{N}_i^{x_i} \cdot \tilde{Y}^{x_1} \cdot \tilde{H})^{\frac{1}{r}}$. Return $\sigma := (R, \tilde{S}) \in \mathbb{G} \times \mathbb{H}$.
- Verify $\Big(\text{vk}, \big((M_1, \tilde{N}_1), \ldots, (M_\ell, \tilde{N}_\ell)\big), \sigma = (R, \tilde{S})\Big)$: Return 1 iff $R \in \mathbb{G}$, $\tilde{S} \in \mathbb{H}$, for all $i \in [\ell] : (M_i, \tilde{N}_i) \in \widehat{\mathbb{GH}}$, and

$$e(R, \tilde{S}) = \prod_{i=1}^\ell e(X_i, \tilde{N}_i) e(X_1, \tilde{Y}) e(G, \tilde{H}) \cdot$$

- Randomize $\Big(\text{vk}, \big((M_1, \tilde{N}_1), \ldots, (M_\ell, \tilde{N}_\ell)\big), \sigma = (R, \tilde{S})\Big)$: Select $r' \leftarrow \mathbb{Z}_p$, and return $\sigma' := (R^{r'}, \tilde{S}^{\frac{1}{r'}})$.

Efficiency of the Scheme. The public key for signing a vector of size ℓ has size $\ell|\mathbb{G}| + |\mathbb{H}|$ whereas the signature is of size $|\mathbb{G}| + |\mathbb{H}|$ regardless of the size of the message vector. Thus, our signatures are shorter than all existing schemes since the best existing optimal schemes for unilateral messages, e.g. [4], have signatures of size $2|\mathbb{G}| + |\mathbb{H}|$. Assuming that the messages are already well-formed, verification requires only a single PPE with $\ell + 2$ pairings where 1 pairing, i.e. the pairing $e(G, \tilde{H})$ can be pre-computed. Hence, we only require $\ell + 1$ pairings for each signature after the first signature. If the messages are already assumed to be well-formed, this compares favourably to existing schemes since the most efficient existing scheme requires 2 PPE for verification. The scheme yields very short proofs of knowledge when combined with Groth-Sahai proofs [34] as one requires a proof for a linear (rather than quadratic) equation. As a result, our scheme outperforms the best existing scheme [29] in this respect. Refer to Sect. 5 for concrete efficiency comparison with existing schemes.

Security of the Scheme. The scheme is perfectly randomizable as the distribution of re-randomized signatures is identical to that of fresh signatures on the same vector. We now prove the following theorem.

Theorem 1. *The scheme is EUF-CMA secure.*

Proof. Correctness of the scheme follows by inspection and is straightforward to verify. The following two lemmata prove unforgeability of the scheme against adaptive chosen-message attacks. Lemma 1 proves that the case when $\ell = 1$ is secure in the generic group model whereas Lemma 2 reduces any attack on the scheme when $\ell > 1$ to the case when $\ell = 1$ which is proved by Lemma 1.

Lemma 1. *The scheme for $\ell = 1$ is EUF-CMA secure in the generic group model.*

Proof. We proceed by proving that no linear combinations (which represent Laurent polynomials in the discrete logarithms) of the group elements the adversary sees in the game correspond to a forgery on a new message.

At the start of the game, the only elements in $\mathbb{H}$ the adversary sees are $\tilde{H}$, $\tilde{Y}$ which correspond to the discrete logarithms 1 and y, respectively. Also, at the start of the game the only elements in $\mathbb{G}$ the adversary sees are G, X which correspond to the discrete logarithms 1 and x, respectively.

At the j-th sign query on the message $(M_j, \tilde{N}_j)$, m_j and n_j (the discrete logarithms of M_j and $\tilde{N}_j$, respectively, can only be a linear combination of the discrete logarithms of the elements in $\mathbb{G}$ and $\mathbb{H}$, respectively, the adversary sees up to that point of time. Thus, we have

$$m_j = a_{m_j} + b_{m_j}x + \sum_{i=1}^{j-1} c_{m_j,i}r_i$$

$$n_j = a_{n_j} + b_{n_j}y + \sum_{i=1}^{j-1} c_{n_j,i}\frac{n_ix + xy + 1}{r_i}$$

For the message to satisfy $(M_j, \tilde{N}_j) \in \widehat{\mathbb{GH}}$, we must have that $m_j = n_j$ and hence we must have that $a_{m_j} = a_{n_j}$, $b_{m_j} = b_{n_j} = 0$ and for all i that $c_{m_j,i} = c_{n_j,i} = 0$. This ensures that the message queried is nothing but a constant polynomial. If the message is well-formed [1], the sign oracle responds with a signature of the form

$$\left(r_j, s_j = \frac{n_jx + xy + 1}{r_j}\right)$$

Since the adversary is generic, she can only construct $\left((M^*, \tilde{N}^*), \sigma^* = (R^*, \tilde{S}^*)\right)$ as a linear combination of the group elements she sees in the game. Thus, we have

$$m^* = a_m + b_mx + \sum_{i=1}^{q} c_{m,i}r_i \qquad r^* = a_r + b_rx + \sum_{i=1}^{q} c_{r,i}r_i$$

$$n^* = a_n + b_ny + \sum_{i=1}^{q} c_{n,i}\frac{n_ix + xy + 1}{r_i} \qquad s^* = a_s + b_sy + \sum_{i=1}^{q} c_{s,i}\frac{n_ix + xy + 1}{r_i}$$

Since the forged message $(M^*, \tilde{N}^*)$ must correspond to a Diffie-Hellman pair, we must have $m^* = n^*$ and thus $a_m = a_n$, $b_m = b_n = 0$ and $c_{m,i} = c_{n,i} = 0$ for all $i \in [q]$ and hence $m^* = n^* = a_m$. For the forgery to be accepted, r^* and s^* must satisfy $r^*s^* = n^*x + xy + 1$. Therefore, we must have

$$\left(a_r + b_rx + \sum_{i=1}^{q} c_{r,i}r_i\right)\left(a_s + b_sy + \sum_{i=1}^{q} c_{s,i}\frac{n_ix + xy + 1}{r_i}\right) = n^*x + xy + 1$$

---

[1] We remark that the scheme remains secure even if the sign oracle only gets $\tilde{N}_j$ as long as the final forgery is on a well-formed message $(M^*, \tilde{N}^*) \in \widehat{\mathbb{GH}}$.

Thus, we must have

$$
a_r a_s + a_r b_s y + \sum_{i=1}^{q} a_r c_{s,i} \frac{n_i x + xy + 1}{r_i}
$$

$$
+ a_s b_r x + b_s b_r xy + \sum_{i=1}^{q} b_r c_{s,i} \frac{n_i x^2 + x^2 y + x}{r_i}
$$

$$
+ a_s \sum_{i=1}^{q} c_{r,i} r_i + b_s y \sum_{i=1}^{q} c_{r,i} r_i + \sum_{i=1}^{q} c_{r,i} r_i \sum_{i=1}^{q} c_{s,i} \frac{n_i x + xy + 1}{r_i}
$$

$$
= n^* x + xy + 1
$$

There is no term in $\frac{xy}{r_i}$ or $\frac{x^2 y}{r_i}$ on the RHS so we must have for all $i \in [q]$ that $a_r c_{s,i} = 0$ and $b_r c_{s,i} = 0$. This means that we either have that $c_{s,i} = 0$ for all $i \in [q]$ or we have $a_r = b_r = 0$.

- Case $a_r = b_r = 0$: In this case we must have

$$
a_s \sum_{i=1}^{q} c_{r,i} r_i + b_s y \sum_{i=1}^{q} c_{r,i} r_i + \sum_{i=1}^{q} c_{r,i} r_i \sum_{i=1}^{q} c_{s,i} \frac{n_i x + xy + 1}{r_i} = n^* x + xy + 1
$$

There are no terms in r_i or $r_i y$ on the RHS so we must have for all $i \in [q]$ that $a_s c_{r,i} = 0$ and $b_s c_{r,i} = 0$. This means that we either have that $c_{r,i} = 0$ for all $i \in [q]$ or we have $a_s = b_s = 0$. The former case cannot occur as otherwise the LHS will not have a term in xy and hence the equality will not hold. So we must have $a_s = b_s = 0$ and hence we must have

$$
\sum_{i=1}^{q} c_{r,i} r_i \sum_{i=1}^{q} c_{s,i} \frac{n_i x + xy + 1}{r_i} = n^* x + xy + 1
$$

There is no term on the RHS of the form $\frac{r_j xy}{r_i}$ for any $i, j \in [q]$ where $i \neq j$. Thus, we must have $c_{r,i} c_{s,j} = 0$ for all $i \neq j$. This means we must have for some $i \in [q]$

$$
c_{r,i} c_{s,i} n_i x + c_{r,i} c_{s,i} xy + c_{r,i} c_{s,i} = n^* x + xy + 1
$$

By the monomial xy, we must have $c_{r,i} c_{s,i} = 1$ from which it is clear that the only way the equality will hold is if $n^* = n_i$ from some $i \in [q]$ which means the forgery is not valid as the signature is on a message that was queried to the sign oracle.

- Case $c_{s,i} = 0$ for all $i \in [q]$: In this case we must have

$$
a_r a_s + a_r b_s y + a_s b_r x + b_s b_r xy + a_s \sum_{i=1}^{q} c_{r,i} r_i + b_s y \sum_{i=1}^{q} c_{r,i} r_i = n^* x + xy + 1
$$

The only term on the LHS with the monomial xy is the term $b_s b_r xy$ thus for the equality to hold we must have that $b_s \neq 0$ and $b_r \neq 0$. There is no term on the RHS with the monomial $r_i y$ and since we cannot have $b_s = 0$, we must have that $c_{r,i} = 0$ for all $i \in [q]$, which means we have:

$$a_r a_s + a_r b_s y + a_s b_r x + b_s b_r xy = n^* x + xy + 1$$

There is no term on the RHS wih the monomial y and since we cannot have $b_s = 0$, we must have that $a_r = 0$ which means we have:

$$a_s b_r x + b_s b_r xy = n^* x + xy + 1$$

which cannot hold.

$\square$

Lemma 2. *The scheme for $\ell > 1$ is EUF-CMA secure.*

Proof. We proceed by showing that any valid forgery in the case $\ell > 1$ can be reduced to a forgery for the case $\ell = 1$.

Let $\mathcal{A}$ be a successful adversary in the $\ell > 1$ case we show how to construct an adversary $\mathcal{B}$ who uses adversary $\mathcal{A}$ to break the scheme for the case $\ell = 1$ which would contradict Lemma 1.

Adversary $\mathcal{B}$ gets $\mathsf{vk}' = (X', \tilde{Y}')$ from her game where she has access to a sign oracle for a single Diffie-Hellman pair. She chooses $x_1, \ldots, x_{\ell-1} \leftarrow \mathbb{Z}_p$ and sets $\tilde{Y} := \tilde{Y}'$, $X_1 := X'$ and $X_i := X'^{x_{i-1}}$ for $i = 2, \ldots, \ell$. She starts $\mathcal{A}$ on the verification key $\mathsf{vk} := (X_1, \ldots, X_\ell, \tilde{Y})$. Note that since $x_1, \ldots, x_{\ell-1}$ are chosen uniformly at random, the verification key vk $\mathcal{A}$ sees is indistinguishable from one she gets from the real signer. When receiving a query on $\boldsymbol{m}_i = \left((M, \tilde{N})_{i,1}, \ldots, (M, \tilde{N})_{i,\ell} \right)$ from $\mathcal{A}$, $\mathcal{B}$ returns $\bot$ if $(M, \tilde{N})_{i,j} \notin \widehat{\mathbb{GH}}$ for any $j \in [\ell]$. Otherwise, she forwards $(M_i', \tilde{N}_i') := \left(M_{i,1} \cdot \prod_{j=2}^{\ell} M_{i,j}^{x_{j-1}}, \tilde{N}_{i,1} \cdot \prod_{j=2}^{\ell} \tilde{N}_{i,j}^{x_{j-1}} \right) \in \widehat{\mathbb{GH}}$ to her sign oracle and returns the signature she gets to $\mathcal{A}$. Such a signature is a valid signature on the message $\boldsymbol{m}_i = \left((M, \tilde{N})_{i,1}, \ldots, (M, \tilde{N})_{i,\ell} \right)$ w.r.t. the verification key $\mathsf{vk} = (X_1, \ldots, X_\ell, \tilde{Y})$.

When $\mathcal{A}$ outputs her forgery σ^* on $\boldsymbol{m}^* = \left((M^*, \tilde{N}^*)_1, \ldots, (M^*, \tilde{N}^*)_\ell \right)$, $\mathcal{B}$ returns $(M', \tilde{N}') := \left(M_1^* \cdot \prod_{j=2}^{\ell} M_j^{*x_{j-1}}, \tilde{N}_1^* \cdot \prod_{j=2}^{\ell} \tilde{N}_j^{*x_{j-1}} \right) \in \widehat{\mathbb{GH}}$ and σ^* as the answer in her game. Thus, $\mathcal{B}$ wins her game with the same advantage as that of $\mathcal{A}$ in her game. $\square$

3.2   Scheme II

We show here that by transposing the signature components of Scheme I, we obtain a scheme with signatures $(S, \tilde{R}) \in \mathbb{G} \times \mathbb{H}$ where $\tilde{R}$ is information-theoretically independent of the message vector. The verification key matches that of Scheme I, i.e. the verification key size is $\ell|\mathbb{G}| + |\mathbb{H}|$. Note that the scheme has the property that signing requires only the $\mathbb{G}$ components of the messages whereas verification requires, besides verifying well-formedness of the messages, only the $\mathbb{H}$ components of the messages. We remark that existing schemes with similar properties have found various applications, see e.g. [13,28].

Given the description of Type-3 bilinear groups $\mathcal{P}$ output by $\mathcal{BG}(1^\kappa)$, the scheme is as follows:

- KeyGen($\mathcal{P}$): Select $x_1, \ldots, x_\ell, y \leftarrow \mathbb{Z}_p$. Set $X_i := G^{x_i}$ for all $i \in [\ell]$, $\tilde{Y} := \tilde{H}^y$, sk $:= (x_1, \ldots, x_\ell, y)$, and vk $:= (X_1, \ldots, X_\ell, \tilde{Y}) \in \mathbb{G}^\ell \times \mathbb{H}$.
- Sign $\left(\text{sk}, \left((M_1, \tilde{N}_1), \ldots, (M_\ell, \tilde{N}_\ell) \right) \right)$: To sign $\left((M_1, \tilde{N}_1), \ldots, (M_\ell, \tilde{N}_\ell) \right) \in \widehat{\mathbb{GH}}^\ell$, select $r \leftarrow \mathbb{Z}_p$ and set $\tilde{R} := \tilde{H}^r$, and $S := (\prod_{i=1}^\ell M_i^{x_i} \cdot X_1^y \cdot G)^{\frac{1}{r}}$. Return $\sigma := (\tilde{R}, S) \in \mathbb{H} \times \mathbb{G}$.
- Verify $\left(\text{vk}, \left((M_1, \tilde{N}_1), \ldots, (M_\ell, \tilde{N}_\ell) \right), \sigma = (\tilde{R}, S) \right)$: Return 1 iff $\tilde{R} \in \mathbb{H}$, $S \in \mathbb{G}$, for all $i \in [\ell] : (M_i, \tilde{N}_i) \in \widehat{\mathbb{GH}}$, and

$$e(S, \tilde{R}) = \prod_{i=1}^\ell e(X_i, \tilde{N}_i)e(X_1, \tilde{Y})e(G, \tilde{H}) \cdot$$

- Randomize $\left(\text{vk}, \left((M_1, \tilde{N}_1), \ldots, (M_\ell, \tilde{N}_\ell) \right), \sigma = (\tilde{R}, S) \right)$: Select $r' \leftarrow \mathbb{Z}_p$, and return $\sigma' := (\tilde{R}^{r'}, S^{\frac{1}{r'}})$.

The scheme has identical efficiency as that of Scheme I.

Security of the Scheme. The scheme is perfectly randomizable as the distribution of re-randomized signatures is identical to that of fresh signatures on the same vector.

Theorem 2. *The scheme is EUF-CMA secure.*

Proof. Correctness of the scheme follows by inspection and is straightforward to verify. The following two lemmata prove unforgeability of the scheme against adaptive chosen-message attacks. Lemma 3 proves that the case when $\ell = 1$ is secure in the generic group model whereas Lemma 4 reduces any attack on the scheme when $\ell > 1$ to the case when $\ell = 1$ which is proved by Lemma 3.

Lemma 3. *The scheme for $\ell = 1$ is EUF-CMA secure in the generic group model.*

Proof. We proceed by proving that no linear combinations (which represent Laurent polynomials in the discrete logarithms) of the group elements the adversary sees in the game correspond to a forgery on a new message.

At the start of the game, the only elements in $\mathbb{H}$ the adversary sees are $\tilde{H}$, $\tilde{Y}$ which correspond to the discrete logarithms 1 and y, respectively. Also, at the start of the game the only elements in $\mathbb{G}$ the adversary sees are G, X which correspond to the discrete logarithms 1 and x, respectively.

At the j-th query on message $(M_j, \tilde{N}_j)$, m_j and n_j which are the discrete logarithm of the message can only be a linear combination of the elements in the respective groups so far. Thus, we have

$$m_j = a_{m_j} + b_{m_j} x + \sum_{i=1}^{j-1} c_{m_j,i} \frac{m_i x + xy + 1}{r_i}$$

$$n_j = a_{n_j} + b_{n_j} y + \sum_{i=1}^{j-1} c_{n_j,i} r_i$$

For the message to satisfy $(M_j, \tilde{N}_j) \in \widehat{\mathbb{GH}}$, we must have that $m_j = n_j$ and hence we must have that $a_{m_j} = a_{n_j}$, $b_{m_j} = b_{n_j} = 0$ and for all i that $c_{m_j,i} = c_{n_j,i} = 0$. This ensures that the message queried is nothing but a constant polynomial.

If the message is well-formed, the sign oracle responds with a signature of the form

$$\left(r_j, s_j = \frac{m_j x + xy + 1}{r_j} \right)$$

Since the adversary is generic, she can only construct $(M^*, \tilde{N}^*)$ and $\sigma^* = (\tilde{R}^*, S^*)$ as a linear combination of the group elements she sees in the game. Thus, we must have

$$m^* = a_m + b_m x + \sum_{i=1}^{q} c_{m,i} \frac{m_i x + xy + 1}{r_i} \qquad r^* = a_r + b_r y + \sum_{i=1}^{q} c_{r,i} r_i$$

$$n^* = a_n + b_n y + \sum_{i=1}^{q} c_{n,i} r_i \qquad s^* = a_s + b_s x + \sum_{i=1}^{q} c_{s,i} \frac{m_i x + xy + 1}{r_i}$$

Since the forged message $(M^*, \tilde{N}^*)$ must correspond to a Diffie-Hellman pair, we must have $m^* = n^*$ and thus $a_m = a_n$, $b_m = b_n = 0$ and $c_{m,i} = c_{n,i} = 0$ for all $i \in [q]$ and hence $m^* = n^* = a_m$. For the forgery to be accepted, r^* and s^* must satisfy $s^* r^* = m^* x + xy + 1$. Therefore, we must have

$$\left(a_r + b_r y + \sum_{i=1}^{q} c_{r,i} r_i \right) \left(a_s + b_s x + \sum_{i=1}^{q} c_{s,i} \frac{m_i x + xy + 1}{r_i} \right) = m^* x + xy + 1$$

Thus, we must have

$$a_r a_s + a_r b_s x + \sum_{i=1}^{q} a_r c_{s,i} \frac{m_i x + xy + 1}{r_i}$$

$$+ a_s b_r y + b_s b_r xy + \sum_{i=1}^{q} b_r c_{s,i} \frac{m_i xy + xy^2 + y}{r_i}$$

$$+ a_s \sum_{i=1}^{q} c_{r,i} r_i + b_s x \sum_{i=1}^{q} c_{r,i} r_i + \sum_{i=1}^{q} c_{r,i} r_i \sum_{i=1}^{q} c_{s,i} \frac{m_i x + xy + 1}{r_i}$$

$$= m^* x + xy + 1$$

There is no term in $\frac{xy}{r_i}$ or $\frac{xy^2}{r_i}$ on the RHS so we must have for all $i \in [q]$ that $a_r c_{s,i} = 0$ and $b_r c_{s,i} = 0$. This means that we either have that $c_{s,i} = 0$ for all $i \in [q]$ or we have $a_r = b_r = 0$.

- Case $a_r = b_r = 0$: Here we must have

$$a_s \sum_{i=1}^{q} c_{r,i} r_i + b_s x \sum_{i=1}^{q} c_{r,i} r_i + \sum_{i=1}^{q} c_{r,i} r_i \sum_{i=1}^{q} c_{s,i} \frac{m_i x + xy + 1}{r_i} = m^* x + xy + 1$$

There is no terms in r_i or $r_i x$ on the RHS so we must have for all $i \in [q]$ that $a_s c_{r,i} = 0$ and $b_s c_{r,i} = 0$. This means that we either have that $c_{r,i} = 0$ for all $i \in [q]$ or we have $a_s = b_s = 0$. The former case cannot occur as otherwise the LHS will not have a term in xy and hence the equality will not hold. So we must have $a_s = b_s = 0$ and hence we have

$$\sum_{i=1}^{q} c_{r,i} r_i \sum_{i=1}^{q} c_{s,i} \frac{m_i x + xy + 1}{r_i} = m^* x + xy + 1$$

There is no term on the RHS of the form $\frac{r_j xy}{r_i}$ for any $i, j \in [q]$ where $i \neq j$. Thus, we must have $c_{r,i} c_{s,i} = 0$ if $i \neq j$. This means we have

$$c_{r,i} c_{s,i} m_i x + c_{r,i} c_{s,i} xy + c_{r,i} c_{s,i} = m^* x + xy + 1$$

By the monomial xy, we must have $c_{r,i} c_{s,i} = 1$ from which it is clear that the only way the equality will hold is if $m^* = m_i$ from some $i \in [q]$ which means the forgery is not valid as the signature is on a message that was queried to the sign oracle.

- Case $c_{s,i} = 0$ for all $i \in [q]$:

Thus, we must have

$$a_r a_s + a_r b_s x + a_s b_r y + b_s b_r xy + a_s \sum_{i=1}^{q} c_{r,i} r_i + b_s x \sum_{i=1}^{q} c_{r,i} r_i = m^* x + xy + 1$$

The only term on the LHS with the monomial xy is the term $b_s b_r xy$ thus for the equality to hold we must have that $b_s \neq 0$ and $b_r \neq 0$. There is no term on the RHS with the monomial $r_i x$ and since we cannot have $b_s = 0$, we must have that $c_{r,i} = 0$ for all $i \in [q]$, which means we have:

$$a_r a_s + a_r b_s x + a_s b_r y + b_s b_r xy = m^* x + xy + 1$$

There is no term on the RHS wih the monomial y and since we cannot have $b_r = 0$, we must have that $a_s = 0$ which means we have:

$$a_r b_s x + b_s b_r xy = m^* x + xy + 1$$

which cannot hold.

$\square$

Lemma 4. *The scheme for $\ell > 1$ is EUF-CMA secure.*

Proof. We proceed by showing that any valid forgery in the case $\ell > 1$ can be reduced to a forgery for the case $\ell = 1$.

Let $\mathcal{A}$ be a successful adversary in the $\ell > 1$ case we show how to construct an adversary $\mathcal{B}$ who uses adversary $\mathcal{A}$ to break the scheme for the case $\ell = 1$ which would contradict Lemma .

Adversary $\mathcal{B}$ gets $\mathsf{vk}' = (X', \tilde{Y}')$ from her game where she has access to a sign oracle for a single Diffie-Hellman pair. She chooses $x_1, \ldots, x_{\ell-1} \leftarrow \mathbb{Z}_p$ and sets $\tilde{Y} := \tilde{Y}'$, $X_1 := X'$ and $X_i := X'^{x_{i-1}}$ for $i = 2, \ldots, \ell$. She starts $\mathcal{A}$ on the verification key $\mathsf{vk} := (X_1, \ldots, X_\ell, \tilde{Y})$. Note that since $x_1, \ldots, x_{\ell-1}$ are chosen uniformly at random, the verification key vk $\mathcal{A}$ sees is indistinguishable from one she gets from the real signer. When receiving a query on $\boldsymbol{m}_i = \left((M, \tilde{N})_{i,1}, \ldots, (M, \tilde{N})_{i,\ell}\right)$ from $\mathcal{A}$, $\mathcal{B}$ returns $\bot$ if $(M, \tilde{N})_{i,j} \notin \widehat{\mathbb{GH}}$ for any $j \in [\ell]$. Otherwise, she forwards $(M'_i, \tilde{N}'_i) := \left(M_{i,1} \cdot \prod_{j=2}^\ell M_{i,j}^{x_{j-1}}, \tilde{N}_{i,1} \cdot \prod_{j=2}^\ell \tilde{N}_{i,j}^{x_{j-1}}\right) \in \widehat{\mathbb{GH}}$ to her sign oracle and returns the signature she gets to $\mathcal{A}$. Such a signature is a valid signature on the message $\boldsymbol{m}_i = \left((M, \tilde{N})_{i,1}, \ldots, (M, \tilde{N})_{i,\ell}\right)$ w.r.t. the verification key $\mathsf{vk} = (X_1, \ldots, X_\ell, \tilde{Y})$.

When $\mathcal{A}$ outputs her forgery σ^* on $\boldsymbol{m}^* = \left((M^*, \tilde{N}^*)_1, \ldots, (M^*, \tilde{N}^*)_\ell\right)$, $\mathcal{B}$ returns $(M', \tilde{N}') := \left(M_1^* \cdot \prod_{j=2}^\ell M_j^{*x_{j-1}}, \tilde{N}_1^* \cdot \prod_{j=2}^\ell \tilde{N}_j^{*x_{j-1}}\right) \in \widehat{\mathbb{GH}}$ and σ^* as the answer in her game. Thus, $\mathcal{B}$ wins her game with the same advantage as that of $\mathcal{A}$ in her game. $\square$

4   Unilateral Scheme for 2 Diffie-Hellman Pairs

We give here a scheme for 2 pairs of Diffie-Hellman messages yielding unilateral signatures of size $3|\mathbb{G}|$. The scheme is an extension of the recent single-message scheme from [29] where we use different randomness for each message. Signatures of this scheme are still shorter than those of all existing optimal Type-3 schemes since the latter require that at least one of the components of σ is from the second base group. The scheme is also more efficient than the single-message scheme from [28]. The verification key of the scheme is of size $3|\mathbb{H}|$, whereas verification of signatures require 1 PPE and 3 pairings, excluding the cost for verifying well-formedness of the messages. Given the description of Type-3 bilinear groups $\mathcal{P}$ output by $\mathcal{BG}(1^\kappa)$, the scheme is as follows:

- KeyGen($\mathcal{P}$): Select $x_1, x_2, y \leftarrow \mathbb{Z}_p$. Set $\mathsf{sk} := (x_1, x_2, y)$ and $\mathsf{vk} := (\tilde{X}_1, \tilde{X}_2, \tilde{Y}) := (\tilde{H}^{x_1}, \tilde{H}^{x_2}, \tilde{H}^y) \in \mathbb{H}^3$.
- Sign $\left(\mathsf{sk}, \left((M_1, \tilde{N}_1), (M_2, \tilde{N}_2)\right)\right)$: To sign $\left((M_1, \tilde{N}_1), (M_2, \tilde{N}_2)\right) \in \widehat{\mathbb{GH}}^2$, select $r_1, r_2 \leftarrow \mathbb{Z}_p$, set $R_1 := G^{r_1}$, $R_2 := G^{r_2}$, $S := ((G^{x_1} \cdot M_1)^{r_1} \cdot (G^{x_2} \cdot M_2)^{r_2})^{\frac{1}{y}}$. Return $\sigma := (R_1, R_2, S) \in \mathbb{G}^3$.

- Verify $\left(\text{vk}, \left((M_1, \tilde{N}_1), (M_2, \tilde{N}_2)\right), \sigma = (R_1, R_2, S)\right)$: Return 1 iff $R_1 \in \mathbb{G}^\times$, $R_2, S \in \mathbb{G}$, $\left((M_1, \tilde{N}_1), (M_2, \tilde{N}_2)\right) \in \widehat{\mathbb{GH}}^2$ and

$$e(S, \tilde{Y}) = e(R_1, \tilde{X}_1 \cdot \tilde{N}_1)e(R_2, \tilde{X}_2 \cdot \tilde{N}_2) \cdot$$

- Randomize $\left(\text{vk}, \left((M_1, \tilde{N}_1), (M_2, \tilde{N}_2)\right), \sigma = (R_1, R_2, S)\right)$: Select $r' \leftarrow \mathbb{Z}_p^\times$, and set $R_1' := R_1^{r'}$, $R_2' := R_2^{r'}$, $S' := S^{r'}$. Return $\sigma' := (R_1', R_2', S')$.

Correctness of the scheme follows by inspection and is straightforward to verify. We remark here that the signer will always be able to link a randomized signature to the original signature from which it was obtained even if we additionally require that $R_2 \neq 1_{\mathbb{G}}$. For instance, the malicious signer can choose $r_2 = -r_1$ which will make all randomized versions of the signature in question satisfy $R_1' \cdot R_2' = 1_{\mathbb{G}}$. Another way the signer can link a randomized signature to its original signature is by using knowledge of the exponents r_1 and r_2 since we will always have that $R_1'^{\frac{1}{r_1}} = R_2'^{\frac{1}{r_2}}$.

We now prove the following theorem.

Theorem 3. *The scheme is EUF-CMA secure in the generic group model.*

Proof. Public elements in $\mathbb{H}$ are $\tilde{H}$, $\tilde{X}_1, \tilde{X}_2$, and $\tilde{Y}$ which correspond to the discrete logarithms 1, x_1, x_2, and y, respectively. At the i-th signing query, we have that $((m_{i,1}, n_{i,1}), (m_{i,2}, n_{i,2}))$, which are the discrete logarithms of the queried message $\left((M_{i,1}, \tilde{N}_{i,1}), (M_{i,2}, \tilde{N}_{i,2})\right)$, must be of the form

$$n_{i,k} = a_{n_{i,k}} + b_{n_{i,k}} x_1 + c_{n_{i,k}} x_2 + d_{n_{i,k}} y$$

$$m_{i,k} = a_{m_{i,k}} + \sum_{j=1}^{i-1} b_{m_{i,k,j}} r_{1j} + \sum_{j=1}^{i-1} c_{m_{i,k,j}} r_{2j} + \sum_{j=1}^{i-1} d_{m_{i,k,j}} \frac{r_{1j} m_{1j} + r_{1j} x_1 + r_{2j} m_{2j} + r_{2j} x_2}{y},$$

for $k = 1, 2$. Since we must have $m_{i,1} = n_{i,1}$ and $m_{i,1} = n_{i,2}$ for the messages to be valid, we have $m_{i,1} = n_{i,1} = a_{m_{i,1}} = a_{n_{i,1}}$ and $m_{i,2} = n_{i,2} = a_{m_{i,2}} = a_{n_{i,2}}$, i.e. the messages queried to the signing oracle correspond to constant polynomials. Note that the sign oracle does not produce any elements in $\mathbb{H}$.

After q signing queries, $((m_1^*, n_1^*), (m_2^*, n_2^*))$, which are the discrete logarithms of the forged Diffie-Hellman pairs $\left((M_1^*, \tilde{N}_1^*), (M_2^*, \tilde{N}_2^*)\right)$, must be of the form

$$n_k^* = a_{n_k} + b_{n_k} x_1 + c_{n_k} x_2 + d_{n_k} y$$

$$m_k^* = a_{m_k} + \sum_{i=1}^{q} b_{m_{k,i}} r_{1i} + \sum_{i=1}^{q} c_{m_{k,i}} r_{2i} + \sum_{i=1}^{q} d_{m_{k,i}} \frac{r_{1i} m_{1i} + r_{1i} x_1 + r_{2i} m_{2i} + r_{2i} x_2}{y},$$

for $k = 1, 2$. Since we must have $m_1^* = n_1^*$ and $m_2^* = n_2^*$ for the forgery to be a valid element of $\widehat{\mathbb{GH}}^2$, we have $m_1^* = n_1^* = a_{m_1} = a_{n_1}$ and $m_2^* = n_2^* = a_{m_2} = a_{n_2}$.

Similarly, the signature (R_1^*, R_2^*, S^*) has the form

$$r_1^* = a_{r_1} + \sum_{i=1}^{q} b_{r_1,i} r_{1_i} + \sum_{i=1}^{q} c_{r_1,i} r_{2_i} + \sum_{i=1}^{q} d_{r_1,i} \frac{r_{1_i} m_{1_i} + r_{1_i} x_1 + r_{2_i} m_{2_i} + r_{2_i} x_2}{y}$$

$$r_2^* = a_{r_2} + \sum_{i=1}^{q} b_{r_2,i} r_{1_i} + \sum_{i=1}^{q} c_{r_2,i} r_{2_i} + \sum_{i=1}^{q} d_{r_2,i} \frac{r_{1_i} m_{1_i} + r_{1_i} x_1 + r_{2_i} m_{2_i} + r_{2_i} x_2}{y}$$

$$s^* = a_s + \sum_{i=1}^{q} b_{s,i} r_{1_i} + \sum_{i=1}^{q} c_{s,i} r_{2_i} + \sum_{i=1}^{q} d_{s,i} \frac{r_{1_i} m_{1_i} + r_{1_i} x_1 + r_{2_i} m_{2_i} + r_{2_i} x_2}{y}$$

For the forgery to be a valid signature, (r_1^*, r_2^*, s^*) must satisfy $s^* y = r_1^* m_1^* + r_1^* x_1 + r_2^* m_2^* + r_2^* x_2$. So we must have

$$\left(a_s + \sum_{i=1}^{q} b_{s,i} r_{1_i} + \sum_{i=1}^{q} c_{s,i} r_{2_i} + \sum_{i=1}^{q} d_{s,i} \frac{r_{1_i} m_{1_i} + r_{1_i} x_1 + r_{2_i} m_{2_i} + r_{2_i} x_2}{y} \right) y$$

$$= \left(a_{r_1} + \sum_{i=1}^{q} b_{r_1,i} r_{1_i} + \sum_{i=1}^{q} c_{r_1,i} r_{2_i} + \sum_{i=1}^{q} d_{r_1,i} \frac{r_{1_i} m_{1_i} + r_{1_i} x_1 + r_{2_i} m_{2_i} + r_{2_i} x_2}{y} \right) (x_1 + m_1^*)$$

$$+ \left(a_{r_2} + \sum_{i=1}^{q} b_{r_2,i} r_{1_i} + \sum_{i=1}^{q} c_{r_2,i} r_{2_i} + \sum_{i=1}^{q} d_{r_2,i} \frac{r_{1_i} m_{1_i} + r_{1_i} x_1 + r_{2_i} m_{2_i} + r_{2_i} x_2}{y} \right) (x_2 + m_2^*)$$

There is no term in y, $r_{1_i} y$ or $r_{2_i} y$ on the RHS so we must have $a_s = 0$ and $b_{s,i} = c_{s,i} = 0$ for all i.

Also, there are no terms in x_1, x_2, $r_{1_i} x_2$, $r_{2_i} x_1$, $\frac{r_{1_i} x_1^2}{y}$, or $\frac{r_{2_i} x_2^2}{y}$ on the LHS so we must have $a_{r_1} = a_{r_2} = 0$ and $c_{r_1,i} = b_{r_2,i} = d_{r_1,i} = d_{r_2,i}$ for all i. Thus, we have

$$\sum_{i=1}^{q} d_{s,i} (r_{1_i} m_{1_i} + r_{1_i} x_1 + r_{2_i} m_{2_i} + r_{2_i} x_2)$$

$$= \sum_{i=1}^{q} b_{r_1,i} r_{1_i} m_1^* + \sum_{i=1}^{q} b_{r_1,i} r_{1_i} x_1 + \sum_{i=1}^{q} c_{r_2,i} r_{2_i} m_2^* + \sum_{i=1}^{q} c_{r_2,i} r_{1_i} x_2$$

Since we must have $r_1^* \neq 0$, it follows that we must have at least for one value of i that $b_{r_1,i} \neq 0$. By the monomial $r_{1_i} x_1$, we have $b_{r_1,i} = d_{s,i}$. Since $d_{s,i} \neq 0$, we also have that $c_{r_2,i} = d_{s,i}$. Now by the monomial r_{1_i}, we have that $b_{r_1,i} m_1^* = d_{s,i} m_{1_i}$ from which it follows that $m_1^* = m_{1_i}$. Similarly, by the monomial r_{2_i}, we have that $c_{r_2,i} m_2^* = d_{s,i} m_{2_i}$ from which it follows that $m_2^* = m_{2_i}$. Thus, the forgery is on a message pair that was queried to the oracle. $\square$

5   Efficiency Comparison

We compare in Table 1 the efficiency of our schemes with that of existing ones.

Table 1. Efficiency comparison between our schemes and existing Type-3 schemes

Scheme	σ		vk		PP		$\mathcal{M}$	Randomizable	Verification Cost			
									1 Signature		n Signatures	
	$\mathbb{G}$	$\mathbb{H}$	$\mathbb{G}$	$\mathbb{H}$	$\mathbb{G}$	$\mathbb{H}$			PPE	Pairing	PPE	Pairing
[3] I	5	2	$8+2\ell$	4	-	-	$\mathbb{G}^\ell$	Partially	2	$6+2\ell+4^\dagger$	$2n$	$6n+2\ell+4^\dagger$
[3] II	2	5	$8+2\ell$	4	-	-	$\mathbb{H}^\ell$	Partially	2	$6+2\ell+4^\dagger$	$2n$	$6n+2\ell+4^\dagger$
[4]	2	1	ℓ	1	-	-	$\mathbb{H}^\ell$	Yes	2	$3+\ell+1^\dagger$	$2n$	$3n+\ell+1^\dagger$
[33] 1	1	2	ℓ	-	-	1	$\mathbb{H}^\ell$	Yes	2	$2+\ell+3^\dagger$	$2n$	$2n+\ell+3^\dagger$
[33] 2	1	2	ℓ	-	-	1	$\mathbb{H}^\ell$	No	2	$3+\ell+3^\dagger$	$2n$	$3n+\ell+3^\dagger$
Ours I	1	1	ℓ	1	-	-	$\widehat{\mathbb{GH}}^\ell$	Yes	$1+\ell^*$ Or $1+1^*$	$1+\ell+1^\dagger+2\ell^*$ Or $1+\ell+1^\dagger+2^*$	$n+\ell^*$ Or $n+1^*$	$n+\ell+1^\dagger+2\ell^*$ Or $n+\ell+1^\dagger+2^*$
Ours II	1	1	ℓ	1	-	-	$\widehat{\mathbb{GH}}^\ell$	Yes	$1+\ell^*$ Or $1+1^*$	$1+\ell+1^\dagger+2\ell^*$ Or $1+\ell+1^\dagger+2^*$	$n+\ell^*$ Or $n+1^*$	$n+\ell+1^\dagger+2\ell^*$ Or $n+\ell+1^\dagger+2^*$

In the table numbers superscripted with † are the number of pairings that can be precomputed, whereas numbers superscripted with ∗ are the cost needed to verify well-formedness of the Diffie-Hellman message. The latter cost is constant when verifying multiple signatures on the same message. Also, as mentioned earlier, one can use techniques from batch verification, e.g. [12,17], to reduce the cost required for verifying the well-formedness of a vector of ℓ Diffie-Hellman pairs to a single PPE and 2 pairings. For our schemes, we give 2 estimations for the efficiency overhead where the first is for the case where no batch verification is applied to verifying the well-formedness of the messages, whereas the second cost is when batch verification is applied in that respect. For all schemes listed, public parameters PP do not include the default group generators. Note that the security of all schemes in the table except for [3] which rely on non-interactive q-type assumptions is proven in the generic group model. For the cost of verification, we give two estimations which are for verifying 1 and n different signatures on the same message vector.

As can be seen from the table, our schemes outperform existing schemes w.r.t signature size. The size of the verification key of our schemes matches the best existing scheme. Also, the verification cost compares favourably especially when verifying various signatures on the same message vector which is the case for many applications, e.g. when the user is required to prove possession of various credentials/attributes from an authority or possibly different authorities.

5.1   Efficiency in the Single Message Setting

The best existing scheme in terms of signature size and verification overhead is the one recently given in [29] which has signatures of size $2|\mathbb{G}|$ and verification key of size $2|\mathbb{H}|$. When used on their own, the scheme in [29] has slightly shorter signatures than ours, whereas schemes I and II of ours have shorter verification key. In fact, the combined size of signatures and verification key in the 3 schemes are identical. Note that the scheme in [29] has the slight non-standard requirement that one needs to check that a signature component (which is information-theoretically independent of the message) is not the trivial element and hence in the case that one needs to commit to that signature component, one needs more expensive alternatives to prove that it conforms to the requirement, which is not the case in our schemes. Let's now compare the verification overhead when verifying n signatures on the same message. Ignoring the cost of checking that $(M, \tilde{N}) \in \widehat{\mathbb{GH}}$, the scheme in [29] would require $2n$ pairings, whereas schemes I and II of ours require only $n + 2$ pairings where one of the pairings, i.e. $e(G, \tilde{H})$ can be pre-computed and used for signatures on other messages, i.e. the cost drops to only $n + 1$ pairings after verifying signatures on the first message. Thus, it is obvious that ours have less computational overhead when verifying multiple signatures on the same message.

Let's now compare the performance of Scheme I of ours and the one in [29] when combined with Groth-Sahai [34] to prove knowledge of a signature on a committed message. We consider the most efficient instantiation of the proofs which relies on the SXDH assumption as noted by [30]. The scheme from [29] has signatures of the form $(R, S) \in \mathbb{G}^2$ and a verification key of the form $(\tilde{X}, \tilde{Y}) \in \mathbb{H}^2$, and verification requires checking that $(M, \tilde{N}) \in \widehat{\mathbb{GH}}$, $R \neq 1_{\mathbb{G}}$, and evaluating the following PPE:

$$e(S, \tilde{Y}) = e(R, \tilde{X} \cdot \tilde{N}) \qquad (2)$$

In the terminology of [34], Equation (2) is a quadratic PPE. When proving knowledge of a signature, one has to commit to M, $\tilde{N}$ and S and thus we need to produce a proof for the satisfiability of (2) as well as the quadratic PPE $e(G, \tilde{N}) = e(M, \tilde{H})$ to prove that $(M, \tilde{N}) \in \widehat{\mathbb{GH}}$. The total size of the Groth-Sahai commitments is $4|\mathbb{G}| + 2|\mathbb{H}|$, whereas the size of the proof for each of the above equations is $4|\mathbb{G}| + 4|\mathbb{H}|$. Thus, the total size of the witness indistinguishable Groth-Sahai proof of knowledge is $12|\mathbb{G}| + 10|\mathbb{H}|$.

Scheme I of ours has signatures of the form $(R, \tilde{S}) \in \mathbb{G} \times \mathbb{H}$ and a verification key of the form $(X, \tilde{Y}) \in \mathbb{G} \times \mathbb{H}$, and verification requires checking that $(M, \tilde{N}) \in \widehat{\mathbb{GH}}$ and evaluating the following PPE:

$$e(R, \tilde{S}) = e(X, \tilde{N} \cdot \tilde{Y})e(G, H) \qquad (3)$$

When proving knowledge, we need to commit to M, $\tilde{N}$ and $\tilde{S}$ and thus we need to produce a proof for the satisfiability of (3), which is a linear PPE since components of the witness are all from the same group, as well as the quadratic PPE to prove that $(M, \tilde{N}) \in \widehat{\mathbb{GH}}$. The total size of the Groth-Sahai commitments is $2|\mathbb{G}| + 4|\mathbb{H}|$. The size of the proof for (3) is $2|\mathbb{G}|$ whereas proving $(M, \tilde{N}) \in \widehat{\mathbb{GH}}$ requires a proof of size $4|\mathbb{G}| + 4|\mathbb{H}|$. Thus, the total size of the witness indistinguishable Groth-Sahai proof of knowledge is $8|\mathbb{G}| + 8|\mathbb{H}|$. From the above, it is obvious when proving knowledge of signatures using Groth-Sahai proofs, which was the main motivation behind introducing the structure-preserving signatures notion, and which is required for the vast majority of applications of the notion, e.g. group, blind, attribute-based signatures, e-cash, etc., our scheme outperforms the best existing scheme. The efficiency gain has implication for various applications.

Acknowledgements. We thank anonymous IMA International Conference on Cryptography and Coding reviewers for valuable comments.

References

1. Abe, M., Chase, M., David, B., Kohlweiss, M., Nishimaki, R., Ohkubo, M.: Constant-size structure-preserving signatures: generic constructions and simple assumptions. In: Wang, X., Sako, K. (eds.) ASIACRYPT 2012. LNCS, vol. 7658, pp. 4–24. Springer, Heidelberg (2012). https://doi.org/10.1007/978-3-642-34961-4_3

2. Abe, M., David, B., Kohlweiss, M., Nishimaki, R., Ohkubo, M.: Tagged one-time signatures: tight security and optimal tag size. In: Kurosawa, K., Hanaoka, G. (eds.) PKC 2013. LNCS, vol. 7778, pp. 312–331. Springer, Heidelberg (2013). https://doi.org/10.1007/978-3-642-36362-7_20

3. Abe, M., Fuchsbauer, G., Groth, J., Haralambiev, K., Ohkubo, M.: Structure-preserving signatures and commitments to group elements. In: Rabin, T. (ed.) CRYPTO 2010. LNCS, vol. 6223, pp. 209–236. Springer, Heidelberg (2010). https://doi.org/10.1007/978-3-642-14623-7_12

4. Abe, M., Groth, J., Haralambiev, K., Ohkubo, M.: Optimal structure-preserving signatures in asymmetric bilinear groups. In: Rogaway, P. (ed.) CRYPTO 2011. LNCS, vol. 6841, pp. 649–666. Springer, Heidelberg (2011). https://doi.org/10.1007/978-3-642-22792-9_37

5. Abe, M., Groth, J., Ohkubo, M.: Separating short structure-preserving signatures from non-interactive assumptions. In: Lee, D.H., Wang, X. (eds.) ASIACRYPT 2011. LNCS, vol. 7073, pp. 628–646. Springer, Heidelberg (2011). https://doi.org/10.1007/978-3-642-25385-0_34

6. Abe, M., Groth, J., Ohkubo, M., Tibouchi, M.: Unified, minimal and selectively randomizable structure-preserving signatures. In: Lindell, Y. (ed.) TCC 2014. LNCS, vol. 8349, pp. 688–712. Springer, Heidelberg (2014). https://doi.org/10.1007/978-3-642-54242-8_29

7. Abe, M., Groth, J., Ohkubo, M., Tibouchi, M.: Structure-preserving signatures from type II pairings. In: Garay, J.A., Gennaro, R. (eds.) CRYPTO 2014. LNCS, vol. 8616, pp. 390–407. Springer, Heidelberg (2014). https://doi.org/10.1007/978-3-662-44371-2_22

8. Abe, M., Kohlweiss, M., Ohkubo, M., Tibouchi, M.: Fully structure-preserving signatures and shrinking commitments. In: Oswald, E., Fischlin, M. (eds.) EUROCRYPT 2015. LNCS, vol. 9057, pp. 35–65. Springer, Heidelberg (2015). https://doi.org/10.1007/978-3-662-46803-6_2

9. Attrapadung, N., Libert, B., Peters, T.: Computing on authenticated data: new privacy definitions and constructions. In: Wang, X., Sako, K. (eds.) ASIACRYPT 2012. LNCS, vol. 7658, pp. 367–385. Springer, Heidelberg (2012). https://doi.org/10.1007/978-3-642-34961-4_23

10. Baldimtsi, F., Chase, M., Fuchsbauer, G., Kohlweiss, M.: Anonymous transferable E-Cash. In: Katz, J. (ed.) PKC 2015. LNCS, vol. 9020, pp. 101–124. Springer, Heidelberg (2015). https://doi.org/10.1007/978-3-662-46447-2_5

11. Barthe, G., Fagerholm, E., Fiore, D., Scedrov, A., Schmidt, B., Tibouchi, M.: Strongly-Optimal structure preserving signatures from Type II pairings: synthesis and lower bounds. In: Katz, J. (ed.) PKC 2015. LNCS, vol. 9020, pp. 355–376. Springer, Heidelberg (2015). https://doi.org/10.1007/978-3-662-46447-2_16

12. Bellare, M., Garay, J.A., Rabin, T.: Fast batch verification for modular exponentiation and digital signatures. In: Nyberg, K. (ed.) EUROCRYPT 1998. LNCS, vol. 1403, pp. 236–250. Springer, Heidelberg (1998). https://doi.org/10.1007/BFb0054130

13. Bernhard, D., Fuchsbauer, G., Ghadafi, E.: Efficient signatures of knowledge and DAA in the standard model. In: Jacobson, M., Locasto, M., Mohassel, P., Safavi-Naini, R. (eds.) ACNS 2013. LNCS, vol. 7954, pp. 518–533. Springer, Heidelberg (2013). https://doi.org/10.1007/978-3-642-38980-1_33

14. Brickell, E., Camenisch, J., Chen, L.: Direct anonymous attestation. In: CCS 2004, ACM, pp. 132–145 (2004)

15. Camenisch, J., Dubovitskaya, M., Haralambiev, K.: Efficient structure-preserving signature scheme from standard assumptions. In: Visconti, I., De Prisco, R. (eds.) SCN 2012. LNCS, vol. 7485, pp. 76–94. Springer, Heidelberg (2012). https://doi.org/10.1007/978-3-642-32928-9_5

16. Camenisch, J., Dubovitskaya, M., Haralambiev, K., Kohlweiss, M.: Composable and modular anonymous credentials: definitions and practical constructions. In: Iwata, T., Cheon, J.H. (eds.) ASIACRYPT 2015. LNCS, vol. 9453, pp. 262–288. Springer, Heidelberg (2015). https://doi.org/10.1007/978-3-662-48800-3_11

17. Camenisch, J., Hohenberger, S., Pedersen, M.Ø.: Batch verification of short signatures. J. Cryptology 25(4), 723–747 (2012)

18. Chase, M., Kohlweiss, M.: A New hash-and-sign approach and structure-preserving signatures from DLIN. In: Visconti, I., De Prisco, R. (eds.) SCN 2012. LNCS, vol. 7485, pp. 131–148. Springer, Heidelberg (2012). https://doi.org/10.1007/978-3-642-32928-9_8

19. Chatterjee, S., Menezes, A.: Type 2 structure-preserving signature schemes revisited. In: Iwata, T., Cheon, J.H. (eds.) ASIACRYPT 2015. LNCS, vol. 9452, pp. 286–310. Springer, Heidelberg (2015). https://doi.org/10.1007/978-3-662-48797-6_13

20. ElGamal, T.: A public key cryptosystem and a signature scheme based on discrete logarithms. IEEE Trans. Inf. Theor. 31(4), 469–472 (1985)

21. El Kaafarani, A., Ghadafi, E., Khader, D.: Decentralized traceable attribute-based signatures. In: Benaloh, J. (ed.) CT-RSA 2014. LNCS, vol. 8366, pp. 327–348. Springer, Cham (2014). https://doi.org/10.1007/978-3-319-04852-9_17

22. Fiat, A., Shamir, A.: How To prove yourself: practical solutions to identification and signature problems. In: Odlyzko, A.M. (ed.) CRYPTO 1986. LNCS, vol. 263, pp. 186–194. Springer, Heidelberg (1987). https://doi.org/10.1007/3-540-47721-7_12

23. Fuchsbauer, G.: Automorphic signatures in bilinear groups and an application to round-optimal blind signatures. In: Cryptology ePrint Archive, Report 2009/320

24. Fuchsbauer, G.: Commuting Signatures and verifiable encryption. In: Paterson, K.G. (ed.) EUROCRYPT 2011. LNCS, vol. 6632, pp. 224–245. Springer, Heidelberg (2011). https://doi.org/10.1007/978-3-642-20465-4_14

25. Fuchsbauer, G., Hanser, C., Slamanig, D.: Practical round-optimal blind signatures in the standard model. In: Gennaro, R., Robshaw, M. (eds.) CRYPTO 2015. LNCS, vol. 9216, pp. 233–253. Springer, Heidelberg (2015). https://doi.org/10.1007/978-3-662-48000-7_12

26. Galbraith, S., Paterson, K., Smart, N.P.: Pairings for cryptographers. Discrete Appl. Math. 156, 3113–3121 (2008)

27. Ghadafi, E.: Formalizing group blind signatures and practical constructions without random oracles. In: Boyd, C., Simpson, L. (eds.) ACISP 2013. LNCS, vol. 7959, pp. 330–346. Springer, Heidelberg (2013). https://doi.org/10.1007/978-3-642-39059-3_23

28. Ghadafi, E.: Short structure-preserving signatures. In: Sako, K. (ed.) CT-RSA 2016. LNCS, vol. 9610, pp. 305–321. Springer, Cham (2016). https://doi.org/10.1007/978-3-319-29485-8_18

29. Ghadafi, E.: More efficient structure-preserving signatures - or: bypassing the Type-III lower bounds. In: Foley, S.N., Gollmann, D., Snekkenes, E. (eds.) ESORICS 2017. LNCS, vol. 10493, pp. 43–61. Springer, Cham (2017). https://doi.org/10.1007/978-3-319-66399-9_3

30. Ghadafi, E., Smart, N.P., Warinschi, B.: Groth–Sahai proofs revisited. In: Nguyen, P.Q., Pointcheval, D. (eds.) PKC 2010. LNCS, vol. 6056, pp. 177–192. Springer, Heidelberg (2010). https://doi.org/10.1007/978-3-642-13013-7_11

31. Green, M., Hohenberger, S.: Universally composable adaptive oblivious transfer. In: Pieprzyk, J. (ed.) ASIACRYPT 2008. LNCS, vol. 5350, pp. 179–197. Springer, Heidelberg (2008). https://doi.org/10.1007/978-3-540-89255-7_12

32. Groth, J.: Simulation-Sound NIZK proofs for a practical language and constant size group signatures. In: Lai, X., Chen, K. (eds.) ASIACRYPT 2006. LNCS, vol. 4284, pp. 444–459. Springer, Heidelberg (2006). https://doi.org/10.1007/11935230_29

33. Groth, J.: Efficient fully structure-preserving signatures for large messages. In: Iwata, T., Cheon, J.H. (eds.) ASIACRYPT 2015. LNCS, vol. 9452, pp. 239–259. Springer, Heidelberg (2015). https://doi.org/10.1007/978-3-662-48797-6_11

34. Groth, J., Sahai, A.: Efficient non-interactive proof systems for bilinear groups. SIAM J. Comput. **41**(5), 1193–1232 (2012)

35. Hofheinz, D., Jager, T.: Tightly secure signatures and public-key encryption. In: Safavi-Naini, R., Canetti, R. (eds.) CRYPTO 2012. LNCS, vol. 7417, pp. 590–607. Springer, Heidelberg (2012). https://doi.org/10.1007/978-3-642-32009-5_35

36. Jutla, C.S., Roy, A.: Improved structure preserving signatures under standard bilinear assumptions. In: Fehr, S. (ed.) PKC 2017. LNCS, vol. 10175, pp. 183–209. Springer, Heidelberg (2017). https://doi.org/10.1007/978-3-662-54388-7_7

37. Kiltz, E., Pan, J., Wee, H.: Structure-preserving signatures from standard assumptions, revisited. In: Gennaro, R., Robshaw, M. (eds.) CRYPTO 2015. LNCS, vol. 9216, pp. 275–295. Springer, Heidelberg (2015). https://doi.org/10.1007/978-3-662-48000-7_14

38. Libert, B., Peters, T., Yung, M.: Short group signatures via structure-preserving signatures: standard model security from simple assumptions. In: Gennaro, R., Robshaw, M. (eds.) CRYPTO 2015. LNCS, vol. 9216, pp. 296–316. Springer, Heidelberg (2015). https://doi.org/10.1007/978-3-662-48000-7_15

39. Maji, H.K., Prabhakaran, M., Rosulek, M.: Attribute-based signatures. In: Kiayias, A. (ed.) CT-RSA 2011. LNCS, vol. 6558, pp. 376–392. Springer, Heidelberg (2011). https://doi.org/10.1007/978-3-642-19074-2_24

40. Maurer, U.: Abstract models of computation in cryptography. In: Smart, N.P. (ed.) Cryptography and Coding 2005. LNCS, vol. 3796, pp. 1–12. Springer, Heidelberg (2005). https://doi.org/10.1007/11586821_1

41. Shoup, V.: Lower bounds for discrete logarithms and related problems. In: Fumy, W. (ed.) EUROCRYPT 1997. LNCS, vol. 1233, pp. 256–266. Springer, Heidelberg (1997). https://doi.org/10.1007/3-540-69053-0_18

42. Wang, Y., Zhang, Z., Matsuda, T., Hanaoka, G., Tanaka, K.: How to obtain fully structure-preserving (automorphic) signatures from structure-preserving ones. In: Cheon, J.H., Takagi, T. (eds.) ASIACRYPT 2016. LNCS, vol. 10032, pp. 465–495. Springer, Heidelberg (2016). https://doi.org/10.1007/978-3-662-53890-6_16

Post-Quantum Cryptography

CAKE: Code-Based Algorithm for Key Encapsulation

Paulo S. L. M. Barreto[1,2], Shay Gueron[3,4], Tim Güneysu[5,6],
Rafael Misoczki[7(✉)], Edoardo Persichetti[8],
Nicolas Sendrier[9], and Jean-Pierre Tillich[9]

[1] University of Washington Tacoma, Tacoma, USA
[2] University of São Paulo, São Paulo, Brazil
[3] University of Haifa, Haifa, Israel
[4] Amazon Web Services, Seattle, USA
[5] University of Bremen, Bremen, Germany
[6] DFKI, Saarbrücken, Germany
[7] Intel Corporation, Hillsboro, USA
`Rafael.Misoczki@intel.com`
[8] Florida Atlantic University, Boca Raton, USA
[9] INRIA, Paris, France

Abstract. Current widely-used key exchange (KE) mechanisms will be vulnerable to quantum attacks when sufficiently strong quantum computers become available. Therefore, devising quantum-resistant replacements that combine efficiency with solid security guarantees is an important and challenging task. This paper proposes several contributions towards this goal. First, we introduce *"CAKE"*, a key encapsulation algorithm based on the QC-MDPC McEliece encryption scheme, with two major improvements: (a) the use of ephemeral keys that defeats a recent reaction attack against MDPC decoding of the corresponding encryption scheme and (b) a highly efficient key generation procedure for QC-MDPC-based cryptosystems. Then, we present an authenticated key exchange protocol based on CAKE, which is suitable for the Internet Key Exchange (IKE) standard. We prove that CAKE is IND-CPA secure, that the protocol is SK-Secure, and suggest practical parameters. Compared to other post-quantum schemes, we believe that CAKE is a promising candidate for post-quantum key exchange standardization.

Keywords: Post-quantum cryptography · Code-based cryptography · Key exchange

1 Introduction

The currently deployed public key cryptosystems rely on the difficulty of number theory problems, e.g. factorization [47] and the discrete logarithm problem [37]. These problems will be efficiently solved by large quantum computers [50], turning those schemes completely useless in a not-so-distant future. Thus, it is of

© Springer International Publishing AG 2017
M. O'Neill (Ed.): IMACC 2017, LNCS 10655, pp. 207–226, 2017.
https://doi.org/10.1007/978-3-319-71045-7_11

great relevance to devise and deploy alternative schemes that can survive the advent of large quantum computers and, ideally, offer reasonable performance.

In this context code-based cryptography is a promising alternative. It relies on the well-known decoding problem [7], believed to be hard even against quantum adversaries [8], and on the indistinguishability of its public key from random, a problem that strongly depends on the code family. The best-known code-based scheme, namely the McEliece encryption scheme [35], suggests binary Goppa codes as the code family. This choice has two main drawbacks: (a) Goppa codes may not be the optimal security choice given a recent distinguisher for certain Goppa codes [18] and (b) they require very large public keys (size of several megabytes).

To address these issues, the QC-MDPC McEliece scheme [39] was introduced replacing Goppa codes by Quasi-Cyclic Moderate-Density Parity-Check (QC-MDPC) codes. This approach led to key sizes that are just a few thousand bits long, and approximated the distinguishing problem to the decoding problem. These features attracted great attention from the community (see [15, 25, 52, 53], just to mention a few) including a mention in the preliminary European recommendations for post-quantum cryptography [30].

Despite their promising features, QC-MDPC codes need to be handled carefully due to the probabilistic nature of MDPC decoding (which is inherited from Low-Density Parity-Check (LDPC) codes [21]): there is some probability that the MDPC decoding may fail. This property can be leveraged to mount an attack on some schemes. Indeed, Guo, Johansson and Stankovski [22] presented an interesting reaction attack (GJS attack) against the QC-MDPC McEliece encryption scheme. In this attack, the adversary carefully crafts error patterns and observes whether (or not) the decoding process fails. The adversary can recover the private key by collecting the decoding failure rate of various error patterns. This is possible only because the parameters suggested in [39] ensured (through exhaustive simulation) a decoding failure rate (DFR) of 10^{-7}. The simplest way to foil this attack is to choose parameters such that $DFR \leq 2^{-\lambda}$, where λ is the security level of the scheme. However, the difficulty with this strategy is to *formally* prove that a given parameter set attains a given DFR. Empirical observations indicate that the DFR of MDPC codes decreases exponentially, and secure parameters could be achieved by increasing the code length of [39] by 30% or 40%. However, with no formal proof for this property, the GJS attack might prevent wide adoption of QC-MDPC McEliece for asymmetric encryption.

Contributions. Thus far neither an MDPC-based key exchange nor any MDPC-based encryption scheme has been proposed that defeats the GJS attack. This work provides several contributions to address this and other problems:

✓ It introduces CAKE, a new key encapsulation mechanism (KEM), based on QC-MDPC codes. It differs from the QC-MDPC McEliece encryption scheme in two respects: (a) the key generation process is significantly faster at the cost of longer public keys, and (b) completely defeats the GJS attack by employing ephemeral keys (i.e., new keys are generated at each key exchange).

✓ It proposes an authenticated key exchange protocol based on CAKE that is suitable for the Internet Key Exchange (IKE), similarly to what was previously done done for lattices [41].

✓ It proves that CAKE is CPA secure and the protocol is SK secure [13].

The full version of this paper will include a discussion of implementation aspects, including strategies to deploy our proposal in an isochronous way.

Related Work. Lattice-based cryptography has a long record of academic works [42], including promising key exchange (KE) protocols. The NewHope scheme [1] provides good performance and is based on the Ring-LWE problem [32] (a ring variant of the Learning-With-Errors (LWE) problem [46]). It improves over previous work by Bos, Costello, Naherig and Stebilla [11] which is an implementation of Peikert's proposal [41] for TLS. Frodo [10] is a key exchange scheme based on the LWE problem itself at the price of larger parameters and worse performance. Cryptography based on isogenies of supersingular elliptic curves seems to be another promising way to devise KE protocols [16,26] offering small public keys but not so attractive latency. There are very few code-based key encapsulation mechanism (KEM) schemes. The best known is McBits [9]which builds on the work of [44], and lives in the classical McEliece setting with binary Goppa codes and enormous public keys. Very recently, Ouroboros scheme [28] has been introduced and seems to be a competitive proposal with security proof advantages. There is another class of related works which is not focused on key exchange but that shares some similarities on the techniques to achieve compact McEliece public key sizes, e.g. the seminal work based on quasi-cyclic codes [20], based on quasi-dyadic codes [14,38,43] and quasi-cyclic low-density parity-check codes [2–5,40].

Organization. This paper is organized as follows. Section 2 presents the preliminary concepts, Sect. 3 introduces CAKE, a new unauthenticated key encapsulation mechanism (KEM) based on QC-MDPC codes, Sect. 4 presents an authenticated key exchange protocol based on CAKE, Sect. 5 proves that CAKE is IND-CPA secure and the corresponding authenticated key exchange protocol is SK secure, Sect. 6 discusses practical security and suggests parameters. Section 7 presents our conclusions.

2 Preliminaries

Definition 1 (Linear codes). *The Hamming weight of a vector $x \in \mathbb{F}_2^n$ is the number $\mathrm{wt}(x)$ of its nonzero components. A binary (n, r)-linear code $\mathcal{C}$ of length n, co-dimension r and dimension $k = (n-r)$ is a k-dimensional vector subspace of $\mathbb{F}_2^n$. It is spanned by the rows of a matrix $G \in \mathbb{F}_2^{k \times n}$, called a generator matrix of $\mathcal{C}$. Equivalently, it is is the kernel of a matrix $H \in \mathbb{F}_2^{r \times n}$, called parity-check matrix, i.e. $\mathcal{C} = \{c \mid Hc^T = 0\}$. The codeword $c \in \mathcal{C}$ of a vector $m \in \mathbb{F}_2^{(n-r)}$ is $c = mG$. The syndrome $s \in \mathbb{F}_2^r$ of a vector $e \in \mathbb{F}_2^n$ is $s^T = He^T$.*

Definition 2 (Quasi-cyclic code). *An (n, r)-linear code is quasi-cyclic (QC) if there is some integer n_0 such that every cyclic shift of a codeword by n_0 places is again a codeword.*

When $n = n_0 r$, for some integer r, it is possible and convenient to have both generator and parity check matrices composed by $r \times r$ circulant blocks. A circulant block is completely described by its first row (or column) and the algebra of $r \times r$ binary circulant matrices is isomorphic to the algebra of polynomials modulo $x^r - 1$ over $\mathbb{F}_2$, enabling efficient computations. For example, a parity-check matrix H of an $(n_0 r, r)$-quasi-cyclic code can be represented as:

$$H = [H_0 | \ldots | H_{n_0 - 1}], \text{ where: } H_i = \begin{pmatrix} h_{i,0} \ldots h_{i,r-1} \\ \vdots \quad \ddots \quad \vdots \\ h_{i,1} \ldots \quad h_{i,0} \end{pmatrix} \in \mathbb{F}_2^{r \times r}$$

Definition 3 (QC-MDPC codes). *An (n_0, r, w)-QC-MDPC code is a quasi-cyclic code of length $n = n_0 r$, co-dimension r admitting a parity-check matrix with constant row weight $w = O(\sqrt{n \log n})$.*

3   CAKE: A QC-MDPC KEM with Fast Key-Generation

In this section we introduce CAKE – an unauthenticated key encapsulation mechanism based on QC-MDPC codes. The strategy to present our scheme as an unauthenticated KEM follows works such as NewHope [10] and BCNS [11]. In this way, authentication and key exchange features are decoupled, allowing flexibility to select (and eventually replace) the choice for each feature. Section 4 describes one way to add the authentication layer on top of CAKE.

CAKE resembles the QC-MDPC McEliece encryption scheme [39] but also has important differences. While QC-MDPC McEliece intends to use long term keys, CAKE relies on ephemeral keys. This means that a new key pair is generated at each key exchange, thus completely defeating the GJS attack [22] which depends on observing a large number of decoding failures for a same private key. Given the new requirement of generating a key pair at every key exchange, a major challenge consisted of investigating novel strategies to accelerate MDPC key generation. To address this issue, we suggest a simple and elegant solution. In contrast to QC-MDPC McEliece (and any quasi-cyclic McEliece variant), CAKE does not compute the inversion of one of its private cyclic blocks and then multiply it by the whole private matrix. Note that this was done to ensure that one of the blocks in the public matrix is the identity block (and thus no need to be transmitted) and to hide the private code structure. Instead, CAKE hides the private code structure by simply multiplying its sparse private matrix by any random, dense cyclic block. This turns CAKE key generation into the most efficient process among key generation, encryption and decryption. It is worth mentioning that the QC-MDPC inversion-based key generation can be up to 21x slower than encryption [33]. Therefore, removing the inversion operation is an excellent strategy to accelerate key generation.

The drawback of this strategy is the doubled public key size since the public key will not have an identity block anymore. We consider that this is an acceptable cost given the significant speedup. Finally, we make use of a simple variant of McEliece, as presented in [14,36], which swaps the roles of message and randomness in the encryption process to avoid a costly polynomial inversion.

A key encapsulation mechanism (KEM) is composed by three algorithms: GEN which outputs a public encapsulation key pk and a private decapsulation key sk, ENCAPS which takes as input an encapsulation key pk and outputs a ciphertext c and a symmetric key K, and DECAPS which takes as input a decapsulation key sk and a cryptogram c and outputs a symmetric key K or a decapsulation failure symbol $\perp$. For more details on KEM definitions, we refer the reader to [17].

For a security level λ, let r be a prime such that $(x^r - 1)/(x - 1) \in \mathbb{F}_2[x]$ is irreducible, d_v be an odd integer and t be an integer such that decoding t errors with a uniformly chosen binary linear error-correcting code of length $n = 2r$ and dimension r, as well as recovering a base of column weight d_v given an arbitrary base of a QC-MDPC code of the same length and dimension, both have a computational cost in $\Omega(\exp(\lambda))$. See Sect. 6 for a detailed discussion on parameters selection. The CAKE algorithms definition is presented next.

Notation: We denote by $\xleftarrow{\$}$ the process of sampling uniformly at random, by $\mathcal{R}$ the ring $\mathbb{F}_2[x]/\langle x^r - 1\rangle$ and by $\mathbf{K} : \{0,1\}^n \to \{0,1\}^{\ell_K}$ the hash function used by encapsulation and decapsulation, where ℓ_K is the desired symmetric key length.

Algorithm 1. CAKE.GEN:

- Input: λ, the target quantum security level.
- Output: the sparse private key (h_0, h_1) and the dense public key (g_0, g_1).

0. Given λ, set the parameters r, d_v, t as described above.
1. Generate $h_0, h_1 \xleftarrow{\$} \mathcal{R}$ both of (odd) weight $\mathsf{wt}(h_0) = \mathsf{wt}(h_1) = d_v$.
2. Generate $g \xleftarrow{\$} \mathcal{R}$ of odd weight (so $\mathsf{wt}(g) \approx r/2$).
3. Compute $(g_0, g_1) \leftarrow (g \cdot h_1^T, g \cdot h_0^T)$.

Let H and G be the quasi-cyclic matrices built from $(r - 1)$ cyclic shifts of (h_0, h_1) and (g_0, g_1) respectively. It is easy to see that $G \cdot H^T = 0$ and therefore they satisfy the condition to be a generator and a parity-check matrix of the given code: $G \cdot H^T = [g \cdot h_1^T \mid g \cdot h_0^T] \cdot [h_0 \mid h_1]^T = g \cdot h_1^T \cdot h_0^T + g \cdot h_0^T \cdot h_1^T = g \cdot (h_1^T \cdot h_0^T + h_0^T \cdot h_1^T) = 2 \cdot g \cdot h_0^T \cdot h_1^T = 0$. It is also important to show that g, as created above, is always invertible (thus not risking to generate a public code which is in fact a sub-code of the private one) and this is proven in Appendix A.

Algorithm 2. CAKE.ENCAPS:

– Input: the dense public key (g_0, g_1).
– Output: the encapsulated key K and the cryptogram c.

1. Generate an error pattern $e = (e_0, e_1) \xleftarrow{\$} \mathcal{R}$ of total weight $\mathsf{wt}(e) = t$.
2. Generate $m \xleftarrow{\$} \mathcal{R}$.
3. Compute $c = (c_0, c_1) \leftarrow (m \cdot g_0 + e_0, m \cdot g_1 + e_1)$.
4. Compute $K \leftarrow \mathbf{K}(e)$.

Algorithm 3. CAKE.DECAPS:

– Input: the sparse private key (h_0, h_1) and the cryptogram c.
– Output: the decapsulated key K or a failure symbol $\perp$.

1. Compute the syndrome $s \leftarrow c_0 \cdot h_0^T + c_1 \cdot h_1^T$.
2. Try to decode s to recover an error vector $e' = (e_0', e_1')$.
3. If $\mathsf{wt}(e') \neq t$ or decoding fails, output $\perp$ and halt.
4. Compute $K \leftarrow \mathbf{K}(e')$.

All public key, private key and cryptogram are n bits long. We remark that e can be represented with only $\lceil \log_2 \binom{n}{t} \rceil$ bits and such a compact representation can be used if memory is the preferred metric of optimization (the hash function $\mathbf{K}$ would need to be changed as well to receive $\lceil \log_2 \binom{n}{t} \rceil$ bits instead of n). Figure 1 illustrates CAKE as a protocol of messages exchanged between an Initiator and a Responder. Table 1 shows the bandwidth cost per message.

Initiator		Responder
$(h_0, h_1, g_0, g_1) \leftarrow$ CAKE.GEN(λ)		
	$\xrightarrow{\quad (g_0,g_1) \quad}$	
		$(K, c) := $ CAKE.ENCAPS(g_0, g_1)
	$\xleftarrow{\quad c \quad}$	
$K/\perp := $ CAKE.DECAPS(h_0, h_1, c)		

Fig. 1. CAKE key encapsulation mechanism

Table 1. Communication bandwidth.

Message flow	Message	Size (bits)
Initiator → Responder	(g_0, g_1)	n
Responder → Initiator	(c_0, c_1)	n

4   An Authenticated Key Exchange Protocol from CAKE

In this section, we discuss one way to extend CAKE to an authenticated key exchange protocol. This discussion intends to demonstrate that CAKE ephemeral keys are not a limitation for its integration into real-world key exchange protocols and also allows us to discuss interesting security properties required in the real world, such as perfect forward secrecy, which are usually managed in levels of abstraction above the simple key encapsulation building block.

The construction here described is based on the well-known SIGn-and-MAc (SIGMA) protocol design [29], which is adopted by the Internet Key Exchange (IKE) protocol [24], part of the IPSec standard [49]. The simplest SIGMA protocol is known as Σ_0 and is proven to be secure (in terms to be discussed in Sect. 5.2) when instantiated with Diffie-Hellman key agreement [13]. Our proposal essentially leverages a result presented by Peikert which demonstrated that Σ_0 can be proven secure with any IND-CPA KEM [41], instead of being restricted to Diffie-Hellman.

As in [41], the key exchange protocol here described is parametrized by an (IND-CPA-secure) key encapsulation mechanism KEM with key space K, a digital signature scheme SIG, a pseudorandom function $f : \mathsf{K} \times \{0,1\} \to \mathsf{K}_0$, and a message authentication code MAC with key space K_0 and message space $\{0,1\}^*$. A successful execution of the protocol outputs a secret key in K_0. In our work, we explicitly defines CAKE as the KEM scheme. For the sake of flexibility, we do not specify any particular signature, MAC or pseudorandom function although they all need to meet some minimum security notion (the signature and MAC must be EUF-CMA secure and f must be a secure pseudorandom function; see Sect. 5). We assume that each party has a long-term signing key for SIG whose corresponding verification key is publicly available and associated to its identity ID. This can be done in terms of certificate authorities and common public key infrastructure.

Key exchange protocols are multiparty protocols activated by messages that are locally processed, leading to new messages being triggered. A session is an invocation of this protocol. Each session is associated to a unique session ID (denoted as sid) and a party can be called the Initiator (with identity ID_I) who first activates the session or the Responder (identity ID_R) who is activated upon receiving a message. For a more detailed discussion on key exchange protocol definitions we refer to [12]. Figure 2 describes how CAKE can be plugged into an authenticated key exchange protocol, similarly as done in [41].

The protocol assumes that Initiator and Responder possess identities ID_I and ID_R, respectively. Initiator generates a unique session identifier sid and a CAKE key pair $(sk = (h_0, h_1), pk = (g_0, g_1))$, and sends (sid, pk) to Responder, who generates a key K and a ciphertext C using the encapsulation method. The pair (K_0, K_1) is generated from K using the pseudorandom function f. The tuple $(1, sid, pk, C)$ is signed using Responder's signing key and a MAC tag is generated from $(1, dif, ID_R)$ using key K_1. The signature, tag, ID_R, sid and C is sent to Initiator, who tries to decapsulate C. In case of success, Initiator

Initiator	Responder
ID_I	ID_R

sid

$(sk, pk) := \text{CAKE.GEN}(\lambda)$

$$\xrightarrow{\quad sid, pk \quad}$$

$$(K, C) := \text{CAKE.ENCAPS}(pk)$$
$$K_0 := f_K(0), \ K_1 := f_K(1)$$
$$\alpha := SIG.Sign_R(1, sid, pk, C)$$
$$\beta := MAC.Tag_{K_1}(1, sid, ID_R)$$

$$\xleftarrow{\quad sid, C, ID_R, \alpha, \beta \quad}$$

k or $\bot := \text{CAKE.DECAPS}(sk, C)$
$K_0 := f_K(0), \ K_1 := f_K(1)$
$\top$ or $\bot := SIG.Verify_R(\alpha)$
$\top$ or $\bot := MAC.Verify_{K_1}(\beta)$
$\gamma := SIG.Sign_I(0, sid, C, pk)$
$\delta := MAC.Tag_{K_1}(0, sid, ID_I)$

$$\xrightarrow{\quad sid, ID_I, \gamma, \delta \quad}$$

$$\top \text{ or } \bot := SIG.Verify_I(\gamma)$$
$$\top \text{ or } \bot := MAC.Verify_{K_1}(\delta)$$

| Public output: (ID_I, sid, ID_R) | Public output: (ID_I, sid, ID_R) |
| Local output: (K_0) | Local output: (K_0) |

Fig. 2. SIGMA-like authenticated key exchange from CAKE KEM

reconstructs (K_0, K_1) and verifies both signature and MAC tag. If it succeeds, Initiator signs the tuple $(0, sid, C, pk)$ and generates a MAC tag for the tuple $(0, sid, ID_I)$. Signature, tag, sid and ID_I are sent to Responder who verifies both signature and tag. If it succeeds, the public output is the tuple (ID_I, sid, ID_R) and the local output is the shared key K_0. If any process fails, the public output is $(abort, ID_I, sid)$ and $(abort, ID_R, sid)$, and the key exchange is restarted.

5   Formal Security Assessment

In this section, we prove that CAKE is IND-CPA secure and that the authenticated key exchange protocol described in Sect. 4 is SK-Secure.

5.1   CAKE IND-CPA Security

In the following definition, we denote by $\mathcal{K}$ the domain of the exchanged symmetric key and by λ the security level of the scheme.

Definition 4. *A key encapsulation mechanism is IND-CPA (passively) secure if the outputs of the two following games are computationally indistinguishable.*

Game 1	Game 2
$(sk, pk) \leftarrow \text{GEN}(\lambda)$	$(sk, pk) \leftarrow \text{GEN}(\lambda)$
$(c, K) \leftarrow \text{ENCAPS}(pk)$	$(c, K) \leftarrow \text{ENCAPS}(pk)$
	$K^* \leftarrow \mathcal{K}$
Output (pp, pk, c, K)	Output (pp, pk, c, K^*)

Proposition 1. *CAKE is IND-CPA secure in the random oracle model assuming that the hash function $\mathbf{K}$ is modeled as a random oracle.*

Proof. It is easy to show that our claim is true. In fact, note that the only difference between the two distributions in Game 1 and Game 2 is the value of K which is replaced by a uniformly random value K^*. Remember that in an honest run of CAKE (i.e. Game 1), the key K is obtained as $\mathbf{K}(e)$. Since $\mathbf{K}$ is modeled as a random oracle, its output is pseudorandom. Thus the only way an attacker could distinguish the two values would be by recovering the vector e. Since this is a passive attack, the attacker can't perform any decryption queries and can only rely on the public data, that is public key and ciphertext. Thus, this is equivalent to decoding the noisy codeword c in the code described by (g_0, g_1). Decoding a random linear code and distinguishing the public code from the private one are both well-known problems which are considered to be hard, and which will be described and discussed extensively in Sect. 6. For now, suffice to say that since the output of $\mathbf{K}$ is pseudorandom and recovering e is infeasible, CAKE satisfies the IND-CPA security notion. ☐

5.2 SK Security of Authenticated Key Exchange from CAKE

The security notion targeted by our SIGMA-like construction and also by [41] is known as SK Secure[1], which stands for *session-key secure* [13]. Informally, this notion translates into: "the adversary does not learn anything about the session key by interacting with the protocol" and enables the establishment of secure channels (usually the ultimate goal of sharing a key). In the following paragraphs, we give an overview on SK Security.

---

[1] This security notion was originally introduced in [12]. The main difference between [12] and [13] is that in the former there was an implicit requirement that the identities of the parties must be known to each other beforehand, while the latter attains a more realistic (internet-oriented) scenario where the identities of the parties are not initially known and only becomes known after the protocol run evolves (this model is called the "post-specified peer model" and is the one used in our proposal).

According to [13], a key exchange protocol is a multiparty protocol where each party runs one or more copies of the protocol. A *session* is a local procedure resulting from a protocol activation at a party. The activation of a protocol at a party has three inputs (P, sid, d): the local party P, the unique session identifier *sid* and the intended peer address d. A party can be activated as an Initiator or as a Responder (upon an incoming message). The output of a session is a public triple (P, sid, Q), where Q is the intended peer identity and a secret *session key*. In case of failure, the output is a special failure symbol. Sessions have a local state which is erased after the session completes. Besides, each party may have an additional long-term state (composed by long-term signing keys, for example) which is visible to multiple sessions and is not erased after session completion.

The adversarial model is called the "unauthenticated-links model (UM)" and allows the attacker to have full control over the communication channel, thus being able to intercept, delay, inject, drop, or change any message exchanged. In short, it is a fully-capable man-in-the-middle attacker. Besides, the attacker is also allowed to start key exchange sessions and, more importantly, is able to perform all three *session exposure* attacks:

- **Session-state reveal**: targets a still incomplete session. The adversary learns the state of that particular session (not including any long-term secrets accessible to all sessions, such as long-term signing keys).
- **Session-key queries**: targets a complete session and allows the adversary to learn its corresponding session key.
- **Party corruption**: the attacker learns all information possessed by the party (including long-term secrets accessible to all sessions, such as long-term signing keys).

An important concept in this model is *session expiration*. When a session expires, the attacker is not allowed to perform session-state reveal or session-key queries, although is fully able to corrupt a party. A key exchange protocol which is secure even after a party corruption is said to enjoy *perfect forward secrecy* (PFS). Another relevant concept is the one of matching session.

Definition 5. *Let (P, sid) be a complete session with public output (P, sid, Q). The session (Q, sid) is called the matching session of (P, sid) if either:*

1. (Q, sid) *is not completed; or*
2. (Q, sid) *is completed and its public output is (Q, sid, P).*

Finally, the actual concept of SK Secure relies on the attacker's ability of distinguishing a session key from random. This is done through the *test session* game that allows the attacker to choose any session which has not been *exposed* (by any of the session exposure attacks above) nor its matching session, and runs the following game used in the formal SK secure definition.

Game 1 (Test Session). *Let $\mathcal{U}$ be an adversary of the key exchange protocol π. In the test-session game, the key exchange protocol oracle toss a coin $b \leftarrow \{0, 1\}$*

and returns a valid session key k if b = 0 or returns a sequence of random bits if b = 1. The experiment finishes by the adversary $\mathcal{U}$ outputting $b' \in \{0, 1\}$, a guess on the value of b.

Definition 6 (SK Secure). *A key exchange protocol π is SK Secure in the post-specified peer model with unauthenticated links if the following holds for any adversary:*

1. *π satisfies that both uncorrupted parties output the same session key.*
2. *The probability that $\mathcal{U}$ guesses b correctly in Game 1 is $\frac{1}{2} + \epsilon$, where ϵ is a negligible fraction in the security parameter.*

Having provided this overview on SK Security, we can finally prove the protocol described in Sect. 4 attains such a security notion.

Theorem 1. *The key exchange protocol described in Sect. 4 is SK Secure in the post-specified peer model with unauthenticated links assuming that:*

1. *The key exchange protocol described in Sect. 4 satisfies that both uncorrupted parties output the same session key;*
2. *CAKE scheme is IND-CPA secure;*
3. *SIG and MAC are existentially unforgeable under chosen message attack and that the function f is a secure pseudorandom function.*

Proof. The proof follows Theorem 6.1 of [41]. The first item is about the correctness of the scheme and boils down to ensure that both parties derive the same session key. This is guaranteed by the correctness of the underlying key encapsulation mechanism (CAKE) and the unforgeability of the signature scheme (see third item below) required to ensure that the key corresponds to the decapsulation of the given ciphertext. As in [41], we remark that the security of the MAC and the pseudorandom function are not needed for such a correctness proof. The second item is achieved by Proposition 1. The third item is achieved by construction, i.e. by selecting a MAC and a signature scheme that are EUF-CMA and the function f that is a secure pseudorandom function.   □

Remark on Perfect Forward Secrecy. Key exchange protocols based on asymmetric encryption, such as key transport protocols, are usually not able to achieve PFS. This happens because if a party is compromised, then its long-term encryption keys are also compromised, allowing the adversary to recover past session keys by decrypting previously exchanged ciphertexts. We remark that this is not the case of the protocol described in Sect. 4 given the fact we use ephemeral asymmetric encryption keys. Since these keys are part of the session state, they will be erased in an event of session expiration. Signing keys are the actual long-term keys in our proposal and their leakage does not affect previous sessions. The same argument holds for our key encapsulation mechanism (CAKE) as long as the ephemeral encryption keys are guaranteed to be erased after key exchange completion.

6 Practical Security Assessment

This section discusses the practical security aspects of our proposal.

6.1 Hard Problems and Security Reduction

Let $\mathcal{R}$ be the ring $\mathbb{F}_2[x]/\langle x^r - 1 \rangle$. For every $h \in \mathcal{R}$ and any positive integer t, let $\mathcal{E}(h, t)$ denote the uniform distribution over $\{e_0 + e_1 h \mid e_0, e_1 \in \mathcal{R}, \mathsf{wt}(e_0) + \mathsf{wt}(e_1) = t\}$. For any positive integer w, let $\mathcal{K}(w)$ denote the uniform distribution over $\{h_1 h_0^{-1} \mid h_0, h_1 \in \mathcal{R}, \mathsf{wt}(h_0) + \mathsf{wt}(h_1) = w\}$.

The KEM of Sect. 3 is secure as long as both distributions $\mathcal{E}(h, t)$ and $\mathcal{K}(w)$ are computationally indistinguishable from the uniform distribution over $\mathcal{R}$. From the practical viewpoint, this means that r, w, t must be chosen such that the following two problems are intractable:

Problem 1. Given $s, h \in \mathcal{R}$, find $e_0, e_1 \in \mathcal{R}$ such that $\mathsf{wt}(e_0) + \mathsf{wt}(e_1) = t$ and $e_0 + e_1 h = s$.

Problem 2. Given $h \in \mathcal{R}$, find $h_0, h_1 \in \mathcal{R}$ such that $\mathsf{wt}(h_0) + \mathsf{wt}(h_1) = w$ and $h_1 + h_0 h = 0$.

Problems 1 and 2 are respectively the problems of decoding t errors and finding a codeword of weight w in an arbitrary quasi-cyclic code of dimension r and length $n = 2r$.

In the current state of the art, the best known techniques for solving those problems are variants of Prange's Information Set Decoding (ISD) [45]. We remark that, though the best attacks consist in solving one of the search problems, the security reduction of our scheme requires the decision version of Problem 2.

6.2 Information Set Decoding

The best asymptotic variant of ISD is due to May and Ozerov [34], but it has a polynomial overhead which is difficult to estimate precisely. In practice, the BJMM variant [6] is probably the best for relevant cryptographic parameters. The work factor for classical (*i.e.* non quantum) computing of any variant $\mathcal{A}$ of ISD for decoding t errors (or finding a word of weight t) in a binary code of length n and dimension k can be written

$$\mathrm{WF}_{\mathcal{A}}(n, k, t) = 2^{ct(1+o(1))}$$

where c depends on the algorithm, on the code rate $R = k/n$ and on the error rate t/N. It has been proven in [51] that, asymptotically, for sublinear weight $t = o(n)$ (which is the case here as $w \approx t \approx \sqrt{n}$), we have $c = \log_2 \frac{1}{1-R}$ for all variants of ISD.

In practice, when t is small, using 2^{ct} with $c = \log_2 \frac{1}{1-R}$ gives a remarkably good estimate for the complexity. For instance, non asymptotic estimates derived from [23] gives $\text{WF}_{\text{BJMM}}(65542, 32771, 264) = 2^{263.3}$ "column operations" which is rather close to 2^{264}. This closeness is expected asymptotically, but is circumstantial for fixed parameters. It only holds because various factors compensate, but it holds for most MDPC parameters of interest.

Exploiting the Quasi-Cyclic Structure. Both codeword finding and decoding are a bit easier (by a polynomial factor) when the target code is quasi-cyclic. If there is a word of weight w in a QC code then its r quasi-cyclic shifts are in the code. In practice, this gives a factor r speedup compared to a random code. Similarly, using Decoding One Out of Many (DOOM) [48] it is possible to produce r equivalent instances of the decoding problem. Solving those r instances together saves a factor $\sqrt{r}$ in the workload.

Exploiting Quantum Computations. As commented in [8], Grover's algorithm fully applies to Prange algorithm. Effectively, this halves the above asymptotic exponent for Prange algorithm. Later, it was proven in [27] that more involved variants of ISD could achieve a better exponent but also the improvement was disappointingly away from the factor 2 that could be expected. In the sequel, we will estimate the quantum security by dividing the classical exponent by two. This is probably conservative but a more precise evaluation would not be significantly different.

Practical Parameter Selection. We denote $\text{WF}(n, k, t)$ the workfactor of the best ISD variant for decoding t errors in a binary code of length n and dimension k. In the following we will consider only codes of transmission rate 0.5, that is length $n = 2r$ and dimension r. In a classical setting, the best solver for Problem 1 has a cost $\text{WF}(2r, r, t)/\sqrt{r}$ and the best solver for Problem 2 has a cost $\text{WF}(2r, r, w)/r$. As remarked above, with $\text{WF}(2r, r, t) \approx 2^t$ we obtain a crude but surprisingly accurate, parameter selection rule. To reach λ bits of quantum security, we choose w, t and r such that

$$\lambda \approx \frac{t - \frac{1}{2}\log_2 r}{2} \approx \frac{w - \log_2 r}{2}. \tag{1}$$

6.3   Defeating the GJS Reaction Attack

Both CAKE and the authenticated key exchange protocol described in Sect. 4 requires ephemeral KEM key pair, i.e. a KEM key generation is performed for each key exchange. As a result, the GJS reaction attack is inherently defeated: a GJS adversary would have (at most) a single opportunity to observe decryption, thus not being able to create statistics about different error patterns. We note that, for efficiency purposes, an initiator may want to precompute KEM key pairs before engaging in key exchange sessions. We remark that policies to securely store the pregenerated KEM key pair must be in place, in order to avoid that an adversary access a KEM key pair to be used in a future communication.

6.4   How to Choose MDPC Parameters

If we denote λ the (quantum) security parameter, then both t and w must be close to 2λ, as in (1). In addition, to ensure decoding, we expect the product tw to grow as $r \log r$. Putting everything together we obtain

$$\begin{cases} t \approx 2\lambda + \log_2(2\lambda) \\ w \approx 2\lambda + 2\log_2(2\lambda) \end{cases}$$

and r will grow as $\lambda^2/\log \lambda$. The exact value of r needs to be checked, by simulation, and increased to a point where the decoding failure rate is acceptable.

Finally, we choose r such that 2 is primitive modulo r. First, this will force r to be prime, thwarting the so-called squaring attack [31]. Also, it implies that $x^r - 1$ only has two irreducible factors (one of them being $x - 1$). This is an insurance against an adversary trying to exploit the structure of $\mathbb{F}_2[x]/\langle x^r - 1\rangle$ when $x^r - 1$ has small factors, other than $x - 1$.

The parameters suggested in Table 2 consider the security attacks discussed in Sect. 6. In addition, the block size r is chosen so that state-of-the-art bit flipping decoding (see [33]; or [15] for a comprehensive assessment) has a failure rate not exceeding 10^{-7} (validated through exhaustive simulation). The last column shows the public and private key size which are both n bits long.

Table 2. QC-MDPC suggested parameters for λ bits of quantum security.

λ	n_0	n	r	w	t	Key size (bits)
128	2	65,542	32,771	274	264	65,542
96	2	39,706	19,853	206	199	39,706
64	2	20,326	10,163	142	134	20,326

7   Conclusion

This paper introduced CAKE, an IND-CPA secure key encapsulation mechanism (KEM) based on QC-MDPC codes. CAKE uses ephemeral keys and therefore inherently defeats the recent GJS attack [22]. Since key generation is performed for every key exchange, we devised an efficient QC-MDPC key generation, which is much faster than the one proposed for the QC-MDPC McEliece encryption scheme [39].

CAKE offers a competitive performance. All public key, private key and cryptogram are n bits long, corresponding to the bandwidth of the messages depicted in Fig. 1. The key generation cost is dominated by two sparse-dense modular polynomial multiplications, and does not require any polynomial inversion as usually seen in code-based cryptosystems. The cost of encapsulation is dominated by the two dense-dense modular polynomial multiplications and a hash computation. The cost of decapsulation is dominated by two sparse-dense polynomial modular multiplications, a decoding attempt, and a hash computation. In summary, besides MDPC decoding, CAKE relies on modular polynomial multiplications and hash computations, so we can expect efficient implementations on a wide range of platforms. A detailed assessment of implementation aspects will be discussed in the full version of this paper.

CAKE compares well with other post-quantum key exchange schemes. Comparing to other code-based schemes, the Goppa-based McBits [9], one of the fewest currently known code based KEM, offers a public key whose size is orders of magnitude greater than the one of CAKE. From a security perspective, [9] does not seem optimal either given a distinguisher for certain (i.e., high-rate) Goppa codes [18]. On the other hand, Ouroboros [28] is a very recent proposal that seems to have interesting security proof properties.

Recent works [16,26] have shown that isogenies in supersingular elliptic curves can be used to devise efficient key exchange mechanisms. In particular, those constructions have the benefit of achieving small public key sizes, but not so attractive latency performance. Note that this is a much more recent trend and caution should be exercised as they have not gone through nearly as similar scrutiny as code-based cryptosystems, first appeared almost 40 years ago.

When comparing with lattice-based schemes, e.g., [1,11] and [10], CAKE and the lattice-based protocols show some similarities. All of them suffer from decoding failures (lattice schemes usually have a lower failure probability though). Also, the use of ephemeral keys for key exchange is not new in the literature; [1] discusses the security loss inherent to key cache ([19] presents a comprehensive analysis on the security impact of key reuse for Ring-LWE). Besides, they offer unbalanced cost between the parties, what may lead to great flexibility (e.g., in a certain application, the role of Initiator/Responder could be predefined depending on the expected computational power of the parties). In terms of total bandwidth cost, CAKE's traffic requires 2/3 of the traffic presented in [10], but is 1.3 and 3 times larger than that of [1] and [11], respectively. While such comparisons are certainly useful, we point out that lattice-based schemes are not the immediate "competitors" of CAKE because they are based on a different class of hard problems. We note that the transition to post-quantum cryptography is an unprecedented move, thus, relying on a single, silver-bullet class of cryptographic problems (e.g., lattices) is a very risky strategy, whilst considering a set of well-studied constructions seems a considerably safer choice in the long term.

This paper also presents an SK secure authenticated key exchange protocol based on CAKE, which is suitable for the Internet Key Exchange (IKE), similarly to [41]. We prove that CAKE is IND-CPA secure, and that the authenticated protocol is SK secure. Moreover, we demonstrate that our proposal achieves perfect forward secrecy, despite the fact it is based on asymmetric encryption (key transport schemes with static keys do not attain PFS, for example).

Taking all these considerations into account, we believe that CAKE is a promising candidate for post-quantum key exchange standardization.

Acknowledgments. Shay Gueron, Tim Güneysu, Nicolas Sendrier and Jean-Pierre Tillich were supported in part by the Commission of the European Communities through the Horizon 2020 program under project number 645622 (PQCRYPTO). Shay Gueron was also partially supported by the Israel Science Foundation (grant No. 1018/16). Paulo S. L. M. Barreto was partially supported by Intel and FAPESP through the project "Efficient Post-Quantum Cryptography for Building Advanced Security Applications" (grant No. 2015/50520-6).

Appendix

A   Efficiently Sampling Invertible Elements from $\mathbb{F}_2[x]/\langle X^r - 1\rangle$

In this section, we prove that one can efficiently sample an invertible element from $\mathbb{F}_2[x]/\langle x^r - 1\rangle$ by taking any polynomial $h \xleftarrow{\$} \mathbb{F}_2[x]/\langle x^r - 1\rangle$ such that $\mathsf{wt}(h)$ is odd.

Lemma 1. *Let $h \in \mathbb{F}_2[x]$ have even weight. Then h is not invertible modulo $x^r - 1$.*

Proof. We show that $(x - 1) \mid h$ by induction on $\mathsf{wt}(h)$. For $\mathsf{wt}(h) = 0$ trivially $(x - 1) \mid h$. Assume that $(x - 1) \mid h$ whenever $\mathsf{wt}(h) = 2k$ for some $k \geqslant 0$. Now consider any $h \in \mathbb{F}_2[x]$ with weight $\mathsf{wt}(h) = 2(k + 1)$, and take two distinct terms x^i, x^j of h such that $i < j$. Define $h' = h - x^i - x^j$, so that $\mathsf{wt}(h') = 2k$. Then $(x - 1) \mid h'$ by induction, i.e. $h' = (x - 1)h''$ for some $h'' \in \mathbb{F}_2[x]$. Hence $h = h' + x^i + x^j = (x-1)h'' + x^i(x^{j-i} + 1) = (x-1)h'' + x^i(x - 1)(x^{j-i-1} + \cdots + 1) = (x - 1)(h'' + x^i(x^{j-i-1} + \cdots + 1))$, and therefore $(x - 1) \mid h$. □

Theorem 2. *Let r a prime such that $(x^r - 1)/(x - 1) \in \mathbb{F}_2[x]$ is irreducible. Then any $h \in \mathbb{F}_2[x]$ with $\deg(h) < r$ is invertible modulo $x^r - 1$ iff $h \neq x^{r-1} + \cdots + 1$ and $\mathsf{wt}(h)$ is odd.*

Proof. Take a term x^i of h. Then $\mathsf{wt}(h + x^i) = \mathsf{wt}(h) - 1$ is even, and by Lemma 1 $(x - 1) \mid (h + x^i)$. Hence $h \bmod (x - 1) = x^i \bmod (x - 1) = 1$, meaning that h is invertible modulo $x - 1$.

Now, because $(x^r - 1)/(x - 1) = x^{r-1} + \cdots + 1$ is irreducible, if $\deg(h) < r - 1$ then $\gcd(h, x^{r-1} + \cdots + 1) = 1$, and if $\deg(h) = r - 1$, then $\gcd(h, x^{r-1} + \cdots + 1) = \gcd(h + x^{r-1} + \cdots + 1, x^{r-1} + \cdots + 1) = 1$, since $\deg(h + x^{r-1} + \cdots + 1) < r - 1$. Hence h is invertible modulo $x^{r-1} + \cdots + 1$.

Therefore, the combination of the inverses of h modulo $x - 1$ and modulo $x^{r-1} + \cdots + 1$ via the Chinese remainder theorem is well defined, and by construction it is the inverse of h modulo $(x - 1)(x^{r-1} + \cdots + 1) = x^r - 1$. □

Corollary 1. *One can efficiently sample an invertible element from $\mathbb{F}_2[x]/\langle x^r - 1\rangle$ by taking any polynomial $h \xleftarrow{\$} \mathbb{F}_2[x]/\langle x^r - 1\rangle$ such that $\mathsf{wt}(h)$ is odd.* □

References

1. Alkim, E., Ducas, L., Pöppelmann, T., Schwabe, P.: Post-Quantum Key Exchange - A New Hope. Cryptology ePrint Archive, Report 2015/1092, http://eprint.iacr.org/2015/1092 (2015)
2. Baldi, M., Bodrato, M., Chiaraluce, F.: A new analysis of the McEliece cryptosystem based on QC-LDPC codes. In: Ostrovsky, R., de Prisco, R., Visconti, I. (eds.) SCN 2008. LNCS, vol. 5229, pp. 246–262. Springer, Heidelberg (2008). https://doi.org/10.1007/978-3-540-85855-3_17
3. Baldi, M., Chiaraluce, F.: Cryptanalysis of a new instance of McEliece cryptosystem based on QC-LDPC codes. In: Proceedings of the IEEE International Symposium on Information Theory (ISIT 2007), pp. 2591–2595, June 2007
4. Baldi, M., Chiaraluce, F., Garello, R.: On the usage of quasi-cyclic low-density parity-check codes in the McEliece cryptosystem. In: Proceedings of the First International Conference on Communication and Electronics (ICEE 2006), pp. 305–310, October 2006
5. Baldi, M., Chiaraluce, F., Garello, R., Mininni, F.: Quasi-cyclic low-density parity-check codes in the McEliece cryptosystem. In: Proceedings of the IEEE International Conference on Communications (ICC 2007), pp. 951–956, June 2007
6. Becker, A., Joux, A., May, A., Meurer, A.: Decoding random binary linear codes in $2^{n/20}$: how $1 + 1 = 0$ improves information set decoding. In: Pointcheval, D., Johansson, T. (eds.) EUROCRYPT 2012. LNCS, vol. 7237, pp. 520–536. Springer, Heidelberg (2012). https://doi.org/10.1007/978-3-642-29011-4_31
7. Berlekamp, E., McEliece, R., van Tilborg, H.: On the inherent intractability of certain coding problems (corresp.). IEEE Trans. Inf. Theory **24**(3), 384–386 (1978)
8. Bernstein, D.J.: Grover vs. McEliece, pp. 73–80. Springer, Berlin (2010)
9. Bernstein, D.J., Chou, T., Schwabe, P.: McBits: fast constant-time code-based cryptography. In: Bertoni, G., Coron, J.-S. (eds.) CHES 2013. LNCS, vol. 8086, pp. 250–272. Springer, Heidelberg (2013). https://doi.org/10.1007/978-3-642-40349-1_15
10. Bos, J., Costello, C., Ducas, L., Mironov, I., Naehrig, M., Nikolaenko, V., Raghunathan, A., Stebila, D.: Frodo: Take off the ring! Practical, Quantum-secure Key Exchange from LWE. Cryptology ePrint Archive, Report 2016/659 (2016). http://eprint.iacr.org/2016/659
11. Bos, J.W., Costello, C., Naehrig, M., Stebila, D.: Post-quantum key exchange for the TLS protocol from the ring learning with errors problem. In: Proceedings of the 2015 IEEE Symposium on Security and Privacy (SP), pp. 553–570. IEEE (2015)
12. Canetti, R., Krawczyk, H.: Analysis of key-exchange protocols and their use for building secure channels. In: Pfitzmann, B. (ed.) EUROCRYPT 2001. LNCS, vol. 2045, pp. 453–474. Springer, Heidelberg (2001). https://doi.org/10.1007/3-540-44987-6_28
13. Canetti, R., Krawczyk, H.: Security analysis of IKE's signature-based key-exchange protocol. In: Yung, M. (ed.) Advances in Cryptology. LNCS, vol. 2442. Springer, Heidelberg (2002)
14. Cayrel, P.-L., Hoffmann, G., Persichetti, E.: Efficient implementation of a CCA2-secure variant of McEliece using generalized Srivastava codes. In: Fischlin, M., Buchmann, J., Manulis, M. (eds.) PKC 2012. LNCS, vol. 7293, pp. 138–155. Springer, Heidelberg (2012). https://doi.org/10.1007/978-3-642-30057-8_9
15. Chaulet, J., Sendrier, N.: Worst case QC-MDPC decoder for McEliece cryptosystem. In: Proceedings of the 2016 IEEE International Symposium on Information Theory (ISIT), pp. 1366–1370. IEEE (2016)

16. Costello, C., Longa, P., Naehrig, M.: Efficient algorithms for supersingular isogeny Diffie-Hellman. In: Robshaw, M., Katz, J. (eds.) CRYPTO 2016. LNCS, vol. 9814, pp. 572–601. Springer, Heidelberg (2016). https://doi.org/10.1007/978-3-662-53018-4_21

17. Cramer, R., Shoup, V.: Design and analysis of practical public-key encryption schemes secure against adaptive chosen ciphertext attack. SIAM J. Comput. **33**(1), 167–226 (2004)

18. Faugere, J.-C., Gauthier-Umana, V., Otmani, A., Perret, L., Tillich, J.-P.: A distinguisher for high-rate McEliece cryptosystems. IEEE Trans. Inf. Theory **59**(10), 6830–6844 (2013)

19. Fluhrer, S.: Cryptanalysis of ring-LWE based key exchange with key share reuse. Cryptology ePrint Archive, Report 2016/085 (2016). http://eprint.iacr.org/2016/085

20. Gaborit, P.: Shorter keys for code based cryptography. In: International Workshop on Coding and Cryptography (WCC 2005), pp. 81–91. ACM Press, Bergen (2005)

21. Gallager, R.G.: Low-density parity-check codes. Ph.D. thesis, M.I.T. (1963)

22. Guo, Q., Johansson, T., Stankovski, P.: A key recovery attack on MDPC with CCA security using decoding errors. In: Cheon, J.H., Takagi, T. (eds.) ASIACRYPT 2016. LNCS, vol. 10031, pp. 789–815. Springer, Heidelberg (2016). https://doi.org/10.1007/978-3-662-53887-6_29

23. Hamdaoui, Y., Sendrier, N.: A non asymptotic analysis of information set decoding. Cryptology ePrint Archive, Report 2013/162 (2013). http://eprint.iacr.org/2013/162

24. Harkins, D., Carrel, D.: RFC 2409: The Internet Key Exchange (IKE). Status: Proposed Standard (1998)

25. Heyse, S., von Maurich, I., Güneysu, T.: Smaller keys for code-based cryptography: QC-MDPC McEliece implementations on embedded devices. In: Bertoni, G., Coron, J.-S. (eds.) CHES 2013. LNCS, vol. 8086, pp. 273–292. Springer, Heidelberg (2013). https://doi.org/10.1007/978-3-642-40349-1_16

26. Jao, D., De Feo, L.: Towards quantum-resistant cryptosystems from supersingular elliptic curve isogenies. In: Yang, B.-Y. (ed.) PQCrypto 2011. LNCS, vol. 7071, pp. 19–34. Springer, Heidelberg (2011). https://doi.org/10.1007/978-3-642-25405-5_2

27. Kachigar, G., Tillich, J.-P.: Quantum information set decoding algorithms. In: Lange, T., Takagi, T. (eds.) PQCrypto 2017. LNCS, vol. 10346, pp. 69–89. Springer, Cham (2017). https://doi.org/10.1007/978-3-319-59879-6_5

28. Kiayias, A., Russell, A., David, B., Oliynykov, R.: Ouroboros: a provably secure proof-of-stake blockchain protocol. In: Katz, J., Shacham, H. (eds.) CRYPTO 2017. LNCS, vol. 10401, pp. 357–388. Springer, Cham (2017). https://doi.org/10.1007/978-3-319-63688-7_12

29. Krawczyk, H.: SIGMA: the 'SIGn-and-MAc' approach to authenticated Diffie-Hellman and its use in the IKE protocols. In: Boneh, D. (ed.) CRYPTO 2003. LNCS, vol. 2729, pp. 400–425. Springer, Heidelberg (2003). https://doi.org/10.1007/978-3-540-45146-4_24

30. Lange, T.: Initial recommendations of long-term secure post-quantum systems. PQCRYPTO. EU. Horizon, 2020 (2015)

31. Lndahl, C., Johansson, T., Koochak Shooshtari, M., Ahmadian-Attari, M., Aref, M.R.: Squaring attacks on McEliece public-key cryptosystems using quasi-cyclic codes of even dimension. Des. Codes Cryptogr. **80**(2), 359–377 (2016)

32. Lyubashevsky, V., Peikert, C., Regev, O.: On ideal lattices and learning with errors over rings. In: Gilbert, H. (ed.) EUROCRYPT 2010. LNCS, vol. 6110, pp. 1–23. Springer, Heidelberg (2010). https://doi.org/10.1007/978-3-642-13190-5_1

33. Von Maurich, I., Oder, T., Güneysu, T.: Implementing QC-MDPC McEliece encryption. ACM Trans. Embed. Comput. Syst. **14**(3), 44:1–44:27 (2015)
34. May, A., Ozerov, I.: On computing nearest neighbors with applications to decoding of binary linear codes. In: Oswald, E., Fischlin, M. (eds.) EUROCRYPT 2015. LNCS, vol. 9056, pp. 203–228. Springer, Heidelberg (2015). https://doi.org/10.1007/978-3-662-46800-5_9
35. McEliece, R.J.: A public-key cryptosystem based on algebraic coding theory. Deep Space Netw. Prog. Rep. **44**, 114–116 (1978)
36. Micciancio, D.: Improving lattice based cryptosystems using the hermite normal form. In: Silverman, J.H. (ed.) CaLC 2001. LNCS, vol. 2146, pp. 126–145. Springer, Heidelberg (2001). https://doi.org/10.1007/3-540-44670-2_11
37. Miller, V.S.: Use of elliptic curves in cryptography. In: Williams, H.C. (ed.) CRYPTO 1985. LNCS, vol. 218, pp. 417–426. Springer, Heidelberg (1986). https://doi.org/10.1007/3-540-39799-X_31
38. Misoczki, R., Barreto, P.S.L.M.: Compact McEliece keys from Goppa codes. In: Jacobson, M.J., Rijmen, V., Safavi-Naini, R. (eds.) SAC 2009. LNCS, vol. 5867, pp. 376–392. Springer, Heidelberg (2009). https://doi.org/10.1007/978-3-642-05445-7_24
39. Misoczki, R., Tillich, J.P, Sendrier, N., Barreto, P.L.S.M.: MDPC-McEliece: new McEliece variants from moderate density parity-check codes. In: Proceedings of the IEEE International Symposium on Information Theory - ISIT 2013, Istambul, Turkey, pp. 2069–2073. IEEE (2013)
40. Monico, C., Rosenthal, J., Shokrollahi, A.: Using low density parity check codes in the McEliece cryptosystem. In: Proceedings of the IEEE International Symposium on Information Theory (ISIT 2000), Sorrento, Italy, p. 215. IEEE (2000)
41. Peikert, C.: Lattice cryptography for the internet. In: Mosca, M. (ed.) PQCrypto 2014. LNCS, vol. 8772, pp. 197–219. Springer, Cham (2014). https://doi.org/10.1007/978-3-319-11659-4_12
42. Peikert, C.: A decade of lattice cryptography. Found. Trends® Theor. Comput. Sci. **10**(4), 283–424 (2016)
43. Persichetti, E.: Compact mceliece keys based on quasi-dyadic Srivastava codes. J. Math. Cryptol. **6**(2), 149–169 (2012)
44. Persichetti, E.: Secure and anonymous hybrid encryption from coding theory. In: Gaborit, P. (ed.) PQCrypto 2013. LNCS, vol. 7932, pp. 174–187. Springer, Heidelberg (2013). https://doi.org/10.1007/978-3-642-38616-9_12
45. Prange, E.: The use of information sets in decoding cyclic codes. IRE Trans. Inf. Theor. **8**, S5–S9 (1962)
46. Regev, O.: On lattices, learning with errors, random linear codes, and cryptography. J. ACM (JACM) **56**(6), 34 (2009)
47. Rivest, R.L., Shamir, A., Adleman, L.M.: A method for obtaining digital signatures and public-key cryptosystems. Commun. ACM **21**(2), 120–126 (1978)
48. Sendrier, N.: Decoding one out of many. In: Yang, B.-Y. (ed.) PQCrypto 2011. LNCS, vol. 7071, pp. 51–67. Springer, Heidelberg (2011). https://doi.org/10.1007/978-3-642-25405-5_4
49. Seo, K., Kent, S.: Security architecture for the internet protocol. Status: Proposed Standard (2005)
50. Shor, P.W.: Polynomial-time algorithms for prime factorization and discrete logarithms on a quantum computer. SIAM J. Comput. **26**(5), 1484–1509 (1997)
51. Canto Torres, R., Sendrier, N.: Analysis of information set decoding for a sub-linear error weight. In: Takagi, T. (ed.) PQCrypto 2016. LNCS, vol. 9606, pp. 144–161. Springer, Cham (2016). https://doi.org/10.1007/978-3-319-29360-8_10

52. Von Maurich, I., Güneysu, T.: Lightweight code-based cryptography: QC-MDPC McEliece encryption on reconfigurable devices. In: Proceedings of the Conference on Design, Automation and Test in Europe. European Design and Automation Association, p. 38 (2014)

53. von Maurich, I., Güneysu, T.: Towards side-channel resistant implementations of QC-MDPC McEliece encryption on constrained devices. In: Mosca, M. (ed.) PQCrypto 2014. LNCS, vol. 8772, pp. 266–282. Springer, Cham (2014). https://doi.org/10.1007/978-3-319-11659-4_16

A Practical Implementation of Identity-Based Encryption Over NTRU Lattices

Sarah McCarthy[✉], Neil Smyth, and Elizabeth O'Sullivan

Centre for Secure Information Technologies (CSIT),
Queen's University Belfast, Belfast, UK
{smccarthy10,n.smyth,e.osullivan}@qub.ac.uk

Abstract. An identity-based encryption scheme enables the efficient distribution of keys in a multi-user system. Such schemes are particularly attractive in resource constrained environments where critical resources such as processing power, memory and bandwidth are severely limited. This research examines the first pragmatic lattice-based IBE scheme presented by Ducas, Lyubashevsky and Prest in 2014 and brings it into the realm of practicality for use on small devices. This is the first standalone ANSI C implementation of all the software elements of the scheme with improved performance. User Key Extraction demonstrates a 180% speed increase and Encrypt and Decrypt demonstrate increases of over 500% and 1200% respectively for 80-bit security on an Intel Core i7-6700 CPU at 4.0 GHz, with similar accelerations for 192-bit security, compared with Prest's NTL proof-of-concept implementation on an Intel Core i5-3210M CPU at 2.5 GHz. In addition, we provide a range of suggestions to further enhance performance.

Keywords: Lattice-based cryptography · Identity-based encryption · NTRU

1 Introduction

Managing keys in systems that use Public Key Cryptography (PKC) as the primary means of authentication is achieved within the established framework of a Public Key Infrastructure (PKI). However, it is widely known that PKI requires an extensive network for operational and certificate management. This imposes significant overheads in resource constrained environments and in practice limits the frequency that PKC can be used for large scale, bandwidth intensive applications requiring real-time performance. As technology progresses to operational landscapes such as the Internet of Things (IoT), the need for alternative PKC schemes comes to the fore. Schemes such as Identity-based Encryption (IBE) have been introduced to overcome the complexity issues associated with traditional PKI based approaches. IBE simplifies key generation and distribution in a multi-user system. In environments with limited resources IBE can offer the potential for PKC to be utilised when it is needed and not just when it can be

© Springer International Publishing AG 2017
M. O'Neill (Ed.): IMACC 2017, LNCS 10655, pp. 227–246, 2017.
https://doi.org/10.1007/978-3-319-71045-7_12

accommodated. In addition to resource efficient schemes, many applications have long-term security requirements. For such applications the threat of quantum attacks must be mitigated [NIST-IR8109]. The formulation of Shor's algorithm over two decades ago has prompted research into mathematical areas which could potentially provide quantum-security. One such area is that of lattices and their associated NP-hard problems. Finding lattice-based schemes analogous to classical schemes such as public key encryption and digital signature schemes is the subject of intense research. One of the main advantages of lattice-based cryptography is that it can also provide quantum-resilient alternatives to today's IBE schemes, traditionally based on pairing. Ducas, Lyubashevsky and Prest proposed such a scheme in 2014 [11], henceforth referred to as DLP-IBE. This research presents a complete standalone ANSI C implementation of this scheme. There has been no prior indication of the practical performance and costs of a lattice-based IBE scheme. This work not only provides a benchmark for this type of scheme, but our efficiency improvements bring it into the realm of practicality for the post-quantum setting.

The paper is organised as follows: Sect. 1 reviews both non-lattice and lattice-based IBE schemes and gives a background of lattice geometry. Section 2 introduces the DLP-IBE scheme, and Sect. 3 describes the proposed software architecture, which includes the functionality of Master Key Generation and Extract algorithms as well as the Encrypt and Decrypt processes. Section 4 gives the conclusions. We acknowledge the major bottlenecks, optimisations and challenges and our methods to address them. Implementation results are also given along with potential extensions of the scheme.

1.1 Identity-Based Encryption

An IBE scheme is one where the user's public key is a piece of meaningful information, such as an email address, or a device identifier. A trusted authority uses a master secret key to compute the user secret key. The authority has a master public key which is also needed to send messages to the user. The use of already established personal information as the user ID removes the need for public key distribution. Elements such as timestamps can be incorporated into the user keys to provide a key refresh mechanism. Additionally, the use of timestamps with the user ID can allow senders to encrypt messages that can only be read in the future. In the generic IBE instantiation the central authority has complete access to keys and can therefore decrypt any message and so should be trusted. Additionally, the communication channels between users and the trusted authority should be secure.

The first notion of identity-based schemes was presented by Shamir in 1984 [26]. The idea was to eliminate the need for a public certificate across email systems. These schemes allowed secure communication without exchanging user keys. Shamir presented a solution for an identity-based signature scheme but it wasn't until 2001 that such an encryption scheme was realised [5]. There are two main threads of constructing traditional IBE schemes; using pairings or quadratic residues. The most prominent schemes are Boneh-Franklin [5],

Cocks [10] and Sakai-Kasahara [25]. Boneh co-founded a start-up company in 2002 called Voltage Security Inc.[1] which currently provides IBE solutions to industry. These include secure email and file transfer applications. However, these schemes are susceptible to quantum attacks due to Shor's algorithm, creating the need for quantum-resilient variants.

The first application of lattices (Sect. 1.2) to IBE schemes was in 2008 by Gentry et al. [14]. The main contribution of this work was a sampling algorithm (known as GPV sampling) which showed how to use a short basis as a trapdoor for generating short lattice vectors. This sampler was then used to construct a lattice-based IBE scheme that resembled Cocks' traditional scheme (due to the use of a trapdoor), and can be considered as the dual of Regev's LWE scheme [23]. However, the security proof was in the random oracle model and the master public key and user secret keys had large sizes of $O(n^2)$ bits. In 2010, Agrawal et al. [1] proposed a Learning With Errors (LWE)-based IBE scheme with a trapdoor structure, with performance comparable to the GPV scheme. It uses a sampling algorithm to obtain a basis with low Gram-Schmidt Norm for the master secret key and forms a lattice family with two associated trapdoors to generate short vectors; one for all lattices in the family and the other for all but one. It improves on previous schemes which process the user identities bit by bit by instead considering them as a whole. The public key is $O(nm)$, where the lattice basis is of size $n \times m$. In 2016, Apon et al. [3] proposed the most efficient *standard* LWE scheme to date with a public key size of $O(2nm\log(q))$. This includes the design of new encoding scheme for identities, incorporating a collision-resistant hash function. The first Ring-LWE based IBE scheme was the DLP-IBE scheme [11]. The use of the ring variant increases efficiency by reducing the public key to a polynomial/vector of $O(n)$ and ciphertext $O(2n)$. However, it makes additional assumptions to standard LWE. In particular, it uses the GPV sampling algorithm on a certain distribution of NTRU lattices to increase its efficiency. Other Ring-LWE schemes have since been proposed, for example in 2016 Katsumata and Yamada [16] introduced a scheme based on Yamada's 2016 standard-LWE scheme [29], and exploits the ring properties and assumes the Ring-LWE problem hardness for fixed polynomial approximation factors. The public parameters in this scheme are of size $O(nl^{1/d}\log(n))$, ciphertext $O(n\log(n))$ and private key $O(n\log(n))$. However, the DLP-IBE scheme is still considered the most efficient scheme to date due to smaller key sizes.

1.2   Lattice-Based Cryptography

Shor's algorithm [27] has prompted the research community to investigate so-called "quantum-resistant" forms of cryptography. One of the strong contenders is lattice-based cryptography. The advantages of this type of cryptography are the associated "worst-case hardness" properties [2], efficiency of implementations and flexibility, as it has potential to be used in both encryption and digital signature schemes, as well as IBE, attribute-based encryption (ABE) and even

---

[1] https://www.voltage.com.

fully homomorphic encryption (FHE), although in general the latter two schemes have not yet demonstrated practicality.

A lattice is a mathematical structure, defined by a collection of vectors called a basis, denoted $\mathcal{B}$. The points v of the lattice are all the possible linear combinations of the basis vectors with integer coefficients:

$$\mathcal{L} = \{v = a_1 b_1 + a_2 b_2 + \ldots + a_n b_n : a_i \in \mathbb{Z}, b_i \in \mathcal{B}\}$$

Informally, this can be thought of as an infinite arrangement of regularly spaced points. The closest vector problem (CVP), which is that of finding the closest lattice point to a given point in the space, is an NP-hard lattice problem. The shortest vector problem (SVP), which is that of finding the shortest vector in a lattice, is also NP-hard under randomised reductions. These and connected problems can be used as the basis of security for cryptographic schemes.

A popular lattice problem is the learning with errors (LWE) problem, formulated by Regev in 2005 [23], and its ideal-lattice-based variant Ring-LWE [18]. Many cryptographic schemes based on these have been proposed, such as the encryption scheme in the original papers, digital signature scheme [19] and other concepts such as e-voting [9]. Adding structure and pattern to the lattice basis aids the working of the scheme. This can also improve memory and efficiency, for example by reducing the amount of basis information that needs to be stored or transported to recover the lattice. The DLP-IBE Scheme uses NTRU lattices for this reason. NTRU lattice bases have a convolutional, modular structure. The trapdoors in this scheme are the polynomials f, g, which allow the user to generate a "nice" basis $\mathcal{B}_{\text{nice}}$ whilst the public only have access to the lattice through a "bad" basis $\mathcal{B}_{\text{bad}}$ defined by polynomial h.

$$\mathcal{B}_{\text{bad}} = \begin{pmatrix} 1 & 0 & \ldots & 0 & h_0 & h_1 & \ldots & h_{N-1} \\ 0 & 1 & \ldots & 0 & -h_{n-1} & h_0 & \ldots & h_{N-2} \\ \vdots & & \ddots & \vdots & \vdots & \vdots & \ddots & \vdots \\ 0 & 0 & \ldots & 1 & -h_1 & -h_2 & \ldots & h_0 \\ 0 & 0 & \ldots & 0 & q & 0 & \ldots & 0 \\ 0 & 0 & \ldots & 0 & 0 & q & \ldots & 0 \\ \vdots & & \ddots & \vdots & \vdots & \vdots & \ddots & \vdots \\ 0 & 0 & \ldots & 0 & 0 & 0 & \ldots & q \end{pmatrix} = \begin{pmatrix} 1 & \mathcal{H} \\ 0 & q \end{pmatrix} \text{ and } \mathcal{B}_{\text{nice}} = \begin{pmatrix} \mathcal{A}(g) & -\mathcal{A}(f) \\ \mathcal{A}(G) & -\mathcal{A}(F) \end{pmatrix},$$

where each $\mathcal{A}(\cdot)$ is an anti-circulant matrix dependent on a polynomial f, g, F or G and is of the form:

$$\mathcal{A}(f) = \begin{pmatrix} f_0 & f_1 & \ldots & f_{N-1} \\ -f_{n-1} & f_0 & \ldots & f_{N-2} \\ \vdots & & \ddots & \vdots \\ -f_1 & -f_2 & \ldots & f_0 \end{pmatrix}$$

The NTRU lattice assumption is that it is a hard problem to recover polynomials f, g from h, where $h = g/f$, i.e. it is hard to obtain $\mathcal{B}_{\text{nice}}$ from $\mathcal{B}_{\text{bad}}$. The original NTRU system used the polynomial ring $\mathbb{Z}_q[x]/(x^N - 1)$, however the DLP-IBE scheme uses the NTRU distribution over the polynomial ring $\mathbb{Z}_q[x]/(x^N + 1)$, as proposed as by Stehlé and Steinfeld in 2011 [28].

2   IBE Scheme Setup

The DLP-IBE scheme was introduced in [11] as the first efficient lattice-based IBE scheme, whereby the underlying computational hardness is the NTRU and the Ring-LWE assumption. The first practical efforts towards executing the DLP-IBE scheme was a Proof-of-Concept (PoC) implementation by the original authors[2]. This implementation is written in C++ and depends on the NTL library; it also relaxes some constraints such as security thresholds for the lattice basis size. Recently, Güneysu and Oder [15] demonstrated the efficiency of the Encrypt and Decrypt components of this scheme on a range of low-cost microcontrollers and reconfigurable hardware. The research in this paper implements and examines the entire scheme in C. In particular our focus is on the computationally intensive tasks of the Key Generation and Extraction algorithms. The design includes the enforcement of the aforementioned security thresholds and, in particular, provides the first indication of practical performance of the overall scheme.

IBE schemes consist of 4 main algorithms:

Master KeyGen: generates the master secret key and the master public key. Here, the private key is an NTRU lattice basis and the public key is an identifier of that lattice, in the form of a polynomial. See Sect. 3.1.

Extract: an algorithm to generate the user secret key, given their identity. It uses the master secret key and a specified hash function to do this. See Sect. 3.2.

Encryption and Decryption: encryption is the process public clients use to encrypt a message to a user. The DLP-IBE uses the generic ring-LWE encryption scheme [18]. The encryption process uniformly samples small error polynomials to encapsulate a uniformly-sampled key, the hash of which is used to one-time-pad the message. To decrypt, the key is recovered by rounding, and this allows the message to be output. See Sect. 3.3.

Table 1 shows the inputs and outputs of each algorithm in the DLP-IBE scheme. In DLP-IBE there is an additional Gaussian sampler algorithm.

Table 1. Algorithm summary

Algorithm	Inputs	Outputs
Master KeyGen	N, q	$\mathbf{B} \in \mathbb{Z}_q^{2N \times 2N}$, $h \in \mathcal{R}_q$
Extract	$\mathbf{B} \in \mathbb{Z}_q^{2N \times 2N}$, $H : \{0,1\}^* \to \mathbb{Z}_q^N$, id	$\mathbf{SK}_{id} \in \mathcal{R}_q$
Encryption	$h \in \mathcal{R}_q$, id, $m \in \{0,1\}^m$,	$(u, v, c) \in \mathcal{R}_q^2$
	$H : \{0,1\}^* \to \mathbb{Z}_q^N$,	
	$H' : \{0,1\}^N \to \{0,1\}^m$	
Decryption	SK_{id}, $(u, v, c) \in \mathcal{R}_q^2$	$m \in \{0,1\}^N$

---

[2] https://github.com/tprest/Lattice-IBE.

2.1   Notation

Throughout the paper, we are working over the polynomial ring modulo $(x^N + 1)$ of integers modulo q, denoted $\mathcal{R}_q = \mathbb{Z}_q[x]/(x^N + 1)$. Here, N is a power of 2 and q is a prime congruent to $1 \mod 2N$. Vectors/polynomials are consider analogous and will be written as v. Matrices will denoted as $\mathbf{M}$. The lattice basis will be denoted by $\mathcal{B}$ or simply $\mathbf{B}$ depending on the context; the Gram-Schmidt Orthogonalisation denoted $\mathbf{B}_{gs}$ with basis vectors $\tilde{b}_i$. The Gaussian distribution over $\mathcal{R}_q$ with standard deviation σ is denoted $\mathcal{D}_{N,\sigma}$.

3   Software Design of the DLP-IBE Scheme

The DLP-IBE scheme is implemented in portable ANSI C. It is intended for general-purpose applications ranging from high-end 64-bit Intel Xeon servers to 32-bit ARM Cortex-M embedded systems. The design presented here focusses on 32-bit and 64-bit x86 processors in an Ubuntu/CentOS Linux environment, with options to configure client compilation on ARM v7 Cortex-A and Cortex-M target platforms. The Autotools build system is used to deliver the scheme as a library within a software distribution that can be suitably adapted to the host system at compile-time, i.e. utilising alternative algorithms for environments with constrained RAM. Additional adaptations can be configured at run-time, such as the selected underlying cryptographic functions (i.e. CSPRNG, hash), NTT optimisations, modular reduction techniques etc.

The proposed architecture considers a range of security levels to suit deployment needs, as in practice it is only possible to deploy particular levels of security on constrained devices, depending upon their capabilities, memory resources and the information being protected. For example, a battery-powered temperature sensor offering a 192-bit security strength would certainly be secure, but the reduced battery life and increased price of more capable hardware that is required are unlikely to appeal to consumers. More powerful devices within an typical IoT architecture may be able to support the full functionality of DLP-IBE, but peripheral devices may only support the much more efficient Encrypt and/or Decrypt functionality. In a standard scenario the peripheral devices could be provided with a user secret key for decryption purposes by one of three means: (a) embedded in firmware, (b) provided during device installation or (c) issued periodically by the DLP-IBE trusted authority. In such a scenario it is possible for DLP-IBE to provide public-key encryption for constrained devices.

The results have been obtained using GNU GCC 5.4.0. An Intel Core i7 6700 with both hyper-threading and TurboBoost disabled has been used, wherein the four CPUs are placed in performance mode at 4 GHz. GNU GMP 6.1.2 has been used to provide multiple precision arithmetic.

3.1   The KeyGen Algorithm

The master key generation (KeyGen) algorithm generates the master keys. This happens once per environment setup. In this scheme, the KeyGen algorithm

(Algorithm 1) requires the degree N of defining polynomials f, g, h and the modulus q and outputs the master secret key $\mathbf{B} \in \mathbb{Z}_q^{2N \times 2N}$ and master public key $h \in \mathcal{R}_q$.

Algorithm 1: Key Generation [11]

  Data: N, q
  Result: $\mathbf{B} \in \mathbb{Z}_q^{2N \times 2N}$, $h \in \mathcal{R}_q$
1 $\sigma_f = 1.17\sqrt{\frac{q}{2N}}$
2 $f, g, \leftarrow \mathcal{D}_{N,\sigma_f}$
3   Norm $\leftarrow max\left(||g, -f||, \left|\left|\left(\frac{q\bar{f}}{f*\bar{f}+g*\bar{g}}, \frac{q\bar{g}}{f*\bar{f}+g*\bar{g}}\right)\right|\right|\right)$
4   **if** $Norm > 1.17\sqrt{q}$ **then** go to Step 2;
5   Compute $\rho_f, \rho_g \in \mathcal{R}$ and $R_f, R_g \in \mathbb{Z}$ such that: $-\rho_f \cdot f = R_f$ and $-\rho_g \cdot g = R_g$
6   **if** $GCD(R_f, R_g) \neq 1$ **or** $GCD(R_f, q) \neq 1$ **then** go to Step 2;
7   Compute $u, v \in \mathbb{Z}$ such that: $u \cdot R_f + v \cdot R_g = 1$
8 $F \leftarrow qv\rho_g$ and $Q \leftarrow -qu\rho_f$
9 $k = \left\lfloor \frac{F*\bar{f}+G*\bar{g}}{f*\bar{f}+g*\bar{g}} \right\rceil \in \mathcal{R}$
10 $F \leftarrow F - k*f$ and $G \leftarrow G - k*g$
11   **return** $h = g * f^{-1}$ mod q
12   and $\mathbf{B} = \begin{pmatrix} \mathcal{A}(g) & -\mathcal{A}(f) \\ \mathcal{A}(G) & -\mathcal{A}(F) \end{pmatrix}$

In Step 1, the standard deviation of the Gaussian distribution from which f, g are generated is set to $\sigma_f = 1.17\sqrt{\frac{q}{2N}}$ and is chosen so that $E[||b_1||] = 1.17\sqrt{q}$. We have used a **CDT Sampler** in Step 2 to generate polynomials f, g from a discrete Gaussian distribution $\mathcal{D}_{N,\sigma_f}$ over $\mathcal{R}_q$. In Step 3, $||\tilde{B}_{f,g}||$, the **Gram-Schmidt Norm** of $B_{f,g}$, is computed, where $B_{f,g}$ is a basis of the NTRU lattice associated to f, g ($h = g * f^{-1}$ mod q). If $||\tilde{B}_{f,g}|| > 1.17\sqrt{q}$, the algorithm returns to Step 2 as the Gram-Schmidt Norm needs to be small enough so the basis can form a short trapdoor for sampling elements. In Step 5 the **Extended Euclidean Algorithm** is used to compute $\rho_f, \rho_g \in \mathcal{R}$ and $R_f, R_g \in \mathbb{Z}$ such that $\rho_f \cdot f = R_f$ and $\rho_g \cdot g = R_g$. If $GCD(R_f, R_g) \neq 1$ or $GCD(R_f, q) \neq 1$, the algorithm returns to Step 2. Next, the algorithm computes $u, v \in \mathbb{Z}$ such that: $u \cdot R_f + v \cdot R_g = 1$. These integers are obtained from the Extended Euclidean algorithm (this extended version keeps track of the coefficients). In step 8, $F = qv\rho_g$ and $Q = -qu\rho_f$ is computed so that $f*G - g*F = q$, a condition needed to find a short basis. Next $k = \left\lfloor \frac{F*\bar{f}+G*\bar{g}}{f*\bar{f}+g*\bar{g}} \right\rceil$ is computed and F and G are reduced: $F = F - k*f$ and $G = G - k*g$. The final steps generate and output the keys. Polynomial $h = g * f^{-1}$ mod q is the master public key and defines a lattice $\Lambda_{h,q}$. Matrix $\mathbf{B} = \begin{pmatrix} \mathcal{A}(g) & -\mathcal{A}(f) \\ \mathcal{A}(G) & -\mathcal{A}(F) \end{pmatrix}$ is the master secret key and is a short basis for $\Lambda_{h,q}$. $\mathcal{A}$ is an anti-circulant matrix defined previously in Sect. 1.2.

Key Generation is the most intensive component of the DLP-IBE scheme due to the arithmetic involving multiple-precision polynomials. The main software operations are generating the basis and multiple-precision arithmetic, using NTT and entropy coding. Optimal performance (i.e. the first f and g polynomials that are randomly selected are within bounds) is now ≈ 0.3 s slower than Prest's PoC implementation (i.e. 2.7 s vs 2.4 s). However, as the PoC was for reference purposes, it does not fully implement the f and g selection, which means that it generates keys that do not meet the security criteria and will not perform many retries for key selection if the bound thresholds are not met. The design proposed here enforces this security threshold.

Throughout the entire implementation, floating-point Barrett reduction is used with a precomputed inverse of q, i.e. multiply by the inverse of q, truncate towards zero and then multiply by q, subtracting the result from the input to obtain the remainder.

Gram-Schmidt Norm. A lattice basis can have the Gram-Schmidt process applied to it. This reduces and shifts the basis vectors in relation to each other so they become shorter and more orthogonal, yet still define the same vector space ($\mathcal{B} \rightarrow \tilde{\mathcal{B}}$ and $Span(\mathcal{B}) = Span(\tilde{\mathcal{B}})$). The Gram-Schmidt Norm is a property of the basis. It is the maximum of the norms (moduli) of the vectors in the Gram-Schmidt orthogonalisation of the basis.

$$\text{GS Norm of } \mathcal{B} = ||\tilde{\mathcal{B}}|| = \max_{i \in I} ||\tilde{b}_i||$$

The obvious way to compute the Gram-Schmidt Norm would be to compute the norms of each of the vectors and take the maximum. However, in the case of the NTRU lattices, it was proved in Sect. 3.2 of [11] that there are only two candidate vectors with the largest norm, namely b_1 and $\tilde{b}_{N+1}$ (with the vectors ordered as in the definition of **B**). Further to this, we can prove that $||\tilde{b}_{N+1}|| = \left|\left|\left(\frac{q\bar{f}}{f*\bar{f}+g*\bar{g}}, \frac{q\bar{g}}{f*\bar{f}+g*\bar{g}}\right)\right|\right|$. It is always the case that $\tilde{b}_1 = b_1$, therefore $||\tilde{b}_1|| = ||b_1||$. In this NTRU lattice basis, $b_1 = $ the top row of $(\mathcal{A}(g), -\mathcal{A}(f)) = (g, -f)$, therefore we can compute the Gram-Schmidt norm solely from f and g and form an alternative definition.

$$\text{GS Norm of } \mathcal{B} = \max_{i \in I} \left\{ ||b_1||, \left|\left|\left(\frac{q\bar{f}}{f*\bar{f}+g*\bar{g}}, \frac{q\bar{g}}{f*\bar{f}+g*\bar{g}}\right)\right|\right| \right\}$$

The Gram-Schmidt Norm computation is the first main bottleneck in the Key Generation algorithm. The b_1 norm calculation is simply placing two vectors in tandem and computing the dot product. However, the $\tilde{b}_{N+1}$ norm computation is more intensive as it involves polynomial multiplication over a ring, with polynomials coefficients being of approximately 2000–4000 bits in length. Therefore, we use the Number Theoretic Transform (NTT) to transform the polynomials into the polynomial ring of integers modulo p, meaning multiplication can be done coefficient-wise by reducing it to a negative wrapped convolution, rather than the more complex classical school-book method.

The Extended Euclidean Algorithm. The Extended Euclidean Algorithm computes the Greatest Common Divisor (GCD) of two numbers (or polynomials) x, y, and the corresponding Bezout coefficients u, v, such that $ux + vy = GCD(x, y)$. Note the "extended" version refers to the algorithm in which the coefficients are both computed and stored. The KeyGen algorithm uses two versions: one for integer inputs and one for polynomial inputs. The Extended Euclidean Algorithm for polynomials is along the same principles as the regular version for integers. The differences are that the variables are polynomials, the input polynomials are divided by their leading coefficients in order to become monic for use in the algorithm, and (the more intensive) polynomial multiplication and division is used.

Step 5 of the Algorithm 1 states that given $f, g \in \mathcal{R}$, find $\rho_f, \rho_g \in \mathcal{R}$ and $R_f, R_g \in \mathbb{Z}$ which satisfy Eqs. 1 and 2.

$$- \rho_f \cdot f = R_f \quad \mathrm{mod} \ (x^N + 1) \tag{1}$$

$$- \rho_g \cdot g = R_g \quad \mathrm{mod} \ (x^N + 1) \tag{2}$$

The Extended Euclidean Algorithm for polynomials is used twice here. The first time, it is used to find the GCD of f and $x^N + 1$. The second time, it is used to find the GCD of g and $x^N + 1$. During the computation, the algorithm holds the coefficients while calculating the GCD of two integers or polynomials. The PoC reference implementation uses the XGCD function from NTL, which selects the most suitable strategy considering polynomial properties such as coefficient bit-length and degree. Here, we have used Brown's Modular GCD for computing GCDs of multi-precision polynomials, which consists of two subroutines. First, it maps the polynomials into the bivariate polynomial ring of integers modulo q, $\mathbb{Z}_q[x, y]$, and then uses the Chinese Remainder Theorem (CRT) to compute the coefficients.

A further subroutine is required to map these polynomials from $\mathbb{Z}_q[x, y] \approx \mathbb{Z}_q[x][y]$ into $\mathbb{Z}_q[x]$, perform the GCD computation and recover the y terms using CRT. The GCD computations within the subroutines are computed using Euclid's algorithm or a variant called Half-GCD, which recursively runs halfway through the Euclidean algorithm and uses the intermediate polynomials to reduce the original ones. Equation 3 illustrates the mathematical problem in the familiar format of $ux + vy = GCD(x, y)$, where u and v are the Bezout coefficients.

$$- \rho_f \cdot f + \triangle \cdot (x^N + 1) = R_f \tag{3}$$

The $\triangle$ represents one of the Bezout coefficients computed during the Extended Euclidean Algorithm but it becomes obsolete as we apply $\mathrm{mod} \ (x^N + 1)$ to each side to obtain Eq. 4.

$$- \rho_f \cdot f = R_f \quad \mathrm{mod} \ (x^N + 1) \tag{4}$$

The useful outputs here are the other Bezout coefficient ρ_f and the greatest common divisor R_f. The second use of the algorithm is similar but for g instead of f to obtain ρ_g and R_g. Currently GMP is used to provide the multiple-precision arithmetic, but this has been segmented in the software to a collection of wrapper functions to allow it to be replaced for future optimisations within the Extended GCD, multiplication and division components.

3.2 Extract

The Extract algorithm generates the user secret key for a given user ID. This algorithm is run once per user. In this scheme, the Extract Algorithm requires the master secret key $\mathbf{B} \in \mathbb{Z}_q^{2N \times 2N}$, a public hash function $H : \{0,1\}^* \to \mathbb{Z}_q^N$ and user identity id. The user identity can be any type of data. For implementation purposes it is considered to be a MAC address, which can be expressed as a 48-bit char array. The random oracle used in the implementation is given as Algorithm 6, using SHA-3 as the hash function[3]. The Extract algorithm outputs the user secret key $\mathbf{SK}_{id} \in \mathcal{R}_q$. The first steps check if $\mathbf{SK}_{id}$ is in local storage; if so then the secret key has already been extracted for this user so we must use this one. Extracting multiple secret keys for the same user would compromise the security of the system by leaking information. If an existing key is not found, the extraction process begins. Extraction begins by hashing the user id to arrive at an integer vector t of length N. The vector t is then concatenated with a zero vector of length N to obtain a $2N$-length vector which will become the centre of the gaussian sample over the lattice. This step uses the **Gaussian Sampler** (see Sect. 7) to sample a vector from the lattice defined by $\mathbf{B}$. This vector is then subtracted from the $(t,0)$ vector to obtain (s_1, s_2) such that $s_1 + s_2 * h = t$. This equality is due to the GPV algorithm. The user secret key $\mathbf{SK}_{id}$ is set to s_2 and this is output and kept in local storage.

Algorithm 2: Extract [11]

Data: $\mathbf{B} \in \mathbb{Z}_q^{2N \times 2N}$, $H : \{0,1\}^* \to \mathbb{Z}_q^N$, id
Result: SK_{id}

1 **if** SK_{id} *is in local storage* **then**
2 $\quad\lfloor$ **return** Output SK_{id} to user id

3 **else**
4 $\quad\mid$ $t \leftarrow H(id)$;
5 $\quad\mid$ $(s_1, s_2) \leftarrow (t,0) - Gaussian(B, \sigma, (t,0))$;
6 $\quad\mid$ $SK_{id} \leftarrow s_2$;
7 $\quad\lfloor$ **return** Output SK_{id} to user id and keep in local storage

---

The software components of the Extract operation described in Algorithm 2 are expanding the basis into its matrix form, the use of the random oracle, hash

---

[3] https://github.com/mjosaarinen/tiny_sha3.

function and CSPRNG, the Gaussian Samplers over integer and the lattice and its required Gram-Schmidt Orthogonalisation, and entropy coding. The process as a whole is computationally simple but requires large memory resources. First the private keys (f, g, F, G) are used to form the polynomial basis $\mathbf{B}$ and its Gram Schmidt orthogonalisation $\mathbf{B}_{gs}$ (both $2N * 2N$ square matrices). Then the user's unique ID is converted into its public key form (a ring polynomial modulo q) using a random oracle. The proposed software architecture for this is described in Algorithm 6 and relies upon a hash function and a CSPRNG. The final and most intensive stage is obtaining the user secret key using Gaussian Sampling over a lattice.

Gram-Schmidt Orthogonalisation. A Gram-Schmidt Orthogonalised (GSO) basis of the lattice is required by the Gaussian Sampler. In order to accelerate this algorithm, our design currently uses Prest's implementation of the algorithm, which is based on improvements proposed in [20]. This uses $O(2N^2)$ floating point operations as opposed to $O(2N^3)$ of the classical algorithm, for a matrix of dimension $2N \times 2N$ and considers the isometric structure of the basis: $\{b, r(b), r^2(b), ..., r^{2N-1}(b)\}$ (the cyclic structure of the NTRU basis). The intuition behind this is that if $\tilde{b_k}$ is the GSO of b_k, then $r(\tilde{b_k})$ is the GSO of b_{k+1}. In fact, this is orthogonal to $b_2, ..., b_k$, but not b_1. It is therefore needed to reduce $r(\tilde{b_k})$ with respect to $b_1 - Proj(b_1, Span(b_2, ..., b_k))$.

Obtaining $\mathbf{B}$ and $\mathbf{B}_{gs}$ is relatively straightforward and fast. Depending upon the size of the modulus q it is possible to store B using 16-bit or 32-bit types to both reduce memory storage and improve speed (reduced memory bandwidth, fewer cache misses etc.). To reduce memory usage we have identified that storing $\mathbf{B}$ and $\mathbf{B}_{gs}$ using 32-bit floating-point types is sufficient. Our current implementation uses 32-bit floats to store both $\mathbf{B}$ and $\mathbf{B}_{gs}$ and thus for $n = 512$ we require 4 MB for each matrix. We propose that $\mathbf{B}$ could alternatively be computed on-the-fly to further reduce memory usage.

Gaussian Sampler. The Gaussian Sampling algorithm given in the paper is a variant of the GPV algorithm [14]. Originally, it was deemed impractical but this distribution of NTRU lattices, along with reducing the standard deviation by a factor of $\sqrt{2}$ due to consideration of Kullback-Leibler Divergence (see Sect. 4 of [11]), improves this. The GPV sampler returns a short lattice vector without revealing the trapdoor. It requires a 1-dimensional Gaussian sampler as a subroutine. A range of algorithms have been presented in the literature for such purposes, for example Bernoulli [12], CDT [21], Ziggurat [7] and Knuth-Yao [17]. This research deploys the CDT method for efficiency purposes. Alternative samplers could also be incorporated within this design and will be considered in future research.

The CDT method gives an efficient form of generating integers according to a Gaussian distribution by reducing the problem to a binary search on precomputed values of the cumulative distribution function. An efficient CDT sampler has been developed in [6,24]. This CDT method requires 16 kB to store the

CDF with 64-bit precision and offers constant-time sampling. A disadvantage of the GPV algorithm is the requirement to sample over varying standard deviations, requiring the re-initialisation of the Gaussian sampler $2N$ times for a ring length of N. We have identified the initialisation time of the Gaussian sampler as a performance bottleneck, and of the range of samplers available to us the CDT method was optimal in this respect. However, we have further modified the sampling scheme to improve performance by reducing the number of re-initialisations from $2N$ to 2. We achieve this by noting that the standard deviation varies insignificantly for the first and latter N samples. This is because it is scaled according to the basis vector modulus, but as this is already capped at $1.17\sqrt{q}$ during basis generation this step has negligible effect. The performance of the Gaussian Sampling algorithm can also be improved by pre-computing the inverse of the norm of the columns of $\mathbf{B}_{gs}$ for a given IBE master key, permitting division to be replaced with faster multiplication.

In terms of side-channel attacks, the Gaussian Sampling algorithm is required only for the server-side operations of Key Generation and Extract. In those applications where the server is vulnerable to physical access by an attacker the constant-time operation of the CDT limits timing analysis.

The GPV samples from a Gaussian distribution with standard deviation that is essentially the length of the Gram-Schmidt Norm. Aside from this, there are no other characteristics of the basis used which could leak information. A better quality (shorter) basis therefore means a narrower Gaussian distribution and the samples are closer to c. The algorithm is a randomised variant of Babai's Nearest Plane [4] for solving (or approaching the solution of) the CVP. Babai's algorithm inductively finds a lattice vector v close to some vector w. To do this, it solves the problem in a lower dimension; specifically, the sub-lattice (or plane) spanned by the first b_{2N-1} basis vectors. This is computed for dimension $2N$ and iterated until dimension 1, when the next "plane" is a vector. The output vectors are summed to "reverse-project" back onto the original lattice. The difference between Babai's algorithm and the GPV sampler is movement to the next plane. Whilst Babai's moves to the nearest plane in each iteration, the GPV sampler chooses the next plane with probability determined by distance to the centre point. The 1-dimensional Gaussian Sampler is used for this plane selection process.

The Gaussian Sampler requires the basis of $2N$-dimensional lattice (the master secret key) $\mathbf{B} \in \mathbb{Z}_q^{2N \times 2N}$, standard deviation $\sigma \gtrless 0$ and centre of the sample $c \in \mathbb{Z}^N$. These input parameters mean the probability of a vector v being sampled is proportional to $exp(-\pi||v - c||^2/2\sigma^2)$. The Gaussian Sampler algorithm outputs a sampled vector v in the Gaussian distribution $\mathcal{D}_{\lambda,\sigma,c}$ over the lattice. The algorithm is presented as Algorithm 3 and is as follows; it iterates through vectors $v_{2N} \rightarrow v_0$ and $c_{2N} \rightarrow c_0$. The vector v_0 is the sample vector output at the end.

To begin, v_{2N} is set to the zero vector and c_{2N} is set to the centre vector c. The algorithm then iterates through i from $i = 2N$ to 1. The projection coefficient of c_i on lower-dimensional plane is computed as $c_i' = \langle c_i, \tilde{b}_i \rangle / ||\tilde{b}_i||^2$, where $\tilde{b}_i$ is the

---

Algorithm 3: Gaussian Sampler [11]

Data: $\mathbf{B}$, $\sigma > 0$, $c \in \mathbb{Z}^n$
Result: $v \in \mathcal{D}_{\lambda,\sigma,c}$

1   $v_{2N} \leftarrow 0$
2   $c_{2N} \leftarrow 0$
3   **for** $i \leftarrow 2N, ..., 1$ **do**
4      $c_i' \leftarrow \langle c_i, \tilde{b}_i \rangle / ||\tilde{b}_i||^2$
5      $\sigma_i' \leftarrow \sigma / ||\tilde{b}_i||$
6      $z_i \leftarrow Gaussian(\sigma_i', c_i')$
7      $c_{i-1} \leftarrow c_i - z_i b_i$ and $v_{i-1} \leftarrow v_i + z_i b_i$

8   **return** v_0

Gram-Schmidt orthogonalisation of the basis vector b_i. In Step 5, the standard deviation is scaled down as $\sigma_i' = \sigma / ||\tilde{b}_i||$. Step 6 calls the Gaussian Sampler over the uniform distribution of integers for each i to obtain $z_i = Gaussian(\sigma_i', c_i')$. The next steps involve the projection of the centre and sample vector onto the next plane. The vector v_{i-1} is the closest vector to the centre in that (randomly sampled) plane: $c_{i-1} = c_i - z_i b_i$ and $v_{i-1} = v_i + z_i b_i$. Finally, at the finish of all the loops, the vector v_0 is output. For a small cost to RAM requirements it is beneficial to store the inverse of $||\tilde{b}_i||$ (see step 4 and 5 of Algorithm 3). The Gaussian Sampler requires repeated division by this norm and its squared value, the performance of which is much improved by precomputing the inverse value and replacing division with faster multiplication. The Gaussian Sampler is also initialised for each sample that must be produced when generating a user secret key; this is quite intensive and can potentially be omitted if the standard deviation does not vary between iterations of the algorithm. In this design, software acceleration of the Extract process is achieved using auto-vectorisation and more efficient use of types within the dot product and other loops in the Gaussian sampler over the lattice. Once the user secret key has been obtained it can be further compressed for storage or transmission. For this, we use Huffman coding.

3.3 Encryption and Decryption

The Encryption and Decryption algorithms of the scheme are given as Algorithms 4 and 5 respectively. These are based on the original R-LWE cryptosystem [18] and are consequently well studied and refined throughout numerous optimisations.

    The Key Generation and Extract components are server-side functions in IBE, whereas Encryption and Decryption are seen as client-side functions and could therefore be implemented in either software or hardware. Therefore we propose the hardware design of [15] could be incorporated with this software design of KeyGen and Extract to create an even faster scheme.

The software procedures needed here are the use of two random oracles $H(id)$ and $H'(k)$, and for each of these, a hash function and CSPRNG are needed. NTT and entropy coding is utilised again.

Algorithm 4: Encrypt [11]

    Data: h, id, m, H, H'.
    Result: (u, v, c)
1   $r, e_1, e_2 \leftarrow \{-1, 0, 1\}^N$, $k \leftarrow \{0, 1\}$;
2   $t \leftarrow H(id)$;
3   $u \leftarrow r * h + e_1 \in \mathcal{R}_q$;
4   $v \leftarrow r * t + e_2 + \lfloor q/2 \rfloor$;
5   Drop the least significant bits of $v : v \leftarrow 2^l \lfloor v/2^l \rfloor$;
6   **return** $(u, v, m \oplus H'(k))$

Algorithm 5: Decrypt [11]

    Data: SK_{id}, (u, v, c)
    Result: $m \in \{0, 1\}^m$
1   $w \leftarrow v - u * s_2$;
2   $k \leftarrow \lfloor \frac{w}{q/2} \rfloor$;
3   **return** $m \leftarrow c \oplus H'(k)$

Encrypt requires two NTT's and two inverse NTT's in order to efficiently perform a number of ring modular multiplications (for smaller moduli, sparse multiplication can be used), while Decrypt requires only a single NTT and inverse NTT. As the master public key and user secret key are repeatedly used for this purpose their NTT representation is precomputed to reduce complexity at the expense of additional storage. Additionally, the Encrypt operation requires two Random Oracles ($H(id)$ and $H'(k)$) while Decrypt requires one ($H'(k)$). How this operation is constructed is not specified in the original work and is implementation dependent. In Algorithm 6 we describe our method for mapping an arbitrary length user ID into a ring polynomial and in Algorithm 7 we describe a similar process where a random bit string is used to generate a one-time pad. These mapping processes both use the hash function SHA-3 and a NIST AES CTR-DRBG. Encrypt benefits greatly from sparse multiplication when calculating $e_3 * h$ and $e_3 * H(id)$ when q is less than 26 bits, but requires less efficient and aggressive NTT multiplication with larger moduli. Decryption is reliable with NTT with less aggressive reduction when q is less than 26 bits, otherwise the more aggressive and costly version needs to be used, as in Encrypt. Additionally, the proposed architecture of Encrypt and Decrypt has been modified to support any length m of the message instead of specifically N bits, at the cost of performance, but it is envisaged that the increased flexibility is more suitable for full scale testing of the practicality of the scheme.

Algorithm 6: Random Oracle H(id) - convert the ID into a unique polynomial

Data: id, N, q
Result: $t \in \mathcal{R}_q$
1 $s \leftarrow H(id)$
2 $t \leftarrow \text{CSRNG}(s) \in \mathbb{Z}_q^N$
3 **return** t

Algorithm 7: Random Oracle $H'(k)$ - create a byte stream to use as a one-time pad

Data: k, N, q
Result: $t \in \{0,1\}^m$
1 $s \leftarrow H'(k)$
2 $t \leftarrow \text{CSRNG}(s) \in \{0,1\}^m$
3 **return** t

3.4   Parameters

One of the main problems surrounding lattice-based cryptography is choosing secure yet efficient parameters. This is due to constantly evolving attacks and the use of bounds rather than concrete estimates in their analysis. The original authors suggest parameters in [11] and these are given in Table 2. The security levels of these parameters are estimated in [11] by considering both key recovery and ciphertext attacks. The encryption component of the scheme is the most vulnerable, so the security level estimations depend on the strongest attack known to recover the small errors e_1 and e_2, which is estimated to reach a root Hermite factor of $\gamma = 1.0075$ for $N = 512$ and $\gamma = 1.0044$ for $N = 1024$. However, due to the use of the NTT in this implementation, the value of N has been changed. To apply the NTT, an $2N^{th}$ root of unity has to be found. We also need the condition $q = 1 \mod 2N$ to be satisfied in order to compute the negative wrapped convolution. Therefore, one of the contributions of this design is the proposal of new parameter sets, given in Table 3. We include a parameter l from the Encryption algorithm, which corresponds to the truncation of the ciphertext vector v. The security level is estimated from the root Hermite factor γ introduced in 2008 [13], which measures the hardness of the underlying lattice problem. For $\gamma \approx 1.004$, we can estimate 80-bit security and for $\gamma < 1.007$, we can estimate 192-bit security. The bit size information for the selected parameter sets is set out in Table 4. Compression uses Huffman coding throughout. The master public key cannot be compressed as the nature of the NTRU assumption requires it to appear random.

3.5   Results

Figures obtained on an Intel Core i7-6700 CPU at 4.0 GHz are shown in Table 5. This design precomputes $\mathbf{B}$, $\mathbf{B}_{gs}$, the inverse of $||\mathbf{B}_{gs}||$ and the NTT representa-

Table 2. IBE scheme original parameters

Security parameter	80-bit	192-bit
Polynomial degree N	512	1024
Modulus q	2^{23} or 2^{24}	2^{27}

Table 3. Proposed IBE scheme parameters

Parameter set	Root hermite factor	Security level	q	q in bits	N	l	$2N^{th}$ root of unity
0	1.0075	80	5767169	23	512	19	971
1	1.0079	80	10223617	24	512	20	3981
2	1.0085	<80	51750913	26	512	23	115658
3	1.0038	192	5767169	23	1024	18	19484
4	1.0039	192	10223617	24	1024	20	6877
5	1.0043	<192	51750913	26	1024	22	36945

tions of the public master key and the user secret key. The random oracles use the SHA-3 hash function and the AES CTR-DRBG random number generator. A CDT Gaussian Sampler is used to randomly sample over the lattices. It should be noted that this performs all necessary tasks and does not require any offline computation. As the Key Generation is only run once per scheme setup, the time in seconds for one run-through is given. The remaining components are called multiple times (Extract once per user, Encrypt/Decrypt once per message) and so we give the number of times each can be run per second. Extract I refers to the original Extract function, while Extract II utilises compression techniques.

For reference, we now give comparable figures from Prest's NTL-based implementation in Table 6 (scaled up to account for differences in CPU). Prest's results were given in ms on an Intel Core i5-3210M laptop with 2.5 GHz CPU and 6GB RAM so we have converted to "per second" to represent how they would look like on our 4 GHz platform: For example, $8.6\,ms = 0.0086\,s$, which means 116.28 per sec at 2.5 GHz, which is equivalent to $116.38/2.5 * 4 = 186.04$ per sec at 4 GHz. We compare Prest's 80-bit and 192-bit security results to our parameter sets 2 and 5 respectively, without compression. It can be seen that the proposed software architecture outperforms the original PoC in all respects, for example for $N = 512, q = 2^{24}$ (or 80-bit security) with NTL, the Extract function can be

Table 4. DLP IBE key and encrypted message bit sizes. All figures are in bits.

Parameter set	Message length	Master public key	Master private key		User secret key		Message
			Uncoded	Compressed	Uncoded	Compressed	
0	512	11776	27648	23650	9216	7576	14336
1	512	12288	27648	23779	9216	7807	14848
2	512	13312	29696	25908	9728	8528	15360
3	1024	23552	51200	43834	17408	15522	29696
4	1024	24576	51200	44161	17408	15702	29696
5	1024	26624	59392	51458	19456	17614	31744

Table 5. DLP IBE performance in terms of KeyGen processing time in seconds and Extract, Encrypt and Verify operations per second on an Intel Core i7 6700 @ 4 GHz with SHA-3, CDT Gaussian Sampling and AES CTR-DRBG

Parameter Set	q	N	KeyGen	Extract I	Extract II	Encrypt	Decrypt
0	5767169	512	2.666	544	521	9726	33070
1	10223617	512	2.74	541	526	9753	33359
2	51750913	512	4.034	537	527	9390	22489
3	5767169	1024	16.860	138	135	4179	17493
4	10223617	1024	23.004	137	133	3854	17568
5	51750913	1024	25.126	137	134	3598	11526

run almost three times as many per second, and the Encrypt/Decrypt over x5 and x12 times respectively. Note that the Master KeyGen timings are not specified here, but as this is only run once per scheme set-up it can be temporarily disregarded.

Table 6. Prest's NTL implementation results comparison, operations per sec

Security level	Extract		Encrypt		Decrypt	
	This work	Prest	This work	Prest	This work	Prest
80-bit	537	186	9725	1758	33070	2580
192-bit	137	49	3598	856	11526	1260

In comparison to classical IBE schemes, the DLP lattice-based IBE scheme also has respectable performance. In 2011, performance testing of the Boneh-Franklin IBE scheme [8] on a Pentium Dual T2330 at 1.60 GHz reported that Extraction could be run at 170.6 ops/s, Encrypt at 1.08 op/s and Decrypt at 1.26 op/s. Therefore, this research shows that replacing current schemes with post-quantum schemes will improve security without impacting efficiency.

4 Conclusions and Further Research

The research presented here demonstrates how a lattice-based IBE scheme performs on software. It can be used as a benchmark for further improvements within the scheme and provides a starting point for further investigation. We have proposed the first working, efficient C implementation of the DLP-IBE scheme with a range of novel software optimisations to enhance performance and have discovered many areas for potential optimisations for a range of targeted devices. The future aim is to consider suitable client-side optimisations for a range of constrained devices, such as those likely to be encountered in IoT, as well as a range of server-side optimisations, such as GPU and multithreading. We intend to carry out a full performance testing of several aspects of the scheme. The Gaussian Sampler is a main bottleneck of the scheme. There is scope to investigate other variants of the GPV sampler, by computing the memory-heavy Gram-Schmidt orthogonalisation on the fly or further acceleration by properties of the NTRU basis structure. We also intend to test different hash functions and Extended Euclidean Algorithms to evaluate the effect on the scheme. Lastly, but perhaps most importantly, is the choice of parameters for the scheme. Currently, we consider 80-bit and 192-bit security levels but it could be insightful to test parameter sets for higher security and determine how they would fare on small devices.

Additionally, the implementation of the scheme opens up other applications for investigation and further research. A hash-and-sign digital signature scheme can use the components of the IBE scheme in a different way. The public verification key corresponds to the master public key, the secret signing key corresponds to the master secret key, messages replace user IDs and signatures replace user secret keys. Secondly, an Authenticated Key Exchange (AKE) scheme can be constructed. This consists of a Key Encapsulation Mechanism (KEM) together with a digital signature scheme. Therefore we can use Pino et al. [22] KEM (based on NTRU) with this digital signature scheme to form a AKE scheme. Both these additional schemes offer the hardness properties and quantum-resilience of lattice-based primitives.

Acknowledgements. The authors would like to thank the anonymous reviewers of SAC 2017 and IMACC 2017 for their careful reading of the paper and their diligent comments. The authors would also like to acknowledge that this work was partially funded by the European Union H2020 SAFEcrypto project (grant no. 644729).

References

1. Agrawal, S., Boneh, D., Boyen, X.: Efficient lattice (H)IBE in the standard model. In: Gilbert, H. (ed.) EUROCRYPT 2010. LNCS, vol. 6110, pp. 553–572. Springer, Heidelberg (2010). https://doi.org/10.1007/978-3-642-13190-5_28
2. Ajtai, M., Dwork, C.: A public-key cryptosystem with worst-case/average-case equivalence. In: Proceedings of the Twenty-Ninth Annual ACM Symposium on Theory of Computing, STOC 1997, pp. 284–293 (1997)
3. Apon, D., Fan, X., Liu, F.H.: Compact identity based encryption from LWE. IACR Cryptology ePrint Archive (2016)
4. Babai, L.: On Lovasz lattice reduction and the nearest lattice point problem. Combinatorica **6**(1), 1–13 (1986)
5. Boneh, D., Franklin, M.: Identity-based encryption from the weil pairing. In: Kilian, J. (ed.) CRYPTO 2001. LNCS, vol. 2139, pp. 213–229. Springer, Heidelberg (2001). https://doi.org/10.1007/3-540-44647-8_13
6. Brannigan, S., Smyth, N., Oder, T., Valencia, F., O'Sullivan, E., Güneysu, T., Regazzoni, F.: An investigation of sources of randomness within discrete Gaussian sampling. Cryptology ePrint Archive, Report 2017/298 (2017). http://eprint.iacr.org/2017/298

7. Buchmann, J., Cabarcas, D., Göpfert, F., Hülsing, A., Weiden, P.: Discrete Ziggurat: a time-memory trade-off for sampling from a gaussian distribution over the integers. In: Lange, T., Lauter, K., Lisoněk, P. (eds.) SAC 2013. LNCS, vol. 8282, pp. 402–417. Springer, Heidelberg (2014). https://doi.org/10.1007/978-3-662-43414-7_20

8. Cheng, P., Gu, Y., Lv, Z., Wang, J., Zhu, W., Chen, Z., Huang, J.: A performance analysis of identity-based encryption schemes. In: Chen, L., Yung, M., Zhu, L. (eds.) INTRUST 2011. LNCS, vol. 7222, pp. 289–303. Springer, Heidelberg (2012). https://doi.org/10.1007/978-3-642-32298-3_19

9. Chillotti, I., Gama, N., Georgieva, M., Izabachène, M.: A homomorphic LWE based e-voting scheme. In: Takagi, T. (ed.) PQCrypto 2016. LNCS, vol. 9606, pp. 245–265. Springer, Cham (2016). https://doi.org/10.1007/978-3-319-29360-8_16

10. Cocks, C.: An identity based encryption scheme based on quadratic residues. In: Honary, B. (ed.) Cryptography and Coding 2001. LNCS, vol. 2260, pp. 360–363. Springer, Heidelberg (2001). https://doi.org/10.1007/3-540-45325-3_32

11. Ducas, L., Lyubashevsky, V., Prest, T.: Efficient Identity-Based Encryption over NTRU Lattices. In: Sarkar, P., Iwata, T. (eds.) ASIACRYPT 2014, Part II. LNCS, vol. 8874, pp. 22–41. Springer, Heidelberg (2014). https://doi.org/10.1007/978-3-662-45608-8_2

12. Ducas, L., Durmus, A., Lepoint, T., Lyubashevsky, V.: Lattice signatures and bimodal gaussians. In: Canetti, R., Garay, J.A. (eds.) CRYPTO 2013, Part I. LNCS, vol. 8042, pp. 40–56. Springer, Heidelberg (2013). https://doi.org/10.1007/978-3-642-40041-4_3

13. Gama, N., Nguyen, P.Q.: Predicting lattice reduction. In: Smart, N. (ed.) EUROCRYPT 2008. LNCS, vol. 4965, pp. 31–51. Springer, Heidelberg (2008). https://doi.org/10.1007/978-3-540-78967-3_3

14. Gentry, C., Peikert, C., Vaikuntanathan, V.: Trapdoors for hard lattices and new cryptographic constructions (2007). http://eprint.iacr.org/

15. Gúneysu, T., Oder, T.: Towards lightweight identity-based encryption for the post-quantum-secure internet of things. In: 2017 18th International Symposium on Quality Electronic Design (ISQED), pp. 319–324 (2017). iD: 1

16. Katsumata, S., Yamada, S.: Partitioning via non-linear polynomial functions: more compact IBEs from ideal lattices and bilinear maps. In: Cheon, J.H., Takagi, T. (eds.) ASIACRYPT 2016, Part II. LNCS, vol. 10032, pp. 682–712. Springer, Heidelberg (2016). https://doi.org/10.1007/978-3-662-53890-6_23

17. Knuth, D.E., Yao, A.C.: The complexity of nonuniform random number generation. In: Algorithms and Complexity: New Directions and Recent Results, pp. 357–428 (1976)

18. Lyubashevsky, V., Peikert, C., Regev, O.: On ideal lattices and learning with errors over rings. J. ACM (JACM) 60(6), 43:1–43:35 (2013)

19. Lyubashevsky, V.: Lattice signatures without trapdoors. In: Pointcheval, D., Johansson, T. (eds.) EUROCRYPT 2012. LNCS, vol. 7237, pp. 738–755. Springer, Heidelberg (2012). https://doi.org/10.1007/978-3-642-29011-4_43

20. Lyubashevsky, V., Prest, T.: Quadratic time, linear space algorithms for gram-schmidt orthogonalization and gaussian sampling in structured lattices. In: Oswald, E., Fischlin, M. (eds.) EUROCRYPT 2015, Part I. LNCS, vol. 9056, pp. 789–815. Springer, Heidelberg (2015). https://doi.org/10.1007/978-3-662-46800-5_30

21. Peikert, C.: An efficient and parallel gaussian sampler for lattices. In: Rabin, T. (ed.) CRYPTO 2010. LNCS, vol. 6223, pp. 80–97. Springer, Heidelberg (2010). https://doi.org/10.1007/978-3-642-14623-7_5

246   S. McCarthy et al.

22. del Pino, R., Lyubashevsky, V., Pointcheval, D.: The whole is less than the sum of its parts: constructing more efficient lattice-based AKEs. In: Zikas, V., De Prisco, R. (eds.) SCN 2016. LNCS, vol. 9841, pp. 273–291. Springer, Cham (2016). https://doi.org/10.1007/978-3-319-44618-9_15
23. Regev, O.: On lattices, learning with errors, random linear codes, and cryptography. J. ACM (JACM) **56**(6), 34:1–34:40 (2009)
24. Saarinen, M.J.O.: Arithmetic coding and blinding countermeasures for lattice signatures. Cryptology ePrint Archive, Report 2016/276 (2016). http://eprint.iacr.org/2016/276
25. Sakai, R., Kasahara, M.: ID based cryptosystems with pairing on elliptic curve. IACR Cryptology ePrint Archive 2003, 54 (2003)
26. Shamir, A.: Identity-based cryptosystems and signature schemes. In: Blakley, G.R., Chaum, D. (eds.) CRYPTO 1984. LNCS, vol. 196, pp. 47–53. Springer, Heidelberg (1985). https://doi.org/10.1007/3-540-39568-7_5
27. Shor, P.W.: Polynomial-time algorithms for prime factorization and discrete logarithms on a quantum computer. SIAM Rev. **41**(2), 303–332 (1999)
28. Stehlé, D., Steinfeld, R.: Making NTRU as secure as worst-case problems over ideal lattices. In: Paterson, K.G. (ed.) EUROCRYPT 2011. LNCS, vol. 6632, pp. 27–47. Springer, Heidelberg (2011). https://doi.org/10.1007/978-3-642-20465-4_4
29. Yamada, S.: Adaptively secure identity-based encryption from lattices with asymptotically shorter public parameters. In: Fischlin, M., Coron, J.-S. (eds.) EUROCRYPT 2016, Part II. LNCS, vol. 9666, pp. 32–62. Springer, Heidelberg (2016). https://doi.org/10.1007/978-3-662-49896-5_2

A Note on the Implementation of the Number Theoretic Transform

Michael Scott[(✉)]

MIRACL.com, Trim, County Meath, Ireland
mike.scott@miracl.com

Abstract. The Number Theoretic Transform (NTT) is a time critical function required by many post-quantum cryptographic protocols based on lattices. For example it is commonly used in the context of the Ring Learning With Errors problem (RLWE), which is a popular basis for post-quantum key exchange, digital signature, and encryption. Here we apply a simple methodology to convert the NTT and its inverse from a mathematically correct (but side-channel vulnerable) description, to an efficient constant-time and side-channel resistant version.

1 Introduction

Often important cryptographic functions are described in the literature without consideration for side-channel vulnerability. Then they are implemented by competent software engineers who produce functionally correct and efficient real-world implementations, unfortunately without eliminating the side-channels. The result is that many widely used cryptographic libraries contain side-channel weaknesses, that are just awaiting a determined attacker. For a recent example see [5].

What is needed is an intermediate version of the function which is side-channel resistant, from which the engineer can go on to produce their real-world implementation. The purpose of this paper is to describe an easy to follow step-by-step methodology which converts that which is mathematically correct, to a constant-time side-channel resistant version with the same functionality. Note that while claiming that our implementation is immune to timing attacks (to the extent that this is achievable in software), we are merely claiming that it is "resistant" to more general side-channel attacks, on the basis that some side-channel weaknesses may not be currently known.

Our particular context is modular arithmetic, that is arithmetic with respect to a prime modulus q. Modular arithmetic is widely used as the basis for many techniques of public key cryptography. Unfortunately it is notoriously hard to implement in constant time, and has been a prime source of side-channel leakage.

In an earlier paper [12] we developed a methodology which we applied to vulnerable functions in the context of elliptic curve cryptography. Here we turn our attention to the NTT transform function (and its inverse), as used by protocols based on the post-quantum Ring Learning with Errors (RLWE) problem.

© Springer International Publishing AG 2017
M. O'Neill (Ed.): IMACC 2017, LNCS 10655, pp. 247–258, 2017.
https://doi.org/10.1007/978-3-319-71045-7_13

2   The Methodology

Our starting point is a mathematically correct implementation of the function, which is "exception-free". This is a higher-level requirement for side-channel resistance and for the possibility of a constant time implementation. Basically it means that at the level above the modular arithmetic there is only a single path through the code, independent of the data it is processing. Fortunately "exception-free" algorithms are commonly available.

Starting with an implementation of such a function, proceed as follows. First identify a modular reduction algorithm that works well with the given prime modulus q. This modular reduction function must operate in constant time, but it is not required to fully reduce its output to be less than q. It is sufficient that the reduction is to a value less that $E.q$, where E is a small positive integer constant. In general it has been observed [8] that such a partial reduction is often easier to achieve than a full reduction, given the constant time constraint. It must also be capable of handling an input significantly greater than q^2, as its input may be a product of two values that are not themselves fully reduced. For example the well-known Montgomery modular reduction algorithm reduces an input less than qR (where R can be significantly greater than q) to a value less than $2q$ [10].

We note in passing that the often suggested alternative reduction method due to Barret [4] does not meet these conditions. Next

- Associate with every finite field element x an "excess" E_x which tracks the extent to which its value may exceed q in the absence of any reduction, under worst case assumptions. So we know that the unreduced $x < E_x.q$. Input values might be assumed to be fully reduced, in which case they can be initialised to have an excess of 1.
- For modular additions, note that for $z = x + y$, then $E_z = E_x + E_y$, and update and record excesses accordingly.
- Consider all modular subtractions as negation followed by addition, and observe that negation calculated as $-x = E_x.q - x$ will not affect the excess of x.
- For modular multiplications, note that for $z = x.y$, then $E_z = E_x.E_y$ that is the product of the excesses of the inputs, and record a worst-case size of the product $E_z.q^2$ which is to undergo reduction. Set the excess of the output to E.

Next execute the program once. Note that as a consequence of being exception-free, there will be only one path through the code, and so excesses recorded as described above will be invariant irrespective of the actual data being processed.

Now, using these recorded excesses, choose a representation of field elements that (a) would not overflow if modular addition were to be replaced with non-modular addition, and (b) could not under worst case assumptions cause an input to the modular reduction algorithm which would violate its conditions for correct operation. The transcript of the excesses provides a proof that integer overflow cannot occur. Next

- Replace all modular additions, with simple non-modular additions.
- Replace all modular subtractions with negation followed by addition, where $-x = E_x.q - x$
- Perform modular multiplications with a simple non-modular multiplication, followed by our modular reduction algorithm.

Note that for modular negation, it appears to be necessary to continue to track excesses. So as a final step, either replace the excesses with the fixed values that apply for each individual occurence, or identify a single worst-case value that can be applied in all cases. Assuming this is possible, excesses have now served their purpose, and can be eliminated from the code. We also note that some post-processing might be required to fully reduce the final outputs of the function (if this is required).

3   The NTT

The NTT is basically a form of Discrete Fast Fourier transformation. Once a pair of polynomials is transformed to the "frequency" domain, their product can be calculated by a simple $\mathcal{O}(n)$ element-by-element product, and the result converted back via the inverse transformation (INTT). Therefore the dominant cost of polynomial multiplication, is the cost of the transformation to and from the frequency domain. Hence the significance of the NTT, which has a complexity of just $\mathcal{O}(n \log n)$.

Now when using Fast Fourier methods to determine the product of two polynomials of degree n, this normally requires them to be first padded to length $2n$. However in the RLWE setting we get around this problem by manipulating our polynomials modulo $x^n + 1$, and using the negative wrapped convolution.

The fixed system parameters for a typical instance of the Ring Learning with Errors problem consist of a prime modulus q and polynomials of degree n where $n = 2^m$, and with coefficients $\in \mathbb{F}_q$. In most cases the prime modulus q is selected such that $q = 1 \mod 2n$, so that the $2n$-th roots of unity exist and can be precalculated. Typical choices might be $q = 12289$, and $n = 1024$, as used in the NewHope proposal [2], in which case a 2048-th root of unity would be 9089, and it is easily confirmed that $9089^{2048} = 1 \mod 12289$. To implement the NTT we will need to precompute a vector of the first n powers of such a root, but stored in bit reverse order. So given a root g, while the natural ordering of its powers would be $[g^0, g^1, g^2, \dots g^{n-1}]$, in bit reverse order the element g^i would actually be stored at an index in the table found by reversing the m bits in i.

Our starting point is the basic NTT algorithm and its inverse, based on its description by Naehrig and Longa [9], which integrates many prior optimizations. A key idea is to use the Cooley Tukey butterfly for the forward transformation, but to switch to the Gentleman-Sande butterfly for the inverse operation. See Algorithms 1 and 2.

Algorithm 1. The Cooley-Tukey NTT algorithm

INPUT: A vector $\boldsymbol{x} = [x_0, \ldots, x_{n-1}]$ where $x_i \in [0, p-1]$ of degree n (a power of 2) and modulus $q = 1 \bmod 2n$
INPUT: Precomputed table of $2n$-th roots of unity $\boldsymbol{g}$, in bit reversed order
OUTPUT: $\boldsymbol{x} \leftarrow NTT(\boldsymbol{x})$

```
 1: function NTT(x)
 2:     t ← n/2
 3:     m ← 1
 4:     while m < n do
 5:         k ← 0
 6:         for i ← 0; i < m; i ← i + 1 do
 7:             S ← g[m + i]
 8:             for j ← k; j < k + t; j ← j + 1 do
```

$$U \leftarrow x[j]$$
$$V \leftarrow x[j+t].S \bmod q$$
$$x[j] \leftarrow U + V \bmod q$$
$$x[j+t] \leftarrow U - V \bmod q$$

```
13:             k ← k + 2t
14:         t ← t/2
15:         m ← 2m
16:     return
```

Algorithm 2. The Gentleman-Sande inverse INTT algorithm

INPUT: A vector $\boldsymbol{x} = [x_0, \ldots, x_{n-1}]$ where $x_i \in [0, p-1]$ of degree n (a power of 2) and modulus $q = 1 \bmod 2n$
INPUT: Precomputed table of inverses of $2n$-th roots of unity $\boldsymbol{g}^{-1}$, in bit reversed order
INPUT: $n^{-1} \bmod q$
OUTPUT: $\boldsymbol{x} \leftarrow INTT(\boldsymbol{x})$

```
 1: function INTT(x)
 2:     t ← 1
 3:     m ← n/2
 4:     while m > 0 do
 5:         k ← 0
 6:         for i ← 0; i < m; i ← i + 1 do
 7:             S ← g⁻¹[m + i]
 8:             for j ← k; j < k + t; j ← j + 1 do
```

$$U \leftarrow x[j]$$
$$V \leftarrow x[j+t]$$
$$x[j] \leftarrow U + V \bmod q$$
$$W \leftarrow U - V \bmod q$$
$$x[j+t] \leftarrow W.S \bmod q$$

```
14:             k ← k + 2t
15:         t ← 2t
16:         m ← m/2
17:     for i ← 0; i < n; i ← i + 1 do
18:         x[i] ← x[i].n⁻¹ mod q
19:     return
```

Our ultimate aim is to eliminate the side channel leakage from the modular arithmetic, that is from those clearly indicated calculations that take place modulo q. One clever optimization that is not shown here, but which we will make use of in all of our implementations, is to merge the last iteration of the main INTT loop with the multiplication of each element of its output by $n^{-1} \bmod q$, which saves $n/2$ modular multiplications. See [9] for details.

3.1   A Naïve Solution

An initial reaction might be that surely we could simply replace modulo q everywhere with %q, and let the processor's built in integer division/remainder instruction take care of it.

But this is a very unsatisfactory solution for a number of reasons. Firstly integer remaindering is not the same as modular reduction, and commonly requires conditional corrections to keep results in range. More importantly integer division is complex to implement in hardware, is rarely a bottleneck calculation in most computer applications, and therefore is not heavily optimized and is thus very slow, and of particular relevance to us, most often not implemented in constant time [6]. That is takes a number of clock cycles that is dependent on the data being processed. Nevertheless this makes a good starting point from which to calculate and record excesses, and to develop better solutions.

We focus on the "butterfly" code in the innermost loops of the NTT and INTT algorithms. Once we move from an algorithmic description to actual code, we need to become aware of the possibility of integer overflow. We will assume two signed integer data types, which we will refer to as int_t and int_dt (wordlength and double-wordlength), where the actual wordlength WL might be 16, 32 or 64 bits. In the C programming language on a 32-bit computer these types might be int32_t and int64_t respectively. We refer to their unsigned equivalents as uint_t and uint_dt. For a particular implementation we assume that the modulus q is globally visible.

Of course polynomials might be transported and stored using a smaller data type, if the modulus q is small. For example the commonly suggested 14-bit prime 12289 will fit comfortably in a 16-bit type irrespective of the wordlength of the processor.

Listing 1.1. Naïve Modular multiplication

```
int_t  modmul( int_t  a , int_t  b)
{
        return  ( int_t ) ((( int_dt ) a*b)%q);
}
```

Listing 1.2. Naïve method for NTT

```
U=x [ j ];
V=modmul(x [ j+t ] , S );
x [ j ] = (U+V)%q;
x [ j+t ] = (U+q-V)%q;
```

Listing 1.3. Naïve method for INTT

```
U=x [ j ];
V=x [ j+t ];
x [ j ] = (U+V)%q;
W=(U+q-V);
x [ j+t ]=modmul(W, S );
```

It becomes immediately obvious that our ability of optimize the code will depend on the extent of the allowable excess that exists, which will allow intermediate values in the butterfly computation to increase outside of the rigid range $0 \rightarrow q$, without overflow. For the above code to function correctly it is already assumed that calculating $U+V$ in Listing 1.3 does not cause an overflow. We will initially assume a signed type of a length at least 2 bits bigger than the prime modulus. Making immediate use of this latitude, observe that in the INTT case we can calculate W without reduction modulo q.

3.2   A Constant Time Solution

However this is not a constant-time solution, and its slow. We need an alternative technique, and Montgomery's method for modular multiplication without division [10], which replaces division by some multiplications, is ideal, widely used in this context, and generically applicable. Note that integer multiplication, unlike division, is heavily optimized for most processors, and usually executes in a fixed number of clock cycles independent of the data being processed, often just 1 or 2. So we can anticipate that such an implementation might even be faster. One downside to Montgomery's method is that we need to convert field elements to and from Montgomery representation before the NTT and after INTT functions. An obvious optimization is to precompute the tables of roots of unity and their inverses in Montgomery format.

The Montgomery method assumes the choice of an alternate modulus R greater than q, which is a simple power of 2, the idea being to replace the modulo q calculation with a much simpler reduction modulo R. For maximum efficiency it is common to choose R to be 2 to the power of the wordlength, and this is what we will use here. The method also requires the precomputed constant $N = 1/(R - q) \bmod R$.

Montgomery's method introduces a modular reduction function redc which reduces an input T to a positive integer t less than $2q$, assuming that $T < qR$. Therefore reduction is not complete. However a simple constant-time augmentation can complete the reduction. Subtract q from t and do an arithmetic shift right by one less than the bitlength of the signed type used for t. If $t - q < 0$ this results in all ones, otherwise all zeros. Perform a logical AND of this bit pattern with q and add it back into t.

Note the condition on the input to redc that it be less than qR. Since in this context one of the inputs is from a precomputed table, and hence less than q, it merely suffices that the other is less than R and is representable as an int_t.

The conversion of x to Montgomery form can be computed by applying the redc function to the product of x and the precomputed constant $R^2 \bmod q$. The conversion back to "normal" form is simply an application of redc [10].

Listing 1.4. redc function with full reduction

```
int_t redc(int_dt T)
{
    uint_t m=(uint_t)T*N;
    int_t V=((uint_dt)m*q+T)>>WL;
    V-=q; V+=(V>>(WL-1))&q;
    return V;
}
```

Listing 1.5. Modular multiplication

```
int_t modmul(int_t a,int_t b)
{
    return redc((int_dt)a*b);
}
```

Listing 1.6. Constant Time method NTT

```
U=x[j];
V=modmul(x[j+t],S);
W=U+V-q;
x[j]=W+((W>>(WL-1))&q);
W=U-V;
x[j+t]=W+((W>>(WL-1))&q);
```

Listing 1.7. Constant Time method INTT

```
U=x[j];
V=x[j+t];
W=U+V-q;
x[j]=W+((W>>(WL-1))&q);
W=U+q-V;
x[j+t]=modmul(W,S);
```

3.3 Lazy Reduction

Next we apply our proposed methodology to make maximum use of delayed reductions. Ideally we will succeed in removing all of the reduction code, other than that implicit in the basic un-augmented redc function. We would expect our ability to achieve this to depend on the detail of the NTT and INTT algorithms, and on the number of excess bits available to us, which will facilitate delayed reduction.

We make a minor change from the description of our methodology above. Since our conversion to Montgomery form now uses the un-augmented redc function, we will assume initial excesses of 2 rather than 1. However we still assume that precomputed values such as the roots of unity are fully reduced.

One immediate and striking observation is that the Cooley-Tukey NTT and Gentleman-Sande INTT butterflies behave very differently. As the iterations progress the excesses get bigger. But whereas the Cooley-Tukey excesses increase only slowly and linearly, the Gentleman-Sande worst case excesses grow much more rapidly.

First examine the Cooley-Tukey butterfly. Observe that x values are incremented by the output of the a modular multiplication, which will have a maximum excess of 2. So the new excesses will be at most 2 bigger than an existing excess. But for the Gentleman-Sande butterfly certain x values may have their excesses doubled by the execution of the equivalent of x[j]=x[j]+x[j+t] in listing 1.10. And this is what we observe.

Recall that there are two places where integer overflow might occur due to excessive excesses, after addition and before modular multiplication. Experimentally we determine that, for polynomials of degree n, for the NTT (based on Cooley-Tukey) the maximum excess is $2. \lg n + 2$, and for the INTT (based on Gentleman-Sande) the maximum excess is $2n$.

Assuming for the moment that these excesses can be accomodated, we can replace the constant time code with the following. Observe that all explicit modular reduction code has been removed. In the case of INTT the worst-case excess for V, which is just the polynomial degree n, is used in the calculation of W in listing 1.10, and so explicit use of the excesses is not required. Obviously $2q$ and nq can be precalculated.

Listing 1.8. redc function incomplete reduction

```
int_t redc(int_dt T)
{
        uint_t m=(uint_t)T*N;
        int_t V=(int_t)(((uint_dt)m*q+T)>>WL);
        return V;
}
```

Listing 1.9. Lazy Reduction method for NTT

```
U=x[j];
V=modmul(x[j+t],S);
x[j]=U+V;
x[j+t]=U+2*q-V;
```

Listing 1.10. Lazy Reduction method for INTT

```
U=x[j];
V=x[j+t];
x[j]=U+V;
W=U+n*q-V;
x[j+t]=modmul(W,S);
```

Finally we need to consider the conditions under which the excesses that might arise, can be safely accomodated. Since the worst case arises for the INTT butterfly, this code will work correctly as long as $2nq$ can be represented in the int_t type. For example on a 32-bit processor, the C language type int32_t can comfortably handle the case of $q = 12289$ and $n = 1024$. However for larger values of q we can expect problems to arise. For example consider the parameters chosen by Güneysu et al. [7], where $q = 8383489$ and $n = 512$. This will cause a problem for our INTT code on a 32-bit processor.

However from our analysis we know exactly where the worst case excesses occur, and so we can compensate for it. By inserting extra reduction code at the appropriate point in the INTT function, it has the effect of suppressing the excesses. Note that reduction of any value can be achieved at any time by multiplying it by the Montgomery representation of unity ($O = R \mod q$). When extra reductions are introduced, the excess transcript can be examined to determine whether or not the correction has succeeded.

Experimentally we have determined that the modified code in listing 1.11 seems to work well. Set L as the smallest power of 2 such that $2(n/L)q < 2^{31}$. For $q = 8383489$, and $n = 512$, then $L = 4$. Since the corrections are only rarely required, the performance impact should be small. However we appreciate that such measures will eventually become less effective as q increases, and the available excess diminishes.

Listing 1.11. Modified Lazy Reduction method for INTT

```
if (m<L && j<k+(L/2*m))
{
        U=modmul(x[j],O);
        V=modmul(x[j+t],O);
}
else
{
        U=x[j];
        V=x[j+t];
}
x[j]=U+V;
W=U+(n/L)*q-V;
x[j+t]=modmul(W,S);
```

We would emphasise that by vigorous loop unrolling all conditional branches can be eliminated from the generated code.

3.4 Special Moduli

Special form moduli can be used and exploited in our framework as long as they obey the same rules as Montgomery arithmetic, that is for an input $< qR$ they produce an output less than $2q$. For example the Fermat prime $2^{16} + 1 = 65537$ which has been proposed for RLWE implementations [11], has a fast reduction, and does not require field elements to be converted to and from Montgomery form, with further savings. See Listing 1.12 for the fast reduction code for a 32-bit processor. Careful analysis confirms that the output will always be positive and less than $2q$.

Listing 1.12. reduction function for Fermat prime 65537

```
int32_t redc(int64_t T)
{
        T=(uint32_t)T+(T>>32);
        return (T&0xFFFF)+q-(T>>16);
}
```

4   Mapping Implementations to Platforms

Our näive and constant time implementations will work immediately on a 16-bit processor, where a int_t is represented by a 16-bit C type like int16_t, and int_dt maps to a int32_t, assuming that the prime modulus q is 14-bits or less. Unfortunately in this setting the available excesses are insufficient for our full lazy reduction approach. But in many cases q is bigger than 16-bits, although usually less than 32-bits, in which case a 32-bit (or 64-bit) processor is really a necessity, where int_t maps to int32_t, and int_dt maps to int64_t. The majority of primes suggested for RLWE range from 13 to 26 bits [1]. In these cases our lazy reduction code will be a good fit on a 32-bit processor.

5   Comparison with Prior Art

In their influential paper Alkim et al. [2] provide a reference C implementation of the NTT, using the Gentleman-Sande approach. Their solution is closer to our constant time solution, and appears to be targeted at a 32-bit architecture, but one without a 32×32 multiplier. Such architectures exist, and a prime example would be the ARM Cortex-M processor, which they specifically targetted in a follow-up paper [3]. By using the 14-bit prime $q = 12289$ and a Montgomery modulus of 2^{18}, they cleverly succeed in squeezing the arithmetic into 32-bits (as $14 + 18 = 32$). As $R = 2^{18}$ is a few bits greater than q a modest amount of lazy reduction then becomes possible.

The paper by Longa and Naehrig [9], which was the starting point for this research, ends up with an implementation not very dissimilar to our own, albeit they come to it by a different route. The main difference is that they choose to use a modular reduction method tailored to the specific types of primes used in RLWE, that is primes such that $q = 1 \bmod 2n$. Therefore they do not use Montgomery reduction, but can hence avoid the transformation to/from Montgomery form, with further savings. Their solution is appropriate to a more conventional 32-bit architecture which allows 64-bit products.

However the Longa and Naehrig implementation is described only in the context of a particular choice of parameters, namely $q = 12289$ and $n = 1024$, as used for the NewHope key exchange protocol described in [2]. Their implementation, like ours, requires extra modular reductions introduced at certain steps in the NTT algorithm and its inverse. The reasoning for the positioning of these extra reductions is not fully explained, and hence it is not clear when they would be required for a different choice of parameters. However we can see now that they are introduced as a mechanism to suppress the excesses from getting too large. Using their special reduction function, it appears that the extra reductions must be introduced into both the NTT and the INTT code, whereas in our implementation our analysis shows that they are not needed at all for the NewHope parameter set, and are only required for the INTT code when q gets much larger.

6   Results

Our code is available here[1].

First we provide some comparative timings, using cycle counts obtained from an Odroid C2 single board computer, as used by Streit and De Santis [13] in their implementation of NewHope on an ARM Cortex-A53 processor. Following their example, we obtain hardware cycle counts using the accurate Linux Kernel performance monitoring system call, using the GCC compiler version 5.4 with maximum optimization. We provide results for all three methods described here, for the parameters $q = 12289, n = 1024$ and $q = 8383489, n = 512$, and $q = 16760833, n = 1024$ [1] to demonstrate that our code is not tied to just one fixed set of parameters. See Table 1.

Table 1. Odroid C2 Cycle counts

Prime q	Degree n	Method	NTT	INTT
12289	1024	Naive	161701	127879
12289	1024	Constant time	102306	91223
12289	1024	Lazy reduction	74174	78108
8383489	512	Naive	96369	74126
8383489	512	Constant time	48478	43273
8383489	512	Lazy reduction	35537	39784
16760833	1024	Naive	196473	133014
16760833	1024	Constant time	102208	91059
16760833	1024	Lazy reduction	74206	84088

For the NewHope parameters we note that our cycle counts are nearly exactly half of those quoted by Streit and De Santis, who used the C reference code from [2]. Using our new counts, it would appear that the advantage of using NEON instructions is not the speed-up of 8.3 as claimed, but is closer to (a still very impressive) 4. We next adapted the Longa and Naehrig code to use the same performance counters, and observed that for the NewHope parameters their code is about as fast as ours (79020 for NTT, 75822 for INTT). However we would contend that our reference code is much more general purpose.

---

[1] http://indigo.ie/~mscott/ntt_ref.c.

Next we performed the same measurements this time using an Intel i5-6400 processor with Turbo Boost disabled, and the GCC version 5.3 compiler (Table 2).

Table 2. Intel i5 Cycle counts

Prime q	Degree n	Method	NTT	INTT
12289	1024	Naive	70327	46997
12289	1024	Constant time	47017	42424
12289	1024	Lazy reduction	34300	35110
8383489	512	Naive	37455	23350
8383489	512	Constant Time	21891	1587
8383489	512	Lazy reduction	15863	16703
16760833	1024	Naive	71800	51446
16760833	1024	Constant time	47392	43160
16760833	1024	Lazy reduction	35165	37655

In this case the Longa and Naehrig code when measured on our compiler/processor combination, was about 5% faster than our lazy reduction code for the NewHope parameters.

We observe that the extra reductions necessary for the INTT code to work correctly for the larger primes 8383489 and 16760833, do not appear to significantly effect the performance.

7   Conclusion

We have described an improved reference C implementation of the Number Theoretic Transform and its inverse, as required for the implementation of post-quantum cryptographic schemes based on the Ring Learning With Errors problem. The implementation is efficient and constant time, and hence a safe starting point for more highly optimized code. It can be used with a range of parameters, and is easily translated to other languages. Our solution uses a methodology which allows the idea of Lazy Reduction to be exploited to the full, with confidence that integer overflow will never occur. Our methodology exposes the surprising observation that the Cooley-Tukey butterfly is much more lazy-reduction-friendly than the Gentleman-Sande alternative.

Another conclusion from our results is that, if one ignores bandwidth considerations, the cost of moving to a larger value for q has only a negligible impact on performance.

Finally we conclude that some performance improvements claimed for assembly code that exploits instruction set extensions like Intel AVX2 and ARM NEON, when compared to compiler-generated C code, while still very impressive, are perhaps not quite as good as originally claimed.

References

1. Ring learning with errors parameters (2017). http://www.ringlwe.info/parameters-for-rlwe.html
2. Alkim, E., Ducas, L., Poppelmann, T., Schwabe, P.: Post-quantum key exchange - a new hope. In: 25th Usenix Security Symposium, pp. 327–343 (2016)
3. Alkim, E., Jakubeit, P., Schwabe, P.: NEWHOPE on ARM Cortex-M. In: Carlet, C., Hasan, M.A., Saraswat, V. (eds.) SPACE 2016. LNCS, vol. 10076, pp. 332–349. Springer, Cham (2016). https://doi.org/10.1007/978-3-319-49445-6_19
4. Barrett, P.: Implementing the Rivest Shamir and Adleman public key encryption algorithm on a standard digital signal processor. In: Odlyzko, A.M. (ed.) CRYPTO 1986. LNCS, vol. 263, pp. 311–323. Springer, Heidelberg (1987). https://doi.org/10.1007/3-540-47721-7_24
5. Bernstein, D., Breitner, J., Genkin, D., Bruinderink, L.G., Heninger, N., Lange, T., van Vredendaal, C., Yarom, Y.: Sliding right into disaster: left-to-right sliding windows leak. Cryptology ePrint Archive, Report 2017/627 (2017). http://eprint.iacr.org/2017/627
6. Fog, A.: Instruction tables: lists of instruction latencies, throughputs and micro-operation breakdowns for intel, AMD and VIA CPUs (2017). http://www.agner.org/optimize/
7. Güneysu, T., Oder, T., Pöppelmann, T., Schwabe, P.: Software speed records for lattice-based signatures. In: Gaborit, P. (ed.) PQCrypto 2013. LNCS, vol. 7932, pp. 67–82. Springer, Heidelberg (2013). https://doi.org/10.1007/978-3-642-38616-9_5
8. Harvey, D.: Faster arithmetic for number-theoretic transforms. J. Symb. Comput. **60**, 113–119 (2014)
9. Longa, P., Naehrig, M.: Speeding up the number theoretic transform for faster ideal lattice-based cryptography. In: Foresti, S., Persiano, G. (eds.) CANS 2016. LNCS, vol. 10052, pp. 124–139. Springer, Cham (2016). https://doi.org/10.1007/978-3-319-48965-0_8
10. Montgomery, P.: Modular multiplication without trial division. Math. Comput. **44**(170), 519–521 (1985)
11. Pöppelmann, T., Güneysu, T.: Towards efficient arithmetic for lattice-based cryptography on reconfigurable hardware. In: Hevia, A., Neven, G. (eds.) LATIN-CRYPT 2012. LNCS, vol. 7533, pp. 139–158. Springer, Heidelberg (2012). https://doi.org/10.1007/978-3-642-33481-8_8
12. Scott, M.: Slothful reduction. Cryptology ePrint Archive, Report 2017/437 (2017). http://eprint.iacr.org/2017/437
13. Streit, S., De Santis, F.: Post-quantum key exchange on ARMv8-A - a new hope for NEON made simple. Cryptology ePrint Archive, Report 2017/388 (2017). http://eprint.iacr.org/2017/388

Homomorphic Signatures

A Linearly Homomorphic Signature Scheme from Weaker Assumptions

Lucas Schabhüser[✉], Johannes Buchmann, and Patrick Struck

Technische Universität Darmstadt, Darmstadt, Germany
{lschabhueser,buchmann}@cdc.informatik.tu-darmstadt.de,
patrick.struck@stud.tu-darmstadt.de

Abstract. In delegated computing, prominent in the context of cloud computing, guaranteeing both the correctness and authenticity of computations is of critical importance. Homomorphic signatures can be used as cryptographic solutions to this problem. In this paper we solve the open problem of constructing a linearly homomorphic signature scheme that is secure against an active adversary under standard assumptions. We provide a construction based on the DL and CDH assumption. Furthermore we show how our scheme can be combined with homomorphic encryption under the framework of Linearly Homomorphic Authenticated Encryption with Public Verifiability. This way we can provide the first such scheme that is context hiding. Furthermore our solution even allows verification in constant time (in an amortized sense).

Keywords: Homomorphic signatures · Homomorphic encryption · Delegated computation · Cloud computing

1 Introduction

1.1 Motivation

Homomorphic signature schemes allow to check the correctness of a computations result without having to perform the computation oneself. This allows a client to delegate computations to a computationally more powerful server, such that the server can verify the result. In this scenario the server is asked to not only perform a computation but also to evaluate this function over the signatures as well. The resulting signature to the output can be used to verify the correctness of the result. There have been multiple schemes proposed for this. Their security however is mostly based on weaker non-standard assumptions. Besides outsourcing of computations, homomorphic signatures offer security in *network coding* [9]. These constructions however do not consider confidentiality, i.e. the client might not be comfortable with the server knowing what data he is computing on. Homomorphic encryption schemes allow the evaluation of functions over encrypted messages. That servers can perform computations, learning neither the input nor the output. However, clients still have to trust the server

© Springer International Publishing AG 2017
M. O'Neill (Ed.): IMACC 2017, LNCS 10655, pp. 261–279, 2017.
https://doi.org/10.1007/978-3-319-71045-7_14

to a degree, as there is no way to check whether the function has been evaluated as claimed. Combining both approaches allows a client to verify the correctness by checking a signature and decrypting the cipher returned by the server. However, naively combining both primitives requires the cipher space of the encryption scheme to be (a subset of) the message space of the homomorphic signature scheme. In the case of Paillier encryption for instance the underlying message space is $\mathbb{Z}_n$ while the cipher space is $\mathbb{Z}_{n^2}$, i.e. a doubling the signature size. Catalano et al. [14] proposed a method which allows to combine the Paillier encryption scheme with a homomorphic signature scheme instantiated to support only the message space of the Paillier encryption scheme. Currently there exists only one instantiation of this, whose security is also based on strong assumptions.

1.2 Related Work

Linearly homomorphic signature schemes: The idea of linearly homomorphic signature schemes was introduced in [16] and later refined in [19]. Freeman proposed stronger security definitions in [17]. An instantiation based on 2-3-Diffie Hellmann was proposed in [9]. Later realizations are based on subgroup decision problems [2,3], the k-Simultaneous Flexible Pairing Problem [4], the RSA problem [18] (offering only security against *weak adversaries*), the strong RSA problem [11], the Flexible DH Inversion problem [10], and the lattice based k-SIS problem [8]. As already mentioned in [17] the construction of such a scheme, that is secure against a strong adversary, and based on weak assumptions, has been solved by using so called *chameleon hash functions*, which are very computationally expensive. Constructing such a scheme without them, has remained an open problem ever since. The idea of homomorphic signatures with efficient verification was introduced in [12]. Intuitively, this means that the outcome of a computation can be checked faster by using the schemes verification algorithm than computing it oneself. However, this only holds in an *amortized* sense, as an expensive preprocessing phase has to be amortized over multiple datasets (see [5,14]).

Authenticated Homomorphic Encryption. An and Bellare [1] introduced a new paradigm called *encryption with redundancy* which allows to achieve both privacy and authentication. In [6] the idea of *authenticated encryption* is formalized. Analogous notions for the homomorphic setting were given in [20] and [14]. In the latter the notion of *linearly homomorphic authenticated encryption with public verifiability (LAEPuV)* was introduced which will be used in this paper. As pointed out in [22], the candidate instantiation of [14] suffers from false negatives however, and an improved version was proposed.

1.3 Contribution and Roadmap

In this paper we propose a linearly homomorphic signature scheme that is unforgeable against strong (adaptive) adversaries under the computational

Diffie-Hellman assumption, which is one of the most well studied cryptographic problems and thereby solve a problem left open in [17]. This scheme has several desirable properties. The size of a signature does not depend on the size of the dataset over which computations are executed, so it is in particular *succinct*, it allows for *efficient verification*, in our case even *constant time verification*, and is *context hiding*, i.e. no information about the input values can be learned from the signature to the output of a computation (not even if the secret key is compromised). We then show how our scheme can be used in conjunction with Paillier encryption [21] in order to instantiate a LAEPuV scheme. This is both the first context hiding construction and the first to support vectors of messages.

We introduce notation and preliminaries in Sect. 2. We present a new homomorphic signature scheme in Sect. 3 and prove its properties, while Sect. 4 shows how our scheme can be combined with homomorphic encryption.

2   Preliminaries

To accurately describe what both correct and legitimate operations for homomorphic signatures are, we will make use of *multi-labeled programs* similar to [5]. On a high level a function is appended by several identifiers, in our case input identifiers and dataset identifiers. Input identifiers label in which order the input values are to be used and dataset identifiers determine which signatures can be homomorphically combined. The idea is that only signatures created under the same dataset identifier can be combined. We will now give formal definitions.

A *labeled program* $\mathcal{P}$ consists of a tuple $(f, \tau_1, \ldots, \tau_k)$, where $f : \mathcal{M}^k \to \mathcal{M}$ is a function with k inputs and $\tau_i \in \mathcal{T}$ is a label for the i-th input of f from some set $\mathcal{T}$. Given a set of labeled programs $\mathcal{P}_1, \ldots, \mathcal{P}_t$ and a function $g : \mathcal{M}^t \to \mathcal{M}$, they can be composed by evaluating g over the labeled programs, i.e. $\mathcal{P}^* = g(\mathcal{P}_1, \ldots, \mathcal{P}_t)$. The identity program with label τ is given by $\mathcal{I}_\tau = (f_{id}, \tau)$, where $f_{id} : \mathcal{M} \to \mathcal{M}$ is the identity function. Note that program $\mathcal{P} = (f, \tau_1, \ldots, \tau_k)$ can be expressed as the composition of k identity programs $\mathcal{P} = f(\mathcal{I}_{\tau_1}, \ldots, \mathcal{I}_{\tau_k})$.

A *multi-labeled program* $\mathcal{P}_\Delta$ is a pair $(\mathcal{P}, \Delta)$ of the labeled program $\mathcal{P}$ and a dataset identifier Δ. Given a set of t multi-labeled programs with the same data set identifier Δ, i.e. $(\mathcal{P}_1, \Delta), \ldots, (\mathcal{P}_t, \Delta)$, and a function $g : \mathcal{M}^t \to \mathcal{M}$, a composed multi-label program $\mathcal{P}_\Delta^*$ can be computed, consisting of the pair $(\mathcal{P}^*, \Delta)$, where $\mathcal{P}^* = g(\mathcal{P}_1, \ldots, \mathcal{P}_t)$. Analogous to the identity program for labeled programs we refer to a multi-labeled identity program by $\mathcal{I}_{(\Delta, \tau)} = ((f_{id}, \tau), \Delta)$.

Definition 1 (Homomorphic Signature Scheme). *A homomorphic signature scheme is a tuple of the following probabilistic polynomial-time algorithms:*

HKeyGen$(1^\lambda, k)$**:** *On input a security parameter λ and an integer k, the algorithm returns a key pair* (sk, pk)*, where* sk *is the secret key kept private and* pk *is the public key which determines the message space $\mathcal{M}$, the signature space $\mathcal{Y}$, and the set $\mathcal{F}$ of admissible labeled programs $\mathcal{P} : \mathcal{M}^k \to \mathcal{M}$.*

HSign(sk, Δ, τ, m): *On input a secret key* sk, *a dataset identifier* Δ, *an input identifier* τ, *and a message* $m \in \mathcal{M}$, *the algorithm returns a signature* $\sigma \in \mathcal{Y}$ *which is the signature for the message labeled by* τ *in the dataset identified by* Δ.

HEval(pk, $\mathcal{P}_\Delta, \boldsymbol{\sigma}$): *On input a public key* pk, *a multi-labeled program* $\mathcal{P}_\Delta$, *and a set of signatures* $\boldsymbol{\sigma} \in \mathcal{Y}^k$, *the algorithm returns a signature* $\sigma' \in \mathcal{Y}$ *for the multi-labeled program* $\mathcal{P}$ *over the (tuple of) signatures* $\boldsymbol{\sigma}$ *identified by* Δ.

HVerify(pk, $\mathcal{P}_\Delta, m, \sigma$): *On input a public key* pk, *a multi-labeled program* $\mathcal{P}_\Delta$, *a message* $m \in \mathcal{M}$, *and a signature* $\sigma \in \mathcal{Y}$, *the algorithm either accepts the signature* σ, *for the multi-labeled program* $\mathcal{P}$ *over the dataset identified by* Δ, *i.e. it returns* 1, *or rejects the signature, i.e. it returns* 0.

We will now define the relevant properties for homomorphic signatures.

Definition 2 (Correctness). *A homomorphic signature scheme* (HKeyGen, HSign, HEval, HVerify) *is called correct, if for any security parameter* λ, *any integer* k, *and any key pair* (sk, pk) $\leftarrow$ HKeyGen($1^\lambda, k$) *the following two conditions are satisfied.*

Condition 1. *For any dataset identifier* Δ, *any input identifier* τ, *and any message* $m \in \mathcal{M}$, *it holds that*

$$\text{HVerify}(\text{pk}, \mathcal{I}_{\Delta,\tau}, m, \text{HSign}(\text{sk}, \Delta, \tau, m)) = 1.$$

Condition 2. *For any dataset identifier* Δ, *any multi-labeled program* $\mathcal{P}_\Delta = ((f_1, \ldots, f_k), \tau_1, \ldots, \tau_k, \Delta)$ *containing a linear function, and any set of messages* $\boldsymbol{m} \in \mathcal{M}^k$ *with* $\boldsymbol{m} = (m_1, \ldots, m_k)$, *it holds that*

$$\text{HVerify}(\text{pk}, \mathcal{P}_\Delta, f(m_1, \ldots, m_k), \text{HEval}(\text{pk}, \mathcal{P}_\Delta, \boldsymbol{\sigma})) = 1$$

where $\boldsymbol{\sigma} = (\sigma_{\tau_1}, \ldots, \sigma_{\tau_k}) \in \mathcal{Y}^k$ *with* $\sigma_\tau \leftarrow \text{HSign}(\text{sk}, \Delta, \tau, m_\tau)$.

Definition 3 (Succinctness). *A homomorphic signature scheme* (HKeyGen, HSign, HEval, HVerify) *is called* succinct *if for a fixed security parameter* λ *the size of the signatures depends at most logarithmically on the dataset size* k.

For the security notion of our homomorphic signature scheme we first provide a definition for *well defined programs* and *forgeries* on these programs. Then, we introduce an experiment the attacker can run in order to make a successful forgery and present a definition for unforgeability based on this experiment.

Definition 4 (Well Defined Program). *A labeled program* $\mathcal{P} = (f, \tau_1, \ldots, \tau_k)$ *is well defined with respect to a list* $\mathcal{L}$ *if one of the two following cases holds: First, there exists exactly one* m_i *such that* $(\tau_i, m_i) \in \mathcal{L} \; \forall i = 1, \ldots, k$. *Second, there is an* $i \in \{1, \ldots, k\}$ *such that* $(\tau_i, \cdot) \notin \mathcal{L}$ *and* $f(\{m_j\}_{(\tau_j, m_j) \in \mathcal{L}} \cup \{\tilde{m}_l\}_{(\tau_l, \cdot) \notin \mathcal{L}})$ *does not depend on the choice of* $\tilde{m}_l \in \mathcal{M}$.

Definition 5 (Forgery). *A forgery is a tuple $(\mathcal{P}_\Delta, m^*, \sigma^*)$ such that* HVerify$(\mathsf{pk}, \mathcal{P}_\Delta, m^*, \sigma^*) = 1$ *holds and one of the following conditions is met:*

Type 1: *The list $\mathcal{L}$ was not initialized during the game, i.e. no message was ever committed under the dataset identifier Δ.*
Type 2: *$\mathcal{P}_\Delta$ is well defined with respect to the list $\mathcal{L}$ and m^* is not the correct output of the computation, i.e. $m^* \neq f(\{m_j\}_{(\tau_j, m_j)\in\mathcal{L}})$.*
Type 3: *$\mathcal{P}_\Delta$ is not well defined with respect to $\mathcal{L}$.*

For the notion of unforgeability we define the following experiments HomUF $-$ CMA$_{\mathcal{A},\mathsf{HomSign}}(\lambda)$ and Weak $-$ HomUF $-$ CMA$_{\mathcal{A},\mathsf{HomSign}}(\lambda)$ between an adversary $\mathcal{A}$ and a challenger $\mathcal{C}$.

HomUF $-$ CMA$_{\mathcal{A},\mathsf{HomSign}}(\lambda)$:
Key Generation. $\mathcal{C}$ calls $(\mathsf{sk}, \mathsf{pk}) \leftarrow_\$ \mathsf{HKeyGen}(1^\lambda, k)$ and gives pk to $\mathcal{A}$.
Queries. $\mathcal{A}$ adaptively submits queries for (Δ, τ, m) where Δ is a dataset, τ is an input identifier, and m is a message. $\mathcal{C}$ proceeds as follows: if (Δ, τ, m) is the first query with dataset identifier Δ, it initializes an empty list $\mathcal{L} = \emptyset$ for Δ. If $\mathcal{L}$ does not contain a tuple $(\tau, \cdot)$, i.e. $\mathcal{A}$ never queried $(\Delta, \tau, \cdot)$, $\mathcal{C}$ calls $\sigma \leftarrow \mathsf{HSign}(\mathsf{sk}, \Delta, \tau, m)$, updates the list $\mathcal{L} = \mathcal{L} \cup (\tau, m)$, and gives σ to $\mathcal{A}$. If $(\tau, m) \in \mathcal{L}$ then $\mathcal{C}$ returns the same signature σ as before. If $\mathcal{L}$ already contains a tuple (τ, m') for $m \neq m'$, $\mathcal{C}$ returns $\bot$.
Forgery. $\mathcal{A}$ outputs a tuple $(\mathcal{P}_\Delta, m, \sigma)$. The experiment outputs 1, if $(\mathcal{P}_\Delta, m, \sigma)$ is a forgery according to Definition 5.

In the following experiment Weak $-$ HomUF $-$ CMA$_{\mathcal{A},\mathsf{HomSign}}(\lambda)$, the adversary has to declare the message components of the later signing queries before the key generation and can later on specify in which dataset Δ_j it wants to query it.

Weak $-$ HomUF $-$ CMA$_{\mathcal{A},\mathsf{HomSign}}(\lambda)$:

Declaration of Messages. $\mathcal{A}$ outputs a list of possible messages $\{m_{\tau,j}\}_{\tau\in\mathcal{L},j=1}^{Q} \subset \mathcal{M}$ where Q is the number of datasets to be queried.
Key Generation. $\mathcal{C}$ calls $(\mathsf{sk}, \mathsf{pk}) \leftarrow \mathsf{HKeyGen}(1^\lambda, k)$ and gives pk to $\mathcal{A}$.
Queries. $\mathcal{A}$ adaptively submits queries for $(\Delta_j, \tau, m_{\tau,j})$ where Δ is a dataset, τ is an identifier, and $m_{\tau,j}$ is a message. $\mathcal{C}$ proceeds as follows: if $(\Delta_j, \tau, m_{\tau,j})$ is the first query with dataset identifier Δ_j, it initializes an empty list $\mathcal{L} = \emptyset$ for Δ_j. If $\mathcal{L}$ does not contain a tuple $(\tau, \cdot)$, i.e. $\mathcal{A}$ never queried $(\Delta_j, \tau, \cdot)$, $\mathcal{C}$ calls $\sigma \leftarrow \mathsf{HSign}(\mathsf{sk}, \Delta_j, \tau, m)$, updates the list $\mathcal{L} = \mathcal{L} \cup (\tau, m_{\tau,j})$, and gives σ to $\mathcal{A}$. If $(\tau, m_{\tau,j}) \in \mathcal{L}$ then $\mathcal{C}$ returns the same signature σ as before. If $\mathcal{L}$ already contains a tuple $(\tau, m'_{\tau,j})$ for $m \neq m'$ $\mathcal{C}$ returns $\bot$.
Forgery. $\mathcal{A}$ outputs a tuple $(\mathcal{P}_\Delta, m, \sigma)$. The experiment outputs 1, if $(\mathcal{P}_\Delta, m, \sigma)$ is a forgery according to Definition 5

Definition 6 (Unforgeability). *A linearly homomorphic signature scheme is* unforgeable *if for any PPT adversary $\mathcal{A}$ we have*

$$Pr[\mathsf{HomUF} - \mathsf{CMA}_{\mathcal{A},\mathsf{HomSign}}(\lambda) = 1] \leq \mathsf{negl}(\lambda).$$

It is weakly unforgeable *if for any PPT adversary $\mathcal{A}$ we have*

$$Pr[\text{Weak} - \text{HomUF} - \text{CMA}_{\mathcal{A},\text{HomSign}}(\lambda) = 1] \leq \text{negl}(\lambda).$$

However any homomorphic signature scheme weakly-unforgeable under a computational assumption can be transformed into one that is unforgeable under the same assumption by [12, Theorem 1].

Additionally we will make use of the following statement.

Lemma 1 (Proposition 2.3 of [17])
   Let $\mathcal{H} = (\text{HKeyGen}, \text{HSign}, \text{HEval}, \text{HVerify})$ be a linearly homomorphic signature scheme over a message space $\mathcal{M} \subset R^T$ for some ring R. If $\mathcal{H}$ is secure against Type 2 forgeries, then $\mathcal{H}$ is also secure against Type 3 forgeries.

Definition 7 (Context-Hiding).   *A homomorphic signature scheme for multi-labeled programs is called* context hiding *if there exist additional PPT procedures $\tilde{\sigma} \leftarrow \text{HHide}(\text{pk}, m, \sigma)$ and $\text{HHideVer}(\text{pk}, \mathcal{P}_\Delta, m, \tilde{\sigma})$ such that:*

Correctness: *For any $(\text{sk}, \text{pk}) \leftarrow \text{HKeyGen}(1^\lambda, k)$ and tuple $(\mathcal{P}_\Delta, m, \sigma)$, such that $\text{HVerify}(\text{pk}, \mathcal{P}_\Delta, m, \sigma) = 1$, and $\tilde{\sigma} \leftarrow \text{HHide}(\text{pk}, m, \sigma)$, it holds that $\text{HHideVer}(\text{pk}, \mathcal{P}_\Delta, m, \tilde{\sigma}) = 1$.*
Unforgeability: *The homomorphic signature scheme is unforgeable (see Definition 6) when replacing the algorithm HVerify with HHideVer in the security experiment.*
Context-Hiding Security: *There is a simulator Sim such that, for any fixed (worst-case) choice of $(\text{sk}, \text{pk}) \leftarrow \text{HKeyGen}(1^\lambda, k)$, any multi-labeled program $\mathcal{P}_\Delta = (f, \tau_1, \ldots, \tau_k, \Delta)$, messages $m_1, \ldots, m_l$, and distinguisher $\mathcal{D}$ there exists a function $\epsilon(\lambda)$ such that the following equation holds:*

$$|Pr[\mathcal{D}(I, \text{HHide}(\text{pk}, m, \sigma) = 1] - Pr[\mathcal{D}(I, \text{Sim}(\text{sk}, \mathcal{P}_\Delta, m)) = 1]| = \epsilon(\lambda)$$

where $I = (\text{sk}, \text{pk}, \mathcal{P}_\Delta, \{m_i, \sigma_i\}_{i=1}^l, m, \sigma)$ for $\sigma_i \leftarrow \text{HSign}(\text{sk}, \Delta, \tau_i, m_i)$, $m \leftarrow f(m_1, \ldots, m_k)$, $\sigma \leftarrow \text{HEval}(\text{pk}, \mathcal{P}_\Delta, \sigma_1, \ldots, \sigma_k)$, and the probabilities are taken over the randomness of $\text{HSign}, \text{HHide}$ and Sim. If $\epsilon(\lambda) \leq \text{negl}(\lambda)$ we call the homomorphic signature scheme statistically context-hiding, if $\epsilon(\lambda) = 0$ we call it perfectly context hiding.

Definition 8 (Efficient Verification).   *A homomorphic signature scheme for multi-labeled programs allows for* efficient verification, *if there exist two additional algorithms $(\text{VerPrep}, \text{EffVer})$ such that:*

$\text{VerPrep}(\text{pk}, \mathcal{P})$**:** *Given a public key pk and a labeled program $\mathcal{P} = (f, \tau_1, \ldots, \tau_k)$, this algorithm generates a concise public key $\text{pk}_\mathcal{P}$. This does not depend on a dataset identifier Δ.*
$\text{EffVer}(\text{pk}_\mathcal{P}, m, \sigma, \Delta)$**:** *Given a concise public key $\text{pk}_\mathcal{P}$, a message m, a signature σ and a dataset Δ, it outputs 1 or 0.*

The above algorithms are required to satisfy the following two properties:

Correctness: *Let* $(\mathsf{sk}, \mathsf{pk}) \leftarrow \mathsf{HKeyGen}(1^\lambda, k)$ *be honestly generated keys and* $(\mathcal{P}, m, \sigma)$ *be a tuple such that for* $\mathcal{P}_\Delta = (\mathcal{P}, \Delta)$ *we have* $\mathsf{HVerify}(\mathsf{pk}, \mathcal{P}_\Delta, m, \sigma) = 1$.

Then for every $\mathsf{pk}_\mathcal{P} \xleftarrow{\$} \mathsf{VerPrep}(\mathsf{pk}, \mathcal{P})$, $\mathsf{EffVer}(\mathsf{pk}_\mathcal{P}, m, \sigma, \Delta) = 1$ *holds except with negligible probability.*

Amortized Efficiency: *Let* $\mathcal{P}$ *be a program,* $m_1, \ldots, m_k$, *be valid input values and let* $t(k)$ *be the time required to compute* $\mathcal{P}(m_1, \ldots, m_k)$. *Then for* $\mathsf{pk}_\mathcal{P} \xleftarrow{\$}$ $\mathsf{VerPrep}(\mathsf{pk}, \mathcal{P})$ *the time required to compute* $\mathsf{EffVer}(\mathsf{pk}_\mathcal{P}, m, \sigma, \Delta)$ *is* $t' = o(t(k))$.

Note that efficiency here is used in an amortized sense. There is a function dependent preprocessing so that the cost of verification amortizes over multiple datasets.

2.1 Notation

Definition 9 (Asymmetric bilinear groups). *An asymmetric bilinear group is a tuple* $\mathsf{bgp} = (q, \mathbb{G}_1, \mathbb{G}_2, \mathbb{G}_T, g_1, g_2, e)$ *such that (1)* $\mathbb{G}_1, \mathbb{G}_2,$ *and* $\mathbb{G}_T$ *are cyclic groups of order* q, *(2) the* Discrete Logarithm Problem *is hard to be computed in* $\mathbb{G}_1, \mathbb{G}_2,$ *and* $\mathbb{G}_T$, *(3)* $e : \mathbb{G}_1 \times \mathbb{G}_2 \to \mathbb{G}_T$ *is bilinear, i.e.* $e(g_1{}^a, g_2{}^b) = e(g_1, g_2)^{ab}$ *holds for all* $g_1 \in \mathbb{G}_1, g_2 \in \mathbb{G}_2$, *and* $a, b \in \mathbb{Z}_q$, *(4)* e *is non-degenerate, i.e.* $e(g_1, g_2) \neq 1$, *and (5)* e *is efficiently computable. The function* e *is called* bilinear map *or* pairing.

During our constructions we will have multiple input messages m_i where the messages are vectors. For reasons of clarity we will make the following convention: m_i will be used to identify a certain message, while $m[j]$ will be used to denote the j-th entry of the message vector m. Thus $m_i[j]$ is the j-th entry of the i-th message.

2.2 Assumptions

Definition 10 *(DL). Let* $\mathbb{G}$ *be a group of order* q *(not necessarily prime): We say the Discrete Logarithm assumption holds in* $\mathbb{G}$. *if there exists no ppt adversary* $\mathcal{A}$ *that given* (g, g^a) *for a random generator* $g \in \mathbb{G}$ *and random* $a \in \mathbb{Z}_q$ *can output* a *with more than negligible probability.*

Note that there exist different variations of Diffie-Hellman assumptions in bilinear groups (see for example [15]). We will use the following definition.

Definition 11 *(CDH in Bilinear Groups [15]). Let* $\mathsf{bgp} = (q, \mathbb{G}_1, \mathbb{G}_2, \mathbb{G}_T, g_1, g_2, e)$ *be a description of a bilinear group. We say the Computational Diffie-Hellman assumption holds in* bgp, *if there exists no ppt adversary* $\mathcal{A}$ *that given* $(\mathsf{bgp}, g_1^a, g_2^b)$ *where* $a, b \xleftarrow{\$} \mathbb{Z}_q$ *can output* g_1^{ab} *with more than negligible probability.*

Definition 12 *(DCRA).* *Let n be the product of two (safe) primes, i.e. $n = pq$. We say the Decisional composite residuosity assumption (DCRA) holds if there exists no ppt adversary $\mathcal{A}$ that can distinguish between an element drawn uniformly random from the set $\mathbb{Z}_{n^2}^*$ and an element from the set $\{z^n | z \in \mathbb{Z}_{n^2}^*\}$, that is the set of the n-th residues modulo n^2.*

3   Construction

In the following we will describe a linearly homomorphic signature scheme HSig = (HKeyGen, HSign, HEval, HVerify) based on CDH in bilinear groups. In this instantiation the input identifiers are simply the integers from 1 to k. Multi-labeled programs contain linear functions f given by their coefficients, i.e. $f = (f_1, \ldots, f_k)$.

HKeyGen($1^\lambda, k, T$): On input a security parameter λ, an integer k, and an integer T, the algorithm runs $\mathcal{G}(1^\lambda)$ to obtain a bilinear group bgp = $(q, \mathbb{G}_1, \mathbb{G}_2, \mathbb{G}_T, g_1, g_2, e)$, and samples $k + T$ elements $R_1, \ldots, R_k, h_1, \ldots, h_T \leftarrow \mathbb{G}_1$. Additionally it generates a key pair (sk', pk') $\leftarrow$ KeyGen'(1^λ) of a regular signature scheme and a key $K \xleftarrow{\$} \mathcal{K}$ for a pseudorandom function PRF : $\mathcal{K} \times \{0,1\}^* \to \mathbb{Z}_q$. It returns the key pair (sk, pk) with sk = (sk', K) and pk = (pk', bgp, $\{h_j\}_{j=1}^T$, $\{R_i\}_{i=1}^k$).

HSign(sk, Δ, i, m): On input a secret key sk, a dataset identifier Δ, an input identifier $i \in [k]$, and a message $m \in \mathbb{Z}_q^T$, the algorithm generates the parameters for the dataset identified by Δ, by running $z \leftarrow \mathrm{PRF}_K(\Delta)$ and computing $Z = g_2^z$. It binds Z to the dataset identifier Δ by using the regular signature scheme, i.e. it sets $\sigma_\Delta \leftarrow$ Sign'(sk', $Z|\Delta$). Then, it computes $\Lambda \leftarrow (R_i \cdot \prod_{j=1}^T h_j^{-m[j]})^z$ and returns the signature $\sigma = (\sigma_\Delta, Z, \Lambda)$.

HEval(pk, $\mathcal{P}_\Delta, \boldsymbol{\sigma}$): On input a public key pk, a multi-labeled program $\mathcal{P}_\Delta$ containing a linear function f, and signatures $\boldsymbol{\sigma} = (\sigma_1, \ldots, \sigma_k)$, where $\sigma_i = (\sigma_{\Delta,i}, Z_i, \Lambda_i)$, the algorithm checks if the signatures share the same public values, i.e. if $\sigma_{\Delta,1} = \sigma_{\Delta,i}$ and $Z_1 = Z_i$ for all $i = 2, \ldots, k$, and the signature for each set of public values is correct and matches the dataset identifier Δ, i.e. Verify'(pk', $Z_i|\Delta, \sigma_{\Delta,i}$) = 1 for any $i = 1, \ldots, k$. If that is not the case the algorithm rejects the signature, otherwise, it proceeds as follows. It computes $m = \sum_{i=1}^k f_i m_i$ and $\Lambda = \prod_{i=1}^k \Lambda_i^{f_i}$, and returns the signature $\sigma = (Z_1, \sigma_{\Delta,1}, \Lambda)$.

HVerify(pk, $\mathcal{P}_\Delta, m, \sigma$): On input a public key pk, a message m, a signature $\sigma = (\sigma_\Delta, Z, \Lambda)$, and a multi-labeled program containing a linear function f, the algorithm returns 1, if Verify'(pk', $Z|\Delta, \sigma_\Delta$) = 1 and $e\left(R \cdot \prod_{j=1}^T h_j^{-m[j]}, Z\right) = e(\Lambda, g_2)$, where $R \leftarrow \prod_{i=1}^k R_i^{f_i}$. Otherwise, it returns 0.

Theorem 1. *HSig is a correct linearly homomorphic signature scheme according to Definition 2.*

Proof. Throughout this proof, let $(\mathsf{sk}, \mathsf{pk}) \leftarrow \mathsf{HKeyGen}(1^\lambda, k, T)$ be an honestly generated key pair with $\mathsf{sk} = (\mathsf{sk}', K)$ and $\mathsf{pk} = (\mathsf{pk}', \mathsf{bgp}, \{h_j\}_{j=1}^T, \{R_i\}_{i=}^k)$.

Condition 1: Let Δ be a dataset identifier, $i \in [k]$ be an input identifier, $m \in \mathbb{Z}_q^T$ be a message, and $\sigma = (\sigma_\Delta, Z, \Lambda) \leftarrow \mathsf{HSign}(\mathsf{sk}, \Delta, i, m)$ be the signature of m. Furthermore, let $\mathcal{I}_{(\Delta, i)}$ be the identity function for the i-th input under the tag Δ. By construction it holds that $\mathsf{Verify}'(\mathsf{pk}', Z | \Delta, \sigma_\Delta) = 1$ and $R = \prod_{i=1}^k R_i^{f_i} = R_i^1 = R_i$, which yields $e\left(R_i \cdot \prod_{j=1}^T h_j^{-m[j]}, Z\right) = e\left(R_i \cdot \prod_{j=1}^T h_j^{-m[j]}, g_2^z\right) = e\left(R_i h_1^{-m}, g_2\right)^z = e\left(\left(R_i \cdot \prod_{j=1}^T h_j^{-m[j]}\right)^z, g_1\right) = e(\Lambda, g_2)$. Thus, we have $\mathsf{HVerify}(\mathsf{pk}, \mathcal{I}_{(\Delta, i)}, m, \sigma) = \mathsf{HVerify}(\mathsf{pk}, \mathcal{I}_{(\Delta, i)}, m, \mathsf{HSign}(\mathsf{sk}, \Delta, i, m)) = 1$.

Condition 2: Let Δ be a dataset identifier, $m_i \in \mathbb{Z}_q^T$ for $i \in [k]$ be messages, $\mathcal{P}_\Delta = ((f_1, \ldots, f_k), 1, \ldots, k, \Delta)$, and $\sigma_i \leftarrow \mathsf{HSign}(\mathsf{sk}, \Delta, i, m_i)$, with $\sigma_i = (\sigma_{\Delta, i}, Z_i, \Lambda_i)$, be a signature of m_i. Furthermore, let $\sigma = (\sigma_\Delta, Z, \Lambda) \leftarrow \mathsf{HEval}(\mathsf{pk}, \mathcal{P}_\Delta, \sigma)$ be the signature obtained by evaluating f over the signatures in the dataset identified by Δ.

By construction we have $Z = Z_1$ and $\sigma_{\Delta, i} = \sigma_{\Delta, 1}$, hence we have $\mathsf{Verify}'(\mathsf{pk}', Z | \Delta, \sigma_\Delta) = 1$. To prove the correctness it remains to show that $e\left(R \cdot \prod_{j=1}^T h_j^{-m[j]}, Z\right) = e(\Lambda, g_2)$, where $R = \prod_{i=1}^k R_i^{f_i}$. It holds that

$$
e\left(R \cdot \prod_{j=1}^T h_j^{-m[j]}, Z\right) = e\left(\prod_{i=1}^k R_i^{f_i} \cdot \prod_{j=1}^T h_j^{-\sum_{i=1}^k f_i m_i[j]}, g_2^z\right)
$$

$$
= e\left(\prod_{i=1}^k R_i^{f_i} \cdot \prod_{i=1}^k (\prod_{j=1}^T h_j^{-m_i[j]})^{f_i}, g_2\right)^z = e\left(\prod_{i=1}^k (R_i \cdot \prod_{j=1}^T h_j^{-m_i[j]})^{f_i}, g_2\right)^z
$$

$$
= e\left(\prod_{i=1}^k ((R_i \cdot \prod_{j=1}^T h_j^{-m_i[j]})^z)^{f_i}, g_2\right) = e\left(\prod_{i=1}^k \Lambda_i^{f_i}, g_2\right) = e(\Lambda, g_2)
$$

hence $\mathsf{HVerify}(\mathsf{pk}, \mathcal{P}_\Delta, f(m_1, \ldots, m_k), \mathsf{HEval}(\mathsf{pk}, \mathcal{P}_\Delta, \sigma)) = 1$.

Theorem 2. *If Sig' is an unforgeable signature scheme, PRF is a pseudorandom function, and the CDH assumption (see Definition 11) holds in bgp, then the signature scheme describe above is a weakly-unforgeable homomorphic signature scheme for linear functions.*

Proof. To prove this Theorem we define a series of games with the adversary $\mathcal{A}$ and we will show that the adversary $\mathcal{A}$ wins, i.e. the game outputs 1, only with negligible probability. Following the notation of [10] we will write $G_i(\mathcal{A})$ to denote that a run of game i with adversary $\mathcal{A}$ returns 1. We will make use of flag values bad_i initially set to false. If at the end of the game any of these flags is set to true, the game simply outputs 0. Let Bad_i denote the event that bad_i is set to true during a game.

Game 1: This is the experiment Weak − HomUF − CMA$_{\mathcal{A},\mathsf{HomSign}}$ (see Definition 6) where $\mathcal{A}$ only outputs Type-1 or Type-2 forgeries.

Game 2: This game is defined as Game 1 apart from the fact that whenever $\mathcal{A}$ outputs a forgery $(\mathcal{P}_\Delta, m^*, \sigma^*)$, where $\sigma^* = (\sigma^*_\Delta, Z^*, \Lambda^*)$ such that Z^* was not generated by the challenger, then Game 2 sets $\mathsf{bad}_2 \leftarrow \mathsf{true}$.

Game 3: This game is the same as Game 2, except that the pseudorandom function of the scheme is replaced with a true random function $\Phi : \{0,1\}^* \to \mathbb{Z}_q$.

Game 4: This game is the same as Game 3, except for an additional check. When given a forgery $(\mathcal{P}^*_{\Delta^*}, m^*, \sigma^*)$ where $\mathcal{P}^*_{\Delta^*} = ((f^*, 1, \ldots, k), \Delta^*)$ the simulator computes $m \leftarrow f^*(m_{1,\Delta}, \ldots, m_{k,\Delta})$. It checks whether $\prod_{j=1}^T h_j^{m[j]} = \prod_{j=1}^T h_j^{m^*[j]}$ holds. If it does it sets $\mathsf{bad}_4 = \mathsf{true}$.

We will first show that these games are computationally indistinguishable under our assumptions and then proceed by showing how to construct a simulator $\mathcal{S}$ which uses an efficient adversary $\mathcal{A}$ against the signature scheme to solve the CDH problem.

Games 1 and 2 are only different if Bad_2 occurs. By constructions this means that $\mathcal{A}$ produced a forgery containing a valid signature σ^*_Δ on $(\Delta^*|Z^*)$ even though no signature has ever been queried for datatset Δ^*. This means that the adversary $\mathcal{A}$ can be used to obtain an existential forgery for the signature scheme Sig'.

If PRF is a pseudorandom function then Game 2 is computationally indistinguishable from Game 3.

We obviously have $|Pr[G_3(\mathcal{A})] - Pr[G_4(\mathcal{A})]| \leq Pr[\mathsf{Bad}_4]$.

In Lemma 3 in the Appendix we show how an adversary $\mathcal{A}$, such that $Pr[\mathsf{Bad}_4]$ is non negligible, can be used to break the DL assumption. Afterwards in Lemma 2 we show how a simulator can use an adversary winning Game 4 to break the CDH assumption.

Theorem 3. *The homomorphic signature scheme* HSig *is succinct.*

Proof. The signature size is independent of the size k of the datasets.

Theorem 4. *The homomorphic signature scheme* HSig *allows for efficient verification.*

Proof. We describe the two algorithms (VerPrep, EffVer).

VerPrep(pk, $\mathcal{P}$)**:** It parses $\mathcal{P} = ((f_1, \ldots, f_k), 1, \ldots, k)$ and takes the R_i for $i \in [k]$ contained in the public key. It computes $R_\mathcal{P} \leftarrow \prod_{i=1}^k R_i^{f_i}$ and outputs $\mathsf{pk}_\mathcal{P} = (\mathsf{pk}', \mathsf{bgp}, \{h_j\}_{j=1}^T, R_\mathcal{P})$ where $\mathsf{pk}', \mathsf{bgp}, \{h_j\}_{j=1}^T$ are taken from pk.

EffVer(pk$_\mathcal{P}$, m, σ, Δ)**:** This algorithm does the same as HVerify only the value R has been precomputed as $R_\mathcal{P}$.

Obviously this satisfies correctness and the running time of EffVer is now independent of k and therefore the runtime complexity of $\mathcal{P}$. Thus our construction is constant time (in an amortized sense).

Theorem 5. *The linearly homomorphic signature scheme* HSig *is perfectly context hiding according to Definition 7 if* Sig' *is a deterministic signature scheme.*

For the proof we refer to the appendix (see Theorem 7).

4 Linearly Homomorphic Authenticated Encryption

We will give the formal definitions for Linearly Homomorphic Authenticated Encryption with Public Verifiability.

Definition 13 *(LAEPuV [14]). A LAEPuV scheme is a tuple of five ppt algorithms* (AKeyGen, AEncrypt, AEval, AVerify, ADecrypt) *such that:*

AKeyGen($1^\lambda, k$)**:** *It takes a security parameter λ and the maximum number k of encrypted messages in each dataset as input. It returns a key pair (sk, pk), where sk is the secret key for encrypting and signing and pk is the public key used for verification and evaluation. The message space $\mathcal{M}$, the cipher space $\mathcal{C}$ and dataset identifier space $\mathcal{D}$ are implicitly defined by the public key pk.*

AEncrypt(sk, Δ, τ, m)**:** *The input is a secret key sk, a dataset identifier Δ, an input identifier τ, and a message m. The output is a cipher c.*

AEval(pk, $\mathcal{P}_\Delta, \{c_i\}_{i=1}^k$)**:** *The input is a public key pk, a multi-labeled program $\mathcal{P}_\Delta$, and a set of k ciphers $\{c_i\}_{i=1...k}$. The output is a cipher c.*

AVerify(pk, $\mathcal{P}_\Delta, c$)**:** *The input is a public key pk, a multi-labeled program $\mathcal{P}_\Delta$ containing a linear function f, and a cipher c. The output is either 1, i.e. the cipher is valid, or 0, i.e. the cipher is invalid.*

ADecrypt(sk, $\mathcal{P}_\Delta, c$)**:** *It gets a secret key sk, a multi-labeled program $\mathcal{P}_\Delta$, and a cipher c as input and outputs a message m if c is valid and $\perp$ if c is invalid, respectively.*

Definition 14 (Correctness). *Let* LAE = (AKeyGen, AEncrypt, AEval, AVerify, ADecrypt) *be a LAEPuV scheme. We say* LAE *is* correct *if the following two conditions all hold.*

1. *For any key pair* (sk, pk) ← AKeyGen($1^\lambda, k$) *and any cipher $c \in \mathcal{C}$ we have*

$$\text{AVerify}(\text{pk}, \mathcal{P}_\Delta, c) = 1 \Leftrightarrow \exists m \in \mathcal{M} : \text{ADecrypt}(\text{sk}, \mathcal{P}_\Delta, c) = m.$$

2. *Let* (sk, pk) ← AKeyGen($1^\lambda, k$) *be a key pair, $\Delta \in \{0,1\}^*$ be any dataset identifier, $m_1, \ldots, m_k \in \mathcal{M}$ be a tuple of messages, and let c_i ← AEncrypt(sk, Δ, τ_i, m_i). For any admissible multi-labeled program $\mathcal{P}_\Delta = ((f_1, \ldots, f_k), \tau_1, \ldots, \tau_k, \Delta)$ it holds that*

$$\text{ADecrypt}(\text{sk}, \mathcal{P}_\Delta, \text{AEval}(\text{pk}, \mathcal{P}_\Delta, \{c_i\}_{i=1}^k)) = f(m_1, \ldots, m_k).$$

Note that in particular, if we have $\mathcal{P}_\Delta = \mathcal{I}_{(\Delta, \tau_i)}$ the identity program, then ADecrypt(sk, $\mathcal{I}_{(\Delta, \tau)}, c_i$) = m_i *holds.*

We will give a security definition for a LAEPuV scheme in the Appendix (Definition 15).

We will now show how our linearly homomorphic signature scheme can be used to instantiate such a LAEPuV scheme LAE = (AKeyGen, AEncrypt, AEval, AVerify, ADecrypt) when using bilinear groups of *composite order*. In [7] it is shown how to construct even asymmetric bilinear groups of composite order $n = pq$. Note that previous instantiations of LAEPuV schemes can only sign messages in $\mathbb{Z}_n$, i.e. vectors of length 1, while we show the first use of LAEPuV for vectors of *polynomial length*. Note again, that in this case the input identifiers are integers $i \in [k]$.

AKeyGen($1^\lambda, k, T$): On input a security parameter λ, an integer k, and an integer T, it chooses two (safe) primes p, q and computes the modulus $n \leftarrow p \cdot q$. It runs $\mathcal{G}(1^\lambda)$ to obtain a bilinear group bgp $= (n, \mathbb{G}_1, \mathbb{G}_2, \mathbb{G}_t, g_1, g_2, e)$ of composite order and samples $k + T$ elements $R_1, \ldots, R_k, h_1, \ldots h_T \leftarrow \mathbb{G}_1$ uniformly at random. Additionally, the algorithm generates a key pair (sk′, pk′) $\leftarrow$ KeyGen′(1^λ) of a regular signature scheme and a key $K \xleftarrow{\$} \mathcal{K}$ for the pseudorandom function PRF. Furthermore it chooses an element $g \in \mathbb{Z}_{n^2}^*$ of order n as well as a hash function $H : \{0,1\}^* \to \mathbb{Z}_{n^2}^*$. It returns the key pair (sk, pk) with sk $= $ (sk′, K, p, q) and pk $= $ (bgp, H, pk′, $g, \{h_j\}_{j=1}^T, \{R_i\}_{i=1}^k$).

AEncrypt(sk, Δ, i, m): On input a secret key sk, a dataset identifier Δ, an input identifier $i \in [k]$, and a message $m \in \mathbb{Z}_n^T$, it chooses β_j uniformly at random from $\mathbb{Z}_{n^2}^*$ for $j \in [T]$. It computes the cipher $C[j] \leftarrow g^{m[j]} \cdot \beta[j]^n \mod n^2$, computes $S[j] \leftarrow H(\Delta|i|j)$ and computes $(a[j], b[j]) \in \mathbb{Z}_n \times \mathbb{Z}_n^*$ such that $g^{a[j]} \cdot b[j]^n = C[j]S[j] \mod n^2$ using the factorization of n (see [21] for a detailed description). It generates the parameters for the dataset identified by Δ, by running $z \leftarrow \mathsf{PRF}_K(\Delta)$ and computing $Z = g_2^z$. It binds Z to the dataset identifier Δ by using the regular signature scheme, i.e. it sets $\sigma_\Delta \xleftarrow{\$} \mathsf{Sign}'(\mathsf{sk}', Z|\Delta)$. Then, it computes $\Lambda \leftarrow (R_i \cdot \prod_{j=1}^T h_j^{-a[j]})^z$ and returns the the cipher $c = (C, a, b, \sigma_\Delta, Z, \Lambda)$.

AEval(pk, $\mathcal{P}_\Delta, \{c_i\}_{i=1}^k$): On input a public key pk, a multi-labeled program $\mathcal{P}_\Delta$, and a set of cipers c_i, it parses $\mathcal{P}_\Delta = ((f_1, \ldots, f_k), 1, \ldots, k, \Delta)$ and $c_i = (C_i, a_i, b_i, \sigma_{\Delta,i}, Z_i, \Lambda_i)$. If $Z_i \neq Z_1$ for any $i \in [k]$, it aborts. Otherwise, it sets

$$C \leftarrow \prod_{i=1}^k C_i^{f_i} \mod n^2 \qquad\qquad a \leftarrow \sum_{i=1}^k f_i a_i \mod n$$

$$b[j] \leftarrow \prod_{i=1}^k b_i[j]^{f_i} \mod n^2, \text{ for } j \in [T] \qquad\qquad \Lambda \leftarrow \prod_{i=1}^k \Lambda_i^{f_i} \mod n$$

It returns the cipher $c = (C, a, b, \sigma_{\Delta,1}, Z_1, \Lambda)$.

AVerify(pk, $\mathcal{P}_\Delta, c$): On input a public key pk, a multi-labeled program $\mathcal{P}_\Delta$, and a cipher c, it parses $\mathcal{P}_\Delta = ((f_1, ..., f_k), \tau_1, \ldots, \tau_k, \Delta)$ and $c = (C, a, b, \sigma_\Delta, Z, \Lambda)$. The algorithm checks whether the following equations hold:

$\mathsf{Verify}'(\mathsf{pk}', Z|\Delta, \sigma_\Delta) = 1$, $e\left(R \cdot \prod_{j=1}^{T} h_j^{-a[j]}, Z\right) = e(\Lambda, g_2)$, and $g^{a[j]} \cdot b[j]^n = C[j] \prod_{i=1}^{k} H(\Delta|i|j)^{f_i} \mod n^2$. If all checks are satisfied, it returns 1. Otherwise, it returns 0.

$\mathsf{ADecrypt}(\mathsf{sk}, \mathcal{P}_\Delta, c)$: Returns $\perp$ if $\mathsf{AVerify}(\mathsf{pk}, \mathcal{P}_\Delta, c) = 0$. Otherwise, compute (m, β) such that $g^{m[j]}\beta[j]^n = C[j] \mod n^2$ and return m.

We will formally show the correctness of LAE in Theorem 8 in the Appendix.

Theorem 6 ([14]). *In the random oracle model, if the DCR Assumption (see Definition 12) and the CDH Assumption (see Definition 11) hold and H is a random oracle the LAEPuV scheme LAE is a LH-IND-CCA secure (see Definition 15) LAEPuV scheme.*

Proof. This is a direct corollary of [14, Theorem 1] and Theorem 2.

5   Conclusion

We provide a new linearly homomorphic signature scheme directly based on the CDH assumption, without using a chameleon hash function thereby solving the problem introduced in [17]. Additionally we provide the first LAEPuV scheme that supports vectors as inputs and hereby give an alternative to the instantiation provided in [22]. Our construction achieves two additional properties, that are constant time verification and context hiding. It would be interesting to see if the security of homomorphic schemes supporting a larger class of computations can also be based on such well studied assumptions.

Acknowledgments. This work has received funding from the European Union's Horizon 2020 research and innovation program under Grant Agreement No 644962.

A   Appendix: Postponed Proofs

Lemma 2. *An efficient adversary $\mathcal{A}$ winning Game 4 in Theorem 2, can be used to break the CDH assumption.*

Proof. We will now show how to construct a simulator $\mathcal{S}$ which uses an efficient adversary $\mathcal{A}$ against Game 4 to solve the CDH problem. Let $\mathsf{bgp} = (q, \mathbb{G}_1, \mathbb{G}_2, \mathbb{G}_T, g_1, g_2, e) \leftarrow \mathcal{G}(1^\lambda)$ be a bilinear group of order q. The simulator $\mathcal{S}$ is given g_1, g_1^a, g_2^b, where $a, b \xleftarrow{\$} \mathbb{Z}_q$, and intends to compute g_1^{ab}.

Initialization: Let Q be the number of datasets in which the adversary makes signature queries. The adversary gives the simulator all messages $\{m_{(i,l)}\}_{i=1}^{k}$, for $l \in [Q]$ on which he makes signature queries.

Setup: The simulator runs the key generation algorithm of the regular signature scheme to obtain a key pair $(\mathsf{sk}', \mathsf{pk}') \leftarrow \mathsf{KeyGen}'(1^\lambda)$ and samples a key $K \xleftarrow{\$}$

$\mathcal{K}$ for the pseudorandom function PRF. The simulator guesses the dataset in which the adversary produces a forgery, in the following identified by the dataset identifier Δ. Then, it chooses $r_i \xleftarrow{\$} \mathbb{Z}_q$ for $i \in [k]$ as well as $s_j \xleftarrow{\$} \mathbb{Z}_q$ for $j \in [T]$. It sets $R_i \leftarrow g_1^{r_i} \cdot g_1^{a \cdot \sum_{j=1}^{T} m_{(i,\Delta)}[j]}$, sets $h_j = (g_1^a)^{s_j}$, and sends the public key $\mathsf{pk} = (\mathsf{pk}', g_1, \{R_i\}_{i=1}^k, \{h_j\}_{j=1}^T)$ to the adversary. Note that since the s_j and r_i are chosen uniformly at random this is perfectly indistinguishable from an honest setup.

Query: While the adversary queries signatures for messages, we distinguish between the following two cases.

- Case I: The adversary queries signatures for the dataset $\Delta_l \neq \Delta$.
- Case II: The adversary queries signatures for the dataset $\Delta_l = \Delta$.

Case I: In this case, the simulator answers the signing queries by the adversary with honestly generated signatures. More precisely, let $m_1, \ldots, m_k$ be the messages and Δ_l be the dataset identifier. The simulator computes $z \leftarrow \mathsf{PRF}_K(\Delta_l)$, sets $Z = g_2^z$, and $\sigma_\Delta \leftarrow \mathsf{Sign}'(\mathsf{sk}', \Delta_l | Z)$. Then, for any $i \in [k]$, it computes $\Lambda_i \leftarrow (R_i \cdot \prod_{j=1}^{T} h_j^{-m_i[j]})^z$ and returns the set of signatures $\boldsymbol{\sigma} = \{(\sigma_{\Delta_l}, Z, \Lambda_i)\}_{i=1}^k$. The validity of the signatures can be easily verified.

Case II: In this case the simulator $\mathcal{A}$ queries signatures in the dataset the simulator expects $\mathcal{A}$ to produce a forgery in. It chooses $u \leftarrow \mathbb{Z}_q$ uniformly at random and sets $Z = (g_2^b)^u$. Let $m_1, \ldots, m_k$ be the messages and Δ be the dataset identifier. The simulator sets $\sigma_\Delta \leftarrow \mathsf{Sign}'(\mathsf{sk}', Z|\Delta)$. Then, for $i = \in [k]$, the simulator computes $\Lambda_i \leftarrow (g_2^b)^{u r_i}$ and returns the signatures $\boldsymbol{\sigma} = (\sigma_1, \ldots, \sigma_k)$, where $\sigma_i = (\sigma_\Delta, Z, \Lambda_i)$. Note that for any $i = 1, \ldots, k$, it holds that

$$
e(R_i \cdot \prod_{j=1}^{T} h_j^{-m_i[j]}, Z) = e(g_1^{r_i} \cdot g_1^{a \cdot s_j \cdot m_i[j]} \cdot (g_1^{a \cdot s_j})^{-m_i[j]}, g_2^{ub})
$$

$$
= e(g_1^{r_i}, g_2)^{ub} = e((g_1^{u r_i})^b, g_2) = e(\Lambda, g_2)
$$

Thus, σ_i is a valid signature for any $i \in [k]$ and the simulated signatures are perfectly indistinguishable from honestly generated signatures.

Challenge. Let $(\mathcal{P}_{\Delta^*}^*, m^*, \sigma^*)$ be the forgery returned by the adversary $\mathcal{A}$. Parse $\sigma^* = (\sigma_{\Delta^*}^*, Z^*, \Lambda^*))$ and $\mathcal{P}_{\Delta^*}^* = (f^*, 1, \ldots, k, \Delta^*)$. If $\Delta^* \neq \Delta$, restart the simulation. Otherwise, the simulator evaluates the function f^* over the dataset identified by Δ, i.e. it computes $m \leftarrow f^*(m_1, ..., m_k)$ and $\sigma = (\sigma_\Delta, Z, \Lambda) \leftarrow \mathsf{HEval}(\mathsf{pk}, \Delta, \boldsymbol{\sigma}, f^*)$. Note that we have $\prod_{j=1}^{T} h_j^{m[j]} \neq \prod_{j=1}^{T} h_j^{m^*[j]}$, since $\mathsf{bad}_4 = \mathsf{false}$ and therefore also $\sum_{j=1}^{T} s_j \cdot m[j] \neq \sum_{j=1}^{T} s_j \cdot m^*[j]$. It returns

$(\Lambda \cdot (\Lambda^*)^{-1})^{(\sum_{j=1}^T s_j(m^*[j]-m[j]))^{-1}}$ as a solution. Let $R \leftarrow \prod_{i=1}^k R_i^{f_i}$. Since Λ and Λ^* are valid signatures for the function f^*, it holds that

$$\Lambda = \left(R \cdot \prod_{j=1}^T h_j^{-m[j]}\right)^{ub} = \left(R^{ub} \cdot (g_1^a)^{-ub(\sum_{j=1}^T s_j m[j])}\right)$$

$$= R^{ub} \cdot g_1^{-(\sum_{j=1}^T s_j m[j])uab}$$

$$\Lambda^* = \left(R \cdot \prod_{j=1}^T h_j^{-m^*[j]}\right)^{ub}$$

$$= R^{ub}(g_1^a)^{-ub(\sum_{j=1}^T s_j m^*[j])} = R^{ub} g_1^{-(\sum_{j=1}^T s_j m^*[j])uab}$$

Therefore, we have

$$\Lambda \cdot (\Lambda^*)^{-1} = \left(R^{ub} \cdot g_1^{-u(\sum_{j=1}^T s_j \cdot m[j])ab}\right) \cdot \left(R^{-ub} \cdot g_1^{u(\sum_{j=1}^T s_j \cdot m^*[j])ab}\right)$$

$$= g_1^{(\sum_{j=1}^T s_j \cdot m^*[j])uab} \cdot g_1^{-(\sum_{j=1}^T s_j \cdot m[j])uab} = g_1^{ab(u\sum_{j=1}^T s_j(m^*[j]-m[j]))}$$

which yields

$$(\Lambda \cdot (\Lambda^*)^{-1})^{\frac{1}{u\sum_{j=1}^T s_j(m^*[j]-m[j])}} = (g_1^{ba})^{\frac{u\sum_{j=1}^T s_j(m^*[j]-m[j])}{u\sum_{j=1}^T s_j(m^*[j]-m[j])}} = g_1^{ab}$$

Since the simulator guesses the right dataset with probability at least $1/Q$, it holds that

$$\Pr[\mathbf{Adv}(\mathcal{S})] \geq \frac{1}{Q} \cdot \Pr[G_4(\mathcal{A})]$$

which proves the statement.

Lemma 3. *Assuming the DL assumption holds in $\mathbb{G}_1$ then $Pr[\mathsf{Bad}_4] \leq \mathsf{negl}(\lambda)$*

Proof. Given $g_1, g_1' \in \mathbb{G}_1$ from bgp we show how to simulate the game in order to break the discrete logarithm in $\mathbb{G}_1$, i.e. computing x for $g_1' = g_1^x$. The simulator chooses an index $\nu \in [T]$. It follows the protocol faithfully except for the generation of the h_j. It chooses $s_j \xleftarrow{\$} \mathbb{Z}_q$. and sets $h_j = g_1^{s_j}$ for all $j \neq \nu$ and sets $h_\nu = g_1'^{s_\nu}$. This is perfectly indistinguishable from a real execution of the game. It answers all queries faithfully. When the adversary returns a forgery $(\mathcal{P}^*_{\Delta^*}, m^*, \sigma^*)$ it checks whether $m[\nu] \neq m^*[\nu]$. If not it restarts the simulation. Otherwise we know that $\prod_{j=1}^T h_j^{m[j]} = \prod_{j=1}^T h_j^{m^*[j]}$ and therefore we have

$$s_\nu m[\nu]x + \sum_{j=1,j\neq\nu}^T s_j m[j] = s_\nu m^*[\nu]x + \sum_{j=1,j\neq\nu}^T s_j m^*[j]$$

$$\Leftrightarrow x = \frac{1}{s_\nu(m[\nu] - m^*[\nu])} \sum_{j=1,j\neq\nu}^T s_j(m^*[j] - m[j])$$

and found the discrete logarithm $g_1^x = g_1'$.

Theorem 7. *The linearly homomorphic signature scheme* HSig *is perfectly context hiding according to Definition 7 if* Sig′ *is a deterministic signature scheme.*

Proof. First we note that in our case the algorithm HHide is just the identity function, i.e. $\sigma \leftarrow$ HHide(pk, m, σ) for all pk, m, σ and we have HHideVer $=$ HVerify. We will show how to construct a simulator Sim that outputs signatures perfectly indistinguishable from the ones obtained by running HEval. Parse the simulator's input as sk $=$ (sk′, K), $\mathcal{P}_\Delta = ((f_1, \ldots, f_k), 1, \ldots, k, \Delta)$, and $\tilde{m} = (\tilde{m}[1], \ldots, \tilde{m}[T])$. With this information the simulator computes the following:

$$Z' = g_2^z \text{ where } z \leftarrow \mathsf{PRF}_K(\Delta)$$
$$\sigma'_\Delta \overset{\$}{\leftarrow} \mathsf{Sign}'(\mathsf{sk}', Z|\Delta)$$
$$\Lambda' = (\textstyle\prod_{i=1}^k R_i^{f_i} \cdot \textstyle\prod_{j=1}^T h_j^{-m[j]})^z$$

The simulator outputs the signature $\sigma' = (\sigma'_\Delta, Z', \Lambda')$.

We will now show that this simulator allows for perfectly context hiding security. We will fix an arbitrary key pair (sk, pk), a multi-labeled program $((f_1, \ldots, f_k), 1, \ldots, k, \Delta)$, and messages $m_1, \ldots, m_k \in \mathbb{Z}_q^T$.
Let $\sigma \leftarrow$ HEval(pk, $\mathcal{P}_\Delta, \boldsymbol{\sigma}$) and parse it as $\sigma = (\sigma_\Delta, Z, \Lambda)$.
We look at each component of the signature.
We have $Z = \mathsf{PRF}_K(\Delta)$ by definition and therefore also $Z = Z'$. In particularly we also have $z = z'$ where $Z = g_2^z$ and $Z' = g_2^{z'}$.
We have $\sigma_\Delta = \mathsf{Sign}'(\mathsf{sk}', Z|\Delta)$ by definition and since $Z = Z'$ therefore also $\sigma_\Delta = \sigma'_\Delta$ since Sign′ is deterministic.
We have $\Lambda = \prod_{i=1}^k (R_i \cdot \prod_{j=1}^T h_j^{-m_i[j]})^{z \cdot f_i} = (\prod_{i=1}^k R_i^{f_i})^z \cdot (\prod_{j=1}^T \prod_{i=1}^k h_j^{-f_i \cdot m_i[j]})^z$
$= (\prod_{i=1}^k R_i^{f_i} \cdot \prod_{j=1}^T h_j^{-m[j]})^z$, where the last equation holds since $m = \sum_{i=1}^k f_i \cdot m_i$. Thus we also have $\Lambda = \Lambda'$.
We can see that we have *identical* elements and therefore even a computationally unbounded distinguisher has no advantage distinguishing the two cases.

Definition 15. (LH-IND-CCA [13]**).** *Let* LAE $=$ (AKeyGen, AEncrypt, AEval, AVerify, ADecrypt) *be a LAEPuV scheme. We define the following experiment* $LH - IND - CCA_{\mathcal{H},\mathcal{A}}(1^\lambda, k)$ *between a challenger* $\mathcal{C}$ *and an adversary* $\mathcal{A}$:

Setup: *The challenger runs* (sk, pk) $\leftarrow$ AKeyGen($1^\lambda, k$). *Then it initializes an empty list* $\mathcal{L}$ *and gives* pk *to the adversary* $\mathcal{A}$.
Queries I: $\mathcal{A}$ *can ask a polynomial number of both encryption and decryption queries. The former are of the form* (m, Δ, τ) *where* $m \in \mathcal{M}$ *is a message,* $\Delta \in \{0, 1\}^*$ *is a dataset identifier, and* $\tau \in \mathcal{T}$ *is an input identifier. The challenger computes* $c \leftarrow$ AEncrypt(sk, Δ, τ, m), *gives* c *to* $\mathcal{A}$ *and updates the list* $\mathcal{L} \leftarrow \mathcal{L} \cup \{(m, \Delta, \tau)\}$. *If* $\mathcal{L}$ *already contains a query* $(\cdot, \Delta, \tau)$ *the challenger* $\mathcal{C}$ *will answer* $\perp$. *The latter queries are of the form* $(\mathcal{P}_\Delta, c)$ *and* $\mathcal{A}$ *receives the output of* ADecrypt(sk, $\mathcal{P}_\Delta, c$). *Note that this can be* $\perp$ *if* c *is not a valid cipher.*
Challenge: $\mathcal{A}$ *produces a challenge tuple* $(m_0, m_1, \Delta^*, \tau^*)$. *If a query of the form* $(\cdot, \Delta^*, \tau^*)$ *is contained in* $\mathcal{L}$, *the challenger returns* $\perp$ *as before.*

The challenger chooses a random bit $b \overset{\$}{\leftarrow} \{0,1\}$ *and gives* $c^* \leftarrow$ AEncrypt(sk, Δ^*, τ^*, m_b) *to* $\mathcal{A}$. *Then it updates the list* $\mathcal{L} \leftarrow \mathcal{L} \cup \{(m_b, \Delta^*, \tau^*)\}$.

Queries II: *This phase is carried out similar to the Queries I phase. Any decryption query* $(\mathcal{P}_{\Delta^*}, c)$ *with* $\mathcal{P}_{\Delta^*} = ((f_1, \ldots, f_k), \tau_1, \ldots, \tau_k, \Delta^*)$ *where* $f_{\tau^*} \neq 0$ *is answered with* $\perp$. *All other queries are answered as in phase Queries I.*

Output: *Finally* $\mathcal{A}$ *outputs a bit* $b' \in \{0,1\}$. *The challenger outputs* 1 *if* $b = b'$ *and* 0 *otherwise.*

We say that a LAEPuV scheme is LH-IND-CCA secure if for any ppt adversary $\mathcal{A}$ *we have*

$$|Pr[LH - IND - CCA_{\mathsf{LAE}, \mathcal{A}}(1^\lambda, k) = 1] - 1/2| \leq \mathsf{negl}(\lambda).$$

Theorem 8. *The LAEPuV scheme* LAE *is correct in the sense of Definition 14.*

Proof. We fix a random key pair $(\mathsf{sk}, \mathsf{pk}) \leftarrow \mathsf{AKeyGen}(1^\lambda, k, T)$, with $\mathsf{sk} = (\mathsf{sk}', K, p, q)$ and $\mathsf{pk} = (\mathsf{bgp}, H, \mathsf{pk}', g, \{h_j\}_{j=1}^T, \{R_i\}_{i=1}^k)$.

1 If $g \in \mathbb{Z}_{n^2}^*$ has order n then the map: $\mathbb{Z}_n \times \mathbb{Z}_n^* \to \mathbb{Z}_{n^2}^*$, $(a, b) \mapsto g^a \cdot b^n$ is an isomorphism (see [21]). If $\mathsf{AVerify}(\mathsf{pk}, \mathcal{P}_\Delta, c) = 1$ holds then we have in particular $g^{a[j]} \cdot b[j]^n = C[j] \prod_{i=1}^k H(\Delta|i|j)^{f_i} \mod n^2$, where each $g^{a[j]} \cdot b[j]^n$ and $H(\Delta|i|j)^{f_i}$ is an element of $\mathbb{Z}_{n^2}^*$. Since this is a group so is every $C[j]$ which means every Paillier decryption yields a valid message m.

2 We choose messages $m_i \overset{\$}{\leftarrow} \mathbb{Z}_n^T$ as well as a dataset identifier $\Delta \in \{0,1\}^*$ and a multi-labeled program $\mathcal{P}_\Delta = ((f_1, \ldots, f_k), \tau_1, \ldots, \tau_k, \Delta)$. Let $c_i \leftarrow \mathsf{AEncrypt}(\mathsf{sk}, \Delta, i, m_i)$ and $c \leftarrow \mathsf{AEval}(\mathsf{pk}, \mathcal{P}_\Delta, \{c_i\}_{i=1}^k)$. By definition we have $c = (C, a, b, \sigma_\Delta, Z, \Lambda)$. Where for each $j \in [T]$ we have

$$C[j] = \prod_{i=1}^k \left(g^{m_i[j]} \beta_i[j]^n\right)^{f_i} = g^{\sum_{i=1}^k f_i m_i[j]} \left(\prod_{i=1}^k \beta_i[j]^{f_i}\right)^n \mod n^2$$

$$g^{a[j]} \cdot b[j]^n = g^{\sum_{i=1}^k f_i a_i[j]} \cdot \left(\prod_{i=1}^k b_i[j]^{f_i}\right)^n = \prod_{i=1}^k \left(C[j]^{f_i} \cdot H(\Delta|i|j)^{f_i}\right)$$

$$= C \cdot \prod_{i=1}^k (H(\Delta|i|j)^{f_i}) \mod n^2$$

$$z = \mathsf{PRF}_K(\Delta), \quad Z = g_2^z, \quad \sigma_\Delta = \mathsf{Sign}'(\mathsf{sk}', Z|\Delta)$$

$$\Lambda = \prod_{i=1}^k \Lambda_i^{f_i} = \left(\prod_{i=1}^k R_i^{f_i} \cdot \prod_{j=1}^T h_j^{-\sum_{i=1}^k f_i a_i[j]}\right)^z = \left(R \cdot \prod_{j=1}^T h_j^{-a[j]}\right)^z$$

Therefore we have $\mathsf{AVerify}(\mathsf{pk}, \mathcal{P}_\Delta, C) = 1$ and due to the first equation Paillier decryption of $C[j]$ yields $\sum_{i=1}^k f_i m_i[j]$ for each $j \in [T]$.

References

1. An, J.H., Bellare, M.: Does encryption with redundancy provide authenticity? In: Pfitzmann, B. (ed.) EUROCRYPT 2001. LNCS, vol. 2045, pp. 512–528. Springer, Heidelberg (2001). https://doi.org/10.1007/3-540-44987-6_31

2. Attrapadung, N., Libert, B.: Homomorphic network coding signatures in the standard model. In: Catalano, D., Fazio, N., Gennaro, R., Nicolosi, A. (eds.) PKC 2011. LNCS, vol. 6571, pp. 17–34. Springer, Heidelberg (2011). https://doi.org/10.1007/978-3-642-19379-8_2

3. Attrapadung, N., Libert, B., Peters, T.: Computing on authenticated data: new privacy definitions and constructions. In: Wang, X., Sako, K. (eds.) ASIACRYPT 2012. LNCS, vol. 7658, pp. 367–385. Springer, Heidelberg (2012). https://doi.org/10.1007/978-3-642-34961-4_23

4. Attrapadung, N., Libert, B., Peters, T.: Efficient completely context-hiding quotable and linearly homomorphic signatures. In: Kurosawa, K., Hanaoka, G. (eds.) PKC 2013. LNCS, vol. 7778, pp. 386–404. Springer, Heidelberg (2013). https://doi.org/10.1007/978-3-642-36362-7_24

5. Backes, M., Fiore, D., Reischuk, R.M.: Verifiable delegation of computation on outsourced data. In: Sadeghi, A., Gligor, V.D., Yung, M. (eds.) ACM CCS. pp. 863–874. ACM (2013)

6. Bellare, M., Namprempre, C.: Authenticated encryption: relations among notions and analysis of the generic composition paradigm. J. Cryptology **21**(4), 469–491 (2008), http://dx.doi.org/10.1007/s00145-008-9026-x

7. Boneh, D., Rubin, K., Silverberg, A.: Finding composite order ordinary elliptic curves using the cocks-pinch method. J. Number Theor. **131**(5), 832-841 (2011), http://www.sciencedirect.com/science/article/pii/S0022314X10001344

8. Boneh, D., Freeman, D.M.: Linearly homomorphic signatures over binary fields and new tools for lattice-based signatures. In: Catalano, D., Fazio, N., Gennaro, R., Nicolosi, A. (eds.) PKC 2011. LNCS, vol. 6571, pp. 1–16. Springer, Heidelberg (2011). https://doi.org/10.1007/978-3-642-19379-8_1

9. Boneh, D., Freeman, D., Katz, J., Waters, B.: Signing a linear subspace: signature schemes for network coding. In: Jarecki, S., Tsudik, G. (eds.) PKC 2009. LNCS, vol. 5443, pp. 68–87. Springer, Heidelberg (2009). https://doi.org/10.1007/978-3-642-00468-1_5

10. Catalano, D., Fiore, D., Nizzardo, L.: Programmable hash functions go private: constructions and applications to (homomorphic) signatures with shorter public keys. In: Gennaro, R., Robshaw, M. (eds.) CRYPTO 2015. LNCS, vol. 9216, pp. 254–274. Springer, Heidelberg (2015). https://doi.org/10.1007/978-3-662-48000-7_13

11. Catalano, D., Fiore, D., Warinschi, B.: Efficient network coding signatures in the standard model. In: Fischlin, M., Buchmann, J., Manulis, M. (eds.) PKC 2012. LNCS, vol. 7293, pp. 680–696. Springer, Heidelberg (2012). https://doi.org/10.1007/978-3-642-30057-8_40

12. Catalano, D., Fiore, D., Warinschi, B.: Homomorphic signatures with efficient verification for polynomial functions. In: Garay, J.A., Gennaro, R. (eds.) CRYPTO 2014. LNCS, vol. 8616, pp. 371–389. Springer, Heidelberg (2014). https://doi.org/10.1007/978-3-662-44371-2_21

13. Catalano, D., Marcedone, A., Puglisi, O.: Authenticating computation on groups: New homomorphic primitives and applications. Cryptology ePrint Archive, Report 2013/801 (2013), http://eprint.iacr.org/2013/801

14. Catalano, D., Marcedone, A., Puglisi, O.: Authenticating computation on groups: new homomorphic primitives and applications. In: Sarkar and Iwata [22], pp. 193–212

15. Chatterjee, S., Hankerson, D., Knapp, E., Menezes, A.: Comparing two pairing-based aggregate signature schemes. Des. Codes Cryptography **55**(2–3), 141–167 (2010), https://doi.org/10.1007/s10623-009-9334-7

16. Desmedt, Y.: Computer security by redefining what a computer is. In: Michael, J.B., Ashby, V., Meadows, C.A. (eds.) NSPW, pp. 160–166. ACM (1993)

17. Freeman, D.M.: Improved security for linearly homomorphic signatures: a generic framework. In: Fischlin, M., Buchmann, J., Manulis, M. (eds.) PKC 2012. LNCS, vol. 7293, pp. 697–714. Springer, Heidelberg (2012). https://doi.org/10.1007/978-3-642-30057-8_41

18. Gennaro, R., Katz, J., Krawczyk, H., Rabin, T.: Secure network coding over the integers. In: Nguyen, P.Q., Pointcheval, D. (eds.) PKC 2010. LNCS, vol. 6056, pp. 142–160. Springer, Heidelberg (2010). https://doi.org/10.1007/978-3-642-13013-7_9

19. Johnson, R., Molnar, D., Song, D., Wagner, D.: Homomorphic signature schemes. In: Preneel, B. (ed.) CT-RSA 2002. LNCS, vol. 2271, pp. 244–262. Springer, Heidelberg (2002). https://doi.org/10.1007/3-540-45760-7_17

20. Joo, C., Yun, A.: Homomorphic authenticated encryption secure against chosen ciphertext attack. In: Sarkar, P., Iwata, T. (eds.) ASIACRYPT 2014. LNCS, vol. 8874, pp. 173–192. Springer, Heidelberg (2014). https://doi.org/10.1007/978-3-662-45608-8

21. Paillier, P.: Public-key cryptosystems based on composite degree residuosity classes. In: Stern, J. (ed.) EUROCRYPT 1999. LNCS, vol. 1592, pp. 223–238. Springer, Heidelberg (1999). https://doi.org/10.1007/3-540-48910-X_16

22. Struck, P., Schabhüser, L., Demirel, D., Buchmann, J.: Linearly homomorphic authenticated encryption with provable correctness and public verifiability. In: El Hajji, S., Nitaj, A., Souidi, E.M. (eds.) C2SI 2017. LNCS, vol. 10194, pp. 142–160. Springer, Cham (2017). https://doi.org/10.1007/978-3-319-55589-8_10

Subset Signatures with Controlled Context-Hiding

Essam Ghadafi[✉]

University of the West of England, Bristol, UK
essam.ghadafi@uwe.ac.uk

Abstract. Subset signatures are a variant of malleable signatures which allow anyone to derive signatures on any subset of previously signed sets in such a way that derived signatures are indistinguishable from new signatures on the subset (i.e. context-hiding). Such a primitive has many applications. In some scenarios, it might be desirable to restrict some elements in the set from preserving the context-hiding property. In other words, it might be desirable to allow the signer, at the time of the signing, to mark specific elements (which we refer to as hereafter as the *restricted subset*) such that the inclusion of any elements from the restricted subset in any derived signatures would violate the context-hiding property and make the derived signature linkable to the original signature. In this paper, we put forward the notion of subset signatures with controlled context-hiding. We propose a security model and a generic construction as well as efficient instantiations which do not rely on random oracles. Our instantiations are structure-preserving and therefore could be useful for other applications. As a special case of our constructions when the restricted subset is empty, we obtain more efficient constructions of standard subset signatures. Our constructions, which satisfy the strongest existing security definitions, have constant-size keys and outperform existing constructions in every respect.

As part of our contribution, we construct a structure-preserving signature scheme with combined unforgeability that signs a vector of group elements while maintaining constant-size signatures. The scheme has some desirable properties and combines nicely with Groth-Sahai proofs, and thus could be of independent interest.

Keywords: Malleable signatures · Subset signatures · Standard model

1 Introduction

Malleable signatures (sometimes also referred to as homomorphic signatures), first suggested by Desmedt [25], allow for computing on authenticated data. Given a message/signature pair (m, σ), anyone can derive a signature σ' on the message $m' = T(m)$ for some "allowable" transformation T. For instance, if m is a document, T could be defined as quoting or redacting from m. Johnson et al. [37] provided security definitions and early realizations of homomorphic

© Springer International Publishing AG 2017
M. O'Neill (Ed.): IMACC 2017, LNCS 10655, pp. 280–304, 2017.
https://doi.org/10.1007/978-3-319-71045-7_15

signatures. Inspired by the advent of fully homomorphic encryption [31] which allowed computing on encrypted data, and motivated by allowing computation on authenticated data, the last few years witnessed the emergence of a long line of research related to malleable signatures. Constructions of malleable signatures for arithmetic functions include [8,14–16,30]. Signature schemes supporting document redaction, i.e. redactable signatures, include [17–19,41]. Other notions permitting other types of allowable transformation, such as append-only signatures and transitive signatures, include [10,20,38–40]. Malleable signature schemes for network coding include [6,21,22,28].

Other variants of malleable signatures include quoting and subset signatures [5]. In the latter, given a signature on some set S, anyone (without knowledge of the secret signing key) can derive signatures on any subsets of S. Subset signatures without the context-hiding requirement were considered earlier by Hevia and Micciancio [36]. Ahn et al. [5] showed that by utilizing a Naor-like transformation [13], which was used to obtain signature schemes from identity-based encryption, some variants of Ciphertext-Policy Attribute-Based Encryption (CP-ABE), e.g. [4], can be used to obtain subset signatures satisfying the context-hiding requirement. As noted, by Attrapadung et al. [7], instantiating the generic idea of [5] with existing compatible CP-ABE schemes has the downside of supporting only bounded-length messages, since the maximal message length, i.e. the cardinality of the sets that can be signed, need to be fixed beforehand. Another downside is that the verification key of such instantiations depends linearly on the maximal length.

Attrapadung et al. [7] combined Groth-Sahai proofs [35], which are randomizable, with the structure-preserving signature scheme of Abe et al. [1] and Waters' signature scheme [43] to obtain an instantiation of subset signatures which do not rely on random oracles [11]. Their construction, which is over Type-1 bilinear groups, inherits the linear dependency between the verification key size and the bit-length of the message space from the underlying Waters' scheme [43].

While useful, the context-hiding property in its entirety might be a bit too strong for some applications. For instance, in some scenarios, it might be desirable for the authenticator of a message/document (or anyone else) to be able to detect if some clearly marked (e.g. sensitive) parts of the document, which we refer to hereafter as "restricted parts", have been included in future derivatives of the document without affecting the unlinkability (i.e. context-hiding) of the remaining parts of the document. In other words, as long as the derivative does not contain restricted parts from the original document, it cannot be linked to the original signature.

The main aims of this work is to generalize the notion of subset signatures to allow for the controlled context-hiding functionality and to obtain efficient constructions of the new variant as well as the original notion which is a special case of the new one.

Our Contribution. We define the notion of subset signatures with controlled context-hiding. We propose a generic construction for the primitive as well as efficient instantiations in the standard model. As a special case of our instantiations when the restricted subset is empty, we obtain more efficient (in every respect) constructions of standard subset signatures than existing constructions. In order to realize our instantiations, we construct a structure-preserving signature scheme with combined unforgeability that signs multiple group elements while maintaining constant-size signatures. Randomization of signatures is done additively and thus the scheme combines nicely with Groth-Sahai proofs. In particular, when proving knowledge of signatures, anyone can randomize the public components of the signature (part of the statement) and adapt the committed components of the signature (part of the witness) as well as the associated Groth-Sahai proofs. The latter observation is of independent interest and might be useful for other applications beyond the scope of this paper. As a special case of the new combined signature scheme, we also obtain a new (optimal) strongly unforgeable structure-preserving signature scheme in Type-3 bilinear groups.

Paper Organization. In Sect. 2, we give some preliminaries. In Sect. 3, we define the notion of subset signatures with controlled context-hiding. We present the building blocks we use in Sect. 4. In Sect. 5, we present our generic construction and provide a proof of its security. In Sect. 6, we present instantiations in the standard model.

Notation. A function $\nu(.) : \mathbb{N} \to \mathbb{R}^+$ is negligible (in n) if for every polynomial $p(.)$ and all sufficiently large values of n, it holds that $\nu(n) < \frac{1}{p(n)}$. Given a probability distribution Y, we denote by $y \leftarrow Y$ the operation of selecting an element according to Y. By PPT we mean running in probabilistic polynomial time in the relevant security parameter. By $[n]$, we denote the set $\{1, \ldots, n\}$. For an algorithm Alg, $y \leftarrow \mathsf{Alg}(x_1, \ldots, x_n; r)$ denotes the process of running Alg with inputs $x_1, \ldots, x_n$ and coins r to get output y. $y \xleftarrow{\$} \mathsf{Alg}(x_1, \ldots, x_n)$ or $\mathsf{Alg}(x_1, \ldots, x_n) \xrightarrow{\$} y$ denote the act of choosing the coin r at random and running $y \leftarrow \mathsf{Alg}(x_1, \ldots, x_n; r)$.

2   Preliminaries

In this section we provide some preliminary definitions.

2.1   Bilinear Groups

A bilinear group is a tuple $\mathcal{P} := (\mathbb{G}, \tilde{\mathbb{G}}, \mathbb{T}, p, G, \tilde{G}, e)$ where $\mathbb{G}$, $\tilde{\mathbb{G}}$ and $\mathbb{T}$ are groups of a prime order p, and G and $\tilde{G}$ generate $\mathbb{G}$ and $\tilde{\mathbb{G}}$, respectively. The function e is an efficient non-degenerate bilinear map $e : \mathbb{G} \times \tilde{\mathbb{G}} \longrightarrow \mathbb{T}$. We use multiplicative notation for all the groups. We let $\mathbb{G}^\times := \mathbb{G} \setminus \{1_\mathbb{G}\}$ and $\tilde{\mathbb{G}}^\times := \tilde{\mathbb{G}} \setminus \{1_{\tilde{\mathbb{G}}}\}$. We limit our attention to the efficient Type-3 setting [29], where $\mathbb{G} \neq \tilde{\mathbb{G}}$ and there is no efficient isomorphism between the groups in either direction. We assume there is an algorithm BG taking as input a security parameter λ and outputting a description of bilinear groups.

2.2 Intractability Assumptions

We list here some existing assumptions.

Definition 1 (Decisional Diffie-Hellman (DDH) Assumption). *The DDH assumption holds w.r.t. a group setup $\mathcal{G}$ if for all PPT adversaries $\mathcal{A}$, there exists a negligible (in λ) function ν s.t.*

$$\Pr\left[\begin{array}{l} (\mathbb{G}, G, p) \xleftarrow{\$} \mathcal{G}(1^\lambda);\ x, y, z \xleftarrow{\$} \mathbb{Z}_p;\ b \xleftarrow{\$} \{0,1\}; \\ X := G^x;\ Y := G^y;\ Z := G^{bxy+(1-b)z}\ : \mathcal{A}(G, X, Y, Z) = b \end{array}\right] \le \frac{1}{2} + \nu(\lambda)\ .$$

Definition 2 (Symmetric External Diffie-Hellman (SXDH) Assumption). *Given a bilinear group $\mathcal{P} := (\mathbb{G}, \tilde{\mathbb{G}}, \mathbb{T}, p, G, \tilde{G}, e)$, the SXDH assumption requires that the DDH assumption holds in both groups $\mathbb{G}$ and $\tilde{\mathbb{G}}$.*

2.3 Combined Digital Signatures

A signature scheme can either satisfy the standard notion of unforgeabiliy or strong unforgeability. In the latter (which implies the former), the adversary wins even if she forges a signature on a message that she obtained a signature on from the oracle. Of course, to obtain both variants simultaneously, one can interleave two different schemes each meeting one of the desired security variants. However, as recently argued by Groth [34], such an approach results in less efficient schemes that are conceptually less elegant than a unified scheme. Groth recently defined a combined notion and gave structure-preserving constructions.

A combined signature scheme over a bilinear group $\mathcal{P}$ generated by BG for a message space $\mathcal{M}$ is a tuple

$$\mathcal{CDS} := (\mathsf{KeyGen}, \mathsf{Sign}_0, \mathsf{Verify}_0, \mathsf{Sign}_1, \mathsf{Verify}_1, \mathsf{Randomize}),$$

where:

$\mathsf{KeyGen}(\mathcal{P})$ outputs a pair of secret/verification keys $(\mathsf{sk}, \mathsf{vk})$.

$\mathsf{Sign}_0(\mathsf{sk}, m)$ on input sk and a message $m \in \mathcal{M}$, outputs a randomizable signature σ.

$\mathsf{Verify}_0(\mathsf{vk}, m, \sigma)$ this deterministic algorithm outputs 1 if σ (produced by Sign_0) is a valid signature on m w.r.t. vk, and 0 otherwise.

$\mathsf{Sign}_1(\mathsf{sk}, m)$ on input sk and a message $m \in \mathcal{M}$, outputs a strongly unforgeable signature σ.

$\mathsf{Verify}_1(\mathsf{vk}, m, \sigma)$ this deterministic algorithm outputs 1 if σ (produced by Sign_1) is a valid signature on m w.r.t. vk, and 0 otherwise.

$\mathsf{Randomize}(\mathsf{vk}, m, \sigma)$ if the valid signature σ was produced by Sign_0, it returns a new randomized signature σ' on m. If σ was produced by Sign_1, the algorithm returns the original signatures σ.

Besides (perfect) correctness, which requires that signatures produced by both modes are accepted, we require the following two properties.

Definition 3 (Combined Existential Unforgeability). *A combined signature scheme* $\mathcal{CDS}$ *over a bilinear group generator* BG *satisfies combined existential unforgeability against adaptive chosen-message attack (CEUF-CMA) if for all* $\lambda \in \mathbb{N}$ *for all PPT adversaries* $\mathcal{A}$*, the following is negligible (in λ)*

$$\Pr \left[\begin{array}{l} \mathcal{P} \xleftarrow{\$} \mathsf{BG}(1^\lambda); (\mathsf{sk}, \mathsf{vk}) \xleftarrow{\$} \mathsf{KeyGen}(\mathcal{P}); \\ (\sigma^*, m^*) \xleftarrow{\$} \mathcal{A}^{\mathsf{Sign}_0(\mathsf{sk}, \cdot), \mathsf{Sign}_1(\mathsf{sk}, \cdot)}(\mathcal{P}, \mathsf{vk}) \\ \quad : (\mathsf{Verify}_0(\mathsf{vk}, m^*, \sigma^*) = 1 \ \wedge \ m^* \notin Q_0) \\ \quad\quad \vee \ (\mathsf{Verify}_1(\mathsf{vk}, m^*, \sigma^*) = 1 \ \wedge \ (m^*, \sigma^*) \notin Q_1) \end{array} \right],$$

where Q_1 *is the set of messages/signatures returned by* Sign_1 *and* Q_0 *is the set of messages queried to* Sign_0*.*

Definition 4 (Perfect Randomizability). *A combined signature scheme* $\mathcal{CDS}$ *over a bilinear group generator* BG *is perfectly randomizable if for all* $\lambda \in \mathbb{N}$ *for all stateful adversaries* $\mathcal{A}$

$$\Pr \left[\begin{array}{l} \mathcal{P} \xleftarrow{\$} \mathsf{BG}(1^\lambda); (\mathsf{sk}, \mathsf{vk}) \xleftarrow{\$} \mathsf{KeyGen}(\mathcal{P}); (\sigma^*, m^*) \xleftarrow{\$} \mathcal{A}(\mathcal{P}, \mathsf{sk}, \mathsf{vk}); \\ b \xleftarrow{\$} \{0,1\}; \sigma_0 \xleftarrow{\$} \mathsf{Sign}_0(\mathsf{sk}, m^*); \sigma_1 \xleftarrow{\$} \mathsf{Randomize}(\mathsf{vk}, m^*, \sigma^*) \\ \quad : \mathsf{Verify}_0(\mathsf{vk}, m^*, \sigma^*) = 1 \ \wedge \ \mathcal{A}(\sigma_b) = b \end{array} \right] = \frac{1}{2}.$$

Note that our randomizability definition is stronger than that of [34] as we allow the adversary to create the original signature σ^*.

2.4   Structure-Preserving Signatures

A structure-preserving signature scheme [1] is a signature scheme defined over bilinear groups where the messages, the verification key and signatures are all group elements and verifying signatures only involves deciding group membership of the signature components and evaluating pairing-product equations. of the form of equation (1).

$$\prod_i \prod_j e(A_i, \tilde{B}_j)^{c_{i,j}} = 1_{\mathbb{T}}, \tag{1}$$

where $A_i \in \mathbb{G}$ and $\tilde{B}_j \in \tilde{\mathbb{G}}$ are group elements appearing in $\mathcal{P}, m, \mathsf{vk}, \sigma$, whereas $c_{i,j} \in \mathbb{Z}_p$ are constants.

3   Subset Signatures with Controlled Context-Hiding

Here we define Subset Signatures with Controlled Context-Hiding (SS-CCH).

For a message space $\mathcal{M}$, we denote by $\mathcal{P}(M)$ its powerset and by $\mathcal{P}^*(M)$ its powerset excluding the empty subset, i.e. $\mathcal{P}^*(\mathcal{M}) = \mathcal{P}(\mathcal{M}) \setminus \emptyset$. A homomorphic signature scheme with controlled context-hiding for a subset predicate for a message space $\mathcal{M}$ is a tuple of polynomial-time algorithms (KeyGen, Sign, Derive, Verify, Link), whose definitions are as follows:

KeyGen$(1^\lambda) \xrightarrow{\$} (\mathsf{sk}, \mathsf{vk})$: is a probabilistic key generation algorithm, which on input a security parameter 1^λ outputs a secret signing/public verification key pair $(\mathsf{sk}, \mathsf{vk})$.

Sign$(\mathsf{sk}, \mathcal{S}, \mathcal{S}_{\mathsf{restrict}}) \xrightarrow{\$} \sigma$: is a probabilistic signing algorithm which on input the signing key sk, a set $\mathcal{S} \in \mathcal{P}^*(\mathcal{M})$ and a possibly empty set $\mathcal{S}_{\mathsf{restrict}} \in \mathcal{P}(\mathcal{M})$, outputs either a signature σ on the set $\mathcal{S}$ or the reject symbol $\perp$ if $\mathcal{S}_{\mathsf{restrict}} \notin \mathcal{P}(\mathcal{S})$, i.e. if $\mathcal{S}_{\mathsf{restrict}} \not\subseteq \mathcal{S}$.

Derive$(\mathsf{vk}, \mathcal{S}, \sigma, \mathcal{S}') \xrightarrow{\$} \sigma'$: on input the verification key vk, a set $\mathcal{S} \in \mathcal{P}^*(\mathcal{M})$, a signature σ on $\mathcal{S}$, and a set $\mathcal{S}' \subseteq \mathcal{S}$, derives a signature on the subset $\mathcal{S}'$. The algorithm returns the reject symbol $\perp$ if $\mathcal{S}' \not\subseteq \mathcal{S}$ or σ is not a valid signature on the set $\mathcal{S}$.

Verify$(\mathsf{vk}, \mathcal{S}, \sigma) \to 0/1$: is a deterministic algorithm which on input the verification key vk, a set $\mathcal{S} \in \mathcal{P}^*(\mathcal{M})$ and a signature σ, outputs either 0 or 1.

IsRestricted$(\mathsf{vk}, \mathcal{S}, \sigma, \mathcal{S}_{\mathbf{R}})$: is an additional deterministic polynomial-time algorithm which is only used in the security definitions to ease composition. It returns 1 if the signature σ is a valid signature on the set $\mathcal{S}$ and there is a subset $\mathcal{S}_{\mathrm{R}'}$ satisfying $\mathcal{S}_{\mathrm{R}'} \subseteq \mathcal{S}_{\mathrm{R}} \subseteq \mathcal{S}$ where the elements of $\mathcal{S}_{\mathrm{R}'}$ marked as restricted elements within the signature σ. If σ does not contain any such restricted elements from $\mathcal{S}_{\mathrm{R}}$, the algorithm returns 0.

Link$(\mathsf{vk}, \mathcal{S}_1, \sigma_1, \mathcal{S}_2, \sigma_2) \to 0/1$: is a deterministic algorithm which on input the verification key vk, two pairs of set/signature $(\mathcal{S}_i, \sigma_i)$, the algorithm outputs 1 if all of the following conditions are satisfied or 0 otherwise:

(i) σ_1 and σ_2 are valid signatures on the sets $\mathcal{S}_1$ and $\mathcal{S}_2$, respectively.

(ii) Either of the following holds:

- $\mathcal{S}_1 \subseteq \mathcal{S}_2$, σ_1 was derived from σ_2 and IsRestricted$(\mathsf{vk}, \mathcal{S}_2, \sigma_2, \mathcal{S}_1) = 1$.
- $\mathcal{S}_1 \supseteq \mathcal{S}_2$, σ_2 was derived from σ_1, and IsRestricted$(\mathsf{vk}, \mathcal{S}_1, \sigma_1, \mathcal{S}_2) = 1$.

(Perfect) correctness requires that for all $(\mathsf{sk}, \mathsf{vk}) \in [\mathsf{KeyGen}(1^\lambda)]$, all sets $\mathcal{S} \in \mathcal{P}^*(\mathcal{M})$, all sets $\mathcal{S}_{\mathsf{restrict}} \in \mathcal{P}(\mathcal{S})$, all sets $\mathcal{S}' \in \mathcal{P}^*(\mathcal{S})$, all signatures $\sigma \in [\mathsf{Sign}(\mathsf{sk}, \mathcal{S}, \mathcal{S}_{\mathsf{restrict}})]$, all sets $\mathcal{S}_{\mathrm{R}} \in \mathcal{P}^*(\mathcal{S})$ satisfying IsRestricted$(\mathsf{vk}, \mathcal{S}, \sigma, \mathcal{S}_{\mathrm{R}}) = 1$, we have that:

$$\Pr\left[\begin{array}{l} \mathsf{Verify}(\mathsf{vk}, \mathcal{S}, \sigma) = 1 \quad \wedge \quad \mathsf{Verify}(\mathsf{vk}, \mathcal{S}', \mathsf{Derive}(\mathsf{vk}, \mathcal{S}, \sigma, \mathcal{S}')) = 1 \\ \wedge \quad \mathsf{Link}(\mathsf{vk}, \mathcal{S}, \sigma, \mathcal{S}_{\mathrm{R}}, \mathsf{Derive}(\mathsf{vk}, \mathcal{S}, \sigma, \mathcal{S}_{\mathrm{R}})) = 1 \end{array}\right] = 1 \,.$$

Security requires *unforgeability*, *privacy* (i.e. *context-hiding*) and *linkability*.

The unforgeability requirement ensures that it is infeasible for an adversary to produce a signature on a new set which is not a subset of any of the sets she obtained signatures on from the signing oracle.

Definition 5 (Unforgeability). *We say the scheme satisfies* unforgeability *if for all $\lambda \in \mathbb{N}$, all PPT adversaries have a negligible advantage in winning the game below in which the following initially empty data structures are maintained:*

- Q_{Sign}: *is a list maintaining input/output of queries to the Sign and Derive oracles.*
- Q_{Reveal}: *is a set whose elements are set-signature pairs from the list Q_{Sign} that have been revealed to the adversary.*

The unforgeability game is as follows:

- *The challenger runs $(\mathsf{sk}, \mathsf{vk}) \xleftarrow{\$} \mathsf{KeyGen}(1^\lambda)$ and gives vk to $\mathcal{A}$. The challenger also initializes a global counter $\mathsf{cnt} = 0$.*
- *$\mathcal{A}$ has an adaptive access to the following oracles:*
  - ***Sign:*** *on input $(\mathcal{S}, \mathcal{S}_{\mathsf{restrict}})$, it runs $\sigma \xleftarrow{\$} \mathsf{Sign}(\mathsf{sk}, \mathcal{S}, \mathcal{S}_{\mathsf{restrict}})$. It increments the counter cnt, sets $Q_{Sign}[\mathsf{cnt}] := (\mathcal{S}, \sigma)$ and returns cnt to $\mathcal{A}$.*
  - ***Derive:*** *on input $(\mathsf{ind}, \mathcal{S}')$, it returns $\bot$ if $\mathsf{ind} \notin [\mathsf{cnt}]$. Otherwise, it parses $Q_{Sign}[\mathsf{ind}]$ as $(\mathcal{S}, \sigma)$ and returns $\bot$ if $\mathcal{S}' \not\subseteq \mathcal{S}$. Otherwise, it runs $\sigma' \xleftarrow{\$} \mathsf{Derive}(\mathsf{vk}, \mathcal{S}, \sigma, \mathcal{S}')$, increments the counter cnt and sets $Q_{Sign}[\mathsf{cnt}] := (\mathcal{S}', \sigma')$ and returns cnt to $\mathcal{A}$.*
  - ***Reveal:*** *on input an index ind, it returns $\bot$ if $\mathsf{ind} \notin [\mathsf{cnt}]$. Otherwise, it updates Q_{Reveal} by computing $Q_{Reveal} := Q_{Reveal} \cup Q_{Sign}[\mathsf{ind}]$, and returns the content of $Q_{Sign}[\mathsf{ind}]$ to $\mathcal{A}$.*
- *Eventually, $\mathcal{A}$ halts by returning a pair $(\mathcal{S}^*, \sigma^*)$.*

The adversary wins if all the following conditions hold:

1. $\mathsf{Verify}(\mathsf{vk}, \mathcal{S}^*, \sigma^*) = 1$.
2. $\mathcal{S}^* \notin \bigcup_{i=1}^{|Q_{Reveal}|} \mathcal{P}^*(\mathcal{S}_i)$, *i.e. $\mathcal{S}^*$ is not a subset of any of the sets $\mathcal{S}_i$ in Q_{Reveal}.*

Linkability ensures that a derived signature on a set containing restricted elements is always linkable to the original signature from which it was derived.

Definition 6 (Linkability). *We say the scheme satisfies* linkability *if for all $\lambda \in \mathbb{N}$, all PPT adversaries have a negligible advantage in winning the following game in which the following initially empty data structures are maintained:*

- *Q_{Sign}: is a list whose entries are triples. The first two components are sets, whereas the last is a signature.*

The linkability game is as follows:

- *The challenger runs $(\mathsf{sk}, \mathsf{vk}) \xleftarrow{\$} \mathsf{KeyGen}(1^\lambda)$ and gives vk to $\mathcal{A}$. The challenger also initializes a global counter $\mathsf{cnt} = 0$.*
- *$\mathcal{A}$ has access to a sign oracle which on input $(\mathcal{S}, \mathcal{S}_{\mathsf{restrict}})$, returns a signature σ on the set $\mathcal{S}$. After each invocation, the oracle increments cnt and updates Q_{Sign} by computing $Q_{Sign}[\mathsf{cnt}] := (\mathcal{S}, \mathcal{S}_{\mathsf{restrict}}, \sigma)$. We will denote the first component of the i-th entry of Q_{Sign}, i.e. $Q_{Sign}[i].\mathcal{S}$, by $\mathcal{S}_i$.*
- *Eventually, $\mathcal{A}$ halts by returning a pair $(\mathcal{S}^*, \sigma^*)$.*

The adversary wins if all the following conditions hold:

1. $\mathsf{Verify}(\mathsf{vk}, \mathcal{S}^*, \sigma^*) = 1$.
2. *For all* $(\mathcal{S}_i, \sigma_i)$ *returned by the sign oracle*, $\mathsf{Link}(\mathsf{vk}, \mathcal{S}_i, \sigma_i, \mathcal{S}^*, \sigma^*) = 0$.
3. $\mathcal{S}^* \in (\mathcal{P}_{\mathsf{all}} \setminus \mathcal{P}_{\mathsf{unrestrict}})$, *where* $\mathcal{P}_{\mathsf{all}} := \cup_{i=1}^{\mathsf{cnt}} \mathcal{P}^*(\mathcal{S}_i)$ *and* $\mathcal{P}_{\mathsf{unrestrict}} := \cup_{i=1}^{\mathsf{cnt}} \mathcal{P}^*(\mathcal{S}_i \setminus \mathcal{S}_{i_{\mathsf{restrict}}})$.

The context-hiding requirement ensures that derived signatures on unrestricted sets are indistinguishable from fresh signatures on those sets. It guarantees that derived signatures cannot be linked to the original signatures from which they were derived. We will define a few variants of this requirement.

Definition 7 (Adaptive Context-Hiding [7]**).** *This requires that for all* $\lambda \in \mathbb{N}$, *all PPT adversaries* $\mathcal{A}$ *have a negligible advantage in the following game:*

- *The challenger runs* $(\mathsf{sk}, \mathsf{vk}) \xleftarrow{\$} \mathsf{KeyGen}(1^\lambda)$ *and gives* $(\mathsf{sk}, \mathsf{vk})$ *to* $\mathcal{A}$.
- $\mathcal{A}$ *outputs a triple* $(\mathcal{S}, \sigma, \mathcal{S}')$ *satisfying the following conditions:*
  - $\mathsf{Verify}(\mathsf{vk}, \mathcal{S}, \sigma) = 1$, $\mathcal{S}' \subseteq \mathcal{S}$ *and* $\mathsf{IsRestricted}(\mathsf{vk}, \mathcal{S}, \sigma, \mathcal{S}') = 0$.
- *The challenger chooses a random bit* $b \xleftarrow{\$} \{0,1\}$ *and responds as follows:*
  - *If* $b = 0$, *she returns* $\sigma' \xleftarrow{\$} \mathsf{Derive}(\mathsf{vk}, \mathcal{S}, \sigma, \mathcal{S}')$.
  - *If* $b = 1$, *she returns* $\sigma' \xleftarrow{\$} \mathsf{Sign}(\mathsf{sk}, \mathcal{S}', \emptyset)$.
- *Eventually,* $\mathcal{A}$ *halts by outputting a bit* b' *as her guess for* b. $\mathcal{A}$'s advantage *in winning the game is defined as* $\mathsf{Adv}_{\mathcal{A}}(\lambda) := |2 \cdot \Pr[b = b'] - 1|$.

The above definition can be strengthened by allowing the adversary to choose the key pair $(\mathsf{sk}, \mathsf{vk})$. We refer to this variant as *Strong Adaptive Context-Hiding*.

Note that both adaptive context-hiding and strong adaptive context-hiding definitions only protect against polynomial-time adversaries. A stronger variant is where the distributions of derived signatures and fresh signatures on unrestricted sets are statistically close.

Definition 8 (Complete Context-Hiding [7]**).** *This requires that for all* $(\mathsf{sk}, \mathsf{vk}) \in [\mathsf{KeyGen}(1^\lambda)]$, *for all sets* $\mathcal{S}, \mathcal{S}' \in \mathcal{P}^*(\mathcal{M})$ *(where* $\mathcal{S}' \subseteq \mathcal{S}$*), for all signatures* $\sigma \in [\mathsf{Sign}(\mathsf{sk}, \mathcal{S}, \cdot)]$ *satisfying* $\mathsf{Verify}(\mathsf{vk}, \mathcal{S}, \sigma) = 1$ *and* $\mathsf{IsRestricted}(\mathsf{vk}, \mathcal{S}, \sigma, \mathcal{S}') = 0$, *the following two distributions, which are taken over the random coins of* Sign *and* Derive, *are statistically close:*

$$\left\{ (\mathsf{sk}, \mathsf{Sign}(\mathsf{sk}, \mathcal{S}', \emptyset)) \right\}_{\mathsf{sk}, \mathcal{S}, \mathcal{S}'}, \quad \left\{ (\mathsf{sk}, \mathsf{Derive}(\mathsf{vk}, \mathcal{S}, \sigma, \mathcal{S}')) \right\}_{\mathsf{sk}, \mathcal{S}, \mathcal{S}'}.$$

4 Building Blocks

In this section we present the building blocks we use in our constructions.

4.1   A New Structure-Preserving Combined Signature Scheme

We give here a new efficient combined structure-preserving signature scheme. The new scheme is an extension of the randomizable signature scheme by Chatterjee and Menezes [23]. We extend their scheme to sign multiple messages and to obtain combined unforgeability without affecting the constant signature size or the number of verification equations. We identify a nice property of the scheme which might be of independent interest and find applications beyond the scope of this paper. We observe that when combined with Groth-Sahai proofs [35], one can re-randomize (the randomizable) signatures and the underlying Groth-Sahai proofs without knowledge of the hidden components of the signature. This leads to much better efficiency as one need not hide all signature components when proving knowledge of signatures.

As a special case of the new combined scheme, we obtain a new (optimal) strongly unforgeable structure-preserving signature scheme in the Type-3 bilinear group setting matching the lower bounds [2]. The new combined scheme is given in Fig. 1.

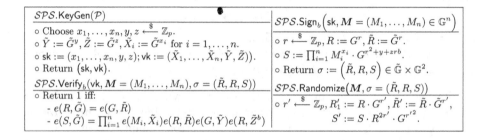

Fig. 1. A Structure-Preserving Signature Scheme with Combined Unforgeability

Correctness of the scheme is straightforward to verify. The signatures produced by Sign_0 are perfectly randomizable as the distribution of randomized signatures is identical to that of fresh signatures on the same message. We now prove the following theorem.

Theorem 1. *The scheme is a secure combined signature scheme in the generic group model* [42].

Proof. Since the adversary is generic, she can only produce linear combinations of the signature elements, verification key elements and public parameters in each of the source groups. The linear combinations represent Laurent polynomials in the discrete logarithm of those elements. We will prove that no linear combinations produce Laurent polynomials corresponding to a forgery on a message that was not queried to the sign oracle.

Public elements in $\tilde{\mathbb{G}}$ are $\tilde{G}$, $\tilde{X}_1$, ..., $\tilde{X}_n$, $\tilde{Y}$, $\tilde{Z}$ which correspond to the discrete logarithms 1, x_1, ..., x_n, y, z, respectively. Thus, this means that at the it-h sign query on M_i, $M_{i,j}$ (for $j = 1, \ldots, n$) can only be a linear combination of $G, \{R_k\}_{k=1}^{i-1}, \{S_k\}_{k=1}^{i-1}$. Thus, we have

$$m_{i,j} = a_{m_{i,j}} + \sum_{k=1}^{i-1} b_{m_{i,j,k}} r_k + \sum_{k=1}^{i-1} c_{m_{i,j,k}} (m_{k,1} x_1 + \ldots + m_{k,n} x_n + r_k^2 + y + b_k r_k z),$$

where $b_k = 1$ if the k-th signing query was for a strongly unforgeable signature (i.e. to Sign_1) and $b_k = 0$ otherwise.

After q signing queries, m^*, which is the discrete logarithm of the forged message M^* must be of the form

$$m_i^* = a_{m_i} + \sum_{k=1}^{q} b_{m_{i,k}} r_k + \sum_{k=1}^{q} c_{m_{i,k}} (m_{k,1} x_1 + \ldots + m_{k,n} x_n + r_k^2 + y + b_k r_k z),$$

for $i = 1, \ldots, n$. Similarly, the (R^*, S^*) components part of the forgery can only be a linear combination of the group elements from $\mathbb{G}$, i.e. a linear combination of $G, \{R_i\}_{i=1}^{q}$ and $\{S_i\}_{i=1}^{q}$ and therefore we have

$$r^* = a_r + \sum_{k=1}^{q} b_{r_k} r_k + \sum_{k=1}^{q} c_{r_k} (m_{k,1} x_1 + \ldots + m_{k,n} x_n + r_k^2 + y + b_k r_k z),$$

$$s^* = a_s + \sum_{k=1}^{q} b_{s_k} r_k + \sum_{k=1}^{q} c_{s_k} (m_{k,1} x_1 + \ldots + m_{k,n} x_n + r_k^2 + y + b_k r_k z),$$

where $b_k = 1$ if the i-th signing query was for a strongly unforgeable signature (i.e. to Sign_1) and $b_k = 0$ otherwise. Analogously, the $\tilde{R}^*$ part of the forgery can only be a linear combination of the elements from $\tilde{\mathbb{G}}$. Therefore, we have

$$\tilde{r}^* = a_{\tilde{r}} + \sum_{k=1}^{q} b_{\tilde{r}_k} \tilde{r}_k + \sum_{i=1}^{n} c_{\tilde{r}_i} x_i + d_{\tilde{r}} y + e_{\tilde{r}} z$$

For the forgery to be a valid signature, r^*, $\tilde{r}^*$ and s^* must satisfy

$$r^* = \tilde{r}^* \tag{2}$$

$$s^* = m_1^* x_1 + \ldots + m_n^* x_n + r^{*2} + y + b^* r^* z, \text{ for } b^* \in \{0,1\} \tag{3}$$

By (2), we must have $d_{\tilde{r}} = e_{\tilde{r}} = 0$ and $c_{\tilde{r}_i} = 0$ for all $i \in [n]$. Also, we must have $a_{\tilde{r}} = a_r$, $b_{\tilde{r}_k} = b_{r_k}$ for all k, and $c_{r_k} = 0$ for all $k \in [q]$. Therefore, have

$$r^* = \tilde{r}^* = a_r + \sum_{k=1}^{q} b_{r_k} r_k$$

By (3), we must have

$$a_s + \sum_{k=1}^{q} b_{s_k} r_k + \sum_{k=1}^{q} c_{s_k} (\sum_{i=1}^{n} m_{k,i} x_i + r_k^2 + y + b_k r_k z)$$

$$= \sum_{i=1}^{n} m_i^* x_i + r^{*2} + y + b^* r^* z$$

Thus, we must have

$$a_s + \sum_{k=1}^{q} b_{s_k} r_k + \sum_{k=1}^{q} c_{s_k} \left(\sum_{i=1}^{n} m_{k,i} x_i + r_k^2 + y + b_k r_k z \right)$$

$$= \sum_{i=1}^{n} m_i^* x_i + \left(a_r + \sum_{k=1}^{q} b_{r_k} r_k \right)^2 + y + \left(a_r + \sum_{k=1}^{q} b_{r_k} r_k \right) b^* z$$

Note that there is no term in z, on the left-hand side so we must have $a_r = 0$. Since now there is no constant term on the right-hand side, we have $a_s = 0$. Thus, we have

$$\sum_{k=1}^{q} b_{s_k} r_k + \sum_{k=1}^{q} c_{s_k} \left(\sum_{i=1}^{n} m_{k,i} x_i + r_k^2 + y + b_k r_k z \right)$$

$$= \sum_{i=1}^{n} m_i^* x_i + \left(\sum_{k=1}^{q} b_{r_k} r_k \right)^2 + y + \left(\sum_{k=1}^{q} b_{r_k} r_k \right) b^* z$$

Note that on the left-hand side there is no term in $r_j r_k$ for all $k \neq j$. This means that on the right-hand side we must have $b_{r_j} b_{r_k} = 0$ for all $k \neq j$ which implies that there is only one value of j such that $b_{r_j} \neq 0$, whereas $b_{r_k} = 0$ for all $k \neq j$. Thus, we have

$$\sum_{k=1}^{q} b_{s_k} r_k + \sum_{k=1}^{q} c_{s_k} \left(\sum_{i=1}^{n} m_{k,i} x_i + r_k^2 + y + b_k r_k z \right)$$

$$= \sum_{i=1}^{n} m_i^* x_i + (b_{r_j} r_j)^2 + y + b_{r_j} r_j b^* z, \text{ for some } j \in [q].$$

For the above two sides to equate, we must have $b_{s_k} = 0$ for all k. Now, rewriting the left-hand side, we have

$$c_{s_j} \sum_{i=1}^{n} m_{j,i} x_i + c_{s_j} r_j^2 + c_{s_j} y + c_{s_j} b_j r_j z = \sum_{i=1}^{n} m_i^* x_i + (b_{r_j} r_j)^2 + y + b_{r_j} r_j b^* z,$$

for some $j \in [q]$. The monomial y implies $c_{s,j} = 1$. Thus, we can rewrite the above as

$$\sum_{i=1}^{n} m_{j,i} x_i + r_j^2 + y + b_j r_j z = \sum_{i=1}^{n} m_i^* x_i + (b_{r_j} r_j)^2 + y + b_{r_j} r_j b^* z, \text{ for some } j \in [q].$$

We now have two cases depending on whether the forgery is a strongly or weakly unforgeable signature, i.e. depending on whether $b^* = 1$ or $b^* = 0$.

- Case $b^* = 0$: This case means the forgery is a randomizable signature. For the two sides to equate, we must also have $b_j = 0$. Therefore, we have

$$\sum_{i=1}^{n} m_{j,i} x_i + r_j^2 + y = \sum_{i=1}^{n} m_i^* x_i + (b_{r_j} r_j)^2 + y, \text{ for some } j \in [q].$$

By the monomial x_i, it is clear that we must have $m_{j,i} = m_i^*$ for all $i \in [n]$ and some $j \in [q]$ which means the forgery is on a message vector that was queried to Sign_0 and hence the adversary does not win.

- Case $b^* = 1$: This case means the forgery is a strongly unforgeable signature. We have

$$\sum_{i=1}^{n} m_{j,i} x_i + r_j^2 + y + b_j r_j z = \sum_{i=1}^{n} m_i^* x_i + (b_{r_j} r_j)^2 + y + b_{r_j} r_j z, \text{ for some } j \in [q].$$

By the monomial r_j^2, we must have $b_{r_j}^2 = 1$. By the monomial $r_j z$ we must have $b_{r_j} = b_j$. This implies that $b_{r_j} = b_j = 1$.

We have

$$\sum_{i=1}^{n} m_{j,i} x_i + r_j^2 + y + r_j z = \sum_{i=1}^{n} m_i^* x_i + (b_{r_j} r_j)^2 + y + r_j z, \text{ for some } j \in [q].$$

The above means that we have $m_i^* = m_{j,i}$ for all $i \in [n]$ and $r^* = r_j$ which means the forgery is a signature that the adversary got from the sign oracle on the message $\boldsymbol{M}_j$ for some $j \in [q]$ and thus the adversary does not win. □

Efficiency of the Scheme. We compare the efficiency of our scheme with Groth's scheme [34] which is also secure in the generic group model. The latter signs messages in $\tilde{\mathbb{G}}^{kn}$ yielding signatures in $\mathbb{G} \times \tilde{\mathbb{G}}^{n+1}$ and requires a verification key (in the case of a single signer) in $\mathbb{G}^k \times \tilde{\mathbb{G}}^n$, and requires $n + 1$ pairing-product verification equations. In our case, by transposing the groups in which S and vk and $\boldsymbol{M}$ lie, for the same message space ours yields signatures in $\mathbb{G} \times \tilde{\mathbb{G}}^2$ and requires a verification key in $\mathbb{G}^{kn+2}$ and 2 pairing-product verification equations. Thus, our scheme compares favorably to [34] w.r.t. the signature size and the cost of verification. The only advantage the scheme in [34] has over ours is that one can reduce the size of the verification key at the expense of longer signatures and more verification equations which is not desirable for the applications in this paper. In addition, randomizability of signatures in [34] is done via exponentiation which means his scheme does not have the same desirable randomization compatibility when combined with Groth-Sahai proofs.

4.2   A Combined Tagged Signature Scheme

Tagged signatures [26] are digital signatures where the signing and verification algorithms take as an additional input a tag τ. As noted by [26], any signature scheme that signs a vector of dimension $k+1$ can be used as a tagged signature to sign a vector of k elements. Following the naming of [26] is merely for easing composition since we need to treat tags differently from the rest of the messages when presenting our generic construction later on.

A combined tagged signature scheme is just a tagged signature scheme with combined unforgeability, i.e. it combines both notions of tagged signatures and combined signatures. The syntax and security of a combined tagged signature scheme for a message space $\mathcal{M}_{CTS}$ and a tag space $\mathcal{T}_{CTS}$ over a bilinear group $\mathcal{P}$ generated by BG is analogous to that of a combined signature scheme with the only difference being that Sign and Verify algorithms take as input an additional tag. Combined existential unforgeability of tagged signatures under adaptive chosen-message-tag attack is similar to the combined existential unforgeability of combined digital signatures.

By setting $n = k+1$ in our combined signature scheme from Sect. 4.1, we obtain a structure-preserving combined tagged signature scheme for tag space $\mathcal{T}_{CTS} := \mathbb{G}$ and message space $\mathcal{M}_{CTS} := \mathbb{G}^k$.

4.3   Randomizable Non-Interactive Witness-Indistinguishable Proofs

Let $\mathcal{R}$ be an efficiently computable relation. For pairs $(x, w) \in \mathcal{R}$, we call x the statement and w the witness. We define the language $\mathcal{L}_\mathcal{R} = \{x | \exists w : (x, w) \in \mathcal{R}\}$, i.e. $\mathcal{L}_\mathcal{R}$ is the set of the statements x in $\mathcal{R}$.

A non-interactive proof system [12] for the relation $\mathcal{R}$ allows a prover to convince a verifier that for some instance $x \in \mathcal{L}_\mathcal{R}$ there is a witness w such that $(x, w) \in \mathcal{R}$.

The proof system is defined by a tuple of algorithms (Setup, Prove, Verify). On input a security parameter 1^λ, Setup outputs a common reference string crs. On input (crs, x, w), Prove outputs a proof π that $(x, w) \in \mathcal{R}$. On input (crs, x, π), Verify outputs 1 if the proof is valid, or 0 otherwise. Informally, completeness of the proof system requires that honest proofs for valid statements are accepted by the verifier. Soundness requires that no prover can convince an honest verifier of an invalid statement $x \notin \mathcal{L}_\mathcal{R}$ (except for a negligible probability). A proof of knowledge [24] guarantees that the prover knows the underlying witness used in the proof. This is formalized by requiring two polynomial-time algorithms (ExtractSetup, Extract); ExtractSetup outputs a common reference string crs' (distributed identically to that output by Setup) and an extraction key xk which allows for witness extraction; On input (crs', xk, x, π), Extract outputs a valid witness.

Witness-Indistinguishability [27] requires that the verifier cannot determine which element of the set $\mathcal{R}(x) = \{w : (x, w) \in \mathcal{R}\}$ was used in the proof.

A proof system is *randomizable* if there exists a PPT algorithm Randomize which on input (crs, x, π), where π is a valid proof for the statement $x \in \mathcal{L}_\mathcal{R}$, produces a new proof π' for the same statement. We require that π' is indistinguishable from a fresh proof for the same statement. For formal definitions refer to [3].

Groth-Sahai Proofs. Groth-Sahai (GS) proofs [35] are efficient randomizable non-interactive proofs in the Common Reference String (CRS) model. The language for the system has the form

$$\mathcal{L} := \{\text{statement} \mid \exists \, \text{witness} : E_i(\text{statement}, \text{witness}) \text{ holds for } i = 1, \ldots, n\} \, ,$$

where E_i can be instantiated using different equation types but for our purpose we only require proofs for the satisfiability of pairing-product equations.

The proof system has perfect completeness, (perfect) soundness, composable witness-indistinguishability/zero-knowledge. Refer to [35] for the formal definitions.

In this paper, we will be using the SXDH-based instantiation [32,35] of Groth-Sahai proofs (see Appendix A) which is the most efficient instantiation of the proof system [32].

5   A Generic Construction of Subset Signatures with Controlled Context-Hiding

For more generality, we present our construction for the case where the elements of the set to be signed are vectors of n elements. The case where the elements of the set are singleton messages is then a special case where $n = 1$. The tools we require for our generic construction are a re-randomizable NIWI proof system $\mathcal{NIWI}$ and a combined tagged signature scheme $\mathcal{CTS}$ which can sign n messages. For the sake of maximizing efficiency, we require that the two primitives are compatible where we can randomize any hidden components of the signature within the NIWI proof.

The verification key vk of the signer contains the CRS for $\mathcal{NIWI}$ crs, the verification key $\text{vk}_{\mathcal{CTS}}$ for $\mathcal{CTS}$, the bilinear group public parameters $\mathcal{P}$, and the security parameter λ, whereas her secret key sk contains the secret signing key $\text{sk}_{\mathcal{CTS}}$ for $\mathcal{CTS}$.

To sign a set $\mathcal{S} = \{m_1, \ldots, m_{|\mathcal{S}|}\}$ with a specified restricted subset $\mathcal{S}_{\text{restrict}} \subseteq \mathcal{S}$, the signer first chooses a random tag $\tau_{\mathcal{S}}$ from the tag space of the combined tagged signature scheme and computes $\sigma_i \xleftarrow{\$} \mathcal{CTS}.\text{Sign}_b$ $(\text{sk}_{\mathcal{CTS}}, \tau_{\mathcal{S}}, m_i)$ for all $m_i \in \mathcal{S}$ where $b = 1$ (i.e. a strongly unforgeable signature) if $m_i \in \mathcal{S}_{\text{restrict}}$ and $b = 0$ (i.e. a rerandomizable signature) otherwise. Note that revealing the whole signature of the tagged signature would allow the original signer to tell if the signature is valid on the set and the tag even if we hide the tag: this is because the tag is chosen by the signer herself. Therefore, we need to hide both the tag as well as the signature components which depend on the tag. We parse σ_i as $\check{\sigma}_i \cup \hat{\sigma}_i$ where $\check{\sigma}_i$ contains the components of σ_i which depend on the tag $\tau_{\mathcal{S}}$ whereas $\hat{\sigma}_i := \sigma_i \setminus \check{\sigma}_i$ contains the rest of the signature components which are independent of the tag. To enforce the controlled context-hiding property, we necessitate that for all $i \in [|\mathcal{S}|]$, $|\hat{\sigma}_i| \geq 1$, i.e. the set is not empty. The signer produces a NIWI proof of knowledge π_{sig} of $\tau_{\mathcal{S}}$ and $\check{\sigma}_i$ such that for all $i \in [\|\mathcal{S}\|]$ it holds that

$$CTS.\mathsf{Verify}_b(\mathsf{vk}_{CTS}, \underline{\tau_{\mathcal{S}}}, m_i, \sigma_i = \underline{\check{\sigma}_i} \cup \hat{\sigma}_i) = 1$$

The signature on the set $\mathcal{S}$ is then $\Sigma := (\{\hat{\sigma}_i\}_{i=1}^{|\mathcal{S}|}, \pi_{\mathsf{sig}})$.

Note that if the randomizable signatures of the combined tagged scheme are only partially randomizable, one needs to hide the non-randomizable components of the signature as part of the witness of the underlying NIWI proof.

To derive a signature on a subset $\mathcal{S}' \subseteq \mathcal{S}$ given a valid signature $\Sigma = (\{\hat{\sigma}_i\}_{i=1}^{|\mathcal{S}|}, \pi_{\mathsf{sig}})$ on the set $\mathcal{S}$, one first omits the signatures $\{\hat{\sigma}_i\}_{m_i \in \mathcal{S} \setminus \mathcal{S}'}$ from Σ and adapts the proof π_{sig} accordingly. Now one re-randomizes all $\{\hat{\sigma}_i\}_{m_i \in \mathcal{S}'}$ to obtain $\{\hat{\sigma}_i'\}_{m_i \in \mathcal{S}'}$ and re-randomizes the proof π_{sig} into π_{sig}' accordingly. The derived signature on the set $\mathcal{S}'$ is then $\Sigma' := (\{\hat{\sigma}_i'\}_{i=1}^{|\mathcal{S}'|}, \pi_{\mathsf{sig}}')$. Note that if $\mathcal{S}' \cap \mathcal{S}_{\mathsf{restrict}} \neq \emptyset$, Σ' and Σ will be linkable as the signatures on the elements in $\mathcal{S}' \cap \mathcal{S}_{\mathsf{restrict}}$ are strongly unforgeable and hence cannot be randomized.

To verify a signature on a set $\mathcal{S}$, one verifies the validity of the proof π_{sig} and the public parts of the signatures, i.e. $\hat{\sigma}_i$.

Note that our approach of using a combined tagged signature yields a more efficient construction than e.g. the approach used by [7] where the signer chooses a random key pair for a digital signature and certifies the verification key using her own long-term secret key and uses the new corresponding signing key to sign the set.

The construction is detailed in Fig. 2 and its security is proven by the following theorem.

Theorem 2. *The construction is secure if CTS satisfies combined existential unforgeability under adaptive chosen-message-tag attack, and the NIWI proof system is sound, witness-indistinguishable and re-randomizable.*

Proof. Correctness follows from the completeness of NIWI and the correctness of CTS and is straightforward to verify. The following 3 lemmata complete the rest of the proof.

Lemma 1. *The construction is completely context-hiding w.r.t. any subset $\mathcal{S} \setminus \mathcal{S}_{\mathsf{restrict}}$ if $\mathcal{NIWI}$ is perfectly witness-indistinguishable and perfectly re-randomizable, and CTS is perfectly re-randomizable.*

Proof. The prefect witness indistinguishability of $\mathcal{NIWI}$ ensures the underlying NIWI poof π_{sig} contained in a derived signature does not reveal which witness used in the proof. If this is not the case, we can construct an adversary against the witness indistinguishability of the NIWI proof system.

The perfect re-randomizability of $\mathcal{NIWI}$ ensures that a re-randomized proof π_{sig}' cannot be linked to the original proof π_{sig}. Thus far we ensured that the proof part of the signature does not help the adversary in winning the context-hiding game.

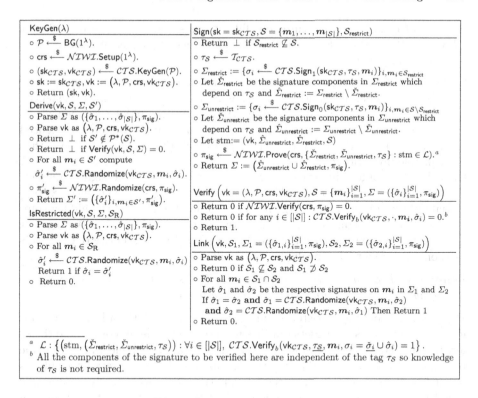

KeyGen(λ)	Sign(sk = $\mathsf{sk}_{CTS}, \mathcal{S} = \{m_1, \ldots, m_{|\mathcal{S}|}\}, \mathcal{S}_{\text{restrict}}$)
$\circ$ $\mathcal{P} \xleftarrow{\$} BG(1^\lambda)$.	$\circ$ Return $\perp$ if $\mathcal{S}_{\text{restrict}} \not\subseteq \mathcal{S}$.
$\circ$ crs $\xleftarrow{\$} \mathcal{NIWI}.\mathsf{Setup}(1^\lambda)$.	$\circ$ $\tau_S \xleftarrow{\$} \mathcal{T}_{CTS}$.
$\circ$ $(\mathsf{sk}_{CTS}, \mathsf{vk}_{CTS}) \xleftarrow{\$} CTS.\mathsf{KeyGen}(\mathcal{P})$.	$\circ$ $\Sigma_{\text{restrict}} := \{\sigma_i \xleftarrow{\$} CTS.\mathsf{Sign}_1(\mathsf{sk}_{CTS}, \tau_S, m_i)\}_{i, m_i \in \mathcal{S}_{\text{restrict}}}$
$\circ$ sk := sk_{CTS}, vk := $(\lambda, \mathcal{P}, \mathsf{crs}, \mathsf{vk}_{CTS})$.	$\circ$ Let $\check{\Sigma}_{\text{restrict}}$ be the signature components in Σ_{restrict} which
$\circ$ Return (sk, vk).	depend on τ_S and $\hat{\Sigma}_{\text{restrict}} := \Sigma_{\text{restrict}} \setminus \check{\Sigma}_{\text{restrict}}$.
Derive(vk, $\mathcal{S}, \Sigma, \mathcal{S}'$)	$\circ$ $\Sigma_{\text{unrestrict}} := \{\sigma_i \xleftarrow{\$} CTS.\mathsf{Sign}_0(\mathsf{sk}_{CTS}, \tau_S, m_i)\}_{i, m_i \in \mathcal{S} \setminus \mathcal{S}_{\text{restrict}}}$
$\circ$ Parse Σ as $(\{\hat{\sigma}_1, \ldots, \hat{\sigma}_{|\mathcal{S}|}\}, \pi_{\text{sig}})$.	$\circ$ Let $\check{\Sigma}_{\text{unrestrict}}$ be the signature components in $\Sigma_{\text{unrestrict}}$ which
$\circ$ Parse vk as $(\lambda, \mathcal{P}, \mathsf{crs}, \mathsf{vk}_{CTS})$.	depend on τ_S and $\hat{\Sigma}_{\text{unrestrict}} := \Sigma_{\text{unrestrict}} \setminus \check{\Sigma}_{\text{unrestrict}}$.
$\circ$ Return $\perp$ if $\mathcal{S}' \notin \mathcal{P}^*(\mathcal{S})$.	$\circ$ Let stm:= (vk, $\check{\Sigma}_{\text{unrestrict}}, \check{\Sigma}_{\text{restrict}}, \mathcal{S})$
$\circ$ Return $\perp$ if $\mathsf{Verify}(\mathsf{vk}, \mathcal{S}, \Sigma) = 0$.	$\circ$ $\pi_{\text{sig}} \xleftarrow{\$} \mathcal{NIWI}.\mathsf{Prove}(\mathsf{crs}, \{\check{\Sigma}_{\text{restrict}}, \check{\Sigma}_{\text{unrestrict}}, \tau_S\} : \text{stm} \in \mathcal{L})$.[a]
$\circ$ For all $m_i \in \mathcal{S}'$ compute	$\circ$ Return $\Sigma := (\hat{\Sigma}_{\text{unrestrict}} \cup \hat{\Sigma}_{\text{restrict}}, \pi_{\text{sig}})$.
$\hat{\sigma}'_i \xleftarrow{\$} CTS.\mathsf{Randomize}(\mathsf{vk}_{CTS}, m_i, \hat{\sigma}_i)$.	
$\circ$ $\pi'_{\text{sig}} \xleftarrow{\$} \mathcal{NIWI}.\mathsf{Randomize}(\mathsf{crs}, \pi_{\text{sig}})$.	Verify $\left(\mathsf{vk} = (\lambda, \mathcal{P}, \mathsf{crs}, \mathsf{vk}_{CTS}), \mathcal{S} = \{m_i\}_{i=1}^{|\mathcal{S}|}, \Sigma = (\{\hat{\sigma}_i\}_{i=1}^{|\mathcal{S}|}, \pi_{\text{sig}})\right)$
$\circ$ Return $\Sigma' := (\{\hat{\sigma}'_i\}_{i, m_i \in \mathcal{S}'}, \pi'_{\text{sig}})$.	$\circ$ Return 0 if $\mathcal{NIWI}.\mathsf{Verify}(\mathsf{crs}, \pi_{\text{sig}}) = 0$.
IsRestricted(vk, $\mathcal{S}, \Sigma, \mathcal{S}_R$)	$\circ$ Return 0 if for any $i \in [|\mathcal{S}|] : CTS.\mathsf{Verify}_b(\mathsf{vk}_{CTS}, \cdot, m_i, \hat{\sigma}_i) = 0$.[b]
$\circ$ Parse Σ as $(\{\hat{\sigma}_1, \ldots, \hat{\sigma}_{|\mathcal{S}|}\}, \pi_{\text{sig}})$.	$\circ$ Return 1.
$\circ$ Parse vk as $(\lambda, \mathcal{P}, \mathsf{crs}, \mathsf{vk}_{CTS})$.	Link $\left(\mathsf{vk}, \mathcal{S}_1, \Sigma_1 = (\{\hat{\sigma}_{1,i}\}_{i=1}^{|\mathcal{S}|}, \pi_{\text{sig}}), \mathcal{S}_2, \Sigma_2 = (\{\hat{\sigma}_{2,i}\}_{i=1}^{|\mathcal{S}|}, \pi_{\text{sig}})\right)$
$\circ$ For all $m_i \in \mathcal{S}_R$	$\circ$ Parse vk as $(\lambda, \mathcal{P}, \mathsf{crs}, \mathsf{vk}_{CTS})$.
$\hat{\sigma}'_i \xleftarrow{\$} CTS.\mathsf{Randomize}(\mathsf{vk}_{CTS}, m_i, \hat{\sigma}_i)$	$\circ$ Return 0 if $\mathcal{S}_1 \not\subseteq \mathcal{S}_2$ and $\mathcal{S}_1 \not\supseteq \mathcal{S}_2$
Return 1 if $\hat{\sigma}_i = \hat{\sigma}'_i$	$\circ$ For all $m_i \in \mathcal{S}_1 \cap \mathcal{S}_2$
$\circ$ Return 0.	Let $\hat{\sigma}_1$ and $\hat{\sigma}_2$ be the respective signatures on m_i in Σ_1 and Σ_2
	If $\hat{\sigma}_1 = \hat{\sigma}_2$ and $\hat{\sigma}_1 = CTS.\mathsf{Randomize}(\mathsf{vk}_{CTS}, m_i, \hat{\sigma}_2)$
	and $\hat{\sigma}_2 = CTS.\mathsf{Randomize}(\mathsf{vk}_{CTS}, m_i, \hat{\sigma}_1)$ Then Return 1
	$\circ$ Return 0.

[a] $\mathcal{L} : \left\{(\text{stm}, (\check{\Sigma}_{\text{restrict}}, \check{\Sigma}_{\text{unrestrict}}, \tau_S)) : \forall i \in [|\mathcal{S}|], CTS.\mathsf{Verify}_b(\mathsf{vk}_{CTS}, \underline{\tau_S}, m_i, \sigma_i = \underline{\check{\sigma}_i} \cup \hat{\sigma}_i) = 1\right\}$.
[b] All the components of the signature to be verified here are independent of the tag τ_S so knowledge of τ_S is not required.

Fig. 2. Our generic construction.

What is left now is to show that the remaining components of the subset signature, i.e. the public randomized components of the tagged signature, which are independent of the tag τ_S, do not help the adversary either. Since the context-hiding requirement excludes restricted elements of the set, we have that all signatures contained in a subset signature Σ are randomizable CTS signatures. The re-randomizability of CTS ensures that re-randomized signatures are indistinguishable from fresh signatures on the same message. Thus, if the public parts of the tagged signature can help the adversary win, we can launch an adversary against the randomizability of the combined tagged signatures. $\square$

Remark 1. If the security properties mandated by the above lemma hold only computationally rather than information-theoretically, the construction satisfies adaptive context-hiding instead.

Lemma 2. *The construction is unforgeable if the proof system $\mathcal{NIWI}$ is sound and CTS satisfies combined existential unforgeability under adaptive chosen-message-tag attack.*

Proof. By the soundness of proof system, the adversary against unforgeability has a negligible advantage in faking proofs for a false statement. This includes the case of combining signatures on different sets, i.e. which are on different $\mathcal{CTS}$ tags. We are now left with two cases in which the adversary can win the unforgeability game:

Case I: The forgery involves a tag that is not used in any of the sign queries. This corresponds to breaking the chosen-message-tag combined existential unforgeability of $\mathcal{CTS}$. By extracting the tag and the hidden components of the signatures from π_{sig}, we can construct an adversary against the existential unforgeability of $\mathcal{CTS}$. By the security of $\mathcal{CTS}$, this is only possible with a negligible probability.

Case II: The forgery involves a tag that is used in one of the signing queries. This also corresponds to breaking the chosen-message-tag combined existential unforgeability of $\mathcal{CTS}$. Again, by extracting the tag and the hidden components of the signatures from π_{sig}, we can construct an adversary against the combined existential unforgeability of $\mathcal{CTS}$. By the security of $\mathcal{CTS}$, this is only possible with a negligible probability.   □

Lemma 3. *The construction is linkable if $\mathcal{CTS}$ satisfies combined existential unforgeability under adaptive chosen-message-tag attack.*

Proof. By the combined existential unforgeability of $\mathcal{CTS}$, the adversary cannot forge new signatures on subsets that has been signed by the sign oracle and therefore it is limited to re-using those it obtained from the sign oracle. Since the game requires that the subset in the forgery is a subset of one of the restricted subsets queried to the sign oracle, the original signature contains strongly unforgeable signatures which cannot be re-randomized. If the latter does not hold, we can break the combined existential unforgeability of the tagged signature scheme. By searching in the list of the signatures returned by the sign oracle, we are guaranteed to be able to find a signature which has the same components as those contained in the forgery.   □

6   Structure-Preserving Instantiations

We instantiate $\mathcal{CTS}$ using our new combined tagged signature scheme from Sect. 4.2 and instantiate $\mathcal{NIWI}$ using the SXDH-based instantiation of the Groth-Sahai proof system [32,35]. To realize the stronger complete context-hiding requirement, we instantiate the proof system in the hiding setting which yields perfectly witness-indistinguishable proofs. If adaptive context-hiding suffices, we can instead instantiate the proof system in the binding setting, in which case the proofs are only computationally witness-indistinguishable.

A combined tagged signature on $m_i \in \mathcal{S}$ is of the form $(\tilde{R}_i, R_i, S_i) \in \tilde{\mathbb{G}} \times \mathbb{G}^2$ where $\tilde{R}_i$ and R_i are independent of the tag $\tau_{\mathcal{S}}$. The signer generates a Groth-Sahai commitment $\mathcal{C}_{\tau_{\mathcal{S}}} \in \mathbb{G}^2$ to the tag $\tau_{\mathcal{S}}$ and for each $m_i \in \mathcal{S}$, it commits to the component S_i of the signature to get a Groth-Sahai commitment $\mathcal{C}_{S_i} \in \mathbb{G}^2$, and produces a proof $\tilde{\pi}_i \in \tilde{\mathbb{G}}^2$ for the following linear pairing-product equation

$$e(\underline{S_i}, \tilde{G})e(\underline{\tau_{\mathcal{S}}}, \tilde{X}_0^{-1}) = \prod_{j=1}^{n} e(M_{i,j}, \tilde{X}_j)e(R_i, \tilde{R}_i \cdot \tilde{Z}^{b_i})e(G, \tilde{Y}),$$

where $b_i = 1$ if $m_i \in S_{\text{restrict}}$ and $b_i = 0$ otherwise. We have $\pi_{\text{sig}} := \Big(\mathcal{C}_{TS},$ $(\mathcal{C}_{S_i}, \tilde{\pi}_i)_{i=1}^{|\mathcal{S}|}\Big)$ and the subset signature is $\Sigma := \Big((R_i, \tilde{R}_i)_{i=1}^{|\mathcal{S}|}, \pi_{\text{sig}}\Big)$. The subset signature size is $(2 + 3|\mathcal{S}|) \cdot |\mathbb{G}| + 3|\mathcal{S}| \cdot |\tilde{\mathbb{G}}|$. When verifying the signature, besides verifying the proof π_{sig}, for each element of the set, the verifier checks that $e(G, \tilde{R}_i) = e(R_i, \tilde{G})$.

We now show how the $\mathcal{NIWI}$ proof as well as the public components of the tagged signatures are randomized which is needed when deriving signatures on subsets. Further details as well as a proof can be found in Appendix B.

The crs is $\Big(\mathcal{U} = (\mathcal{U}_1, \mathcal{U}_2), \tilde{\mathcal{V}} = (\tilde{\mathcal{V}}_1, \tilde{\mathcal{V}}_2)\Big) \in \mathbb{G}^4 \times \tilde{\mathbb{G}}^4$ and the proof system uses the maps $\iota : \mathbb{G} \to \mathbb{G}^2$ and $\tilde{\iota} : \tilde{\mathbb{G}} \to \tilde{\mathbb{G}}^2$. For details of the Groth-Sahai SXDH-instantiation see Appendix A.

We randomly choose $\gamma_i \xleftarrow{\$} \mathbb{Z}_p$ and set $R_i' := R_i \cdot G^{\gamma_i}$ and $\tilde{R}_i' := \tilde{R}_i \cdot \tilde{G}^{\gamma_i}$. To randomize the (committed) signature component S_i, we compute $\mathcal{C}_{S_i} := \mathcal{C}_{S_i} \cdot \iota_{\mathbb{G}}\big(R_i^{2\gamma_i} \cdot G^{\gamma_i^2}\big)$. What is left now is to re-randomize the Groth-Sahai commitments and proofs so that they are unlinkable to the original ones. We choose $r_0' = (r_{0,1}', r_{0,2}') \xleftarrow{\$} \mathbb{Z}_p^2$ and $r_i' = (r_{i,1}', r_{i,2}') \xleftarrow{\$} \mathbb{Z}_p^2$ for $i = 1, \ldots, |\mathcal{S}|$ and randomize the Groth-Sahai commitments by computing $\mathcal{C}_{TS}' := \mathcal{C}_{TS} \cdot \mathcal{U}^{r_0'}$ and $\mathcal{C}_{S_i}' := \mathcal{C}_{S_i} \cdot \mathcal{U}^{r_i'}$. Providing that all r_i' for $i = 0, \ldots, |\mathcal{S}|$ are chosen at random, the new commitments are uniformly distributed over $\mathbb{G}^2$ and are thus independent of the original ones. To re-randomize proof $\tilde{\pi}_i$, we let $\tilde{\pi}_i' := \tilde{\pi}_i \cdot \tilde{\iota}(\tilde{H})^{r_i'^T} \cdot \tilde{\iota}(\tilde{X}_0^{-1})^{r_0'^T}$. Again, providing that all r_i' for $i = 0, \ldots, |\mathcal{S}|$ are chosen at random, the new proof is uniformly distributed and is thus independent of the original one.

The proof of the following theorem follows from that of theorem 2.

Theorem 3. *The instantiation is a secure subset signature with controlled complete context-hiding if the SXDH assumption holds and the combined tagged signature scheme from Sect. 4.2 is secure.*

6.1 Efficiency Comparison

We compare in Table 1 the efficiency of our scheme for the case of traditional subset signatures (i.e. where the restricted subset is empty) with the most efficient existing scheme [7].

Table 1. Efficiency comparison between our instantiations and existing schemes.

Scheme	$|\Sigma|$	$|\text{vk}|$	$|\text{sk}|$	Model	Setting
[7]	$(22 + 7|\mathcal{S}|) \cdot |\mathbb{G}|$	$(|\mathcal{M}| + 16) \cdot$ $|\mathbb{G}| + 2 \cdot |\mathbb{T}|$	$6 \cdot |\mathbb{Z}_p|$	STD	Type-1
Ours	$(2 + 3|\mathcal{S}|) \cdot$ $|\mathbb{G}| + 3|\mathcal{S}| \cdot |\tilde{\mathbb{G}}|$	$4 \cdot |\mathbb{G}| + 7 \cdot |\tilde{\mathbb{G}}|$	$3 \cdot |\mathbb{Z}_p|$	STD	Type-3

Besides enjoying much shorter signatures, our scheme also has shorter (constant-size) keys. Our scheme being in the most efficient Type-3 setting enjoys shorter group elements' sizes than those in Type-1 setting. Also, note that after the recent advances in solving the discrete logarithm problem in finite fields of small characteristic, e.g. [9,33], it is nowadays recommended [9,33] to base Type-1 instantiations on large-characteristic bilinear groups which means much larger group elements. For the sake of comparison, note that, for example, at 128-bit security level, elements of $\mathbb{G}$ and $\tilde{\mathbb{G}}$ in Type-3 are 256 and 512 bits long, respectively, whereas their small-characteristic and large-characteristic Type-1 counterparts have sizes 512 and 1536, respectively. Therefore, it is clear that our instantiations outperform existing ones. The only component of our scheme that is not based on a standard (static) intractability assumption is the tagged signature. Note that the security of [7] also relies on a non-standard q-type assumption (the q-SFP assumption [1]).

A   SXDH-Based Groth-Sahai Proofs

Here we give the SXDH-instantiation of Groth-Sahai proofs [32,35].

Let $\mathbb{B} := \mathbb{G}^2$, $\tilde{\mathbb{B}} := \tilde{\mathbb{G}}^2$ and $\mathbb{H} := \mathbb{T}^4$, with all operations performed componentwise. Define

$$F : \begin{cases} \mathbb{B} \times \tilde{\mathbb{B}} & \longrightarrow \mathbb{H} \\ (X_1, Y_1), (\tilde{X}_2, \tilde{Y}_2) & \longmapsto \left(e(X_1, \tilde{X}_2),\ e(X_1, \tilde{Y}_2),\ e(Y_1, \tilde{X}_2),\ e(Y_1, \tilde{Y}_2) \right) \end{cases}.$$

We will use the $\bullet$ notation instead of F for vectors. To generate the crs, the trusted party randomly chooses $a_i, t_i \xleftarrow{\$} \mathbb{Z}_p^\times$ for $i = 1, 2$ and computes $Q := G^{a_1}$, $U := G^{t_1}$, $V := Q^{t_1}$, $\tilde{Q} := \tilde{G}^{a_2}$, $\tilde{U} := \tilde{G}^{t_2}$, $\tilde{V} := \tilde{Q}^{t_2}$. We now set

$$\mathcal{U}_1 = (G, Q) \in \mathbb{B},$$
$$\mathcal{U}_2 = \begin{cases} \mathcal{U}_1^{t_1} & = (U, V) & \text{Binding Setting} \\ \mathcal{U}_1^{t_1} \cdot (1_\mathbb{G}, G^{-1}) = (U, V \cdot G^{-1}) & \text{Hiding Setting} \end{cases} \in \mathbb{B}.$$

$$\tilde{\mathcal{V}}_1 = (\tilde{G}, \tilde{Q}) \in \tilde{\mathbb{B}},$$
$$\tilde{\mathcal{V}}_2 = \begin{cases} \tilde{\mathcal{V}}_1^{t_2} & = \left(\tilde{U}, \tilde{V}\right) & \text{Binding Setting} \\ \tilde{\mathcal{V}}_1^{t_2} \cdot (1_{\tilde{\mathbb{G}}}, \tilde{G}^{-1}) = \left(\tilde{U}, \tilde{V} \cdot \tilde{G}^{-1}\right) & \text{Hiding Setting} \end{cases} \in \tilde{\mathbb{B}}.$$

The crs is then the set $(\mathcal{U}, \mathcal{V})$ where $\mathcal{U} = (\mathcal{U}_1, \mathcal{U}_2) \in \mathbb{B}^2$ and $\tilde{\mathcal{V}} = \left(\tilde{\mathcal{V}}_1, \tilde{\mathcal{V}}_2\right) \in \tilde{\mathbb{B}}^2$. Under the SXDH assumption, one cannot tell a binding key from a hiding key.

To define the commitment schemes used by the proof system, we need the two maps $\iota : \mathbb{G} \to \mathbb{B}$ and $\tilde{\iota} : \tilde{\mathbb{G}} \to \tilde{\mathbb{B}}$ which are defined as follows:

$$\iota : \begin{cases} \mathbb{G} \longrightarrow \mathbb{B} \\ X \longmapsto (1_\mathbb{G}, X) \end{cases} \qquad\qquad \tilde{\iota} : \begin{cases} \tilde{\mathbb{G}} \longrightarrow \tilde{\mathbb{B}} \\ \tilde{X} \longmapsto (1_{\tilde{\mathbb{G}}}, \tilde{X}) \end{cases}$$

To commit to a group element $X \in \mathbb{G}$, the commitment algorithm $\mathsf{GSCommit}_\mathbb{G}$ chooses $r = (r_1, r_2) \xleftarrow{\$} \mathbb{Z}_p^2$ and computes $\mathcal{C}_X := \iota(X) \cdot \mathcal{U}^r$. We have

$$\mathcal{C}_X = \begin{cases} \left(G^{(r_1+t_1 r_2)}, X \cdot Q^{(r_1+t_1 r_2)}\right) & \text{Binding Setting} \\ \left(G^{(r_1+t_1 r_2)}, X \cdot Q^{(r_1+t_1 r_2)} \cdot G^{-r_2}\right) & \text{Hiding Setting} \end{cases}$$

Similarly, to commit to a group element $\tilde{X} \in \tilde{\mathbb{G}}$, the commitment algorithm $\mathsf{GSCommit}_{\tilde{\mathbb{G}}}$ chooses $s = (s_1, s_2) \xleftarrow{\$} \mathbb{Z}_p^2$ and computes $\mathcal{C}_{\tilde{X}} := \tilde{\iota}(\tilde{X}) \cdot \tilde{\mathcal{V}}^s$. We have

$$\mathcal{C}_{\tilde{X}} = \begin{cases} \left(\tilde{G}^{(s_1+t_2 s_2)}, \tilde{X} \cdot \tilde{Q}^{(s_1+t_2 s_2)}\right) & \text{Binding Setting} \\ \left(\tilde{G}^{(s_1+t_2 s_2)}, \tilde{X} \cdot \tilde{Q}^{(s_1+t_2 s_2)} \cdot \tilde{G}^{-s_2}\right) & \text{Hiding Setting} \end{cases}$$

We now define the map ι_T as follows:

$$\iota_T : \begin{cases} \mathbb{T} \longrightarrow & \mathbb{H} \\ \zeta \longmapsto & (1_\mathbb{T}, 1_\mathbb{T}, 1_\mathbb{T}, \zeta) \end{cases}$$

The equations we prove are pairing-product equations of the form:

$$\prod_{j=1}^{n} e(A_j, \underline{\tilde{Y}_j}) \prod_{i=1}^{m} e(\underline{X_i}, \tilde{B}_i) \prod_{i=1}^{m} \prod_{j=1}^{n} e(\underline{X_i}, \underline{\tilde{Y}_j})^{\alpha_{i,j}} = t_T \qquad (4)$$

In fact, all the equations we prove are linear equations (Eq. 5) where $\alpha_{i,j} = 0$ for all i, j.

$$\prod_{j=1}^{n} e(A_j, \underline{\tilde{Y}_j}) \prod_{i=1}^{m} e(\underline{X_i}, \tilde{B}_i) = t_T \qquad (5)$$

B   More Details of the Instantiation

Each signature in the set contains a proof for the following linear equation

$$e(\underline{S_i}, \tilde{G}) e(\tau_{\underline{S}}, \tilde{X}_0^{-1}) = \prod_{i=j}^{n} e(M_{i,j}, \tilde{X}_j) e(R_i, \tilde{R}_i \cdot \tilde{Z}^{b_i}) e(G, \tilde{Y}) \qquad (6)$$

We have

$$\mathcal{C}_{\tau_S} := \mathsf{GSCommit}_\mathbb{G}(\tau_S) = \iota(\tau_S) \cdot \mathcal{U}^{r_0} = \left(G^{(r_{0,1}+t_1 r_{0,2})}, \tau_S \cdot Q^{(r_{0,1}+t_1 r_{0,2})}\right)$$
$$\mathcal{C}_{S_i} := \mathsf{GSCommit}_\mathbb{G}(S_i) = \iota(S_i) \cdot \mathcal{U}^{r_i} = \left(G^{(r_{i,1}+t_1 r_{i,2})}, S_i \cdot Q^{(r_{i,1}+t_1 r_{i,2})}\right)$$

The proof for the above linear equation is given by

$$\tilde{\pi}_i := \tilde{\iota}(\tilde{G})^{r_i^T} \cdot \tilde{\iota}(\tilde{X}_0^{-1})^{r_0^T} = \left(\left(1_{\tilde{\mathbb{G}}}, \tilde{G}^{r_{i,1}} \cdot \tilde{X}_0^{-r_{0,1}}\right), \left(1_{\tilde{\mathbb{G}}}, \tilde{G}^{r_{i,2}} \cdot \tilde{X}_0^{-r_{0,2}}\right)\right) \in \tilde{\mathbb{B}}^2$$

As noted in [35], we can omit the $1_{\tilde{G}}$ components from the proof which halves the size of the proof into $\tilde{G}^2$. To verify the proof, one needs to check the following equation:

$$F(\mathcal{C}_{S_i}, \iota(\tilde{G}))F(\mathcal{C}_{\tau_S}, \iota(\tilde{X}_0^{-1})) = \iota_T\Big(\prod_{j=1}^{n} e(M_{i,j}, \tilde{X}_j)e(R_i, \tilde{R}_i \cdot \tilde{Z}^{b_i})e(G, \tilde{Y})\Big)\Big(\mathcal{U} \bullet \tilde{\pi}_i\Big)$$

$$(7)$$

We show now how to randomize the public components of the signature, i.e. R_i and $\tilde{R}_i$ (which are part of the statement) and the Groth-Sahai commitments and proof accordingly. One chooses $\gamma_i \xleftarrow{\$} \mathbb{Z}_p$ and sets $R_i' := R_i \cdot G^{\gamma_i}$ and $\tilde{R}_i' := \tilde{R}_i \cdot \tilde{G}^{\gamma_i}$. We also randomize the (committed) signature component S_i using the same randomness γ_i as follows:

$$\mathcal{C}_{S_i} := \mathcal{C}_{S_i} \cdot \iota\big(R_i^{2\gamma_i} \cdot G^{\gamma_i^2}\big) = \Big(G^{(r_{i,1}+t_1 r_{i,2})}, S_i \cdot R_i^{2\gamma_i} \cdot G^{\gamma_i^2} \cdot Q^{(r_{i,1}+t_1 r_{i,2})}\Big)$$

We now re-randomize the Groth-Sahai commitments and proofs to make them unlinkable to the original ones. We choose $r_0' = (r_{0,1}', r_{0,2}') \xleftarrow{\$} \mathbb{Z}_p^2$ and $r_i' = (r_{i,1}', r_{i,2}') \xleftarrow{\$} \mathbb{Z}_p^2$ for $i = 1, \ldots, |\mathcal{S}|$ and compute

$$\mathcal{C}_{\tau_S}' := \mathcal{C}_{\tau_S} \cdot \mathcal{U}^{r_0'}$$
$$= \Big(G^{\big((r_{0,1}+r_{0,1}')+t_1(r_{0,2}+r_{0,2}')\big)}, \tau_S \cdot Q^{\big((r_{0,1}+r_{0,1}')+t_1(r_{0,2}+r_{0,2}')\big)}\Big)$$
$$\mathcal{C}_{S_i}' := \mathcal{C}_{S_i} \cdot \mathcal{U}^{r_i'}$$
$$= \Big(G^{\big((r_{i,1}+r_{i,1}')+t_1(r_{i,2}+r_{i,2}')\big)}, S_i \cdot R_i^{2\gamma_i} \cdot G^{\gamma_i^2} \cdot Q^{((r_{i,1}+r_{i,1}')+t_1(r_{i,2}+r_{i,2}'))}\Big)$$

Providing that all r_i' for $i = 0, \ldots, |\mathcal{S}|$ are chosen at random, the new commitments are uniformly distributed over $\mathbb{B}$ and are thus independent of the original ones. We now show how to re-randomize proof $\tilde{\pi}_i$ into $\tilde{\pi}_i'$ accordingly.

$$\tilde{\pi}_i' := \tilde{\pi}_i \cdot \iota(\tilde{G})^{r_i'^T} \cdot \iota(\tilde{X}_0^{-1})^{r_0'^T}$$
$$= \Big(\big(1_{\tilde{G}}, \tilde{G}^{r_{i,1}+r_{i,1}'} \cdot \tilde{X}_0^{-(r_{0,1}+r_{0,1}')}\big), \big(1_{\tilde{G}}, \tilde{G}^{r_{i,2}+r_{i,2}'} \cdot \tilde{X}_0^{-(r_{0,2}+r_{0,2}')}\big)\Big)$$

Since r_i' for $i = 0, \ldots, |\mathcal{S}|$ are chosen at random, the new proof is uniformly distributed and is thus independent of the original one. To verify the proof, one needs to check the following equation:

$$F(\mathcal{C}_{S_i}', \iota(\tilde{G}))F(\mathcal{C}_{\tau_S}', \iota(\tilde{X}_0^{-1})) = \iota_T\Big(\prod_{j=1}^{n} e(M_{i,j}, \tilde{X}_j)e(R_i', \tilde{R}_i' \cdot \tilde{Z}^{b_i})e(G, \tilde{Y})\Big)\Big(\mathcal{U} \bullet \tilde{\pi}_i'\Big)$$

$$(8)$$

We now show that the new proofs will be accepted by the verify algorithm.

Lemma 4. *The randomized proof $\tilde{\pi}_i'$ verifies correctly.*

Proof. Our proof is for a binding CRS. The proof for a hiding CRS is very similar.

By expanding the left-hand side of the verification equation (Eq. 8), we have

$$F\big(c'_{S_i}, \iota(\tilde{G})\big)F\big(c'_{\tau_S}, \iota(\tilde{X}_0^{-1})\big)$$

$$= F\Big(\big(G^{((r_{i,1}+r'_{i,1})+t_1(r_{i,2}+r'_{i,2}))}, S_i \cdot R_i^{2\gamma_i} \cdot G^{\gamma_i^2} \cdot Q^{((r_{i,1}+r'_{i,1})+t_1(r_{i,2}+r'_{i,2}))}\big), (1_{\tilde{G}}, \tilde{G})\Big)$$

$$F\Big(\big(G^{((r_{0,1}+r'_{0,1})+t_1(r_{0,2}+r'_{0,2}))}, \tau_S \cdot Q^{((r_{0,1}+r'_{0,1})+t_1(r_{0,2}+r'_{0,2}))}\big), (1_{\tilde{G}}, \tilde{X}_0^{-1})\Big)$$

$$= \Big(1_{\mathbb{T}}, e(G^{((r_{i,1}+r'_{i,1})+t_1(r_{i,2}+r'_{i,2}))}, \tilde{G}), 1_{\mathbb{T}}, e(S_i \cdot R_i^{2\gamma_i} \cdot G^{\gamma_i^2} \cdot Q^{((r_{i,1}+r'_{i,1})+t_1(r_{i,2}+r'_{i,2}))}, \tilde{G})\Big)$$

$$\Big(1_{\mathbb{T}}, e\big(G^{((r_{0,1}+r'_{0,1})+t_1(r_{0,2}+r'_{0,2}))}, \tilde{X}_0^{-1}\big), 1_{\mathbb{T}}, e\big(\tau_S \cdot Q^{((r_{0,1}+r'_{0,1})+t_1(r_{0,2}+r'_{0,2}))}\big), \tilde{X}_0^{-1}\big)\Big)$$

$$= \Big(1_{\mathbb{T}}, e(G^{((r_{i,1}+r'_{i,1})+t_1(r_{i,2}+r'_{i,2}))}, \tilde{G})1_{\mathbb{T}}, e(S_i \cdot R_i^{2\gamma_i} \cdot G^{\gamma_i^2}, \tilde{G})e(Q^{((r_{i,1}+r'_{i,1})+t_1(r_{i,2}+r'_{i,2}))}, \tilde{G})\Big)$$

$$\Big(1_{\mathbb{T}}, e(G^{((r_{0,1}+r'_{0,1})+t_1(r_{0,2}+r'_{0,2}))}, \tilde{X}_0^{-1}), 1_{\mathbb{T}}, e(\tau_S, \tilde{X}_0^{-1})e(Q^{((r_{0,1}+r'_{0,1})+t_1(r_{0,2}+r'_{0,2}))}, \tilde{X}_0^{-1})\Big)$$

Similarly, by expanding the right-hand side of Eq. 8, we have

$$\iota_T\Big(\prod_{j=1}^{n} e(M_{i,j}, \tilde{X}_j)e(R'_i, \tilde{R}'_i \cdot \tilde{Z}^{b_i})e(G, \tilde{Y})\Big)\big(\mathcal{U} \bullet \tilde{\pi}'_i\big)$$

$$= \iota_T\Big(\prod_{j=1}^{n} e(M_{i,j}, \tilde{X}_j)e(R'_i, \tilde{R}'_i \cdot \tilde{Z}^{b_i})e(G, \tilde{Y})\Big)$$

$$\big((G, Q), (G^{t_1}, Q^{t_1})\big) \bullet \Big(\big(1_{\tilde{G}}, \tilde{G}^{r_{i,1}+r'_{i,1}} \cdot \tilde{X}_0^{-(r_{0,1}+r'_{0,1})}\big),$$

$$\big(1_{\tilde{G}}, \tilde{G}^{r_{i,2}+r'_{i,2}} \cdot \tilde{X}_0^{-(r_{0,2}+r'_{0,2})}\big)\Big)\Big)$$

$$= \Big(1_{\mathbb{T}}, 1_{\mathbb{T}}, 1_{\mathbb{T}}, \prod_{j=1}^{n} e(M_{i,j}, \tilde{X}_j)e(R'_i, \tilde{R}'_i \cdot \tilde{Z}^{b_i})e(G, \tilde{Y})\Big)$$

$$\Big(1_{\mathbb{T}}, e(G, \tilde{G}^{r_{i,1}+r'_{i,1}} \cdot \tilde{X}_0^{-(r_{0,1}+r'_{0,1})}), 1_{\mathbb{T}}, e(Q, \tilde{G}^{r_{i,1}+r'_{i,1}} \cdot \tilde{X}_0^{-(r_{0,1}+r'_{0,1})})\Big)$$

$$\Big(1_{\mathbb{T}}, e(G^{t_1}, \tilde{G}^{r_{i,2}+r'_{i,2}} \cdot \tilde{X}_0^{-(r_{0,2}+r'_{0,2})}), 1_{\mathbb{T}}, e(Q^{t_1}, \tilde{G}^{r_{i,2}+r'_{i,2}} \cdot \tilde{X}_0^{-(r_{0,2}+r'_{0,2})})\Big)$$

$$= \Big(1_{\mathbb{T}}, 1_{\mathbb{T}}, 1_{\mathbb{T}}, \prod_{j=1}^{n} e(M_{i,j}, \tilde{X}_j)e(R'_i, \tilde{R}'_i \cdot \tilde{Z}^{b_i})e(G, \tilde{Y})\Big)$$

$$\Big(1_{\mathbb{T}}, e(G, \tilde{G}^{r_{i,1}+r'_{i,1}} \cdot \tilde{X}_0^{-(r_{0,1}+r'_{0,1})})e(G^{t_1}, \tilde{G}^{r_{i,2}+r'_{i,2}} \cdot \tilde{X}_0^{-(r_{0,2}+r'_{0,2})}),$$

$$1_{\mathbb{T}}, e(Q, \tilde{G}^{r_{i,1}+r'_{i,1}} \cdot \tilde{X}_0^{-(r_{0,1}+r'_{0,1})})e(Q^{t_1}, \tilde{G}^{r_{i,2}+r'_{i,2}} \cdot \tilde{X}_0^{-(r_{0,2}+r'_{0,2})})\Big)$$

$$= \Big(1_{\mathbb{T}}, 1_{\mathbb{T}}, 1_{\mathbb{T}}, \prod_{j=1}^{n} e(M_{i,j}, \tilde{X}_j)e(R'_i, \tilde{R}'_i \cdot \tilde{Z}^{b_i})e(G, \tilde{Y})\Big)$$

$$\Big(1_{\mathbb{T}}, e(G, \tilde{G}^{r_{i,1}+r'_{i,1}})e(G, \tilde{G}^{t_1(r_{i,2}+r'_{i,2})})e(G, \tilde{X}_0^{-(r_{0,1}+r'_{0,1})})e(G, \tilde{X}_0^{-t_1(r_{0,2}+r'_{0,2})}),$$

$$1_{\mathbb{T}}, e(Q, \tilde{G}^{r_{i,1}+r'_{i,1}})e(Q, \tilde{G}^{t_1(r_{i,2}+r'_{i,2})})e(Q, \tilde{X}_0^{-(r_{0,1}+r'_{0,1})})e(Q, \tilde{X}_0^{-t_1(r_{0,2}+r'_{0,2})})\Big)$$

It is clear both sides equate and hence the proof $\tilde{\pi}'_i$ verifies correctly. This concludes the proof. □

References

1. Abe, M., Fuchsbauer, G., Groth, J., Haralambiev, K., Ohkubo, M.: Structure-preserving signatures and commitments to group elements. In: Rabin, T. (ed.) CRYPTO 2010. LNCS, vol. 6223, pp. 209–236. Springer, Heidelberg (2010). https://doi.org/10.1007/978-3-642-14623-7_12

2. Abe, M., Groth, J., Haralambiev, K., Ohkubo, M.: Optimal structure-preserving signatures in asymmetric bilinear groups. In: Rogaway, P. (ed.) CRYPTO 2011. LNCS, vol. 6841, pp. 649–666. Springer, Heidelberg (2011). https://doi.org/10.1007/978-3-642-22792-9_37

3. Belenkiy, M., Camenisch, J., Chase, M., Kohlweiss, M., Lysyanskaya, A., Shacham, H.: Randomizable proofs and delegatable anonymous credentials. In: Halevi, S. (ed.) CRYPTO 2009. LNCS, vol. 5677, pp. 108–125. Springer, Heidelberg (2009). https://doi.org/10.1007/978-3-642-03356-8_7

4. Bethencourt, J., Sahai, A., Waters, B.: Ciphertext-policy attribute-based encryption. In: S&P 2007, pp. 321–334. IEEE (2007)

5. Ahn, J.H., Boneh, D., Camenisch, J., Hohenberger, S., shelat, A., Waters, B.: Computing on authenticated data. In: Cramer, R. (ed.) TCC 2012. LNCS, vol. 7194, pp. 1–20. Springer, Heidelberg (2012). https://doi.org/10.1007/978-3-642-28914-9_1

6. Attrapadung, N., Libert, B.: Homomorphic network coding signatures in the standard model. In: Catalano, D., Fazio, N., Gennaro, R., Nicolosi, A. (eds.) PKC 2011. LNCS, vol. 6571, pp. 17–34. Springer, Heidelberg (2011). https://doi.org/10.1007/978-3-642-19379-8_2

7. Attrapadung, N., Libert, B., Peters, T.: Computing on authenticated data: new privacy definitions and constructions. In: Wang, X., Sako, K. (eds.) ASIACRYPT 2012. LNCS, vol. 7658, pp. 367–385. Springer, Heidelberg (2012). https://doi.org/10.1007/978-3-642-34961-4_23

8. Attrapadung, N., Libert, B., Peters, T.: Efficient completely context-hiding quotable and linearly homomorphic signatures. In: Kurosawa, K., Hanaoka, G. (eds.) PKC 2013. LNCS, vol. 7778, pp. 386–404. Springer, Heidelberg (2013). https://doi.org/10.1007/978-3-642-36362-7_24

9. Barbulescu, R., Gaudry, P., Joux, A., Thomé, E.: A heuristic quasi-polynomial algorithm for discrete logarithm in finite fields of small characteristic. In: Nguyen, P.Q., Oswald, E. (eds.) EUROCRYPT 2014. LNCS, vol. 8441, pp. 1–16. Springer, Heidelberg (2014). https://doi.org/10.1007/978-3-642-55220-5_1

10. Bellare, M., Neven, G.: Transitive signatures based on factoring and RSA. In: Zheng, Y. (ed.) ASIACRYPT 2002. LNCS, vol. 2501, pp. 397–414. Springer, Heidelberg (2002). https://doi.org/10.1007/3-540-36178-2_25

11. Bellare, M., Rogaway, P.: Random oracles are practical: a Paradigm for Designing Efficient Protocols. In: ACM-CCS 1993, pp. 62–73. ACM (1993)

12. Blum, M., Feldman, P., Micali, S.: Non-interactive zero-knowledge and its applications. In: STOC 1988, pp. 103–112 (1988)

13. Boneh, D., Franklin, M.: Identity-based encryption from the weil pairing. In: Kilian, J. (ed.) CRYPTO 2001. LNCS, vol. 2139, pp. 213–229. Springer, Heidelberg (2001). https://doi.org/10.1007/3-540-44647-8_13

14. Boneh, D., Freeman, D.M.: Linearly homomorphic signatures over binary fields and new tools for lattice-based signatures. In: Catalano, D., Fazio, N., Gennaro, R., Nicolosi, A. (eds.) PKC 2011. LNCS, vol. 6571, pp. 1–16. Springer, Heidelberg (2011). https://doi.org/10.1007/978-3-642-19379-8_1

15. Boneh, D., Freeman, D.M.: Homomorphic signatures for polynomial functions. In: Paterson, K.G. (ed.) EUROCRYPT 2011. LNCS, vol. 6632, pp. 149–168. Springer, Heidelberg (2011). https://doi.org/10.1007/978-3-642-20465-4_10

16. Boneh, D., Freeman, D., Katz, J., Waters, B.: Signing a linear subspace: signature schemes for network coding. In: Jarecki, S., Tsudik, G. (eds.) PKC 2009. LNCS, vol. 5443, pp. 68–87. Springer, Heidelberg (2009). https://doi.org/10.1007/978-3-642-00468-1_5

17. Brzuska, C., Busch, H., Dagdelen, O., Fischlin, M., Franz, M., Katzenbeisser, S., Manulis, M., Onete, C., Peter, A., Poettering, B., Schröder, D.: Redactable signatures for tree-structured data: definitions and constructions. In: Zhou, J., Yung, M. (eds.) ACNS 2010. LNCS, vol. 6123, pp. 87–104. Springer, Heidelberg (2010). https://doi.org/10.1007/978-3-642-13708-2_6

18. Brzuska, C., Fischlin, M., Freudenreich, T., Lehmann, A., Page, M., Schelbert, J., Schröder, D., Volk, F.: Security of sanitizable signatures revisited. In: Jarecki, S., Tsudik, G. (eds.) PKC 2009. LNCS, vol. 5443, pp. 317–336. Springer, Heidelberg (2009). https://doi.org/10.1007/978-3-642-00468-1_18

19. Brzuska, C., Fischlin, M., Lehmann, A., Schröder, D.: Unlinkability of sanitizable signatures. In: Nguyen, P.Q., Pointcheval, D. (eds.) PKC 2010. LNCS, vol. 6056, pp. 444–461. Springer, Heidelberg (2010). https://doi.org/10.1007/978-3-642-13013-7_26

20. Camacho, P., Hevia, A.: Short transitive signatures for directed trees. In: Dunkelman, O. (ed.) CT-RSA 2012. LNCS, vol. 7178, pp. 35–50. Springer, Heidelberg (2012). https://doi.org/10.1007/978-3-642-27954-6_3

21. Catalano, D., Fiore, D., Warinschi, B.: Adaptive pseudo-free groups and applications. In: Paterson, K.G. (ed.) EUROCRYPT 2011. LNCS, vol. 6632, pp. 207–223. Springer, Heidelberg (2011). https://doi.org/10.1007/978-3-642-20465-4_13

22. Catalano, D., Fiore, D., Warinschi, B.: Efficient network coding signatures in the standard model. In: Fischlin, M., Buchmann, J., Manulis, M. (eds.) PKC 2012. LNCS, vol. 7293, pp. 680–696. Springer, Heidelberg (2012). https://doi.org/10.1007/978-3-642-30057-8_40

23. Chatterjee, S., Menezes, A.: Type 2 structure-preserving signature schemes revisited. In: Iwata, T., Cheon, J.H. (eds.) ASIACRYPT 2015. LNCS, vol. 9452, pp. 286–310. Springer, Heidelberg (2015). https://doi.org/10.1007/978-3-662-48797-6_13

24. De Santis, A., Di Crescenzo, G., Persiano, G.: Necessary and sufficient assumptions for non-interactive zero-knowledge proofs of knowledge for all NP relations. In: Montanari, U., Rolim, J.D.P., Welzl, E. (eds.) ICALP 2000. LNCS, vol. 1853, pp. 451–462. Springer, Heidelberg (2000). https://doi.org/10.1007/3-540-45022-X_38

25. Desmedt, Y.: Computer security by redefining what a computer is. In: NSPW 1993, pp. 160–166 (1993)

26. El Kaafarani, A., Ghadafi, E., Khader, D.: Decentralized traceable attribute-based signatures. In: Benaloh, J. (ed.) CT-RSA 2014. LNCS, vol. 8366, pp. 327–348. Springer, Cham (2014). https://doi.org/10.1007/978-3-319-04852-9_17

27. Fiat, A., Shamir, A.: Witness indistinguishable and witness hiding protocols. In: STOC 1990, pp. 416–426 (1990)

28. Freeman, D.M.: Improved security for linearly homomorphic signatures: a generic framework. In: Fischlin, M., Buchmann, J., Manulis, M. (eds.) PKC 2012. LNCS, vol. 7293, pp. 697–714. Springer, Heidelberg (2012). https://doi.org/10.1007/978-3-642-30057-8_41

29. Galbraith, S., Paterson, K., Smart, N.P.: Pairings for cryptographers. Discrete Appl. Math. **156**, 3113–3121 (2008)

30. Gennaro, R., Katz, J., Krawczyk, H., Rabin, T.: Secure network coding over the integers. In: Nguyen, P.Q., Pointcheval, D. (eds.) PKC 2010. LNCS, vol. 6056, pp. 142–160. Springer, Heidelberg (2010). https://doi.org/10.1007/978-3-642-13013-7_9

31. Gentry, C.: Fully homomorphic encryption using ideal lattices In: STOC 2009, pp. 169–178. ACM (2009)

32. Ghadafi, E., Smart, N.P., Warinschi, B.: Groth–Sahai proofs revisited. In: Nguyen, P.Q., Pointcheval, D. (eds.) PKC 2010. LNCS, vol. 6056, pp. 177–192. Springer, Heidelberg (2010). https://doi.org/10.1007/978-3-642-13013-7_11

33. Granger, R., Kleinjung, T., Zumbrägel, J.: Breaking '128-bit Secure' Supersingular Binary Curves (or how to solve discrete logarithms in $\mathbb{F}_{2^{4 \cdot 1223}}$ and $\mathbb{F}_{2^{12 \cdot 367}}$). In: Cryptology ePrint Archive, Report 2014/119, http://eprint.iacr.org/2014/119.pdf

34. Groth, J.: Efficient fully structure-preserving signatures for large messages. In: Iwata, T., Cheon, J.H. (eds.) ASIACRYPT 2015. LNCS, vol. 9452, pp. 239–259. Springer, Heidelberg (2015). https://doi.org/10.1007/978-3-662-48797-6_11

35. Groth, J., Sahai, A.: Efficient non-interactive proof systems for bilinear groups. SIAM J. Comput. **41**(5), 1193–1232 (2012)

36. Hevia, A., Micciancio, D.: The provable security of graph-based one-time signatures and extensions to algebraic signature schemes. In: Zheng, Y. (ed.) ASIACRYPT 2002. LNCS, vol. 2501, pp. 379–396. Springer, Heidelberg (2002). https://doi.org/10.1007/3-540-36178-2_24

37. Johnson, R., Molnar, D., Song, D., Wagner, D.: Homomorphic signature schemes. In: Preneel, B. (ed.) CT-RSA 2002. LNCS, vol. 2271, pp. 244–262. Springer, Heidelberg (2002). https://doi.org/10.1007/3-540-45760-7_17

38. Kiltz, E., Mityagin, A., Panjwani, S., Raghavan, B.: Append-only signatures. In: Caires, L., Italiano, G.F., Monteiro, L., Palamidessi, C., Yung, M. (eds.) ICALP 2005. LNCS, vol. 3580, pp. 434–445. Springer, Heidelberg (2005). https://doi.org/10.1007/11523468_36

39. Libert, B., Joye, M., Yung, M., Peters, T.: Secure efficient history-hiding append-only signatures in the standard model. In: Katz, J. (ed.) PKC 2015. LNCS, vol. 9020, pp. 450–473. Springer, Heidelberg (2015). https://doi.org/10.1007/978-3-662-46447-2_20

40. Micali, S., Rivest, R.L.: Transitive signature schemes. In: Preneel, B. (ed.) CT-RSA 2002. LNCS, vol. 2271, pp. 236–243. Springer, Heidelberg (2002). https://doi.org/10.1007/3-540-45760-7_16

41. Miyazaki, K., Hanaoka, G., Imai, H.: Digitally signed document sanitizing scheme based on bilinear maps. In: ASIACCS 2006, pp. 343–354. ACM (2006)

42. Shoup, V.: Lower bounds for discrete logarithms and related problems. In: Fumy, W. (ed.) EUROCRYPT 1997. LNCS, vol. 1233, pp. 256–266. Springer, Heidelberg (1997). https://doi.org/10.1007/3-540-69053-0_18

43. Waters, B.: Efficient identity-based encryption without random oracles. In: Cramer, R. (ed.) EUROCRYPT 2005. LNCS, vol. 3494, pp. 114–127. Springer, Heidelberg (2005). https://doi.org/10.1007/11426639_7

Symmetric Cryptography

Orthogonal MDS Diffusion Matrices over Galois Rings

Chik How Tan$^{(\boxtimes)}$ and Theo Fanuela Prabowo

Temasek Laboratories, National University of Singapore,
5A Engineering Drive 1, #09-02, Singapore 117411, Singapore
{tsltch,tsltfp}@nus.edu.sg

Abstract. MDS matrices are important components in block cipher algorithm design, which provide diffusion of input bits. Recently, many constructions of MDS matrices focused on lightweight constructions. All MDS matrices constructions were over Galois field. In this paper, we give new construction of MDS matrices which is over Galois ring $GR(2^n, k) = \mathbb{Z}_{2^n}[x]/(f(x))$, where $f(x)$ is a basic irreducible polynomial of degree k over $\mathbb{Z}_{2^n}$. We first construct Hadamard matrices over $U(GR(2^n, k))$ by adding some signs on the entries of the matrices (i.e. performing entry-wise multiplication with enabling Hadamard $(1, -1)$-matrices). We give complete enumerations of 4×4 and 8×8 enabling Hadamard $(1, -1)$-matrices. We prove that there is no 2×2 orthogonal MDS matrix over Galois ring $GR(2^n, k)$ and construct 4×4 orthogonal MDS matrices over $GR(2^n, k)$.

Keywords: Cryptography · Diffusion matrices · MDS matrices · Orthogonal matrices · Galois rings

1 Introduction

It is well-known that MDS matrices are used for diffusion in the design of block cipher algorithms, for example, AES, other AES-like block ciphers and authenticated encryption algorithms use MDS matrices to mix the input bits to achieve diffusion of bits. Recently, the construction of MDS matrices is an active area of research. Most of the research focuses on the construction of lightweight MDS matrices [6–8,10–12]. While some constructions of MDS matrices are from BCH codes [1], algebraic-geometry codes [2], Gabidulin codes [3], polynomials [9] and compact Cauchy matrices [5], etc., all these constructions are over Galois field $(\mathbb{F}_{2^k} = \mathbb{F}_2[x]/(\bar{f}(x))$, where $\bar{f}(x)$ is an irreducible polynomial of degree k over $\mathbb{F}_2$). The problem with these constructions is that to mix more bits, it is required to construct bigger MDS matrices, e.g. 16×16 or 32×32 MDS matrices over $\mathbb{F}_{2^k}$. In order to solve this problem, we propose constructing MDS matrices over Galois ring $(GR(2^n, k) = \mathbb{Z}_{2^n}[x]/(f(x))$, where $f(x)$ is a basic irreducible polynomial of degree k over $\mathbb{Z}_{2^n}$).

© Springer International Publishing AG 2017
M. O'Neill (Ed.): IMACC 2017, LNCS 10655, pp. 307–330, 2017.
https://doi.org/10.1007/978-3-319-71045-7_16

The algebraic structure of Galois ring $GR(2^n, k)$ is different from that of Galois field $\mathbb{F}_{2^k}$, for example, not all the nonzero elements in $GR(2^n, k)$ are invertible, which is not the case in $\mathbb{F}_{2^k}$. So, we first need to study and prove some properties of Galois ring $GR(2^n, k)$, especially, which elements of $GR(2^n, k)$ are unit elements and square elements, etc. Using these properties, we will construct MDS matrices over $GR(2^n, k)$ via Hadamard matrices and construct orthogonal MDS matrices.

The organization of this paper is as follows. In Sect. 2, we give some properties of Galois ring $GR(2^n, k)$. These properties will be used to construct MDS matrices. In order to construct orthogonal MDS matrices, we first construct Hadamard matrices over $GR(2^n, k)$ in Sect. 3. In Sect. 4, we give a definition of MDS matrices over $GR(2^n, k)$ and prove the necessary and sufficient condition between MDS matrices over $GR(2^n, k)$ and $\mathbb{F}_{2^k}$. In Sect. 5, we construct 4×4 orthogonal MDS matrices over $GR(2^n, k)$ and prove that there is no 2×2 orthogonal MDS matrix over $GR(2^n, k)$. Finally, we give a conclusion in Sect. 6.

2   Preliminaries

In this section, we will briefly discuss the properties of Galois ring, especially unit elements and square elements in Galois ring; and also the relation via an epimorphism between Galois ring and finite field.

Let $n \geq 3$ and $k \geq 2$ be positive integers, $\mathbb{F}_2$ be the finite field of 2 elements and $\mathbb{Z}_{2^n}$ be the ring of integers modulo 2^n. Let $\mathbb{F}_2[x]$ and $\mathbb{Z}_{2^n}[x]$ be the polynomial rings over $\mathbb{F}_2$ and $\mathbb{Z}_{2^n}$ respectively. Suppose $\bar{f}(x)$ is an irreducible polynomial of degree k over $\mathbb{F}_2$ and $f(x)$ is a basic irreducible polynomial of degree k over $\mathbb{Z}_{2^n}$ with $\bar{f}(x) \equiv f(x) \bmod 2$. Then finite field is $\mathbb{F}_{2^k} = \mathbb{F}_2[x]/(\bar{f}(x))$ and Galois ring is $GR(2^n, k) = \mathbb{Z}_{2^n}[x]/(f(x))$; and there is an epimorphism μ from $GR(2^n, k)$ to $\mathbb{F}_{2^k}$ such that $\mu(\alpha) = \bar{\alpha}$ where α and $\bar{\alpha}$ are the root of $f(x)$ and $\bar{f}(x)$ respectively. That is,

$$\mu : GR(2^n, k) = \mathbb{Z}_{2^n}[x]/(f(x)) \longrightarrow \mathbb{F}_{2^k} = \mathbb{F}_2[x]/(\bar{f}(x))$$

$$\mu(\sum_{i=0}^{k-1} a_i \alpha^i) = \sum_{i=0}^{k-1} \bar{a}_i \bar{\alpha}^i,$$

where $a_i \in \mathbb{Z}_{2^n}$ and $\bar{a}_i \equiv a_i \bmod 2$ for $i = 0, \cdots, k-1$.

As μ is an epimorphism, then for any $\beta, \gamma \in GR(2^n, k)$, one has
(a) $\mu(0) = 0$,   (c) $\mu(\beta + \gamma) = \mu(\beta) + \mu(\gamma)$,
(b) $\mu(1) = 1$,   (d) $\mu(\beta\gamma) = \mu(\beta)\mu(\gamma)$.
Note: For other representation of elements in Galois ring $GR(2^n, k)$, please refer to [4].

We first give a definition of unit element in $GR(2^n, k)$ and find the total number of unit elements in $GR(2^n, k)$.

Definition 1. An element β is called unit element if there exists an element $\gamma \in GR(2^n, k)$ such that $\beta\gamma = 1$, otherwise, β is called a non-unit element. We denote the units of $GR(2^n, k)$ by $U(GR(2^n, k))$.

Lemma 1. *If $\beta \in GR(2^n, k)$ is a unit element, then $\mu(\beta)$ is a unit element in $\mathbb{F}_{2^k}$. Furthermore, $|U(GR(2^n, k))| = 2^{(n-1)k}(2^k - 1)$.*

Proof. As β is a unit element, there exists $\gamma \in GR(2^n, k)$ such that $\beta\gamma = 1$. Hence, $\mu(\beta\gamma) = 1$ and $\mu(\beta\gamma) = \mu(\beta)\mu(\gamma) = 1$. That is, there is an element $\mu(\gamma) \in \mathbb{F}_{2^k}$ such that $\mu(\beta)\mu(\gamma) = 1$. Therefore, $\mu(\beta)$ is a unit element in $\mathbb{F}_{2^k}$.

If $\mathbf{a} = \sum_{i=0}^{k-1} a_i\alpha^i \in GR(2^n, k)$ is a non-unit element, then all a_i are even integers and the total number of non-unit elements is $2^{k(n-1)}$. Therefore, $|U(GR(2^n, k))| = 2^{kn} - 2^{k(n-1)} = 2^{k(n-1)}(2^k - 1)$. $\qquad\square$

Now, we define a square element in $U(GR(2^n, k))$ and prove that certain elements of $U(GR(2^n, k))$ are non-square elements.

Definition 2. *An element β is called a square element if there exists an element $\gamma \in GR(2^n, k)$ such that $\beta = \gamma^2$, otherwise, β is called a non-square element.*

Remark 1. 1 is a square element in $U(GR(2^n, k))$ as $1^2 = 1$.

Lemma 2. *If $\mathbf{a}$ and $\mathbf{b}$ are non-square and square elements in $U(GR(2^n, k))$ respectively, then $\mathbf{ab}$ is a non-square in $U(GR(2^n, k))$.*

Proof. Assume that $\mathbf{ab}$ is a square in $U(GR(2^n, k))$, then there exists $\mathbf{c} \in U(GR(2^n, k))$ such that $\mathbf{c}^2 = \mathbf{ab}$. As $\mathbf{b}$ is a square in $U(GR(2^n, k))$, we have $\mathbf{b} = \mathbf{d}^2$ for some $\mathbf{d} \in U(GR(2^n, k))$. Therefore, $\mathbf{a} = (\mathbf{cd}^{-1})^2$. This implies that $\mathbf{a}$ is a square, contradicting the assumption that $\mathbf{a}$ is a non-square. Hence, we proved the lemma. $\qquad\square$

Lemma 3. *For $n \geq 3$, any square element in $U(GR(2^n, k))$ has exactly 2^{k+1} square roots. If $\beta \in U(GR(2^n, k))$, then the 2^{k+1} square roots of β^2 are $\pm\beta + \sum_{i=0}^{k-1} 2^{n-1}\delta_i\alpha^i$, where $\delta_i \in \{0, 1\}$ for $0 \leq i \leq k-1$. Furthermore, the number of square elements in $U(GR(2^n, k))$ is $2^{k(n-2)-1}(2^k - 1)$.*

Proof. Let $\beta, \gamma \in U(GR(2^n, k))$ be such that $\beta^2 = \gamma^2$. We shall show that $\gamma = \pm\beta + \sum_{i=0}^{k-1} 2^{n-1}\delta_i\alpha^i$ for some $\delta_i \in \{0, 1\}$. As $\beta^2 = \gamma^2$, we have $(\gamma - \beta)(\gamma + \beta) = 0$. Let 2^{j_1} (resp. 2^{j_2}) be the highest power of 2 that divides $\beta - \gamma$ (resp. $\beta + \gamma$). Then $j_1, j_2 \geq 0$, and $\gamma - \beta = 2^{j_1}u_1$ and $\gamma + \beta = 2^{j_2}u_2$ for some $u_1, u_2 \in U(GR(2^n, k))$. As $(\gamma - \beta)(\gamma + \beta) = 0$, we must have $j_1 + j_2 \geq n$.

Suppose $j_1, j_2 \geq 2$. Then $2\gamma = (\gamma - \beta) + (\gamma + \beta) = 2^{j_1}u_1 + 2^{j_2}u_2$, so that $2 = (2^{j_1}u_1 + 2^{j_2}u_2)\gamma^{-1} = 4(2^{j_1-2}u_1 + 2^{j_2-2}u_2)\gamma^{-1}$. But this implies that $1 \equiv 2(2^{j_1-2}u_1 + 2^{j_2-2}u_2)\gamma^{-1} \bmod 2^{n-1}$, a contradiction. Thus, it is not the case that $j_1, j_2 \geq 2$, i.e. one of them must be ≤ 1. Assume that $j_1 \leq 1$. Then $j_2 \geq n - 1$ as $j_1 + j_2 \geq n$. So, $\gamma + \beta = 2^{j_2}u_2 = 2^{n-1}v_2$ for some $v_2 \in GR(2^n, k)$. Note that $2^{n-1}v_2$ is of the form $\sum_{i=0}^{k-1} 2^{n-1}\delta_i\alpha^i$ for some $\delta_i \in \{0, 1\}$. Thus, $\gamma = -\beta + 2^{n-1}v_2 = -\beta + \sum_{i=0}^{k-1} 2^{n-1}\delta_i\alpha^i$ if $j_1 \leq 1$. Similarly, one can show that if $j_2 \leq 1$, then $\gamma = \beta + \sum_{i=0}^{k-1} 2^{n-1}\delta_i\alpha^i$.

We have shown that if $\beta^2 = \gamma^2$, then $\gamma = \pm\beta + \sum_{i=0}^{k-1} 2^{n-1}\delta_i\alpha^i$ for some $\delta_i \in \{0, 1\}$. This implies that a square element in $U(GR(2^n, k))$ has at most

2^{k+1} square roots. To show that in fact a square element has exactly 2^{k+1} square roots, in the following we verify that any γ of this form satisfies $\gamma^2 = \beta^2$.

$$
\gamma^2 = (\pm\beta + \sum_{i=0}^{k-1} 2^{n-1}\delta_i\alpha^i)^2
$$

$$
= \beta^2 + \sum_{i=0}^{k-1} 2^{2n-2}\delta_i^2\alpha^{2i} + 2\sum_{i=0,j=0,i\neq j}^{k-1} 2^{2n-2}\delta_i\delta_j\alpha^{i+j} + 2\beta\sum_{i=0}^{k-1} 2^{n-1}\delta_i\alpha^i
$$

$$
= \beta^2. \qquad (\text{as } 2^{2n-2} \equiv 0 \bmod 2^n)
$$

We also note that the elements of the form $\pm\beta + \sum_{i=0}^{k-1} 2^{n-1}\delta_i\alpha^i$ with $\delta_i \in \{0,1\}$ are pairwise distinct. It is clear that elements of the form $\beta + \sum_{i=0}^{k-1} 2^{n-1}\delta_i\alpha^i$ (resp. $-\beta + \sum_{i=0}^{k-1} 2^{n-1}\delta_i\alpha^i$) are pairwise distinct. Now, suppose $\beta + \sum_{i=0}^{k-1} 2^{n-1}\delta_i\alpha^i = -\beta + \sum_{i=0}^{k-1} 2^{n-1}\delta_i'\alpha^i$. Then $2\beta = \sum_{i=0}^{k-1} 2^{n-1}(\delta_i' - \delta_i)\alpha^i$, or equivalently $\beta \equiv \sum_{i=0}^{k-1} 2^{n-2}(\delta_i' - \delta_i)\alpha^i \bmod 2^{n-1}$. Note that 2^{n-2} is even as $n \geq 3$. Thus, all coefficients of β are even and so β is not a unit, contradiction. We conclude that the elements of the form $\pm\beta + \sum_{i=0}^{k-1} 2^{n-1}\delta_i\alpha^i$ with $\delta_i \in \{0,1\}$ are pairwise distinct. Hence, a square element in $U(GR(2^n, k))$ has exactly 2^{k+1} square roots.

Define a function θ from $U(GR(2^n, k))$ to $U(GR(2^n, k))$ by $\theta(z) = z^2$ for $z \in U(GR(2^n, k))$. For each $\theta(z)$, there are exactly 2^{k+1} preimages that map to $\theta(z)$. Hence, $|\text{Im } \theta| = 2^{k(n-1)}(2^k - 1)/2^{k+1} = 2^{k(n-2)-1}(2^k - 1)$. □

Lemma 4. *Let j and l be integers such that $0 \leq j < \frac{k}{2}$ and $0 \leq l < 2^{n-2}$. If $2 \mid c_i$, for all $i \neq 2j, i \leq k-1$, then $-5^l\alpha^{2j} + \sum_{i\neq 2j, i\leq k-1} c_i\alpha^i$ is not a square in $U(GR(2^n, k))$.*

Proof. Let μ be the epimorphism from $GR(2^n, k)$ to $\mathbb{F}_{2^k}$. Assume that $-5^l\alpha^{2j} + \sum_{i\neq 2j, i\leq k-1} c_i\alpha^i$ is a square in $U(GR(2^n, k))$, then there exists $\mathbf{a} \in U(GR(2^n, k))$ such that $\mathbf{a}^2 = -5^l\alpha^{2j} + \sum_{i\neq 2j, i\leq k-1} c_i\alpha^i$ and $\mathbf{a} = \sum_{i=0}^{k-1} a_i\alpha^i$. Then, we have $\mu(\mathbf{a})^2 = \mu(\mathbf{a}^2) = \bar{\alpha}^{2j}$ and so $\mu(\mathbf{a}) = \bar{\alpha}^j$. This implies that $\mathbf{a} = (2a_j' + 1)\alpha^j + 2\sum_{i\neq j, i\leq k-1} a_i'\alpha^i$, where $a_j = 2a_j' + 1$ and $a_i = 2a_i'$ for $i \neq j, i \leq k-1$. Thus,

$$
\mathbf{a}^2 = (1 + 4a_j' + 4(a_j')^2)\alpha^{2j} + 4a_j\sum_{i\neq j, i\leq k-1} a_i'\alpha^i + 4\left(\sum_{i\neq j, i\leq k-1} a_i'\alpha^i\right)^2
$$

$$
= -5^l\alpha^{2j} + \sum_{i\neq 2j, i\leq k-1} c_i\alpha^i. \tag{1}
$$

As $5^l \equiv 1 \bmod 4$, there exists $u \in \mathbb{Z}$ such that $5^l = 4u + 1$. Then (1) becomes

$$(-2 - 4u)\alpha^{2j} = (4a'_j + 4(a'_j)^2)\alpha^{2j} + 4 \left[a_j \sum_{i \neq j,\, i \leq k-1} a'_i \alpha^i + \left(\sum_{i \neq j,\, i \leq k-1} a'_i \alpha^i \right)^2 \right]$$
$$- \sum_{i \neq 2j,\, i \leq k-1} c_i \alpha^i.$$

Thus,

$$2\alpha^{2j} \equiv \sum_{i \neq 2j,\, i \leq k-1} \bar{c}_i \alpha^i \bmod 4,$$

where $\bar{c}_i \equiv c_i \bmod 4$ for $i \neq 2j, i \leq k - 1$. Note that the left hand side has the term α^{2j}, while the right hand side does not. This is a contradiction. Therefore, we conclude that $-5^l \alpha^{2j} + \sum_{i \neq 2j,\, i \leq k-1} c_i \alpha^i$ is not a square in $U(GR(2^n, k))$. $\square$

Corollary 1. -1 *is a non-square element in* $U(GR(2^n, k))$.

3 Hadamard Matrices

In this section, we will construct Hadamard matrices over $U(GR(2^n, k))$ by considering Hadamard matrices over $\mathbb{F}_{2^k}$ and introducing some signs on the entries of the matrices. We first give a definition of Hadamard matrices as follows.

Definition 3. An $m \times m$ matrix M is called Hadamard matrix if $MM^T = cI_m$, where c is a constant, M^T is the transpose of M and I_m is the identity matrix. Furthermore,

(1) If $c = 1$, then M is called orthogonal matrix.
(2) If $c = 1$ and $M^T = M$, then M is called involutory matrix.

Definition 4. Let R be a ring. A 2×2 matrix of the form $\begin{bmatrix} a_0 & a_1 \\ a_1 & a_0 \end{bmatrix}$, where $a_0, a_1 \in R$, is called 2×2 pseudo Hadamard matrix over R and is denoted by $\mathrm{PHD}(a_0, a_1)$. For $r \geq 2$, define a $2^r \times 2^r$ matrix M over R by $M = \begin{bmatrix} M_1 & M_2 \\ M_2 & M_1 \end{bmatrix}$, where M_i is a $2^{r-1} \times 2^{r-1}$ pseudo Hadamard matrix over R for $i = 1, 2$. The matrix M is called $2^r \times 2^r$ pseudo Hadamard matrix over R. We denote M by $\mathrm{PHD}(a_0, \cdots, a_{2^r-1})$, where $M_1 = \mathrm{PHD}(a_0, \cdots, a_{2^{r-1}-1})$ and $M_2 = \mathrm{PHD}(a_{2^{r-1}}, \cdots, a_{2^r-1})$.

Any 2×2 pseudo Hadamard matrix over $\mathbb{F}_{2^k}$ is a Hadamard matrix, but a pseudo Hadamard matrix $M = \begin{bmatrix} a_0 & a_1 \\ a_1 & a_0 \end{bmatrix}$ over $U(GR(2^n, k))$ may not always be a Hadamard matrix as $MM^T \neq (a_0^2 + a_1^2)I_2$ if $2a_0a_1 \neq 0$ in $GR(2^n, k)$. But, the matrix M over $U(GR(2^n, k))$ can be made into a Hadamard matrix by adding some signs on the entries of the matrix M as follows.

$$\begin{bmatrix} a_0 & a_1 \\ a_1 & -a_0 \end{bmatrix}, \qquad \begin{bmatrix} a_0 & a_1 \\ -a_1 & a_0 \end{bmatrix}.$$

It is easy to check that the above two matrices are 2×2 Hadamard matrices over $U(GR(2^n, k))$. This construction of adding signs on the entries of matrix M can be considered as entry-wise multiplying a pseudo Hadamard matrix with a $(1, -1)$-matrix, that is, a matrix whose entries are either 1 or -1.

Notation: We denote $\odot$ as the entry-wise multiplication of two $m \times m$ matrices $M = (m_{ij})$ and $S = (s_{ij})$, that is, $M \odot S = (m_{ij} s_{ij})$.

With this notation, the above 2×2 Hadamard matrices can be written as follows:

$$\begin{bmatrix} a_0 & a_1 \\ a_1 & -a_0 \end{bmatrix} = \begin{bmatrix} a_0 & a_1 \\ a_1 & a_0 \end{bmatrix} \odot \begin{bmatrix} 1 & 1 \\ 1 & -1 \end{bmatrix}, \qquad \begin{bmatrix} a_0 & a_1 \\ -a_1 & a_0 \end{bmatrix} = \begin{bmatrix} a_0 & a_1 \\ a_1 & a_0 \end{bmatrix} \odot \begin{bmatrix} 1 & 1 \\ -1 & 1 \end{bmatrix}.$$

Therefore, a pseudo Hadamard matrix can be made into a Hadamard matrix by performing entry-wise multiplication with a $(1, -1)$-matrix.

Definition 5. Let R be a commutative ring with unity of characteristic $\neq 2$. If S is a $(1, -1)$-matrix such that $\mathrm{PHD}(a_0, \cdots, a_{m-1}) \odot S$ is Hadamard for any $a_0, a_1, \cdots, a_{m-1} \in R$, then we call S an enabling Hadamard $(1, -1)$-matrix with respect to R. We denote the Hadamard matrix $\mathrm{PHD}(a_0, \cdots, a_{m-1}) \odot S$ by $\mathrm{HD}(a_0, \cdots, a_{m-1}; S)$.

Remark 2. If R is a commutative ring with unity of characteristic 2 (e.g. $\mathbb{F}_{2^k}$), then $m \times m$ pseudo Hadamard matrix $\mathrm{PHD}(a_0, \cdots, a_{m-1})$ over R is always a Hadamard matrix and is denoted by $\mathrm{HD}(a_0, \cdots, a_{m-1}; \mathbb{I})$, where $\mathbb{I}$ is the $(1, -1)$-matrix whose entries are all 1.

For the rest of the paper, we will always assume that R is a commutative ring with unity of characteristic $\neq 2$, and we say that a $(1, -1)$-matrix is an enabling Hadamard $(1, -1)$-matrix if it is an enabling Hadamard $(1, -1)$-matrix with respect to R.

In the following, we construct 2×2 Hadamard matrices over R by listing eight 2×2 enabling Hadamard $(1, -1)$-matrices.

Proposition 1. *The following eight matrices are enabling Hadamard $(1, -1)$-matrices*

$$\begin{bmatrix} 1 & 1 \\ 1 & -1 \end{bmatrix}, \begin{bmatrix} 1 & 1 \\ -1 & 1 \end{bmatrix}, \begin{bmatrix} 1 & -1 \\ 1 & 1 \end{bmatrix}, \begin{bmatrix} -1 & 1 \\ 1 & 1 \end{bmatrix}, \begin{bmatrix} -1 & -1 \\ -1 & 1 \end{bmatrix}, \begin{bmatrix} -1 & -1 \\ 1 & -1 \end{bmatrix}, \begin{bmatrix} -1 & 1 \\ -1 & -1 \end{bmatrix}, \begin{bmatrix} 1 & -1 \\ -1 & -1 \end{bmatrix}.$$

Proof. Let M be a 2×2 matrix $M = \begin{bmatrix} a_0 & a_1 \\ a_1 & a_0 \end{bmatrix}$ over R. It is easy to check that if S is any of the above eight matrices, then $M \odot S$ are Hadamard matrices over R. $\square$

By observing the eight 2×2 enabling Hadamard $(1, -1)$-matrices in Proposition 1, we have the following lemma.

Lemma 5. *If* $\begin{bmatrix} a_1 & b_1 \\ b_2 & a_2 \end{bmatrix}$ *is a* 2×2 *enabling Hadamard* $(1, -1)$-*matrix, then,*

(a) $a_1 b_1 = -a_2 b_2$,   (b) $a_1 b_2 = -a_2 b_1$,   (c) $a_1 a_2 = -b_1 b_2$.

Proof. It is easy to check that the eight 2×2 enabling Hadamard $(1, -1)$-matrices in Proposition 1 satisfy all the equations above.   □

3.1 4×4 Hadamard Matrices

In Proposition 1, we constructed 2×2 enabling Hadamard $(1, -1)$-matrices. Now, we will construct all 4×4 enabling Hadamard $(1, -1)$-matrices in the following proposition.

Proposition 2. *Let* S *be a* 4×4 $(1, -1)$-*matrix, i.e.*

$$S = \begin{bmatrix} a_1 & b_1 & c_1 & d_1 \\ b_2 & a_2 & d_2 & c_2 \\ c_3 & d_3 & a_3 & b_3 \\ d_4 & c_4 & b_4 & a_4 \end{bmatrix} = \begin{bmatrix} S_1 & S_2 \\ S_3 & S_4 \end{bmatrix},$$

where each S_i *is a* 2×2 $(1, -1)$-*matrix for* $1 \le i \le 4$. *Then* S *is a* 4×4 *enabling Hadamard* $(1, -1)$-*matrix if and only if* S_1, S_2, S_3, S_4 *are* 2×2 *enabling Hadamard* $(1, -1)$-*matrices and the following system of equations holds:*

$$\begin{array}{lll} c_3 = b_1 b_2 c_2 d_1 d_3, & b_3 = -b_1 d_1 d_3, & a_3 = -a_1 c_1 c_3, \\ c_4 = b_1 b_2 c_1 d_2 d_4, & b_4 = -b_2 d_2 d_4, & a_4 = -a_2 c_2 c_4. \end{array} \tag{2}$$

Moreover, there are 256 4×4 *enabling Hadamard* $(1, -1)$-*matrices.*

Proof. Let R be a commutative ring with unity of characteristic $\ne 2$ and $\mathbf{a}, \mathbf{b}, \mathbf{c}, \mathbf{d}$ be arbitrary elements of R. Suppose

$$M := \mathrm{HD}(\mathbf{a}, \mathbf{b}, \mathbf{c}, \mathbf{d}; S) = \begin{bmatrix} \mathbf{a_1} & \mathbf{b_1} & \mathbf{c_1} & \mathbf{d_1} \\ \mathbf{b_2} & \mathbf{a_2} & \mathbf{d_2} & \mathbf{c_2} \\ \mathbf{c_3} & \mathbf{d_3} & \mathbf{a_3} & \mathbf{b_3} \\ \mathbf{d_4} & \mathbf{c_4} & \mathbf{b_4} & \mathbf{a_4} \end{bmatrix} = \begin{bmatrix} M_1 & M_2 \\ M_3 & M_4 \end{bmatrix},$$

where $\mathbf{z}_i$ is either $\mathbf{z}$ or $-\mathbf{z}$ for $1 \le i \le 4$ and $\mathbf{z} \in \{\mathbf{a}, \mathbf{b}, \mathbf{c}, \mathbf{d}\}$. As M is Hadamard, we have

$$MM^T = \begin{bmatrix} M_1 M_1^T + M_2 M_2^T & M_1 M_3^T + M_2 M_4^T \\ (M_1 M_3^T + M_2 M_4^T)^T & M_3 M_3^T + M_4 M_4^T \end{bmatrix} = (\mathbf{a}^2 + \mathbf{b}^2 + \mathbf{c}^2 + \mathbf{d}^2) I_4.$$

Thus, S is enabling Hadamard $(1, -1)$-matrix if and only if $M_1 M_1^T + M_2 M_2^T = (\mathbf{a}^2 + \mathbf{b}^2 + \mathbf{c}^2 + \mathbf{d}^2) I_2 = M_3 M_3^T + M_4 M_4^T$ and $M_1 M_3^T + M_2 M_4^T = 0$ for any $\mathbf{a}, \mathbf{b}, \mathbf{c}, \mathbf{d} \in R$.

We first examine the condition that $M_1 M_1^T + M_2 M_2^T = (a^2 + b^2 + c^2 + d^2)I_2 = M_3 M_3^T + M_4 M_4^T$. As a, b, c, d could be arbitrary, we may take $c = 0 = d$ (in this case $M_2 = 0$) to see that $M_1 = HD(a, b; S_1)$ is Hadamard. Thus, S_1 is a 2×2 enabling Hadamard $(1, -1)$-matrix. Similarly, S_2, S_3, and S_4 are 2×2 enabling Hadamard $(1, -1)$-matrices. Conversely, assuming S_1, S_2, S_3, S_4 are 2×2 enabling Hadamard $(1, -1)$ matrices, it is easy to check that $M_1 M_1^T + M_2 M_2^T = (a^2 + b^2 + c^2 + d^2)I_2 = M_3 M_3^T + M_4 M_4^T$. Hence, $M_1 M_1^T + M_2 M_2^T = (a^2 + b^2 + c^2 + d^2)I_2 = M_3 M_3^T + M_4 M_4^T$ holds if and only if S_1, S_2, S_3, S_4 are 2×2 enabling Hadamard $(1, -1)$-matrices.

Now we shall consider the condition $M_1 M_3^T + M_2 M_4^T = 0$, or equivalently

$$a_1 c_3 + b_1 d_3 + c_1 a_3 + d_1 b_3 = 0, \quad a_1 d_4 + b_1 c_4 + c_1 b_4 + d_1 a_4 = 0,$$
$$b_2 c_3 + a_2 d_3 + d_2 a_3 + c_2 b_3 = 0, \quad b_2 d_4 + a_2 c_4 + d_2 b_4 + c_2 a_4 = 0.$$

Note that a, b, c, d are arbitrary. So, we may set $b = 0$ (this implies that $b_1 = b_3 = 0$) in the first equation to get $a_1 c_3 + c_1 a_3 = 0$. Similarly, one may set $a = 0$ (this implies that $a_1 = a_3 = 0$) to obtain $b_1 d_3 + d_1 b_3 = 0$. Using similar argument, we conclude that

$$a_1 c_3 + c_1 a_3 = b_1 d_3 + d_1 b_3 = a_1 d_4 + d_1 a_4 = b_1 c_4 + c_1 b_4 = 0$$
$$b_2 c_3 + c_2 b_3 = a_2 d_3 + d_2 a_3 = b_2 d_4 + d_2 b_4 = a_2 c_4 + c_2 a_4 = 0.$$

As $a_i = a a_i$ for $1 \leq i \leq 4$ (and the same holds whenever a is replaced by b or c or d), we note that the above system of equations holds if and only if the following holds (note that the following system of equations holds in R if and only if it holds in $\mathbb{Z}$ as $char(R) \neq 2$):

$$\begin{array}{ll} a_1 c_3 + c_1 a_3 = 0, & a_1 d_4 + d_1 a_4 = 0, \\ b_1 d_3 + d_1 b_3 = 0, & b_1 c_4 + c_1 b_4 = 0, \\ b_2 c_3 + c_2 b_3 = 0, & b_2 d_4 + d_2 b_4 = 0, \\ a_2 d_3 + d_2 a_3 = 0, & a_2 c_4 + c_2 a_4 = 0. \end{array}$$

These equations can be expressed in the following matrix form.

$$\begin{bmatrix} c_1 & 0 & a_1 & 0 \\ 0 & d_1 & 0 & b_1 \\ 0 & c_2 & b_2 & 0 \\ d_2 & 0 & 0 & a_2 \end{bmatrix} \begin{bmatrix} a_3 \\ b_3 \\ c_3 \\ d_3 \end{bmatrix} = \begin{bmatrix} 0 \\ 0 \\ 0 \\ 0 \end{bmatrix}, \quad \begin{bmatrix} c_2 & 0 & a_2 & 0 \\ 0 & d_2 & 0 & b_2 \\ 0 & c_1 & b_1 & 0 \\ d_1 & 0 & 0 & a_1 \end{bmatrix} \begin{bmatrix} a_4 \\ b_4 \\ c_4 \\ d_4 \end{bmatrix} = \begin{bmatrix} 0 \\ 0 \\ 0 \\ 0 \end{bmatrix}.$$

We will simplify the equation on the left by performing elementary row operations as follows.

$$\mathbf{L} = \begin{bmatrix} c_1 & 0 & a_1 & 0 \\ 0 & d_1 & 0 & b_1 \\ 0 & c_2 & b_2 & 0 \\ d_2 & 0 & 0 & a_2 \end{bmatrix} \longrightarrow \begin{bmatrix} 1 & 0 & \frac{a_1}{c_1} & 0 \\ 0 & 1 & 0 & \frac{b_1}{d_1} \\ 0 & 1 & \frac{b_2}{c_2} & 0 \\ 1 & 0 & 0 & \frac{a_2}{d_2} \end{bmatrix} \longrightarrow \begin{bmatrix} 1 & 0 & \frac{a_1}{c_1} & 0 \\ 0 & 1 & 0 & \frac{b_1}{d_1} \\ 0 & 0 & \frac{b_2}{c_2} & -\frac{b_1}{d_1} \\ 0 & 0 & \frac{a_1}{c_1} & -\frac{a_2}{d_2} \end{bmatrix} \longrightarrow$$

$$\begin{bmatrix} 1 & 0 & \frac{a_1}{c_1} & 0 \\ 0 & 1 & 0 & \frac{b_1}{d_1} \\ 0 & 0 & 1 & -\frac{c_2 b_1}{b_2 d_1} \\ 0 & 0 & 1 & -\frac{c_1 a_2}{a_1 d_2} \end{bmatrix} \longrightarrow \begin{bmatrix} 1 & 0 & \frac{a_1}{c_1} & 0 \\ 0 & 1 & 0 & \frac{b_1}{d_1} \\ 0 & 0 & 1 & -\frac{c_2 b_1}{b_2 d_1} \\ 0 & 0 & 0 & \frac{c_1 a_2}{a_1 d_2} - \frac{c_2 b_1}{b_2 d_1} \end{bmatrix}.$$

By Lemma 5(a), we have $\frac{a_2}{a_1} = -\frac{b_1}{b_2}$ and $c_1 d_1 + c_2 d_2 = 0$. Hence,

$$\frac{c_1 a_2}{a_1 d_2} - \frac{c_2 b_1}{b_2 d_1} = \frac{a_2}{a_1}\left(\frac{c_1 d_1 + c_2 d_2}{d_1 d_2}\right) = 0.$$

Therefore, the equation $\mathbf{L} \cdot (a_3, b_3, c_3, d_3)^T = 0$ holds if and only if $c_3 - \frac{c_2 b_1}{b_2 d_1} \cdot d_3 = 0$ (i.e. $c_3 = b_1 b_2 c_2 d_1 d_3$) and $b_3 = -b_1 d_1 d_3$ and $a_3 = -a_1 c_1 c_3$.

By similar computation, we may perform elementary row operations on the right matrix as follows.

$$\mathbf{R} = \begin{bmatrix} c_2 & 0 & a_2 & 0 \\ 0 & d_2 & 0 & b_2 \\ 0 & c_1 & b_1 & 0 \\ d_1 & 0 & 0 & a_1 \end{bmatrix} \longrightarrow \cdots \longrightarrow \begin{bmatrix} 1 & 0 & \frac{a_2}{c_2} & 0 \\ 0 & 1 & 0 & \frac{b_2}{d_2} \\ 0 & 0 & 1 & -\frac{c_1 b_2}{b_1 d_2} \\ 0 & 0 & 0 & \frac{c_2 a_1}{a_2 d_1} - \frac{c_1 b_2}{b_1 d_2} \end{bmatrix}.$$

By Lemma 5(a), we have $\frac{a_1}{a_2} = -\frac{b_2}{b_1}$ and $c_1 d_1 + c_2 d_2 = 0$. Hence,

$$\frac{c_2 a_1}{a_2 d_1} - \frac{c_1 b_2}{b_1 d_2} = \frac{a_1}{a_2}\left(\frac{c_1 d_1 + c_2 d_2}{d_1 d_2}\right) = 0.$$

Therefore, the equation $\mathbf{R} \cdot (a_4, b_4, c_4, d_4)^T = 0$ holds if and only if $c_4 = b_1 b_2 c_1 d_2 d_4$ and $b_4 = -b_2 d_2 d_4$ and $a_4 = -a_2 c_2 c_4$. Thus, the condition $M_1 M_3^T + M_2 M_4^T = 0$ holds if and only if (2) holds.

Hence, S is a 4×4 enabling Hadamard $(1, -1)$-matrix if and only if (2) holds and S_1, S_2, S_3, S_4 are 2×2 enabling Hadamard $(1, -1)$-matrices. From these conditions, we observe that to construct a 4×4 enabling Hadamard $(1, -1)$-matrix S, one may choose S_1 (and also S_2) to be any 2×2 enabling Hadamard $(1, -1)$-matrix (there are 8 possible choices each for S_1 and S_2) and d_3 (and also d_4) can be chosen to be either 1 or -1 (so there are 2 choices each for d_3 and d_4). Once S_1, S_2, d_3, d_4 are fixed, the remaining values (i.e. $c_3, b_3, a_3, c_4, b_4, a_4$) are uniquely determined by (2). Note that by construction, (2) is satisfied and S_1, S_2 are 2×2 enabling Hadamard $(1, -1)$-matrices. Moreover, it is easy to check that S_3 and S_4 are 2×2 enabling Hadamard $(1, -1)$-matrices. Therefore, S is a 4×4 enabling Hadamard $(1, -1)$-matrix. Hence, in total, there are $8 * 8 * 2 * 2 = 256$ enabling Hadamard $(1, -1)$-matrices of dimension 4×4.   □

From Proposition 2 above, we give a detailed algorithm for constructing 4×4 enabling Hadamard $(1, -1)$-matrices in Appendix A. Below we list some 4×4 enabling Hadamard $(1, -1)$-matrices.

$$
\begin{bmatrix} 1 & 1 & 1 & 1 \\ -1 & 1 & -1 & 1 \\ -1 & 1 & 1 & -1 \\ -1 & -1 & 1 & 1 \end{bmatrix},
\begin{bmatrix} 1 & 1 & 1 & 1 \\ -1 & 1 & 1 & -1 \\ -1 & -1 & 1 & 1 \\ -1 & 1 & -1 & 1 \end{bmatrix},
\begin{bmatrix} 1 & -1 & -1 & -1 \\ 1 & 1 & -1 & 1 \\ 1 & 1 & 1 & -1 \\ 1 & -1 & 1 & 1 \end{bmatrix},
\begin{bmatrix} -1 & 1 & 1 & 1 \\ -1 & -1 & -1 & 1 \\ -1 & 1 & -1 & -1 \\ -1 & -1 & 1 & -1 \end{bmatrix}.
$$

3.2 8×8 Hadamard Matrices

In this subsection, we shall construct all possible 8×8 enabling Hadamard $(1, -1)$-matrices.

Let S be an 8×8 $(1, -1)$-matrix, say

$$
S = \begin{bmatrix}
a_1 & b_1 & c_1 & d_1 & e_1 & f_1 & g_1 & h_1 \\
b_2 & a_2 & d_2 & c_2 & f_2 & e_2 & h_2 & g_2 \\
c_3 & d_3 & a_3 & b_3 & g_3 & h_3 & e_3 & f_3 \\
d_4 & c_4 & b_4 & a_4 & h_4 & g_4 & f_4 & e_4 \\
e_5 & f_5 & g_5 & h_5 & a_5 & b_5 & c_5 & d_5 \\
f_6 & e_6 & h_6 & g_6 & b_6 & a_6 & d_6 & c_6 \\
g_7 & h_7 & e_7 & f_7 & c_7 & d_7 & a_7 & b_7 \\
h_8 & g_8 & f_8 & e_8 & d_8 & c_8 & b_8 & a_8
\end{bmatrix} = \begin{bmatrix} S_1 & S_2 \\ S_3 & S_4 \end{bmatrix}, \tag{3}
$$

where S_1, S_2, S_3, S_4 are 4×4 $(1, -1)$-matrices.

Lemma 6. *If S_1 and S_2 are two fixed enabling Hadamard $(1, -1)$-matrices in (3) and $\frac{a_1 b_3}{a_4 b_2} = \frac{e_4 f_1}{e_2 f_3}$, then there are 16 possible choices for S_3, S_4 such that S is an enabling Hadamard $(1, -1)$-matrix.*

Proof. The proof is given in Appendix B.   □

Proposition 3. *There are $2^{19} = 524288$ 8×8 enabling Hadamard $(1, -1)$-matrices.*

Proof. The matrix S_1 can be chosen to be any 4×4 enabling Hadamard $(1, -1)$-matrix. By Proposition 2, there are 256 choices for S_1. The matrix S_2 is also a 4×4 enabling Hadamard $(1, -1)$-matrix. However, we must choose S_2 such that the condition in Lemma 6 is satisfied, that is $\frac{a_1 b_3}{a_4 b_2} = \frac{e_4 f_1}{e_2 f_3}$. Thus, the number of choices for S_2 is $\frac{1}{2} * 256 = 128$. For each choices of S_2, there are 16 choices for S_3 and S_4. Hence, in total, there are $256 * 128 * 2^4 = 2^{19} = 524288$ enabling Hadamard $(1, -1)$-matrices of dimension 8×8.   □

From Lemma 6, we give a detailed algorithm for constructing 8×8 enabling Hadamard $(1, -1)$-matrices in Appendix C. Some examples of 8×8 enabling Hadamard $(1, -1)$-matrices obtained from this algorithm are given in Appendix D.

4 MDS Matrices

In this section, we will define MDS matrices over $U(GR(2^n, k))$ and examine some of their properties.

Definition 6. Let F be either finite field or Galois ring. Let M be an $m \times m$ matrix over F. If every $r \times r$ submatrix of M is non-singular for all $1 \le r \le m$, then M is an MDS matrix.

Remark 3. A square matrix over a ring is non-singular if and only if its determinant is a unit.

Lemma 7. *Let μ be the epimorphism from $GR(2^n, k)$ to $\mathbb{F}_{2^k}$ and $M = (a_{ij})$ be an $m \times m$ matrix over $U(GR(2^n, k))$, where $a_{ij} \in U(GR(2^n, k))$ is the (i, j)-entry of the matrix. Suppose $\bar{M} := \mu(M) = (\mu(a_{ij}))$ over $\mathbb{F}_{2^k}$. Then, $\mu(\det(M)) = \det(\bar{M})$, where $\det(M)$ is the determinant of M.*

Proof. This is true as μ is a ring homomorphism and the computation of determinant of a matrix only involves addition and multiplication of its entries. □

Theorem 1. *Let μ be the epimorphism from $GR(2^n, k)$ to $\mathbb{F}_{2^k}$. An $m \times m$ matrix $M = (a_{ij})$ over $U(GR(2^n, k))$ is MDS if and only if $\bar{M} = \mu(M) = (\bar{a}_{ij})$ is an $m \times m$ MDS matrix over $\mathbb{F}_{2^k}$, where $\bar{a}_{ij} := \mu(a_{ij})$.*

Proof. ($\Longrightarrow$) Suppose M is an MDS matrix over $U(GR(2^n, k))$. Assume that $\bar{M}$ is not MDS over $\mathbb{F}_{2^k}$. Then, there exists $r \times r$ submatrix $\bar{S}$ of $\bar{M}$ such that $\det(\bar{S}) = 0$ in $\mathbb{F}_{2^k}$. Let S be the corresponding $r \times r$ submatrix of M. Then, by Lemma 7, we have $\det(S) \notin U(GR(2^n, k))$. This contradicts the fact that M is an MDS matrix over $U(GR(2^n, k))$. Hence, $\bar{M}$ is MDS over $\mathbb{F}_{2^k}$.

($\Longleftarrow$) Suppose $\bar{M}$ is an MDS matrix over $\mathbb{F}_{2^k}$. Assume that M is not MDS over $U(GR(2^n, k))$, then, there exists $r \times r$ submatrix S of M such that $\det(S) \notin U(GR(2^n, k))$. Consider the corresponding submatrix $\bar{S} = \mu(S)$ of $\bar{M}$. By Lemma 7, we have $\det(S) = 0$ in $\mathbb{F}_{2^k}$. This contradicts the fact that $\bar{M}$ is an MDS matrix over $\mathbb{F}_{2^k}$. Hence, M is MDS over $U(GR(2^n, k))$. □

By the above theorem, every MDS matrices over $\mathbb{F}_{2^k}$ can be easily extended to MDS matrices over $U(GR(2^n, k))$. We give a proposition on how to ensure that a Hadamard matrix is an MDS matrix.

Proposition 4 (Proposition 4 of [12]). *Given an $m \times m$ Hadamard matrix M over $\mathbb{F}_{2^k}^* = \mathbb{F}_{2^k} \setminus \{0\}$ with the sum of the first row of M being not equal to 0. If all submatrices of M of order less than or equal to $\frac{m}{2}$ are non-singular, then M is MDS.*

Proposition 5. *Given a 4×4 Hadamard matrix M over $\mathbb{F}_{2^k}^* = \mathbb{F}_{2^k} \setminus \{0\}$ with the first row of M being $[u_1, u_2, u_3, u_4]$ such that $u_i \ne u_j$ for $i \ne j$ and $\sum_{i=1}^{4} u_i \ne 0$. If $u_i u_j \ne u_s u_t$ for $(i, j) \ne (s, t)$, where $1 \le i, j, s, t \le 4$, then M is MDS.*

Proof. By Proposition 4, we only need to check that all 1×1 and 2×2 submatrices of M are non-singular. It is clear that all 1×1 submatrices of M are non-singular as $u_i \neq 0$ for all $1 \leq i \leq 4$. Since M is Hadamard, then any 2×2 submatrix $S = \begin{bmatrix} a & b \\ c & d \end{bmatrix}$ of M falls into one of the following two cases.

(1) $a = d, b = c$: Then $\det(S) = a^2 + b^2 = (a+b)^2$. Since a $\neq$ b, therefore, $\det(S) \neq 0$.

(2) a, b, c, d are distinct: Then $\det(S) = ad + bc$. Since $ad \neq bc$ for $a, b, c, d \in \{u_1, \cdots, u_4\}$, then we have $\det(S) \neq 0$.

Combining the two cases above, all 2×2 submatrices of M are non-singular. Hence, M is MDS. $\qquad\square$

5   Orthogonal MDS Matrices

In order to have the same MDS matrix structure for encryption and decryption, it is necessary to convert an $m \times m$ Hadamard MDS matrix M ($MM^T = cI_m$) to an orthogonal MDS matrix ($\tilde{M}\tilde{M}^T = I_m$), where $\tilde{M} = \frac{1}{\sqrt{c}}M$ and $\tilde{M}^T = \frac{1}{\sqrt{c}}M^T$. In this section, we will examine the existence and construction of 2×2 and 4×4 orthogonal MDS matrices.

Lemma 8. *If* $\mathbf{a}, \mathbf{b} \in U(GR(2^n, k))$ *and* $\mathbf{a}^2 + \mathbf{b}^2 \in U(GR(2^n, k))$, *then* $\mathbf{a}^2 + \mathbf{b}^2$ *is not a square in* $U(GR(2^n, k))$.

Proof. The proof is given in Appendix E. $\qquad\square$

Corollary 2. *There is no* 2×2 *orthogonal MDS matrix over* $U(GR(2^n, k))$.

Proof. Assume that there exists 2×2 orthogonal MDS matrix over $U(GR(2^n, k))$, say $M = \begin{bmatrix} \mathbf{a} & \mathbf{b} \\ \mathbf{c} & \mathbf{d} \end{bmatrix}$. Then, we have $\mathbf{a}^2 + \mathbf{b}^2 = 1 \in U(GR(2^n, k))$. By Lemma 8, $\mathbf{a}^2 + \mathbf{b}^2$ is a non-square. This is a contradiction. Therefore, there is no 2×2 orthogonal MDS matrix over $U(GR(2^n, k))$. $\qquad\square$

Now, we will construct 4×4 orthogonal MDS matrices of the form $M = HD(\mathbf{a}, \mathbf{b}, \mathbf{c}, \mathbf{d}; S)$ over $U(GR(2^n, k))$, where S is a 4×4 enabling Hadamard $(1, -1)$-matrix. We note that $\mathbf{a}^2 + \mathbf{b}^2 + \mathbf{c}^2 + \mathbf{d}^2 = 1$ and $\mathbf{a}, \mathbf{b}, \mathbf{c}, \mathbf{d}$ must be distinct. First, we construct 4×4 orthogonal MDS matrices over $\mathbb{F}_{2^k}$ as follows.

Proposition 6. *Let* k *be even integer and* $\xi \in \mathbb{F}_{2^k}$ *such that* $\mathbb{F}_{2^k}^* = \{1, \xi, \cdots, \xi^{2^k - 2}\}$. *Let* $\omega = \xi^{(2^k - 1)/3}$ *and* $z \in \mathbb{F}_{2^k}^* \setminus \{1, \omega, \omega^2\}$. *Then the* 4×4 *Hadamard matrix* $M = HD(1, z, z\omega, z\omega^2; \mathbb{I})$ *is an orthogonal MDS matrix over* $\mathbb{F}_{2^k}$, *where* $\mathbb{I}$ *is the* $(1, -1)$*-matrix whose entries are all* 1.

Proof. Since $\omega^3 = 1$, then we have

$$1 + z^2 + (z\omega)^2 + (z\omega^2)^2 = 1 + z^2(1 + \omega + \omega^2) = 1.$$

Hence, M is an orthogonal matrix. By Proposition 4, we only need to check that all 1×1 and 2×2 submatrices of M are non-singular. It is clear that all 1×1 submatrices of M are non-singular as $1, z, z\omega, z\omega^2 \neq 0$. There are $C_2^4 \times C_2^4 = 36$ 2×2 submatrices of M (not necessarily distinct), which are listed as follows.

$$\begin{bmatrix} 1 & z \\ z & 1 \end{bmatrix}, \begin{bmatrix} 1 & z\omega \\ z & z\omega^2 \end{bmatrix}, \begin{bmatrix} 1 & z\omega^2 \\ z & z\omega \end{bmatrix}, \begin{bmatrix} z & z\omega \\ 1 & z\omega^2 \end{bmatrix}, \begin{bmatrix} z & z\omega^2 \\ 1 & z\omega \end{bmatrix}, \begin{bmatrix} z\omega & z\omega^2 \\ z\omega^2 & z\omega \end{bmatrix},$$

$$\begin{bmatrix} 1 & z \\ z\omega & z\omega^2 \end{bmatrix}, \begin{bmatrix} 1 & z\omega \\ z\omega & 1 \end{bmatrix}, \begin{bmatrix} 1 & z\omega^2 \\ z\omega & z \end{bmatrix}, \begin{bmatrix} z & z\omega \\ z\omega^2 & 1 \end{bmatrix}, \begin{bmatrix} z & z\omega^2 \\ z\omega^2 & z \end{bmatrix}, \begin{bmatrix} z\omega & z\omega^2 \\ 1 & z \end{bmatrix},$$

$$\begin{bmatrix} 1 & z \\ z\omega^2 & z\omega \end{bmatrix}, \begin{bmatrix} 1 & z\omega \\ z\omega^2 & z \end{bmatrix}, \begin{bmatrix} 1 & z\omega^2 \\ z\omega^2 & 1 \end{bmatrix}, \begin{bmatrix} z & z\omega \\ z\omega & 1 \end{bmatrix}, \begin{bmatrix} z & z\omega^2 \\ z\omega & 1 \end{bmatrix}, \begin{bmatrix} z\omega & z\omega^2 \\ z & 1 \end{bmatrix},$$

$$\begin{bmatrix} z & 1 \\ z\omega & z\omega^2 \end{bmatrix}, \begin{bmatrix} z & z\omega^2 \\ z\omega & 1 \end{bmatrix}, \begin{bmatrix} z & z\omega \\ z\omega & z \end{bmatrix}, \begin{bmatrix} 1 & z\omega^2 \\ z\omega^2 & 1 \end{bmatrix}, \begin{bmatrix} 1 & z\omega \\ z\omega^2 & z \end{bmatrix}, \begin{bmatrix} z\omega^2 & z\omega \\ 1 & z \end{bmatrix},$$

$$\begin{bmatrix} z & 1 \\ z\omega^2 & z\omega \end{bmatrix}, \begin{bmatrix} z & z\omega^2 \\ z\omega^2 & z \end{bmatrix}, \begin{bmatrix} z & z\omega \\ z\omega^2 & 1 \end{bmatrix}, \begin{bmatrix} 1 & z\omega^2 \\ z\omega & z \end{bmatrix}, \begin{bmatrix} 1 & z\omega \\ z\omega & 1 \end{bmatrix}, \begin{bmatrix} z\omega^2 & z\omega \\ z & 1 \end{bmatrix},$$

$$\begin{bmatrix} z\omega & z\omega^2 \\ z\omega^2 & z\omega \end{bmatrix}, \begin{bmatrix} z\omega & 1 \\ z\omega^2 & z \end{bmatrix}, \begin{bmatrix} z\omega & z \\ z\omega^2 & 1 \end{bmatrix}, \begin{bmatrix} z\omega^2 & 1 \\ z\omega & z \end{bmatrix}, \begin{bmatrix} z\omega^2 & z \\ z\omega & 1 \end{bmatrix}, \begin{bmatrix} 1 & z \\ z & 1 \end{bmatrix}.$$

By computing the determinants of all the 36 submatrices, their determinants are as follows.

$$1 + z^2, z^2\omega + z\omega^2, z\omega + z^2\omega^2, z^2\omega + z^2\omega^2,$$
$$1 + z^2\omega^2, 1 + z^2\omega, z + z^2, z^2 + z^2\omega, z^2 + z^2\omega^2.$$

Since $z \neq 1, \omega, \omega^2$; $\omega \neq 1$ and $\omega^2 \neq 1$, therefore, all of the above are non-zero. Hence, M is an orthogonal MDS matrix over $\mathbb{F}_{2^k}$. □

In the following, we will construct two types of 4×4 orthogonal MDS matrices over $U(GR(2^n, k))$. First, we recall the general setting of $U(GR(2^n, k))$ and $\mathbb{F}_{2^k}$.

Let $n \geq 3$, $k \geq 4$ even and $GR(2^n, k) = \mathbb{Z}_{2^n}[x]/(f(x))$ be a Galois ring, where $f(x)$ is a basic irreducible polynomial of degree k over $\mathbb{Z}_{2^n}$. Let $\mathbb{F}_{2^k} = \mathbb{F}_2[x]/(\bar{f}(x))$, where $\bar{f}(x) \equiv f(x) \bmod 2$ and α be a root of $f(x)$, μ is an epimorphism from $GR(2^n, k)$ to $\mathbb{F}_{2^k}$ such that $\bar{\alpha} := \mu(\alpha)$ is a primitive element in $\mathbb{F}_{2^k}$.

Theorem 2. *Let $\omega \in \mathbb{F}_{2^k}$ such that $\omega^3 = 1$. Let $\mathbf{z}, \mathbf{c}, \mathbf{d} \in U(GR(2^n, k))$ such that $\mu(\mathbf{z}) \in \mathbb{F}_{2^k} \setminus \{1, \omega, \omega^2\}$, $\omega = \mu(\mathbf{c})$ and $\omega^2 = \mu(\mathbf{d})$. Then a 4×4 Hadamard matrix $M = \mathrm{HD}(1, \mathbf{z}, \mathbf{zc}, \mathbf{zd}; S)$ is an orthogonal MDS matrix over $U(GR(2^n, k))$, where S is an enabling Hadamard $(1, -1)$-matrix if one of the following holds:*

(1) $k = 4$, $f(x) = x^4 + x + 1$, $\mathbf{c} = \alpha^2 + \alpha$, $\mathbf{d} = \alpha^2 - \alpha - 1$,
(2) $k = 6$, $f(x) = x^6 + x^5 + 1$, $\mathbf{c} = \alpha^5 + \alpha^4 + \alpha^3 + 1$, $\mathbf{d} = \alpha^5 + \alpha^4 - \alpha^3$,
(3) $k = 8$, $f(x) = x^8 + x^7 + x^2 + x + 1$, $\mathbf{c} = \alpha^7 - \alpha^5 - \alpha^3 + \alpha$, $\mathbf{d} = \alpha^7 - \alpha^5 + \alpha^3 + \alpha + 1$,
(4) $k = 10$, $f(x) = x^{10} + x^5 + x^2 + x + 1$, $\mathbf{c} = \alpha^5 - \alpha$, $\mathbf{d} = \alpha^5 + \alpha + 1$.

Proof. By Proposition 6, in order to show that M is an orthogonal MDS matrix over $U(GR(2^n, k))$, it suffices to show that $\mu(\mathbf{c})^3 = 1$, $\mu(\mathbf{d}) = \mu(\mathbf{c})^2$ and $\mathbf{z}^2 + (\mathbf{zc})^2 + (\mathbf{zd})^2 = 0$ in $GR(2^n, k)$. First, it is easy to check that $\mu(\mathbf{c})^3 = 1$ and $\mu(\mathbf{d}) = \mu(\mathbf{c})^2$ are true for (1)-(4). To show $\mathbf{z}^2 + (\mathbf{zc})^2 + (\mathbf{zd})^2 = 0$, it suffices to show that $s := 1 + \mathbf{c}^2 + \mathbf{d}^2 = 0$. We show this as follows.

$$
\begin{aligned}
(1)\ s\ &=\ 1 + (\alpha^2 + \alpha)^2 + (\alpha^2 - \alpha - 1)^2 \\
&=\ 1 + (\alpha^4 + \alpha^2 + 2\alpha^3) + (\alpha^4 + \alpha^2 + 1 - 2\alpha^3 - 2\alpha^2 + 2\alpha) \\
&=\ 2(\alpha^4 + \alpha + 1) \\
&=\ 0. \quad (\text{as } \alpha^4 + \alpha + 1 = 0)
\end{aligned}
$$

$$
\begin{aligned}
(2)\ s\ &=\ 1 + (\alpha^5 + \alpha^4 + \alpha^3 + 1)^2 + (\alpha^5 + \alpha^4 - \alpha^3)^2 \\
&=\ 2(\alpha^{10} + \alpha^8 + \alpha^6 + 1) + 4\alpha^9 + 2(\alpha^5 + \alpha^4 + \alpha^3).
\end{aligned}
$$

Since $\alpha^6 = -\alpha^5 - 1$, $\qquad\qquad \alpha^9 = \alpha^5 - \alpha^3 + \alpha^2 - \alpha + 1$,
$\alpha^7 = \alpha^5 - \alpha + 1$, $\qquad\qquad \alpha^{10} = -\alpha^5 - \alpha^4 + \alpha^3 - \alpha^2 + \alpha - 1$,
$\alpha^8 = -\alpha^5 - \alpha^2 + \alpha - 1$,

it follows that $s = 0$.

$$
\begin{aligned}
(3)\ s\ &=\ 1 + (\alpha^7 - \alpha^5 - \alpha^3 + \alpha)^2 + (\alpha^7 - \alpha^5 + \alpha^3 + \alpha + 1)^2 \\
&=\ 2(\alpha^{14} + \alpha^{10} + \alpha^6 + \alpha^2 + 1) + 4(-\alpha^{12} + \alpha^8 - \alpha^6) + 2(\alpha^7 - \alpha^5 + \alpha^3 + \alpha) \\
&=\ 2[(\alpha^{14} + \alpha^{10} - \alpha^6 + \alpha^2 + 1 + \alpha^7 - \alpha^5 + \alpha^3 + \alpha) + 2(-\alpha^{12} + \alpha^8)].
\end{aligned}
$$

Since $\alpha^8 = -\alpha^7 - \alpha^2 - \alpha - 1$, $\qquad \alpha^{12} = -\alpha^7 - \alpha^6 - \alpha^4 + \alpha^3 - \alpha^2 - 1$,
$\alpha^{10} = -\alpha^7 - \alpha^4 - \alpha^2 - 1$, $\qquad \alpha^{14} = -\alpha^6 + \alpha^5 - \alpha^4 + \alpha^3 + \alpha$,

it follows that $s = 0$.

$$
\begin{aligned}
(4)\ s\ &=\ 1 + (\alpha^5 - \alpha)^2 + (\alpha^5 + \alpha + 1)^2 \\
&=\ 2(\alpha^{10} + \alpha^2) + 2(\alpha^5 + 2\alpha) \\
&=\ 2(\alpha^{10} + \alpha^5 + \alpha^2 + \alpha + 1) \\
&=\ 0. \quad (\text{as } \alpha^{10} + \alpha^5 + \alpha^2 + \alpha + 1 = 0)
\end{aligned}
$$

Hence, the Hadamard matrices given in (1)-(4) are orthogonal MDS matrices over $U(GR(2^n, k))$. $\qquad\qquad\qquad\qquad\qquad\qquad\qquad\qquad\qquad\square$

Theorem 3. *Let $4 \mid k$. Let β be a primitive element of subfield of $\mathbb{F}_{2^k}$ of 2^4 elements such that $\sum_{i=0}^{3} \beta^{2^i} = 1$. Let $\mathbf{z}_i \in U(GR(2^n, k))$ such that $\mu(\mathbf{z}_i) = \beta^{2^i} \in \mathbb{F}_{2^k}$ for $0 \le i \le 3$. Then a 4×4 Hadamard matrix $M = \mathrm{HD}(\mathbf{z}_0, \mathbf{z}_1, \mathbf{z}_2, \mathbf{z}_3; S)$ is an orthogonal MDS matrix over $U(GR(2^n, k))$, where S is an enabling Hadamard $(1, -1)$-matrix if one of the following holds*
(1) $k = 4$, $f(x) = x^4 + x + 1$, $\mathbf{z}_0 = \alpha^3 + \alpha + 1$, $\mathbf{z}_1 = \alpha^3 - 1$, $\mathbf{z}_2 = \alpha^3 + \alpha^2 + 1$, $\mathbf{z}_3 = \alpha^3 - \alpha^2 - \alpha$,
(2) $k = 8$, $f(x) = x^8 + x^7 + x^6 + x^5 + x^2 + x + 1$, $\mathbf{z}_0 = \alpha^7 - \alpha^6 - \alpha^5 - \alpha^4 - \alpha^3 - \alpha$, $\mathbf{z}_1 = \alpha^7 + \alpha^6 - \alpha^3 + \alpha + 1$, $\mathbf{z}_2 = \alpha^6 - \alpha^5 - \alpha^4 + \alpha^3 + \alpha^2 + \alpha + 1$, $\mathbf{z}_3 = \alpha^6 - \alpha^3 + \alpha^2 + \alpha + 1$,

(3) $k = 16$, $f(x) = x^{16} + x^{15} + x^{10} + x^9 + x^4 + x^3 + 1$,
$\quad \mathbf{z}_0 = \alpha^{15} + \alpha^{14} + \alpha^{13} - \alpha^9 + \alpha^8 - \alpha^6 + \alpha^4 + \alpha^2 + 1$,
$\quad \mathbf{z}_1 = \alpha^{14} + \alpha^{13} + \alpha^{12} + \alpha^{10} + \alpha^9 + \alpha^5 - \alpha^2 + \alpha + 1$,
$\quad \mathbf{z}_2 = \alpha^{14} - \alpha^{11} + \alpha^8 + \alpha^7 + \alpha^4 + \alpha^2 - 1$,
$\quad \mathbf{z}_3 = \alpha^{15} + \alpha^{14} - \alpha^{12} - \alpha^{11} + \alpha^{10} + \alpha^7 + \alpha^6 - \alpha^5 + \alpha^2 + \alpha$.

Proof. By Proposition 5, in order to show that M is an orthogonal MDS matrix over $U(GR(2^n, k))$, it suffices to show that $\mu(\mathbf{z}_i) = \mu(\mathbf{z}_0)^{2^i}$ for $1 \leq i \leq 3$, $\sum_{i=0}^3 \mu(\mathbf{z}_i) = 1$ and $\sum_{i=0}^3 \mathbf{z}_i^2 = 1$ in $U(GR(2^n, k))$. First, it is easy to check that $\mu(\mathbf{z}_i) = \mu(\mathbf{z}_0)^{2^i}$ for $1 \leq i \leq 3$ and $\sum_{i=0}^3 \mu(\mathbf{z}_i) = 1$ are true for (1)-(3). Now, we show that $s := \mathbf{z}_0^2 + \mathbf{z}_1^2 + \mathbf{z}_2^2 + \mathbf{z}_3^2 = 1$ as follows.

(1) $s = (\alpha^3 + \alpha + 1)^2 + (\alpha^3 - 1)^2 + (\alpha^3 + \alpha^2 + 1)^2 + (\alpha^3 - \alpha^2 - \alpha)^2$
$\quad = (\alpha^6 + \alpha^2 + 1 + 2\alpha^4 + 2\alpha^3 + 2\alpha) + (\alpha^6 + 1 - 2\alpha^3) + (\alpha^6 + \alpha^4$
$\quad\quad + 1 + 2\alpha^5 + 2\alpha^3 + 2\alpha^2) + (\alpha^6 + \alpha^4 + \alpha^2 - 2\alpha^5 - 2\alpha^4 + 2\alpha^3)$
$\quad = 3 + 4\alpha^6 + 2\alpha^4 + 4\alpha^3 + 4\alpha^2 + 2\alpha$
$\quad = 1 \quad$ (as $4\alpha^6 = -4\alpha^3 - 4\alpha^2$, $2\alpha^4 = -2\alpha - 2$)

(2) $s = (\alpha^7 - \alpha^6 - \alpha^5 - \alpha^4 - \alpha^3 - \alpha)^2 + (\alpha^7 + \alpha^6 - \alpha^3 + \alpha + 1)^2$
$\quad\quad + (\alpha^6 - \alpha^5 - \alpha^4 + \alpha^3 + \alpha^2 + \alpha + 1)^2 + (\alpha^6 - \alpha^3 + \alpha^2 + \alpha + 1)^2$
$\quad = 1$

(3) $s = (\alpha^{15} + \alpha^{14} + \alpha^{13} - \alpha^9 + \alpha^8 - \alpha^6 + \alpha^4 + \alpha^2 + 1)^2$
$\quad\quad + (\alpha^{14} + \alpha^{13} + \alpha^{12} + \alpha^{10} + \alpha^9 + \alpha^5 - \alpha^2 + \alpha + 1)^2$
$\quad\quad + (\alpha^{14} - \alpha^{11} + \alpha^8 + \alpha^7 + \alpha^4 + \alpha^2 - 1)^2$
$\quad\quad + (\alpha^{15} + \alpha^{14} - \alpha^{12} - \alpha^{11} + \alpha^{10} + \alpha^7 + \alpha^6 - \alpha^5 + \alpha^2 + \alpha)^2$
$\quad = 1$.

Hence, the Hadamard matrices given in (1)-(3) are orthogonal MDS matrices over $U(GR(2^n, k))$. □

6   Conclusion

In this paper, we worked on MDS matrices over Galois ring $(GR(2^n, k))$ which are different from the MDS matrices over Galois field $(\mathbb{F}_{2^k})$. For the construction of MDS matrix over $U(GR(2^n, k))$, first, we studied the properties of Galois ring and investigated what are the unit elements and square elements in $GR(2^n, k)$. Secondly, we gave a proof of necessary and sufficient conditions between MDS matrices over $\mathbb{F}_{2^k}$ and $U(GR(2^n, k))$. This result enables us to extend MDS matrices from $\mathbb{F}_{2^k}$ to $U(GR(2^n, k))$. Thirdly, in order to construct orthogonal MDS matrices over $U(GR(2^n, k))$, we constructed Hadamard matrices over $U(GR(2^n, k))$ by adding some signs on the entries of the matrices (i.e. performing entry-wise multiplication with enabling Hadamard $(1, -1)$-matrices). We gave complete enumerations of 4×4 and 8×8 enabling Hadamard $(1, -1)$-matrices. Then, we consider those Hadamard matrices which are MDS matrices. Fourthly, we proved that there is no 2×2 orthogonal MDS matrix over $U(GR(2^n, k))$ and constructed some 4×4 orthogonal MDS matrices over $U(GR(2^n, k))$. In the future work, we will construct 8×8 orthogonal MDS matrices over $U(GR(2^n, k))$.

Acknowledgment. The authors would like to thank the anonymous reviewers for insightful comments and invaluable suggestions, which help us to improve this paper.

Appendices

A   Algorithm for Constructing 4×4 Enabling Hadamard $(1, -1)$-matrices

---

Algorithm 1. Constructing 4×4 enabling Hadamard $(1, -1)$-matrix

---

1. Randomly choose $a_1, b_1, b_2, c_1, d_1, d_2, d_3, d_4 \in \{1, -1\}$
2. Set $a_2 = -a_1 b_1 b_2$
3. Set $c_2 = -c_1 d_1 d_2$
4. Set $c_3 = b_1 b_2 c_2 d_1 d_3$, $b_3 = -b_1 d_1 d_3$, $a_3 = -a_1 c_1 c_3$
5. Set $c_4 = b_1 b_2 c_1 d_2 d_4$, $b_4 = -b_2 d_2 d_4$, $a_4 = -a_2 c_2 c_4$

B   Proof of Lemma 6

To prove Lemma 6, we first prove the following two lemmas.

Let R be a commutative ring with unity of characteristic $\neq 2$ and $\mathbf{a}, \mathbf{b}, \cdots, \mathbf{h}$ be arbitrary elements of R. Suppose

$$
M := \mathrm{HD}(\mathbf{a}, \mathbf{b}, \cdots, \mathbf{h}; S) =
\begin{bmatrix}
a_1 & b_1 & c_1 & d_1 & e_1 & f_1 & g_1 & h_1 \\
b_2 & a_2 & d_2 & c_2 & f_2 & e_2 & h_2 & g_2 \\
c_3 & d_3 & a_3 & b_3 & g_3 & h_3 & e_3 & f_3 \\
d_4 & c_4 & b_4 & a_4 & h_4 & g_4 & f_4 & e_4 \\
e_5 & f_5 & g_5 & h_5 & a_5 & b_5 & c_5 & d_5 \\
f_6 & e_6 & h_6 & g_6 & b_6 & a_6 & d_6 & c_6 \\
g_7 & h_7 & e_7 & f_7 & c_7 & d_7 & a_7 & b_7 \\
h_8 & g_8 & f_8 & e_8 & d_8 & c_8 & b_8 & a_8
\end{bmatrix}
= \begin{bmatrix} M_1 & M_2 \\ M_3 & M_4 \end{bmatrix}, \quad (4)
$$

where z_i is either $\mathbf{z}$ or $-\mathbf{z}$ for $1 \leq i \leq 8$ and $\mathbf{z} \in \{\mathbf{a}, \mathbf{b}, \cdots, \mathbf{h}\}$.

Lemma 9. *Suppose S_1, S_2, S_3, S_4 are 4×4 enabling Hadamard $(1, -1)$-matrices. Then S is an 8×8 enabling Hadamard $(1, -1)$-matrix if and only if the following conditions hold:*

(a1) $-\frac{a_4}{a_3}\frac{g_3}{h_4} + \frac{d_1}{d_2}\frac{g_2}{h_1} = 0$,   (a2) $-\frac{c_4}{c_3}\frac{e_3}{f_4} + \frac{b_1}{b_2}\frac{e_2}{f_1} = 0$,

(b1) $-\frac{a_3}{a_4}\frac{g_4}{h_3} + \frac{d_2}{d_1}\frac{g_1}{h_2} = 0$,   (b2) $-\frac{c_3}{c_4}\frac{e_4}{f_3} + \frac{b_2}{b_1}\frac{e_1}{f_2} = 0$,

(c1) $-\frac{a_2}{a_1}\frac{g_1}{h_2} + \frac{d_3}{d_4}\frac{g_4}{h_3} = 0$,   (c2) $-\frac{c_2}{c_1}\frac{e_1}{f_2} + \frac{b_3}{b_4}\frac{e_4}{f_3} = 0$, (d1) $-\frac{a_1}{a_2}\frac{g_2}{h_1} + \frac{d_4}{d_3}\frac{g_3}{h_4} = 0,$ (d2) $-\frac{c_1}{c_2}\frac{e_2}{f_1} + \frac{b_4}{b_3}\frac{e_3}{f_4} = 0;$

(e) $g_5 = a_3 a_4 g_3 h_4 h_5,$ $f_5 = b_1 b_3 f_1 h_3 h_5,$ $e_5 = c_3 c_4 e_3 f_4 f_5,$
   $d_5 = -d_1 h_1 h_5,$ $c_5 = -c_1 g_1 g_5,$ $b_5 = -b_1 f_1 f_5,$ $a_5 = -a_1 e_1 e_5,$

(f) $g_6 = a_4 a_3 g_4 h_3 h_6,$ $f_6 = b_2 b_4 f_2 h_4 h_6,$ $e_6 = c_4 c_3 e_4 f_3 f_6,$
   $d_6 = -d_2 h_2 h_6,$ $c_6 = -c_2 g_2 g_6,$ $b_6 = -b_2 f_2 f_6,$ $a_6 = -a_2 e_2 e_6,$

(g) $g_7 = a_1 a_2 g_1 h_2 h_7,$ $f_7 = b_3 b_1 f_3 h_1 h_7,$ $e_7 = c_1 c_2 e_1 f_2 f_7,$
   $d_7 = -d_3 h_3 h_7,$ $c_7 = -c_3 g_3 g_7,$ $b_7 = -b_3 f_3 f_7,$ $a_7 = -a_3 e_3 e_7,$

(h) $g_8 = a_2 a_1 g_2 h_1 h_8,$ $f_8 = b_4 b_2 f_4 h_2 h_8,$ $e_8 = c_2 c_1 e_2 f_1 f_8,$
   $d_8 = -d_4 h_4 h_8,$ $c_8 = -c_4 g_4 g_8,$ $b_8 = -b_4 f_4 f_8,$ $a_8 = -a_4 e_4 e_8.$

Proof. Note that $MM^T = \begin{bmatrix} M_1 M_1^T + M_2 M_2^T & M_1 M_3^T + M_2 M_4^T \\ (M_1 M_3^T + M_2 M_4^T)^T & M_3 M_3^T + M_4 M_4^T \end{bmatrix}$. As $S_1, S_2,$
S_3, S_4 are 4×4 enabling Hadamard $(1, -1)$-matrices, we have $M_1 M_1^T + M_2 M_2^T = (\mathbf{a}^2 + \mathbf{b}^2 + \cdots + \mathbf{h}^2) I_4 = M_3 M_3^T + M_4 M_4^T$. Thus, S is an enabling Hadamard $(1, -1)$-matrix if and only if $M_1 M_3^T + M_2 M_4^T = 0$ for any $\mathbf{a}, \mathbf{b}, \cdots, \mathbf{h}$. The last equations are equivalent to the following system of sixteen equations:

$$a_1 e_5 + b_1 f_5 + c_1 g_5 + d_1 h_5 + (e_1 a_5 + f_1 b_5 + g_1 c_5 + h_1 d_5) = 0,$$
$$b_2 e_5 + a_2 f_5 + d_2 g_5 + c_2 h_5 + (f_2 a_5 + e_2 b_5 + h_2 c_5 + g_2 d_5) = 0,$$
$$c_3 e_5 + d_3 f_5 + a_3 g_5 + b_3 h_5 + (g_3 a_5 + h_3 b_5 + e_3 c_5 + f_3 d_5) = 0,$$
$$d_4 e_5 + c_4 f_5 + b_4 g_5 + a_4 h_5 + (h_4 a_5 + g_4 b_5 + f_4 c_5 + e_4 d_5) = 0,$$

$$\vdots$$

$$a_1 h_8 + b_1 g_8 + c_1 f_8 + d_1 e_8 + (e_1 d_8 + f_1 c_8 + g_1 b_8 + h_1 a_8) = 0,$$
$$b_2 h_8 + a_2 g_8 + d_2 f_8 + c_2 e_8 + (f_2 d_8 + e_2 c_8 + h_2 b_8 + g_2 a_8) = 0,$$
$$c_3 h_8 + d_3 g_8 + a_3 f_8 + b_3 e_8 + (g_3 d_8 + h_3 c_8 + e_3 b_8 + f_3 a_8) = 0,$$
$$d_4 h_8 + c_4 g_8 + b_4 f_8 + a_4 e_8 + (h_4 d_8 + g_4 c_8 + f_4 b_8 + e_4 a_8) = 0.$$

Note that $\mathbf{a}, \mathbf{b}, \cdots, \mathbf{h}$ are arbitrary. So, we may set $\mathbf{b} = \mathbf{c} = \mathbf{d} = 0$ (this implies that $b_1 = b_5 = c_1 = c_5 = d_1 = d_5 = 0$) in the first equation to obtain $a_1 e_5 + e_1 a_5 = 0$. Using similar argument, we conclude that the first four equations are equivalent to

$$
\begin{array}{ll}
a_1 e_5 + e_1 a_5 = 0, & c_3 e_5 + e_3 c_5 = 0, \\
b_1 f_5 + f_1 b_5 = 0, & d_3 f_5 + f_3 d_5 = 0, \\
c_1 g_5 + g_1 c_5 = 0, & a_3 g_5 + g_3 a_5 = 0, \\
d_1 h_5 + h_1 d_5 = 0, & b_3 h_5 + h_3 b_5 = 0, \\
b_2 e_5 + e_2 b_5 = 0, & d_4 e_5 + e_4 d_5 = 0, \\
a_2 f_5 + f_2 a_5 = 0, & c_4 f_5 + f_4 c_5 = 0, \\
d_2 g_5 + g_2 h_5 = 0, & b_4 g_5 + g_4 b_5 = 0, \\
c_2 h_5 + h_2 c_5 = 0, & a_4 h_5 + h_4 a_5 = 0.
\end{array}
$$

As $\mathbf{a}_i = aa_i$ for $1 \leq i \leq 8$ (and the same holds whenever a is replaced by $b, c, d, e, f, g,$ or h), we note that the above system of equations holds for any $\mathbf{a}, \mathbf{b}, \cdots, \mathbf{h}$ if and only if the following system of equation holds (note that the following system of equations holds in R if and only if it holds in $\mathbb{Z}$ as $char(R) \neq 2$):

$$
\begin{aligned}
a_1 e_5 + e_1 a_5 &= 0, & c_3 e_5 + e_3 c_5 &= 0, \\
b_1 f_5 + f_1 b_5 &= 0, & d_3 f_5 + f_3 d_5 &= 0, \\
c_1 g_5 + g_1 c_5 &= 0, & a_3 g_5 + g_3 a_5 &= 0, \\
d_1 h_5 + h_1 d_5 &= 0, & b_3 h_5 + h_3 b_5 &= 0, \\
b_2 e_5 + e_2 b_5 &= 0, & d_4 e_5 + e_4 d_5 &= 0, \\
a_2 f_5 + f_2 a_5 &= 0, & c_4 f_5 + f_4 c_5 &= 0, \\
d_2 g_5 + g_2 h_5 &= 0, & b_4 g_5 + g_4 b_5 &= 0, \\
c_2 h_5 + h_2 c_5 &= 0, & a_4 h_5 + h_4 a_5 &= 0.
\end{aligned}
$$

These equations can be expressed in the following matrix form

$$
W^{(5)} \cdot (a_5, b_5, c_5, d_5, e_5, f_5, g_5, h_5)^T = 0,
$$

where

$$
W^{(5)} := \begin{bmatrix}
e_1 & 0 & 0 & 0 & a_1 & 0 & 0 & 0 \\
0 & f_1 & 0 & 0 & 0 & b_1 & 0 & 0 \\
0 & 0 & g_1 & 0 & 0 & 0 & c_1 & 0 \\
0 & 0 & 0 & h_1 & 0 & 0 & 0 & d_1 \\
0 & e_2 & 0 & 0 & b_2 & 0 & 0 & 0 \\
f_2 & 0 & 0 & 0 & 0 & a_2 & 0 & 0 \\
0 & 0 & 0 & g_2 & 0 & 0 & d_2 & 0 \\
0 & 0 & h_2 & 0 & 0 & 0 & 0 & c_2 \\
g_3 & 0 & 0 & 0 & 0 & 0 & a_3 & 0 \\
0 & h_3 & 0 & 0 & 0 & 0 & 0 & b_3 \\
0 & 0 & e_3 & 0 & c_3 & 0 & 0 & 0 \\
0 & 0 & 0 & f_3 & 0 & d_3 & 0 & 0 \\
h_4 & 0 & 0 & 0 & 0 & 0 & 0 & a_4 \\
0 & g_4 & 0 & 0 & 0 & b_4 & 0 & 0 \\
0 & 0 & f_4 & 0 & 0 & c_4 & 0 & 0 \\
0 & 0 & 0 & e_4 & d_4 & 0 & 0 & 0
\end{bmatrix}
\longrightarrow
\begin{bmatrix}
1 & 0 & 0 & 0 & \frac{a_1}{e_1} & 0 & 0 & 0 \\
0 & 1 & 0 & 0 & 0 & \frac{b_1}{f_1} & 0 & 0 \\
0 & 0 & 1 & 0 & 0 & 0 & \frac{c_1}{g_1} & 0 \\
0 & 0 & 0 & 1 & 0 & 0 & 0 & \frac{d_1}{h_1} \\
0 & 0 & 0 & 0 & 1 & -\frac{c_4 e_3}{c_3 f_4} & 0 & 0 \\
0 & 0 & 0 & 0 & 0 & 1 & 0 & -\frac{b_3 f_1}{b_1 h_3} \\
0 & 0 & 0 & 0 & 0 & 0 & 1 & -\frac{a_4 g_3}{a_3 h_4} \\
0 & 0 & 0 & 0 & \frac{b_1 e_2}{b_2 f_1} & -\frac{c_4 e_3}{c_3 f_4} & 0 & 0 \\
0 & 0 & 0 & 0 & 0 & 0 & \frac{d_1 g_2}{d_2 h_1} & -\frac{a_4 g_3}{a_3 h_4} \\
0 & 0 & 0 & 0 & 0 & 0 & 0 & 0 \\
\vdots & \vdots & \vdots & \vdots & \vdots & \vdots & \vdots & \vdots \\
0 & 0 & 0 & 0 & 0 & 0 & 0 & 0
\end{bmatrix}.
$$

The matrix on the right above (called $\widetilde{W}^{(5)}$) is obtained by performing elementary row operations to $W^{(5)}$. Thus, $W^{(5)} \cdot (a_5, b_5, \cdots, h_5)^T = 0$ if and only if conditions (a1), (a2), and (e) hold. Summarizing what we have done so far, recall that S is an enabling Hadamard $(1, -1)$-matrix if and only if $M_1 M_3^T + M_2 M_4^T = 0$. Using this matrix equation, we derive the equation $W^{(5)} \cdot (a_5, b_5, \cdots, h_5)^T = 0$, which is equivalent to $\widetilde{W}^{(5)} \cdot (a_5, \cdots, h_5)^T = 0$. Similarly, from $M_1 M_3^T + M_2 M_4^T = 0$, we may derive $W^{(i)} \cdot (a_i, b_i, \cdots, h_i)^T = 0$, for $i = 6, 7, 8$, where $W^{(i)}$ are as follows.

i	$W^{(i)}$ by replacing index in $W^{(5)}$
6	$1 \rightarrow 2$, $2 \rightarrow 1$, $3 \rightarrow 4$ and $4 \rightarrow 3$
7	$1 \rightarrow 3$, $2 \rightarrow 4$, $3 \rightarrow 1$ and $4 \rightarrow 2$
8	$1 \rightarrow 4$, $2 \rightarrow 3$, $3 \rightarrow 2$ and $4 \rightarrow 1$

For each $6 \leq i \leq 8$, using elementary row operations similar to those being performed to $W^{(5)}$, we show that $W^{(i)} \cdot (a_i, b_i, \cdots, h_i)^T = 0$ holds if and only if $\widetilde{W}^{(i)} \cdot (a_i, b_i, \cdots, h_i)^T = 0$. Finally, we observe that the last equation holds if and only if conditions (b1), (b2), and (f) are satisfied when $i = 6$. Similarly, when $i = 7$ (resp. 8), the equation is equivalent to conditions (c1), (c2), and (g) (resp. (d1), (d2), and (h)). Hence, S is an 8×8 enabling Hadamard $(1, -1)$-matrix if and only if conditions (a)–(h) hold. $\Box$

Lemma 10. *In Lemma 9, the four conditions (a1) – (d1) and (a2) – (d2) are equivalent to* $\frac{a_1 b_3}{a_4 b_2} = \frac{e_4 f_1}{e_2 f_3}$.

Proof. (i) We first prove that conditions (a1) and (a2) are equivalent to $\frac{a_1 b_3}{a_4 b_2} = \frac{e_4 f_1}{e_2 f_3}$. It is clear that (a1) is equivalent to $\frac{a_4 d_2}{a_3 d_1} = \frac{g_2 h_4}{g_3 h_1}$ and (a2) is equivalent to $\frac{b_1 c_3}{b_2 c_4} = \frac{e_3 f_1}{e_2 f_4}$. We then note that

$$
\begin{aligned}
\frac{a_4 d_2}{a_3 d_1} &= -\frac{a_4 d_3}{a_2 d_1} \; \left(\text{as } \frac{d_2}{d_3} = -\frac{d_3}{a_2}\right) \\
&= \frac{a_4 b_3}{a_2 b_1} \; \left(\text{as } \frac{d_3}{d_1} = -\frac{b_3}{b_1}\right) \\
&= -\frac{a_4 b_3}{a_1 b_2} \; \left(\text{as } \frac{a_2}{b_2} = -\frac{a_1}{b_1}\right) \\
&= -\frac{a_1 b_3}{a_4 b_2}
\end{aligned}
\qquad
\begin{aligned}
\frac{b_1 c_3}{b_2 c_4} &= -\frac{b_1 d_3}{b_2 d_4} \; \left(\text{as } \frac{c_3}{c_4} = -\frac{d_3}{d_4}\right) \\
&= \frac{b_3 d_1}{b_2 d_4} \; \left(\text{as } \frac{d_3}{b_3} = -\frac{d_1}{b_1}\right) \\
&= -\frac{a_1 b_3}{a_4 b_2} \; \left(\text{as } \frac{d_1}{d_4} = -\frac{a_1}{a_4}\right)
\end{aligned}
$$

$$
\begin{aligned}
\frac{g_2 h_4}{g_3 h_1} &= -\frac{f_2 h_4}{f_3 h_1} \; \left(\text{as } \frac{g_2}{g_3} = -\frac{f_2}{f_3}\right) \\
&= \frac{f_2 e_4}{f_3 e_1} \; \left(\text{as } \frac{h_4}{h_1} = -\frac{e_4}{e_1}\right) \\
&= -\frac{f_1 e_4}{f_3 e_2} \; \left(\text{as } \frac{f_2}{e_1} = -\frac{f_1}{e_2}\right)
\end{aligned}
\qquad
\begin{aligned}
\frac{e_3 f_1}{e_2 f_4} &= -\frac{e_4 f_1}{e_2 f_3} \; \left(\text{as } \frac{e_3}{f_4} = -\frac{e_4}{f_3}\right)
\end{aligned}
$$

Hence, (a1) is equivalent to $\frac{a_4 d_2}{a_3 d_1} = \frac{g_2 h_4}{g_3 h_1}$, which in turn is equivalent to $\frac{a_1 b_3}{a_4 b_2} = \frac{e_4 f_1}{e_2 f_3}$. Also, (a2) is equivalent to $\frac{b_1 c_3}{b_2 c_4} = \frac{e_3 f_1}{e_2 f_4}$, and so it is also equivalent to $\frac{a_1 b_3}{a_4 b_2} = \frac{e_4 f_1}{e_2 f_3}$.

(ii) We now prove that (b1) and (b2) are equivalent to $\frac{a_1 b_3}{a_4 b_2} = \frac{e_4 f_1}{e_2 f_3}$. It is clear that (b1) is equivalent to $\frac{a_3 d_1}{a_4 d_2} = \frac{g_1 h_3}{g_4 h_2}$ and (b2) is equivalent to $\frac{b_1 c_3}{b_2 c_4} = \frac{e_1 f_3}{e_4 f_2}$.

Note that

$$\frac{a_3 d_1}{a_4 d_2} = \frac{a_4 d_2}{a_3 d_1}$$
$$= -\frac{a_4 b_3}{a_1 b_2} \text{ (by (i))}$$
$$\frac{g_1 h_3}{g_4 h_2} = -\frac{g_2 h_3}{g_4 h_1} \left(\text{as } \frac{g_1}{h_2} = -\frac{g_2}{h_1}\right)$$
$$= \frac{g_2 h_4}{g_3 h_1} \left(\text{as } \frac{h_3}{g_4} = -\frac{h_4}{g_3}\right)$$
$$= -\frac{f_1 e_4}{f_3 e_2} \text{ (by (i))}$$

$$\frac{b_1 c_3}{b_2 c_4} = -\frac{a_1 b_3}{a_4 b_2} \text{ (by (i))}$$
$$\frac{e_1 f_3}{e_4 f_2} = -\frac{e_2 f_3}{e_4 f_1} \left(\text{as } \frac{e_1}{f_2} = -\frac{e_2}{f_1}\right)$$
$$= -\frac{e_4 f_1}{e_2 f_3}$$

Hence, both (b1) and (b2) are equivalent to $\frac{a_1 b_3}{a_4 b_2} = \frac{e_4 f_1}{e_2 f_3}$.

(iii) We now prove that (c1) and (c2) are equivalent to $\frac{a_1 b_3}{a_4 b_2} = \frac{e_4 f_1}{e_2 f_3}$. Clearly, (c1) is equivalent to $\frac{a_2 d_4}{a_1 d_3} = \frac{g_4 h_2}{g_1 h_3}$ and (c2) is equivalent to $\frac{b_4 c_2}{b_3 c_1} = \frac{e_4 f_2}{e_1 f_3}$. Note that

$$\frac{a_2 d_4}{a_1 d_3} = \frac{d_2 d_4}{a_3 a_1} \left(\text{as } \frac{a_2}{a_3} = -\frac{d_2}{a_3}\right)$$
$$= \frac{a_4 d_2}{a_3 d_1} \left(\text{as } \frac{d_4}{a_1} = -\frac{a_4}{d_1}\right)$$
$$= -\frac{a_4 b_3}{a_1 b_2} \text{ (by (i))}$$
$$\frac{g_4 h_2}{g_1 h_3} = -\frac{g_4 h_1}{g_2 h_3} \left(\text{as } \frac{h_2}{g_1} = -\frac{h_1}{g_2}\right)$$
$$= \frac{g_3 h_1}{g_2 h_4} \left(\text{as } \frac{g_4}{h_3} = -\frac{g_3}{h_4}\right)$$
$$= \frac{g_2 h_4}{g_3 h_1}$$
$$= -\frac{f_1 e_4}{f_3 e_2} \text{ (by (i))}$$

$$\frac{b_4 c_2}{b_3 c_1} = -\frac{b_1 c_2}{b_3 c_4} \left(\text{as } \frac{b_4}{c_1} = -\frac{b_1}{c_4}\right)$$
$$= \frac{b_1 c_3}{b_2 c_4} \left(\text{as } \frac{c_2}{b_3} = -\frac{c_3}{b_2}\right)$$
$$= -\frac{a_1 b_3}{a_4 b_2} \text{ (by (i))}$$
$$\frac{e_4 f_2}{e_1 f_3} = \frac{e_1 f_3}{e_4 f_2}$$
$$= -\frac{e_4 f_1}{e_2 f_3} \text{ (by(ii))}$$

Hence, both (c1) and (c2) are equivalent to $\frac{a_1 b_3}{a_4 b_2} = \frac{e_4 f_1}{e_2 f_3}$.

(iv) Finally, we prove that (d1) and (d2) are equivalent to $\frac{a_1 b_3}{a_4 b_2} = \frac{e_4 f_1}{e_2 f_3}$. Clearly, (d1) is equivalent to $\frac{a_1 d_3}{a_2 d_4} = \frac{g_3 h_1}{g_2 h_4}$ and (d2) is equivalent to $\frac{b_3 c_1}{b_4 c_2} = \frac{e_3 f_1}{e_2 f_4}$. By (iii), $\frac{a_1 d_3}{a_2 d_4} = \frac{g_3 h_1}{g_2 h_4}$ is equivalent to $\frac{a_1 b_3}{a_4 b_2} = \frac{e_4 f_1}{e_2 f_3}$ and $\frac{b_3 c_1}{b_4 c_2} = \frac{e_3 f_1}{e_2 f_4}$ is equivalent to $\frac{a_1 b_3}{a_4 b_2} = \frac{e_4 f_1}{e_2 f_3}$. Hence, both (d1) and (d2) are equivalent to $\frac{a_1 b_3}{a_4 b_2} = \frac{e_4 f_1}{e_2 f_3}$. Therefore, we complete the proof of the Lemma. □

Lemma 6 can now be obtained as a corollary of Lemmas 9 and 10.

Proof of Lemma 6. By Lemma 10, conditions (a)–(d) in Lemma 9 are satisfied. Thus, S is an 8×8 enabling Hadamard $(1, -1)$-matrix as long as S_3 and S_4 satisfy conditions (e)–(h) in Lemma 9. Note that in these conditions, there is no restriction on h_5, h_6, h_7, h_8. Thus, each h_i can be chosen to be either 1 or -1 (for $5 \le i \le 8$). So, there are $2^4 = 16$ possible ways to choose h_5, h_6, h_7, h_8. Once they are fixed, the other entries of S_3 and S_4 are uniquely determined by conditions (e)–(h) of Lemma 9. Hence, there are 16 possible choices for S_3, S_4 such that S is an enabling Hadamard $(1, -1)$-matrix. □

C   Algorithm for Constructing 8 × 8 Enabling Hadamard $(1, -1)$-matrices

---

Algorithm 2. Constructing 8 × 8 enabling Hadamard $(1, -1)$-matrices

A. Generating S_1 which is the same as Algorithm 2 for constructing 4 × 4 enabling Hadamard $(1, -1)$- matrices

B. Generating S_2: Randomly choose $e_1, f_1, f_2, g_1, h_1, h_2, h_3 \in \{-1, 1\}$
   Compute
   1. $e_2 = -e_1 f_1 f_2, g_2 = -g_1 h_1 h_2$
   2. $g_3 = f_1 f_2 g_2 h_1 h_3, f_3 = -f_1 h_1 h_3, e_3 = -e_1 g_1 g_3$
   3. $h_4 = a_3 a_4 d_1 d_2 g_2 g_3 h_1$
   4. $g_4 = f_1 f_2 g_1 h_2 h_4, f_4 = -f_2 h_2 h_4, e_4 = -e_2 g_2 g_4$

C. Generating S_3, S_4
   5. Constructing 5th-row of S: Randomly choose $h_5 \in \{-1, 1\}$
      Compute
      (i) $g_5 = a_3 a_4 g_3 h_4 h_5,\ f_5 = b_1 b_3 f_1 h_3 h_5,\ e_5 = c_3 c_4 e_3 f_4 f_5$
      (ii) $d_5 = -d_1 h_1 h_5,\ c_5 = -c_1 g_1 g_5,\ b_5 = -b_1 f_1 f_5,\ a_5 = -a_1 e_1 e_5$
   6. Constructing 6th-row of S: Randomly choose $h_6 \in \{-1, 1\}$
      Compute
      (i) $g_6 = a_4 a_3 g_4 h_3 h_6,\ f_6 = b_2 b_4 f_2 h_4 h_6,\ e_6 = c_4 c_3 e_4 f_3 f_6$
      (ii) $d_6 = -d_2 h_2 h_6,\ c_6 = -c_2 g_2 g_6,\ b_6 = -b_2 f_2 f_6,\ a_6 = -a_2 e_2 e_6$
   7. Constructing 7th-row of S: Randomly choose $h_7 \in \{-1, 1\}$
      Compute
      (i) $g_7 = a_1 a_2 g_1 h_2 h_7,\ f_7 = b_3 b_1 f_3 h_1 h_7,\ e_7 = c_1 c_2 e_1 f_2 f_7$
      (ii) $d_7 = -d_3 h_3 h_7,\ c_7 = -c_3 g_3 g_7,\ b_7 = -b_3 f_3 f_7,\ a_7 = -a_3 e_3 e_7$
   8. Constructing 8th-row of S: Randomly choose $h_8 \in \{-1, 1\}$
      Compute
      (i) $g_8 = a_2 a_1 g_2 h_1 h_8,\ f_8 = b_4 b_2 f_4 h_2 h_8,\ e_8 = c_2 c_1 e_2 f_1 f_8$
      (ii) $d_8 = -d_4 h_4 h_8,\ c_8 = -c_4 g_4 g_8,\ b_8 = -b_4 f_4 f_8,\ a_8 = -a_4 e_4 e_8$

D   Examples of 8 × 8 Enabling Hadamard $(1, -1)$-matrices

In the following, we list some 8 × 8 enabling Hadamard $(1, -1)$-matrices obtained from Algorithm 2.

$$
\begin{bmatrix}
1 & 1 & 1 & 1 & 1 & 1 & 1 & 1 \\
1 & -1 & 1 & -1 & 1 & -1 & 1 & -1 \\
-1 & 1 & 1 & -1 & -1 & 1 & 1 & -1 \\
1 & 1 & -1 & -1 & -1 & -1 & 1 & 1 \\
1 & -1 & -1 & 1 & -1 & 1 & 1 & -1 \\
1 & 1 & 1 & 1 & -1 & -1 & -1 & -1 \\
-1 & 1 & -1 & 1 & 1 & -1 & 1 & -1 \\
1 & 1 & -1 & -1 & 1 & 1 & -1 & -1
\end{bmatrix},
\begin{bmatrix}
1 & 1 & 1 & 1 & 1 & 1 & 1 & 1 \\
1 & -1 & 1 & -1 & 1 & -1 & 1 & -1 \\
-1 & 1 & 1 & -1 & -1 & 1 & 1 & -1 \\
1 & 1 & -1 & -1 & -1 & -1 & 1 & 1 \\
1 & -1 & -1 & 1 & -1 & 1 & 1 & -1 \\
1 & 1 & 1 & 1 & -1 & -1 & -1 & -1 \\
-1 & 1 & -1 & 1 & 1 & -1 & 1 & -1 \\
-1 & -1 & 1 & 1 & -1 & -1 & 1 & 1
\end{bmatrix},
$$

$$\begin{bmatrix} 1 & 1 & 1 & 1 & 1 & 1 & 1 & 1 \\ 1 & -1 & 1 & -1 & 1 & -1 & 1 & -1 \\ -1 & 1 & 1 & -1 & -1 & 1 & 1 & -1 \\ 1 & 1 & -1 & -1 & -1 & -1 & 1 & 1 \\ 1 & -1 & -1 & 1 & -1 & 1 & 1 & -1 \\ 1 & 1 & 1 & 1 & -1 & -1 & -1 & -1 \\ 1 & -1 & 1 & -1 & -1 & 1 & -1 & 1 \\ 1 & 1 & -1 & -1 & 1 & 1 & -1 & -1 \end{bmatrix}, \quad \begin{bmatrix} 1 & 1 & 1 & 1 & 1 & 1 & 1 & 1 \\ 1 & -1 & 1 & -1 & 1 & -1 & 1 & -1 \\ -1 & 1 & 1 & -1 & -1 & 1 & 1 & -1 \\ 1 & 1 & -1 & -1 & -1 & -1 & 1 & 1 \\ 1 & -1 & -1 & 1 & -1 & 1 & 1 & -1 \\ 1 & 1 & 1 & 1 & -1 & -1 & -1 & -1 \\ 1 & -1 & 1 & -1 & -1 & 1 & -1 & 1 \\ -1 & -1 & 1 & 1 & -1 & -1 & 1 & 1 \end{bmatrix},$$

$$\begin{bmatrix} 1 & 1 & 1 & 1 & 1 & 1 & 1 & 1 \\ 1 & -1 & 1 & -1 & 1 & -1 & 1 & -1 \\ -1 & 1 & 1 & -1 & -1 & 1 & 1 & -1 \\ 1 & 1 & -1 & -1 & -1 & -1 & 1 & 1 \\ 1 & -1 & -1 & 1 & -1 & 1 & 1 & -1 \\ -1 & -1 & -1 & -1 & 1 & 1 & 1 & 1 \\ -1 & 1 & -1 & 1 & 1 & -1 & 1 & -1 \\ 1 & 1 & -1 & -1 & 1 & 1 & -1 & -1 \end{bmatrix}, \quad \begin{bmatrix} 1 & 1 & 1 & 1 & 1 & 1 & 1 & 1 \\ 1 & -1 & 1 & -1 & 1 & -1 & 1 & -1 \\ -1 & 1 & 1 & -1 & -1 & 1 & 1 & -1 \\ 1 & 1 & -1 & -1 & -1 & -1 & 1 & 1 \\ 1 & -1 & -1 & 1 & -1 & 1 & 1 & -1 \\ -1 & -1 & -1 & -1 & 1 & 1 & 1 & 1 \\ -1 & 1 & -1 & 1 & 1 & -1 & 1 & -1 \\ -1 & -1 & 1 & 1 & -1 & -1 & 1 & 1 \end{bmatrix}.$$

E   Proof of Lemma 8

Proof of Lemma 8. Let $\gamma = \mathbf{a}^2 + \mathbf{b}^2$. If γ is a square in $U(GR(2^n, k))$, then there is a $\beta \in U(GR(2^n, k))$ such that $\beta^2 = \gamma$. We have $(\beta^{-1}\mathbf{a})^2 + (\beta^{-1}\mathbf{b})^2 = 1$. Therefore, it is sufficient to show that there does not exist $\mathbf{a}, \mathbf{b} \in U(GR(2^n, k))$ such that $\mathbf{a}^2 + \mathbf{b}^2 = 1$.

Let $\mathbf{a} = \sum_{i=0}^{k-1} a_i \alpha^i$ and $\mathbf{b} = \sum_{i=0}^{k-1} b_i \alpha^i$. Let μ be the epimorphism from $GF(2^n, k)$ to $\mathbb{F}_{2^k}$. Assume that $\mathbf{a}^2 + \mathbf{b}^2 = 1$, then $\mu(\mathbf{a}^2) + \mu(\mathbf{b}^2) = 1$, which implies that $\mu(\mathbf{a}) + \mu(\mathbf{b}) = 1$. Thus, the parity of a_i and b_i are the same (i.e. $a_i \equiv b_i \bmod 2$) for $1 \leq i \leq k - 1$; and exactly one of a_0 and b_0 is odd, while the other is even. Without loss of generality, assume that b_0 is odd. Then, a_0 is even. Let $\mathbb{A} = \{0, 1, \cdots, k - 1\}$, $\mathbb{O} = \{i \mid a_i \text{ odd}\}$ and $\mathbb{E} = \mathbb{A} \setminus \mathbb{O}$. Let $\mathbf{a}_o = \sum_{i \in \mathbb{O}} a_i \alpha^i$, $\mathbf{a}_e = \sum_{i \in \mathbb{E}} a_i \alpha^i$, $\mathbf{b}_o = \sum_{i \in \mathbb{O}} b_i \alpha^i$ and $\mathbf{b}_e = \sum_{i \in \mathbb{E} \setminus \{0\}} b_i \alpha^i$. Then we have

$$\left(\sum_{i=0}^{k-1} a_i \alpha^i \right)^2 + \left(\sum_{i=0}^{k-1} b_i \alpha^i \right)^2 = 1$$

$$(\mathbf{a}_o + \mathbf{a}_e)^2 + (\mathbf{b}_0 + \mathbf{b}_o + \mathbf{b}_e)^2 = 1$$

$$(\mathbf{a}_o^2 + \mathbf{a}_e^2 + 2\mathbf{a}_o\mathbf{a}_e) + (b_0^2 + \mathbf{b}_o^2 + \mathbf{b}_e^2 + 2b_0\mathbf{b}_o + 2b_0\mathbf{b}_e + 2\mathbf{b}_o\mathbf{b}_e) = 1$$

$$\mathbf{a}_o^2 + \mathbf{b}_o^2 + b_0^2 + 2b_0\mathbf{b}_o \equiv 1 \bmod 4,$$

where $\mathbf{a}_e^2 \equiv 0 \bmod 4$, $2\mathbf{a}_o\mathbf{a}_e \equiv 0 \bmod 4$, $\mathbf{b}_e^2 \equiv 0 \bmod 4$, $2b_0\mathbf{b}_e \equiv 0 \bmod 4$, $2\mathbf{b}_o\mathbf{b}_e \equiv 0 \bmod 4$.

Since $b_0^2 \equiv 1 \bmod 4$ and $2b_0 \equiv 2 \bmod 4$, then we have

$$\mathbf{a}_o^2 + \mathbf{b}_o^2 + 2\mathbf{b}_o \equiv 0 \bmod 4$$

$$\left(\sum_{i\in\mathbb{O}} a_i\alpha^i\right)^2 + \left(\sum_{i\in\mathbb{O}} b_i\alpha^i\right)^2 + 2\sum_{i\in\mathbb{O}} b_i\alpha^i \equiv 0 \bmod 4$$

$$\sum_{i\in\mathbb{O}} a_i^2\alpha^{2i} + \sum_{i\in\mathbb{O}} b_i^2\alpha^{2i} + 2\sum_{i\in\mathbb{O},\, i\neq j}(a_ia_j + b_ib_j)\alpha^{i+j} + 2\sum_{i\in\mathbb{O}} b_i\alpha^i \equiv 0 \bmod 4$$

$$\sum_{i\in\mathbb{O}}(a_i^2 + b_i^2)\alpha^{2i} + 2\sum_{i\in\mathbb{O},\, i\neq j}(a_ia_j + b_ib_j)\alpha^{i+j} + 2\sum_{i\in\mathbb{O}} b_i\alpha^i \equiv 0 \bmod 4.$$

Note that $a_i^2 + b_i^2 \equiv 2 \bmod 4$, $a_ia_j + b_ib_j \equiv 2 \bmod 4$ and $2b_i \equiv 2 \bmod 4$ for $i, j \in \mathbb{O}$ with $i \neq j$. Hence, we have

$$2\sum_{i\in\mathbb{O}}\alpha^{2i} + 2\sum_{i\in\mathbb{O}}\alpha^i \equiv 0 \bmod 4$$

$$2\left(\sum_{i\in\mathbb{O}}\alpha^{2i} + \sum_{i\in\mathbb{O}}\alpha^i\right) \equiv 0 \bmod 4.$$

This implies that all coefficients of α^i in $\sum_{i\in\mathbb{O}}\alpha^{2i} + \sum_{i\in\mathbb{O}}\alpha^i$ are even, or equivalently, $\mu(\sum_{i\in\mathbb{O}}\alpha^{2i} + \sum_{i\in\mathbb{O}}\alpha^i) = 0$, i.e.

$$\sum_{i\in\mathbb{O}}\bar{\alpha}^{2i} + \sum_{i\in\mathbb{O}}\bar{\alpha}^i = 0, \tag{5}$$

where $\bar{\alpha} = \mu(\alpha)$. We may also compute $\sum_{i\in\mathbb{O}}\bar{\alpha}^{2i} + \sum_{i\in\mathbb{O}}\bar{\alpha}^i$ in $\mathbb{F}_{2^k}$ as follows.

$$\sum_{i\in\mathbb{O}}\bar{\alpha}^{2i} + \sum_{i\in\mathbb{O}}\bar{\alpha}^i = \left(\sum_{i\in\mathbb{O}}\bar{\alpha}^i\right)^2 + \sum_{i\in\mathbb{O}}\bar{\alpha}^i$$

$$= \left(\sum_{i\in\mathbb{O}}\bar{\alpha}^i\right)\left(1 + \sum_{i\in\mathbb{O}}\bar{\alpha}^i\right)$$

$$\neq 0. \quad \left(\text{as } \sum_{i\in\mathbb{O}}\bar{\alpha}^i \neq 0 \text{ and } 1 + \sum_{i\in\mathbb{O}}\bar{\alpha}^i \neq 0\right)$$

This contradicts (5). Therefore, we conclude that $\mathbf{a}^2 + \mathbf{b}^2$ is a non-square in $U(GR(2^n, k))$. $\qquad\square$

References

1. Augot, D., Finiasz, M.: Direct construction of recursive MDS diffusion layers using shortened BCH codes. In: Cid, C., Rechberger, C. (eds.) FSE 2014. LNCS, vol. 8540, pp. 3–17. Springer, Heidelberg (2015). https://doi.org/10.1007/978-3-662-46706-0_1

2. Augot, D., Fouque, P.-A., Karpman, P.: Diffusion matrices from algebraic-geometry codes with efficient SIMD implementation. In: Joux, A., Youssef, A. (eds.) SAC 2014. LNCS, vol. 8781, pp. 243–260. Springer, Cham (2014). https://doi.org/10.1007/978-3-319-13051-4_15

3. Berger, T.P.: Construction of recursive MDS diffusion layers from gabidulin codes. In: Paul, G., Vaudenay, S. (eds.) INDOCRYPT 2013. LNCS, vol. 8250, pp. 274–285. Springer, Cham (2013). https://doi.org/10.1007/978-3-319-03515-4_18

4. Bini, G., Flamini, F.: Finite Commutative Rings and Their Applications, Kluwer International Series in Engineering and Computer Science 680. Kluwer Academic Publishers, Dordrecht (2002)

5. Cui, T., Jin, C.I., Kong, Z.: On compact Cauchy matrices for substitution permutation networks. IEEE Trans. Comput. **64**(7), 2098–2102 (2015). https://doi.org/10.1109/TC.2014.2346180

6. Chand Gupta, K., Ghosh Ray, I.: On constructions of involutory MDS matrices. In: Youssef, A., Nitaj, A., Hassanien, A.E. (eds.) AFRICACRYPT 2013. LNCS, vol. 7918, pp. 43–60. Springer, Heidelberg (2013). https://doi.org/10.1007/978-3-642-38553-7_3

7. Gupta, K.C., Ray, I.G.: Cryptographically significant MDS matrices based on circulant and circulant-like matrices for lightweight applications. Crypt. Commun. **7**, 257–287 (2015). https://doi.org/10.1007/s12095-014-0116-3

8. Gupta, K.C., Pandey, S.K., Venkateswarlu, A.: On the direct construction of recursive MDS matrices. Des. Codes Crypt. **82**(1–2), 77–94 (2017). https://doi.org/10.1007/s10623-016-0233-4

9. Gupta, K.C., Pandey, S.K., Venkateswarlu, A.: Towards a general construction of recursive MDS diffusion layers. Des. Codes Crypt. **82**(1–2), 179–195 (2017). https://doi.org/10.1007/s10623-016-0261-0

10. Li, Y., Wang, M.: On the construction of lightweight circulant involutory MDS matrices. In: Peyrin, T. (ed.) FSE 2016. LNCS, vol. 9783, pp. 121–139. Springer, Heidelberg (2016). https://doi.org/10.1007/978-3-662-52993-5_7

11. Sajadieh, M.I., Dakhilalian, M., Mala, H., Omoomi, B.: On construction of involutory MDS matrices from Vandermonde matrices in $GF(2^q)$. Des. Codes Crypt. **64**(3), 287–308 (2012). https://doi.org/10.1007/s10623-011-9578-x

12. Sim, S.M., Khoo, K., Oggier, F., Peyrin, T.: Lightweight MDS involution matrices. In: Leander, G. (ed.) FSE 2015. LNCS, vol. 9054, pp. 471–493. Springer, Heidelberg (2015). https://doi.org/10.1007/978-3-662-48116-5_23. Extended version is in Cryptology ePrint Archive, Report 2015/258 (2015). http://eprint.iacr.org/

Cryptanalysis

MILP-Based Cube Attack
on the Reduced-Round WG-5 Lightweight
Stream Cipher

Raghvendra Rohit$^{(\boxtimes)}$, Riham AlTawy, and Guang Gong

Department of Electrical and Computer Engineering, University of Waterloo,
Waterloo, Ontario N2L 3G1, Canada
{rsrohit,raltawy,ggong}@uwaterloo.ca

Abstract. The cube attack is a powerful cryptanalytic tool for the analysis of stream ciphers, which until recently were investigated in a blackbox scenario with a minimal consideration to their internal and polynomial structures. In this paper, we analyze the lightweight stream cipher WG-5, which offers 80-bit security, using cube attacks in a non-blackbox polynomial setting employing the division property. WG-5 is a lightweight instantiation of the eSTREAM submission Welch-Gong stream cipher which provides mathematically proven random properties for its generated keystream. Our cube attack is automated using Mixed Integer Linear Programming models to theoretically bound the complexity of the superpoly recovery. The results of such an attack enable us to recover the secret key of WG-5 after 24 rounds of initialization utilizing $2^{6.32}$ keystream bits in $2^{76.81}$ time. Our attack on WG-5 has significantly lower data complexity than the algebraic attacks presented in the literature, albeit higher in computational complexity, it fits a more realistic scenario where large amount of data is hard to collect in lightweight constrained applications. Moreover, our attack is the first one to investigate the nonlinear feedback-based initialization phase of WG-5. Hence, such results are considered the best cryptanalytic ones in the case that the cipher runs a nonlinear key generation phase. Finally, our results are interesting in the sense that they enable us to argue how the design choices of WG-5 hinder the extension of cube attacks to more rounds in contrast to Grain 128a and Trivium, where such attacks can cover more than half of the number of initialization rounds.

Keywords: Welch-Gong stream cipher · Cube attacks · Division property · MILP · Lightweight stream ciphers

1 Introduction

The eSTREAM project [3] which was launched in 2004 is one of the first initiative that aimed to identify and recommend stream ciphers that fall under two profiles, (I) software oriented and (II) hardware efficient designs, for standardization.

© Springer International Publishing AG 2017
M. O'Neill (Ed.): IMACC 2017, LNCS 10655, pp. 333–351, 2017.
https://doi.org/10.1007/978-3-319-71045-7_17

Profile II category received 25 submissions and the project was finalized after three phases of analysis by recommending the three stream ciphers Grain v.1 [14], Trivium [8], and Mickey 2.0 [7]. Following the finale of the eSTREAM project, the work on stream cipher design has slowed for a while, however, it is revived again by the current NIST lightweight standardization competition [17].

By investigating most of the recent stream cipher proposals such as Sprout [5], Fruit [27], Lizard [13], Plantlet [19], and Flip [18], one can easily spot that there is a noticeable class of them that follow a Grain-like structure where two Feedback Shift Registers (FSRs) are used to provide a guarantee on minimum periodicity. While some of them opt for utilizing one Linear Feedback Shift Register (LFSR) with a primitive polynomial to prove a minimum bound on the period of the keystream sequence, others employ one Non-Linear Feedback Shift Register (NLFSR) with known maximum periodicity. Nevertheless, all the previously mentioned proposals fail to provide guarantees for other important randomness criteria such as runs, t-tuple distribution, and ideal 2-level autocorrelation [12]. On the other hand, another class of cipher such as the eSTREAM profile II submission Welch-Gong (WG) cipher [20] follows a more rigorous approach to provide mathematically proven randomness properties which are not provided by other ciphers. More precisely, WG adopts only one LFSR that produces m-*sequences* followed by the Welch-Gong filtering transformation during keystream generation. Such a transformation is theoretically proven to generate a balanced keystream with long period, large and exact linear complexity, t-tuple distribution, and ideal 2-level autocorrelation. However, such desirable randomness properties which are provided by filtering m-*sequences* generated by the LFSR come with the price of the feasibility of a range of algebraic attacks [21,23], which are not applicable on other ciphers that employ NLFSRs during keystream generation. Nevertheless, in both classes of ciphers, NLFSRs are utilized during the state initialization phase and accordingly, the analysis of such phase provides better comparison to their resistance to attacks targeting their non-linear feedback-based state initialization.

In this paper, we investigate the security of the nonlinear initialization phase of WG-5 [4] which is a lightweight version of the eSTREAM submission WG [20]. WG-5 is a word oriented stream cipher that provides all the aforementioned randomness criteria. WG resists time-memory-data trade-off attacks by utilizing a state size that is double the size of the offered security, thus having a hardware footprint that ranges between 1229 and 1235 GEs for a throughput of 100 kbps. The best cryptanalytic result available for WG-5 is a univariate algebraic attack over the extension field $\mathbb{F}_{2^5}$ that recovers the secret key using around 2^{15} keystream bits in 2^{33} time [23]. Such attack [23] is applicable on WG-5 only when it runs a linear feedback keystream generation phase. The results of this paper are summarized as follows.

Our contributions. We analyze WG-5 with respect to non-blackbox polynomial-based cube attacks. More precisely, given the complicated structures of stream ciphers, conventional cube attacks always regard them as blackbox functions, and the attack was only proven feasible if its complexity falls within the practical experimental range. In our analysis, we adopt the techniques from [25] which takes the polynomial structure of the analyzed stream cipher into consideration by tracing the propagation of a specific division property [24] through the initialization rounds. Accordingly, the propagation of the division property offers a theoretically proven bound on the number of key bits involved in the superpoly and the complexity of its recovery. Moreover, we further automate our attacks by proposing Mixed Integer Linear Programming (MILP) models for the division trails and then feed them to another MILP model for the whole attack. In what follows, we list our contributions.

- For the 24-round reduced initialization phase of WG-5, we model the division trail through the WG-5 permutation as an Sbox trail propagation which reduces the number of MILP inequalities and increases the solver chances in optimizing our model. We also provide the algorithmic description of all the proposed MILP models that we employ in our attack. The optimization of such models leads to a full key recovery when given $2^{6.32}$ keystream bits with $2^{76.81}$ time complexity.
- We present an argument which shows that the design choices in terms of feedback and filtering tap positions of WG-5 offer more security against cube attacks than Grain 128a and Trivium where such attacks break more than half the number of rounds of their initialization phases.

The rest of the paper is organized as follows. In Sect. 2, we recall the principals of the cube attack, division property, and how to model division trails using MILP. The specification of the WG-5 stream cipher is given in Sect. 3. In Sect. 4, we explain the details of the attack on the initialization phase of the WG-5 stream cipher, and how we model the WG-5 permutation as an Sbox to further reduce the number of MILP variables. Moreover, we give an algorithmic description of all MILP models used in our analysis and list the cube attack results and complexities. Furthermore, we compare our results on WG-5 to other cryptanalytic results available in the literature. In Sect. 5, we give an argument on the relation between the design parameters of WG-5 and the applicability of the cube attack, and further contrast such parameters to those of Grain and Trivium where cube attacks cover more than half the number of rounds of their initialization phases. Finally, the paper is concluded in Sect. 6.

2   Cube Attacks and the Division Property

In [25], Todo *et al.* proposed a method to apply cube attacks on stream ciphers employing the propagation of specific division trails. The consequence of their technique is that the application of the cube attack does not have to consider the analyzed cipher as a blackbox in order to recover its superpoly (the most difficult step in cube attacks) because the utilization of some specific division trails exploit the polynomial structure of the stream cipher. More precisely, since the cube attack is a kind of higher-order differential attack [16] and the division property is a technique to find higher-order differential trails, then the division property can be used to analyze the Algebraic Normal Form (ANF) of the superpoly by investigating multiple division trails corresponding to a given cube. In order to better understand how we utilize this method in our analysis of the initialization phase of WG-5, in what follows, we recall the concepts and definitions related to the cube attack and division property.

2.1   Cube Attack

The cube attack [9] is based on higher-order differential cryptanalysis to recover the secret key of the investigated primitive by analyzing the ANF of the summation of a set of its outputs corresponding to a set of inputs. Unlike block ciphers, stream ciphers are easily evaluated in the forward direction to compute their output keystream and very hard to invert them. Accordingly, the cube attack has been extensively used in the analysis of stream ciphers [6,10,11,25] because the attacker has to manipulate the input and analyze the output without evaluating the cipher in the backward direction. More formally, let the analyzed stream cipher take an n-bit secret key $k = (k_0, k_1, \cdots, k_{n-1})$ and an m-bit $IV = (v_0, v_1, \cdots, v_{m-1})$, then, the first keystream bit is given by the polynomial $f(k, v)$ which operates on $n + m$ bits to output 1 bit. After sufficiently enough initialization rounds, the polynomial $f(k, v)$ becomes very complicated, thus the role of the cube attack is to simplify it by computing the higher-order differential of this polynomial which results in what is called the *superpoly*, that is the result of summing a set of polynomials $\bigoplus f(k, v)$ corresponding to a cube. Such a cube is a set of different public input variables taking all possible values and is denoted by C_I. If the structure of the superpoly is simple enough (e.g., linear or quadratic), then its ANF can be analyzed and secret variables can be recovered. Formally, let the set of public indices $I = \{i_1, i_2, \cdots, i_{|I|}\} \subset \{0, 1, \cdots, m-1\}$ denote the cube indices, then the polynomial $f(k, v)$ can be represented as:

$$f(k, v) = t_I \cdot p(k, v) + q(k, v),$$

where $t_I = v_{i_1} v_{i_2} \cdots v_{i_{|I|}}$, $p(k, v)$ is a polynomial that does not contain any of the cube indices variables $(v_{i_1}, v_{i_2}, \cdots, v_{i_{|I|}})$, and $q(k, v)$ is independent of at least one variable from $(v_{i_1}, v_{i_2}, \cdots, v_{i_{|I|}})$.

Let the cube C_I denote the set of all the possible $2^{|I|}$ values of $(v_{i_1}, v_{i_2}, \cdots, v_{i_{|I|}})$, and the remaining input $n + m - |I|$ variables are set to some constant values, then the summation of $f(k, v)$ over all values of the cube C_I is given by

$$\bigoplus_{C_I} f(k, v) = \bigoplus_{C_I} t_I \cdot p(k, v) + \bigoplus_{C_I} q(k, v).$$

Since such summation reduces t_I to 1 because the set C_I has only one possibility where all the $|I|$ variables are equal to 1, and $q(k, v)$ vanishes because it misses at least one variable from the cube variables, then the above equation denotes the *superpoly* which is given by

$$superpoly : \bigoplus_{C_I} f(k, v) = p(k, v).$$

If the ANF of the superpoly is simple enough, then an attacker can query the encryption oracle with the chosen cube C_I. Hence, the returned first keystream bits are summed to evaluate the right-hand side of the superpoly and accordingly, secret variables can be recovered by solving a system of equations.

2.2   Division Property

The division property [24] is a generalization of the integral attacks [15] and a method to find higher-order differential trails. Moreover, a more refined bit-based division property is proposed in [26] and is defined as follows

Definition 1 (Bit-based division property [26]). *Let* $\mathbb{X}$ *be a multiset whose elements take a value of* $\mathbb{F}_2^n$*. Let* $\mathbb{W}$ *be a set whose elements take an n-dimensional vector of binary elements. The multiset* $\mathbb{X}$ *has the division property* $\mathcal{D}_{\mathbb{W}}^{1,n}$ *if it fulfills the following conditions[1]:*

$$\bigoplus_{x \in \mathbb{X}} \pi_u(x) = \begin{cases} unknown & if there exists w \in \mathbb{W} \ s.t \ u \succeq w, \\ 0 & otherwise, \end{cases}$$

where $u, w, x \in \mathbb{F}_2^n$*,* $\pi_u(x) = \prod_{i=0}^{n-1} x_i^{u_i}$ *and* $u \succeq w$ *if* $u_i \geq w_i$ *for all i.*

An attacker selects a set of chosen messages with a specific division property and traces its propagation until it reaches a round from where onwards the division property can not propagate. Accordingly, in the case of a cube attack, one prepares a set of $2^{|I|}$ chosen IVs where the variables $(v_{i_1}, v_{i_2}, \cdots, v_{i_{|I|}})$ take all the possible values. The division property of such a chosen set is $\mathcal{D}_v^{1,n}$, where $v_i = 1$ if $i \in \{i_1, i_2, \cdots, i_{|I|}\}$ and $v_i = 0$ for all remaining indices. Then one evaluates the propagation of this division property $\mathcal{D}_v^{1,n}$ for r rounds. We denote by $\{v\} \overset{def}{=} \mathbb{W}_0 \rightarrow \mathbb{W}_1 \rightarrow \cdots \rightarrow \mathbb{W}_r$ a r round division property propagation where $\mathbb{W}_i \subseteq \mathbb{F}_2^n$ for $0 \leq i \leq r$. Furthermore, we call $(w_0, w_1, \ldots, w_r) \in \mathbb{W}_0 \times \mathbb{W}_1 \times \ldots \times \mathbb{W}_r$ a r round division trail if w_{i-1} can propagate to w_i by division property propagation rules for all $i \in \{1, 2, \ldots, r\}$ [26,28]. The i-th bit at round r is balanced if $\mathbb{W}_r$ does not contain a unit vector whose i-th element is 1.

MILP models for division property. The propagation of the division property becomes infeasible when the input block size increases because the size of the corresponding $\mathbb{W}_i$ increases too. Particularly, in order to determine if the i-th bit at round r is balanced, one has to try all possible division trails with a given input division property and prove that there is no division trail that leads to a division property at round r with a unit vector where the i-th bit equals 1. However, in [28], a MILP-based method was proposed that allowed the efficient propagation of the division property for larger input spaces. More precisely, a MILP solver [1] is used to efficiently evaluate the feasibility of all division trails that cover the analyzed r rounds which are modeled by specific MILP models, and a higher-order differential trail is found if the solver determines that there

---

[1] "unknown" in Definition 1 means the xor sum can be 0 or 1 with probability $p \neq 1$.

is no division trail. MILP models that describe the propagation of the division property through different ciphers utilize the following three models [25,28]. Note that we refer to '+' as integer addition in all the MILP models.

- *MILP model for Copy.* Let the division trail through a copy be denoted by $a \rightarrow (b_1, b_2, \ldots, b_m)$, then the following inequalities are used to model such propagation:

$$M.var \leftarrow a, b_1, b_2, \ldots, b_m \text{ as binary.}$$
$$M.con \leftarrow a = b_1 + b_2 + \ldots + b_m.$$

- *MILP model for XOR.* Let $(a_1, a_2, \cdots, a_m) \rightarrow b$ denote the division trail of XOR, then the following inequalities are sufficient to describe the propagation of the division property:

$$M.var \leftarrow a_1, a_2, \cdots a_m, b \text{ as binary.}$$
$$M.con \leftarrow a_1 + a_2 + \cdots + a_m = b.$$

- *MILP model for AND.* Let $(a_1, a_2, \cdots, a_m) \rightarrow b$ denote the division trail for AND, then the following inequalities are used to describe the propagation:

$$M.var \leftarrow a_1, a_2, \cdots a_m, b \text{ as binary.}$$
$$M.con \leftarrow b \geq a_i \text{ for } i = 1, 2, \cdots, m.$$

In what follows, we give the description of the WG-5 stream cipher and how we use the division property to launch a cube attack on its initialization phase.

3   Specification of the WG-5 Stream Cipher

WG-5 [4] is a lightweight instantiated version of the eSTREAM submission word oriented WG stream cipher. It utilizes an 80-bit secret key, an 80-bit initialization vector and a 32-stage LFSR defined over the extension field $\mathbb{F}_{2^5}$. As depicted in Fig. 1, the LFSR is defined using the primitive polynomial $x^{32} + x^7 + x^6 + x^4 + x^3 + x^2 + \gamma$, where the polynomial belongs to $\mathbb{F}_{2^5}[x]$, $\gamma = \alpha^4 + \alpha^3 + \alpha^2 + \alpha + 1$, and α is a root of $x^5 + x^4 + x^2 + x + 1$ with its polynomial $\in \mathbb{F}_2[x]$. We denote the state of WG-5 at i-th round by $S^i = S^i[0] || S^i[1] || \ldots || S^i[31]$, where $S^i[j] = (s_{5j}^i, s_{5j+1}^i, s_{5j+2}^i, s_{5j+3}^i, s_{5j+4}^i)$ for $0 \leq j \leq 31$. The 80-bit secret key $(k_0, k_1, \ldots, k_{79})$ and 80-bit initialization vector $(v_0, v_1, \ldots, v_{79})$ are denoted by $K[0] || K[1] || \ldots || K[15]$ and $IV[0] || IV[1] || \ldots || IV[15]$, respectively. The cipher runs in two phases: initialization and keystream generation (KSG) phase. The initialization phase runs for 64 rounds with the output of WG-permutation (WGP) feedback into the state, whereas the non-linear feedback is not used during the KSG phase. We now formally describe the WG-5 cipher. Initially, the state is loaded with K and IV as follows:

$$S^0[j] = \begin{cases} K[j \bmod 2], & \text{if } j \equiv 0 \bmod 2 \\ IV[j \bmod 2], & \text{if } j \not\equiv 0 \bmod 2 \end{cases}$$

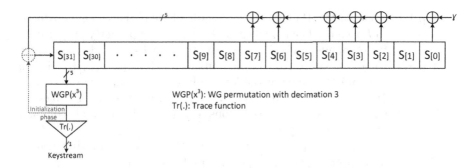

Fig. 1. Structure of WG-5

We use WG-5 with decimation 3 in our analysis[2]. The state update function is given by $S^{i+1}[j] = S^i[j+1], 0 \leq j \leq 30$ and $S^{i+1}[31] = \gamma S^i[0] \oplus S^i[2] \oplus S^i[3] \oplus S^i[4] \oplus S^i[6] \oplus S^i[7] \oplus \text{WGP}((S^i[31])^3)$. During the KSG phase, the keystream bit is given by $z_{i-64} = Tr(\text{WGP}(S^i[31])^3)$, where $Tr : \mathbb{F}_{2^5} \to \mathbb{F}_2$ denotes the Trace function. The corresponding boolean representation of keystream bit is given by $z_{i-64} = s^i_{155} + s^i_{156} + s^i_{157} + s^i_{158} + s^i_{159} + s^i_{155}s^i_{156} + s^i_{155}s^i_{157} + s^i_{155}s^i_{159} + s^i_{156}s^i_{158} + s^i_{156}s^i_{159} + s^i_{155}s^i_{156}s^i_{157} + s^i_{155}s^i_{157}s^i_{158} + s^i_{155}s^i_{157}s^i_{159} + s^i_{155}s^i_{158}s^i_{159} + s^i_{156}s^i_{157}s^i_{158} + s^i_{156}s^i_{158}s^i_{159}$. The state is then updated as follows:

$$S^{i+1}[j] = S^i[j + 1], 0 \leq j \leq 30 \text{ and}$$

$$S^{i+1}[31] = \gamma S^i[0] \oplus S^i[2] \oplus S^i[3] \oplus S^i[4] \oplus S^i[6] \oplus S^i[7], \text{ for } i \geq 64.$$

In the following section, we describe our attack on the initialization phase of WG-5, and explain all the proposed MILP models used in our analysis. More detailed explanation is provided in the full paper [22].

4   Cube Attack on WG-5

We adopt the techniques presented in [25, 28] to propose the cube attack on WG-5. The attack procedure consists of two phases: *offline phase* and *online phase*.

1. **Offline phase.** The goal of this phase is to recover a superpoly that is almost balanced[3] for a given cube C_I. It consists of three steps:

---

[2] We use decimation 3 as the degree of each of the component functions for WGP is 4, whereas it is 3 for decimation 1.

[3] $f : \mathbb{F}_2^n \to \mathbb{F}_2$ is almost balanced if $f = 0$ for $\approx 2^{n-1}$ values and $f = 1$ for the remaining values.

Step 1.1: Create a MILP model M for WG-5 whose initialization is reduced to R rounds. The model encodes the division property propagation for R rounds to check the feasibility of all R-round division trails.

Step 1.2: Choose a cube C_I by flipping bits in $I = \{i_1, i_2, \ldots, i_{|I|}\}$ and then evaluate the secret variables involved in the superpoly. Let $J = \{k_{j_1}, k_{j_2}, \ldots, k_{j_{|J|}}\}$ denotes the set of involved secret variables[4].

Step 1.3: Choose a value in the constant part of IV and compute $\oplus_{C_I} f(k, v) = p(\bar{k}, \bar{v})$, where $\bar{k} = \{k_{j_1}, k_{j_2}, \ldots, k_{j_{|J|}}\}$, $\bar{v} = \{(v_0, v_1, \ldots, v_{79}) - (v_{i_1}, v_{i_2}, \ldots, v_{i_{|I|}})\}$ and all the possible combinations of $k_{j_1}, k_{j_2}, \ldots, k_{j_{|J|}}$ are tried out, then $p(\bar{k}, \bar{v})$ is recovered and stored in a list for all values of $\bar{k}$. Assuming the best case that we can recover the balanced superpoly in a single trial, the time complexity of this phase is bounded by $2^{|I|+|J|}$. However, if N cubes are used, the time complexity is given by $N2^{|I|+|J|}$.

2. **Online phase.** The goal of this phase is to recover the entire secret key. This phase is further divided into two steps.

Step 2.1: Use the balanced superpoly recovered in the *offline phase* and query the cube C_I to the encryption oracle to obtain the value of $p(\bar{k}, \bar{v})$ which is then compared to the previously stored values. Then one bit is recovered from J as $p = 0$ for $2^{|J|-1}$ values and $p = 1$ for the remaining half values. To recover more than 1 bit we use multiple cubes.

Step 2.2: Guess the remaining secret key values.

In what follows, we describe all the steps of the attack.

4.1   Automating the Cube Attack on WG-5 Using MILP

We start by modelling the division property propagation for each of the functions used in WG-5. We use COPY, XOR and AND operations described in Sect. 2 to model all the functions in the initialization and key generation phases.

MILP model for the WG-permutation (WGP). To model the WG-permutation, we can use its boolean representation which is given in Sect. 5. However, this approach results in large number of MILP variables and constraints due to its high non-linearity and involvement of terms of up to degree 4 in each of the component function. Hence, we use an alternative approach, we treat WGP as a 5-bit Sbox. Let $(x_0, x_1, x_2, x_3, x_4)$ and $(y_0, y_1, y_2, y_3, y_4)$ be the input and output of the WGP Sbox, respectively. We use the *inequality_generator()* function in Sage [2] and Algorithms 1 and 2 in [28], and consequently find that only 12 inequalities are sufficient to model the division property propagation through the WGP Sbox. The inequalities are given by:

---

[4] Step 1.2 is computationally feasible because of MILP.

$$\begin{cases}
2x_0 + 2x_1 + 2x_2 + 2x_3 + 6x_4 - 3y_0 - 3y_1 - 3y_2 - 3y_3 - 3y_4 \geq -1 \\
4x_3 - y_0 - y_1 - y_2 - y_3 - y_4 \geq -1 \\
4x_0 - y_0 - y_1 - y_2 - y_3 - y_4 \geq -1 \\
-x_0 - x_2 - x_3 - y_0 + 4y_1 - y_2 - y_3 - 2y_4 \geq -4 \\
-6x_0 - 3x_1 - 6x_3 - 6x_4 + 2y_0 - 4y_1 + 3y_2 - y_3 + 2y_4 \geq -19 \\
-3x_0 - x_1 - x_2 - 3x_3 - 2x_4 + 9y_0 + 7y_1 + 8y_2 + 9y_3 + 9y_4 \geq 0 \\
x_0 + x_1 + x_2 + x_3 + x_4 - 3y_0 - 3y_1 - 3y_2 - 3y_3 + 5y_4 \geq -2 \\
-x_0 - 3x_2 - 3x_3 - 2x_4 + y_0 + y_2 + y_3 - 2y_4 \geq -8 \\
-x_0 - x_1 + 2x_2 - x_3 - x_4 - y_0 - 2y_1 - 2y_2 + 3y_3 - y_4 \geq -5 \\
-x_0 - 2x_1 - 2x_2 - 2x_3 - x_4 - 2y_0 - y_1 - y_2 - y_3 + 5y_4 \geq -8 \\
-2x_0 - x_1 - 2x_2 - 2x_4 + y_0 + y_1 - y_2 + y_4 \geq -6 \\
-x_0 - x_2 - x_3 + y_0 - y_4 \geq -3.
\end{cases}$$

Algorithm 2 describes the MILP model for the WG-permutation.

MILP model for the feedback function (FBK). The function FBK in Algorithm 3 generates the MILP variables and constraints for the feedback function $\gamma S^i[0] \oplus S^i[2] \oplus S^i[3] \oplus S^i[4] \oplus S^i[6] \oplus S^i[7]$. Since $\gamma = (1, 1, 1, 1, 1)$, we model $\gamma S^i[0]$ as $S^i[0]$.

MILP model for KSG. The function KSG in Algorithm 4 creates the MILP variables and constraints for the keystream bit $z = s_{155}^R + s_{156}^R + s_{157}^R + s_{158}^R + s_{159}^R + s_{155}^R s_{156}^R + s_{155}^R s_{157}^R + s_{155}^R s_{159}^R + s_{156}^R s_{158}^R + s_{156}^R s_{159}^R + s_{155}^R s_{156}^R s_{157}^R + s_{155}^R s_{157}^R s_{158}^R + s_{155}^R s_{157}^R s_{159}^R + s_{155}^R s_{158}^R s_{159}^R + s_{156}^R s_{157}^R s_{158}^R + s_{156}^R s_{158}^R s_{159}^R$. Furthermore, the bitwise AND and XOR operations are modeled using Algorithm 5.

We now present the MILP model for WG-5 in Algorithm 1. The function WG5EVAL evaluates all division trails for WG-5 whose initialization rounds are reduced to R. The number of MILP variables and constraints required in each function are given in Table 1.

Table 1. WG-5: MILP variables and constraints

Function	# of variables	# of constraints
WGP	15	17
FBK	65	35
KSG	79	63
R round of WG-5	160+159R + 5R	161 + 115R + 10R

4.2 Evaluating Involved Secret Variables and Superpoly Recovery

We prepare a cube C_I by flipping bits in $I = \{i_1, i_2, \ldots, i_{|I|}\}$ and then, we evaluate the involved secret variables in superpoly using the generic algorithm

Algorithm 1. MILP model for the initialization of WG-5

```
 1: function WG5EVAL(R)
 2:     Prepare empty MILP Model M
 3:     M.var ← S⁰[j] for 0 ≤ j ≤ 31
 4:     for i = 1 to R do
 5:         (M, S', a) = WGP(Sⁱ⁻¹)
 6:         (M, S'', b) = FBK(S', [0, 2, 3, 4, 6, 7])
 7:         for j = 0 to 30 do
 8:             Sⁱ[j] = S''[j + 1]
 9:         end for
10:         M.con ← S''[0] = 0
11:         M.var ← Sⁱ[31] as binary
12:         M.con ← Sⁱ[31] = a + b
13:     end for
14:     (M, S''', z) = KSG(Sᴿ)
15:     for j = 0 to 31 do
16:         S'''[j] = 0
17:     end for
18:     M.con ← z = 1
19: end function
```

proposed in [25]. We have given the description of the utilized algorithm (Algorithm 6) in Appendix B for the sake of completeness. The inputs to Algorithm 6 are the cube indices set I and the MILP model M for WG-5. The model M evaluates all the division trails for R rounds with input division property given by $v_i = 1$ for $i \in I$ and $v_i = 0$ for $i \in \{(0, 1, \ldots, 79) - I\}$. The reader is referred to [25] for the detailed explanation of Algorithm 6.

Searching cubes. We limit our search for the cubes to indices I such that $2^{|I|+|J|} < 2^{80}$. Table 2 lists the cubes we found that satisfies the above condition. Note that searching all $\binom{80}{|I|}$ cubes is infeasible and the cubes in Table 2 are the best so far for WG-5 according to our experimental results.

Recovering a balanced superpoly. We choose a value in the constant part of the IV and vary all $2^4 \times 2^{70}$ values to recover $p(k_5, k_6, \ldots, k_{74}, \bar{v})$ where $\bar{v} = (\{v_0, v_1, \ldots, v_{79}\} - \{v_j | j \in I_i\})$ for $1 \leq i \leq 5$ and $R = 24$. We also store 2^{70} values of $p(\bar{k}, \bar{v})$ as they will be used again in the online phase. We assume that we can recover a balanced superpoly in 1 trial for each of the cubes in Table 2. We expect that such an assumption holds with a high probability as there are $80 - |I_i| = 76$ values in the constant part of IV.

4.3   Key Recovery for 24 Rounds

We use the balanced superpolys recovered in offline phase for cubes I_1, I_2, I_3, I_4 and I_5 (see Table 2) in the online phase. We query the cube C_{I_i} to the encryption oracle and compute the sum $\oplus_{C_{I_i}} f(k, v)$. We then compare this sum with $\oplus_{C_{I_i}} f(k, v) = p(k_5, k_6, \ldots, k_{74}, \bar{v})$ stored in the offline phase for all possible

Table 2. Involved secret variables in superpoly for cube indices $I \in \{I_1, I_2, I_3, I_4, I_5\}$

Rounds	Involved secret variables J	Time complexity $log_2(.)$
15	$\{k_5, k_6, \ldots, k_{54}\}$	54
16	$\{k_5, k_6, \ldots, k_{54}\}$	54
17	$\{k_5, k_6, \ldots, k_{59}\}$	59
18	$\{k_5, k_6, \ldots, k_{59}\}$	59
19	$\{k_5, k_6, \ldots, k_{64}\}$	64
20	$\{k_5, k_6, \ldots, k_{64}\}$	64
21	$\{k_5, k_6, \ldots, k_{69}\}$	69
22	$\{k_5, k_6, \ldots, k_{69}\}$	69
23	$\{k_5, k_6, \ldots, k_{74}\}$	74
24	$\{k_5, k_6, \ldots, k_{74}\}$	74

$I_1 = \{0, 1, 2, 3\}, I_2 = \{0, 1, 2, 4\}, I_3 = \{0, 1, 3, 4\}, I_4 = \{0, 2, 3, 4\}, I_5 = \{1, 2, 3, 4\}$.
Here, time complexity means the complexity to recover the superpoly.

combinations of $\{k_5, k_6, \ldots, k_{74}\}$. We discard the values of $\{k_5, k_6, \ldots, k_{74}\}$ for which the sum is different. Since, we are using a balanced superpoly, $p(k_5, k_6, \ldots, k_{74}, \bar{v}) = 0$ for 2^{69} values and equals 1 for the remaining 2^{69} values. Thus, one bit of secret information can always be recovered. We use cubes I_1, I_2, I_3, I_4 and I_5 in our attack and hence can recover 5 secret variables. We then guess remaining 75 bits to recover the entire secret key. The attack time complexity for 24 rounds is then given by $5 \times 2^{74} + 2^{75} \approx 2^{76.81}$.

4.4   Attack Comparison with Algebraic Attacks

The univariate algebraic attacks [23] exploits the fact that WG-5 is updated linearly during the keystream generation phase. Hence, using the trace representation of z_t, it is possible to find a multiple g (also known as annihilator) of filtering function f i.e. $fg = 0$ and g contains only one term of hamming weight 3. This lowers the data and time complexity of the conventional algebraic attack to 2^{15} and 2^{33}, respectively. The applicability of such attacks does not hold if the nonlinear WGP is feedback into the state during KSG phase because the concept of annihilator functions no longer exists. On the other hand, the attack proposed in this paper is not affected by the nonlinear feedback of WGP into state during KSG phase. Moreover, our attack requires significantly low data complexity which enables a more realistic attack scenario in constrained applications where the available online data that may be queried by an adversary under a given key is usually limited by the running protocol. In summary, we can attack 24 rounds of the initialization phase of WG-5 with data and time complexity of $2^{6.32}$ and $2^{76.81}$, respectively.

5   Comparison of the Initialization Phase of WG-5 with Those of Grain128a and Trivium

In this section, we present an argument to show how the initialization phase of WG-5 is more resistant to cube attacks than those of Grain128a and Trivium. We particularly choose Grain128a and Trivium because both are eSTREAM finalists and also they offer the same level of security as WG-5. We give a brief description of both stream ciphers in Appendix C.

We now look at the state update functions of both Grain128a and Trivium more carefully and deduce the following observations:

– *For Trivium, the degree of z is 3 after 81 rounds.* The algebraic degree of z can only be increased by AND terms $s_{90}s_{91}$, $s_{174}s_{175}$ and $s_{285}s_{286}$. Thus, the round at which the degree of z equals 3 is $\min(90, 174 - 93, 285 - 177) = 81$.
– *For Grain128a, the degree of z is 6 after 32 rounds.* The maximum index in h function is 95 (for b_{95} term). At round 32 (127-95) only the degree of b_{95} is 4 and the remaining terms are of degree 1. Hence, the degree of z is 6 because of $b_{12}b_{95}s_{94}$ term.

On the other hand, for WG-5 we find that the *degree of z is 6 in 1 round only*. The degree of each component of $S^1[31] = \gamma S^0[0] \oplus S^0[2] \oplus S^0[3] \oplus S^0[4] \oplus S^0[6] \oplus S^0[7] \oplus \mathrm{WGP}((S^0[31])^3) = (s_{155}^1, s_{156}^1, s_{157}^1, s_{158}^1, s_{159}^1)$ equals 4. This can be deduced from the boolean representation of the component functions of the WG-permutation given below.

$$y_0 = x_0x_1x_3x_4 + x_0x_1x_4 + x_0x_2x_3x_4 + x_0x_2x_3 + x_0x_2x_4 + x_0x_4 + x_0$$
$$+ x_1x_2x_3 + x_1x_2 + x_1x_3 + x_3x_4$$

$$y_1 = x_0x_1x_2x_3 + x_0x_1x_2x_4 + x_0x_1x_2 + x_0x_1x_3 + x_0x_1x_4 + x_0x_1$$
$$+ x_0x_2x_4 + x_0x_2 + x_0x_3x_4 + x_0x_4 + x_1x_2x_3x_4 + x_1x_4 + x_1$$
$$+ x_2x_4 + x_2 + x_3x_4$$

$$y_2 = x_0x_1x_2x_3 + x_0x_1x_4 + x_0x_1 + x_0x_2 + x_0x_3x_4 + x_1x_2x_3x_4 + x_1x_2$$
$$+ x_1x_4 + x_2x_3x_4 + x_2x_3 + x_2x_4 + x_2 + x_3x_4 + x_3 + x_4$$

$$y_3 = x_0x_1x_2x_3 + x_0x_1x_3 + x_0x_1 + x_0x_2x_3x_4 + x_0x_2x_3 + x_0x_2x_4$$
$$+ x_0x_3x_4 + x_0x_4 + x_1x_2x_4 + x_1x_3x_4 + x_1x_3 + x_1$$

$$y_4 = x_0x_1x_2x_4 + x_0x_1x_2 + x_0x_1x_3x_4 + x_0x_1 + x_0x_2x_3x_4 + x_0x_2$$
$$+ x_0x_3x_4 + x_0x_3 + x_0x_4 + x_1x_2x_3 + x_1x_2x_4 + x_1x_2 + x_1x_3$$
$$+ x_1x_4 + x_1 + x_2x_3x_4 + x_2x_3 + x_2x_4 + x_4$$

Since z at round 1 is given by $s_{155}^1 + s_{156}^1 + s_{157}^1 + s_{158}^1 + s_{159}^1 + s_{155}^1 s_{156}^1 + s_{155}^1 s_{157}^1 + s_{155}^1 s_{159}^1 + s_{156}^1 s_{158}^1 + s_{156}^i s_{159}^1 + s_{155}^1 s_{156}^1 s_{157}^1 + s_{155}^1 s_{157}^1 s_{158}^1 + s_{155}^1 s_{157}^1 s_{159}^1 + s_{155}^1 s_{158}^1 s_{159} + s_{156}^1 s_{157}^1 s_{158}^1 + s_{156}^1 s_{158}^1 s_{159}^1$, then the degree of z is 6.

Based on the degree comparison of 32 rounds of Grain128a and 81 rounds of Trivium with 1 round of WG-5, we see that degree in WG-5 grows much faster.

We also observe that all the 5 bits processed by WGP at the i-th round are used to generate the keystream bit at round $(i + 1)$ along with $5 \times 6 = 30$ new bits from the feedback function. This is not the same case with Grain128a because the updated bits b_{127} and s_{127} in i-th round are used in keystream bit at $i + 32$ and $i + 33$, respectively. Similarly, for Trivium the values of t_1, t_2 and t_3 at i-th round are used in keystream bit at $i + 90, i + 81$ and $i + 108$ rounds, respectively. Thus, cubes of higher dimension whose superpoly involves few secret variables exist for both Grain128a and Trivium. For example, Todo *et al.* [25] experimentally found 92 dimension cube for 183 rounds Grain128a whose superpoly involves 16 secret key bits. Also, for Trivium reduced to 832 rounds, they found a 72 dimension cube which has only 5 secret variables in its superpoly. We tried some cubes of higher dimension for WG-5 and found that all the 80 secret variables are involved in the superpoly. The best cubes we have found are listed in Table 2 and they can cover 24 rounds of WG-5. Thus, based on the above observations, we conclude that the initialization phase of WG-5 is more stronger than those of Grain128a and Trivium with respect to cube attacks.

6   Conclusion

In this paper, we have investigated the lightweight stream cipher WG-5 with respect to non-blackbox cube attacks. Specifically, we have utilized the division property to find higher-order differential trails corresponding to a set of chosen initial values generated from specific cubes, and consequently the structure of the superpoly is recovered. Moreover, we have automated the process of the propagation of the division property by proposing MILP models for the WG-5 initialization and keystream generation phases. We have further modeled the WG permutation as an Sbox to reduce the number of variables and inequalities in the model which raises the chances of the MILP solver to find a feasible solution. The results of our cube attack reveals low data complexity requirements which when compared to the existing algebraic attacks, offer a more realistic attack scenario for lightweight constrained applications where the amount of data available to attacker under a given key is restricted by the running protocol. Also, unlike algebraic attacks, our attack is applicable on WG-5 whether it runs a linear or nonlinear keystream generation phase. Finally, the findings of our analysis enable us to argue that the WG-5 design parameters in terms of feedback and filtering tapping positions inhibit the extension of the cube attack to more rounds, in contrast to Grain128a and Trivium where such an attack covers more than half of the rounds of their initialization phases. Thus, we conclude that the initialization phase of WG-5 is more resistant to cube attacks than Grain's and Trivium's.

Acknowledgment. We would like to thank the reviewers of IMACC 2017 for their valuable comments that helped improve the quality of the paper. This work is supported by the National Institute of Standards and Technology (NIST) and Natural Sciences and Engineering Research Council of Canada (NSERC).

A   MILP Models for WG-5 Components

Algorithm 2. MILP model for WGP

1: **function** WGP(S)   ▷ $S = (s_0, s_1, \ldots, s_{159})$
2:     $M.var \leftarrow s'_{155+i}, x_i, y_i$ as binary for $0 \leq i \leq 4$
3:     $M.con \leftarrow s_{155+i} = s'_{155+i} + x_i$ for $0 \leq i \leq 4$
4:     Add constraints to M according to the WGP inequalities 4.1
5:     **for** $j = 0$ to 30 **do**
6:         $S'[j] = S[j]$ ▷ $S'[j] = (s'_{5j}, s'_{5j+1}, s'_{5j+2}, s'_{5j+3}, s'_{5j+4})$
7:     **end for**
8:     return $(M, S', [y_0, y_1, y_2, y_3, y_4])$
9: **end function**

Algorithm 3. MILP model for the FBK function in WG-5

1: **function** FBK(S, I)
2:     **for** $i \in I$ **do**
3:         $M.var \leftarrow s'_{5i+j}, x_{5i+j}$ as binary for $0 \leq j \leq 4$
4:     **end for**
5:     $M.var \leftarrow y_i$ as binary for $0 \leq i \leq 4$
6:     **for** $i \in I$ **do**
7:         $M.con \leftarrow s_{5i+j} = s'_{5i+j} + x_{5i+j}$ for $0 \leq j \leq 4$
8:     **end for**
9:     **for** $j = 0$ to 4 **do**
10:         $temp = 0$
11:         **for** $i \in I$ **do**
12:             $temp = temp + x_{5i+j}$
13:         **end for**
14:         $M.con \leftarrow y_j = temp$
15:     **end for**
16:     **for** $j \in \{0, 1, \ldots, 31\} - I$ **do**
17:         $S'[j] = S[j]$
18:     **end for**
19:     return $(M, S', [y_0, y_1, y_2, y_3, y_4])$
20: **end function**

Algorithm 4. MILP model for the KSG operation in WG-5

1: **function** KSG(S)
2:     $(M, S_1, a_1) = \text{AND}(S, [155, 156])$
3:     $(M, S_2, a_2) = \text{AND}(S_1, [155, 157])$
4:     $(M, S_3, a_3) = \text{AND}(S_2, [155, 159])$
5:     $(M, S_4, a_4) = \text{AND}(S_3, [156, 158])$
6:     $(M, S_5, a_5) = \text{AND}(S_4, [156, 159])$
7:     $(M, S_6, a_6) = \text{AND}(S_5, [155, 156, 157])$
8:     $(M, S_7, a_7) = \text{AND}(S_6, [155, 157, 158])$
9:     $(M, S_8, a_8) = \text{AND}(S_7, [155, 157, 159])$
10:     $(M, S_9, a_9) = \text{AND}(S_8, [155, 158, 159])$
11:     $(M, S_{10}, a_{10}) = \text{AND}(S_9, [156, 157, 158])$
12:     $(M, S_{11}, a_{11}) = \text{AND}(S_{10}, [156, 158, 159])$
13:     $(M, S_{12}, a_{12}) = \text{XOR}(S_{11}, [155, 156, 157, 158, 159])$
14:     $M.var \leftarrow z$ as binary
15:     $M.con \leftarrow z = \sum_{i=1}^{12} a_i$
16:     **return** (M, S_{12}, z)
17: **end function**

Algorithm 5. MILP model for AND and XOR operations in WG-5

1: **function** AND(S, I)
2:     $M.var \leftarrow s'_i, x_i$ as binary for i in I
3:     $M.var \leftarrow y$ as binary
4:     $M.con \leftarrow s_i = s'_i + x_i$ for i in I
5:     $M.con \leftarrow y \geq x_i$ for i in I
6:     **for** $i \in \{(0, 1, \ldots, 159) - I\}$ **do**
7:         $s'_i = s_i$
8:     **end for**
9:     **return** (M, S', y)
10: **end function**
11: **function** XOR(S, I)
12:     $M.var \leftarrow s'_i, x_i$ as binary for i in I
13:     $M.var \leftarrow y$ as binary
14:     $M.con \leftarrow s_i = s'_i + x_i$ for i in I
15:     $temp = 0$
16:     **for** $i \in I$ **do**
17:         $temp = temp + x_i$
18:     **end for**
19:     $M.con \leftarrow y = temp$
20:     **for** i in $\{(0, 1, \ldots, 159) - I\}$ **do**
21:         $s'_i = s_i$
22:     **end for**
23:     **return** (M, S', y)
24: **end function**

B A Generic Algorithm for the Evaluation of the Involved Secret Variables in a Superpoly [25]

Algorithm 6. MILP model to find involved secret variables in superpoly

---

1: **function** EXTRACTSECRETVARIABLES(MILP model M, Cube Indices I)
2:     $M.var \leftarrow k_i$ as binary for $0 \le i \le n - 1$, $\triangleright$ $k_0, k_1, \ldots, k_{n-1}$ are secret variables
3:     $M.var \leftarrow v_i$ as binary for $0 \le i \le m - 1$, $\triangleright$ $v_0, v_1, \ldots, v_{m-1}$ are public variables
4:     $M.con \leftarrow v_i = 1$ for $i \in I$
5:     $M.con \leftarrow v_i = 0$ for $i \in \{(0, 1, \ldots, m - 1) - I\}$
6:     $M.con \leftarrow \sum_{i=0}^{n-1} k_i = 1$
7:     **do**
8:         solve MILP model M
9:         **if** M is feasible **then**
10:             pick $j \in \{0, 1, \ldots, n - 1\}$ s.t $k_j = 1$
11:             $J = J \cup \{j\}$
12:             $M.con \leftarrow k_j = 0$
13:         **end if**
14:     **while** M is feasible
15:     **return** J
16: **end function**

C Description of Grain128a and Trivium

Grain128a is a NLFSR based stream cipher of Grain family with two 128-bit states represented by $(b_0, b_1, \ldots, b_{127})$ and $(s_0, s_1, \ldots, s_{127})$. The state is loaded with 128-bit key and 96-bit IV as follows $(b_0, b_1, \ldots, b_{127}) = (k_0, k_1, \ldots, k_{127})$ and $(s_0, s_1, \ldots, s_{127}) = (iv_0, iv_1, \ldots, iv_{95}, 1, \ldots, 1, 0)$. The initialization phase runs for 256 rounds with the state update function given by

$$g \leftarrow b_0 + b_{26} + b_{56} + b_{91} + b_{96} + b_3 b_{67} + b_{11} b_{13}$$
$$+ b_{17} b_{18} + b_{27} b_{59} + b_{40} b_{48} + b_{61} b_{65} + b_{68} b_{84}$$
$$+ b_{88} b_{92} b_{93} b_{95} + b_{22} b_{24} b_{25} + b_{70} b_{78} b_{82}$$
$$f \leftarrow s_0 + s_7 + s_{38} + s_{70} + s_{81} + s_{96}$$
$$h \leftarrow b_{12} s_8 + s_{13} s_{20} + b_{95} s_{42} + s_{60} s_{79} + b_{12} b_{95} s_{94}$$
$$z \leftarrow h + s_{93} + b_2 + b_{15} + b_{36} + b_{45} + b_{64} + b_{73} + b_{89}$$
$$(b_0, b_1, \ldots, b_{127}) \leftarrow (b_1, b_2, \ldots, b_{127}, g + s_0 + z)$$
$$(s_0, s_1, \ldots, s_{127}) \leftarrow (s_1, s_2, \ldots, s_{127}, f + z).$$

During the KSG phase, z is not feedback to the state and directly used as the keystream bit.

Trivium is also an NLFSR based stream cipher with state size 288. The 80-bit key and 80-bit IV are loaded into the state as follows $(s_0, s_1, \ldots, s_{92}) = (k_0, k_1, \ldots, k_{79}, 0, \ldots, 0)$, $(s_{93}, s_{94}, \ldots, s_{176}) = (iv_0, iv_1, \ldots, iv_{79}, 0, \ldots, 0)$ and $(s_{177}, s_{178}, \ldots, s_{287}) = (0, 0, \ldots, 0, 1, 1, 1)$. The state update function of Trivium is given by

$$t_1 \leftarrow s_{65} + s_{92}$$

$$t_2 \leftarrow s_{161} + s_{176}$$

$$t_3 \leftarrow s_{242} + s_{287}$$

$$z \leftarrow t_1 + t_2 + t_3$$

$$t_1 \leftarrow t_1 + s_{90}s_{91} + s_{170}$$

$$t_2 \leftarrow t_2 + s_{174}s_{175} + s_{263}$$

$$t_3 \leftarrow t_3 + s_{285}s_{286} + s_{68}$$

$$(s_0, s_1, \ldots, s_{92}) \leftarrow (t_3, s_0, \ldots, s_{91})$$

$$(s_{93}, s_1, \ldots, s_{176}) \leftarrow (t_1, s_{93}, \ldots, s_{175})$$

$$(s_{177}, s_1, \ldots, s_{287}) \leftarrow (t_2, s_{177}, \ldots, s_{286}).$$

The initialization phase runs for 1152 rounds without producing an output while z is used as the keystream bit during KSG phase.

References

1. Gurobi: MILP optimizer. http://www.gurobi.com/
2. SageMath. http://www.sagemath.org/
3. eSTREAM: the ECRYPT stream cipher project (2008)
4. Aagaard, M.D., Gong, G., Mota, R.K.: Hardware implementations of the WG-5 cipher for passive rfid tags. In: 2013 IEEE International Symposium on Hardware-Oriented Security and Trust (HOST), pp. 29–34 (2013)
5. Armknecht, F., Mikhalev, V.: On lightweight stream ciphers with shorter internal states. In: Leander, G. (ed.) FSE 2015. LNCS, vol. 9054, pp. 451–470. Springer, Heidelberg (2015). https://doi.org/10.1007/978-3-662-48116-5_22
6. Aumasson, J.-P., Dinur, I., Meier, W., Shamir, A.: Cube testers and key recovery attacks on reduced-round MD6 and trivium. In: Dunkelman, O. (ed.) FSE 2009. LNCS, vol. 5665, pp. 1–22. Springer, Heidelberg (2009). https://doi.org/10.1007/978-3-642-03317-9_1
7. Babbage, S., Dodd, M.: The MICKEY stream ciphers. In: Robshaw, M., Billet, O. (eds.) New Stream Cipher Designs. LNCS, vol. 4986, pp. 191–209. Springer, Heidelberg (2008). https://doi.org/10.1007/978-3-540-68351-3_15
8. De Cannière, C.: TRIVIUM: a stream cipher construction inspired by block cipher design principles. In: Katsikas, S.K., López, J., Backes, M., Gritzalis, S., Preneel, B. (eds.) ISC 2006. LNCS, vol. 4176, pp. 171–186. Springer, Heidelberg (2006). https://doi.org/10.1007/11836810_13
9. Dinur, I., Shamir, A.: Cube attacks on tweakable blackbox polynomials. In: Joux, A. (ed.) EUROCRYPT 2009. LNCS, vol. 5479, pp. 278–299. Springer, Heidelberg (2009)
10. Dinur, I., Shamir, A.: Breaking Grain-128 with dynamic cube attacks. In: Joux, A. (ed.) FSE 2011. LNCS, vol. 6733, pp. 167–187. Springer, Heidelberg (2011). https://doi.org/10.1007/978-3-642-21702-9_10

11. Fouque, P.-A., Vannet, T.: Improving key recovery to 784 and 799 rounds of trivium using optimized cube attacks. In: Moriai, S. (ed.) FSE 2013. LNCS, vol. 8424, pp. 502–517. Springer, Heidelberg (2014). https://doi.org/10.1007/978-3-662-43933-3_26

12. Gong, G., Youssef, A.M.: Cryptographic properties of the Welch-Gong transformation sequence generators. IEEE Trans. Inf. Theor. **48**(11), 2837–2846 (2002)

13. Hamann, M., Krause, M., Meier, W.: Lizard: a lightweight stream cipher for power-constrained devices. IACR Trans. Symmetric Crypt. **2017**(1), 45–79 (2017)

14. Hell, M., Johansson, T., Maximov, A., Meier, W.: A stream cipher proposal: Grain-128. In: IEEE International Symposium on Information Theory, pp. 1614–1618 (2006)

15. Knudsen, L., Wagner, D.: Integral cryptanalysis. In: Daemen, J., Rijmen, V. (eds.) FSE 2002. LNCS, vol. 2365, pp. 112–127. Springer, Heidelberg (2002). https://doi.org/10.1007/3-540-45661-9_9

16. Lai, X.: Higher order derivatives and differential cryptanalysis. In: Blahut, R.E., Costello, D.J., Maurer, U., Mittelholzer, T. (eds.) Communications and Cryptography 1994. LNCS, vol. 276, pp. 227–233. Springer, MA (1994). https://doi.org/10.1007/978-1-4615-2694-0_23

17. McKay, K., Bassham, L., Sönmez Turan, M., Mouha, N.: Report on lightweight cryptography (NISTIR8114) (2017)

18. Méaux, P., Journault, A., Standaert, F.-X., Carlet, C.: Towards stream ciphers for efficient FHE with low-noise ciphertexts. In: Fischlin, M., Coron, J.-S. (eds.) EUROCRYPT 2016, Part I. LNCS, vol. 9665, pp. 311–343. Springer, Heidelberg (2016). https://doi.org/10.1007/978-3-662-49890-3_13

19. Mikhalev, V., Armknecht, F., Müller, C.: On ciphers that continuously access the non-volatile key. IACR Trans. Symmetric Crypt. **2017**(2), 52–79 (2017)

20. Nawaz, Y., Gong, G.: Wg: a family of stream ciphers with designed randomness properties. Inf. Sci. **178**(7), 1903–1916 (2008)

21. Orumiehchiha, M.A., Pieprzyk, J., Steinfeld, R.: Cryptanalysis of WG-7: a lightweight stream cipher. Crypt. Commun. **4**(3–4), 277–285 (2012)

22. Rohit, R., AlTawy, R., Gong, G.: MILP-based cube attack on the reduced-round WG-5 lightweight stream sipher. The University of Waterloo CACR Archive, Technical report CACR 2017-06 (2017). http://cacr.uwaterloo.ca/techreports/2017/cacr2017-06.pdf

23. Rønjom, S.: Improving algebraic attacks on stream ciphers based on linear feedback shift register over $\mathbb{F}_{2^K}$. Des. Codes Crypt. **82**(1–2), 27–41 (2017)

24. Todo, Y.: Structural evaluation by generalized integral property. In: Oswald, E., Fischlin, M. (eds.) EUROCRYPT 2015, Part I. LNCS, vol. 9056, pp. 287–314. Springer, Heidelberg (2015). https://doi.org/10.1007/978-3-662-46800-5_12

25. Todo, Y., Isobe, T., Hao, Y., Meier, W.: Cube attacks on non-blackbox polynomials based on division property. In: Katz, J., Shacham, H. (eds.) CRYPTO 2017, Part III. LNCS, vol. 10403, pp. 250–279. Springer, Cham (2017). https://doi.org/10.1007/978-3-319-63697-9_9

26. Todo, Y., Morii, M.: Bit-based division property and application to SIMON family. In: Peyrin, T. (ed.) FSE 2016. LNCS, vol. 9783, pp. 357–377. Springer, Heidelberg (2016). https://doi.org/10.1007/978-3-662-52993-5_18

27. Vahid Amin Ghafari, H.H., Chen, Y.: Fruit: Ultra-lightweight stream cipher with shorter internal state. Cryptology ePrint Archive, Report 2016/355 (2016). http://eprint.iacr.org/2016/355
28. Xiang, Z., Zhang, W., Bao, Z., Lin, D.: Applying MILP method to searching integral distinguishers based on division property for 6 lightweight block ciphers. In: Cheon, J.H., Takagi, T. (eds.) ASIACRYPT 2016, Part I. LNCS, vol. 10031, pp. 648–678. Springer, Heidelberg (2016). https://doi.org/10.1007/978-3-662-53887-6_24

Lattice Attacks on Pairing-Based Signatures

Thierry Mefenza[1,2] and Damien Vergnaud[3,4(✉)]

[1] Département d'informatique de l'ENS, École normale supérieure, CNRS,
PSL Research University, 75005 Paris, France
[2] INRIA, Paris, France
[3] Sorbonne Universités, UPMC, CNRS, LIP6, Équipe Almasty, Paris, France
[4] Institut Universitaire de France, Paris, France
damien.vergnaud@ens.fr

Abstract. Practical implementations of cryptosystems often suffer from critical information leakage through side-channels (such as their power consumption or their electromagnetic emanations). For public-key cryptography on embedded systems, the core operation is usually group exponentiation – or scalar multiplication on elliptic curves – which is a sequence of group operations derived from the private-key that may reveal secret bits to an attacker (on an unprotected implementation).

We present lattice-based polynomial-time (heuristic) algorithms that recover the signer's secret in popular pairing-based signatures when used to sign several messages under the assumption that blocks of consecutive bits of the corresponding exponents are known by the attacker. Our techniques relies upon Coppersmith method and apply to all signatures in the so-called *exponent-inversion* framework in the standard security model (*i.e.* Boneh-Boyen and Gentry signatures) as well as in the random oracle model (*i.e.* Sakai-Kasahara signatures).

Keywords: Cryptanalysis · Side-channel attacks · Lattice attacks · Coppersmith's methods · Pairing-based signatures · Boneh-Boyen signatures · Gentry signatures · Modular Inversion Hidden Number Problem

1 Introduction

Pairing-based signatures. An identity-based encryption (IBE) scheme is a public key encryption scheme in which a user public key is its identity which may be an arbitrary string such as an email address, a phone number or any other identifier and the user private key is generated by a trusted authority called the private-key generator. In their seminal paper proposing the first IBE scheme, Boneh and Franklin [5] mentioned an interesting transform from an IBE scheme to a signature scheme (whose observation was attributed to Naor). The transformation is as follows: the private-key generator public key and secret key correspond to the public key and secret key of the signature scheme and the user private

© Springer International Publishing AG 2017
M. O'Neill (Ed.): IMACC 2017, LNCS 10655, pp. 352–370, 2017.
https://doi.org/10.1007/978-3-319-71045-7_18

key generation correspond to signatures generation. The well-known short signature scheme proposed by Boneh, Lynn and Shacham [7,8] can be seen as an application of Naor transformation to Boneh and Franklin IBE [5].

Pairings (or bilinear maps) are powerful mathematical constructs which have been used since 2000 to design numerous complex cryptographic protocols. There are three known pairing-based approaches to design IBE schemes [9]: *full-domain-hash* [5], *commutative-blinding* [3] and *exponent-inversion* [2–4]. We focus on the latter framework which gives rise to several short signature schemes thanks to Naor transformation.

Embedded devices and side-channel attacks. The pairing-based signature schemes are very well-suited for resource-limited devices since they produce short signatures and their generation involves only one scalar multiplication on an elliptic curve. In the recent years, theoretical attacks against elliptic curves have shown little improvements whereas *side-channel attacks* became a major threat against elliptic curves implementations [19,20]. These attacks are based on information gained from the physical leakage of a cryptosystem implementation (such as timing information, power consumption or electromagnetic leaks).

For elliptic-curve cryptography, the core operation is scalar multiplication which is usually computed with the binary method: the binary representation of the (secret) exponent is scanned; for the bit-value zero, a point-doubling is computed, whereas a point-doubling and a point-addition are calculated when the bit-value is one. Distinguishing point-doubling from point-addition in power traces can thus reveal the secret exponent. Classical countermeasures to this *simple power analysis* consist of using regular algorithms for scalar multiplication. In the more involved *differential power analysis*, the idea is to guess the secret bit-by-bit, and try to confirm or infirm the guess for each bit thanks to statistical analysis of several power traces. This approach requires that the same secret is used to perform several cryptographic operations but since pairing-based signatures in the exponent-inversion framework use a different exponent for each new signature, they seem immune to differential power analysis.

In [10], Chari, Rao and Rohatgi introduced the so-called *template attacks* which aim at exploiting side-channel information when only a limited number of leakage traces is available. These attacks require that the attacker is able to perform a profiling of the side-channel leakage. Countermeasures against simple power analysis attacks might not prevent such template-based attacks since they exploit data dependent leakages and not only operation dependent leakages. For pairing-based signatures in the exponent-inversion framework, the signature generation consists of a single scalar multiplication of a fixed base point where the exponent depends algebraically on the secret key, the message and some public randomness. Since the base point is fixed, the first bits of these variable exponents that are processed during the signature computation can only lead to a small set of points and we only need to build templates for the points in this (small) set. In this paper, we show that only a small number of bits of several such exponents is sufficient to determine the secret key via lattice attacks.

This approach is similar to lattice attacks [17,24,25] combined with template attacks [23] that were proposed against the standardized signature scheme DSA and ECDSA.

Contributions of the Paper

We consider several pairing-based signature schemes in the exponent-inversion framework. In [26], Sakai and Kasahara presented the first such scheme (whose security was analyzed in the random oracle model by Zhang, Safavi-Naini and Susilo in [27]). Boneh and Boyen [2] then presented the first pairing-based signature whose security can be proven in the standard security model. In 2006, Gentry [14] proposed yet another scheme using the exponent-inversion paradigm, with a tighter security proof than the earlier proposals.

   These schemes can be described in a general simplified form as follows. Let $\mathbb{G}$ and $\mathbb{G}_T$ be two cyclic groups of the same prime order p and let g be a generator of $\mathbb{G}$. We suppose that $(\mathbb{G}, \mathbb{G}_T)$ are equipped with an efficiently computable bilinear map $e : \mathbb{G} \times \mathbb{G} \to \mathbb{G}_T$. Let $\mathcal{H} : \{0,1\}^* \to \mathbb{Z}_q$ be a collision-resistant hash function. Let $f, g \in \mathbb{Z}_p[X, Y, M, R]$ be two polynomials of degree at most one in X and Y. The key generation picks uniformly at random two integers $(x, y) \in \mathbb{Z}_p$ as the signing secret key and outputs $(g^x, g^y) \in \mathbb{G}^2$ as the public-key. To sign a message $m \in \{0,1\}^*$, the signer picks uniformly at random $r \in \mathbb{Z}_p$, computes

$$\sigma = g^{f(x,y,\mathcal{H}(m),r)/g(x,y,\mathcal{H}(m),r)}$$

and outputs the pair (σ, r) as the signature. The validity of a signature is checked by verifying whether the following equality holds:

$$e(\sigma, g^{g(x,y,\mathcal{H}(m),r)}) = e(g^{f(x,y,\mathcal{H}(m),r)}, g)$$

where the elements $g^{f(x,y,\mathcal{H}(m),r)}$ and $g^{g(x,y,\mathcal{H}(m),r)}$ can be computed publicly from g^x, g^y, m and r. The three schemes use the following specific polynomials:

- **Sakai-Kasahara** [26]: $f(X,Y,M,R) = 1$, $g(X,Y,M,R) = X + M$
- **Boneh-Boyen** [2]: $f(X,Y,M,R) = 1$, $g(X,Y,M,R) = X + M + YR$
- **Gentry** [14]: $f(X,Y,M,R) = Y + R$, $g(X,Y,M,R) = X + M$

   We present lattice-based polynomial-time algorithms that recover the signer's secret $(x, y) \in \mathbb{Z}_p^2$ in these pairing-based signatures when used to sign a constant number of messages under the assumption that blocks of consecutive bits of the corresponding exponents $f(x, y, \mathcal{H}(m), r)/g(x, y, \mathcal{H}(m), r)$ modulo p are known by the attacker. We consider known-message attacks and chosen-message attacks (*i.e.* where the attacker is allowed to choose the message m). The method of this paper is heuristic and uses Coppersmith's lattice technique. Let ℓ denote the bit-length of p and N denote the number of unknown blocks of each signing exponent. In a nutshell, we show that one can recover the secret key if the number of consecutive bits of each unknown block is smaller than the following theoretical values:

- **Sakai-Kasahara:** $\ell/2N^2$
- **Boneh-Boyen:** $\ell/2N^2$
- **Gentry:** ℓ/N

provided that the number of signatures is sufficiently large (see the corresponding sections in the paper for more precise bounds). It is interesting to note, that Gentry scheme which provides the best classical security (tight security reduction in the standard security model), is the weakest against our class of attacks.

More generally, our lattice-based algorithms can be seen as methods to solve variants of the *modular inversion hidden number problem* which was introduced by Boneh, Halevi and Howgrave-Graham in 2001 [6]. This problem is to find a hidden number given several integers and partial bits of the corresponding modular inverse integers of the sums of the known integers and that unknown integer. It was used in [6] to built a pseudo-random number generator and a message authentication code scheme. In [22], the authors mentioned that it is interesting to study a general problem of recovering of an unknown rational function. One can see our results as a first step towards solving this problem.

The efficiency of our (heuristic) attacks has been validated experimentally.

2   Coppersmith Method

We provide a short description of the Coppersmith method [11,12] for finding small roots of a multivariate modular polynomial system of equations modulo an integer p. We refer the reader to [18] for details and proofs.

Problem Definition. Let $f_1(y_1, \ldots, y_n), \ldots, f_s(y_1, \ldots, y_n)$ be irreducible multivariate polynomials defined over $\mathbb{Z}$, having a root $(x_1, \ldots, x_n)$ modulo a known integer p namely for $i \in \{1, \ldots, s\}$, we have $f_i(x_1, \ldots, x_n) \equiv 0 \mod p$. Our goal is to recover the desired root $(x_1, \ldots, x_n)$. This problem is generally intractable but becomes solvable (under some conditions) in polynomial time $\log(p)^{O(1)}$ (for constant n and constant total degree of the input polynomials) if the root $(x_1, \ldots, x_n)$ is upper-bounded by some values $(X_1, \ldots, X_n)$ that depends on p and the degree of the polynomials $f_1, \ldots, f_s$.

Polynomials Collection. In a first step, one generates a larger collection $\mathfrak{P}$ of polynomials $\{\tilde{f}_1, \ldots, \tilde{f}_r\}$ linearly independent having $(x_1, \ldots, x_n)$ as a root modulo p^m, for some positive integer m. Usually, the technique consists in taking product of powers of the modulus p, the polynomials f_i for $i \in \{1, \ldots, s\}$ and some well-chosen monomials, such as

$$\tilde{f}_\ell = p^{m - \sum_{j=1}^{s} k_{j,\ell}} y_1^{\alpha_{1,\ell}} \cdots y_n^{\alpha_{n,\ell}} f_1^{k_{1,\ell}} \cdots f_s^{k_{s,\ell}}$$

for some positive integers $\alpha_{1,\ell}, \ldots, \alpha_{n,\ell}, k_{1,\ell}, k_{s,\ell}$. These polynomials satisfy $\tilde{f}_\ell(x_1, \ldots, x_n) \equiv 0 \mod p^m$.

Lattice Construction. In a second step, one denotes as $\mathfrak{M}$ the set of monomials appearing in collection of polynomials $\mathfrak{P}$, and one writes the polynomials $\tilde{f}_i(y_1 X_1, \ldots, y_n X_n)$ for $i \in \{1, \ldots, r\}$ as a vector $b_i \in (\mathbb{Z})^\omega$, where $\omega = \sharp\mathfrak{M}$. One then constructs a lattice $\mathcal{L}$ generated by the vectors $b_1, \ldots, b_r$ and computes its reduced basis using the LLL algorithm [21].

Lemma 1. *Let $\mathcal{L}$ be a lattice of dimension ω. In polynomial time, the LLL algorithm given as input of basis of $\mathcal{L}$ outputs a reduced basis of $\mathcal{L}$ formed by vectors v_i, $1 \leqslant i \leqslant \omega$ that satisfy:*

$$\|v_1\| \leqslant \|v_2\| \leqslant \ldots \leqslant \|v_2\| \leqslant 2^{\frac{\omega(\omega-1)}{4(\omega+1-i)}} \det(L)^{\frac{1}{\omega+1-i}}.$$

Generating New Polynomials. In a third step of the method, one combines Lemma 2 below (from [16]) and Lemma 1 to obtain n multivariate polynomials $g_1(y_1, \ldots, y_n), \ldots, g_n(y_1, \ldots, y_n)$ having $(x_1, \ldots, x_n)$ as a root over the integers.

Lemma 2 (Howgrave-Graham). *Let $h(y_1, \ldots, y_n)$ be a polynomial over $\mathbb{Z}$ having at most ω monomials. Suppose that:*

1. *$h(x_1, \ldots, x_n) = 0 \bmod W$ for some $|x_1| < X_1, \ldots, |x_n| < X_n$ and,*
2. *$\|h(X_1 y_1, \ldots, X_n y_n)\| \leqslant \frac{W}{\sqrt{\omega}}$. Then $h(x_1, \ldots, x_n) = 0$ holds over the integers.*

The LLL algorithm run on the lattice $\mathcal{L}$ to obtain n reduced vectors v_i, $i \in \{1, \ldots, n\}$ that we see as some polynomials $\tilde{h}_i(y_1 X_1, \ldots, y_n X_n)$, $i \in \{1, \ldots, n\}$. One can see that for $i \in \{1, \ldots, n\}$, $\tilde{h}_i(x_1, \ldots, x_n) = 0 \bmod p^m$, since $\tilde{h}_i$ is a linear combination of $\tilde{f}_1, \ldots, \tilde{f}_r$. Then if the following condition holds:

$$2^{\frac{r(r-1)}{4(r+1-n)}} \det(L)^{\frac{1}{r+1-n}} < \frac{p^m}{\sqrt{\omega}},$$

by Lemmas 1 and 2, $\tilde{h}_i(x_1, \ldots, x_n) = 0$, $i \in \{1, \ldots, n\}$ holds over the integers and we then obtain n polynomials having $(x_1, \ldots, x_n)$ as a root over the integers.

Condition. In our attacks, the number of polynomials in the first step is equal to the number of monomials that appears in the collection, so $r = \omega = \sharp\mathfrak{M}$. In the analysis, we let (as usual in this setting) terms that do not depend on p contribute to an error term ε, and the simplified condition becomes:

$$\det(L) < p^{m(\omega+1-n)}.$$

Under the (heuristic) assumption that all created polynomials in the third step define an algebraic variety of dimension 0, the previous system can be solved (e.g., using elimination techniques such as resultant computation or Gröbner basis) and the desired root recovered in polynomial time[1] $\log(p)^{O(1)}$ (for constant

---

[1] It is well known that the computational complexity of Gröbner basis algorithm may be exponential or even doubly exponential. In our setting, the number of variables and the total degree of the input polynomials are fixed and the theoretical complexity is polynomial in the field size (and thus in the security parameter).

n and constant total degree of the input polynomials). In this paper, we assume that these polynomials define an algebraic variety of dimension 0 and we justify the validity of our attacks by computer experiments.

3 Lattice Attack on Gentry Signatures

3.1 Gentry Signatures

As mentioned in the introduction, Gentry introduced in [14] an IBE scheme without random oracles with short public parameters and tight security reduction in the standard security model. In this paragraph, we describe the signature scheme obtained by applying Naor transformation to Gentry's IBE. The resulting scheme achieves existential unforgeability under chosen-message attacks in the standard security model.

Let $\mathbb{G}$ and $\mathbb{G}_T$ be two cyclic groups of the same prime order p (where $p > 2^{2\lambda}$ for a security parameter λ) and let g be a generator of $\mathbb{G}$. We suppose that $(\mathbb{G}, \mathbb{G}_T)$ are equipped with an efficient computable bilinear map $e : \mathbb{G} \times \mathbb{G} \to \mathbb{G}_T$. Let $\mathcal{H} : \{0,1\}^* \to \mathbb{Z}_q$ be a collision-resistant hash function. Gentry signature scheme is defined by the three following algorithms:

- **Key generation.** The user picks uniformly at random $(x, y) \in \mathbb{Z}_p^2$, computes $h_1 = g^x$ and $h_2 = g^y$ and sets $\mathsf{sk} = (x, y)$ and $\mathsf{pk} = (h_1, h_2) \in \mathbb{G}^2$.
- **Signature generation.** Given a message $m \in \{0,1\}^*$, the user computes its hash value $\mathcal{H}(m)$, and picks uniformly at random $r \in \mathbb{Z}_p$. It computes the *signing exponent* $\sigma = (y + r)/(x + \mathcal{H}(m)) \bmod p$ and the group element $s = g^\sigma$. The signature is the pair $(r, s) \in \mathbb{Z}_p \times \mathbb{G}$.
- **Signature verification.** Given $(r, s) \in \mathbb{Z}_p \times \mathbb{G}$, a verifier accepts it as a signature on $m \in \{0,1\}^*$ if and only if the following equality holds:

$$e(s, h_2 g^r) \overset{?}{=} e\left(g, h_1 g^{\mathcal{H}(m)}\right)$$

3.2 Description of the Attack

In this section, we use Coppersmith's methods to attack Gentry's signatures when the attacker learns some blocks of consecutive bits of the signing exponents.

Let $n \geqslant 1$ be some integer. We suppose that the attacker is given $(n + 2)$ message/signature pairs $(m_i, (r_i, s_i))_{i \in \{0, \dots, n+1\}}$ as described above (where n does not depend on the security parameter λ). To simplify the notation in the following, instead of the hash values $\mathcal{H}(m_i)$, we assume that the m_i belongs to $\mathbb{Z}_p$ (for $i \in \{0, \dots, n+1\}$).

We assume that the attacker knows some blocks of consecutive bits of the corresponding signing exponents σ_i for $i \in \{0, \dots, n+1\}$ and its goal is to recover the secret keys x and y. From the knowledge of two different signing exponents σ_i and σ_j for integers $i, j \in \{0, \dots, n+1\}$ with $i \neq j$, the attacker can actually recover the secrets x and y. Its goal is therefore to recover the hidden bits of two σ_i's in order to obtain x and y.

We have $\sigma_i = (y + r_i)/(x + m_i) \bmod p$ for $i \in \{0, \ldots, n+1\}$ which can be rewritten as:

$$\sigma_i(x + m_i) - y - r_i = 0 \bmod p, \quad i \in \{0, \ldots, n+1\}.$$

We consider a chosen-message attack where the attacker uses an arbitrary unique message m for all signatures (i.e. $m_i = m$ for all $i \in \{0, \ldots, n+1\}$). Eliminating x and y, in the previous equation, we obtain for $a, b, i \in \{0, \ldots, n+1\}$ with $0 \leqslant a < b < i \leqslant n+1$:

$$(r_a - r_b)\sigma_i + (r_i - r_a)\sigma_b + (r_b - r_i)\sigma_a = 0 \bmod p$$

Putting $\sigma_i = \sum_{j=1}^{N} x_{i,j} 2^{k_{i,j}} + \gamma_i$, $i \in \{0, \ldots, n+1\}$, where γ_i is known to the attacker and $x_{i,j}, j \in \{1, \ldots, N\}$ are unknown and $|x_{i,j}| < 2^{\mu_{i,j}}$ for some integer $\mu_{i,j}$ and with the choice $a = 0$, $b = 1$, we obtain a polynomial

$$f_i(z_{0,1}, \ldots, z_{0,N}, \ldots, z_{n+1,1}, \ldots, z_{n+1,N})$$

having as root $X_0 = (x_{0,1}, \ldots, x_{0,N}, \ldots, x_{n+1,1}, \ldots, x_{n+1,N})$ modulo p with:

$$f_i = z_{i,N} + \sum_{j=1}^{N-1} a_{i,j} z_{i,j} + \sum_{j=1}^{N} b_{i,j} z_{1,j} + \sum_{j=1}^{N} c_{i,j} z_{0,j} + \gamma_i(r_0 - r_1) + d_i \bmod p$$

for $i \in \{2, \ldots, n+1\}$, where

$$\begin{cases} a_{i,j} = 2^{k_{i,j}}/2^{k_{i,N}} \bmod p \\ b_{i,j} = 2^{k_{1,j}}(r_i - r_0)/((r_0 - r_1)2^{k_{i,N}}) \bmod p \\ c_{i,j} = 2^{k_{0,j}}(r_1 - r_i)/((r_0 - r_1)2^{k_{i,N}}) \bmod p \\ d_i = (\gamma_i(r_0 - r_1) + \gamma_1(r_i - r_0) + \gamma_0(r_1 - r_i))/((r_0 - r_1)2^{k_{i,N}}) \bmod p \end{cases}$$

for $i \in \{2, \ldots, n+1\}$ and $j \in \{1, \ldots, N\}$.

We consider the following collection of polynomials (parameterized by some integer $m \in \mathbb{N}$ that does not depend on the security parameter λ):

$$\mathfrak{P}_m = \left\{ f_{i_{0,1}, \ldots, i_{n+1,1}, i_{0,2}, \ldots, i_{n+1,2}, \ldots, i_{0,N}, \ldots, i_{n+1,N}} \right\},$$

for all vectors of integers $(i_{0,1}, \ldots, i_{n+1,1}, i_{0,2}, \ldots, i_{n+1,2}, \ldots, i_{0,N}, \ldots, i_{n+1,N})$ verifying

$$0 \leqslant i_{0,1} + \cdots + i_{n+1,1} + \cdots + i_{0,N}, \ldots, i_{n+1,N} \leqslant m$$

and where the polynomial $f_{i_{0,1}, \ldots, i_{n+1,1}, i_{0,2}, \ldots, i_{n+1,2}, \ldots, i_{0,N}, \ldots, i_{n+1,N}}$ is defined by:

$$z_{0,1}^{i_{0,1}} \cdots z_{n+1,1}^{i_{n+1,1}} \cdots z_{0,N-1}^{i_{0,N-1}} \cdots z_{n+1,N-1}^{i_{n+1,N-1}} z_{0,N}^{i_{0,N}} z_{1,N}^{i_{1,N}} f_2^{i_{2,N}} \cdots f_{n+1}^{i_{n+1,N}} p^{m-(i_{2,N}+\cdots+i_{n+1,N})}.$$

One can see that $f_{i_{0,1}, \ldots, i_{n+1,1}, i_{0,2}, \ldots, i_{n+1,2}, \ldots, i_{0,N}, \ldots, i_{n+1,N}}(X_0) = 0 \bmod p^m$ for all such vector of integers.

If we use for instance the lexicographical monomial order (with $z_{i,j} < z_{i',j'}$ if $(j < j'$ or $(j = j'$ and $i < i'))$ on the set of monomials, we can define an order over the set of polynomials as:

$$f_{i_{0,1}, \ldots, i_{n+1,1}, i_{0,2}, \ldots, i_{n+1,2}, \ldots, i_{0,N}, \ldots, i_{n+1,N}} < f_{i'_{0,1}, \ldots, i'_{n+1,1}, i'_{0,2}, \ldots, i'_{n+1,2}, \ldots, i'_{0,N}, \ldots, i'_{n+1,N}}$$

if $z_{0,1}^{i_{0,1}} \cdots z_{n+1,1}^{i_{n+1,1}} \cdots z_{0,N}^{i_{0,N}} \cdots z_{n+1,N}^{i_{n+1,N}} < z_{0,1}^{i'_{0,1}} \cdots z_{n+1,1}^{i'_{n+1,1}} \cdots z_{0,N}^{i'_{0,N}} \cdots z_{n+1,N}^{i'_{n+1,N}}$.

Using this order, we can write $\mathfrak{P}_m = \{\tilde{f}_i, i \in \{1,\ldots,\omega\}\}$, with $\tilde{f}_1 < \tilde{f}_2 < \cdots < \tilde{f}_\omega$ where ω is the number of polynomials. Putting $U = 2^{\max_{i,j} \mu_{i,j}}$, we define the lattice $\mathcal{L}$ generated by $b_1,\ldots,b_\omega$, where for $i \in \{1,\ldots,\omega\}$, b_i is the coefficient vector of the polynomial $\tilde{f}_i(U z_{0,1}, \ldots, U z_{n+1,1}, \ldots, U z_{0,N}, \ldots, U z_{n+1,N})$.

One can easily verify that the basis matrix is lower triangular and the diagonal elements are $U^a p^{m-(i_{2,N}+\cdots+i_{n+1,N})}$, where the integer a is equal to $i_{0,1} + \cdots + i_{n+1,1} + i_{0,N} + \cdots + i_{n+1,N}$. The number of variables is $N(n+2)$ and the success condition of Coppersmith's method is $\det(\mathcal{L}) < p^{m(\omega-N(n+2))}$, where $\omega = \sum_{i \in I} 1$ is the dimension of the lattice with

$$I = \{\mathbf{i} = (i_{0,1}, \ldots, i_{0,N}, \ldots, i_{n+1,N}) | 0 \leqslant i_{0,1} + \cdots + i_{n+1,N} \leqslant m\}.$$

We have $\det(\mathcal{L}) = U^\eta p^{m\omega} p^{-\mu}$ with

$$\mu = \sum_{i \in I} i_{2,N} + \cdots + i_{n+1,N} \text{ and } \eta = \sum_{i \in I} i_{0,1} + \cdots + i_{n+1,N}.$$

If m is large, we can neglect the $N(n+2)$ term in Coppersmith success condition and the asymptotic condition becomes:

$$U^\eta < p^\mu.$$

Using analytic combinatorics methods (see for instance [1] and the references therein), one can verify that when m tends to ∞, we have $\eta = N(n+2)\beta(m,N,n)$ and $\mu = n\beta(m,N,n)$, with

$$\beta(m,N,n) = \frac{m^{N(n+2)+1}}{(N(n+2)+1)!} + o(m^{N(n+2)+1}).$$

Therefore, the attacker can recover x and y as long as the sizes of each unknown block in the signatures σ_i for $i \in \{0,\ldots,n+1\}$ satisfies:

$$U < p^{\frac{n}{(n+2)N}} \underset{n \to \infty}{\longrightarrow} p^{\frac{1}{N}}.$$

We can thus heuristically recover (using large[2] constant parameters n and m) the secret key (x,y) if the number of consecutive bits of each unknown block is smaller than $\lceil \log_2(p) \rceil / N$.

3.3   Experimental Results

We have implemented the attack in Sage 7.6 on a MacBook Air laptop computer (2,2 GHz Intel Core i7, 4 Gb RAM 1600 MHz DDR3, Mac OSX 10.10.5). Table 1

---

[2] In order to reach this asymptotic bound, the constructed matrix is of huge dimension and the resulting polynomial system has a very large number of variables and the computation which is theoretically polynomial-time becomes in practice prohibitive.

lists the theoretical bound $\delta_{\text{theo}} = \frac{n}{(n+2)N}$ and an experimental bound δ_{exp} for a 512-bit prime p (corresponding to a 256-bit security level) with $(n+2)$ signatures (for $n \in \{1, 3, 5\}$) and a few number of unknown blocks ($N \leqslant 2$). We consider the family of polynomials $\mathfrak{P}_m$ with $m = 4$ and $m = 2$. We ran 2^7 experiments for all parameters and Table 1 gives the average running time (in seconds) of the LLL algorithm and the Gröbner basis computation.

Table 1. Lattice Attack on Gentry signatures. Average running time (in seconds) of the LLL algorithm and the Gröbner basis computation.

N	n	δ_{theo}	δ_{exp}	Dimension	m	LLL time(s)	Gröbner basis time(s)
1	1	0.333	0.32	35	4	3.804	4.603
1	3	0.6	0.49	21	2	0.250	0.699
1	5	0.714	0.49	36	2	0.871	38.374
2	1	0.166	0.16	28	2	1.438	0.650
2	5	0.33	0.29	91	2	191.906	556.715

We denote α the maximum number of least significant bits that the attacker knows in each signature σ_j, for all $j \neq 0$ (for instance $\alpha = 0$ means that it does not know any least significant bits of the signatures σ_j, for all $j \in \{1, \ldots, n+1\}$). If we know at least $\delta_{\text{exp}} \lceil \log_2(p) \rceil + \alpha$ least significant bits of the signature σ_0 then the Gröbner basis always gives us a system of dimension 0 and we are able to find the N unknown block of sizes $p^{\delta_{\text{exp}}}$ in each signature σ_i for $i \in \{0, \ldots, n+1\}$. Otherwise, Gröbner basis computations gives us a system of dimension 1 and we are *a priori* unable to find the unknown blocks (though it is possible in some cases to obtain additional information). This system of dimension 1 occurs because the constructed system admits a large number of "small" solutions. We give an example of this in Appendix A. However, If the condition mentioned above is satisfied, we obtain for $N = 1$ and $n + 2 = 3$, the success rates given in Table 2 (over 250 attacks performed for each parameter pair (m, δ_{exp})).

Table 2. Lattice attack on Gentry signatures. Success rates (over 250 attacks performed for each parameter pair (m, δ_{exp})

	$m = 2$	$m = 3$	$m = 4$
$\delta_{\text{exp}} = 0.3225$	100	100	100
$\delta_{\text{exp}} = 0.3250$	98.4	98.4	99.2
$\delta_{\text{exp}} = 0.3275$	90.4	92.8	94.4
$\delta_{\text{exp}} = 0.3300$	66.0	65.2	72.8
$\delta_{\text{exp}} = 0.3325$	10.0	15.2	17.2
$\delta_{\text{exp}} = 0.3350$	0	0	0

4   Lattice Attack on Boneh-Boyen Signatures

4.1   Boneh-Boyen Signatures

Two years before the proposal of Gentry's IBE, Boneh and Boyen proposed two IBE schemes in [2] and described one signature scheme obtained using the Naor transformation in [3]. Their scheme has comparable efficiency properties and also achieves existential unforgeability under chosen-message attacks in the standard security model.

With the same notation as above, Boneh-Boyen signature scheme is defined by the three following algorithms:

- **Key generation.** The user picks uniformly at random $(x, y) \in \mathbb{Z}_p^2$, computes $h_1 = g^x$ and $h_2 = g^y$ and sets $\mathsf{sk} = (x, y)$ and $\mathsf{pk} = (h_1, h_2) \in \mathbb{G}^2$.
- **Signature generation.** Given a message $m \in \{0, 1\}^*$, the user computes its hash value $\mathcal{H}(m)$, and picks uniformly at random $r \in \mathbb{Z}_p$. It computes the *signing exponent* $s = 1/(x + \mathcal{H}(m) + yr) \bmod p$ and the group element $\sigma = g^s$. The signature is the pair $(r, \sigma) \in \mathbb{Z}_p \times \mathbb{G}$.
- **Signature verification.** Given $(r, \sigma) \in \mathbb{Z}_p \times \mathbb{G}$, a verifier accepts it as a signature on $m \in \{0, 1\}^*$ if and only if the following equality holds:

$$e(\sigma, h_1 \cdot g^{\mathcal{H}(m)} \cdot h_2^r) \stackrel{?}{=} e(g, g)$$

4.2   Description of the Attack

In this section, we use the Coppersmith's methods to attack Boneh-Boyen's signature. Let $n \geqslant 1$ be some integer. We suppose that the attacker is given $(n + 2)$ message/signature pairs $(m_i, (r_i, s_i))_{i \in \{0, \ldots, n+1\}}$ as described above (where n does not depend on the security parameter λ). As above, to simplify the notation, we replace $\mathcal{H}(m_i)$ by $m_i \in \mathbb{Z}_p$ (for $i \in \{0, \ldots, n+1\}$). We assume that the attacker knows some blocks of consecutive bits of the corresponding signing exponents $\sigma_i = 1/(x + m + yr_i) \bmod p$, for $i \in \{0, \ldots, n\}$, where p, r_i and m_i are known to the attacker and x and y are kept secret.

As for Gentry signatures, from the knowledge of two different signing exponents, the attacker can actually recover the secrets x and y and its goal is to recover the hidden bits of two σ_i's in order to recover x and y.

We have $\sigma_i = 1/(x + m_i + yr_i) \bmod p$ for $i \in \{0, \ldots, n+1\}$ and we have:

$$x + m_i + yr_i - \frac{1}{\sigma_i} = 0 \bmod p, \quad i \in \{0, \ldots, n+1\}.$$

Eliminating x and y and assuming again that the attacker chooses a unique message m (namely $m_i = m$, for all $i \in \{0, \ldots, n+1\}$), we obtain, for $a, b, i \in \{0, \ldots, n+1\}$ with $0 \leqslant a < b < i \leqslant n+1$:

$$(r_b - r_i)\sigma_i\sigma_b + (r_i - r_a)\sigma_i\sigma_a + (r_a - r_b)\sigma_a\sigma_b = 0 \bmod p.$$

Putting $\sigma_i = \sum_{j=1}^{N} x_{i,j} 2^{k_{i,j}} + \gamma_i$, $i \in \{0, \ldots, n+1\}$, where γ_i is known to the attacker and $x_{i,j}$, $j \in \{1, \ldots, N\}$ are unknown with $|x_{i,j}| < 2^{\mu_{i,j}}$ for some integer $\mu_{i,j}$ and $a = 0$, we obtain a polynomial $f_{0,b,i}(z_{0,1}, \ldots, z_{0,N}, \ldots, z_{n+1,1}, \ldots, z_{n+1,N})$ having as "small" root $X_0 = (x_{0,1}, \ldots, x_{0,N}, \ldots, x_{n+1,1}, \ldots, x_{n+1,N})$ modulo p, where:

$$f_{0,b,i} = \sum_{j=1}^{N}\sum_{k=1}^{N} \alpha_{b,i,j,k} z_{i,j} z_{b,k} + \sum_{j=1}^{N}\sum_{k=1}^{N} \alpha_{0,i,j,k} z_{i,j} z_{0,k} + \sum_{j=1}^{N}\sum_{k=1}^{N} \alpha_{0,b,j,k} z_{b,j} z_{0,k}$$

$$+ \sum_{j=1}^{N} \alpha_{0,b,i,j} z_{i,j} + \sum_{j=1}^{N} \beta_{0,b,i,j} z_{b,j} + \sum_{j=1}^{N} \gamma_{0,b,i,j} z_{0,j} + \delta_{0,b,i} \bmod p$$

for $b, i \in \{1, \ldots, n+1\}$, $b < i$ and with known coefficients, where $\alpha_{b,i,N,N} = 1$. The set of monomials appearing in the polynomials $f_{0,b,i}$ is:

$$\mathfrak{M} = \left\{ 1, z_{a,j} z_{b,k}, z_{i,j} : i \in \{0, \ldots, n+1\} \middle| \begin{matrix} a, b \in \{0, \ldots, n+1\}; a < b \\ j, k \in \{0, \ldots, N\} \end{matrix} \right\}.$$

We consider the following set of polynomials:

$$\mathfrak{P} = \{p\tilde{m}, \tilde{m} \in \mathfrak{M}_1\} \cup \{f_{0,b,i} : b, i \in \{1, \ldots, n+1\}; b < i\},$$

where $\mathfrak{M}_1 = \mathfrak{M} \setminus \mathfrak{M}_2$ with $\mathfrak{M}_2 = \{z_{b,N} z_{i,N} : b, i \in \{1, \ldots, n+1\}; b < i\}$. One can see that for any polynomial $\tilde{f} \in \mathfrak{P}$, $\tilde{f}(X_0) = 0 \bmod p$. We can define an order on the set of monomials such that all the monomials in $\mathfrak{M}_1$ are smaller than any monomial in $\mathfrak{M}_2$ and for $z_{b,N} z_{i,N}, z_{b',N} z_{i',N} \in \mathfrak{M}_2$, $z_{b,N} z_{i,N} < z_{b',N} z_{i',N}$ if $(b < b'$ or $(b = b'$ and $i < i'))$.

Using that order, we can order the set of polynomials from the smallest element to the greatest as follows:

$$\mathfrak{P} = \{p\tilde{m}_1, \ldots, p\tilde{m}_{\omega_1}, f_{0,1,2}, \ldots, f_{0,1,n+1}, f_{0,2,3}, \ldots, f_{0,2,n+1}, \ldots, f_{0,n,n+1}\}$$
$$= \{\tilde{f}_1, \ldots, \tilde{f}_\omega\}$$

where $\tilde{m}_1 < \cdots < \tilde{m}_{\omega_1}$, ω_1 is the cardinality of $\mathfrak{M}_1$ and ω is the cardinality of $\mathfrak{M}$.

Putting $U = 2^{\max_{i,j} \mu_{i,j}}$, we define the lattice $\mathcal{L}$ generated by $b_1, \ldots, b_\omega$, where for each $i \in \{1, \ldots, \omega\}$, b_i is the coefficient vector of the polynomial

$$\tilde{f}_i(U z_{0,1}, \ldots, U z_{0,N}, \ldots, U z_{n+1,1}, \ldots, U z_{n+1,N}).$$

One can verify that the basis matrix is lower triangular. The number of variables is $N(n+2)$ and the success condition for the Coppersmith's method is:

$$\det(\mathcal{L}) < p^{\omega - N(n+2)+1}, \text{ with } \omega = \sharp \mathfrak{M} = N^2 \frac{(n+1)(n+2)}{2} + (n+2)N + 1.$$

We have $\det(\mathcal{L}) = U^{2N^2 \frac{(n+1)(n+2)}{2} + (n+2)N} p^{\omega - \frac{n(n+1)}{2}}$ and the success condition becomes:

$$U < p^{\frac{\frac{n(n+1)}{2} - N(n+2) + 1}{2N^2 \frac{(n+1)(n+2)}{2} + (n+2)N}}.$$

If n is large and since N is small, we can neglect $-N(n+2)+1$ which contribute to a small error term. So the attacker can recover x and y as long as the sizes of each unknown block in the signatures σ_i, $i \in \{0, \dots, n+1\}$ satisfies:

$$U < p^{\frac{n(n+1)}{2N^2(n+1)(n+2)+2(n+2)N}} \xrightarrow[n \to \infty]{} p^{\frac{1}{2N^2}}.$$

We can thus heuristically recover the secret key if the number of consecutive bits of each unknown block is smaller than $\lceil \log_2(p) \rceil / (2N^2)$.

4.3   Experimental Results

Table 3 lists the theoretical bound $\delta_{\text{theo}} = \frac{n(n+1)}{2N^2(n+1)(n+2)+2(n+2)N}$ and an experimental bound δ_{exp} for a 512-bit prime p with $(n+2)$ signatures for a few values of $n \in \{4, 6, 10\}$ and one or two unknown blocks per signatures.

Table 3. Lattice Attack on Boneh-Boyen signatures. Average running time (in seconds) of the LLL algorithm and the Gröbner basis computation.

N	n	δ_{theo}	δ_{exp}	dimension	LLL time(s)	Gröbner basis time(s)
1	4	0.277	0.293	22	0.205	0.048
1	6	0.306	0.31	29	1.961	1.008
1	10	0.382	0.38	79	75.086	39.669
2	4	0.076	0.08	73	9.185	3.078
2	6	0.087	0.09	129	232.698	397.900

We ran 2^7 experiments for all parameters and in all cases (for the bound δ_{exp}), the assumption that the created polynomials define an algebraic variety of dimension 0 was verified. The constructed system was solved using Gröbner basis and the desired root recovered. Table 3 gives the average running time (in seconds) of the LLL algorithm and the Gröbner basis computation (using the same configuration as above).

5   Lattice Attack on Sakai-Kasahara Signatures

5.1   Sakai-Kasahara Signatures

In [26], Sakai and Kasahara presented the first pairing-based signature scheme in the exponent-inversion framework. Their scheme is very close to Boneh-Boyen signature schemes but produces shorter signatures (at the cost of relying on the random oracle heuristic [27]).

With the same notation as above, Sakai-Kasahara signature scheme is defined by the three following algorithms:

- **Key generation.** The user picks uniformly at random $x \in \mathbb{Z}_p$, computes $h = g^x$ and sets $\mathsf{sk} = x$ and $\mathsf{pk} = h \in \mathbb{G}$.
- **Signature generation.** Given a message $m \in \{0,1\}^*$, the user computes its hash value $\mathcal{H}(m)$. It computes the *signing exponent* $s = 1/(x + \mathcal{H}(m)) \bmod p$ and the group element $\sigma = g^s$. The signature is the group element $\sigma \in \mathbb{G}$.
- **Signature verification.** Given $\sigma \in \mathbb{G}$, a verifier accepts it as a signature on $m \in \{0,1\}^*$ if and only if the following equality holds:

$$e(\sigma, h \cdot g^{\mathcal{H}(m)}) \stackrel{?}{=} e(g,g)$$

We present in the following an attack on this scheme when the attacker learns some blocks of consecutive bits of the signing exponents. This computational problem is related to the Modular Inversion Hidden Number Problem which was introduced in 2001 by Boneh, Halevi and Howgrave-Graham [6]. In this problem, the attacker does not know exactly one block of least significant bits of the signing exponents σ_i while our attack considers the setting where the attacker does not know $N \geqslant 1$ different blocks in each σ_i (for any N).

5.2   Description of the Attack

In this section, we use the Coppersmith's methods to attack Sakai-Kasahara signatures. Let $n \geqslant 1$ be some integer. We suppose that the attacker is given $(n+1)$ message/signature pairs $(m_i, s_i)_{i \in \{0,\ldots,n+1\}}$ as described above (where n does not depend on the security parameter λ). Again, to simplify the notation, we replace $\mathcal{H}(m_i)$ by $m_i \in \mathbb{Z}_p$ (for $i \in \{0,\ldots,n+1\}$). We assume that the attacker knows some blocks of consecutive bits of the corresponding signing exponents $\sigma_i = 1/(x + m_i) \bmod p$ for $i \in \{0,\ldots,n\}$ and its goal is to recover x. One can see that from the knowledge of a value σ_i, the attacker can actually recover the hidden number x and it is thus sufficient to recover the hidden bits of a single σ_i's in order to recover x.

We have $\sigma_i = 1/(x + m_i) \bmod p$ for $i \in \{0,\ldots,n\}$ which can be rewritten as:

$$x + m_i - \frac{1}{\sigma_i} = 0 \bmod p, \quad i \in \{0,\ldots,n\}.$$

Eliminating x, we obtain:

$$(m_i - m_a)\sigma_i\sigma_a + \sigma_i - \sigma_a = 0 \bmod p \quad a, i \in \{0,\ldots,n\}, 0 \leqslant a < i \leqslant n.$$

Putting, for $i \in \{0,\ldots,n+1\}$, $\sigma_i = \sum_{j=1}^{N} x_{i,j} 2^{k_{i,j}} + \gamma_i$, where γ_i is known to the attacker and $x_{i,j}$ for $j \in \{1,\ldots,N\}$ are unknown with $|x_{i,j}| < 2^{\mu_{i,j}}$ for some integer $\mu_{i,j}$, we obtain a polynomial $f_{a,i}(z_{0,1}, \ldots, z_{0,N}, \ldots, z_{n,1}, \ldots, z_{n,N})$ having as root $X_0 = (x_{0,1}, \ldots, x_{0,N}, \ldots, x_{n,1}, \ldots, x_{n,N})$ modulo p with:

$$f_{a,i} = \sum_{j=1}^{N}\sum_{k=1}^{N} \alpha_{a,i,j,k} z_{i,j} z_{a,k} + \sum_{j=1}^{N} \beta_{a,i,j} z_{i,j} + \sum_{j=1}^{N} \gamma_{a,i,j} x_{a,j} + \delta_{a,i} \bmod p$$

for $a, i \in \{0, \ldots, n\}$, $a < i$ and with known coefficients, where $\alpha_{a,i,N,N} = 1$. The set of monomials appearing in the polynomials $f_{a,i}$ is:

$$\mathfrak{M} = \{1, z_{a,j} z_{b,k}, z_{i,j} : i \in \{0, \ldots, n\}; a, b \in \{0, \ldots, n\}; a < b; j, k \in \{1, \ldots, N\}\}.$$

We consider the following set of polynomials:

$$\mathfrak{P} = \{p\tilde{m}, \tilde{m} \in \mathfrak{M}_1\} \cup \{f_{a,i} : a, i \in \{0, \ldots, n\}; a < i\},$$

where $\mathfrak{M}_1 = \mathfrak{M} \setminus \mathfrak{M}_2$ with $\mathfrak{M}_2 = \{z_{a,N} z_{i,N} : a, i \in \{0, \ldots, n\}; a < i\}$. One can see that for any polynomial $\tilde{f} \in \mathfrak{P}$, $\tilde{f}(X_0) = 0 \bmod p$. We can define an order on the set of monomials such that all the monomials in $\mathfrak{M}_1$ are smaller than any monomial in $\mathfrak{M}_2$ and for $z_{a,N} z_{i,N}, z_{a',N} z_{i',N} \in \mathfrak{M}_2$, $z_{a,N} z_{i,N} < z_{a',N} z_{i',N}$ if $(a < a'$ or $(a = a'$ and $i < i'))$.

Using that order, we can order the set of polynomials from the smallest element to the greatest as follows:

$$\mathfrak{P} = \{p\tilde{m}_1, \ldots, p\tilde{m}_{\omega_1}, f_{0,1}, \ldots, f_{0,n}, f_{1,2}, \ldots, f_{1,n}, \ldots, f_{n-1,n}\} = \{\tilde{f}_1, \ldots, \tilde{f}_\omega\}$$

where $\tilde{m}_1 < \cdots < \tilde{m}_{\omega_1}$, ω_1 is the cardinality of $\mathfrak{M}_1$ and ω is the cardinality of $\mathfrak{M}$. Putting $U = 2^{\max_{i,j} \mu_{i,j}}$, we define the lattice $\mathcal{L}$ generated by $b_1, \ldots, b_\omega$, where b_i is the coefficient vector of $\tilde{f}_i(Uz_{0,1}, \ldots, Uz_{0,N}, \ldots, Uz_{n,1}, \ldots, Uz_{n,N})$ for $i \in \{1, \ldots, \omega\}$,. One can easily verify that the basis matrix is lower triangular. The number of variables is $N(n+1)$ and the success condition for the Coppersmith's method is:

$$\det(\mathcal{L}) < p^{\omega - N(n+1)+1},$$

with $\omega = \sharp\mathfrak{M} = N^2 \frac{n(n+1)}{2} + (n+1)N + 1$ and $\det(\mathcal{L}) = U^{2N^2 \frac{n(n+1)}{2} + (n+1)N} p^{\omega - \frac{n(n+1)}{2}}$. The success condition then becomes:

$$U < p^{\frac{\frac{n(n+1)}{2} - N(n+1)+1}{2N^2 \frac{n(n+1)}{2} + (n+1)N}}.$$

If n is large and since N is small, we can neglect $-N(n+1)+1$ which contributes to a small error. The attacker can recover x and y as long as the sizes of each unknown block in the signatures σ_i, $i \in \{0, \ldots, n\}$ satisfies:

$$U < p^{\frac{n(n+1)}{2N^2 n(n+1)) + 2(n+1)N}} \underset{n\to\infty}{\longrightarrow} p^{\frac{1}{2N^2}}.$$

We can heuristically recover the secret key of Sakai-Kasahara signatures if the number of consecutive bits of each unknown block is smaller than $\lceil \log_2(p) \rceil / (2N^2)$.

5.3 Experimental Results

Table 4 gives the theoretical bound $\delta_{\text{theo}} = \frac{n(n+1)}{2N^2n(n+1))+2(n+1)N}$ and an experimental bound δ_{exp} for a 512-bit prime p with $(n+1)$ signatures for a few values of $n \in \{4, 6, 10\}$ and one or two unknown blocks per signatures.

Table 4. Lattice Attack on Sakai-Kasahara signatures. Average running time (in seconds) of the LLL algorithm and the Gröbner basis computation.

N	n	δ_{theo}	δ_{exp}	dimension	LLL time(s)	Gröbner basis time(s)
1	4	0.4	0.39	16	0.015	0.009
1	6	0.4285	0.425	29	0.934	0.267
1	10	0.4545	0.45	67	5.082	4.247
2	4	0.1111	0.1111	51	0.728	0.292
2	6	0.1153	0.1153	99	15.308	14.482

We ran 2^7 experiments for all parameters. As in the attack on Boneh-Boyen signatures, the assumption that the created polynomials define an algebraic variety of dimension 0 was verified (in all cases for the bound δ_{exp}) and the constructed system was solved using Gröbner basis and the desired root recovered. Table 4 gives the average running time (in seconds) of the LLL algorithm and the Gröbner basis computation (using the same configuration as above).

6   Conclusion and Open Questions

We presented lattice-based polynomial-time algorithms that recover the signer's secret in popular pairing-based signatures when used to sign several messages under the assumption that blocks of consecutive bits of the corresponding exponents are known by the attacker. This partial information can be obtained in practice easily through side-channels (such as the power consumption or the electromagnetic emanations of the device generating the signature).

In order to prevent the leakage of partial information on the exponent, it is customary to use a probabilistic algorithm to encode the sensitive values such that the cryptographic operations only occur on randomized data. In [13], Coron proposed notably to randomize the exponent and the projective coordinates of the base point. It is an interesting question to extend our attacks in such setting (as it was done recently for ECDSA in [15]). It is also interesting to study the security against side-channel attacks of the pairing-based signatures whose design does not rely on the exponent inversion framework (i.e. based on the full domain hash framework and the commutative blinding framework).

Our attacks are heuristic and it would be very interesting to provide proven versions of them (as it was done in [24,25] for ECDSA signatures). It is also interesting to study further the attack against Gentry signatures when the unknown blocks of consecutive bits overlap. Finally, it would be nice to improve our attacks on Boneh-Boyen and Sakai-Kasahara signatures.

A   Concrete Attack Examples Against Gentry Signatures

In this section, we present two attack examples on Gentry signatures for a 256-bit prime p with 3 signatures (r_0, σ_0), (r_1, σ_1) and (r_2, σ_2) and one T-bit unknown block in each signature, with $T = \lfloor 0.3 \log_2(p) \rfloor$.

We recall that for $i \in \{0, 1, 2\}$, $\sigma_i = g^{s_i}$ where $s_i = (y + r_i)/(x + m) \bmod p$, x and y are the secret keys and p, m and r_i, $i \in \{0, 1, 2\}$ are public information. In this example, we took the following random values:

- $p = $ 9b814891e89496e776bfeeebcac5c74130862914fe2b928d40c3a88323dcbaaf
- $m = $ 440f4a9df2936c4aad3856ed0ea5cf3d131ef658fc36c2fa56763373288d5519
- $x = $ 57a7b0913f5202e31555ec9538ff90f38a5e6c53b359edfe1106c8ee9518029a
- $y = $ 259b67be7de53e0546860379bc31ab9bb30caf68c314a956a1719e18d4a24ae2
- $r_0 = $ 75c471becf6a9d86aa5480985a95702617892ba84b7662d6bdf3a3c1931abf3b
- $r_1 = $ 675e28ffbf96b29365ebda463c3a0a4290a284f9fed9ddd0ccdada587c1f0152
- $r_2 = $ 7961b0df3f0a286547f25da59a7c2a7c28764f4335a0aa2cd5a72ba2393a6cd3
- $s_0 = $ 45f185a8ce35c2b95b3e1aef9fc516ec9e840c9a5b6b36c70532b10145790401
- $s_1 = $ 8f63fe87fd0d67f6594ff44ba86a2755b2b6ad6a0b7ab4aafecae41fca50c713
- $s_2 = $ 57de02b444bb7716c021d21162c3727ba904ae6e4d44aca2ad9f4406669e8744

and $T = \lfloor 0.3 \log_2(p) \rfloor = 76$.

In the first case, we suppose that we do not know any least significant bits of each signature and show that we are unable to find the unknown blocks since the Gröbner basis gives us a system of dimension 1.

In the second case, we suppose that we know $T + 2$ least significant bits of σ_0 but do not know any least significant bits of s_1, and s_2. We also suppose that we do not know T intermediate bits of s_0 and we show that in this case we are able to find the unknown blocks since the Gröbner basis gives us a system of dimension 0.

First Case

- We can write the signatures as:

$$s_0 = 2^T \cdot \text{45f185a8ce35c2b95b3e1aef9fc516ec9e840c9a5b6b3} + z_0,$$

$$s_1 = 2^T \cdot \text{8f63fe87fd0d67f6594ff44ba86a2755b2b6ad6a0b7ab} + z_1,$$

$$s_2 = 2^T \cdot \text{57de02b444bb7716c021d21162c3727ba904ae6e4d44a} + z_2,$$

where the T-bit numbers z_0, z_1 and z_2 are the unknown blocks.
- We get the polynomial $f(y_0, y_1, y_2)$ defined by:

$$y_2 + \text{86acc2de9d15dab4df6a8114243623f246376c1103c29ee97a0dd7490f87eb33}\, y_1$$

$$+ \text{14d485b34b7ebc3297556dd7a68fa34eea4ebd03fa68f3a3c6b5d13a1454cf7b}\, y_0$$

$$+ \text{11f10fbe97565b062acfb71c6d98f596de6c1e236edaa9168d891d78d66e8c4a}$$

having as root (z_0, z_1, z_2) modulo p.

– Constructing the lattice with $m = 4$, after the LLL reduction and the Gröbner basis computation, we obtain the system of polynomials

$$\begin{cases} f_1(y_0, y_1, y_2) = y_2 - y_0 - \texttt{5dba86c930521258343} \\ f_2(y_0, y_1, y_2) = y_1 - y_0 + \texttt{21c0667cce17b283cee} \end{cases}$$

having indeed (z_0, z_1, z_2) as root over the integers. However, the dimension of the system is 1 and then we are *a priori* unable to find the unknown blocks.

Second Case

– We can write the signatures as:

$$s_0 = \texttt{36c70532b10145790401} + 2^{79} \cdot z_0 + 2^{79+T} \cdot \texttt{8be30b519c6b8572b67c35df3}$$

$$s_1 = 2^{T} \cdot \texttt{8f63fe87fd0d67f6594ff44ba86a2755b2b6ad6a0b7ab} + z_1$$

$$s_2 = 2^{T} \cdot \texttt{57de02b444bb7716c021d21162c3727ba904ae6e4d44a} + z_2$$

where the T-bit numbers z_0, z_1 and z_2 are the unknown blocks.
– If one proceeds like in the attack, we obtain the polynomial $f(y_0, y_1, y_2)$ defined by

$$y_2 + \texttt{86acc2de9d15dab4df6a8114243623f246376c1103c29ee97a0dd7490f87eb33}\, y_1$$

$$+ \texttt{78836c7dbcc6bee53ea07b359a07fa111e09607336b452976acd0f0ec2a0c985}\, y_0$$

$$+ \texttt{77b82eec348f27f19cb7a6c1cc895cf7261093b80d067ea4eb7b8da90e1ae306}$$

having as root (z_0, z_1, z_2) modulo p.
– Constructing the lattice with $m = 4$, after the LLL reduction and the Gröbner basis computation, one obtains the system of polynomials

$$\begin{cases} f_1(y_0, y_1, y_2) = y_2 - \texttt{ca2ad9f4406669e8744} \\ f_2(y_0, y_1, y_2) = y_1 - \texttt{4aafecae41fca50c713} \\ f_3(y_0, y_1, y_2) = y_0 - \texttt{f8a2dd93d081934b6d6} \end{cases}$$

having (z_0, z_1, z_2) as root over the integers. The dimension of the system is 0 and one finds readily the unknown blocks.

References

1. Benhamouda, F., Chevalier, C., Thillard, A., Vergnaud, D.: Easing Coppersmith methods using analytic combinatorics: applications to public-key cryptography with weak pseudorandomness. In: Cheng, C.M., Chung, K.M., Persiano, G., Yang, B.Y. (eds.) PKC 2016: 19th International Conference on Theory and Practice of Public Key Cryptography, Part II. LNCS, vol. 9615, pp. 36–66. Springer, Heidelberg (2016)
2. Boneh, D., Boyen, X.: Efficient selective-ID secure identity based encryption without random oracles. In: Cachin, C., Camenisch, J. (eds.) Advances in Cryptology - EUROCRYPT 2004. LNCS, vol. 3027, pp. 223–238. Springer, Heidelberg (2004)

3. Boneh, D., Boyen, X.: Short signatures without random oracles. In: Cachin, C., Camenisch, J.L. (eds.) EUROCRYPT 2004. LNCS, vol. 3027, pp. 56–73. Springer, Heidelberg (2004). https://doi.org/10.1007/978-3-540-24676-3_4

4. Boneh, D., Boyen, X.: Short signatures without random oracles and the SDH assumption in bilinear groups. J. Cryptol. 21(2), 149–177 (2008)

5. Boneh, D., Franklin, M.: Identity-based encryption from the Weil pairing. In: Kilian, J. (ed.) CRYPTO 2001. LNCS, vol. 2139, pp. 213–229. Springer, Heidelberg (2001). https://doi.org/10.1007/3-540-44647-8_13

6. Boneh, D., Halevi, S., Howgrave-Graham, N.: The modular inversion hidden number problem. In: Boyd, C. (ed.) ASIACRYPT 2001. LNCS, vol. 2248, pp. 36–51. Springer, Heidelberg (2001). https://doi.org/10.1007/3-540-45682-1_3

7. Boneh, D., Lynn, B., Shacham, H.: Short signatures from the Weil pairing. In: Boyd, C. (ed.) ASIACRYPT 2001. LNCS, vol. 2248, pp. 514–532. Springer, Heidelberg (2001). https://doi.org/10.1007/3-540-45682-1_30

8. Boneh, D., Lynn, B., Shacham, H.: Short signatures from the Weil pairing. J. Cryptol. 17(4), 297–319 (2004)

9. Boyen, X.: A tapestry of identity-based encryption: practical frameworks compared. IJACT 1(1), 3–21 (2008)

10. Chari, S., Rao, J.R., Rohatgi, P.: Template attacks. In: Kaliski, B.S., Koç, K., Paar, C. (eds.) CHES 2002. LNCS, vol. 2523, pp. 13–28. Springer, Heidelberg (2003). https://doi.org/10.1007/3-540-36400-5_3

11. Coppersmith, D.: Finding a small root of a bivariate integer equation; factoring with high bits known. In: Maurer, U. (ed.) EUROCRYPT 1996. LNCS, vol. 1070, pp. 178–189. Springer, Heidelberg (1996). https://doi.org/10.1007/3-540-68339-9_16

12. Coppersmith, D.: Finding a small root of a univariate modular equation. In: Maurer, U. (ed.) EUROCRYPT 1996. LNCS, vol. 1070, pp. 155–165. Springer, Heidelberg (1996). https://doi.org/10.1007/3-540-68339-9_14

13. Coron, J.-S.: Resistance against differential power analysis for elliptic curve cryptosystems. In: Koç, Ç.K., Paar, C. (eds.) CHES 1999. LNCS, vol. 1717, pp. 292–302. Springer, Heidelberg (1999). https://doi.org/10.1007/3-540-48059-5_25

14. Gentry, C.: Practical identity-based encryption without random oracles. In: Vaudenay, S. (ed.) EUROCRYPT 2006. LNCS, vol. 4004, pp. 445–464. Springer, Heidelberg (2006). https://doi.org/10.1007/11761679_27

15. Goudarzi, D., Rivain, M., Vergnaud, D.: Lattice attacks against elliptic-curve signatures with blinded scalar multiplication. In: Avanzi, R., Heys, H. (eds.) Selected Areas in Cryptography - SAC 2016–23rd International Conference, St. John's, NL, Canada, August 9–12, 2016, Revised Selected Papers. LNCS. Springer (2017, to appear)

16. Howgrave-Graham, N.: Finding small roots of univariate modular equations revisited. In: Darnell, M. (ed.) Cryptography and Coding 1997. LNCS, vol. 1355, pp. 131–142. Springer, Heidelberg (1997). https://doi.org/10.1007/BFb0024458

17. Howgrave-Graham, N., Smart, N.P.: Lattice attacks on digital signature schemes. Des. Codes Cryptography 23(3), 283–290 (2001)

18. Jochemsz, E., May, A.: A strategy for finding roots of multivariate polynomials with new applications in attacking RSA variants. In: Lai, X., Chen, K. (eds.) ASIACRYPT 2006. LNCS, vol. 4284, pp. 267–282. Springer, Heidelberg (2006). https://doi.org/10.1007/11935230_18

19. Kocher, P.C.: Timing attacks on implementations of Diffie-Hellman, RSA, DSS, and other systems. In: Koblitz, N. (ed.) CRYPTO 1996. LNCS, vol. 1109, pp. 104–113. Springer, Heidelberg (1996). https://doi.org/10.1007/3-540-68697-5_9

20. Kocher, P., Jaffe, J., Jun, B.: Differential power analysis. In: Wiener, M. (ed.) CRYPTO 1999. LNCS, vol. 1666, pp. 388–397. Springer, Heidelberg (1999). https://doi.org/10.1007/3-540-48405-1_25

21. Lenstra, A.K., Lenstra, H.W.J., Lovász, L.: Factoring polynomials with rational coefficients. Math. Ann. **261**, 515–534 (1982)

22. Ling, S., Shparlinski, I.E., Steinfeld, R., Wang, H.: On the modular inversion hidden number problem. J. Symb. Comput. **47**(4), 358–367 (2012)

23. De Mulder, E., Hutter, M., Marson, M.E., Pearson, P.: Using Bleichenbacher's solution to the hidden number problem to attack nonce leaks in 384-Bit ECDSA. In: Bertoni, G., Coron, J.-S. (eds.) CHES 2013. LNCS, vol. 8086, pp. 435–452. Springer, Heidelberg (2013). https://doi.org/10.1007/978-3-642-40349-1_25

24. Nguyen, P.Q., Shparlinski, I.: The insecurity of the digital signature algorithm with partially known nonces. J. Cryptol. **15**(3), 151–176 (2002)

25. Nguyen, P.Q., Shparlinski, I.E.: The insecurity of the elliptic curve digital signature algorithm with partially known nonces. Des. Codes Cryptography **30**(2), 201–217 (2003)

26. Sakai, R., Kasahara, M.: ID based cryptosystems with pairing on elliptic curve. Cryptology ePrint Archive, Report 2003/054 (2003). http://eprint.iacr.org/2003/054

27. Zhang, F., Safavi-Naini, R., Susilo, W.: An efficient signature scheme from bilinear pairings and its applications. In: Bao, F., Deng, R., Zhou, J. (eds.) PKC 2004. LNCS, vol. 2947, pp. 277–290. Springer, Heidelberg (2004). https://doi.org/10.1007/978-3-540-24632-9_20

Lattice Reductions over Euclidean Rings with Applications to Cryptanalysis

Taechan Kim[1(✉)] and Changmin Lee[2]

[1] NTT Secure Platform Laboratories, Tokyo, Japan
taechan.kim@lab.ntt.co.jp
[2] Seoul National University, Seoul, Korea
cocomi11@snu.ac.kr

Abstract. Lattices over number fields arise from various fascinating applications in cryptography. In this paper, we present two algorithms that find a nice, short basis of lattices over arbitrary Euclidean domains. One of the algorithms finds a reduced basis of lattices over biquadratic Euclidean rings with overwhelming probability. We prove that its output is bounded by a constant that depends only on the lattices.

The second algorithm applies to arbitrary norm-Euclidean domain. It is given without the proof of the output quality, nevertheless, we experimentally verify that the algorithm outputs a reasonably good basis and it conjecturally supports the quality of our algorithm.

We also show that the proposed algorithms can be used in various cryptanalytic applications. As a concrete example, we discuss how our algorithm improves special-$\mathfrak{q}$ descent step in tower number field sieve method, which is one of the best known algorithms to solve the discrete logarithm problem over finite fields.

Keywords: Lattices · Cryptanalysis · Number field sieve · LLL algorithm · Discrete logarithm problems

1 Introduction

Lattices are, frequently considered as, free $\mathbb{Z}$-modules.[1] Any free module has a basis, thus, for a lattice M and a positive integer d, there exists a set $(\mathbf{b}_1, \ldots, \mathbf{b}_d)$ of elements in M such that $M = \oplus_{i=1}^{d} \mathbb{Z}\mathbf{b}_i$. The integer d is called the rank or the dimension of M and it does not depend on the choice of a basis. A lattice has infinitely many bases, but some of them are more useful than others. In many cryptographic applications, it is crucial to obtain a good basis of M and the goal of lattice reduction is to find a such interesting basis consisting of reasonably small and almost orthogonal vectors. There have been many approaches

---

C. Lee—Supported by Next-Generation Information Computing Development Program through the National Research Foundation of Korea(NRF) funded by the Ministry of Science, ICT & Future Planning (NRF-2016M3C4A7937116).

[1] For a commutative ring R, an R-module is a finitely generated set of elements that is closed under additions and scalar multiplication by R.

© Springer International Publishing AG 2017
M. O'Neill (Ed.): IMACC 2017, LNCS 10655, pp. 371–391, 2017.
https://doi.org/10.1007/978-3-319-71045-7_19

to find a good reduced basis including the celebrating LLL algorithm [21], BKZ algorithms [27,28], to name a few.

Let K be a number field and $\mathbb{Z}_K$ be its ring of integers. Similar to the classical $\mathbb{Z}$-lattice, we call any $\mathbb{Z}_K$-module M a $\mathbb{Z}_K$-lattice. Throughout this paper, we mainly consider a number field K whose ring of integers is a principal ideal domain (PID). Since any modules over PID are free modules, bases of M are always well-defined. As for $\mathbb{Z}$-lattices, finding a good basis of a $\mathbb{Z}_K$-lattice is of prime importance in many applications, which is our main object in this paper.

Motivations. Lattices over non-integer rings arise from many attractive applications in cryptography. As any integral ideals in number fields being also $\mathbb{Z}$-modules (which we call ideal-lattices), the ideal-lattices are more frequently used than general lattices. It is not only for the case of lattice-based cryptography [6,7,13,14,29], but also the case of various cryptanalysis such as number field sieve method [4,15,16,18,19].

On the other hand, number fields, where the ideals are defined over, are usually chosen so that they contain proper subfields, for instance, power-of-prime cyclotomic fields. For those cases, an integral ideal in a number field L is not only a $\mathbb{Z}$-lattice, but also a $\mathbb{Z}_K$-lattice, where $\mathbb{Z}_K$ is a ring of integers of a subfield $K \subset L$. Then it is often desirable to consider a lattice reduction algorithm directly over $\mathbb{Z}_K$ rather than $\mathbb{Z}$. This approach has a potential advantage since it is possible to deal with lattices of smaller dimensions. For instance, the dimension is reduced to $[L : K]$ over $\mathbb{Z}_K$ instead of $[L : \mathbb{Q}]$ over $\mathbb{Z}$. Remarkably, even a small decrease in the dimensions makes lattices easier to handle.

Related Works. There have been several attempts [10–12,25] to generalize the LLL algorithm. Napias [25] proposed an analogue of the LLL algorithm that can be applied to lattices over five imaginary number fields $K = \mathbb{Q}(\sqrt{-\alpha})$ for $\alpha = 1, 2, 3, 7, 11$. An interesting observation of this approach is that the algebraic norm $N_{K/\mathbb{Q}}(a + b\sqrt{-\alpha})$ coincides with the square of the Euclidean norm $\|(a, b\sqrt{\alpha})\|^2 = a^2 + \alpha b^2$. Then the algebraic norm takes the place of the Euclidean norm which plays a crucial role to prove the bound of the output.

The work in [12] considers the reduction of lattices over complex numbers whose idea is basically the same as Napias's approach. A naive generalization of those works to the case of arbitrary number fields is seemingly not obvious. One might consider an element in a number field as a complex number and try to apply the techniques above. Then the output by the reduction only yields a vector whose entries are complex numbers with small real and imaginary parts. However, since our goal is to obtain a vector of entries in number fields with small coefficients with respect to a given basis, it is unsatisfactory to apply the above techniques directly.

Independently, Fieker and Pohst [10] attempted to generalize the LLL algorithm to any lattices over Dedekind domain. Similarly in [25], they suggested to use either the trace $Tr_{K/\mathbb{Q}}$ or the norm $N_{N/\mathbb{Q}}$ as a replacement of the Euclidean norm. However, their approach gives no guarantee on the output bound.

Fieker and Stehlé [11] suggested an algorithm by viewing the $\mathbb{Z}_K$-module as a high-dimensional $\mathbb{Z}$-lattice. However, this approach is unsatisfactory for our original motivation, since it works with a high-dimensional lattice.

Our Contributions. In this paper, we propose two analogues of the LLL algorithm. One of our algorithms applies to biquadratic fields $K = \mathbb{Q}(\sqrt{-\alpha}, \sqrt{\beta})$ such that $\mathbb{Z}_K$ is an Euclidean domain with respect to the algebraic norm (we call it norm-Euclidean ring). To be precise, let θ be a generator of the Galois group $Gal\big(K/\mathbb{Q}(\sqrt{-\alpha})\big) \cong \mathbb{Z}_2$. Given the input lattice M in K^n, let $(c_1, \ldots, c_n) \in K^n$ be an output vector by our algorithm. Then it satisfies

$$N_{\mathbb{Q}(\sqrt{-\alpha})/\mathbb{Q}} \left(\sum_{i=1}^{n} c_i \theta(c_i) \right) \leq 2^{n-1} N_{K/\mathbb{Q}}\big(\det(M) \big)^{1/n}.$$

This algorithm might abort, but the probability is negligible.

As a second contribution, we revisit the algorithm by Fieker and Pohst [10]. In its original paper, they considered the size reduction step[2] with respect to the trace map. However, it is impossible in general, given $a \in K$, to find $q \in \mathbb{Z}_K$ such that $Tr_{K/\mathbb{Q}}((a - q)\overline{(a - q)})$ is small enough. We observe that, replacing $Tr_{K/\mathbb{Q}}$ by $N_{K/\mathbb{Q}}$, it is possible to find efficiently $q \in \mathbb{Z}_K$ such that $N_{K/\mathbb{Q}}(a - q)$ is small enough, when $\mathbb{Z}_K$ is a norm-Euclidean ring.

Although the output bound has also been unproven, we provide experimental evidences showing the quality of our algorithms. Our implementation has been done over lattices of the form that frequently appears in cryptanalysis. Let $\mathbf{c} := (c_1, \ldots, c_n) \in K^n$ be an output vector of our algorithm, our implementation heuristically shows that

$$\|\mathbf{c}\|_\infty \lesssim C^d N_{K/\mathbb{Q}}(\det(M))^{1/d},$$

where $C \approx 1.02$ and $d = [K : \mathbb{Q}] \cdot n$ is the dimension of M over $\mathbb{Z}$. Taking it into account with $\|\mathbf{c}\|_2 \leq \sqrt{d} \cdot \|\mathbf{c}\|_\infty$ (by abusing the notation $\|\mathbf{c}\|_2$ denotes the Euclidean norm of $\mathbf{c}$ considered as a vector in $\mathbb{Z}^d$), the Hermite's constant of our reduction is bounded by $C \cdot d^{1/2d}$. It is remarkable that this constant is less than the worst case Hermite factor $(4/3)^{1/4} \approx 1.075$ whenever $d \geq 33$ and rapidly becomes close to the average Hermite factor ≈ 1.02 as d grows.

As an application, we discuss how to improve the special-q descent in the tower number field sieve (TNFS) algorithms [4,18,19]. Pairing-based cryptography has recently suffered a significant loss in security level due to these works.

Organization. In Sect. 2, we briefly recall some backgrounds on lattices and algebraic number theory. In Sect. 3.1, we present a sub-algorithm required to run our main algorithms that will be described in Sects. 3.2 and 3.3, respectively. We show that our algorithms can be applied to some cryptanalysis in Sect. 4 and verify our algorithms experimentally in Appendix A.

---

[2] In the classical case, it corresponds to, given $a \in \mathbb{Q}$, find $q \in \mathbb{Z}$ such that $|a - q| \leq 1/2$.

2   Preliminaries

2.1   Number Fields

Throughout this paper, let K be a number field over $\mathbb{Q}$ of degree m and L be its extension of degree n. Denote $\mathbb{Z}_K$ (resp. $\mathbb{Z}_L$) by ring of integers of K (resp. L). As usual, we simply denote $\mathbb{Z}$ by the ring of integers of rational numbers $\mathbb{Q}$.

A number field K of degree m is defined by an irreducible polynomial $h \in \mathbb{Q}[t]$ of the same degree, i.e. $K = \mathbb{Q}(\iota) = \mathbb{Q}[t]/h(t)$, where ι is a root of h in the complex field. Denoting by $(\iota_1, \ldots, \iota_m)$ the distinct complex roots of h, each embedding $\sigma_i : K \to \mathbb{C}$ is the evaluation of $a \in K$, viewed as a polynomial modulo h, at the root ι_i, i.e. $\sigma_i : a \mapsto a(\iota_i)$. Let r_1 be the number of real roots and r_2 be the number of pairs of complex roots so that $m = r_1 + 2r_2$. Then we have a canonical embedding $\sigma : K \to \mathbb{R}^{r_1} \times \mathbb{C}^{r_2}$ defined by $\sigma : a \mapsto (\sigma_1(a), \ldots, \sigma_{r_1+r_2}(a))$, where the first r_1's are the real embeddings and $\sigma_{r_1+r_2+j}(a)$ is the complex conjugation of $\sigma_{r_1+j}(a)$. The number field K is viewed as Euclidean space endowed with the inner product $\langle a, b \rangle = \sum_{i=1}^{m} \sigma_i(a)\overline{\sigma_i}(b)$. The algebraic norm is defined as $N_{K/\mathbb{Q}}(a) = \prod_{i=1}^{m} \sigma_i(a)$.

Proposition 1. Let $K = \mathbb{Q}(\iota) = \mathbb{Q}[t]/h(t)$ be a number field of degree m and $a(\iota) = \sum_{i=0}^{\tau} a_i \iota^i$ be an element in K for a positive integer $\tau \leq m - 1$. Then we have

$$|N_{K/\mathbb{Q}}(a)| \leq (m+1)^{\tau/2}(\tau+1)^{m/2}\|h\|_\infty^\tau \|a\|_\infty^m,$$

where $\|\cdot\|_\infty$ denotes the maximal absolute value of the coefficients.

Euclidean Number Fields. In this paper, we are particularly interested in a ring of integers that is also an Euclidean domain.

Definition 1. A commutative ring R is said to be **Euclidean** if there is a map $\phi : R\backslash\{0\} \to \mathbb{N}$ such that $\phi(a) \leq \phi(ab)$ for any nonzero $a, b \in R$ and there exist q and r in R such that $a = bq + r$ with $r = 0$ or $\phi(r) < \phi(b)$. Furthermore, a number field K is said to be **norm-Euclidean** if its ring of integers $\mathbb{Z}_K$ is Euclidean with respect to the absolute value of the usual field norm $N_{K/\mathbb{Q}}$.

When the field K is either cyclotomic or of low-dimensional, then we have a perfect classification of which number fields are norm-Euclidean. We present some lists that we are interested in.

Proposition 2 ([20]). Let $\mathbb{Q}(\sqrt{-\alpha}, \sqrt{\beta})$ be a biquadratic field, then it is norm-Euclidean if and only if

$$\alpha = 1, \quad \beta = 2, 3, 5, 7;$$
$$\alpha = 2, \quad \beta = -3, 5;$$
$$\alpha = 3, \quad \beta = 2, 5, -7, -11, 17, -19;$$
$$\alpha = 7, \quad \beta = 5.$$

Proposition 3. *Let* $\mathbb{Q}(\zeta_k)$ *be the* k-*th cyclotomic field, then it is norm-Euclidean if*

$$k \in \{1, 3, 4, 5, 7, 8, 9, 11, 12, 15, 16, 20, 24\}.$$

Proof. To see this, refer to [22, 24, 26].

The norm-Euclideanity of R is equivalent to check, for any a/b in its fractional field K, whether there exists an algebraic integer $q \in R$ such that $\left|N_{K/\mathbb{Q}}\left(\frac{a}{b} - q\right)\right| < 1$. It is natural to consider the Euclidean minimum which is defined below.

Definition 2 (Euclidean minimum). *For any* $\xi \in K$, *the value* $m_K(\xi) := \min_{q \in \mathbb{Z}_K} |N_{K/\mathbb{Q}}(\xi - q)|$ *is called the Euclidean minimum of* ξ *and* $\mathfrak{M}(K) := \max_{\xi \in K} (m_K(\xi))$ *is called the Euclidean minimum of* K.

As an easy example, we have $\mathfrak{M}(\mathbb{Q}) = 1/2$. In particular, the Euclidean minima of the fields listed in Proposition 2 and Proposition 3 are known [20, 23] (Tables 1 and 2).

Table 1. Euclidean minimum of k-th cyclotomic fields [23]

k	1	3	4	5	7	8	9	12	15	16	20	24
$\mathfrak{M}(\mathbb{Q}(\zeta_k))$	$\frac{1}{2}$	$\frac{1}{3}$	$\frac{1}{2}$	$\frac{1}{5}$	$\frac{1}{7}$	$\frac{1}{2}$	$\frac{1}{3}$	$\frac{1}{4}$	$\frac{1}{16}$	$\frac{1}{2}$	$\frac{1}{5}$	$\frac{1}{4}$

Table 2. Euclidean minimum of biquadratic fields [20]

(α, β)	(1,2)	(1,3)	(1,5)	(1,7)	(2,-3)	(2,5)	(3,2)
$\mathfrak{M}(\mathbb{Q}(\sqrt{-\alpha}, \sqrt{\beta}))$	$\frac{1}{2}$	$\frac{1}{4}$	$\frac{5}{16}$	$\frac{1}{2}$	$\frac{1}{3}$	$\frac{11}{16}$	$\geq \frac{1}{4}$
(α, β)	(3,5)	(3,-7)	(3,-11)	(3,17)	(3,-19)	(7,5)	
$\mathfrak{M}(\mathbb{Q}(\sqrt{-\alpha}, \sqrt{\beta}))$	$\frac{1}{4}$	$\frac{4}{9}$	≤ 0.46	$\frac{13}{16}$	< 0.95	$\frac{9}{16}$	

2.2 Lattices

The classical LLL-algorithm returns a basis called LLL-reduced for any given $\mathbb{Z}$-basis of the lattice M. We briefly recall the notion of the LLL-reduced basis.

Let $\langle \cdot, \cdot \rangle$ be the inner product in a vector space $\mathbb{R}^d$. Denote $\|\cdot\|$ by the Euclidean norm in $\mathbb{R}^d$. Given a basis $(\mathbf{b}_1, \dots, \mathbf{b}_d)$ of a $\mathbb{Z}$-lattice $M \subseteq \mathbb{Q}^d$, let $(\mathbf{b}_1^*, \dots, \mathbf{b}_d^*)$ be the Gram-Schmidt orthogonalization, i.e. $\mathbf{b}_1^* = \mathbf{b}_1$ and $\mathbf{b}_i^* = \mathbf{b}_i - \sum_{j=1}^{i-1} \mu_{i,j} \mathbf{b}_j^*$ $(2 \leq i \leq d)$, where $\mu_{i,j} = \langle \mathbf{b}_i, \mathbf{b}_j^* \rangle / \langle \mathbf{b}_j^*, \mathbf{b}_j^* \rangle$.

Definition 3. *A basis* $(\mathbf{b}_1, \dots, \mathbf{b}_d)$ *of a* $\mathbb{Z}$-*lattice* M *is called LLL-reduced with respect to* $\delta > 0$ *if it satisfies*

$$|\mu_{i,j}| \leq 1/2 \text{ for } 1 \leq j < i \leq d \, (\text{size reduced})$$

and

$$\|\mathbf{b}_i^*\|^2 \geq \left(\delta - \mu_{i,i-1}^2\right) \|\mathbf{b}_{i-1}^*\|^2 \text{ for } 1 < i \leq d \, (\text{Lovasz condition}).$$

Algorithm 1. Rounding algorithm for norm-Euclidean rings

Input: A norm-Euclidean number field K, its Euclidean minimum $\mathfrak{M}(K)$, the unit
   group $K^\times$ of K, and an element $a \in K$
Output: $q \in \mathbb{Z}_K$ such that $N_{K/\mathbb{Q}}(a - q) \leq \mathfrak{M}(K)$
1: Compute $r := a - \lfloor a \rceil$
2: **if** $N_{K/\mathbb{Q}}(r) \leq \mathfrak{M}(K)$ **then**
3:     **return** $q := \lfloor a \rceil$
4: **else**
5:     **repeat**
6:         $u \leftarrow_\$ K^\times$
7:     **until** $N_{K/\mathbb{Q}}(ur - \lfloor ur \rceil) \leq \mathfrak{M}(K)$
8: **end if**
9: **return** $q := \lfloor a \rceil + u^{-1}\lfloor ur \rceil$

Observe that the constant $1/2$ in the size reduced condition is the same as the
Euclidean minimum $\mathfrak{M}(\mathbb{Q})$. The LLL-reduced condition implies that the LLL
algorithm outputs a reasonably small vector in a lattice.

Proposition 4. *Let* $(\mathbf{b}_1, \ldots, \mathbf{b}_d)$ *be a LLL-reduced* $\mathbb{Z}$-*basis of a lattice* M *with
respect to* $\delta = 3/4$, *then*

$$\|\mathbf{b}_1\| \leq 2^{(d-1)/4} \det(M)^{1/d}.$$

3   Lattice Reduction Algorithms over Euclidean Rings

3.1   Euclidean Algorithm

Assume that the value of the Euclidean minimum of K, $\mathfrak{M}(K)$, is known. In
this section, we propose a simple algorithm that, given an element $a \in K$,
finds an algebraic integer $q \in \mathbb{Z}_K$ such that $|N_{K/\mathbb{Q}}(a - q)| \leq \mathfrak{M}(K)$. If $K = \mathbb{Q}$, we have $\mathfrak{M}(\mathbb{Q}) = 1/2$ and the algorithm simply corresponds to take the
rounding of elements, i.e. $\lfloor a \rceil$ is an integer such that $|a - \lfloor a \rceil| \leq 1/2$ for any
$a \in \mathbb{Q}$. By abusing the notation, define $\lfloor a \rceil := \sum_{i=0}^{m-1} \lfloor a_i \rceil \iota^i \in \mathbb{Z}_K$ for some
$a = \sum_{i=0}^{m-1} a_i \iota^i \in K$. Unfortunately, $|N_{K/\mathbb{Q}}(a - \lfloor a \rceil)| \leq \mathfrak{M}(K)$ does not hold
in general. However, in some cases of norm-Euclidean cyclotomic fields, it is
shown [17] that $|N_{K/\mathbb{Q}}(a - \lfloor a \rceil)| \leq \mathfrak{M}(K) + \epsilon_K$, where ϵ_K is a small positive
constant only depends on K. For instance, $\epsilon_{\mathbb{Q}(\zeta_4)} = 0$, $\epsilon_{\mathbb{Q}(\zeta_3)} = 1/24$, and $\epsilon_{\mathbb{Q}(\zeta_8)} = 1/64$.

Motivated from this observation, we propose Algorithm 1. The idea is simple.
First, one computes $r := a - \lfloor a \rceil$. If $N_{K/\mathbb{Q}}(r) \leq \mathfrak{M}(K)$, it is done. Otherwise,
repeat computing $u \cdot r$ for an unit $u \in K^\times$ chosen uniformly at random until
$N_{K/\mathbb{Q}}(ur - \lfloor ur \rceil) \leq \mathfrak{M}(K)$. Then, the algorithm outputs $\lfloor a \rceil + u^{-1}\lfloor ur \rceil$. Its
running time depends on the distribution of $r = \sum_i r_i \iota^i \in K$ $(-1/2 \leq r_i \leq 1/2)$
such that $N_{K/\mathbb{Q}}(r) \leq \mathfrak{M}(K)$.

To show the running time of the algorithm, we need the following lemma.
Then Theorem 1 is its simple corollary.

Lemma 1. *With the above notations, the probability of* $r = \sum_{i=0}^{m-1} r_i \iota^i \in K = \mathbb{Q}[t]/h(t)$ $(-1/2 \leq r_i \leq 1/2)$ *uniformly chosen at random satisfying* $N_{K/\mathbb{Q}}(r) \leq \mathfrak{M}(K)$ *is at least* $\frac{2^m \mathfrak{M}(K)}{(m+1)^m \|h\|_\infty^{m-1}}$.

Proof. It is obvious from Proposition 1, since $|N_{K/\mathbb{Q}}(r)| \leq \mathfrak{M}(K)$ for any r such that $\|r\|_\infty \leq \frac{\mathfrak{M}(K)^{1/m}}{(m+1)\cdot\|h\|_\infty^{(m-1)/m}}$.

Theorem 1. *Algorithm 1 returns the output with the expected running time of* $\frac{(m+1)^m \|h\|_\infty^{m-1}}{2^m \mathfrak{M}(K)}$ *multiplications by units and the same amount of norm computations.*

The running time of the algorithm is seemingly huge. In practice, however, we mainly focus on the norm-Euclidean cyclotomic/biquadratic fields and in such cases $m = \deg(K) \leq 8$ and $\|h\|_\infty = O(1)$ so that the running time is small enough. Furthermore, our probability estimation in Lemma 1 is crude and implementation results show that simply rounding the element a gives the desired output with very high probability.

On the other hand, taking a random unit u (in step 6) can be simply replaced by deriving it from the fundamental units of K and test the condition with u^i for incremental $i = 1, 2, \dots$. To give a concrete example, we tested our algorithm with $K = \mathbb{Q}(\zeta_{16})$ using the SAGE computer algebra system [30]. Among randomly chosen 200,000 elements of $r = \sum_i r_i \zeta_{16}^i$ with $|r_i| \leq 1/2$, about 97% of them have the norm less than $1/2$. For the remains, it was enough to consider $u^i r$ where $u = \zeta_{16}^6 + \zeta_{16}^4 + \zeta_{16}^2$ and i is running over $1 \leq i \leq 3$.

This algorithm may not terminate if the unit u is repeatedly chosen so that $N_{K/\mathbb{Q}}(ur - \lfloor ur \rceil) > \mathfrak{M}(K)$, although we observed experimentally that it is unlikely to happen.

3.2 LLL Algorithm over Biquadratic Euclidean Rings

In the classical LLL algorithm, the Gram-Schmidt orthogonalization is a crucial part of the algorithm and it necessarily requires an inner product in a vector space $\mathbb{R}^d$. Similarly, for $\mathbb{Z}_K$-lattices, it is also important to define an inner product on K^n to process the orthogonalization.

In this section, we focus on the lattice reduction over $K = \mathbb{Q}(\sqrt{-\alpha}, \sqrt{\beta})$ that are listed in Proposition 2. We define an inner product over K^n as follows. First of all, observe that K contains a subfield $K_0 := \mathbb{Q}(\sqrt{-\alpha})$ that is a norm-Euclidean quadratic imaginary field.

Definition 4. *With the above notations, let θ be a generator of the Galois group* $\mathrm{Gal}(K/K_0) \cong \mathbb{Z}_2$. *Let* $\mathbf{v} = (v_1, \dots, v_n)$ *and* $\mathbf{w} = (w_1, \dots, w_n)$ *be vectors in K^n. We define a bilinear map $B : K^n \times K^n \to K$ by*

$$(\mathbf{v}, \mathbf{w}) \mapsto \sum_{i=1}^n v_i \theta(w_i).$$

The bilinearity of the map is obvious since θ is an endomorphism on K. The map is θ-conjugate symmetric, i.e. $B(\mathbf{v}, \mathbf{w}) = \theta(B(\mathbf{w}, \mathbf{v}))$. Although it is possibly $B(\mathbf{v}, \mathbf{v}) = 0$ for a nonzero $\mathbf{v} \in K^n$, we observe that the set $\{v \neq 0 \in K^n : B(\mathbf{v}, \mathbf{v}) = 0\} \subset K^n$ is of measure 0 in K^n (when K^n is viewed as a dense subset of $\mathbb{R}^{3n}$, the set is contained in a subspace of dimension at most $3n - 2$). Thus, the probability of randomly chosen $\mathbf{v}$ satisfying $B(\mathbf{v}, \mathbf{v}) = 0$ is negligible. In our proof, it is essential that $B(\mathbf{v}, \mathbf{v}) \in K_0$ for any $\mathbf{v} \in K^n$ and $\|(a, b\sqrt{\alpha})\|^2 = N_{K_0/\mathbb{Q}}(a + b\sqrt{-\alpha})$. For $a + b\sqrt{-\alpha} \in K_0$, we abuse the notation so that $\|a + b\sqrt{-\alpha}\|^2 = N_{K_0/\mathbb{Q}}(a + b\sqrt{-\alpha})$.

Let $(\mathbf{b}_1, \ldots, \mathbf{b}_n)$ be a set of vectors in K^n. Let $(\mathbf{b}_1^*, \ldots, \mathbf{b}_n^*)$ be the Gram-Schmidt orthogonalization with respect to the bilinear map B, i.e. $\mathbf{b}_1^* = \mathbf{b}_1$ and $\mathbf{b}_i^* = \mathbf{b}_i - \sum_{j=1}^{i-1} \mu_{i,j} \mathbf{b}_j^*$ ($2 \leq i \leq n$), where $\mu_{i,j} = B(\mathbf{b}_i, \mathbf{b}_j^*)/B(\mathbf{b}_j^*, \mathbf{b}_j^*)$.

Definition 5. *With the above notations, let $\{\mathbf{b}_1, \ldots, \mathbf{b}_n\}$ be a $\mathbb{Z}_K$-basis of a lattice M. Denote $\mathfrak{M}(K)$ by the Euclidean minimum of K. Let δ be a positive constant such that $\mathfrak{M}(K) < \delta^2 < 1$. The basis is called $\mathbb{Z}_K$-LLL-reduced with respect to δ, if it satisfies*

$$\|\mu_{i,j} \cdot \theta(\mu_{i,j})\|^2 = N_{K/\mathbb{Q}}(\mu_{i,j}) \leq \mathfrak{M}(K) \text{ for } 1 \leq j < i \leq n \,(size \, reduced)$$

and

$$\|B_i\| \geq (\delta - \|\mu_{i,i-1} \cdot \theta(\mu_{i,i-1})\|) \|B_{i-1}\| \text{ for } 1 < i \leq n \,(Lovasz \, condition),$$

where $B_i = B(\mathbf{b}_i^*, \mathbf{b}_i^*) \in K_0$. We further require $B_i \neq 0$ for all $1 \leq i \leq n$.

From the definition, we have the following theorem.

Theorem 2. *Let $\{\mathbf{b}_1, \ldots, \mathbf{b}_n\}$ be a $\mathbb{Z}_K$-LLL-reduced basis for a lattice M with respect to δ. Then we have*

1. $\|B_j\| \leq (\delta - \mathfrak{M}(K)^{1/2})^{j-i} \cdot \|B_i\|$ *for $1 \leq j \leq i \leq n$;*
2. $\|B_1\| \leq (\delta - \mathfrak{M}(K)^{1/2})^{-(n-1)/2} \cdot N_{K/\mathbb{Q}}(\det M)^{1/n}.$

Proof. From the definition of the LLL-reduced basis, we have $\|B_j\| \geq (\delta - \mathfrak{M}(K)^{1/2}) \cdot \|B_{j-1}\|$. Then the first statement directly follows from the induction. Applying this result with $j = 1$, we have

$$\begin{aligned}
\|B_1\|^n &\leq \prod_{i=1}^{n} (\delta - \mathfrak{M}(K)^{1/2})^{1-i} \cdot \|B_i\| \\
&= (\delta - \mathfrak{M}(K)^{1/2})^{-n(n-1)/2} \cdot \|\prod_{i=1}^{n} B_i\| \\
&= (\delta - \mathfrak{M}(K)^{1/2})^{-n(n-1)/2} \cdot \|\det(M) \cdot \theta(\det(M))\| \\
&= (\delta - \mathfrak{M}(K)^{1/2})^{-n(n-1)/2} \cdot N_{K/\mathbb{Q}}(\det M).
\end{aligned}$$

The multiplicativity of $\|\cdot\|$ comes from that of $N_{K_0/\mathbb{Q}}(\cdot)$. □

For instance, if $K = \mathbb{Q}(\sqrt{-1}, \sqrt{3})$, we can make a choice of $\delta = 3/4$ so that $\|B_1\| \leq 2^{n-1} N_{K/\mathbb{Q}}(\det M)^{1/n}$.

Now we present Algorithm 2. It is conceptually the same as the classical case. The algorithm aborts when $B_j = 0$ for some j, but it happens only with negligible probability (See the discussion below Definition 4). We show in Theorem 3 that our algorithm always terminates unless it aborts.

Algorithm 2. LLL algorithm over biquadratic Euclidean rings

Input: a basis $\{\mathbf{b}_1, \cdots, \mathbf{b}_n\}$ of $M \subset \mathbb{Z}_K^n$, Euclidean minimum $\mathfrak{M}(K)$, the unit group $K^\times$, and a constant factor δ.

Output: LLL-reduced basis $\{\mathbf{b}_1, \cdots, \mathbf{b}_n\}$.

1: Compute the Gram-Schmidt basis $\{\mathbf{b}_1^*, \cdots, \mathbf{b}_n^*\}$ with respect to the bilinear map $B(\cdot, \cdot)$

2: Compute the coefficients $\mu_{i,j} = B(\mathbf{b}_i, \mathbf{b}_j^*)/B(\mathbf{b}_j^*, \mathbf{b}_j^*)$ for $1 \leq j < i \leq n$ and $B_i = B(\mathbf{b}_i^*, \mathbf{b}_i^*)$ for $1 \leq i \leq n$.

3: Set $k = 2$

4: **while** $k \leq n$ **do**

5:     **for** $j = k - 1$ **to** 1 **do**

6:         Compute $q_j \in \mathbb{Z}_K$ such that $N_{K/\mathbb{Q}}(\mu_{k,j} - q_j) \leq \mathfrak{M}(K)$ using Algorithm 1

7:         Set $\mathbf{b}_k = \mathbf{b}_k - q_j \cdot \mathbf{b}_j$

8:         Update $\mu_{k,j} = B(\mathbf{b}_k, \mathbf{b}_j^*)/B(\mathbf{b}_j^*, \mathbf{b}_j^*)$ and B_k for $1 \leq j \leq k$

9:     **end for**

10:    **if** $\|B_k\| \geq \left(\delta - N_{K/\mathbb{Q}}(\mu_{k,k-1})^{1/2}\right) \cdot \|B_{k-1}\|$ **then**

11:       $k = k + 1$

12:    **else**

13:       Swap $\mathbf{b}_k$ and $\mathbf{b}_{k-1}$

14:       Update $\mathbf{b}_k^*, \mathbf{b}_{k-1}^*, B_k, B_{k-1}$, and $\mu_{i,j}$ for $1 \leq i, j \leq s$

15:       $k = \min\{2, k - 1\}$

16:    **end if**

17: **end while**

Theorem 3. *Let M be a $\mathbb{Z}_K$-lattice in $\mathbb{Z}_K^n$ and $\{\mathbf{b}_1, \cdots, \mathbf{b}_n\}$ be its basis. Let $X \in \mathbb{Z}$ be a such that $\|B_i\| \leq X$ for $1 \leq i \leq n$. Then Algorithm 2 terminates and performs $O(n^2 \log X)$ iterations, unless $B_j = 0$ for some j.*

Proof. The proof is similar to that of the classical case. All we need to show that is the number of swap is finite. For $0 \leq i \leq n$, set $d_i = \prod_{1 \leq j \leq i} \|B_j\|$ and $D = \prod_{1 \leq i \leq n-1} d_i$. Suppose the swap happened for some k. It is straightforward to check that d_i are unchanged for $i < k - 1$ and $i \geq k$. By the Lovasz condition, we observe that d_{k-1} is multiplied by a factor at most equal to δ. Thus, D is reduced by a factor at most equal to δ. On the other hand, we have $D \geq 1$ since M is integral. Thus the number of swap must be finite. It is easy to check that the number of swap is bounded by $\log_\delta(X^{(n-1)n}) = O(n^2 \log X)$. $\qquad\square$

3.3 LLL Algorithm over General Norm-Euclidean Domains

In this section, we propose another lattice reduction algorithm over general norm-Euclidean domains. It uses a Hermitian-type bilinear map over K^n for the Gram-Schmidt orthogonalization.

Definition 6. *For $a \in K$, let $a \mapsto \bar{a}$ be the complex conjugation induced by $K \subset \mathbb{C}$. Let $\mathbf{v} = (v_1, \ldots, v_n)$ and $\mathbf{w} = (w_1, \ldots, w_n)$ be vectors in K^n. We define*

a bilinear map $H : K^n \times K^n \to K$ *by*

$$(\mathbf{v}, \mathbf{w}) \mapsto \sum_{i=1}^{n} v_i \overline{w_i}.$$

The map is bilinear and conjugate-symmetric. Consider the canonical embedding $\sigma = (\sigma_1, \ldots, \sigma_{r_1+r_2}) : K \to \mathbb{R}^{r_1} \times \mathbb{C}^{r_2}$. Then the bilinear map induced by $\sigma_i(H)$ is simply the classical Hermitian inner product on either $\mathbb{R}^n$ or $\mathbb{C}^n$. Thus it is natural to say that H is positive-definite iff $\sigma_i(H)$ is positive-definite for all $1 \leq i \leq r_1 + r_2$. Similar to Sect. 3.2, we define the Gram-Schmidt orthogonalization $\{\mathbf{b}_1^*, \ldots, \mathbf{b}_n^*\}$ with respect to the bilinear map H.

Definition 7. *With the above notations, the basis* $\{\mathbf{b}_1, \ldots, \mathbf{b}_n\}$ *is called* $\mathbb{Z}_K$-*LLL-reduced with respect to* $0 < \delta < 1$ *if it satisfies*

$$N_{K/\mathbb{Q}}(\mu_{i,j}) \leq \mathfrak{M}(K) \text{ for } 1 \leq j < i \leq n \, (size \, reduced)$$

and

$$N_{K/\mathbb{Q}}\big(B_i + \mu_{i,i-1}\overline{\mu_{i,i-1}}B_{i-1}\big) \geq \delta \cdot N_{K/\mathbb{Q}}(B_{i-1}) \text{ for } 1 < i \leq n \, (Lovasz \, condition),$$

where $B_i = H(\mathbf{b}_i^*, \mathbf{b}_i^*)$.

The Lovasz condition is crucial for the proof that the algorithm terminates. Note that the condition is not equivalent to $N_{K/\mathbb{Q}}(B_i) \geq \big(\delta - N_{K/\mathbb{Q}}(\mu_{i,i-1} \cdot \overline{\mu_{i,i-1}})\big) N_{K/\mathbb{Q}}(B_{i-1})$ unlike as the classical case.

In Theorem 4, we show that Algorithm 3 always terminates and runs in a polynomial time.

Theorem 4. *Let* M *be a* $\mathbb{Z}_K$-*lattice in* $\mathbb{Z}_K^n$ *and* $\{\mathbf{b}_1, \cdots, \mathbf{b}_n\}$ *be its basis. Let* $X \in \mathbb{Z}$ *be a such that* $N_{K/\mathbb{Q}}(B_i) \leq X$ *for* $1 \leq i \leq n$. *Then Algorithm 3 terminates and performs* $O(n^2 \log X)$ *iterations.*

Proof. For $0 \leq i \leq n$, set $d_i = \prod_{1 \leq j \leq i} N_{K/\mathbb{Q}}(B_j)$ and $D = \prod_{1 \leq i \leq n-1} d_i$. The remain of the proof is similar as before. $\square$

Although it was impossible to theoretically guarantee the output bound, we experimentally show that the algorithm outputs a reasonably small basis in Appendix A.

4   Cryptographic Applications

4.1   Special-q in TNFS Methods

In this section, we discuss how our algorithm can lead practical improvements on the computation in tower number field sieve (TNFS). The TNFS method [4,18,19] is a recent variant of the number field sieve (NFS) and its target is solving the discrete logarithm problem (DLP) over finite fields. In particular,

Algorithm 3. LLL algorithm over general norm-Euclidean domains

Input: a basis $\{\mathbf{b}_1, \cdots, \mathbf{b}_n\}$ of $M \subset \mathbb{Z}_K^n$, Euclidean minimum $M(K)$, the unit group $K^\times$, and a constant factor δ.
Output: LLL-reduced basis $\{\mathbf{b}_1, \cdots, \mathbf{b}_n\}$.
1: Compute the Gram-Schmidt basis $\{\mathbf{b}_1^*, \cdots, \mathbf{b}_n^*\}$ with respect to the bilinear map $H(\cdot, \cdot)$
2: Compute the coefficients $\mu_{i,j} = H(\mathbf{b}_i, \mathbf{b}_j^*)/H(\mathbf{b}_j^*, \mathbf{b}_j^*)$ for $1 \leq j < i \leq n$ and $B_i = H(\mathbf{b}_i^*, \mathbf{b}_i^*)$ for $1 \leq i \leq n$.
3: Set $k = 2$
4: **while** $k \leq n$ **do**
5:     **for** $j = k - 1$ to 1 **do**
6:         Compute $q_j \in \mathbb{Z}_K$ such that $N_{K/\mathbb{Q}}(\mu_{k,j} - q_j) \leq \mathfrak{M}(K)$ using Algorithm 1
7:         Set $\mathbf{b}_k = \mathbf{b}_k - q_j \cdot \mathbf{b}_j$
8:         Update $\mu_{k,j} = H(\mathbf{b}_k, \mathbf{b}_j^*)/H(\mathbf{b}_j^*, \mathbf{b}_j^*)$ and B_k for $1 \leq j \leq k$
9:     **end for**
10:     **if** $N_{K/\mathbb{Q}}(B_k + \mu_{k,k-1}\overline{\mu_{k,k-1}}B_{k-1}) \geq \delta \cdot N_{K/\mathbb{Q}}(B_{k-1})$ **then**
11:         $k = k + 1$
12:     **else**
13:         Swap $\mathbf{b}_k$ and $\mathbf{b}_{k-1}$
14:         Update $\mathbf{b}_k^*, \mathbf{b}_{k-1}^*, B_k, B_{k-1}$, and $\mu_{i,j}$ for $1 \leq i, j \leq s$
15:         $k = \min\{2, k - 1\}$
16:     **end if**
17: **end while**

pairing-based cryptography has suffered a significant security loss due to these works. See [3,4,18,19] for more details.

In the setting of TNFS, the target is a finite field of form $\mathbb{F}_{p^{mn}}$ (m and n are positive integers greater than or equal to 1) and it is represented as a composition of field extensions, i.e. $\mathbb{F}_{p^m} = \mathbb{F}_p[t]/h(t)$ and $\mathbb{F}_{p^{mn}} = \mathbb{F}_{p^m}[x]/\varphi(x)$. The polynomial h can be chosen by an attacker with several restrictions that it is irreducible over $\mathbb{Z}[t]$, its coefficients are small (typically we expect $\|h\|_\infty = 1$), and p is inert in $\mathbb{Z}[\iota] := \mathbb{Z}[t]/h(t)$. For instance, h can be a cyclotomic polynomial of degree m satisfying the other conditions. Then the attacker selects two irreducible polynomials f and g in $\mathbb{Z}[\iota][x]$ so that $\gcd(f, g) \bmod p = \varphi$ using the methods discussed in the literatures.

Lattice reduction techniques particularly play a key role in two steps called relation collection step and individual logarithm step, using special-$\mathfrak{q}$ method. Recall how the special-$\mathfrak{q}$ method is done. Consider two number fields $K = \mathbb{Q}(\iota) = \mathbb{Q}[t]/h(t)$ and $L_f = K(\alpha_f) = K[x]/f(x)$ (we can choose g instead). Let $\mathfrak{Q}$ be a prime ideal in $\mathbb{Z}_{L_f}$. Given $\mathfrak{Q}$, the task of the special-$\mathfrak{q}$ algorithm is to collect a tuple $(a_0, \ldots, a_{\tau-1}) \in \mathbb{Z}[\iota]^\tau$ such that

- the ideal $\left(\sum_{i=0}^{\tau-1} a_i \alpha_f\right)/\mathfrak{Q}$ factors into prime ideals of norm less than $N_{L_f/\mathbb{Q}}(\mathfrak{Q})^c$ for a constant $0 < c < 1$;
- the principal ideal $\left(\sum_{i=0}^{\tau-1} a_i \alpha_g\right)$ factors into prime ideals of norm less than $N_{L_f/\mathbb{Q}}(\mathfrak{Q})^c$,

and the pairs have the coefficients bounded by a constant parameter. Then a main concern turns out to consider the lattice

$$M_{\mathfrak{Q}} := \left\{ (a_0, \ldots, a_{\tau-1}) \in \mathbb{Z}[\iota]^\tau : \left(\sum_{i=0}^{\tau-1} a_i \alpha_f \right) \equiv 0 \bmod \mathfrak{Q} \right\}, \qquad (1)$$

and try to obtain a basis of small coefficients. A naive approach is to consider $M_{\mathfrak{Q}}$ as a $\mathbb{Z}$-lattice and running the LLL-algorithm (cf. Appendix 7.1 in [4]). However, since $M_{\mathfrak{Q}}$ is naturally a $\mathbb{Z}[\iota]$-module, hence our lattice reduction algorithm can be applied to speed up in finding a reduced basis of $M_{\mathfrak{Q}}$.

The Case When $\mathbb{Z}_K$ is a Norm-Euclidean Ring. Recall that a prime ideal $\mathfrak{Q}$ in $\mathbb{Z}_{L_f}$ is of the form $\langle \mathfrak{q}, T(\alpha_f) \rangle$, where $\mathfrak{q}$ is a prime ideal in $\mathbb{Z}_K$ and T is an irreducible factor of f in $(\mathbb{Z}_K/\mathfrak{q})[x]$ (cf. Proposition 2.3.9 in [9]). Typically, $\mathfrak{Q}$ is a prime ideal of norm less than a prescribed smoothness bound, but large enough. In a such case, prime ideals of degree (which is the same as $\deg(T)$) more than 1 are less numerous than those of degree 1, so it suffices to consider prime ideals $\mathfrak{Q}$ of the form $\langle \mathfrak{q}, \alpha_f - \gamma \rangle$, where $f(\gamma) \equiv 0 \bmod \mathfrak{q}$.

As $\mathbb{Z}_K$ being an Euclidean domain, it is also a principal ideal domain. Assume a generator $q \in \mathbb{Z}_K$ of the ideal $\mathfrak{q}$ is known.[3] Define the matrix of dimension τ with the coefficients in $\mathbb{Z}_K$,

$$\Lambda_{\mathfrak{Q}} := \begin{pmatrix} q & 0 & \cdots & 0 \\ -\gamma & 1 & & \\ & & \ddots & \\ & & -\gamma & 1 \end{pmatrix}. \qquad (2)$$

One can check that the rows of the matrix $\Lambda_{\mathfrak{Q}}$ form a $\mathbb{Z}_K$-basis of the lattice $M_{\mathfrak{Q}}$. By using Algorithm 3, we find a reduced basis. The output quality is reasonably good as shown in Appendix A.

When $\mathbb{Z}_K$ is Gaussian integers and $\tau = 2$, finding a $\mathbb{Z}_K$-reduced basis of $\Lambda_{\mathfrak{Q}}$ was discussed in [4, Appendix 7.1] using the extended Euclidean algorithm. Our algorithm is a generalization of this approach. To get a better intuition, let us see in detail the following example.

Example 1. We consider an example to target a finite field $\mathbb{F}_{p^{12}}$ for the BN curve [5]. The prime parameter is chosen as $p = P(u)$, where $P(x) = 36x^4 +$

---

[3] This can always be done since we are working with the Euclidean domain. Given a prime ideal of the form $\mathfrak{q} = \langle \pi, S(\iota) \rangle$ (as usual π is a prime integer and S is a factor of h modulo π), a generator q is the greatest common divisor of π and $S(\iota)$.

$36x^3 + 24x^2 + 6x + 1$ and $u = 2^{158} - 2^{128} - 2^{68} + 1$ (See [2, Section 6.].). Let us take a polynomial $h(t) = \Phi_5(t) = t^4 + t^3 + t^2 + t + 1$, so that $\mathbb{Z}_K = \mathbb{Z}[\zeta_5]$, where ζ_5 is a 5-th primitive root of unity. Using the SexTNFS method in [18, Section 4.1.], take for example, $f(x) = \varphi(x) = x^3 - x^2 - u$ and $g(x) = P(x^3 - x^2)$. Check that h is irreducible over $\mathbb{F}_p$ since $p \equiv 3 \mod 5$ and f, g and φ satisfy the conditions to be used in exTNFS method.

Take a prime ideal $\mathfrak{Q} = \langle \mathfrak{q}, \alpha_f - \gamma \rangle \subset L_f$ of the norm size $\log_2(N_{L_f/\mathbb{Q}}(\mathfrak{Q})) = 74.29$ (we extrapolate this value due to the record of [1], see [18, Sect. 5.]). Our choice was

$$\mathfrak{q} = (q) = \left(-461479\zeta_5^3 - 383970\zeta_5^2 - 265505\zeta_5 - 303923 \right)$$

and

$$\gamma = 16946578643505257763313.$$

We ran Algorithm 3 on the $\mathbb{Z}_K$-lattice $M_{\mathfrak{Q}}$ that is generated by the rows of the matrix $\Lambda_{\mathfrak{Q}}$ (2). As a result, for instance, when $\tau = 2$, we obtained a $\mathbb{Z}_K$-LLL reduced basis

$$\text{LLL}(\Lambda_{\mathfrak{Q}}) = \begin{pmatrix} 532\zeta_5^3 + 850\zeta_5^2 + 179\zeta_5 - 464 & 224\zeta_5^3 + 132\zeta_5^2 - 13\zeta_5 + 367 \\ -649\zeta_5^3 + 186\zeta_5^2 + 661\zeta_5 + 73 & 11\zeta_5^3 - 264\zeta_5^2 + 35\zeta_5 - 71 \end{pmatrix}.$$

Note that the largest coefficients in the entries of the reduced basis is 850 and $\log_2(850) \approx 9.73$. This is compatible with $\log_2\left(N_{K/\mathbb{Q}}(q)^{\frac{1}{\tau m}}\right) \approx 9.29$ which is an approximation of the size when the reduction is done over $\mathbb{Z}$. Furthermore, the running time is faster than using the classical algorithm (see Appendix A).

Appendix

A   Simulation Results

To verify the quality of the output size of our algorithms, we implemented our algorithm using the SAGE computer algebra system [30] and carried out simulations on a desktop PC with Intel Xeon E5 CPU cores at 3.7 GHz. We also adapted a variant (cf. Algorithm 2.6.3 in [8]) for efficient implementations. We experimented lattice bases generated by the rows of the following shape.

$$\begin{pmatrix} q & 0 & \cdots & \cdots & 0 \\ \gamma_1 & 1 & \cdots & \cdots & 0 \\ \gamma_2 & 0 & 1 & \ddots & 0 \\ \vdots & \vdots & \vdots & \ddots & \vdots \\ \gamma_{n-1} & 0 & \cdots & \cdots & 1 \end{pmatrix},$$

where q and γ_i's are uniformly randomly chosen algebraic integers in $\mathbb{Z}_K$. This HNF type of bases has potential cryptographic applications, for instance, as shown in Sect. 4.1. Recall that the above lattice with $\gamma_i \equiv \gamma^i \mod q$ is equivalent to the lattice generated by Eq. (2).

Let M be a $\mathbb{Z}$-lattice of dimension d. When dealing with the quality of outputs by lattice reduction, one mainly consider the Hermite factor, $\|\mathbf{b}_1\| / \mathrm{vol}(M)^{1/d}$. Let us now consider M as a $\mathbb{Z}_K$-lattice of dimension n (i.e. $[\mathbb{Z}_K : \mathbb{Z}] = d/n$). Let $\mathbf{c}_1 = (c_{1,1}, \ldots, c_{1,n}) \in \mathbb{Z}_K^n$ be an output by the reduction and define by $\|\mathbf{c}_1\|_\infty := \max_{1 \le j \le n} \|c_{1,j}\|_\infty$. In our experiments, we will consider a factor $C := \|\mathbf{c}_1\|_\infty / \mathrm{vol}(M)^{1/d}$ to measure the quality of outputs. Then the classical Hermite's constant by our reduction is bounded by $C^{1/d} \cdot d^{1/2d}$. Note that $\mathrm{vol}(M) = N_{K/\mathbb{Q}}(\det(M)) = N_{K/\mathbb{Q}}(q)$.

We randomly sampled q so that its coefficients are of 100 bits and chose γ_i so that its coefficients are of smaller bitsize than that of q. We carried out our lattice reduction on many lattices sampled in that way and computed the average of the factor C. As the classical case, we can say that the output quality is good enough if $C^{1/d}$ is small.

Output Quality of Algorithm 3. We experimented Algorithm 3 with a hundred of n-dimensional $\mathbb{Z}[\zeta_k]$-lattices for each $10 \le n \le 50$ and $k = 5, 8$ and 16. Surprisingly, the factor $C^{1/d}$ seems to behave consistently. In other words, it seems that the factor C depends only (exponentially) on the dimension n (see Fig. 1) and $C^{1/d}$ is well-bounded by a small constant. To give a concrete example, consider 50-dimensional lattices over $\mathbb{Z}[\zeta_8]$. By running the algorithm over hundreds of lattices of the above form, we obtained $C^{1/d} = C^{1/4n} \approx 1.02$ on average. The classical Hermite's constant is then bounded by $C^{1/d} \cdot d^{1/2d} \approx 1.0335$ which is smaller than the worst case bound of Hermite factor $(4/3)^{1/4} \approx 1.0754$. As shown in Fig. 2, we observe that $C^{1/d}$ belongs in the range between 1.01 and 1.05 regardless the dimension of the lattices. As a remark, we used the parameter $\mathfrak{M}(K) = 1/2$ or $1/5$ corresponding to K and chose $\delta = 3/4$.

Timing Results of Algorithm 3. All of the $\mathbb{Z}_K$-lattices considered above are also considered as $\mathbb{Z}$-lattices with corresponding dimensions. We compared the speed of our algorithm with the classical LLL-algorithm. Since our implementation is far from being well-optimized yet, we avoid to use the internal LLL function in SAGE for the consistency of the comparison. We tried to use equivalently optimized code implementation for the classical LLL algorithm and our algorithm. For the completeness, we include our codes in Appendix B.

To give a concrete example, let $K = \mathbb{Q}(\zeta_8)$ and consider a $\mathbb{Z}_K$-lattice of dimension 20. Then it translates to a $\mathbb{Z}$-lattice of dimension 80. To get a reduced basis, on average, it took 20.40 s over $\mathbb{Z}_K$ which was much faster than 75.40 s running over $\mathbb{Z}$. We present the comparison of the average running time in Fig. 3 for $\mathbb{Z}_K = \mathbb{Z}[\zeta_5]$ and $\mathbb{Z}[\zeta_8]$.

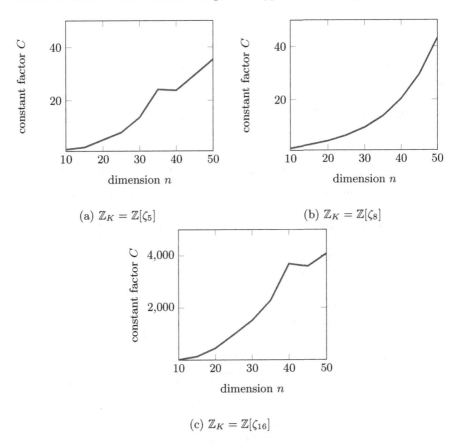

(a) $\mathbb{Z}_K = \mathbb{Z}[\zeta_5]$ (b) $\mathbb{Z}_K = \mathbb{Z}[\zeta_8]$

(c) $\mathbb{Z}_K = \mathbb{Z}[\zeta_{16}]$

Fig. 1. Average Hermite factor by Algorithm 3 over $\mathbb{Z}_K$-lattices

Comparison of Algorithm 2 and 3 over $\mathbb{Z}[\zeta_8]$-Lattices. The 8-th cyclotomic fields $K = \mathbb{Q}(\zeta_8)$ is also a biquadratic field since $\mathbb{Q}(\zeta_8) = \mathbb{Q}(\sqrt{-1}, \sqrt{2})$. Thus both of our proposed algorithms can be applied. We experimented both algorithms. As a result, it appears that Algorithm 3 performs better than Algorithm 2. To give a concrete example, for 10-dimensional lattices, the average of the constant for Algorithm 3 was $C^{1/d} \approx 1.012$. On the other hand, we have $C^{1/d} \approx 2.976$ on average for Algorithm 2. Algorithm 3 was also better than Algorithm 2 with respect to the practical running time.

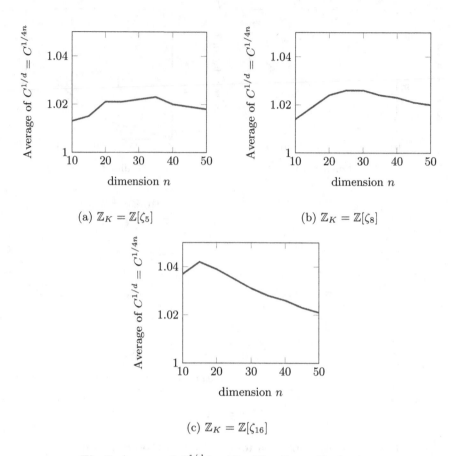

(a) $\mathbb{Z}_K = \mathbb{Z}[\zeta_5]$

(b) $\mathbb{Z}_K = \mathbb{Z}[\zeta_8]$

(c) $\mathbb{Z}_K = \mathbb{Z}[\zeta_{16}]$

Fig. 2. Average of $C^{1/d}$ by Algorithm 3 over $\mathbb{Z}_K$-lattices

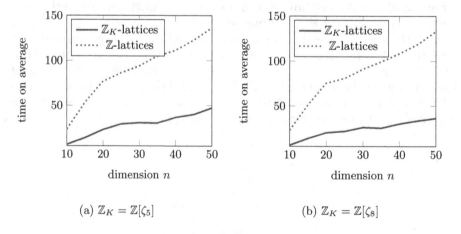

(a) $\mathbb{Z}_K = \mathbb{Z}[\zeta_5]$

(b) $\mathbb{Z}_K = \mathbb{Z}[\zeta_8]$

Fig. 3. Time comparison of running time

B   SAGE Implementation

```
 1  def RLLL(b, delta=3/4, ee=1/2):
 2    K=b.base_ring()
 3    d=K.degree()
 4    z=K.gen()
 5    O=K.maximal_order()
 6    n=b.nrows()
 7    assert n>=1 and b.is_square()
 8    F=b.base_ring().fraction_field()
 9    d=F.degree()
10
11    G=F.galois_group()
12    g=G.complex_conjugation()
13
14    bstar=matrix(F,n,n)
15    mu=matrix(F,n,n)
16    B=[F(0) for _ in range(n)]
17
18    def rnd(vv):
19      ww=K(0)
20      for i in range(d):
21        ww+=round(vv[i])*z^i
22      return ww
23
24    def euc(a,mk=1/2):
25      u=K.units()
26      u0=u[0]
27      tu=u0
28      l=len(u)
29      q=rnd(a)
30      r=a-q
31      if norm(r)<=mk:
32        return q
33      else:
34        while True:
35          na=tu*r
36          nq=rnd(na)
37          nr=na-nq
38          if norm(nr)<=mk:
39            return q+tu^(-1)*nq
40          else:
41            tu*=u0
42
43    def dot(v, w):
44      res=K(0)
45      for i in range(n):
46        res+=v[i]*g(w[i])
47      return res
48
49    def reduce(kk,ll):
50      if norm(mu[kk,ll])>ee:
51        qq=euc(mu[kk,ll],ee)
52        b[kk]-=qq*b[ll]
53        mu[kk,ll]-=qq
54        for i in [0..ll-1]:
55          mu[kk,i]-=qq*mu[ll,i]
56
57    def swap(kk):
58      b[kk],b[kk-1]=b[kk-1],b[kk]
59      if kk>1:
60        for j in [0..kk-2]:
61          mu[kk,j],mu[kk-1,j]=mu[kk-1,j],mu[kk,j]
62      tmu=mu[kk,kk-1]
63      tmubar=g(tmu)
64      tB=B[kk]+tmu*tmubar*B[kk-1]
65      mu[kk,kk-1]=tmubar*B[kk-1]/tB
```

```
66          tb=bstar[kk-1]
67          bstar[kk-1]=bstar[kk]+tmu*tb
68          bstar[kk]=-mu[kk,kk-1]*bstar[kk]+(B[kk]/tB)*tb
69          B[kk]=B[kk-1]*B[kk]/tB
70          B[kk-1]=tB
71          for i in [kk+1..kmax]:
72            t=mu[i,kk]
73            mu[i,kk]=mu[i,kk-1]-tmu*t
74            mu[i,kk-1]=t+mu[kk,kk-1]*mu[i,kk]
75
76      k=1
77      kmax=0
78      bstar[0]=b[0]
79      B[0]=dot(b[0],b[0])
80
81   while k<n:
82      # incremental gram-schmidt
83      if k>kmax:
84        kmax=k
85        bstar[k]=b[k]
86        for j in [0..k-1]:
87          mu[k,j]=dot(b[k],bstar[j])/B[j]
88          bstar[k]-=mu[k,j]*bstar[j]
89        B[k]=dot(bstar[k],bstar[k])
90        assert B[k]!=0
91      # LLL-reduced condition
92      else:
93        while True:
94          reduce(k,k-1)
95          # Lovasz condition
96          if (B[k] + mu[k,k-1]*g(mu[k,k-1])*B[k-1]).norm()<(delta* (B[k
   -1]).norm()):
97            swap(k)
98            k=max(1,k-1)
99          else:
100             for l in [k-2,k-3,..,0]:
101               reduce(k,l)
102             k+=1
103             break
104  return b
```

Listing 1.1. SAGE impelementation of Algorithm 3

```
1 # the classical LLL implementation with delta=3/4
2
3 def ZLLL(b):
4   n=b.nrows()
5   assert n>=1 and b.is_square()
6   F=b.base_ring().fraction_field()
7
8   bstar=matrix(F,n,n)
9   mu=matrix(F,n,n)
10  B=[F(0) for _ in range(n)]
11
12  def reduce(kk,ll):
13    if abs(mu[kk,ll])>0.5:
14      q=round(mu[kk,ll])
15      b[kk]-=q*b[ll]
16      mu[kk,ll]-=q
17      for i in [0..ll-1]:
18        mu[kk,i]-=q*mu[ll,i]
19
20  def swap(kk):
21    b[kk],b[kk-1]=b[kk-1],b[kk]
22    if kk>1:
23      for j in [0..kk-2]:
24        mu[kk,j],mu[kk-1,j]=mu[kk-1,j],mu[kk,j]
25    tmu=mu[kk,kk-1]
```

```
26    tB=B[kk]+tmu^2*B[kk-1]
27    mu[kk,kk-1]=tmu*B[kk-1]/tB
28    tb=bstar[kk-1]
29    bstar[kk-1]=bstar[kk]+tmu*tb
30    bstar[kk]=-mu[kk,kk-1]*bstar[kk]+(B[kk]/tB)*tb
31    B[kk]=B[kk-1]*B[kk]/tB
32    B[kk-1]=tB
33    for i in [kk+1..kmax]:
34        t=mu[i,kk]
35        mu[i,kk]=mu[i,kk-1]-tmu*t
36        mu[i,kk-1]=t+mu[kk,kk-1]*mu[i,kk]
37
38    k=1
39    kmax=0
40    bstar[0]=b[0]
41    B[0]=b[0]*b[0]
42
43    while k<n:
44    # incremental gram-schmidt
45    if k>kmax:
46        kmax=k
47        bstar[k]=b[k]
48        for j in [0..k-1]:
49            mu[k,j]=b[k]*bstar[j]/B[j]
50            bstar[k]-=mu[k,j]*bstar[j]
51        B[k]=bstar[k]*bstar[k]
52        assert B[k]!=0
53    # LLL-reduced condition
54    else:
55        while True:
56            reduce(k,k-1)
57            if B[k]<((3/4-mu[k,k-1]^2)*B[k-1]):
58                swap(k)
59                k=max(1,k-1)
60            else:
61                for l in [k-2,k-3,..,0]:
62                    reduce(k,l)
63                k+=1
64                break
65
66    return b
```

Listing 1.2. SAGE implementation for the classical LLL algorithm

References

1. Aoki, K., Franke, J., Kleinjung, T., Lenstra, A.K., Osvik, D.A.: A kilobit special number field sieve factorization. In: Kurosawa, K. (ed.) ASIACRYPT 2007. LNCS, vol. 4833, pp. 1–12. Springer, Heidelberg (2007). https://doi.org/10.1007/978-3-540-76900-2_1

2. Aranha, D.F., Fuentes-Castañeda, L., Knapp, E., Menezes, A., Rodríguez-Henríquez, F.: Implementing pairings at the 192-bit security level. In: Abdalla, M., Lange, T. (eds.) Pairing 2012. LNCS, vol. 7708, pp. 177–195. Springer, Heidelberg (2013). https://doi.org/10.1007/978-3-642-36334-4_11

3. Barbulescu, R., Duquesne, S.: Updating key size estimations for pairings. IACR Cryptology ePrint Archive 2017:334 (2017)

4. Barbulescu, R., Gaudry, P., Kleinjung, T.: The tower number field sieve. In: Iwata, T., Cheon, J.H. (eds.) ASIACRYPT 2015. LNCS, vol. 9453, pp. 31–55. Springer, Heidelberg (2015). https://doi.org/10.1007/978-3-662-48800-3_2

5. Barreto, P.S.L.M., Naehrig, M.: Pairing-friendly elliptic curves of prime order. In: Preneel, B., Tavares, S. (eds.) SAC 2005. LNCS, vol. 3897, pp. 319–331. Springer, Heidelberg (2006). https://doi.org/10.1007/11693383_22

6. Bauch, J., Bernstein, D.J., de Valence, H., Lange, T., van Vredendaal, C.: Short generators without quantum computers: the case of multiquadratics. In: Coron, J.-S., Nielsen, J.B. (eds.) EUROCRYPT 2017. LNCS, vol. 10210, pp. 27–59. Springer, Cham (2017). https://doi.org/10.1007/978-3-319-56620-7_2

7. Biasse, J.-F., Espitau, T., Fouque, P.-A., Gélin, A., Kirchner, P.: Computing generator in cyclotomic integer rings. In: Coron, J.-S., Nielsen, J.B. (eds.) EUROCRYPT 2017. LNCS, vol. 10210, pp. 60–88. Springer, Cham (2017). https://doi.org/10.1007/978-3-319-56620-7_3

8. Cohen, H.: A Course in Computational Algebraic Number Theory, New York, NY, USA (1993)

9. Cohen, H.: Advanced Topics in Computational Number Theory. Graduate Texts in Mathematics, New York, NY, Berlin, Heidelberg (2000)

10. Fieker, C., Pohst, M.E.: On lattices over number fields. In: Cohen, H. (ed.) ANTS 1996. LNCS, vol. 1122, pp. 133–139. Springer, Heidelberg (1996). https://doi.org/10.1007/3-540-61581-4_48

11. Fieker, C., Stehlé, D.: Short bases of lattices over number fields. In: Hanrot, G., Morain, F., Thomé, E. (eds.) ANTS 2010. LNCS, vol. 6197, pp. 157–173. Springer, Heidelberg (2010). https://doi.org/10.1007/978-3-642-14518-6_15

12. Gan, Y.H., Ling, C., Mow, W.H.: Complex lattice reduction algorithm for low-complexity full-diversity mimo detection. Trans. Sig. Proc. **57**(7), 2701–2710 (2009)

13. Garg, S., Gentry, C., Halevi, S.: Candidate multilinear maps from ideal lattices. In: Johansson, T., Nguyen, P.Q. (eds.) EUROCRYPT 2013. LNCS, vol. 7881, pp. 1–17. Springer, Heidelberg (2013). https://doi.org/10.1007/978-3-642-38348-9_1

14. Gentry, C.: Fully homomorphic encryption using ideal lattices. In: Proceedings of the 41st Annual ACM Symposium on Theory of Computing, STOC 2009, Bethesda, MD, USA, 31 May–2 June 2009, pp. 169–178 (2009)

15. Gordon, D.M.: Discrete logarithms in $GF(p)$ using the number field sieve. SIAM J. Discret. Math. **6**(1), 124–138 (1993)

16. Joux, A., Lercier, R., Smart, N., Vercauteren, F.: The number field sieve in the medium prime case. In: Dwork, C. (ed.) CRYPTO 2006. LNCS, vol. 4117, pp. 326–344. Springer, Heidelberg (2006). https://doi.org/10.1007/11818175_19

17. Kaiblinger, N.: Cyclotomic rings with simple euclidean algorithm. JP J. Algebra Number Theory Appl. **23**(1), 61–76 (2011)

18. Kim, T., Barbulescu, R.: Extended tower number field sieve: a new complexity for the medium prime case. In: Robshaw, M., Katz, J. (eds.) CRYPTO 2016. LNCS, vol. 9814, pp. 543–571. Springer, Heidelberg (2016). https://doi.org/10.1007/978-3-662-53018-4_20

19. Kim, T., Jeong, J.: Extended tower number field sieve with application to finite fields of arbitrary composite extension degree. In: Fehr, S. (ed.) PKC 2017. LNCS, vol. 10174, pp. 388–408. Springer, Heidelberg (2017). https://doi.org/10.1007/978-3-662-54365-8_16

20. Lemmermeyer, F.: Euclid's algorithm in quartic CM-fields. arXiv preprint arXiv:1108.6215 (2011)

21. Lenstra, A.K., Lenstra, H.W., Lovasz, L.: Factoring polynomials with rational coefficients. Math. Ann. **261**, 515–534 (1982)

22. Lenstra, H.W.: Euclid's algorithm in cyclotomic fields. J. London Math. Soc. **s2-10**(4), 457–465 (1975)

23. Lezowski, P.: Computation of the euclidean minimum of algebraic number fields. Math. Comput. **83**, 1397–1426 (2014). 30 pages, shorter version, with many typos fixed

24. Masley, J.M.: On Euclidean rings of integers in cyclotomic fields. Journal für die reine und angewandte Mathematik (Crelles Journal) **272**, 45–48 (1975)
25. Napias, H.: A generalization of the LLL-algorithm over Euclidean rings or orders. Journal de théorie des nombres de Bordeaux **8**(2), 387–396 (1996)
26. Ojala, T.: Euclid's algorithm in the cyclotomic field $Q(\zeta_{16})$. Math. Comput. **31**(137), 268–273 (1977)
27. Schnorr, C.P., Hörner, H.H.: Attacking the chor-rivest cryptosystem by improved lattice reduction. In: Guillou, L.C., Quisquater, J.-J. (eds.) EUROCRYPT 1995. LNCS, vol. 921, pp. 1–12. Springer, Heidelberg (1995). https://doi.org/10.1007/3-540-49264-X_1
28. Schnorr, C.-P., Euchner, M.: Lattice basis reduction: improved practical algorithms and solving subset sum problems. Math. Program. **66**(1–3), 181–199 (1994)
29. Smart, N.P., Vercauteren, F.: Fully homomorphic encryption with relatively small key and ciphertext sizes. In: Nguyen, P.Q., Pointcheval, D. (eds.) PKC 2010. LNCS, vol. 6056, pp. 420–443. Springer, Heidelberg (2010). https://doi.org/10.1007/978-3-642-13013-7_25
30. Stein, W., et al.: Sage Mathematics Software (Version 5.11). The Sage Development Team (2013), http://www.sagemath.org

Author Index

Printed in the United States
By Bookmasters